Engaging Inquiry
Research and Writing in the Disciplines

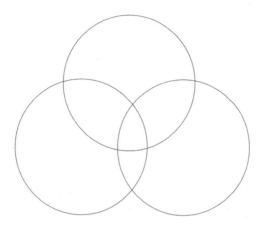

Judy Kirscht

Mark Schlenz

Prentice
Hall

Upper Saddle River, New Jersey 07458

Library of Congress Cataloging-in-Publication Data

Kirscht, Judy
    Engaging inquiry : research and writing in the disciplines / by Judy Kirscht & Mark Schlenz.
        p. cm.
    Includes bibliographical references and index.
    ISBN 0-13-011699-8
        1. English language—Rhetoric. 2. Interdisciplinary approach in education. 3.
    Research—Methodology. 4. Academic writing. I. Schlenz, Mark. II. Title.

PE1408.K672 2002
800'.042—dc 21   00-053051

AVP, Editor-in-chief: Leah Jewell
Acquisitions Editor: Corey Good
Assistant Editor: Vivian Garcia
Editorial Assistant: Jennifer Collins
Managing Editor: Mary Rottino
Production Liaison: Fran Russello
Editorial/Production Supervision: Marianne Hutchinson (Pine Tree Composition, Inc.)
Prepress and Manufacturing Buyer: Mary Ann Gloriande
Art Director: Jayne Conte
Cover Designer: Bruce Kenselaar
Director, Image Resource Center: Melinda Lee Reo
Manager, Rights & Permissions: Kay Dellosa
Image Specialist: Beth Boyd
Marketing Manager: Brandy Dawson

This book was set in 11/13 New Caledonia by Pine Tree Composition, Inc., and was printed and bound by R. R. Donnelley & Sons Company. The cover was printed by Jaguar Advanced Graphics.

© 2002 by Pearson Education, Inc.
Upper Saddle River, NJ 07458

Printed in the United States of America
10 9 8 7 6 5 4 3 2 1

ISBN   0-13-011699-8

Prentice-Hall International (UK) Limited, *London*
Prentice-Hall of Australia Pty. Limited, *Sydney*
Prentice-Hall Canada Inc., *Toronto*
Prentice-Hall Hispanoamericana, S. A., *Mexico*
Prentice-Hall of India Private Limited, *New Delhi*
Prentice-Hall of Japan, Inc., *Tokyo*
Pearson Education Asia Pte. Ltd. *Singapore*
Editora Prentice-Hall do Brasil, Ltda., *Rio de Janeiro*

Brief Contents

Contents

P A R T   I
The Sciences   9

1 Inquiry and Writing in the Sciences   11

2   Readings in the Sciences   53

PART II
The Social Sciences   109

P A R T   I I I

The Humanities   321

6 Readings in the Humanities   361

PART IV

Critical Applications   419

7 Critical Applications   421

List of Figures

Preface

TO THE INSTRUCTOR

Engaging Inquiry creates a framework that joins writing and disciplinary inquiry processes and so introduces academic argument as an integral part of the creation of knowledge. The book is intended as scaffolding for designing cross-disciplinary writing courses at many levels and of varying lengths. We have chosen the creation of knowledge as our central theme because we believe that theme (What should we believe? What is true?) undergirds all others, not only in academic but in public and personal spheres, as well. Three basic questions guide the text—What is it? How does it develop or change over time? How does it function? These questions guide inquiry on many subjects, from mental illness to cloning to sexuality to controversies over the local landfill, which can be and are studied from scientific, social science, and humanities perspectives. Though we developed the book from our work with students at the university level, we believe the model of inquiry can be adapted and applied in any college level course as a standard for argument.

We have included sufficient readings to implement the framework in a number of different configurations (outlined at the beginning of the chapters on readings) and certainly more readings than can be accommodated in any single course. Their purpose is to demonstrate the level of difficulty of university-level content course readings and the way two or three readings can be grouped to create a thematic focus. We hope teachers will complement these readings with other more accessible material from the public domain or find comparable readings to develop their own thematically unified courses. We have found the readings most successful when combined with readings on issues and events from the current press addressing issues in the local community or specific campus and so have not included very many such readings here. When so combined, however, the units relate the academic texts to the "real world" very effectively and demonstrate to students the complexity of knowledge-making in any field, and its relevance to the study of current issues. The articles on coyotes and anemone in the science section, for example, echo environmental issues frequently in the Santa Barbara press; similar studies on other animals would certainly be more appropriate in Kansas City or Tucson. The theories on in-group behavior might be applied to dorm life, ethnic groups, or workplace behavior, depending on the student population. The only constraint on such themes is that they be on subjects appropriate for study in all three divisions: natural sciences, social sciences, and humanities and that writing assignments arise from academic questions raised by the readings. Many familiar composition themes such as capital punishment, abortion, or euthanasia must be translated into more abstract topics, such as violence or population control, to raise questions appropriate to all three divisions.

We have found most writing teachers think of disciplinary differences in terms of the differing written genres. For us the importance of disciplinary distinctions among forms lies in the inquiry processes they reflect and reinforce, not in the conventions and forms as separate and separable entities. The science report, for example, takes its form from the constraints and rigors of scientific study; if severed from the scientific method it reflects, the form becomes a formalistic exercise without any obvious purpose. The critical difference of the inquiry approach, for us, is that it begins with questions, not beliefs—that in the university, argument begins with inquiry, results from inquiry, and sparks further inquiry. Truth claims are tested, not simply defended. The written forms grow out of that inquiry and emphasize important aspects of it; as such they reinforce the critical thinking and linguistic requirements of the discipline and teach thinking habits that students can apply to any topic. Thus the subject matter and history of different disciplines gives rise to differing modes of inquiry and those give rise to differing standards for knowledge claims and different written forms; if students understand both the basic principles of inquiry and the differences between modes, they will better understand both the forms and the standards of argument in different fields. If, in other words, they know what it is to "think like a scientist " or a sociologist or a historian, they can develop and evaluate arguments within those realms, and the forms of writing will make sense. Finally process is a model for critical inquiry that can be applied to public (and later professional) issues and discourses.

We also, paradoxically perhaps, believe that the central principles of good argument and good writing cross all boundaries—between disciplines within the academy, between academic and public, between academic and workplace. We believe that sound logic is sound logic anywhere and clarity is a universal principle of good communication. Therefore teachers of classical argument will find little in these chapters that is not familiar. However, we have found that inquiry-based argument, because it proceeds inductively, avoids many of the hazards of arguing from preexisting claims. It also provides nonconfrontational sites for examining other principles of sound argument: accurate observation, sound induction, specificity of claims, and examination of other interpretations. When we begin teaching the essay with thesis formation, we are asking for the formulation of belief; when we ask for support, we are asking for justification; when we ask for critical examination, we threaten belief systems that give order to students' lives. It is little wonder we are so rarely satisfied with the results. If, on the other hand, students see the disciplines as places where we study what we do not understand, not places with a storehouse of answers to be learned, they learn the process of inquiry as methods of reaching belief. Those who believe, for example, that students in general are politically apathetic and indifferent to public issues will, in a conventional composition class, find ample evidence for their position; students who actually survey their peers find many who are far less apathetic than they thought. To arrive at a thesis, they must dig deeper into student attitudes for cause, using theories provided by their readings. Thus they understand the thesis itself as a qualitatively different sort of claim.

We realize that at the introductory level many students are not yet prepared to do advanced field research, that lower-division courses in the disciplines do not often ask them to do so, and that a writing course cannot be a methods course and still attend to matters of writing. We also realize that the students using the book will be at different levels, the courses of different lengths, and that differing paper assignments are therefore appropriate. The chapters, therefore, offer field exercises and assignments of varying complexity and are intended for teachers to use selectively and modify according to the needs of their students. There is no need to assign every reading or every inquiry exercise in this textbook; on the other hand, many such exercises can be developed into formal papers if that is the level most appropriate to a given group of students. The student papers included at the end of each chapter are intended for revision workshop using the tools provided in the chapters and *not* as models for imitation. They illustrate both what students can achieve and their areas of greatest difficulty. Because many of the assignments are unfamiliar to many teachers, we believe the papers can be useful illustrations, but we do most emphatically warn against students' tendency to use them as formulaic templates.

We hope these assignments generate innovation and creativity on the part of both teachers and students. Their central quality is exposure to observation and inference as the grounds for claims or as a way of testing the claims of others; such exposure changes students' perspective on knowledge, language, and argument in important ways. They recognize, because they have generated and handled the data themselves, the following characteristics of good thinking and writing that have been difficult to bring home in the "standard" composition classroom:

- Representation of observed phenomena requires precise word choice and sentence structure.
- Inference from data is complex and fraught with error.
- Expression of ideas in academic debate requires precise modification and distinction of subtle differences; these, in turn, require complex sentences and correct citation.
- Disciplinary perspectives and underlying belief systems shape the very questions we see as important to ask; therefore, identification of underlying assumptions is a key skill in academic argument.
- The essay requires formulation of one's own ideas in interaction with the ideas of others; it is, therefore, one of the more difficult forms to execute well.

We have also found that the differing focuses and subject matter of the disciplines refine different aspects of logic and language, and therefore make excellent sites for developing those language and thinking skills while at the same time educating students in the principles and expectations of the field. Although careful observation and precise description of the world or its representation is central to all disciplines, the natural sciences' emphasis on objectivity simply make it an excellent arena to contrast the language of representation with the language of expression. Science is similarly an easy place to examine the way we make inferences and create theories, simply because students are not as emotionally invested; engagement in this field comes chiefly from curiosity. If scientific method is understood as a requirement that we test our inferences continuously, it becomes a model for academic argument that distinguishes it from most argument found in the public domain.

The creation and testing of theories is similarly central to all fields and indeed to all prediction and problem solving in any domain. The social sciences are an excellent arena for students to learn to participate in this process simply because there are so many theories and they are so frequently the center of debate. Any composition teacher knows the struggle of getting students to genuinely test their personal theories of the world and that most of these theories remain untouched by their academic course work. Bringing the personal and the academic into interaction is a major struggle for most of us. To the traditional method of "read-understand-apply-evaluate," we have added "raise questions-hypothesize-test." The resulting argument is perforce databased, making it very different from most personal belief essays in ways students find both difficult and memorable.

By the time writing instructors arrive "home" to the humanities, their students have already discovered how critical observation is, how problematic most data, how much every claim depends on the questions asked, and how the questions depend on the theories and perspectives of the researchers. To now study interpretation itself, the many ways humans make meaning, is simply to articulate processes they have already experienced and experienced without direct confrontation with their own belief systems. The careful observation applied to the world in science is now applied to texts, be they poems, advertisements, or film, and precise description is no less important. The role of theory, already studied in the venue of human behavior, a venue very accessible to students, can now move to the more abstract arena of interpretive theory or ethics.

Finally we have found the inquiry process greatly facilitates the relinquishing of certainty, reduces the need to hold opinion as inviolate, and frequently arouses genuine curiosity—all intellectual goals long cherished by writing teachers and educators across all disciplines alike. We believe that it does so in part because it begins away from the students' value systems, the home of most humanities study, while at the same time engaging the issues of their lives. There is a world of difference between studying why people take drugs and arguing whether they should be free to take drugs. The first gives insight, the second, even in the hands of the best of teachers, generates defense and attack. By the time the class addresses the ethical issue, their views are informed by study of the physical and behavioral issues involved. By the time they address the underlying value systems that shape attitudes to drugs, they realized the importance of all three dimensions to any complete study or resolution of the human problem. If there is a belief system guiding this book, and of course there is, it is that none of the disciplinary perspectives is adequate in itself; the quality of thinking that underlies good writing requires everything these disciplinary modes of inquiry can provide—and then some—to resolve the problems our students must face.

ACKNOWLEDGMENTS

The ideas and approaches inspiring this text rose out of a community of composition teachers at the University of California, Santa Barbara Writing Program, a community faced with the challenge of developing an independent program committed to teaching writing across the disciplines. We are therefore indebted to former Program Director Muriel Zimmerman and Advisory Committee Chair, Charles Bazerman for their programmatic leadership and direction, as well for their comments on the text itself. We also want to acknowledge our indebtedness to Charles Bazerman for his contribution to the theoretical foundations of the work.

Because of the collaborative nature of curriculum development at UCSB, virtually everyone in the Writing Program has contributed to the development of this approach to writing across the disciplines through service on curriculum committees, classroom teaching, or through ongoing debate among the faculty at large. Among the many who have contributed directly to this project, we wish to acknowledge, in particular, lecturers and teaching assistants who served with us on curriculum committees over the years developing instructional objectives, piloting readings, and generating classroom materials, including Michael Reese, Betina Calouri, Laura Butcher Holliday, Laura Adams, Patrick Sharp, Kathryn McClymond, Kim Stone, J.D. Applen, Bonnie Beedles, Ashley Tidey, Marty Williams, and Nick Tingle. The following teaching assistants received grants from the UCSB Office of Instructional Development to generate and implement classroom materials for instructional units: Rose Hentschell, Christopher Schedler, Patricia Marby, Kathryn McClymond, and Ellen Posman. For other kinds of insight and advice, we would like to thank Vince Willoughby, Lawrence Behrens, Max Leeming, and the faculty of the UCSB Environmental Studies Program. We would also like to thank the members of the 1997 UCSB Writing Program external review team—Louise Wetherbee-Phelps, Gregory Colomb, and James Kinneavy—who endorsed the epistemological principles underlying this approach and gave valuable critique on its development.

Many hundreds of students have struggled with the challenges posed by this approach at various stages in its development; their trials and triumphs have greatly contributed to the final product offered here. In addition the following students graciously allowed us to include their writing as examples for revision workshop: Eric Morris, Nick Chapman, Kendall Wright, Christal Cobb, Danielle Paddock, Vazgen Khankaldyyan, and Sara Twogood. Our colleagues, Madeleine Sorapure, George Yatchisin, and Pamela Inglesby, also contributed their article on Web literacy.

For their invaluable assistance in production of the manuscript itself, we thank the following outside reviewers, whose careful reading and generous comments guided our revision process: Nancy Lusignan Schultz (Salem State College), Ann Larabee (Michigan State University), Susan F. Stone (California State University-Bakersfield), Mary Ann Ruday, Ph.D. (Chadron State College), James Allen (College of DuPage), Elizabeth Metzger (University of South Florida), Margaret Colavelli (Northwood University), Michael Flanigan (University of Oklahoma), Mary Tobin (Rice University), Joan Graham (University of Washington), Eileen Thompson (Lane Community College), and Emily Thrush (University of Memphis). Thanks also to Jane Freeburg for her professional editorial assistance and to Geoffrey Bateman for his assistance with manuscript preparation. Finally thanks to Jane Freeburg and Joyce Kleinholz for keeping us sane and helping us see the project through.

Judy Kirscht   *Mark Schlenz*

Introduction

Welcome to the universe of knowledge and to the experience of writing within the community of knowledge seekers, whether at college, in the university, or in the workplace.

What does that mean?
What is going on?
How is writing different here?
How will my writing fit in?

It means, simply, that humans shape language to their needs, their communities, and their jobs, and college people are no different. Language gives humans the power to express experience—to reflect, to predict, and to plan. The miracle of language is its flexibility, its ability to adapt to so many kinds of human experience, to so many human purposes. You have already shaped your individual style of writing to many purposes; the language of the note scribbled to a friend, the letter to your grandmother, the angry letter to the newspaper editor, the cover letter on your job application were not the same. You modified your language to suit the purpose at hand. The purpose of this book is to give you enough understanding of the way language adapts to different tasks, so that you can shape your own language effectively in your college, university, or professional work.

To accomplish this you will first need a conception of language that extends beyond correctness of grammar, syntax and diction, though those are the basic tools of meaning-making. A musician must know how to read music to play a flute concerto, but the ability to read notes on a page alone cannot give the musician a sense of the range and subtleties of the flute or of the power of music to create meaning. We assume you come to this book with basic competence in the language, whether gained through experience and use or through technical instruction; we wish to show you how grammar and syntax shape thoughts and mold them for different purposes.

Much of the work of this book consists of making you conscious of and refining the language and thinking processes you already use naturally; humans do what they have to without any particular consciousness of the mental processes they bring to their tasks. When European settlers brought English to a new world, they lacked words for many elements of their new experience. They "borrowed" what they needed from the Native Americans ("canoe," "moccasin," "mackinaw," etc.), from Mexican Spanish ("rodeo," "avocado," "coyote," etc.), and from other Europeans ("stoop," "waffle," "filibuster" from the Dutch, for example). Thus grew a language that was American rather than European because it expressed the American experience, a language that carries with it the history of those settlers in their interaction with other cultures. When Americans of the last thirty years crossed the new frontier into cyberspace, they again needed language. They both borrowed words from existing language ("to boot," "to crash," "Web," "surf," etc.) and created new technical language ("byte," "Internet," "cyberspace," etc.). In so doing they made a new, overwhelming, and sometimes alien space familiar and tangible; words created a reality we could get our minds around. We can now "surf the Web" for recreation and enjoyment, taking pride in our ability to get around in a place that language has created for us. We may not have the expertise of a "web-master" (or hacker), but at least we are becoming comfortable. We can continue to act and to explore as long as the "platforms," "servers," "files, "folders," "Web sites," and "nets" give physical attributes to otherwise unfathomable space. Years from now electronic language, which seems very new and raw today, will carry with it the story of our struggles to adapt to this new territory. More important the language itself will shape the way we think about that territory, and we will begin to apply those conceptions of space and time to other aspects of our lives. Language and thought are inseparable.

We refer to the "culture" of the computer world or the "world" of car racers or professors; those words carry with them an understanding that people consciously or unconsciously shape their language to their environment and indeed shape the thought content of the environment itself. We know that if we walk into a roomfull of hackers or car racers or nurses or professors that we may not understand a good deal of what is being said. To become members of those communities, we must learn what members do, and in learning what they do, we learn their language. Also, as you will see as you move through this book, language will encourage some kinds of thinking and exclude others. Language flows naturally from activity, and that is as true of colleges and universities as of any other community or job site you will encounter. Learn what the people of these institutions do, and the language will follow.

The work of the university is to increase our knowledge, to search for truth, and to pass on both the knowledge and the search to successive generations. The work of the college is to prepare students for further academic work or to apply the knowledge gained by researchers to many occupations and professions. Those applying the knowledge to the practical tasks of life pass that knowledge, revised by experience, back to the universities and colleges. Higher education, in other words, teaches you to participate in the continuous process of making, applying, and revising truth. We all want "the truth," whether about the latest rumor heard in school, the latest auto sales pitch, or global warming, and most of us are wary about the clothing "truth" wears in the first two cases, but are bewildered and confused by conflicting accounts of global warming. This last is the scientific domain—a domain we believe produces certainties. Until we have been a part of the process of knowledge-making, we have little sense of how the knowledge in lectures and textbooks comes to be or why it can be contradictory, temporary, or confused. Texts present the latest best explanations as information, and many students believe that if they simply absorb enough information they ought to be equipped to deal with their work after college; thus arises a great misunderstanding. No carpenter's apprentice would believe that if the number of fasteners—nails, screws, bolts, and so on—were cataloged then that person would become a good carpenter. If the apprentice memorized what jobs require, he or she might get by until a job arose that didn't fit the categories. But to move beyond that point, the apprentice must be able to solve, using technical knowledge, the new and unexpected problems that present themselves. To know a screw is to know nothing without the job it is being given to do. The carpenter's apprentice must know, however intuitively, the physics of the situation and how to apply his or her knowledge to it. The apprentice also knows that however complete that knowledge seems, experience can prove it wrong. Similarly memorizing information and imitating language may get you through the examination of any given course, but it will not give you the kind of knowledge you can apply to a new situation; it will not make you a solver of problems in any field. When people complain that college didn't prepare them for their work, they often mean that it did not provide prepackaged solutions to the problems they encountered in their work beyond college. No such solutions exist; what training in analytical writing can provide is the ability to ask the right questions, identify the problem, research the solutions of others, and adapt them successfully to your specific situation, thereby contributing to the ever-evolving knowledge of your field.

Students must understand the changing nature of knowledge by understanding how it evolves, by understanding the inquiry process. They will also learn to adapt their language by performing the tasks, by writing the process of inquiry rather than through the dangerous and misleading process of imitation. Professors certainly want to know that you have understood the material in the readings and lectures, but that is not enough. They want to know that you have thought about it and more: They want to know that you have thought about it using the methods that in their field make thinking rigorous, systematic, and reliable. The knowledge evolved through the inquiry process is deserving of our trust because it has been arrived at through careful observation and rigorous analysis, not because it is permanent or absolute. The language of university and college communities has been honed to the job of reporting observation precisely and accurately and of performing careful analysis of thinking. It is the language of argument, but argument in the Greek philosophers' sense—the examination of observation and reasoning to arrive at truth—not argument to defend one's own position or persuade others to our beliefs. This key difference between personal belief and researched claim becomes evident as you participate in the research and reasoning activities yourself and discover the way they modify your beliefs, as well as your writing.

The belief in the kind of knowledge that comes from observation and reason dates from the Greek philosophers, defines the Western tradition, and is the common root of the inquiry processes across the disciplines of the colleges and universities. The empirical tradition, the tradition that relies on evidence from the external world, shapes the model of inquiry: from observation we draw theories, which must then be tested through further observation and application, which revises our theories and raises new questions. Whether you are developing or applying theories, researching the interaction of groups or applying the theory developed in a nurses' training program, developing a theory of stress or applying the theory to a bridge design, you must evaluate concrete results. This much remains the same; however, the results of the process vary greatly, depending on the discipline. How can this be? It happens because observation does not happen in a vacuum; it is always done with some purpose, to answer some question. Social science researchers are looking for a solution to group conflict; physicists are looking for ways to measure stress. Those who apply the theories are looking for answers to their own questions—sustaining morale in intensive care wards, preventing the reoccurrence of bridge failures. In all these cases, observation is shaped by the questions of the observer.

Questions are shaped by the discipline and vary first of all by subject matter. Traditionally subject matter is divided into three categories: the natural sciences, which seek to understand physical systems; the social sciences, which seek to understand human behavior; and the humanities, which seek to understand the systems humans use to create meaning and value. Within these broad divisions, the subject matter is further divided into disciplines: the natural sciences into chemistry, biology, and physics; the social sciences into political science, economics, anthropology, sociology, psychology, and sometimes history;

and the humanities into literature, languages, arts, religious studies, philosophy, and sometimes history.

There is nothing absolute or "natural" about the three divisions. As creations of the human mind, the creations of language, in fact, their boundaries evolve and shift over time and with the emergence of new understandings and interests. Historians, for example, may view themselves as social scientists or humanists depending on whether their goal is to make generalizations about the course of human societies or trace the development of ideas or varying interpretations of events. Some types of psychology, such as experimental psychology, fall into the natural sciences, whereas others, social psychology, for example, reside in the social sciences. In addition new understanding of the impact of human behavior on the physical environment, of the influence of biochemistry on behavior, of the importance of interpretation in law, or of the role of culture in knowledge development bring many disciplines together to study specific issues. If you look at the catalog of your school, you will see a variety of "interdisciplinary" departments, such as Environmental Studies, Asian or Afro-American Studies, whose activities cross divisional lines, bringing together scholars from many fields of study. Similarly a nursing program applies knowledge developed in biology, psychology, and sociology, and an engineering school from physics, chemistry, and environmental science. Categories, as we said before, are useful, but growth inevitably blurs and dissolves their boundaries. The Venn diagram (Figure 1) illustrates the interrelationship of the major divisions of the college and university.

To illustrate, imagine yourself standing in the center of campus (where you see the "I" on the diagram) with researchers from the disciplines viewing you as their object of study. Each would ask the same questions:

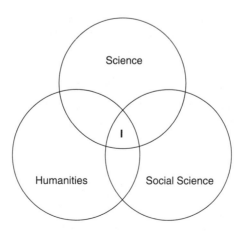

Figure 1   The Disciplines

What is it?

How does it change over time?

*Of what system(s) is it a part and how does
it interact with that (those) system(s)?*

Each, however, would gaze through a different lens. For the psychologist, you are a system in your own right, a dynamic of drives, appetites, needs, a self entering a new stage of autonomy. For the biologist, you are a biological specimen, the result of evolution, of the survival of genetic traits, interacting in a new environment, vulnerable to a host of new organisms, facing the need to adapt. For the sociologist, you are a new member of the student body, searching for congenial in-groups that will give you stability and help develop your future identity. For the political scientist, you are a new member of an institution that trains the nation's leaders, a future power-holder. For the historian, you are a member of that group that will carry the ideas and institutions of the twentieth century forward into the twenty-first millennia. For the anthropologist, you are a product of the culture or mix of cultures you have been a part of, and you are confronting the culture of the twenty-first-century American college or university.

The answers each of the disciplines gives to the question "What is it?" are shaped by the interests, and values and methods of their individual disciplines. Each discipline has developed theories, frequently competing or contradictory theories, to explain what you are, what you are doing here, and how you will interact with and adapt to the institution; those theories shape their questions. Exploring questions from many perspectives will give you a richer, more complete sense of the complexity of the world and a deeper sense of what is known and what is not yet understood.

More important for our purposes, it will give you an organic sense of the way language both gives us the power to create these categories—to reflect upon our world—and to adapt to the assumptions, values, and processes of users in specific fields and occupations. Inevitably that adaptation will itself shape our thinking. Inquiry writing in science, social science, and the humanities will focus, in turn, on different thinking and writing skills, develop different muscles, and extend your thinking and writing in new directions. Science's emphasis on observation and objectivity and the rigor with which it dissects thinking make an excellent introduction to your own observation and thinking processes. When you ask your writing to express that accuracy and rigor, your language will develop new levels of precision and clarity. As you move to the disciplines that study human behavior, with all of the ambiguity that brings with it, we will ask you to think and write about theories—applying them to your own experience, developing your own views. As your thinking becomes more complex, your understanding of sentence structure must grow to keep up. By the time you reach the humanities, you will already understand the amount of interpretation necessary to make sense of the world; studying the ways humans create meaning will therefore seem a natural extension of activities already begun. Because the subject matter of the humanities is perhaps the least tangible of all, you will practice one of the most difficult of writing skills—making the abstract concrete and creating form from ideas alone. You will, in short, move through the thinking and writing roles diagrammed in Figure 2. This progression is not intended to suggest that theory is not involved in science or that interpretation is not involved in social science and science. All three thinking processes are involved in every act we undertake to understand and verbalize; the differing emphases of the inquiry activities simply provide excellent arenas for developing particular skills.

At the end of the book, we bring you back to the world of everyday life and contemporary problems, within the university and beyond, and ask you to apply your newly developed thinking and writing skills beyond the confines of the writing course. We hope that you will find that you read the world quite differently, whether you are deciphering your paper assignments in other courses, the Internet, or the assortment of scientific, social, and ethical problems bombarding you daily at work or in the media. You will undoubtedly write in all of these areas, and we hope you will do so with a new confidence and a deepened respect for the power, importance, and, above all, the versatility of your own written language.

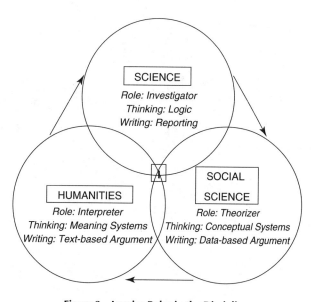

Figure 2   Inquiry Roles in the Disciplines

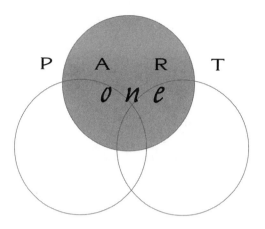

PART
one

The Sciences

one

Inquiry and Writing
in the Sciences

Why is the sky blue?
Why are there so many animals?
Why does that light bend?
Why do birds sing at dawn?
What started that fire?

GOALS AND PURPOSES

The questions of science are questions about the physical universe. From small child to scientist, humans share the need to know why things happen, and embedded in that irresistible spirit of inquiry is the belief that we live in an orderly universe, that events have causes, that life has meaning and purpose. Every known civilization has sought to explain, through religion, myth, or science, the order of their world, the cause of events, and the place of humans in the universe. Western civilization dates its birth from the philosophers of ancient Greece who, in the midst of a civilization that looked to the gods for answers, claimed that humans could discover nature's order through careful observations and reasoning. Though for centuries religious belief supplanted the rationality of Aristotle and Plato, their belief in the power of reason reemerged during the Enlightenment. Seventeenth-century thinkers such as Francis Bacon, rekindling the spirit of inquiry, held that humans, through careful observation and reason, could come to understand the laws of God, or, to put it in secular terms, knowledge uncorrupted by human bias. True scientists, Bacon argued, must cleanse themselves of the effects of human nature and society and approach the world with the attitude of the child (p. 294)—the curious, questioning, open child suggested by the questions at the head of this chapter.

Though modern science's view of the laws of nature and our ability to discern them are far more sophisticated now, Bacon's careful articulation of the varieties of human bias and procedures necessary to eliminate them in the quest of objective truth became cornerstones of scientific methods and of our culture's belief in objective truth. We have become so accustomed to this system that we often view knowledge as an ever-increasing body of certainties flowing from the laboratories of science, so we feel betrayed when medicine causes birth defects or when faulty breast implants poison their recipients. This feeling of betrayal arises from a greatly constricted view of the scientific process—a process that actually begins not in the laboratory, but in the field—and a superficial understanding of the nature of the knowledge it produces. Observation plays as important a role as experimentation in science, and observed "facts" depend on theories, on our conception of systems, to give them meaning. Thus, in "Storm over the Amazon," we find Edward O. Wilson, eminent twentieth-century biologist, sitting in the Amazon jungle, listening to the creatures of the night, trying to discover some pattern in what he hears, some regularity of form that suggests how sounds (facts) relate to each other.

> I would have been happy with any pattern. The best of science doesn't consist of mathematical models and experiments, as textbooks make it seem. Those come later. It springs fresh from a more primitive mode of thought, wherein the hunter's mind weaves ideas from old facts and fresh metaphors and the scrambled crazy images of things recently seen. To move forward is to concoct new patterns of thought, which in turn dictate the design of the models and experiments. Easy to say, difficult to achieve. (p. 52D)

Wilson's statements show the distance our understanding of natural systems, including human thought processes, has traveled since Bacon's day. Gribbin's history of the theories of light included in the readings that follow illustrates the way theories evolve, enlarging our sense of the complexity of nature and of the role of human perception. Wilson, a contemporary scientist, therefore gives a far greater role to the human imagination in the perception of new patterns and sees knowledge-making as an eternal process with no endpoint—no ultimate certainty. However, all three authors find the age-old spirit of inquiry spurred by the need to make order and meaning of chaos and to do so by remaining forever observant, curious, and questioning.

We ask that you join in this essentially human quest by becoming questioning observers as we take you systematically through the inquiry process, the scientific method used, as Jacob Bronowski said, to "turn the products of the imagination into fact" (p. 1). The process begins with observation and moves to

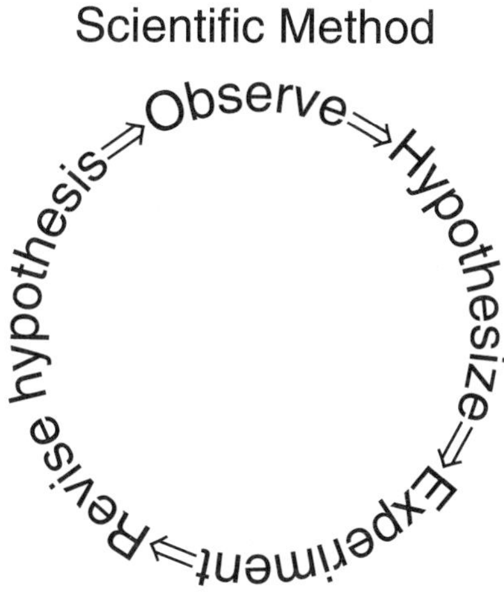

Scientific Method

Figure 3   Scientific Method

questioning, hypothesizing, testing, revising hypotheses (as illustrated in Figure 3) and continues this cycle indefinitely. Knowledge is accumulated through the repeated testing of hypotheses by many scientists; scientific knowledge is communal.

THE INQUIRY-WRITING PROCESS

We have made both informal and formal writing a part of the inquiry process throughout this chapter (and book) to give you an understanding of the way knowledge-making activity shapes both form and style in scientific writing. The notebook or log is the constant companion of any researcher, and in the writing class it is the arena for asking questions, developing thought, and practicing skills—in short it is the primary scene for inquiry. In these first informal inquiries, we use language as a tool of the observer and examine its relationship to objectivity through an exploration of Bacon's analysis of human bias. Though any of this informal writing may be developed into papers for a composition class, in the following sections, we explore the formal scientific studies and consequent reports that emerge at three different points in the inquiry cycle:

- Observation study and report
- Literature review study and report
- Experimental study and report

Whether you actually perform the entire cycle, you will be able to see clearly where the papers fit and how they arise out of the work of inquiry in progress. Because stages of inquiry are cumulative, each depends on understanding the prior stage; the discussions of form, language, and style are also cumulative, the description of each depending on understanding of the formal features of scientific papers at the previous stage.

Observation and Objectivity

Observation in the spirit of inquiry does not occur in a vacuum; it is driven by the need to understand, the need to know—driven, in other words, by questions. We use, as examples, objects for study in three broad areas:

- natural objects and phenomena
- interaction between humans and physical environments
- human technology

Choose one of these areas and follow the appropriate procedures in the inquiries below in order to understand language as an integral part of the observation process.

INQUIRY 1.1: OBSERVING AND DESCRIBING

Step One

Option 1a: Natural Objects and Phenomena

With a partner, wander about in some natural area relatively typical of your geographic region (shorelines, fields, mountains, streams, woods, etc.) until something (animal, vegetable, or mineral) catches your attention. Choose something other than human artifacts for the purpose of this inquiry. Agree with your partner on an object of study, then sit down together and watch it. Ask yourself what it is and why it is the way it is: Why is there a hole in that rock? Why is the trunk of that tree bent the way it is? What is that in the tide pool, clinging to the rock? Is that a beetle? Make notes of your observations and questions. Do not share your questions or notes with your partner and do not interfere with the object or phenomena—simply watch.

Option 1b: Interaction between Human and Physical Environment

With a partner, wander about your campus or neighborhood until you notice evidence of interaction between humans and their physical environment; this can be an interaction in either direction—of nature on human artifacts (rust, cracks, etc.) or of humans on natural features (paths, drains, smoke, etc.). Agree on an object of study, then sit and study it; challenge yourself to define the interaction and its effects precisely and consider various explanations. Make notes on these speculations, but do not share these with your partner and do not interfere with the object or interaction—simply watch.

Option 1c: Technology

With a partner, wander about one of your living areas until some piece of human technology or product of technology rouses your curiosity. Why has that bread turned moldy so soon? Was that tape player really a good buy? What makes that brand of pen your favorite? Agree on an object to study, then sit down and study it, asking yourself what it is and how it came to be. Make notes on your questions and speculations, but do not share these with your partner and do not interfere with the object or phenomena—simply watch.

Step Two

Each of you write an independent description of the object of study.

Example, Option a:

While walking along the beach, a unique shape caught my eye where it lay at the edge of the tide. It was a lovely shell, an elegant swirl of ruffled white edges against a soft brown patterned background rising to a peak. As I pulled it out from where it lay half buried in the sand, it reminded me of a sultan's turban. It is about two and a half inches in diameter, rising about two inches to its peak. The softness of the brown background, I discovered on looking more closely, is caused by hairy fibers clinging to the surface of the shell. These fibers had been worn off toward the peak, leaving the pearly white of the shell itself exposed. On the underside, concentric ridges of white dots formed the floor, swirling into the opening, a pearly passage giving a glimpse of the mysterious interior. Then suddenly, startled, I dropped it. It wasn't empty; a tiny hermit crab appeared, disturbed by my rough handling and scampered away into the water. I gazed at it, wondering what animal had departed this lovely shell, leaving it as a home for hermit crabs at the water's edge. Soon the waves will wash it up the beach where the sand will dull its finish, wear down its edges, and the sun will bleach it until its color is lost and it crumbles into sand itself.

Example, Option b:

The woods that lie between the main campus and the dorms are scarred by footpaths carved by students who won't take time to use the sidewalks provided. The paths are between two- and six-feet wide and most have been worn bare; cracked earth, light brown ruts are made bumpy by the rivulets of water that run down these same paths each time it rains. Sometimes, particularly in the spring, the earth in revenge turns muddy and slippery, waiting to suck in the trespassers; however, the wary students just circle the edges, widening the paths through the defeated forest. The newer paths are narrow, and on these the plants of the woodland floor—sparse, beaten down, and yellowed—still struggle to survive. We have so little respect for the beauty of God's order.

Example, Option c:

My Walkman™ is a new age shape, a silver oval, 2.5″ × 4″ with blips of color marking its controls. It fits into the pocket of my running shorts, out of my way and weightless. Its comfy headset has another set of controls so that I can switch channels or turn up the volume with a flick of the wrist. Neat. No need to fish the Walkman out of my pocket and fiddle while I run, tripping over a crack in the road because I wasn't looking.

Step Three

Exchange your descriptions. Have you written about the same details? Noticed the same features? Asked the same questions? Describe the similarities and differences in yours and your partner's descriptions.

Bacon's Idols

Seventeenth-century philosopher Francis Bacon would expect you and your partner to see different things and respond to them very differently also. However, though we might, today, call these differences evidence of our unique perceptions of the world, he saw them as the human tendency to distort reality in various ways (which he called idols). To catalog these human impediments to objectivity, he began with an examination of human nature itself and proceeded through an examination of the influence of individual experience, of membership in particular groups, of participation in inherited belief systems—all that we today would call socialization and acculturation—to exploration of the lack of precision of language itself. He argued that through rigorous training of our perceptions and reasoning, humans could eliminate all of these errors; whether we agree with this philosophy today (and it is still a matter of strenuous debate), Bacon's list of human idols or subjective tendencies makes us critically aware of our thinking processes of the multiple, complex ways we construct meaning and make sense of the world; further they demonstrate the inseparability of language and thought.

INQUIRY 1.2: EXPLORING BACON'S IDOLS

Try to find examples of Bacon's idols, quoted below, either in the descriptions you just wrote or in the way people make judgments in everyday life. To begin consider the examples below.

Idols of the Tribe

A. "Human understanding is like a false mirror, which, receiving rays irregularly, distorts and discolors the nature of things by mingling its own nature with it."

Example: Math is boring (i.e., boredom is not a quality of mathematics, but of the student).

Examine your descriptions for signs of this idol. For example, in the seashell description, the passage to the interior is described as "mysterious." Who is mystified? In the second description, the woods are given human traits (vengeful, defeated). In the Walkman description, is it the headset that feels "comfy" or the wearer? Mark these elements, then identify them in your logs.

B. "The human understanding is of its own nature prone to suppose the existence of more order and regularity in the world than it finds."

Example: Trouble happens to those who go looking for it (i.e., following the rules keeps us safe).

Examine your descriptions for signs of this idol. For instance, in Option a, there is a suggestion that the crab that surprised the viewer was not in the shell by accident—it had found a home there. The writer of the Option b example suggests that the woods have an order that has been disrupted by humans. And in the Option c description, there is an implication that having the right radio will keep the runner from tripping. In your logs, identify any underlying assumptions about order in your descriptions.

C. "The human understanding when it has once adopted an opinion . . . draws all things else to support and agree with it. And though there be a greater number and weight of instances to be found on the other side yet these it either neglects and despises, or else by some distinction sets aside and rejects; in order that by this great and pernicious predetermination the authority of its former conclusions may remain inviolate."

Example: College students will cheat if they can get away with it (i.e., humans are bad; the only thing that keeps them good is punishment).

Examine your descriptions for signs of this idol. For example, would the describer of the shell be easily persuaded that the original occupant of that shell was an invader in the tide pool and a hazard to its natural ecology? Would the author of the Option b example believe that some of the paths made by humans were beneficial to the woods? That the paths were made by animals in search of food? Would the wearer of the Walkman™ be easily convinced that its workmanship was inferior? In your logs, identify such subtle attitudes in your descriptions (both partners) and give the words, phrases, and so on that convey them.

> **D.** "The human understanding is moved by those things most which strike and enter the mind simultaneously and suddenly, and so fill the imagination; and then it feigns and supposes all other things to be somehow, though it cannot see how, similar to those few things with which it is surrounded."
>
> **Example:** Look at those bodies on the beach. College kids don't study anymore (i.e., the few on the beach represent the whole).

Your descriptions may or may not show indications of this tendency, but you can easily imagine what conclusions a viewer might draw about the world, the makeup of tide pools, the impact of humans on the environment, and the essential function of radios that Bacon would find faulty. In your log, draw some of these conclusions and describe the problem Bacon would find with them.

> **E.** "The human understanding is no dry light, but receives an infusion from the will and affections; whence proceed sciences which may be called as one would 'sciences.' For what a man had rather were true he more readily believes."
>
> **Example:** Anyone who works can make it (i.e., self-reliance produces success in all cases).

Again you probably need to look at inferences that might be drawn from the descriptions you have written. For example, do the descriptions for Options a and b imply that nature is harmonious—the empty shells of dead animals providing homes for live ones, forest thriving where they are untrammeled by humans? In your log, write as many of these as you and your partner can think of, giving the problem with each.

> **F.** "But by far the greatest hindrance and aberration of the human understanding proceeds from the dullness, incompetency, and deceptions of the senses, in

that things which strike the senses outweigh things which do not immediately strike them, though they be more important."

> **Example:** The stores at the mall are jammed, which shows that in the United States everyone is prosperous (i.e., the shoppers around us are more real than the millions unseen in the inner city).

Suppose you were to read in your local newspaper an account of your object of study which differs from your observed phenomena: an account describing the absence of life in the tide pools, the beauty of the natural areas of campus, a condemnation of the shabbily made "new age" radios. Think of such an account. Which would be more credible to the observers above, the accounts or their descriptions? Write a log response on this.

Idols of the Cave

". . . are idols of the individual man. For everyone (besides the errors common to human nature in general) has a cave or den of his own, which refracts and discolors the light of nature owing either to his own proper and peculiar nature, or to his education and conversation with others; or to the reading of books and the authority of those whom he esteems and admires, or to the differences of impressions, accordingly as they take place in a mind preoccupied and predisposed or in a mind indifferent and settled, or the like. . . . whence it was well observed by Heraclitus that men look for sciences in their own lesser worlds, and not in the greater or common world."

> **Example:** Experience is the best teacher (i.e., what we have lived is "truer" than what we have not).

Can you identify any element in your description that relates back to an individual experience, interest, or other quality uniquely your own? These elements can include the reason the object attracted your attention in the first place, your positive or negative attitude toward it, the words you chose to describe it. Mark them and describe the experiences behind your choices.

Idols of the Marketplace

"It is by discourse that men associate, and words are imposed according to the apprehension of the vulgar. And therefore the ill and unfit choice of words wonderfully obstructs the understanding. . . . But words plainly force and overrule the understanding, and throw all into confusion and lead men away into numberless empty controversies and idle fantasies."

> **Example:** Liberate the people of Kuwait! Save them from the Hitler of the Middle East! (i.e., "liberate the people" paired with Hitler makes the Gulf War like World War II).

In the preceding inquiries, you have already discovered that words are alive with far more than descriptions of the objects they refer to. Words carry the histories of the attitudes derived from your experiences and from the lives of those who have used them before you. They carry associations to other domains (i.e., "silky" brings with it images of richness, elegance, whereas "new age" connotes both a style and the pleasure of the author in being up-to-date. This unfixed and unfixable quality of meaning in language, the prismatic quality of meaning that changes with the light, is the very stuff that delights poets, and is the medium of their art. These are the qualities of language we explore further in the humanities section. But these same qualities make language problematic for science which seeks single, fixed meanings agreed on by all observers. The specific language problems Bacon refers to are (1) our habit of using the same word to mean many things (think, for example, of the number of meanings of the word "class," or "know"), and (2) words that have no concrete physical referent (beauty, love, hatred, etc.). See whether you can find such words in your descriptions.

Idols of the Theater

"In my judgment all the received systems [dogmas of philosophies] are but so many stage-plays, representing worlds of their own creation after an unreal and scenic fashion."

> **Example:** Doesn't make sense to me, but that's the way those (Muslims, Christians, Greeks, Marxists, Conservatives, Feminists, Mexicans, French) see it (i.e., "my" way of seeing it is not distorted by any such belief system as theirs is").

Underline words or phrases that associate the object with a religious belief, lifestyle, and so on. For example, the shell's association with the "sultan's hat," the radio's "new age" shape, "the beauty of God's order" disturbed by the footpath.

Objective Language

By now your descriptions should be thoroughly marked up with evidence of personal and social attitudes shaped by language. You are also undoubtedly aware of the way language shapes perception itself. Though we have inherited (probably from Bacon) the notion that "objective" is true and "subjective" is false, it is not necessary (nor our intention) to condemn subjectivity as Bacon did. Practicing objective language simply focuses our perceptions on the object we are studying, eliminating all other concerns as much as possible in order to answer scientific questions. To arrive at neutral or "objective" language (i.e., referring to qualities in the object of study only), language that means the same to everyone, is not a simple matter. The inquiry below will give you practice at developing more objective description and, at the same time, more objective perception.

INQUIRY 1.3: PRACTICING OBJECTIVE LANGUAGE

Return once again to the description you wrote and analyzed in the previous inquiries. Review once again to mark any words that suggest attitudes of the observer rather than qualities of the observed (the italicized words and phrases in the examples below). Change all italicized words to more neutral synonyms and remove phrases referring to the observer or to the observer's reactions. Now rewrite the description using neutral language.

Example, Version a:

While walking along the beach, a *unique* shape *caught my eye* where it lay at the edge of the tide. It was a *lovely* shell, an *elegant* swirl of ruffled white edges against a **soft**(?) brown patterned background rising to a peak. *As I pulled it out from where* it lay half buried in the sand, *it reminded me of a sultan's turban.* It is about two and a half inches in diameter, rising about two inches to its peak. The softness of the brown background, *I discovered on looking more closely*, is caused by hairy fibers clinging to the surface of the shell. These had been worn off towards the peak, leaving the **pearly**(?) white of the shell itself exposed. On the underside, concentric ridges of white dots formed the floor, swirling into the opening, a pearly passage giving a glimpse of the *mysterious* interior. Then *suddenly, startled, I dropped it.* It wasn't empty; a tiny hermit crab appeared, *disturbed by my rough handling and* scampered away into the water. *I gazed at it, wondering* what animal had departed this *lovely home*, leaving it as a *home* for hermit crabs at the water's edge. **Soon the waves will wash it up the beach where the sand will dull its finish, wear down its edges, and the sun will bleach it until its color is lost and it crumbles into sand itself. (?)**

Example, Version b:

The woods that lie between the main campus and the dorms are *scarred by footpaths carved by students who won't take time to use the sidewalks provided.* The paths are between two- and six feet-wide and most **have been**

worn bare; cracked earth, light brown are made bumpy **by the rivulets of water that run down these same paths each time it rains. Sometimes, particularly in the spring, the earth** *in revenge* **turns muddy and slippery,** *waiting to suck in the trespassers;* however, the *wary* **students just circle the edges, widening the paths through the** *defeated* **forest(?).** The *newer* paths are **narrow(?),** and on these the plants of the woodland floor—sparse, **beaten down,** and **yellowed**—*still struggle to survive. We have so little respect for the beauty of God's order.*

Example, Version c:
My Walkman™ is a *new age* shape, a silver oval, 2.5″ × 4″ with *blips* of color marking its controls. It fits into the pocket of *my* running shorts, *out of my way* and *weightless.* Its *comfy* headset has another set of controls so that *I* can switch channels or turn up the volume with a flick of the wrist. *Neat.* **No need to fish the Walkman™ out of my pocket** and *fiddle while I run, tripping over a crack in the road because I wasn't looking.*

You may now have a fairly "objective" description. However, to eliminate all observer influence, you would have to eliminate all references to actions not actually observed and all use of prior knowledge by the observer; such elements are in bold print in the sample descriptions above. If you review your description closely for these elements, you will find that the very act of naming involves reference to the familiar (turban-shaped, for example), and that it is sometimes difficult to separate the quality of the object from the reaction to it (i.e., "soft" brown color). The very difficulty we encounter in neutralizing those qualities, reducing the description to only qualities of the object immediately before our eyes, demonstrates how unconsciously we reshape the world to fit our preexisting systems, as Bacon warned. Indeed, such reshaping may be so much a part of identification that it is not possible to separate language from experience.

You will also notice, particularly in the technology description, that the observer selected details according to criteria he or she had not really examined. The radio's features, as described in the example, include nothing about the quality of the sound or the batteries needed to make it run. Convenience to the consumer seems the paramount consideration.

Thus the inquiry shows that to observe and to use language at all means to select features deemed important and to make abstractions that join the observed to the known—to name. Free descriptions, such as the ones above, illustrate Bacon's argument that our vision is both distorted and incomplete, but his idols also make us aware of the complexity of our meaning-making system, of our imaginative and associative as well as our logical processes. Observation and logic, then, do not in themselves give us objectivity; they make us aware of the inferences we have drawn, inferences that may be the source of error and therefore need to be tested if we are to approach objectivity.

The observer in Option b inferred from prior observation that the paths were made by students; that inference then becomes a hypothesis to be tested against further observation. The scientific methods developed since Bacon strive to do two things:

- To make observation systematic, so that all observers take note of the same features
- To design methods for making and testing hypotheses

INQUIRY 1.4: READING SCIENCE #1

Reread the John Gribbin chapter, "Light," and mark the following places in the experimental designs:

- The question to be tested and the hypothesis
- Procedures to ensure observation will be systematic
- Procedures to rule out all inferences but the one hypothesized
- Discussion and analysis of inferences

METHODICAL OBSERVATION IN THE SCIENCES

The purpose of an observation study and report is to continuously compare the evidence of the world with existing theory and knowledge in order to confirm or raise questions; scientific knowledge is in a constant state of revision. Observation studies are most appropriate for studying natural phenomena (Option a or b) because they do not subject the objects of study to any disturbance. They may seem less valuable for the products of technology (Option c), where the goal of the study is to assess performance, but they nonetheless provide valuable analytical thinking and writing inquiries for these subjects as well.

The purpose of this first study and report, then, is to contribute to or revise existing knowledge about your chosen object or phenomena. The following observation/description procedures should help you explore those questions as objectively and systematically as possible.

Systematic Observation

To observe "systemically" means to follow guidelines to ensure that we see all dimensions of the objects we are observing. John Gribbin's account of the evolving theories of light demonstrates how profoundly perspective affects what we look for and what we see. Newton "saw" particles; Huygens "saw" waves. Huygens's theory won out because it explained more phenomena, until quantum physics, viewing light as a function of a system replaced both (pp. 8–18). We include that history in the readings not only to illustrate the power of perspective, but also to show how complex answering the simple question "What is it?" has become in science. Indeed the three stages of the evolution of light theory—particle, wave, and field—have become a model for scientific observation. The model asks you to look in the mirror, see the unique bit of physical reality that is you, and to recognize that you exist as you see yourself for only a moment in time, that you are a system continuously interacting with your surrounding environment. The trimodal descriptions below respond to Bacon's admonition that our interests shape what we see; the method consciously shapes and re-shapes our vision so that we "see" systems by asking the questions basic to scientific inquiry:

What is it?

How does it move or change?

How does it function?

INQUIRY 1.5: READING SCIENCE #2

Reread E. O. Wilson's "Storm over the Amazon," and mark places where he considers identity questions, "St"; questions of change and development, "D"; and questions of systemic function, "Sys." Now mark places where he answers questions (presents knowledge) "Th" and places where he discusses what he does not know "Unk." Inquiries below ask you to revise your previous description by focusing on these three different aspects of your object. Revisit your object to observe it again as needed.

What Is It? Observation for Identification

These observations focus on those features that will help identify the object and distinguish it from similar objects.

Static Description describes the physical properties of the object in isolation from its surroundings, ignoring changes in time or similarity to other objects.

INQUIRY 1.6A: STATIC OBSERVATION AND DESCRIPTION

Your revised description in Inquiry 1.2 should be a static description. Reexamine it to eliminate any reference to its age, function, behavior, or to the purpose of any of its characteristics. Remove all reference to events prior to or after the period of observation.

Example, Option a:

This pyramid shaped shell spirals up from a flat circular base about 3.5″ in circumference to a height of approximately 2.5″. The ribbon of the spiral is marked with lateral ridges, which break up into bumps toward the outer edge of the spiral, which is fluted. On the under side, the spiral becomes a passageway to the interior of the shell. The overall color is coral, most predominant on the ridges and at the tips of the flutes and fading to a polished, pearly white at the peak of the shell. Many of the peaks of the flutes are chipped and broken, showing the pearly white interior surface and making it evident that this is a two-layered shell. The larger, lower portion of the spiral is coated with a gray-brown hairy substance, so that only the peaks and ridges show color. The whole is slightly rough in texture. The underside of the shell becomes pearly white and very smooth as it moves into the interior. The general shape and spiral appearance of this shell has given it its name—turban.

Example, Option b:

The woods, roughly one acre of maple, ash, and pine trees, that lie between the main campus and the dormitories are traversed by paths that range from two- to six-feet wide. Most are bare of vegetation; the light brown earth is dry and uneven, marked with troughs from an inch to three-inches deep. Some of the narrower paths are sparsely covered with matted, dry, yellowish growth.

Example, Option c:

This is a small (2.5″ × 4″) portable radio known as a Walkman™, a flat silver oval, about 1.5″ thick, with a headset connected to the main unit by a 6″ cord. The main unit is made of a light metal, weighing approximately 2 ounces. The controls on the case are color coded, red for power, green for volume, black for tuning, and there is a second set of controls in the headset, which are distinguished by shape: round for power, triangles pointing up and down for volume, and a notched gear wheel for tuning.

How Has It Come to Be? Observation for Development and Change

These observations focus on the growth and development of the object and on changes to adapt to its environment.

Dynamic description describes the object as existing in its present form only for a moment in time. It identifies those components of the object which give it its name and notes spatial, chronological, or conceptual change or variation. The purpose may be to describe short-term change—the object's life cycle—or long-term change, or evolutionary adaptation—its varieties. What are its boundaries? What characteristics are essential to the genus name you have given it? (When does a shell become a "nonshell"? How many trees in how much space are needed to qualify for the name "woods"? How does a "woods" differ from a "park"? When does a Walkman™ cease to be just a radio? In what ways can a turban shell vary and still remain a "turban"? How do Walkman™ type radios vary? What makes the identification of "Walkman"™ still legitimate?)

INQUIRY 1.6B: DYNAMIC OBSERVATION AND DESCRIPTION

Write another description of your object that focuses on evidence of its developmental stage, on observable changes, and on comparison with other similar objects in the observation area (as in the italicized elements below).

Example, Option a:

This coral-tipped pyramid-shaped shell has grown to *medium* size, roughly 3.5″ in circumference by 2.5″ high. *Turbans along the shore vary from 1″ to 6″ in circumference and from a rich brown to sun bleached white.* The shell *is empty, its snail having died, but is still in fairly good shape*—its spiral is intact, though the peaks of the whorls have been *chipped* and the protective coating *has worn away* from its tip. *Over time, as indicated by other shells on the beach, the sun will bleach out its color and the constant grinding of water and rocks will slowly reduce it to sand.*

Example, Option b:

Paths of varying ages cross the one acre of woods that lie between the main campus and the dormitories. The *narrower* paths are two-feet wide or less and sparsely covered with vegetation; the wider paths are up to six-feet across and *have been worn bare;* the light brown earth is dry and *marked by the rivulets of water that run down these same paths each time it rains.*

Example, Option c:

This 2.5″ × 4″ Walkman radio is *medium* sized, but *thinner (0.5″) than the average* by .33.″ The shape of the case and the color coding of the controls suggest that *it was manufactured recently,* but its cover is *dented* along one side and the color on its controls has *chipped away* in several places, *indicating considerable use.* All of the controls *still function* accurately, though the volume increase control in the headset *emits sudden bursts of sound when touched rather than increasing gradually.* This control also *wobbles* slightly under the fingers when being adjusted.

How Does It Survive? Observation for Function

These observations focus on the interaction of the object with its environment to determine its function and mode of survival.

> *Systemic description* describes the object as a system in its own right or as occupying a place in a larger system. The purpose here is to observe the way it interacts with and functions in the system of which it is a part.

INQUIRY 1.6C: SYSTEMIC OBSERVATION AND DESCRIPTION

Write a systemic description of your object focusing on the object's location, interaction with other objects, behavior, and so on.

Example, Option a:

This shell, home to a snail, lies in a tide pool along with anemone, barnacles, hermit crabs, and many other smaller shells. The pool is located in a rocky outcropping known as Campus Point on the South Coast of California. The sides of the rocks are coated with algae and the whole lies under water except at dead low tide.

Example, Option b:

The one acre of woods, maple, pine, and ash trees, that lie between the main campus of the Northern Michigan university and the dormitories are crossed by footpaths carved by students using it as a shortcut to class. The paths are between two- and six-feet wide and most have been worn bare, exposing the earth to the sun. The dry, light brown earth is carved by the troughs left by the rivulets that run down these paths when it rains. In the spring, when the earth turns muddy the students walk along the dry edges, widening the paths. The newer paths are narrower, and on these sparse, matted, yellowish growth still survives.

Example, Option c:

The size and oval shape of this Walkman™ radio allows the user to slip it in and out of the average running shorts pocket without snagging sharp corners on the material. The separate controls in the headset allow the runner to adjust the station and volume without removing the main unit from the pocket. The color-coded controls permit the runner to identify them without reading. The "U" shape of the headset can be adjusted to fit a range of different head sizes and to fit snuggly so that it won't become dislodged while running.

As you pick out the features of the dynamic and systemic observations, ask yourself how many of those features you can actually see at the time of observation. How many of your statements are actually inferences? How much and what kind of prior knowledge must you have to make the dynamic and systemic observations included in your description? Try to limit your dynamic and systemic descriptions to features that could be observed over time. You will discover that the viewer needs prior knowledge and experience to make even the simplest inferences about time, age, and interaction. Even systematic observation does not eliminate the human thought processes or communal knowledge; each of the perspectives, in fact, makes us aware of different aspects of our inference processes—of the way in which we name, locate objects (and ourselves) in time, and place objects into larger systems. Your descriptions, therefore, should make you sensitive to the accuracy of the words you use and to the inferences you make; you need also to become aware that even "cut-and-dried," "straightforward" prose includes many logical inferences that require testing for accuracy.

INQUIRY 1.7: READING SCIENCE #3

Read Timothy Quinn's article on coyote food habits and the Martin, Lawson, and Engebretson article on the effect of stormwater runoff on anemone populations, marking the following elements as you did in the Wilson article:

- Places where the authors consider identity questions
- Places where they consider dynamic questions
- Places where they consider systemic questions

Identify the hypotheses of the articles. What kind of questions are they?

Analyzing Inferences, Developing Hypotheses

Inference is simply the reasoning process you use every day to fit new experience into your preexisting knowledge system, your understanding of the world. In the earlier examples, the observer fit the shell into an already existing experience of the seashore for the same reason. She already knew the identity of the creature that crawled out of the shell and knew that hermit crabs make their homes in vacant shells. Thus we use prior knowledge to identify and explain new experience. Her description also suggests that she has seen shells of similar shape bleached out by the sun on the beach. In the environmental description, the author was already familiar with the changes in the paths over time and with the effects of the seasons on them. In the product description, the author compared the Walkman™ implicitly to other radios, radios that were heavier, bulkier, less convenient to use.

But relying on preexisting knowledge may also lead to misnaming and misclassifying. Categorizing people according to shared characteristics, for example, we call stereotyping, a word that clearly conveys our awareness of the hazards of such activity. By becoming aware of our own logical processes, we become aware of knowledge we have taken for granted without questioning— our assumptions—and of the logic we use in drawing inferences about identity, classification, and causation. Scientific methods of observational inquiry give us procedures for catching our mistakes by first turning inferences into questions, analyzing the reasoning for our choices, then developing hypotheses for testing, both against existing knowledge and through experiment. The inquiry below takes you through this process.

INQUIRY 1.8: QUESTIONING, ANALYZING, HYPOTHESIZING

1. Questioning

Examine your descriptions and turn all of your inferences into questions. You will notice that each description raises its own type of question:

Static: Identity Questions

> **Examples:** Is it a shell? Is the animal that jumped out of the shell a crab? Is that a woodland, a footpath? Is this a radio?

Dynamic: Developmental and Evolutionary Questions

> **Examples:** Do chips (in the shell) bare earth (of the paths), and dents (on the radio) denote age? Does the wobble in the controls reflect wear?

Systemic: Function and Interaction Questions

> **Examples:** Was the passageway home to the crab? Were the footpaths made by humans? Does foot traffic damage growth? Is function (of radio controls) easier to identify by color than by words?

2. Analyzing

Identification

What else might it be? To develop an "operational" definition of your object of study, make a list of the characteristics essential to your identification, characteristics that distinguish your object from similar ones.

> **Examples:** What distinguishes a snail shell from a mollusk? What distinguishes a footpath from a waterway? What distinguishes a Walkman™ radio from a portable radio?

Refine your list of characteristics so that it rules out similar phenomena or objects.

Development

How did you identify age? List the evidence of age. Could those features be caused by anything else?

Examples: Could chips on the shell be caused by attack? Could the dents in the radio come from being dropped? Could the small size of the shell be from mal-nourishment? Could the paths be narrower because the terrain is more difficult?

Look for additional evidence that will help distinguish cause.

Examples: The chips are all over the shell and are small, smooth sided, indicating gradual occurrence over time. There are many other shells with similar markings of wear. There is a patina of faint scratches on the metal of the radio, indicating wear rather than accident. Size is relative to age in all developing species.

Variation

What distinguishes a variety from a different species? Check the list of characteristics in your Identity entry, then make a list of characteristics that can vary without changing the identifying name.

Examples: The size, color, and external shape of a snail shell, but it must retain an internal passageway.

The length and width, of a footpath, but it must be bare of growth and flatter than a waterway.

The color, material, and shape of a Walkman™ radio, but it must be within a certain weight and size range and have a headset.

Function and Interaction

What is the evidence for your inferences on function? Could that evidence be caused by anything else? A sign of any other function? Consider each of the basic functions of living things: nourishment, protection of self and young, reproduction.

Examples: The location of the shell (evidence) means that the tide pool is its habitat (function). Could it have been dropped there? Could the path have any function other than as a short-cut? Food gathering? Protection? Is the shape of the radio influenced by factors other than convenience?

List the other possible functions and give your evidence and reasoning for your choice.

Example: There are other similar shells in the tide pool, indicating it was not dropped there. The citizens of this neighborhood feed in the dorms. The campus is protected by gateways.

3. Developing Hypotheses

Now give what you believe is the best or most probable answer to each question, spelling out the evidence and logic supporting your choice. Such answers may be based on prior knowledge ("because we studied hermit crabs in Biology"), observation ("I've watched the paths widen over time"), or reasoning (sun bleaches lawn furniture, my hair, everything I see around me on the beach). They should also, however, result from your careful reexamination of your choices above.

These well-reasoned but untested answers become either the evidence for your claims in the observation report below or hypotheses for further testing against existing knowledge and through experiment. You should now be ready to share the results of your observation study with other scientists.

FORMAL WRITING IN THE SCIENCES

If you keep in mind that formal science reports are the means of sharing the results of research with other scientists and of discussing the significance of findings in relation to the findings of others, you will find the conventions and formal requirements much more understandable. If you fall back into your more "normal" mode of student following instructions, you will find the job much more confusing and difficult. You are a scientist reporting to other scientists studying related phenomena.

The Formal Observation Report

We will discuss the form and content of the reports at three levels:

- *Global* level, describing principles that shape the overall form and logic to the report;
- *Local* level, describing features of the individual sections of the reports and the logic guiding paragraph organization and content;
- *Surface* level, describing the characteristics of the prose.

The interdependence of these levels as well as their dependence on the inquiry process that shapes the whole will become evident as we move through them.

Global Features

The overall focus, form, and tone of any piece of writing is shaped by the following factors:

- Purpose
- Audience
- Activity

Purpose   The observation report compares your observations and hypotheses with those of other scientists in order to confirm or raise questions about existing knowledge in the basic areas defined in the observation inquiries:

- Identification
- Development and change
- Systemic interaction and function

Audience   Other scientists interested in the same phenomena. Though it may be that the questions above can only be finally answered in the laboratory, much of what we know from encyclopedias and field guides comes from naturalists in the field, from the pooled observations of hundreds of scientists working in differing locations and times. Your observations, therefore, add to or raise questions about knowledge accumulated by others.

Form   Remember an old adage—form follows function. Keep that in mind and you will master composition, along with many other arts and sciences.

The form of this paper is a report shaped by the scientific method of the observation study, each section comprising a separate stage in the inquiry process. Therefore, the report uses headings, so that researchers can find the stage of inquiry they wish quickly. You can visualize the overall form as answering the following series of questions:

Question	*Section*
What object and issue are under study?	Title
What type of study, object, issue, method, results?	Abstract
What are you studying and why?	Introduction
What did you do?	Method
What did you find out (see)?	Results
What do results mean?	Discussion
What should be done next?	Conclusion
Where did prior knowledge come from?	References

Use headings to separate the sections and use running heads and page numbers.

INQUIRY 1.9: READING FOR GLOBAL FEATURES

Identify the global elements in the Quinn and Martin articles.

Local Features

Each section of the report deals with a different stage of the inquiry process and performs a distinct function, as follows:

Title Page
Titles in science and most social science writing are descriptive rather than rhetorical, that is, they are designed to give information, not to attract attention or to create dramatic or persuasive effect.

> **Example**
> *Descriptive:* "Turban Population Decrease on the Southern California Coastline."
> *Rhetorical:* "Our Withering Coastlines," or "Death in the Tide Pools."

INQUIRY 1.10: SCIENTIFIC AND RHETORICAL TITLES

1. Rewrite the title of the Quinn and Martin articles as rhetorical titles.
2. What kind of a title is E. O. Wilson's *Why?*

Abstract
An overview of the whole. A *concise* statement of the *type* of study, its *purpose, method,* and *results.*

   The abstract gives researchers a quick overview of your work so that they can see at a glance its relevance to their own work. Writing the abstract is an excellent exercise in compression, but since it is a freeze-dried version of the whole, you will find it easier to write when you have finished at least the first draft of the report as a whole.

> **Example**
> SYMBIOSIS BETWEEN A SEA ANEMONE AND A SCAPHOPOD:
> REDUCING THE DIFFICULTY OF DEEP SEA LIFE?
>
> A. K. Wakefield Pagels and D. G. Fautin, University Kansas, Lawrence.
>
> At the site 4100 m deep and 200 km off the California coast, a sea anemone occurs only on shells of living scaphopods; most scaphopods have or have had an anemone. The scaphopod belongs to a new species or possibly a new genus;

taxonomy of the anemone is under study. In this soft-bottom[ed] habitat, the shell provides a firm substratum for anemone attachment, and the scaphopod may transport the anemone to food. The anemone may protect the mollusc from predation, and may prevent sea water from contacting the shell, which can dissolve readily at this site near the calcium carbonate compensation depth. Because the scaphopod is trawled, we infer it is atypical in living on the surface rather than burrowing into the sediment. This inference is consistent with the anemone's being wrapped around the shell—carrying the anemone through sediment would be a drag.

Introduction

A statement of the object and purpose of your study and the specific questions on identification, behavior, variation, and interaction that you sought to answer should comprise the introduction.

If you read about your object of study before doing your observation study, you would cite here what is already known about the phenomenon, what questions have been raised by others, and what gaps in knowledge you are trying to fill. You would, in short, write a literature review as described in Section V below. (See that section for further directions). If you began your study with experiential knowledge only, simply state what you are trying to discover.

Method

A description of your observation activities should be in the method, given precisely enough so that scientists reading your paper could duplicate your activities exactly.

Remember, observation is a method which can be replicated if done systematically according to accepted scientific standards. The trimodal observation technique is one such standard, but you must describe the rules for each of the three types of description. Include any activities that might have influenced your results. Does it matter that you searched the beach for an hour before spotting the shell you chose for study? Does it matter that it was low tide? That the wind was blowing at 35 mph? That it was June 21st? That you were cold? Does it matter where you were located?

Results

In an observation study, your trimodal descriptions constitute your results. They describe what you saw as thoroughly and completely and objectively as your chosen method can.

The function of the descriptions you have written earlier is to convey the appearance of your object so clearly that another scientist could pick the object out of a field of similar objects and study the relationships you have reported.

The form, the paragraph, and the paragraph breaks in the earlier inquiries distinguish one type of description from another. The sequence of the text in each description must give readers information in an order they can process easily and in a way that will give them a clear image of the object.

- Begin with the overall shape of the object (readers need this in order to relate the parts to the whole).
- Relate the parts to the overall shape.
- Be specific about dimensions, color, and texture.
- Include all features relevant to that descriptive mode.
- Stay focused on the object of study.
- Give *information from direct observation only*, saving all inference, prior knowledge, and so on for the next two sections.

To test your paragraphs read them to a classmate other than your study partner and see if he or she can draw a picture of the object in its environment from your description.

Discussion

What do your observations mean? Organize this section according to the static, dynamic, and systemic questions and hypotheses you developed in Inquiry 1.4. Draft separate paragraphs on identity, development, adaptation, systemic interaction, and hypothesizing and explain the reasoning behind your hypotheses. Draw this information from Inquiry 1.4.

> **Example**
>
> This spiral shell is almost certainly the shell of a sea-going snail. Although the external shape and texture and color are unusual, the internal passageway is identical, in both shape, color, and texture to other known snail shells. Several other shells of the same shape and markings but of varying sizes were found along the shore, along with many other snail shells, again leading to the conclusion that this too is a snail.
>
> Exploration of surrounding tide pools revealed shells of this variety ranging in size from ¾″ to 5″. The colors on the smaller shells were darker than that of the object of study, while the larger shells varied from similar to the study shell but bleached almost white. The bleached shell was up from the high tide line and pock marked with holes and scratches. This evidence suggests that the study shell, which is medium sized and colored and fairly undamaged is from the middle of the lifespan of this animal and has not been out of the water for very long. All the shells of this type found on shore were empty, suggesting that the animal doesn't actually live in the tide pools where we found them (i.e., that the shells only wash ashore when empty).

Though in its native habitat, presumably on the ocean bed, the shell clearly functions as protection for some variety of snail, in the tide pool its function seems to provide protection for small crabs. Hermit crabs were observed scampering in and out of these shells in several tide pools. Some old shells had barnacles growing on them, suggesting that they function as anchor surfaces for these animals as well. Since the snail itself was missing from all of the shells observed, we have no further knowledge of its eating or mating habits.

Conclusion

From the uncertainties of your Discussion section, gather questions for further study.

Example

This variety of shell seems common to this location, but further study is needed to determine whether the snail itself is native to this environment or whether the number of such shells on the beach is caused by some change in ocean conditions. More research is also needed to learn more about its native habitat and habits.

Surface Features

"Elegance" in science is that explanation that accounts for the most with the least. Sensitivity to the prose principles of precision, clarity, and efficiency described and developed in this section will lead you toward that kind of elegance in your writing. These principles apply to all writing, but scientific writing is an excellent place to develop an eye for these characteristics; not only do they represent prime values in science, but they are also central to the structure of language. Your purpose, in this paper and in most scientific writing, is to render the external world as clearly and precisely as you can in answering the following questions: What is it? What is it doing? What is its effect? These questions serve the most basic of human language needs: naming things, describing action, and relating things to each other. This also, not at all accidentally, describes the basic function of the sentence: clear, precise word choice and a sentence structure focused on the actions of or relationships between objects.

Word Choice

Word choice has already received a great deal of attention earlier in this chapter when we discussed objectivity and the amount of subjective content in our natural language. Review that examination by doing the revision inquiry below.

INQUIRY 1.11: WORD CHOICE

Connotation

In Inquiry 1.3, you replaced subjective references with more objective terms. Go back through your first unrevised description and make a list of all of the words your partner underlined as suggesting the reactions of the observer. Next to each word, put a "+" or "−" indicating whether you think the word has a positive or negative connotation. Recheck the neutral synonym you used in your revision. Now go through your trimodal descriptions, doing the same thing.

Sentence Structure: Focus, Efficiency, and Precision

Sentences structure meaning. Too often, when students concentrate on "correctness," grammar becomes separated from meaning so that the rules seem arbitrary, and their application becomes mechanical. The rules then seem pointless because they have become separated from their function. The purpose of the sentence inquiries below is to reunite grammar and meaning, using a few basic structural principles.

>   *Focus*
>   - The power and clarity of the sentence reside in the central meaning-making unit, the base clause consisting of:
>   Subject—verb
>   Subject—verb—object or
>   Subject—verb—subject complement
>   - The order of these elements determines the focus, also known as "voice."
>   - The Active Voice order:
>   Subject—verb
>   Subject—verb—object or
>   Subject—verb—complement, focuses on the subject
>   - The Passive Voice order
>   Object—verb—subject focuses on the object

Whether you call this basic unit of the sentence the base clause or the main clause, the core of meaning lies here; everything else in the sentence is related to these key elements. For strength and clarity, the grammatical and meaning centers of a sentence should be one and the same. If they are not, your focus will be fuzzy. Figure 4 illustrates the difference.

In Focus		

Active Voice

Subject	Verb	Object or Complement
Words	*cut.*	
The projectile	*hit*	*the target* at 45 mph.
The light	*refracted* at a 45° angle.	
Submersion in water	*opened*	*the* anemone's tentacles.

Passive Voice

Object	Verb	Subject
The radio	*was*	*silver.*
John	*was cut*	by Sue's *words.*
The target	*was hit*	by *the projectile* at 45 mph.
The angle of refraction	*was*	*45°.*
The anemone's *tentacles*	*were opened* by *submersion* in water.	

Out of Focus		

He	*told*	*me* that Sue's words cut.
He	*estimated* that the projectile hit the target at 45 mph.	
The refraction *factor* of the light *was 45°.*		
It	*was reported* that submersion in water causes the tentacles of the anemone to open.	
The color of the radio	*was*	*silver.*

Figure 4   Sentence Focus

Note that it takes many more words to complete an out-of-focus sentence and that the words that convey the central meaning of the sentences have faded into the background. Note also that most of the words chosen as grammatical subjects convey only secondary meaning or no meaning at all; they are doing little or no work. The scientific standards of precision and efficiency can be applied here to good effect.

Efficiency
- The most efficient constructions are those where meaning is clearly focused on the grammatical subject—verb—object string and where each word works.
- Compression of meaning by removing excess words clarifies key relationships.

Use verbs that work.   Note how often, in the out-of-focus sentences in Figure 4 the verb is reduced to the verb "to be" or "to have." These verbs describe no action at all; they mean "to exist" and "to possess"—that's all—and are appropriately used either as auxiliary to other verbs ("I am writing;" "he is talking;" "I have written") or as subject complements to identify objects or describe characteristics of objects.

Examples

The shell	is	a turban.
The stone	is	limestone.
The radio	is	a Walkman.
The shell	has	many bumps.
The Walkman	has	few controls.

Sample Description

This *shell* is pyramid shaped. *It has* a flat circular base. *It has* lateral ridges running around the spiral. Toward the outer edge of the spiral these *ridges become* bumps. The *outer edge is* fluted. On the underside *there is* a passageway. The *passage goes* into the interior of the shell.

Compress meaning.   One characteristic of "to-be" sentences, such as those above, is that they say very little. By the standard of saying the most with the fewest words, they clearly fail. Once the sentence is properly focused on the subject and verb, however, it will carry a great deal of weight; try turning information into adjectives, where appropriate. You will also find that if you use active verbs, you can include more information in a single sentence rather than breaking your prose into separate information bits, as in the example below. In the sample revision below, the subject and verb are in bold italics, the adjectives underlined.

Example

Original

This *shell is* pyramid shaped. *It has* a flat circular base. *It has* lateral ridges running around the spiral. Toward the outer edge of the spiral these *ridges become* bumps. The *outer edge is* fluted. On the underside *there is* a passageway. The *passage goes* into the interior of the shell.

Revision

This *pyramid-shaped shell spirals* up from a *flat circular* base, 5.4cm in circumference, to a height of approximately 3cm. The *lateral ridges* which make the spiral ribbon *break up* into bumps toward their fluted outer edge. On the underside, the *spiral becomes* a *passageway* to the interior of the shell.

If the original version looks familiar, it may be because we often draft in the passive voice, bit by bit as we notice features, and must concentrate to convert our prose into a more condensed and active form.

Add words for meaning only.   Think about what you mean and your writing is likely to be clear and natural; think about how you sound and you are likely to start adding words to "sound more educated." Scientific writing, and academic writing in general, does sound wordy to the uninitiated, but, as you may have noticed from the inquiries above, much of the "wordiness" is detail needed for precision, not for "sound." It is also true that much academic writing is written for "sound"; the need to fit in is powerful in all groups, including the academic communities. The only inoculation against this very prevalent academic discourse disease is to structure your sentences to focus on your central point and then to add words only when necessary for meaning.

Examples

Active: Though she tried to soften them, Sue's **words,** because they were so unexpected, **cut** John more deeply than he would admit.

Passive: **John,** caught completely unaware, **was** deeply **cut** by Sue's **words,** despite her gentle tone.

Active: The **projectile,** the latest in the XXY series, **hit** the **target,** a rotating disk designed to elude it, at 500 mph, 50 mph faster than any previous test.

Passive: The **target,** a rotating disk designed to elude radar detection, **was hit** only by the last and fastest **projectile,** which was travelling at 500 mph.

INQUIRY 1.12. PRACTICING EFFICIENCY

Go through your descriptions and mark all uses of the verb "to be." Now go through again and identify all use that is not as an auxiliary verb. Go through a third time, examining sentences where the verb to be is the main verb and determine whether it is used appropriately—for example, to identify, as in the examples above. First identify the "real" subjects, the thing you are talking about (the "words" rather than the "effect," the "refraction" rather than the "factor," etc.). Then ask yourself what that true subject is doing—find verbs that describe action. Now rewrite your paragraph, using adjectives to condense as many features as possible.

Voice

Because English speakers are accustomed to hearing the subject (or focus) of the sentence at the front of the sentence, that spot is the natural, or expected, focus point. Sentences written in the passive voice place the object of the action in the lead chair instead of the subject. This structure is appropriate if you *intend* your focus to be on the receiver of the action rather than on the agent. The in-focus passive voice sentences in Figure 4 illustrate the effect of the inversion. Note that the passive voice would be the preferred construction if "John," "the target," "the angle," or "the tentacles" were the intended focus. If not, use the "natural" active voice structure where the agent of the action is at the head of the sentence. The central point is intention; make your choices actively, not out of habit or because one "sounds" more like college writing—to do the latter is to catch the academic wordiness disease. Use the active voice unless you *intend* to focus on the object of study rather than the agent of the action. This grammatical issue of style is most likely to arise in the Methods section, which describes the actions of the observer or researcher. Below is a Methods paragraph written first in the active voice and then in the passive.

Example

Active Voice

I went to the tide pools at Goleta Point on the Santa Barbara coastline on Saturday, January 10th at 2:30 P.M. The weather was cloudy, about 65° and the tide was low (−1.75). I observed a sand crab located in a tide pool for 30 minutes. During this time I did a field drawing and wrote a trimodal description, as follows: first, I described the physical characteristics in isolation from the surroundings; this is known as a static description. Next, I described evidence of the crab's developmental stage, any changes observed, and, after walking around the nearby tide pools, a description of the variety of crabs present. This is a dynamic description. Finally, I described the environment, including other animals, plant life, rock and water action, and the interaction of the crab with these elements. This is known as a systemic description.

Passive Voice

A sand crab was observed in a tide pool at Goleta Point on the Santa Barbara coastline on Saturday, January 10th at 2:30 P.M. The weather was cloudy, about 65° and the tide was low (−1.75). The crab was observed for 30 minutes. A field drawing was made, and three descriptions were written, as follows: a static description, giving the physical details in isolation from the surroundings; a dynamic description, giving developmental characteristics, changes observed; and, after examination of nearby pools, the number and variety of similar species in the area. Lastly, a systemic description recorded the interaction of the crab with animals, plants, water, and other environmental elements.

You may find the first easier to read and understand (a characteristic of the active voice), but the second stays focused on the object of study, giving the reader a clear picture of whether it is being manipulated or interfered with in any way. Thus there are good arguments for either version, and scientific communities frequently prefer the second, particularly in experimental reports where the object of study is being subjected to manipulation by the experimenters.

Literature Reviews

Literature reviews examine the state of knowledge on specific issues by reviewing the work of other scientists. Study the references to other scientists' work in the Quinn and Martin articles as models of this activity. The purpose of such reviews is to discover gaps and uncertainties in need of further testing. The form and placement of such reviews depend on where they stand in relation to the study you have done, and, indeed, on whether you have done a study at all or simply raised questions for research. If you have undertaken your observation study with experiential knowledge alone, the next step in the inquiry process is to compare your observation results with the knowledge gathered by other scientists. In this case you would discuss the result of such comparisons in the Discussion section of the report, as described in Example 1 below. If, on the other hand, you researched existing knowledge on your subject before you did your observation study, if the literature review produced the questions for research, you would review the literature in the Introduction of your report and then return to it in the Discussion section, as described in Example 2. If, finally, you are reviewing the literature independently of any study of your own, the review would become a separate article, not in study report form, as described in Example 3.

In Discussion Section of a Study Report

The literature review does not alter the global and local features of the report; the form and content remain as described earlier. However, instead of reporting the meaning of the observations alone in the Discussion section, compare the observations to existing knowledge, citing according to APA or CBE style, as described in the Appendix. Such knowledge can be found in field guides, textbooks, disciplinary encyclopedias, and on-line databases. Consult your reference librarian for sources specific to the field, either in the library or on the Internet; be warned, however, that general encyclopedias (whether on-line or in print) will not give you enough information. You need to explore disciplinary-based encyclopedias. Do not simply record the information you find. Instead read through the information and examine pictures in the field guides in order to test your inferences and hypotheses on the identity, development, and function of your object of study. Your paragraphs should discuss both the similarities and the differences between your observations and the reported information and draw new conclusions or hypotheses from this comparison. You may, as the first sample paragraph below illustrates, have more difficulty than you expected identifying your specimen. Don't let this complication prevent you from researching the other elements; frequently, as illustrated in the second paragraph, information on reproduction, growth, and habitat will help to confirm or refute your identification.

Example 1
These shells match those in *Peterson's Guide* to Pacific Coast Shells in shape, but are tan to white in color, rather than purple (p.). Mussels of the color most closely matching the study shells are found along the coast of Mexico, rather than Cali-

fornia. The study shells were clustered, as described in the guide and their location on the protected sides of tidal rocks matches those in the guide. We therefore will identify the study shells as mussels, but further study needs to be done on the variations in the California mussel and the range of the Mexico variety.

Example 2

We hypothesized that because the mussels found clinging to the rocks in the tide pool were smaller than the ones usually served in area restaurants they were therefore younger. However, the X Encyclopedia of Marine Biology states that mussel size is related to the depth and temperature of the water, which affects the food supply. Mussels in the warmer shallow water near shore have less food available and are therefore smaller (p. xx). Therefore, it appears that the size of our study mussels may be related more to their location than their age. More study would be needed to see whether age was also a factor. It would also be interesting to see whether the size of mussels in the Santa Barbara Channel increased during the 1997 El Nino weather conditions when the temperature of the water increased by some 5–10 degrees.

Your paragraphs should still be organized according to identity, development and function, and your conclusion will still draw together questions for further research. Once again, be sure to cite your sources according to APA style (Appendix) and add a reference page, giving the sources you used.

Study Report Introduction and Discussion Sections

If you have researched your object of study in the library in encyclopedias and articles prior to your study, you need to synthesize what is known in the Introduction in order to lead to the questions you are trying to answer in your research. This is not simply a summary of the information you found; in order to raise research questions, to ascertain what is known and what is still uncertain, you need to draw together information from all sources on the basic questions: identity, development and change, interaction, and function of systems. In other words use the questions as organizing principles both for your synthesis and for writing the introductory section of your report. Be sure to cite all sources according to the principles and style discussed in the Appendix under APA style. In the concluding paragraphs of the Introduction, draw together the questions you have raised in the course of your discussion in such a way that they lead to the questions addressed in your individual study. Also give the hypothesis(es) you have developed and the rationale supporting it, as developed in Inquiry 1.4.

Following your study, in the Discussion section, you will need to compare your results with the literature you have discussed in the Introduction section. The basic questions can again be used as organizing principles for your discussion, and you will need to conclude each section with an evaluation of what you have added to existing knowledge, what you have confirmed, and questions your research raises. Be careful, once again, to cite all sources as described in the Appendix.

Literature Review Article

The third option takes you beyond reference works to scientific study reports and articles; for this type of article, focus on one or two aspects or questions and read a series of studies to discover what is known about that aspect. Such research may take place as the result of field research or without such research. As a result of field research, for example, students might read about the effect of water temperature changes on tide pool life, the recovery time of newly protected lands, or the reasons why study specimen seem out of their natural habitat. On one field trip, for example, the class found the beach covered with ladybugs. "What are they doing here?" they asked. The students' surprise was itself evidence that the beach is not the normal habitat for these insects, and several members of the class took them as their study objects. Only after library research on the habits of ladybugs did they discover that the high winds that had driven the students off the beach were probably also responsible for blowing the migrating ladybugs out to sea. Their own observations then became interesting data on the ability of ladybugs to survive such an adventure. A group studying the environmental impact issues might, on the other hand, read in the campus paper about a proposal to put a railing along the main path through the woods as a way of controlling traffic. Have similar solutions been tried? What has been their success? Finally, those evaluating technological products can pursue questions in standard reference works such as *Consumer Reports*, which reports on performance across several brands and types of equipment.

Once you have read several articles on your topic, you can relate the results of your own observations to the literature, and you are ready to write a literature review article according to the following guidelines.

If you have not done field research, simply select such issues from the literature itself and apply them to your own experience with the objects of study to arrive at confirmation or questions, following the guidelines below.

Global Features

Purpose
The purpose of the review article is to join a discussion on a given topic. It is *not* to report on a study, but to ask the question: "What is the state of knowledge on this question?" In the ladybug example above, the results of their observation research will help the students assess the knowledge they find in the

literature. They will ask, for example, whether the migration habits reported truly explain their findings, whether anyone has studied the survival of seagoing ladybugs, whether their findings match such research, or whether more study needs to be done.

Audience

The audience is once again the scientists involved in research on the species or question.

Form

This is an essay, the form generally used for the discussion of ideas, not a study report. It differs from essays in the humanities, which you are probably more familiar with, in that it answers the question, "What is the state of knowledge?" rather than the question, "What do I believe?" and consists of a summary and evaluation of existing knowledge, pointing out areas for further research. If you have personal convictions on your subject (the likely success of railings on a path, the virtues of your Walkman™ radio), turn them into questions—ask whether the data give satisfactory answers—but *do not* write an essay on your convictions. Like most essays there is a great deal of freedom on the form, but as a literature review, its focus must be on the literature. To help cross the bridge between the personal opinion essay and the literature review, we will provide more structure than would be necessary for experienced professionals in the field by dividing the paper into sections as follows:

Introduction
Summary
Discussion
Conclusion

Headings are optional, but the content below is not.

Local Features

Title Page

As in the observation study, the title page should be descriptive rather than rhetorical.

Abstract

As in the observation study, the abstract is a one-paragraph summary of the paper. For the literature review, this paragraph should include the issue under study, the confirmed and/or ambiguous aspects of the topic, and the questions for further study.

Introduction
The introduction gives the issue under study, its interest and significance, a brief statement of whether researchers have studied it or the way they have approached it. The thesis gives your evaluation of the state of the knowledge and what needs further study.

Summary of Literature
The summary of the literature pulls together the literature and organizes it according to the issues or aspects studied, the accepted findings, the controversial findings, the areas as yet unanswered. Do not simply summarize each study; focus the topic sentences of your paragraphs on the knowledge presented on specific issues, not on the authors. You may critique methods used or the nature of the results, but not in this section. As in the study report, keep your evaluation separate from the knowledge itself. Your sources, of course, should be fully cited, according to APA style of documentation.

Discussion
The discussion section evaluates the knowledge above and compares it to your own observations in order to confirm the knowledge or raise questions for further research. Such discussion may include evaluation of the completeness of the aspects studied (perhaps no one has studied the survival of the ladybugs), the methods used, or the fit of the results with your own observations. Raise questions for further study as you go along.

Conclusion
The conclusion summarizes the knowledge confirmed and explores the areas requiring further research.

References
The reference page lists the works studied according to APA style of documentation.

Surface Features

The standards of "elegance"—precision, clarity, and efficiency—hold here as well as in the scientific observation study. Reporting on the work of others, however, adds a dimension to the art of focusing and sentence construction for meaning: emphasis.

Emphasis
Focus on the issue under discussion emphasizes the knowledge; focus on the author emphasizes debate. Choose the focus you want and *embed* the other dimension.

Examples

Issue Focus

The *migration paths* of ladybugs, *as studied by Richard Brown, vary* according to climactic conditions.

Author focus

Richard Brown's studies indicate that migration paths vary by climactic conditions; Albert Denker, on the other hand, *did not find that path variation correlated with climate change.*

The Experimental Study and Report

Experiments are tightly controlled by ethical guidelines in virtually all institutions; please observe the following guidelines:

- Experiments on natural phenomena *must be hypothetical only. Do not disturb or perform experiments* on these objects of study or otherwise disturb them unless under the supervision of a scientifically trained researcher.
- Any experiments involving human behavior are actually social science experiments and are subject to rigorous ethical guidelines and protocols. We discuss these in the social science chapter, but do not design studies which do more than observe human behavior in environmental interactions until we discuss ethics in that section.
- Experimental design is appropriate for testing hypotheses on technological objects, so long as such experiments do not involve human behavior or subject humans to risk. The effects of alcohol and drugs, for instance, are therefore not acceptable objects of study for such experiments.
- All study designs should have the approval of your instructor.

Designing the Experiment

Research design requires rigorous thinking, for it determines, to a large extent, the value of your results. The exercise below only illustrates and introduces you to the kind of thinking required, so that you have an insider's view of the process.

INQUIRY 1.13: DESIGNING THE EXPERIMENTAL STUDY

(for Option a, b [hypothetical], or c [technological products])

1. First, decide on a research question. What do you want to know about your product? Do we, for example, wish to test the performance of the radio? Or, for natural processes, what do you want to know about the footpath through

the woods? How long it would take to recover if foot traffic were to stop? What plants were most vulnerable to traffic? The long-term effects of erosion?

2. Develop a hypothesis, using the method described above.

3. Record the specific, observable data that supports your hypothesis. What specific qualities of the music or voice tone are you judging? What observable evidence of wear and growth lead to your estimate of recovery time?

4. Describe the logic you will use in making inferences and judgments of the data. Enter the premises behind your inferences. In the case of the radio test, these would be the qualities of "good" sound (accuracy of pitch, tone, clarity, consistency across the tone range, volume control, etc). For the footpath study, the qualities would be the conditions that support plant growth in your climate.

5. Make four columns labeled, "Data, Researcher, Logic, Claim," and answer the questions under each:

Data	Researcher	Logic	Claim
Sufficient?	Manipulated object?	Other conditions?	Need qualifying?
Relevant?	Subjective criteria?	Other causes?	Too broad?
Measurable?	Influenced results?	Other criteria?	

6. Design an experiment to satisfy the criteria:
   - Produces sufficient, relevant, measurable data to justify your generalizations
   - Uses objective criteria and avoids manipulating the results
   - Controls for other variables (other causes and conditions that might influence the results)

7. Once you have designed the experiment, you will probably find it necessary to modify your claim or hypothesis so that it is not too broad.

Example

To test the radio's sound quality would require either a mechanical means of recording sound fidelity, tone, and volume or a wide range of listeners uninstructed by the researcher. Listeners would be provided a set of criteria and an answer sheet and rank the sound from 1 to 10 for each quality, probably comparing two or three other radios of the same size and type to the test radio. The radios would be played under identical temperature conditions, and play identical pieces of music, which would cover the full range of sound response equally. If the experiment takes place in a closed room, the claim would be modified to reflect those conditions and the specific type of radio tested.

The Experiment Report

Once you have completed your experiment and charted your results, you are ready to report to your fellow scientists.

Global Features

The report of an experiment has the same global features as the observational report and is divided into the same sections that respond to the same questions. The difference is that it reports the results of an experiment done to test a hypothesis.

Local Features

The content of the sections is as follows:

Title Page
As in the observational study report, the title should be descriptive rather than rhetorical.

Abstract
A brief paragraph giving the information itemized in the observational study report.

Introduction
A statement of the object and purpose of your study and the specific questions you sought to answer, the hypothesis you were testing and the rationale for (reasoning behind) your hypothesis.

Method
A description of your procedures, given precisely enough so that scientists reading your paper could duplicate your experiment exactly. Be sure to include the following elements:

- A precise account of the object being tested and objects being compared to it
- What you are measuring and how you are measuring it
- The experimental conditions (time, temperature, size of room, etc.) and be sure to include anything that might influence results

Results
A statement on whether your hypothesis was supported, followed by the numerical results, using tables, charts and graphs to present your results.

Discussion
A discussion of the significance of your results. Begin with a discussion of your hypothesis, but continue with other patterns your results show. Remember studies that do not support their hypotheses but instead report "negative findings" are just as interesting as those that do—perhaps more so. If your hypothe-

sis was not supported, what might be wrong with the logic behind it? Do your data show factors you hadn't considered? Does your study object differ from the norm in some way? How so? What difference might that make? *Explore* your data. *Speculate* on reasons for differences. Finally include a critique of your study design and the effect certain conditions or defects might have had on the results.

Conclusion

Raise questions for further research and suggest improvement in the methods of research. Conclude with a summary of what you know, what you find open to question, and what further research you recommend.

References

If you have consulted reference works or other sources, list them here and cite them fully in the text.

Surface Features

Strive for the precision, clarity, neutrality, and directness you have practiced in all of the inquiries of this chapter. Conventions on the use of "I" will vary from field to field and even from journal to journal, as shown by the readings of the chapter; however, the focus of your prose should be on the object of study and the logic of your inferences and claims, not on yourself as researcher. The Method section alone may focus on you as the researcher because it concerns your actions on the object of study. Don't make the mistake of trying to "sound" scientific or overly formal; the result will most assuredly be a fog of words that makes meaning obscure. Work to make your prose transparent to meaning, which means focusing on the meaning, not the sound.

MOVING ON

As we leave the sciences, we hope you will carry with you an insider's view of the ways scientists look at the world, the ways knowledge is developed in science disciplines, and the ways these attitudes and methods shape both the writing of scientists and their expectations of you. Many of the attitudes and values expressed in this chapter are shared by all of the disciplines within the university community as well. Your professors will know you through your writing, and they will seek, above all, students who are:

- **Curious.** Students who question their world, who want to know how things work, why things are as they are, and why they have the consequences that they do.
- **Observant.** Students who are alive to the elusive elements of whatever world they have chosen to study.

- **Open.** Students who understand the role of perception and perspective (both their own and others) in the formation of belief and are open to change.
- **Analytical.** Students who understand logic, the relationship between data, inference, and claim—in short, the nature of academic argument.
- **Collaborative.** Students who understand that knowledge is developed by many minds in concert.

Students frequently do not understand how clearly these attitudes come across (or fail to come across) in their responses to written assignments or that they distinguish top-quality students from those who simply follow instructions. These attitudes breathe life into your writing. What distinguishes the scientific attitude from the other disciplines has historically been its standards of objectivity, its belief that scientific method, if applied well, can eliminate human subjectivity. Other disciplines, particularly those where the subject matter itself is human belief, do not necessarily share science's unanimity on this subject, and, indeed, scientific opinion is itself now mixed on the subject.

In addition to the attitudes just described, the analytical mode of critical thinking will remain paramount throughout your studies. The central premise of this mode is simply that all belief must be tested against evidence. The nature of the evidence will change when drawn from the physical world or from human behavior or from the products of human thought, but data drawn from any object of study are still evidence and the rules of logic laid out in this chapter apply across the disciplines. University scholars are particularly aware of our resistance to data and ideas that conflict with our existing belief systems (Bacon's idol of the theater); openness to change is far easier to praise than to achieve, so the commitment to require and respect evidence is paramount. The model for argument used in this chapter, with its emphasis on the examination of the perspective of the researcher, the sufficiency and relevance of the data, and the internal logic of inference process will remain the model for argument throughout our explanations of the social sciences and humanities as well. The experimental sciences differ from other disciplines in their attempt to limit knowledge to the results of laboratory experiment, a reliance that simply cannot be shared by disciplines that study political systems, extinct civilizations, or poetry. Inquirers in these fields must rely much more heavily on the analysis of logic. Subject matter, then, dictates method to a large degree, but in all fields of inquiry, the examination of logic is critical.

Finally we trust that it has also become clear through the readings that theories—conceptual understandings of how systems work—are developed through the thinking of many heads. The scientists quoted in the Gribbin article on light, for example, possessed the genius to create a new understanding—to change the very grounds of the thinking in their fields—but they, too, were working in collaboration and in competition with many other critical thinkers as were Darwin, Einstein, Keppler, Watson and all of the other geniuses of science. Bacon's ideas about the possibility of objective thinking mark the opening days of scientific investigation; time now allows scientists to look back at the evolution of their knowledge and to accept the changes wrought by these geniuses as a natural and inevitable part of the scientific process itself. They also now have a far greater understanding of the role of theory. The evolutionary questions in the physical objects option of this unit, for instance, are based on Darwin's theory as are Wilson's and Quinn's questions. The points in the Wilson article that you marked "Th" represent tenets of evolutionary theory, the ground of Wilson's work. Topics in physics are similarly based on Einstein's theory. Because science agrees on a standard method for testing the validity of theories, including the universal standard of judging a theory by the amount it explains, theories win far broader acceptance in science than in other disciplines. Thus the controversy over the dependence (of the questions asked in biology, for example) on theory may not be evident in scientific writing. Though Wilson appears to treat evolutionary principles as truths, his studies in fact test them continuously and will inevitably change the theory over time.

As we move our explanation of inquiry and writing into the social sciences, however, neither the subject matter nor the systems under study are so clearly defined. As a result multiple methods and theories have developed in response to the difficulties inherent in the study of human behavior. Theory, therefore, will become a central focus rather than an underlying assumption as we move into our study on inquiry writing in social science.

t w o

Readings in the Sciences

INTRODUCTION

The readings in the science chapter introduce the goals of scientific thinking and writing, as well as the primary themes that will continue through the other units: identity, development (or change), and interdependence (or systems). Bacon introduces the key concept of "objectivity" by categorizing the ways humans distort "truth" and proposing careful observation and induction as the cure—or the way to objective knowledge. Edward O. Wilson presents a more contemporary version of the same principles. Wilson also stresses careful observation, but seeks patterns and views science as a continuously changing conception of systems rather than a body of certainties. Gribbin, in his essay, describes such changes in his history of theories of light; his movement from light as particle, through light as wave, to light as a variable in an interdependent system sets the framework used for all observation exercises of this book. The last two readings, the Quinn and Martin studies, apply the scientific method to specific environmental problems, problems involving the interaction of biologic and human systems. Together, the readings achieve the following ends:

- Ground scientific method in observation and induction
- Introduce the effect of changing perspectives systematically
- Introduces the key themes of identity, change, and interdependence as rooted in science
- Present science as an ever-changing system rather than a body of certainties
- Explore the nature of objectivity, revealing is complexity
- Introduce both theory and application in their appropriate writing genres
- Provide models for various forms of science writing

Perhaps most importantly the readings all present science as question driven, the product of active curiosity about the world. The rigors of observation, experimentation, and reporting shape and control the results of the quest but have little to do with the attitude of the scientist. The student paper selected for revision workshop demonstrates the spirit of personal curiosity, engagement with the spirit of scientific inquiry, and grasp of assignment's purpose, but offers opportunities for sentence-level work.

Idols of the Mind

Francis Bacon

Biography: *Sir Francis Bacon (1561–1626), a leading figure of the Enlightenment, was a lawyer, philosopher, and statesman. He is considered the originator of modern scientific method because of his insistence on observation and experimentation as a means to knowledge.*

Bacon argues that humans can achieve truth by drawing conclusions from observation using reason alone and avoiding human tendencies toward distortion and error. He claims these tendencies, or "idols," arise from (1) human nature (Tribe), (2) individual experience and taste (Cave), (3) the fuzziness of language (Marketplace), and (4) belief systems (Theater). The reading provides a historical grounding for science's goals and a framework for exploring the subjective/objective dichotomy. Though the language, being four centuries old, is a challenge, the reading is an example of theoretical writing.

APHORISMS
concerning
THE INTERPRETATION OF NATURE
and
THE KINGDOM OF MAN

APHORISM

I

Man, being the servant and interpreter of Nature, can do and understand so much and so much only as he has observed in fact or in thought[1] of the course of nature; beyond this he neither knows anything nor can do anything.

From *The Advancement of Learning, and Novum Organum.* New York: Wiley, 1944.
[1]By observation or reflection on observations.

II

Neither the naked hand nor the understanding left to itself can effect much. It is by instruments and helps that the work is done, which are as much wanted for the understanding as for the hand. And as the instruments of the hand either give motion or guide it, so the instruments of the mind supply either suggestions for the understanding or cautions.

III

Human knowledge and human power meet in one, for where the cause is not known the effect cannot be produced. Nature to be commanded must be obeyed,[1] and that which in contemplation is as the cause is in operation as the rule.

IV

Towards the effecting of works, all that man can do is to put together or put asunder natural bodies. The rest is done by nature working within.

V

The study of nature with a view to works is engaged in by the mechanic, the mathematician, the physician, the alchemist, and the magician, but by all (as things now are) with slight endeavour and scanty success.

VI

It would be an unsound fancy and self-contradictory to expect that things which have never yet been done can be done except by means which have never yet been tried.

VII

The productions of the mind and hand seem very numerous in books and manufactures. But all this variety lies in an exquisite subtlety and derivations from a few things already known; not in the number of axioms.[2]

[1]Followed.
[2]Principles.

VIII

Moreover the works already known are due to chance and experiment rather than to sciences, for the sciences we now possess are merely systems for the nice ordering and setting forth of things already invented; not methods of invention or directions for new works.

IX

The cause and root of nearly all evils in the sciences is this, that while we falsely admire and extol the powers of the human mind we neglect to seek for its true helps.

X

The subtlety of nature is greater many times over than the subtlety of the senses and understanding, so that all those specious meditations, speculations, and glosses in which men indulge are quite from the purpose, only there is no one by to observe it.

XI

As the sciences which we now have do not help us in finding out new works, so neither does the logic[1] which we now have help us in finding out new sciences.

XII

The logic now in use serves rather to fix and give stability to the errors which have their foundation in commonly received notions than to help the search after truth. So it does more harm than good.

XIII

The syllogism is not applied to the first principles of sciences, and is applied in vain to intermediate axioms, being no match for the subtlety of nature. It commands assent therefore to the proposition, but does not take hold of the thing.

---

[1]Syllogistic logic, the efficacy of which depends upon the truth of its major premises. In other words, it presupposes the truth of general principles, and so does not call for the discovery of new principles. Thus it could make no additions to the sciences. Inasmuch as most of the received principles were false, this logic only confirmed error.

XIV

The syllogism consists of propositions, propositions consist of words, words are symbols of notions. Therefore if the notions themselves (which is the root of the matter) are confused and overhastily abstracted from the facts, there can be no firmness in the superstructure. Our only hope therefore lies in a true induction.

XIX

There are and can be only two ways of searching into and discovering truth. The one flies from the senses and particulars to the most general axioms, and from these principles, the truth of which it takes for settled and immovable, proceeds to judgement and to the discovery of middle axioms. And this way is now in fashion. The other derives axioms from the senses and particulars, rising by a gradual and unbroken ascent, so that it arrives at the most general axioms last of all. This is the true way, but as yet untried.

XX

The understanding left to itself takes the same course (namely, the former) which it takes in accordance with logical order. For the mind longs to spring up to positions of higher generality, that it may find rest there; and so after a little while wearies of experiment. But this evil is increased by logic because of the order and solemnity of its disputations.

XXI

The understanding left to itself, in a sober, patient, and grave mind, especially if it be not hindered by received doctrines, tries a little that other way, which is the right one, but with little progress, since the understanding, unless directed and assisted, is a thing unequal and quite unfit to contend with the obscurity of things.

XXII

Both ways set out from the senses and particulars, and rest in the highest generalities, but the difference between them is infinite. For the one just glances at experiment and particulars in passing, the other dwells duly and orderly among them. The one, again, begins at once by establishing certain abstract and useless generalities,[1] the other rises by gradual steps to that which is prior and better known in the order of nature.

---

[1]Fowler gives as examples: "Nature does nothing in vain"; "Nature abhors a vacuum"; "each body has only one proper motion."

XXII

There is a great difference between the Idols of the human mind and the Ideas of the divine. That is to say, between certain empty dogmas and the true signatures and marks set upon the works of creation as they are found in nature.

XXIV

It cannot be that axioms established by argumentation should avail for the discovery of new works, since the subtlety of nature is greater many times over than the subtlety of argument. But axioms duly and orderly formed from particulars easily discover the way to new particulars, and thus render sciences active.

XXXVIII

The idols and false notions which are now in possession of the human understanding, and have taken deep root therein, not only so beset men's minds that truth can hardly find entrance, but even after entrance obtained, they will again in the very instauration of the sciences meet and trouble us, unless men being forewarned of the danger fortify themselves as far as may be against their assaults.

XXXIX

There are four classes of Idols[1] which beset men's minds. To these for distinction's sake I have assigned names, calling the first class *Idols of the Tribe;* the second, *Idols of the Cave;* the third, *Idols of the Market-place;* the fourth, *Idols of the Theatre.*

XL

The formation of ideas and axioms by true induction is no doubt the proper remedy to be applied for the keeping off and clearing away of idols. To point them out, however, is of great use, for the doctrine of Idols is to the Interpretation of Nature what the doctrine of the refutation of Sophisms[2] is to common Logic.

---

[1] Phantoms or apparitions; not false gods as in the Bible. The word is derived from the Greek word εἴδωλα, meaning spectres. That Bacon considered his doctrine of Idols exceedingly important is revealed by the fact that he has touched upon them in the *Advancement of Learning* and several other works, but nowhere has he treated them as thoroughly as here.

[2] Detection of fallacies.

XLI

The Idols of the Tribe have their foundation in human nature itself and in the tribe or race of men. For it is a false assertion that the sense of man is the measure of things.[1] On the contrary, all perceptions as well of the sense as of the mind are according to the measure of the individual and not according to the measure of the universe. And the human understanding is like a false mirror, which, receiving rays irregularly, distorts and discolours the nature of things by mingling its own nature with it.

XLII

The Idols of the Cave are the idols of the individual man. For every one (besides the errors common to human nature in general) has a cave or den of his own, which refracts and discolours the light of nature, owing either to his own proper and peculiar nature, or to his education and conversation with others, or to the reading of books, and the authority of those whom he esteems and admires, or to the differences of impressions, accordingly as they take place in a mind preoccupied and predisposed or in a mind indifferent and settled, or the like. So that the spirit of man (according as it is meted out to different individuals) is in fact a thing variable and full of perturbation, and governed as it were by chance. Whence it was well observed by Heraclitus[2] that men look for sciences in their own lesser worlds and not in the greater or common world.

XLIII

There are also Idols formed by the intercourse and association of men with each other, which I call Idols of the Marketplace on account of the commerce and consort of men there. For it is by discourse that men associate, and words are imposed according to the apprehension of the vulgar. And therefore the ill and unfit choice of words wonderfully obstructs the understanding. Nor do the definitions or explanations, wherewith in some things learned men are wont to guard and defend themselves, by any means set the matter right. But words plainly force and overrule the understanding, and throw all into confusion, and lead men away into numberless empty controversies and idle fancies.

XLIV

Lastly, there are Idols which have immigrated into men's minds from the various dogmas of philosophies and also from wrong laws of demonstration.

---

[1]This is a faulty interpretation of a saying attributed to Protagoras: man is the measure of all things—in which Protagoras implied reason as well as sensuous perception. Plato discusses the idea in his *Theaetetus*.

[2]See *supra*, p. 212, note 1.

These I call Idols of the Theatre, because in my judgment all the received systems are but so many stage-plays, representing worlds of their own creation after an unreal and scenic fashion. Nor is it only of the systems now in vogue or only of the ancient sects and philosophics that I speak, for many more plays of the same kind may yet be composed and in like artificial manner set forth, seeing that errors the most widely different have nevertheless causes for the most part alike. Neither again do I mean this only of entire systems, but also of many principles and axioms in science, which by tradition, credulity, and negligence have come to be received.

But of these several kinds of Idols I must speak more largely and exactly, that the understanding may be duly cautioned.

XLV

The human understanding is of its own nature prone to suppose the existence of more order and regularity in the world than it finds. And though there be many things in nature which are singular and unmatched, yet it devises for them parallels and conjugates and relatives which do not exist. Hence the fiction that all celestial bodies move in perfect circles, spirals and dragons[1] being (except in name) utterly rejected. Hence too the element of Fire with its orb[2] is brought in, to make up the square with the other three which the sense perceives. Hence also the ratio of density of the so-called elements is arbitrarily fixed at ten to one. And so on of other dreams. And these fancies affect not dogmas only, but simple notions also.

XLVI

The human understanding when it has once adopted an opinion (either as being the received opinion or as being agreeable to itself) draws all things else to support and agree with it. And though there be a greater number and weight of instances to be found on the other side, yet these it either neglects and despises, or else by some distinction sets aside and rejects, in order that by this great and pernicious predetermination the authority of its former conclusions may remain inviolate. And therefore it was a good answer that was made by one[3] who when they showed him hanging in a temple a picture of those who

---

[1] I have been unable to discover the meaning Bacon gives this word here. He uses it elsewhere (see p. 410 below), but we learn only that it signifies to him a kind of curve.

[2] According to the Aristotelian philosophy the four elements of which all things are constituted are earth, water, air, and fire, each of which has its natural place or orb. The orb of fire was placed highest and out of sight.

[3] Diagoras, surnamed the Atheist, a Melian philosopher of the fifth century B.C. *Cf. Cicero De Natura Rerum,* III, 37.

had paid their vows as having escaped shipwreck, and would have him say whether he did not now acknowledge the power of the gods. "Aye," asked he again, "but where are they painted that were drowned after their vows?" And such is the way of all superstition, whether in astrology, dreams, omens, divine judgements, or the like, wherein men, having a delight in such vanities, mark the events where they are fulfilled, but where they fail, though this happen much oftener, neglect and pass them by. But with far more subtlety does this mischief insinuate itself into philosophy and the sciences, in which the first conclusion colours and brings into conformity with itself all that come after, though far sounder and better. Besides, independently of that delight and vanity which I have described, it is the peculiar and perpetual error of the human intellect to be more moved and excited by affirmatives than by negatives; whereas it ought properly to hold itself indifferently disposed towards both alike. Indeed in the establishment of any true axiom, the negative instance is the more forcible of the two.

XLVII

The human understanding is moved by those things most which strike and enter the mind simultaneously and suddenly, and so fill the imagination; and then it feigns and supposes all other things to be somehow, though it cannot see how, similar to those few things by which it is surrounded. But for that going to and fro to remote and heterogeneous instances, by which axioms are tried as in the fire, the intellect is altogether slow and unfit, unless it be forced thereto by severe laws and overruling authority.

XLVIII

The human understanding is unquiet; it cannot stop or rest, and still presses onward, but in vain. Therefore it is that we cannot conceive of any end or limit to the world, but always as of necessity it occurs to us that there is something beyond. Neither again can it be conceived how eternity has flowed down to the present day, for that distinction which is commonly received of infinity in time past and in time to come can by no means hold, for it would thence follow that one infinity is greater than another, and that infinity is wasting away and tending to become finite. The like subtlety arises touching the infinite divisibility of lines, from the same inability of thought to stop. But this inability interferes more mischievously in the discovery of causes, for although the most general principles in nature ought to be held merely positive, as they are discovered, and cannot with truth be referred to a cause, nevertheless the human understanding being unable to rest still seeks something prior in the order of nature. And then it is that in struggling towards that which is further off it falls back upon that which is more nigh at hand; namely, on final causes, which have relation clearly to the nature of man rather than to the nature of the universe, and from this source have strangely defiled philosophy.[1] But he is no less an unskilled and shallow philosopher who seeks causes of that which is most general, than he who in things subordinate and subaltern omits to do so.

XLIX

The human understanding is no dry light, but receives an infusion from the will and affections; whence proceed sciences which may be called "sciences as one would." For what a man had rather were true he more readily believes. Therefore he rejects difficult things from impatience of research, sober things because they narrow hope, the deeper things of nature from superstition, the light of experience from arrogance and pride, lest his mind should seem to be occupied with things mean and transitory, things not commonly believed, out of deference to the opinion of the vulgar. Numberless, in short, are the ways, and sometimes imperceptible, in which the affections colour and infect the understanding.

L

But by far the greatest hindrance and aberration of the human understanding proceeds from the dulness, incompetency, and deceptions of the senses; in that things which strike the sense outweigh things which do not immediately strike it, though they be more important. Hence it is that speculation commonly ceases where sight ceases; insomuch that of things invisible there is little or no observation. Hence all the working of the spirits[2] inclosed in tangible bodies lies hid and unobserved of men. So also all the more subtle changes of form in the parts of coarser substances (which they commonly call alteration, though it is in truth local motion through exceedingly small spaces) is in like manner unobserved. And yet unless these two things just mentioned be searched out and brought to light, nothing great can be achieved in nature, as far as the production of works is concerned. So again the essential nature of our common air and of all bodies less dense than air (which are very many) is almost unknown. For the sense by itself is a thing infirm and erring; neither can instruments for enlarging or sharpening the senses do much; but all the truer

---

[1]A final cause is the end which anything subserves, that for which anything exists. Bacon insisted that final causes be ruled out of science, for to interpret nature in this way would be for man to measure God's purposes by what he himself would do, and he would thus make nature correspond to his own ideas, instead of adapting his ideas to nature.

[2]Bacon believed that a subtle, invisible fluid, which he calls spirit, permeates all matter, animate and inanimate, but is perceptible only in its operations.

kind of interpretation of nature is effected by instances and experiments fit and apposite; wherein the sense decides touching the experiment only, and the experiment touching the point in nature and the thing itself.

LI

The human understanding is of its own nature prone to abstractions and gives a substance and reality to things which are fleeting. But to resolve nature into abstractions is less to our purpose than to dissect her into parts, as did the school of Democritus,[1] which went further into nature than the rest. Matter rather than forms should be the object of our attention, its configurations and changes of configuration, and simple action, and law of action or motion, for forms[2] are figments of the human mind, unless you will call those laws of action forms.

LII

Such then are the idols which I call *Idols of the Tribe,* and which take their rise either from the homogeneity of the substance of the human spirit,[3] or from its preoccupation, or from its narrowness, or from its restless motion, or from an infusion of the affections, or from the incompetency of the senses, or from the mode of impression.

LIII

The *Idols of the Cave* take their rise in the peculiar constitution, mental or bodily, of each individual, and also in education, habit, and accident. Of this kind there is a great number and variety, but I will instance those the pointing out of which contains the most important caution, and which have most effect in disturbing the clearness of the understanding.

LIV

Men become attached to certain particular sciences and speculations, either because they fancy themselves the authors and inventors thereof, or because they have bestowed the greatest pains upon them and become most

---

[1]Democritus was the most important of the ancient Greek atomists who believed that all the phenomena of the universe were created by the fortuitous concourse of atoms in a void. Bacon says it is better to dissect by analysis actual material objects than to deduce from nature abstract general principles, which are almost sure to be wrong.

[2]In the Aristotelian philosophy form was that which makes anything, material or immaterial, what it is.

[3]This clause refers to Aph. 45, and seems to mean that the perfect nature of the human soul renders it prone to suppose more order and regularity in the universe than exist.

habituated to them. But men of this kind, if they betake themselves to philosophy and contemplations of a general character, distort and colour them in obedience to their former fancies, a thing especially to be noticed in Aristotle, who made his natural philosophy a mere bond-servant to his logic, thereby rendering it contentious and well nigh useless. The race of chemists[1] again out of a few experiments of the furnace have built up a fantastic philosophy, framed with reference to a few things, and Gilbert[2] also, after he had employed himself most laboriously in the study and observation of the loadstone, proceeded at once to construct an entire system in accordance with his favourite subject.

LV

There is one principal and as it were radical distinction between different minds in respect of philosophy and the sciences, which is this: that some minds are stronger and apter to mark the differences of things, others to mark their resemblances. The steady and acute mind can fix its contemplations and dwell and fasten on the subtlest distinctions, the lofty and discursive mind recognises and puts together the finest and most general resemblances. Both kinds however easily err in excess, by catching the one at gradations the other at shadows.

LVI

There are found some minds given to an extreme admiration of antiquity, others to an extreme love and appetite for novelty, but few so duly tempered that they can hold the mean, neither carping at what has been well laid down by the ancients, nor despising what is well introduced by the moderns. This however turns to the great injury of the sciences and philosophy, since these affectations of antiquity and novelty are the humours of partisans rather than judgements; and truth is to be sought for not in the felicity of any age, which is an unstable thing, but in the light of nature and experience, which is eternal. These factions therefore must be abjured, and care must be taken that the intellect be not hurried by them into assent.

LVII

Contemplations of nature and of bodies in their simple form break up and distract the understanding, while contemplations of nature and bodies in their composition and configuration overpower and dissolve the understanding, a

---

[1]See *supra*, p. 231, note 1.
[2]See *supra*, p. 212, note 6.

distinction well seen in the school of Leucippus and Democritus as compared with the other philosophies. For that school is so busied with the particles that it hardly attends to the structure, while the others are so lost in admiration of the structure that they do not penetrate to the simplicity of nature. These kinds of contemplation should therefore be alternated and taken by turns, that so the understanding may be rendered at once penetrating and comprehensive, and the inconveniences above mentioned, with the idols which proceed from them, may be avoided.

LVIII

Let such then be our provision and contemplative prudence for keeping off and dislodging the *Idols of the Cave,* which grow for the most part either out of the predominance of a favourite subject, or out of an excessive tendency to compare or to distinguish, or out of partiality for particular ages, or out of the largeness or minuteness of the objects contemplated. And generally let every student of nature take this as a rule, that whatever his mind seizes and dwells upon with peculiar satisfaction is to be held in suspicion, and that so much the more care is to be taken in dealing with such questions to keep the understanding even and clear.

LIX

But the *Idols of the Market-place* are the most troublesome of all, idols which have crept into the understanding through the alliances of words and names. For men believe that their reason governs words, but it is also true that words react on the understanding, and this it is that has rendered philosophy and the sciences sophistical and inactive. Now words, being commonly framed and applied according to the capacity of the vulgar, follow those lines of division which are most obvious to the vulgar understanding. And whenever an understanding of greater acuteness or a more diligent observation would alter those lines to suit the true divisions of nature, words stand in the way and resist the change. Whence it comes to pass that the high and formal discussions of learned men end oftentimes in disputes about words and names, with which (according to the use and wisdom of the mathematicians) it would be more prudent to begin, and so by means of definitions reduce them to order. Yet even definitions cannot cure this evil in dealing with natural and material things; since the definitions themselves consist of words, and those words beget others, so that it is necessary to recur to individual instances, and those in due series and order, as I shall say presently when I come to the method and scheme for the formation of notions and axioms.

LX

The idols imposed by words on the understanding are of two kinds. They are either names of things which do not exist (for as there are things left unnamed through lack of observation, so likewise are there names which result from fantastic suppositions and to which nothing in reality corresponds), or they are names of things which exist, but yet confused and ill-defined and hastily and irregularly derived from realities. Of the former kind are Fortune, the Prime Mover,[1] Planetary Orbits,[2] Element of Fire, and like fictions which owe their origin to false and idle theories. And this class of idols is more easily expelled, because to get rid of them it is only necessary that all theories should be steadily rejected and dismissed as obsolete.

But the other class, which springs out of a faulty and unskilful abstraction, is intricate and deeply rooted. Let us take for example such a word as *humid*, and see how far the several things which the word is used to signify agree with each other; and we shall find the word *humid* to be nothing else than a mark loosely and confusedly applied to denote a variety of actions which will not bear to be reduced to any constant meaning. For it both signifies that which easily spreads itself round any other body; and that which in itself is indeterminate and cannot solidise; and that which readily yields in every direction; and that which easily divides and scatters itself; and that which easily unites and collects itself; and that which readily flows and is put in motion; and that which readily clings to another body and wets it; and that which is easily reduced to a liquid, or being solid easily melts. Accordingly when you come to apply the word, if you take it in one sense, flame is humid; if in another, air is not humid; if in another, fine dust is humid; if in another, glass is humid. So that it is easy to see that the notion is taken by abstraction only from water and common and ordinary liquids without any due verification.

There are however in words certain degrees of distortion and error. One of the least faulty kinds is that of names of substances, especially of lowest species and well-deduced (for the notion of *chalk* and of *mud* is good, of *earth* bad); a more faulty kind is that of actions, as *to generate, to corrupt, to alter;* the most faulty is of qualities (except such as are the immediate objects of the sense) as *heavy, light, rare, dense,* and the like. Yet in all these cases some notions are of necessity a little better than others, in proportion to the greater variety of subjects that fall within the range of the human sense.

---

[1]The *primum mobile*, or outermost sphere, which gave motion to the other celestial spheres.
[2]The spheres to which the planets were supposed to be attached.

LXI

But the *Idols of the Theatre* are not innate, nor do they steal into the understanding secretly, but are plainly impressed and received into the mind from the play-books of philosophical systems and the perverted rules of demonstration. To attempt refutations in this case would be merely inconsistent with what I have already said, for since we agree neither upon principles nor upon demonstrations there is no place for argument. And this is so far well, inasmuch as it leaves the honour of the ancients untouched. For they are no wise disparaged, the question between them and me being only as to the way. For as the saying is, the lame man who keeps the right road outstrips the runner who takes a wrong one. Nay, it is obvious that when a man runs the wrong way, the more active and swift he is the further he will go astray.

But the course I propose for the discovery of sciences is such as leaves but little to the acuteness and strength of wits, but places all wits and understandings nearly on a level. For as in the drawing of a straight line or a perfect circle much depends on the steadiness and practice of the hand, if it be done by aim of hand only, but if with the aid of rule or compass, little or nothing; so is it exactly with my plan. But though particular confutations would be of no avail, yet touching the sects and general divisions of such systems I must say something, something also touching the external signs which show that they are unsound, and finally something touching the causes of such great infelicity and of such lasting and general agreement in error, that so the access to truth may be made less difficult, and the human understanding may the more willingly submit to its purgation and dismiss its idols.

LXII

Idols of the Theatre, or of Systems, are many, and there can be and perhaps will be yet many more. For were it not that now for many ages men's minds have been busied with religion and theology, and were it not that civil governments, especially monarchies, have been averse to such novelties, even in matters speculative, so that men labour therein to the peril and harming of their fortunes, not only unrewarded but exposed also to contempt and envy, doubtless there would have arisen many other philosophical sects like to those which in great variety flourished once among the Greeks. For as on the phenomena of the heavens many hypotheses may be constructed, so likewise (and more also) many various dogmas may be set up and established on the phenomena of philosophy. And in the plays of this philosophical theatre you may observe the same thing which is found in the theatre of the poets, that stories invented for the stage are more compact and elegant, and more as one would wish them to be than true stories out of history.

In general however there is taken for the material of philosophy either a great deal out of a few things, or a very little out of many things, so that on both sides philosophy is based on too narrow a foundation of experiment and natural history, and decides on the authority of too few cases. For the Rational School of philosophers snatches from experience a variety of common instances, neither duly ascertained nor diligently examined and weighed, and leaves all the rest to meditation and agitation of wit.

There is also another class of philosophers, who having bestowed much diligent and careful labour on a few experiments, have thence made bold to educe and construct systems, wresting all other facts in a strange fashion to conformity therewith.

And there is yet a third class, consisting of those who out of faith and veneration mix their philosophy with theology and traditions, among whom the vanity of some has gone so far aside as to seek the origin of sciences among spirits and genii. So that this parent stock of errors—this false philosophy—is of three kinds: the Sophistical, the Empirical, and the Superstitious.

LXVIII

So much concerning the several classes of Idols, and their equipage: all of which must be renounced and put away with a fixed and solemn determination, and the understanding thoroughly freed and cleansed; the entrance into the kingdom of man, founded on the sciences, being not much other than the entrance into the kingdom of heaven, whereinto none may enter except as a little child. &

QUESTIONS FOR THOUGHT AND STUDY

Explore the questions in Inquiry 1.2

Storm over the Amazon

Edward O. Wilson

Biography: *Edward O. Wilson, Professor of Science and Curator en Entomology, Museum of Comparative Zoology, Harvard University, is an evolutionary biologist who has spent his career studying the social and adaptive habits of ants. His groundbreaking book,* Sociobiology, *was the first to propose that social behavior is genetically programmed and evolutionarily adaptive. In* The Diversity of Life, *Wilson defines a new environmental ethic, arguing that we must rescue whole ecosystems, not just individual species.*

This introductory essay to Wilson's book emphasizes that science begins with observation of nature, not experimentation, and that the goal of such observation is the quest for patterns, which then become theories to be tested. The piece is a short, lively antidote to the notion that science is a storehouse of "facts" gained through experiment. The shift to patterns also updates Bacon's "pure" induction. It is the introduction to a textbook and therefore an example of a scientist writing to a nontechnical audience.

CHAPTER ONE

In the Amazon Basin the greatest violence sometimes begins as a flicker of light beyond the horizon. There in the perfect bowl of the night sky, untouched by light from any human source, a thunderstorm sends its premonitory signal and begins a slow journey to the observer, who thinks: the world is about to change. And so it was one night at the edge of rain forest north of Manaus, where I sat in the dark, working my mind through the labyrinths of field biology and ambition, tired, bored, and ready for any chance distraction.

Each evening after dinner I carried a chair to a nearby clearing to escape the noise and stink of the camp I shared with Brazilian forest workers, a place called Fazenda Dimona. To the south most of the forest had been cut and burned to create pastures. In the daytime cattle browsed in remorseless heat bouncing off the yellow clay and at night animals and spirits edged out onto the ruined land. To the north the virgin rain forest began, one of the great surviving wildernesses of the world, stretching 500 kilometers before it broke apart and dwindled into gallery woodland among the savannas of Roraima.

Enclosed in darkness so complete I could not see beyond my outstretched hand, I was forced to think of the rain forest as though I were seated in my library at home, with the lights turned low. The forest at night is an experience in sensory deprivation most of the time, black and silent as the midnight zone of a cave. Life is out there in expected abundance. The jungle teems, but in a manner mostly beyond the reach of the human senses. Ninety-nine percent of

From *The Diversity of Life.* New York: W. W. Norton, 1992, pp. 3–15.

the animals find their way by chemical trails laid over the surface, puffs of odor released into the air or water, and scents diffused out of little hidden glands and into the air downwind. Animals are masters of this chemical channel, where we are idiots. But we are geniuses of the audiovisual channel, equaled in this modality only by a few odd groups (whales, monkeys, birds). So we wait for the dawn, while they wait for the fall of darkness; and because sight and sound are the evolutionary prerequisites of intelligence, we alone have come to reflect on such matters as Amazon nights and sensory modalities.

I swept the ground with the beam from my headlamp for signs of life, and found—diamonds! At regular intervals of several meters, intense pinpoints of white light winked on and off with each turning of the lamp. They were reflections from the eyes of wolf spiders, members of the family Lycosidae, on the prowl for insect prey. When spotlighted the spiders froze, allowing me to approach on hands and knees and study them almost at their own level. I could distinguish a wide variety of species by size, color, and hairiness. It struck me how little is known about these creatures of the rain forest, and how deeply satisfying it would be to spend months, years, the rest of my life in this place until I knew all the species by name and every detail of their lives. From specimens beautifully frozen in amber we know that the Lycosidae have survived at least since the beginning of the Oligocene epoch, forty million years ago, and probably much longer. Today a riot of diverse forms occupy the whole world, of which this was only the minutest sample, yet even these species turning about now to watch me from the bare yellow clay could give meaning to the lifetimes of many naturalists.

The moon was down, and only starlight etched the tops of the trees. It was August in the dry season. The air had cooled enough to make the humidity pleasant, in the tropical manner, as much a state of mind as a physical sensation. The storm I guessed was about an hour away. I thought of walking back into the forest with my headlamp to hunt for new treasures, but was too tired from the day's work. Anchored again to my chair, forced into myself, I welcomed a meteor's streak and the occasional courtship flash of luminescent click beetles among the nearby but unseen shrubs. Even the passage of a jetliner 10,000 meters up, a regular event each night around ten o'clock, I awaited with pleasure. A week in the rain forest had transformed its distant rumble from an urban irritant into a comforting sign of the continuance of my own species.

But I was glad to be alone. The discipline of the dark envelope summoned fresh images from the forest of how real organisms look and act. I needed to concentrate for only a second and they came alive as eidetic images, behind closed eyelids, moving across fallen leaves and decaying humus. I sorted the memories this way and that in hope of stumbling on some pattern not obedient to abstract theory of textbooks. I would have been happy with *any* pattern. The best of science doesn't consist of mathematical models and experiments, as textbooks make it seem. Those come later. It springs fresh from a more primitive mode of thought, wherein the hunter's mind weaves ideas from old facts and fresh metaphors and the scrambled crazy images of things recently seen. To move forward is to concoct new patterns of thought, which in turn dictate the design of the models and experiments. Easy to say, difficult to achieve.

The subject fitfully engaged that night, the reason for this research trip to the Brazilian Amazon, had in fact become an obsession and, like all obsessions, very likely a dead end. It was the kind of favorite puzzle that keeps forcing its way back because its very intractability makes it perversely pleasant, like an overly familiar melody intruding into the relaxed mind because it loves you and will not leave you. I hoped that some new image might propel me past the jaded puzzle to the other side, to ideas strange and compelling.

Bear with me for a moment while I explain this bit of personal esoterica; I am approaching the subject of central interest. Some kinds of plants and animals are dominant, proliferating new species and spreading over large parts of the world. Others are driven back until they become rare and threatened by extinction. Is there a single formula for this biogeographic difference, for all kinds of organisms? The process, if articulated, would be a law or at least a principle of dynastic succession in evolution. I was intrigued by the circumstance that social insects, the group on which I have spent most of my life, are among the most abundant of all organisms. And among the social insects, the dominant subgroup is the ants. They range 20,000 or more species strong from the Arctic Circle to the tip of South America. In the Amazon rain forest they compose more than 10 percent of the biomass of all animals. This means that if you were to collect, dry out, and weigh every animal in a piece of forest, from monkeys and birds down to mites and roundworms, at least 10 percent would consist of these insects alone. Ants make up almost half of the insect biomass overall and 70 percent of the individual insects found in the treetops. They are only slightly less abundant in grasslands, deserts, and temperate forests throughout the rest of the world.

It seemed to me that night, as it has to others in varying degrees of persuasion many times before, that the prevalence of ants must have something to do with their advanced colonial organization. A colony is a superorganism, an assembly of workers so tightly knit around the mother queen as to act like a single, well-coordinated entity. A wasp or other solitary insect encountering a worker ant on its nest faces more than just another insect. It faces the worker and all her sisters, united by instinct to protect the queen, seize control of territory, and futher the growth of the colony. Workers are little kamikazes, prepared—eager—to die in order to defend the nest or gain control of a food source. Their deaths matter no more to the colony than the loss of hair or a claw tip might to a solitary animal.

There is another way to look at an ant colony. Workers foraging around their nest are not merely insects searching for food. They are a living web cast out by the superorganism, ready to congeal over rich food finds or shrink back from the most formidable enemies. Superorganisms can control and dominate the ground and treetops in competition with ordinary, solitary organisms, and that is surely why ants live everywhere in such great numbers.

I heard around me the Greek chorus of training and caution: *How can you prove that is the reason for their dominance? Isn't the connection just another shaky conclusion that because two events occur together, one causes the other? Something else entirely different might have caused both. Think about it— greater individual fighting ability? Sharper senses? What?*

Such is the dilemma of evolutionary biology. We have problems to solve, we have clear answers—too many clear answers. The difficult part is picking out the right answer. The isolated mind moves in slow circles and breakouts are rare. Solitude is better for weeding out ideas than for creating them. Genius is the summed production of the many with the names of the few attached for easy recall, unfairly so to other scientists. My mind drifted into the hourless night, no port of call yet chosen.

The storm grew until sheet lightning spread across the western sky. The thunderhead reared up like a top-heavy monster in slow motion, tilted forward, blotting out the stars. The forest erupted in a simulation of violent life. Lightning bolts broke to the front and then closer, to the right and left, 10,000 volts dropping along an ionizing path at 800 kilometers an hour, kicking a countersurge skyward ten times faster, back and forth in a split second, the whole perceived as a single flash and crack of sound. The wind freshened, and rain came stalking through the forest.

In the midst of chaos something to the side caught my attention. The lightning bolts were acting like strobe flashes to illuminate the wall of the rain forest. At intervals I glimpsed the storied structure: top canopy 30 meters off the ground, middle trees spread raggedly below that, and a lowermost scattering of shrubs and small trees. The forest was framed for a few moments in this theatrical setting. Its image turned surreal, projected into the unbounded wildness of the human imagination, thrown back in time 10,000 years. Somewhere close I knew spear-nosed bats flew through the tree crowns in search of fruit, palm vipers, coiled in ambush in the roots of orchids, jaguars walked the river's edge; around them eight hundred species of trees stood, more than are native to all of North America; and a thousand species of butterflies, 6 percent of the entire world fauna, waited for the dawn.

About the orchids of that place we knew very little. About flies and beetles almost nothing, fungi nothing, most kinds of organisms nothing. Five thousand kinds of bacteria might be found in a pinch of soil, and about them we knew absolutely nothing. This was wilderness in the sixteenth-century sense, as it must have formed in the minds of the Portuguese explorers, its interior still largely unexplored and filled with strange, myth-endangering plants and animals. From such a place the pious naturalist would send long respectful letters to royal patrons about the wonders of the new world as testament to the glory of God. And I thought: there is still time to see this land in such a manner.

The unsolved mysteries of the rain forest are formless and seductive. They are like unnamed islands hidden in the blank spaces of old maps, like dark shapes glimpsed descending the far wall of a reef into the abyss. They draw us forward and stir strange apprehensions. The unknown and prodigious are drugs to the scientific imagination, stirring insatiable hunger with a single taste. In our hearts we hope we will never discover everything. We pray there will always be a world like this one at whose edge I sat in darkness. The rain forest in its richness is one of the last repositories on earth of that timeless dream.

That is why I keep going back to the forests forty years after I began, when I flew down to Cuba, a graduate student caught up in the idea of the "big" tropics, free at last to look for something hidden, as Kipling had urged, something lost behind the Ranges. The chances are high, in fact certain, of finding a new species or phenomenon within days or, if you work hard, hours after arrival. The hunt is also on for rare species already discovered but still effectively unknown—represented by one or two specimens placed in a museum drawer fifty or a hundred years ago, left with nothing but a locality and a habitat note handwritten on a tiny label ("Santarém, Brazil, nest on side of tree in swamp forest"). Unfold the stiff yellowing piece of paper and a long-dead biologist speaks: I was there, I found this, now you know, now move on.

There is still more to the study of biological richness. It is a microcosm of scientific exploration as a whole, refracting hands-on experience onto a higher plane of abstraction. We search in and around a subject for a concept, a pattern, that imposes order. We look for a way of speaking about the rough unmapped terrain, even just a name or a phrase that calls attention to the object of our attention. We hope to be the first to make a connection. Our goal is to capture and label a process, perhaps a chemical reaction or behavior pattern driving an ecological change, a new way of classifying energy flow, or a relation between predator and prey that preserves them both, almost anything at all. We will settle for just one good question that starts people thinking and talking: Why are there so many species? Why have mammals evolved more quickly than reptiles? Why do birds sing at dawn?

These whispering denizens of the mind are sensed but rarely seen. They rustle the foliage, leave behind a pug mark filling with water and a scent, excite us for an instant and vanish. Most ideas are waking dreams that fade to an emotional residue. A first-rate scientist can hope to capture and express only several in a lifetime. No one has learned how to invent with any consistent success the equations and phrases of science, no one has captured the metaformula of scientific research. The conversion is an art aided by a stroke of luck in minds set to receive them. We hunt outward and we hunt inward, and the value of the quarry on one side of that mental barrier is commensurate with the value of the quarry on the other side. Of this dual quality the great chemist Berzelius wrote in 1818 and for all time:

> All our theory is but a means of consistently conceptualizing the inward processes of phenomena, and it is presumable and adequate when all scientifically known

facts can be deduced from it. This mode of conceptualization can equally well be false and, unfortunately, presumably is so frequently. Even though, at a certain period in the development of science, it may match the purpose just as well as a true theory. Experience is augmented, facts appear which do not agree with it, and one is forced to go in search of a new mode of conceptualization within which these facts can also be accommodated; and in this manner, no doubt, modes of conceputalization will be altered from age to age, as experienced is broadened, and the complete truth may perhaps never be attained.

The storm arrived, racing from the forest's edge, turning from scattered splashing drops into sheets of water driven by gusts of wind. It forced me back to the shelter of the corrugated iron roof of the open-air living quarters, where I sat and waited with the *mateiros*. The men stripped off their clothing and walked out into the open, soaping and rinsing themselves in the torrential rain, laughing and singing. In bizarre counterpoint, leptodactylid frogs struck up a loud and monotonous honking on the forest floor close by. They were all around us. I wondered where they had been during the day. I had never encountered a single one while sifting through the vegetation and rotting debris on sunny days, in habitats they are supposed to prefer.

Farther out, a kilometer or two away, a troop of red howler monkeys chimed in, their chorus one of the strangest sounds to be heard in all of nature, as enthralling in its way as the songs of humpback whales. A male opened with an accelerating series of deep grunts expanding into prolonged roars and was then joined by the higher-pitched calls of the females. This far away, filtered through dense foliage, the full chorus was machine-like: deep, droning, metallic.

Such raintime calls are usually territorial advertisements, the means by which the animals space themselves out and control enough land to forage and breed. For me they were a celebration of the forest's vitality: *Rejoice! The powers of nature are within our compass, the storm is part of our biology!*

For that is the way of the nonhuman world. The greatest powers of the physical environment slam into the resilient forces of life, and nothing much happens. For a very long time, 150 million years, the species within the rain forest evolved to absorb precisely this form and magnitude of violence. They encoded the predictable occurrence of nature's storms in the letters of their genes. Animals and plants have come to use heavy rains and floods routinely to time episodes in their life cycle. They threaten rivals, mate, hunt prey, lay eggs in new water pools, and dig shelters in the rain-softened earth.

On a larger scale, the storms drive change in the whole structure of the forest. The natural dynamism raises the diversity of life by means of local destruction and regeneration.

Somewhere a large horizontal tree limb is weak and vulnerable, covered by a dense garden of orchids, bromeliads, and other kinds of persuasion many times before, that the prevalence of ants must have something to do with their advanced colonial organization. A colony is a superorganism, an assembly of workers so tightly knit around the mother queen as to act like a single, well-coordinated entity. A wasp or other solitary insect encountering a worker ant on its nest faces more than just another insect. It faces the worker and all her sisters, united by instinct to protect the queen, seize control of territory, and further the growth of the colony. Workers are little kamikazes, prepared—eager—to die in order to defend the nest or gain control of a food source. Their deaths matter no more to the colony than the loss of hair or a claw tip might to a solitary animal.

There is another way to look at an ant colony. Workers foraging around their nest are not merely insects searching for food. They are a living web cast out by the superorganism, ready to congeal over rich food finds or shrink back from the most formidable enemies. Superorganisms can control and dominate the ground and treetops in competition with ordinary, solitary organisms, and that is surely why ants live everywhere in such great numbers.

I heard around me the Greek chorus of training and caution: *How can you prove that is the reason for their dominance? Isn't the connection just another shaky conclusion that because two events occur together, one causes the other? Something else entirely different might have caused both. Think about it—greater individual fighting ability? Sharper senses? What?*

Such is the dilemma of evolutionary biology. We have problems to solve, we have clear answers—too many clear answers. The difficult part is picking out the right answer. The isolated mind moves in slow circles and breakouts are rare. Solitude is better for weeding out ideas than for creating them. Genius is the summed production of the many with the names of the few attached for easy recall, unfairly so to other scientists. My mind drifted into the hourless night, no port of call yet chosen.

The storm grew until sheet lightning spread across the western sky. The thunderhead reared up like a top-heavy monster in slow motion, tilted forward, blotting out the stars. The forest erupted in a simulation of violent life. Lightning bolts broke to the front and then closer, to the right and left, 10,000 volts dropping along an ionizing path at 800 kilometers an hour, kicking a counter-surge skyward ten times faster, back and forth in a split second, the whole perceived as a single flash and crack of sound. The wind freshened, and rain came stalking through the forest.

In the midst of chaos something to the side caught my attention. The lightning bolts were acting like strobe flashes to illuminate the wall of the rain forest. At intervals I glimpsed the storied structure: top canopy 30 meters off the ground, middle trees spread raggedly below that, and a lowermost scattering of shrubs and small trees. The forest was framed for a few moments in this theatrical setting. Its image turned surreal, projected into the unbounded wildness of the human imagination, thrown back in time 10,000 years. Somewhere close I knew spear-nosed bats flew through the tree crowns in search of fruit, palm vipers coiled in ambush in the roots of orchids, jaguars walked the river's edge; around them eight hundred species of trees stood, more than are native to all of North America; and a thousand species of butterflies, 6 percent of the entire world fauna, waited for the dawn.

About the orchids of that place we knew very little. About flies and beetles almost nothing, fungi nothing, most kinds of organisms nothing. Five thousand kinds of bacteria might be found in a pinch of soil, and about them we knew absolutely nothing. This was wilderness in the sixteenth-century sense, as it must have formed in the minds of the Portuguese explorers, its interiors still largely unexplored and filled with strange, myth-engendering plants and animals. From such a place the pious naturalist would send long respectful letters to royal patrons about the wonders of the new world as testament to the glory of God. And I thought: there is still time to see this land in such a manner.

The unsolved mysteries of the rain forest are formless and seductive. They are like unnamed islands hidden in the blank spaces of old maps, like dark shapes glimpsed descending the far wall of a reef into the abyss. They draw us forward and stir strange apprehensions. The unknown and prodigious are drugs to the scientific imagination, stirring insatiable hunger with a single taste. In our hearts we hope we will never discover everything. We pray there will always be a world like this one at whose edge I sat in darkness. The rain forest in its richness is one of the last repositories on earth of that timeless dream.

That is why I keep going back to the forests forty years after I began, when I flew down to Cuba, a graduate student caught up in the idea of the "big" tropics, free at last to look for something hidden, as Kipling had urged, something lost behind the Ranges. The chances are high, in fact certain, of finding a new species or phenomenon within days or, if you work hard, hours after arrival. The hunt is also on for rare species already discovered but still effectively unknown—represented by one or two specimens placed in a museum drawer fifty or a hundred years ago, left with nothing but a locality of plants that grow on trees. The rain fills up the cavities enclosed by the axil sheaths of the epiphytes and soaks the humus and clotted dust around their roots. After years of growth the weight has become nearly unsupportable. A gust of wind whips through or lightning strikes the tree trunk, and the limb breaks and plummets down, clearing a path to the ground. Elsewhere the crown of a giant tree emergent above the rest catches the wind and the tree sways above the rain-soaked soil. The shallow roots cannot hold, and the entire tree keels over. Its trunk and canopy arc downward like a blunt ax, shearing through smaller trees and burying understory bushes and herbs. Thick lianas coiled through the limbs are pulled along. Those that stretch to other trees act as hawsers to drag down still more vegetation. The massive root system heaves up to create an instant mound of bare soil. At yet another site, close to the river's edge, the rising water cuts under an overhanging bank to the critical level of gravity, and a 20-meter front collapses. Behind it a small section of forest floor slides down, toppling trees and burying low vegetation.

Such events of minor violence open gaps in the forest. The sky clears again and sunlight floods the ground. The surface temperature rises and the humidity falls. The soil and ground litter dries out and warms up still more, creating a new environment for animals, fungi, and microorganisms of a different kind from those in the dark forest interior. In the following months pioneer plant species take seed. They are very different from the young shade-loving saplings and understory shrubs of the prevailing old-stand forest. Fast-growing, small in stature, and short-lived, they form a single canopy that matures far below the upper crowns of the older trees all around. Their tissue is soft and vulnerable to herbivores. The palmate-leaved trees of the genus *Cecropia,* one of the gap-filling specialists of Central and South America, harbor vicious ants in hollow internodes of the trunk. These insects, bearing the appropriate scientific name *Azteca,* live in symbiosis with their hosts, protecting them from all predators except sloths and a few other herbivores specialized to feed on *Cecropia.* The symbionts live among new assemblages of species not found in the mature forest.

All around the second-growth vegetation, the fallen trees and branches rot and crumble, offering hiding places and food to a vast array of basidiomycete fungi, slime molds, ponerine ants, scolytid beetles, bark lice, earwigs, embiopteran webspinners, zorapterans, entomobryomorph springtails, japygid diplurans, schizomid arachnids, pseudoscorpions, real scorpions, and other forms that live mostly or exclusively in this habitat. They add thousands of species to the diversity of the primary forest.

Climb into the tangle of fallen vegetation, tear away pieces of rotting bark, roll over logs, and you will see these creatures teeming everywhere. As the pioneer vegetation grows denser, the deepening shade and higher humidity again favor old-forest species, and their saplings sprout and grow. Within a hundred years the gap specialists will be phased out by competition for light, and the tall storied forest will close completely over.

In the succession, pioneer species are the sprinters, old-forest species the long-distance runners. The violent changes and a clearing of space bring all the species briefly to the same starting line. The sprinters dash ahead, but the prolonged race goes to the marathoners. Together the two classes of specialists create a complex mosaic of vegetation types across the forest which, by regular tree falls and landslides, is forever changing. If square kilometers of space are mapped over decades of time, the mosaic turns into a riotous kaleidoscope whose patterns come and go and come again. A new marathon is always beginning somewhere in the forest. The percentages of successional vegetation types are consequently more or less in a steady state, from earliest pioneer species through various mixes of pioneer and deep-forest trees to stands of the most mature physiognomy. Walk randomly on any given day for one or two kilometers through the forest, and you will cut through many of these successional stages and sense the diversity sustained by the passage of storms and the fall of forest giants.

It is diversity by which life builds and saturates the rain forest. And diversity has carried life beyond, to the harshest environments on earth. Rich assemblages of animals swarm in the shallow bays of Antarctica, the coldest marine habitats on earth. Perch-like notothenioid fishes swim there in temperatures just above the freezing point of salt water but cold enough to turn ordinary blood to ice, because they are able to generate glycopeptides in their tissues as antifreeze and thrive where other fish cannot go. Around them flock dense populations of active brittlestars, krill, and other invertebrate animals, each with protective devices of its own.

In a radically different setting, the deep unlighted zone of caves around the world, blind white springtails, mites, and beetles feed on fungi and bacteria growing on rotting vegetable matter washed down through ground water. They are eaten in turn by blind white beetles and spiders also specialized for life in perpetual darkness.

Some of the harshest deserts of the world are home to unique ensembles of insects, lizards, and flowering plants. In the Namib of southwestern Africa, beetles use leg tips expanded into oarlike sandshoes to swim down through the shifting dunes in search of dried vegetable matter. Others, the swiftest runners of the insect world, race over the baking hot surface on bizarre stilt legs.

Archaebacteria, one-celled microorganisms so different from ordinary bacteria as to be candidates for a separate kingdom of life, occupy the boiling water of mineral hot springs and volcanic vents in the deep sea. The species composing the newly discovered genus *Methanopyrus* grow in boiling vents at the bottom of the Mediterranean Sea in temperatures up to 110°C.

Life is too well adapted in such places, out to the edge of the physical envelope where biochemistry falters, and too diverse to be broken by storms and other ordinary vagaries of nature. But diversity, the property that makes resilience possible, is vulnerable to blows that are greater than natural perturbations. It can be eroded away fragment by fragment, and irreversibly so if the abnormal stress is unrelieved. This vulnerability stems from life's composition as swarms of species of limited geographical distribution. Every habitat, from Brazilian rain forest to Antarctic bay to thermal vent, harbors a unique combination of plants and animals. Each kind of plant and animal living there is linked in the food web to only a small part of the other species. Eliminate one species, and another increases in number to take its place. Eliminate a great many species, and the local ecosystem starts to decay visibly. Productivity drops as the channels of the nutrient cycles are clogged. More of the biomass is sequestered in the form of dead vegetation and slowly metabolizing, oxygen-starved mud, or is simply washed away. Less competent pollinators take over as the best-adapted bees, moths, birds, bats, and other specialists drop out. Fewer seeds fall, fewer seedlings sprout. Herbivores decline, and their predators die away in close concert.

In an eroding ecosystem life goes on, and it may look superficially the same. There are always species able to recolonize the impoverished area and exploit the stagnant resources, however clumsily accomplished. Given enough time, a new combination of species—a reconstituted fauna and flora—will reinvest the habitat in a way that transports energy and materials somewhat more efficiently. The atmosphere they generate and the composition of the soil they enrich will resemble those found in comparable habitats in other parts of the world, since the species are adapted to penetrate and reinvigorate just such degenerate systems. They do so because they gain more energy and materials and leave more offspring. But the restorative power of the fauna and flora of the world as a whole depends on the existence of enough species to play that special role. They too can slide into the red zone of endangered species.

Biological diversity—"biodiversity" in the new parlance—is the key to the maintenance of the world as we know it. Life in a local site struck down by a passing storm springs back quickly because enough diversity still exists. Opportunistic species evolved for just such an occasion rush in to fill the spaces. They entrain the succession that circles back to something resembling the original state of the environment.

This is the assembly of life that took a billion years to evolve. It has eaten the storms—folded them into its genes—and created the world that created us. It holds the world steady. When I rose at dawn the next morning, Fazenda Dimona had not changed in any obvious way from the day before. The same high trees stood like a fortress along the forest's edge; the same profusion of birds and insects foraged through the canopy and understory in precise individual timetables. All this seemed timeless, immutable, and its very strength posed the question: how much force does it take to break the crucible of evolution? ✆

QUESTIONS FOR THOUGHT AND STUDY

1. What question is Wilson pursuing?
2. Mark three places where Wilson uses fact. How does Wilson use them?
3. Does Wilson have a theory about the natural world?
4. How does Wilson's view of the natural world compare with Bacon's?
5. Translate the following quote into your own words and explain Wilson's meaning: ". . . because sight and sound are the evolutionary prerequisites of intelligence, we alone have come to reflect on such matters as Amazon nights and sensory modalities."
6. Translate into your own words, the second paragraph on page 71 ("The subject fitfully engaged that night. . . ."). What does this paragraph say about the pursuit of science?
7. What is Wilson's view of collective versus solitary life?
8. Mark places where Wilson uses the static perspective, the dynamic, and the systemic.

Light

John Gribbin

Biography: *John Gribbin (1946–), an astrophysicist in the Science Policy Research Unit of the University of Sussex, England, currently studies the effect of climate change on world food supplies. He has written twenty-seven books, ranging in subject from astronomy to geophysics and from climate change to evolution. His primary interest is the puzzle of gravity and warped space-time.*

Gribbin gives a historical account of theories of light, moving from particle to wave to field theory. He then argues that all three theories are valid in some circumstances and that all three views are necessary for a complete understanding. He presents the theoretical basis for the trimodal (static, dynamic, systemic) observation used throughout the text and an excellent example of the evolution of theory, reinforcing a dynamic view of science. The reading provides an example of historical and theoretical writing in physics.

CHAPTER ONE

Isaac Newton invented physics, and all of science depends on physics. Newton certainly built upon the work of others, but it was the publication of his three laws of motion and theory of gravity, almost exactly three hundred years ago, that set science off on the road that has led to space flight, lasers, atomic energy, genetic engineering, an understanding of chemistry, and all the rest. For two hundred years, Newtonian physics (what is now called "classical" physics) reigned supreme; in the twentieth century revolutionary new insights took physics far beyond Newton, but without those two centuries of scientific growth those new insights might never have been achieved. This book is not a history of science, and it is concerned with the new physics—quantum physics—rather than with those classical ideas. But even in Newton's work three centuries ago there were already signs of the changes that were to come—not from his studies of planetary motions and orbits, or his famous three laws, but from his investigations of the nature of light.

Newton's ideas about light owed a lot to his ideas about the behavior of solid objects and the orbits of planets. He realized that our everyday experiences of the behavior of objects may be misleading, and that an object, a particle, free from any outside influences must behave very differently from such a particle on the surface of the earth. Here, our everyday experience tells us that things tend to stay in one place unless they are pushed, and that once you stop pushing them they soon stop moving. So why don't objects like planets, or the moon, stop moving in their orbits? Is something pushing them? Not at all. It is the planets that are in a natural state, free from outside interference, and the

From *In Search of Schrodinger's Cat: Quantum Physics and Reality,* New York: Bantam Books, 1984, pp. 7–18.

objects on the surface of the earth that are being interfered with. If I try to slide a pen across my desk, my push is opposed by the friction of the pen rubbing against the desk, and that is what brings it to a halt when I stop pushing. If there were no friction, the pen would keep moving. This is Newton's first law: every object stays at rest, or moves with constant velocity, unless an outside force acts on it. The second law tells us how much effect an outside force—a push—has on an object. Such a force changes the velocity of the object, and a change in velocity is called acceleration; if you divided the force by the mass of the object the force is acting upon, the result is the acceleration produced on that body by that force. Usually, this second law is expressed slightly differently: force equals mass times acceleration. And Newton's third law tells us something about how the object reacts to being pushed around: for every action there is an equal and opposite reaction. If I hit a tennis ball with my racket, the force with which the racket pushes on the tennis ball is exactly matched by an equal force pushing back on the racket; the pen on my desk top, pulled down by gravity, is pushed against with an exactly equal reaction by the desk top itself; the force of the explosive process that pushes the gases out of the combustion chamber of a rocket produces an equal and opposite reaction force on the rocket itself, which pushes it in the opposite direction.

These laws, together with Newton's law of gravity, explained the orbits of the planets around the sun, and the moon around the earth. When proper account was taken of friction, they explained the behavior of objects on the surface of the earth as well, and formed the foundation of mechanics. But they also had puzzling philosophical implications. According to Newton's laws, the behavior of a particle could be exactly predicted on the basis of its interactions with other particles and the forces acting on it. If it were ever possible to know the position and velocity of every particle in the universe, then it would be possible to predict with utter precision the future of every particle, and therefore the future of the universe. Did this mean that the universe ran like clockwork, wound up and set in motion by the Creator, down some utterly predictable path? Newton's classical mechanics provided plenty of support for this deterministic view of the universe, a picture that left little place for human free will or chance. Could it really be that we are all puppets following our own preset tracks through life, with no real choice at all? Most scientists were content to let the philosophers debate that question. But it returned, with full force, at the heart of the new physics of the twentieth century.

WAVES OR PARTICLES

With his physics of particles such a success, it is hardly surprising that when Newton tried to explain the behavior of light he did so in terms of particles. After all, light rays are observed to travel in straight lines, and the way light bounces off a mirror is very much like the way a ball bounces off a hard wall. Newton built the first reflecting telescope, explained white light as a superposition of all the colors of the rainbow, and did much more with optics, but always his theories rested upon the assumption that light consisted of a stream of tiny particles, called corpuscles. Light rays bend as they cross the barrier between a lighter and a denser substance, such as from air to water or glass (which is why a swizzle stick in a gin and tonic appears to be bent), and this refraction is neatly explained on the corpuscular theory provided the corpuscles move faster in the more "optically dense" substance. Even in Newton's day, however, there was an alternative way of explaining all of this.

The Dutch physicist Christiaan Huygens was a contemporary of Newton, although thirteen years older, having been born in 1629. He developed the idea that light is not a stream of particles but a wave, rather like the waves moving across the surface of a sea or lake, but propagating through an invisible substance called the "luminiferous ether." Like ripples produced by a pebble dropped into a pond, light waves in the ether were imagined to spread out in all directions from a source of light. The wave theory explained reflection and refraction just as well as the corpuscular theory. Although it said that instead of speeding up the light waves moved more slowly in a more optically dense substance, there was no way of measuring the speed of light in the seventeenth century, so this difference could not resolve the conflict between the two theories. But in one key respect the two ideas did differ observably in their predictions. When light passes a sharp edge, it produces a sharply edged shadow. This is exactly the way streams of particles, traveling in straight lines, ought to be-

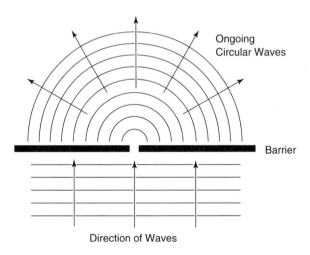

Figure 1   Parallel water waves passing through a small hole in a barrier spread out in circles from the hole, leaving no "shadow."

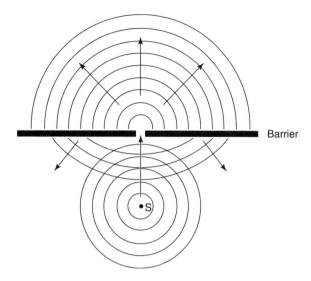

Figure 2   Circular ripples, like the ones produced by a stone dropped in a pond, also spread as circular waves centered on the hole when they pass through a narrow opening (and, of course, the waves that hit the barrier are reflected back again).

have. A wave tends to bend, or diffract, some of the way into the shadow (think of the ripples on a pond, bending around a rock). Three hundred years ago, this evidence clearly favored the corpuscular theory, and the wave theory, although not forgotten, was discarded. By the early nineteenth century, however, the status of the two theories had been almost completely reversed.

In the eighteenth century, very few people took the wave theory of light seriously. One of the few who not only took it seriously but wrote in support of it was the Swiss Leonard Euler, the leading mathematician of his time, who made major contributions to the development of geometry, calculus and trigonometry. Modern mathematics and physics are described in arithmetical terms, by equations; the techniques on which that arithmetical description depends were largely developed by Euler, and in the process he introduced shorthand methods of notation that survive to this day—the name "pi" for the ratio of the circumference of a circle to its diameter; the letter i to denote the square root of minus one (which we shall meet again, along with pi); and the symbols used by mathematicians to denote the operation called integration. Curiously, though, Euler's entry in the *Encyclopaedia Britannica* makes no mention of his views on the wave theory of light, views which a contemporary said were not held "by a single physicist of prominence."* About the only prominent contemporary of Euler

---

*Quote from page 2 of *Quantum Mechanics,* by Ernest Ikenberry; see bibliography.

who did share those views was Benjamin Franklin; but physicists found it easy to ignore them until crucial new experiments were performed by the Englishman Thomas Young just at the beginning of the nineteenth century, and by the Frenchman Augustin Fresnel soon after.

WAVE THEORY TRIUMPHANT

Young used his knowledge of how waves move across the surface of a pond to design an experiment that would test whether or not light propagates in the same way. We all know what a water wave looks like, although it is important to think of a ripple, rather than a large breaker, to make the analogy accurate. The distinctive feature of a wave is that it raises the water level up slightly, then depresses it, as the wave passes; the height of the crest of the wave above the undisturbed water level is its amplitude, and for a perfect wave this is the same as the amount by which the water level is pushed down as the wave passes. A series of ripples, like the ones from our stone dropped into the pond, follow one another with a regular spacing, called the wavelength, which is measured from one crest to the next. Around the point where our pebble drops into the water, the waves spread out in circles, but the waves on the sea, or ripples produced on a lake by the blowing wind, may run forward as a series of straight lines, parallel waves, one behind the other. Either way, the number of wave crests passing by some fixed point—like a rock—in each second tells us the frequency of

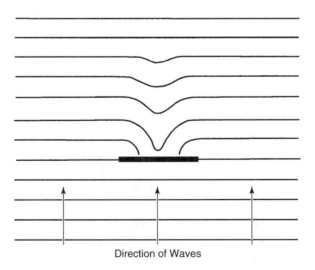

Direction of Waves

Figure 3 **The ability of waves to bend around corners also means that they can quickly fill in the shadow behind an obstacle, provided the obstacle is not much bigger than the wavelength of the waves.**

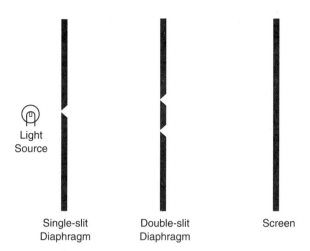

Light
Source

Single-slit   Double-slit   Screen
Diaphragm   Diaphragm

Figure 4   The ability of light to diffract around corners and through small holes can be tested using a single slit to make a circular wave and a double slit to produce interference.

the wave. The frequency is the number of wavelengths passing each second, so the velocity of the wave, the speed with which each crest advances, is the wavelength multiplied by the frequency.

The crucial experiment starts out with parallel waves, rather like the lines of waves advancing toward a beach before they break. You can imagine these as the waves produced by dropping a very large object into the water a very long way away. The "ripples" spreading out in ever-growing circles look like parallel, or plane, waves if you are far enough away from the source of the ripples, because it is difficult to detect the curvature of the very large circle centered on the spot where the disturbances started. It is easy to investigate what happens to such plane waves in a tank of water when an obstacle is placed in their path. If the obstacle is small, the waves bend around it and fill in behind by diffraction, leaving very little "shadow"; but if the obstruction is very large compared with the wavelength of the ripples, then they only bend slightly into the shadow behind it, leaving a region of undisturbed water. If light is a wave, it is still possible to have sharp-edged shadows, provided the wavelength of light is very small compared with the size of the object casting the shadow.

Now turn the idea around. Imagine a nice set of plane waves progressing across our tank of water and coming up to, not an obstruction surrounded by water but a complete wall across their path, with a gap in the middle. If the gap is much larger than the wavelength of the disturbance, just the portion of the wave that is lined up with the gap gets through, spreading out slightly but leaving most of the water on the other side of the barrier undisturbed—like the waves arriving at the entrance to a harbor wall. But if the hole in the wall is very

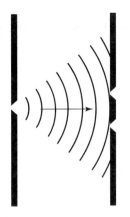

Figure 5   Like water ripples passing through a hole, the light waves spread out in circles from the first slit, moving "in step" with one another.

small, the hole acts as a new source of circular waves, as if pebbles were being dropped into the water at that spot. On the far side of the wall, this circular (or, more accurately, semicircular) wave spreads out across the water surface, leaving no part undisturbed.

So far, so good. Now, at last, we come to Young's experiment. Imagine the same setup as before, a water tank with parallel waves coming to a barrier, but this time a barrier with *two* small holes in it. Each of the holes acts like a new source of semicircular waves in the region of the tank beyond the wall, and because these two sets of waves are being produced by the same parallel waves on the other side of the wall, they move exactly in step, or in phase. Now, we have two sets of ripples spreading out across the water, and this produces a more complicated pattern of ripples on its surface. Where both waves are lifting the water surface upward, we get a more pronounced crest; where one wave is trying to create a crest and the other is trying to create a trough the two cancel out and the water level is undisturbed. The effects are called constructive and destructive interference, and are easy to see, in a cruder way, by dropping two pebbles into a pond at once. If light is a wave, then an equivalent experiment should be able to produce similar interference among light waves, and that is exactly what Young discovered.

He shone a light upon an obstructing screen in which there were two narrow slits. Behind this obstruction, light from the two slits spread out and interfered. If the analogy with water waves was correct, there ought to be a pattern of interference behind the obstruction producing alternate zones of bright light and darkness, caused by constructive and destructive interference of waves from each slit. When Young placed a white screen behind the slits, that is exactly what he found—alternate bands of light and shade striping the screen.

But Young's experiment didn't exactly set the world of science on fire, especially in Britain. The scientific establishment there regarded opposition to any idea of Newton's as almost heretical, and certainly unpatriotic. Newton had

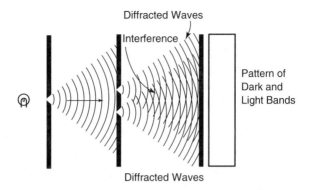

Figure 6 Circular waves advancing from *each* of the holes in the doubly slitted screen interfere to produce a pattern of light and shade on the viewing screen—clear proof that, as far as this experiment is concerned, light behaves as a wave.

only died in 1727, and in 1705—less than a hundred years before Young announced his discoveries—had been the first man to receive a knighthood for his scientific works. It was too soon for the idol to be dethroned in England, so perhaps it was appropriate at that time of the Napoleonic wars that it was a Frenchman, Augustin Fresnel, who took up this "unpatriotic" idea and eventually established the wave explanation of light. Fresnel's work, although a few years later than Young's, was more complete, offering a wave explanation of virtually all aspects of the behavior of light. Among other things, he accounted for a phenomenon familiar to all of us today, the beautifully colored reflections produced when light shines on a thin film of oil. The process is again caused by interference of waves. Some light is reflected from the top of the film of oil, but some passes through and is reflected back from the bottom surface of the layer. So there are two different reflected beams, which interfere with one another. Because each color of light corresponds to a different wavelength, and white light is composed of a superposition of all the colors of the rainbow, the reflections of a white light from an oil film will produce a mass of colors as some waves (colors) interfere destructively and some constructively, depending on just where your eye is in relation to the film.

By the time Léon Foucault, the French physicist famous for the pendulum that bears his name, established in the middle of the nineteenth century that, contrary to the predictions of Newton's corpuscular theory, the speed of light is less in water than in air, this was no more than any reputable scientist expected. By then "everybody knew" that light was a form of wave motion propagated through the ether, whatever that might be. Still, however, it would be nice to know exactly what is "waving" in a beam of light. In the 1860s and 1870s, the theory of light seemed at last to have been completed when the great

Scottish physicist James Clerk Maxwell established the existence of waves involving changing electric and magnetic fields. This electromagnetic radiation was predicted by Maxwell to involve patterns of stronger and weaker electric and magnetic fields in the same way that water waves involve crests and troughs in the height of the water. In 1887—only a hundred years ago—Heinrich Hertz succeeded in transmitting and receiving electromagnetic radiation in the form of radio waves, which are similar to light waves but have much longer wavelengths. At last the wave theory of light was complete—just in time to be overturned by the greatest revolution in scientific thinking since the time of Newton and Galileo. By the end of the nineteenth century, only a genius or a fool would have suggested that light is corpuscular. His name was Albert Einstein; but before we can understand why he took this bold step we need a little more background concerning the ideas of nineteenth-century physics. ☻

QUESTIONS FOR THOUGHT AND STUDY

1. What, according to Gribbin, is the relationship between ordinary experience and scientific investigation. Would Bacon agree?

2. Gribbin, on page 81, calls Newton's theory "deterministic." Can you tell from the context alone what deterministic means?

3. What is the force(s) that causes theories of light to change?

4. What does this article say about the course and nature of science in general?

5. The scientists whose work Gribbin is describing draw their hypotheses on the behavior of light by drawing an analogy to the behavior of water. Would Bacon think this a valid way to create a hypothesis? How do the scientists check the validity of their analogy?

6. Compare the shifting of perspective caused by the changing theories of light to the trimodal observation method.

Coyote (Canis latrans) Food Habits in Three Urban Habitat Types of Western Washington

Timothy Quinn

Biography: *Timothy Quinn conducted and reported this study as a graduate student in the College of Forest Resources, University of Washington.*

In search of an explanation for the increase in coyote populations around urban habitats, Quinn compares the coyote feces of urban to rural habitats and finds significantly more protein in the urban feces. Quinn suggests that the ease of obtaining small animals, particularly cats, around human populations may explain the phenomenon. The article provides an accessible scientific study of a phenomenon students are familiar with and a professional model of science report form.

ABSTRACT

The coyote (*Canis latrans*) is a common resident in urban areas throughout the United States, yet little is known about coyote diets in these environments. I characterized the annual diet of coyotes in an urban environment of western Washington by analyzing their scat from three areas representing typical patterns of human occupation and density: residential (1413 humans/km^2), mixed agricultural-residential (348 humans/km^2), and mixed forest-residential (126 humans/km^2). Coyote scats were collected twice a month for 1 year (Nov. 1989–Oct. 1990) in each habitat type. Fruits and mammals were the largest classes of food items in all habitat types and their seasonal use was similar among habitats. Apple (*Malus* spp.) and cherry (*Prunus* spp.) were the most abundant fruits in the scats, and ranged from 22–41% and 9–13% of the annual diet, respectively. Vole (*Microtus* spp.) was the most abundant mammalian food item (41.7%) of coyotes in mixed agricultural-residential habitat while house cat (*Felis catus*) and squirrel (*Sciurus* spp. and *Tamiasciurus* spp.) were the two most abundant mammalian food items (13.1 and 7.8%, respectively) of coyotes in residential habitat. No single mammalian species made up >6.0% of the coyote diet in mixed forest-residential habitat. Coyotes in my western Washington study area rely on foods that result from human activity but those foods, particularly mammals, may change as land use patterns change.

INTRODUCTION

Coyotes (*Canis latrans*) are becoming increasingly common in human modified habitats throughout North America (Atkinson and Shackleton 1991, MacCracken 1982). One possible explanation for this trend is that human-dominated areas produce abundant food sources for coyotes. Coyotes living in urban habitats have relatively small home ranges (Atkinson and Shackleton 1991, Shargo 1988), which may indicate abundant food resources. However, little is known about the diet of coyotes in these areas. MacCracken's (1982) description of the annual diet of coyotes in residential habitat was based on a small number of scats (*n* = 97) collected during a single month. Atkinson and Shackleton (1991)

From *Northwest Science*, 71, no. 1 (1997): 1–5.

89

described the diet of coyotes in an area that was mostly agricultural (>50% of the study area) and Shargo's (1988) description of urban coyote diet was based on 22 scats. Additionally, none of these studies looked at diet as a function of human density.

Coyotes may play an important role in human modified landscapes. Soulé et al. (1988) suggested that coyotes may reduce the abundance of house cats (*Felis catus*) and other small mammalian carnivores that prey on song birds and thus indirectly contribute to the maintenance of native avifauna. My objectives were to document the annual diet of coyotes in three types of urban habitat of western Washington and to qualitatively assess how coyote diets changed as a function of land use patterns and human density.

STUDY AREA

The study area, located in the low elevation (<200 m) region of King and Snohomish counties, was bordered on the west by Puget Sound and on the east by foothills of the Cascade Mountains. This portion of Washington lies in the wetter region of the Western Hemlock Zone (Franklin and Dyrness 1984). The study area was logged at the turn of the 19th century. Much of the land has been developed for urban and agricultural uses but there are numerous patches of 40–80 year-old naturally regenerated forest dominated by Douglas-fir (*Pseudotsuga menziesii*), western hemlock (*Tsuga heterophylla*), western red cedar (*Thuja plicata*), red alder (*Alnus rubra*), and maple (*Acer* spp; Franklin and Dyrness 1984).

Urban areas are mosaics of habitat patches differing in size and intensity of human use. I chose three habitat types in which to establish permanent scat collection routes (hereafter routes): residential habitat, mixed agricultural-residential (hereafter mixed agricultural) habitat, and mixed forest-residential (hereafter mixed forest) habitat. I described coyote diets in these habitats, which represented the typical range of different land uses in urban western Washington. I characterized habitat types on the basis of human density (Census Population and Housing 1990, Seattle, Wash., unpubl. data). I calculated the density of humans within census tracts in which the route was located and census tracts which were within 1 km of a route. I included density figures from census tracks within 1 km routes to help characterize the area from which coyotes likely would have foraged. Despite efforts to characterize collection areas, coyotes may have deposited scats in habitats very different from where they foraged. Census tracts are areas of similar land use and human density patterns for which human demographic statistics are calculated (Census Population and Housing 1990, Seattle, Wash., unpubl. data).

Residential habitat, which was predominantly single family housing development, represented the most urbanized edge of the coyote's range in King County (Quinn 1991) with a mean density of 1412.72 (SE = 260.12) humans/km^2. Coyotes in this habitat type were closely associated with remnant patches of second growth forest found in parks and riparian areas (Quinn 1995). Mixed agricultural habitat had a density of 347.97 (SE = 51.52) humans/km^2 and was predominantly pasture land supporting dairy farms. Mixed forest habitat had a density of 125.66 (SE = 17.74) humans/km^2 and was predominantly second growth forest with interspersed single family housing developments.

To minimize the chance of encountering scats from midsized carnivores other than coyotes, I located routes in regions of relatively high coyote density (Quinn 1992, 1995), outside the range of the indigenous red fox (*Vulpes vulpes cascadensis,* Aubry 1984), and in areas where bobcats (*Felix rufus*) and introduced red fox (*Vulpes vulpes*) were extremely rare (D. A. Ware, Wash. Dept. Wildl. unpubl. data; J. R. Consolini, Wash. State Trappers Assoc., pers. comm.). There was no evidence of feral dogs (*Canis familiaris*) near any of the routes based on personal records of an animal damage control trapper who has worked in these areas for the past three years (J. R. Consolini, Wash. State Trappers Assoc., pers. comm.). My field observations were consistent with these assumptions.

METHODS AND MATERIALS

I cleared all scats from routes, which consisted of unpaved trails, in October 1989. From November 1989 through October 1990, I collected all scats at 2-week intervals from each route. Routes were 5–9 km in total length but were discontinuous because of the patchy nature of coyote habitat and suitable scat collection areas. The residential route was composed of 6 segments, totaling 9 km in length, and located near the northern border of Seattle. All segments were within 0.5–8.0 km of each other and were in patches of second growth forest surrounded by residential housing developments. The mixed agricultural route, totaling 5 km in length, was composed of 3 segments separated from each other by 0.3–0.5 km. This route was located 5 km north of Redmond in the Sammamish River flood plain. The flood plain was predominantly pasture land surrounding small farms. The adjacent uplands consisted of housing developments and patches of second growth forest. The mixed forest route was 5 km in length and located on Novelty Hill 12 km northeast of Redmond. This route was composed of 2 segments separated by approximately 0.5 km along a power line right-of-way off Novelty Hill road. Except for blackberry (*Rubus* spp.) and grasses directly below the power lines, the area was predominantly second growth forest with interspersed housing developments.

I identified scats by their physical appearance, including size (Danner and Dodd 1982) and shape (Murie 1954). As an added safeguard against including dog scats in the samples I assumed that scats composed of >50% commercial dog food (estimated visually) originated from dog. Commercial dog food was easily identified under low magnification by the abundance of grain particles.

Collected scats were individually bagged and dried at 50°C for 48 hours. Food items in dried feces were separated manually and identified by comparison with reference collections of mammal skeletons and guard hairs, and with hair medulla (Moore et al. 1974) and plant seed keys (Martin 1961).

I used Knowlton's (1964) method for estimating coyote diet because it produces an easily understood qualitative measure of food importance. I visually estimated the volume of each individual food item to the nearest 5% of each scat. I counted only the major food item (>40% by volume) of each fecal specimen (Andelt 1985, Knowlton 1964). When two items each composed >40% of fecal volume, I assigned a 0.5 count to each.

Because I did not sample from replicate habitat types, I made only qualitative comparisons among habitat types. I defined seasons as: spring (1 Apr.–30 Jun.), summer (1 Jul.–30 Sep.), fall (1 Oct.–31 Dec.), and winter (1 Jan.–31 Mar.).

RESULTS

I collected a total of 1435 coyote scats from all habitat types (735 from residential, 449 from mixed agricultural, and 251 from mixed forest). From 88 to 91% of scats from each habitat consisted of a single food item as defined in the methods. Fruits and mammals were the two most abundant classes of food items in scats from all habitats (Table 1). Apple (*Malus* spp.), cherry and plum

Table 1. *Food items by percent, in the annual diet (1989–90) of western Washington coyotes (Canis latrans) from residential habitat, mixed agricultural—residential habitat (mixed agric), mixed forest—residential habitat (mixed forest), and all habitats combined (pooled).*

	Habitat Type			
Food Item	Residential	Mixed Agric	Mixed Forest	Pooled
Fruit				
Apple (*Malus* spp.)	29.4	21.7	40.6	29.1
Cherry (*Prunus* spp.)	9.7	12.8	9.4	10.6
Other/unknown	3.5	2.7	7.0	3.9
Total fruit	42.6	37.2	57.0	43.6
Mammal				
Vole (*Microtus* spp.)	3.3	41.7	5.7	15.9
Squirrel (*Sciurus/Tamiasciurus* spp.)	7.9	1.4	1.1	4.6
Cat (*Felis catus*)	13.1	2.3	3.3	7.8
Mountain beaver (*Aplodontia rufa*)	3.9	0.5	5.4	3.1
Other	7.8	8.3	12.8	8.9
Unknown	2.3	0.8	3.6	2.1
Total mammal	38.3	55.0	31.9	42.4
Miscellaneous				
Bird/reptile	2.7	1.6	2.8	2.4
Grass/other vegetation	4.0	2.3	3.4	3.4
Garbage	1.4	1.1	1.4	1.3
Dogfood	4.5	1.8	1.5	3.1
Unknown	6.4	1.1	2.0	3.9

(*Prunus* spp.), vole (predominantly *Microtus*), and house cat each comprised >10% of the diet in one or more habitat types. Bird, reptile, insect, livestock, and vegetation other than fruit were minor components (<3%) of the diet in each habitat type (Table 1).

Coyotes in mixed agricultural habitat had the highest proportion of mammals in the diet followed by the residential habitat (Table 1). Vole was the most abundant mammalian food item in the diet of coyotes in mixed agricultural habitat. Cat was the most abundant mammalian food item (13.1%) in residential habitat followed by squirrel (*Sciurus* spp. and *Tamiasciurus* spp.) at 7.9% of the annual diet. With the exception of muskrat (*Ondatra zibethica*), which was not found in scats from residential habitat, and dog, coyote, and raccoon (*Procyon lotor*), which were found only in scats from residential diets, diets in all habitat types contained the same mammal species. Muskrat, dog, coyote and raccoon each made up <3.0% of the diet in each habitat. Mammals made up the majority of the spring diet (>58.0%) in all habitat types. For the remainder of the year, mammals were a fairly consistent proportion of the diet (approx. 30.0%) except in the mixed agricultural habitat. During winter, coyote diets in mixed agricultural habitat contained twice as much mammal as in other habitat types (Figure 1).

Coyotes in mixed forest habitat had the highest proportion of fruits in the diet followed by coyotes in residential habitat (Table 1). Cherry and plum were the first dietary fruits to appear in the summer followed by berry (*Rubus* spp.). Apple, the most abundant dietary fruit in all habitat types (Table 1), generally

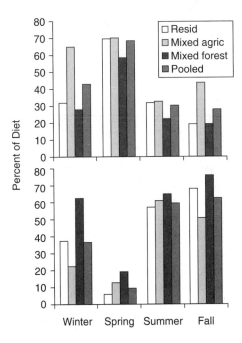

Figure 1 Percentages of mammals (top panel) and fruits (lower panel) in the seasonal diet of coyotes from three habitat types in western Washington, 1989–90: residential habitat (resid), mixed agricultural-residential habitat (mixed agric), mixed forest-residential habitat (mixed forest), and all habitats combined (pooled). I defined seasons as winter (1 Jan.–31 Mar.), spring (1 Apr.–30 Jun.), summer (1 Jul.–30 Sep.), and fall (1 Oct.–31 Dec.).

did not appear in the diet until the fall but remained an important food item into the winter. The greatest proportion of dietary fruits occurred in the summer or fall in all habitat types (Figure 1). The higher annual proportion of fruits in mixed forest habitat was primarily the result of high winter consumption of fruits in that habitat type (Figure 1).

DISCUSSION

The diets of coyotes in all three habitat types were similar in composition for the major food classes (mammals and fruits). Coyotes in all habitat types took advantage of the seasonal availability of mammals and fruits. The winter/spring peak of mammals in the diet corresponded to the time when the availability of fruits was probably at its annual low. Fruits became an important class of coyote food in June and remained important until January. This study was consistent with other studies that have shown fruits to be important dietary components in many coyote populations throughout North America (Dibello et al. 1990, Mac-Cracken 1982), Toweill and Anthony 1988). Apple was the most important fruit in the diet of coyotes in my study area because it was available at times of the year when mammals and other fruits were relatively scarce. Apple ripens later in the year than other fruits and cooler fall and winter temperatures slow the decomposition of apples and make them available for relatively longer periods. Although fruit was a major component of the coyote diets in this study, its importance may be overestimated. Diets containing large quantities of fruit may increase the rate of scat deposition (Andelt and Andelt 1984). In addition, conclusions about dietary preference or the importance of particular food items to coyote fitness should be made cautiously because coyote diet was not assessed in terms of food item availability.

While mammals were important components of the diet in all habitat types, there was considerable variation in proportions of individual mammal species. Coyotes in mixed forest habitat had the lowest proportion of mammals in the diet and no single species of mammal made up >6% of the annual diet. Voles dominated the mammalian portion of coyote diets in the mixed agricultural habitat. This is consistent with Atkinson and Shackleton's (1991) study of coyote food habits in a predominantly agricultural habitat in Canada where voles made up nearly 70% (by volume) of the coyote diet. Cat was the most abundant mammalian food item for coyotes in the residential habitats. In 1991, the Humane Society of the United States (R. Lamb, Humane Soc. of the U.S., pers. comm.) estimated that there were approximately one cat per three households in the U.S. Clearly, cats represent an abundant resource for predators such as the coyote, particularly in areas with high human density. Shargo (1998) found 13.6% occurrence of cat in 22 scats collected in his urban study area, which was most similar to my residential habitat type. However, cat was absent and only a minor food item (<3% frequency of occurrence) of urban/rural coyotes in British Columbia (Atkinson and Shackleton 1991) and urban coyotes in California (MacCracken 1982), respectively.

One major consequence of human activity is the creation of food sources that are readily exploited by coyotes (Gier 1975). Human alteration, particularly logging and the clearing of land for agriculture, may have facilitated the colonization of Oregon, Washington, and British Columbia by coyotes (Dalquest 1948). In western Oregon, many important food items of coyotes were associated with clear-cut areas rather than the surrounding forest (Toweill and Anthony 1988). In British Columbia, coyotes fed primarily (>70% by volume) on meadow voles (*Microtus* spp.) living in agricultural lands that were previously forested (Atkinson and Shackleton 1991). My study suggested that coyotes in western Washington eat large quantities of food that result from human activity and that coyote diet may change as a function of human density and land-use.

ACKNOWLEDGEMENTS

This study was conducted in partial fulfillment of the requirements for a Ph.D. at the University of Washington. I thank the Washington Department of Fish and Wildlife and the College of Forest Resources at the University of Washington for providing funding. I also thank D. Pike, S. Joneson, and D. Peterson for assisting in scat analysis, and S. D. West and P. M. Kareiva for reviewing the manuscript.

LITERATURE CITED

Andelt, W. F. 1985. Behavioral ecology of coyotes in south Texas. Wildl. Monog. 94.

————., and S. H. Andelt. 1984. Diet bias in scat deposition-rate surveys of coyote density. Wildl. Soc. Bull. 12:74–77.

Atkinson, K. T., and D. M. Shackleton. 1991. Coyote, *Canis latrans*, ecology in a rural-urban environment. Can. Field-Nat. 105:49–54.

Aubry, K. B. 1984. The recent history and present distribution of the red fox in Washington. Northw. Sci. 58:69–79.

Dalquest, W. W. 1948. Mammals of Washington. University of Kansas. Publication of Natural History No. 2.

Danner, D. A., and N. Dodd. 1982. Comparison of coyote and gray fox scat diameters. J. Wildl. Manage. 46:240–241.

Dibello, F. J., S. M. Arthur, and W. B. Krohn. 1990. Food habits of sympatric coyotes, *Canis latrans*, red foxes, *Vulpes vulpes*, and bobcats, *Lynx rufus*, in Maine. Can. Field-Nat. 104:403–408.

Franklin, J. F., and C. T. Dyrness. 1984. Natural vegetation of Oregon and Washington. Oregon State University Press, Corvallis.

Gier, H. T. 1975. Ecology and social behavior of the coyote. *In* M. W. Fox (ed.). The wild canids. Van Nostrand Reinhold, New York, New York, Pp. 247–262.

Knowlton, F. F. 1964. Aspects of coyote predation in south Texas with special reference to white-tailed deer. Purdue University, Lafayette, Indiana. Ph.D. Dissertation.

MacCracken, J. G. 1982. Coyote food in a southern California suburb. Wildl. Soc. Bull. 10: 280–281.

Martin, A. C. 1961. Seed identification manual. University of California Press, Berkeley.

Moore, T. D., L. E. Spence, and C. E. Dugnolle. 1974. Identification of the dorsal guard hairs of some mammals of Wyoming. Wyoming Game and Fish Department Bulletin 14, 177 p.

Murie, O. J. 1954. A field guide to animal tracks. Houghton Mifflin Co., Boston, Massachusetts.

Quinn, T. 1991. Distribution and habitat associations of coyotes in Seattle, Washington. In L. W. Adams and D. L. Leedy (eds.), Proceedings of a national symposium on urban wildlife. National Institute for Urban Wildlife, Columbia, Maryland. Pp. 47–51.

———. 1992. The distribution, movements, and diet of coyotes in urban areas of western Washington. University of Washington, Seattle. Ph.D. Dissertation.

———. 1995. Using public sightings to investigate coyote use of urban habitat. J. Wildl. Manage. 59:238–245.

Shargo, E. S. 1988. Home range, movement and activity patterns of coyotes (*Canis latrans*) in a Los Angeles suburb. University of California, Los Angeles. Ph.D. Dissertation.

Soulé, M. E., D. T. Bolger, A. C. Alberts, J. Wright, M. Sorice, and S. Hill. 1988. Reconstructed dynamics of rapid extinctions of chaparral-requiring birds in urban habitat islands. Conserv. Biol. 2:75–92.

Toweill, D. E., and R. G. Anthony. 1988. Coyote foods in a coniferous forest in Oregon. J. Wildl. Manage. 52: 507–512. ☣

QUESTIONS FOR THOUGHT AND STUDY

1. What questions are Quinn and his fellow scientists trying to answer?

2. Does the research question arise from a static, dynamic, or systemic perspective?

3. What is the purpose of the detailed geographic description in the Methods and Materials section?

4. What is the relationship between Table 1 and the text of the Results section? The text of the Discussion section? What is the relationship of Table 1 to Figure 1? Of Figure 1 to the Results section? To the Discussion section?

5. Are the inferences sound? What mistakes might there be in the inferences drawn? How does Quinn guard against mistaken inferences?

6. What conclusion does Quinn draw from his study? Does he answer his research question in its entirety?

7. What inferences does Quinn draw from observable evidence?

Adverse Effects of Hyposalinity from Stormwater Runoff on the Aggregating Anemone

K. L. M. Martin, M. C. Lawson, and H. Engebretson

Biography: *Karen L. M. Martin and her colleagues reported this study at the Symposium on Coastal Watersheds and Their Effects on the Ocean Environment, held in Los Angeles, California, in May of 1995. Dr. Martin received her Ph.D. from University of California, Los Angeles in 1990 and is now on the faculty of the Natural Sciences Division of Pepperdine University. She has also written* Aerial Respiration in Marine Intertidal Fishes, *which explores the possible evolution of air-breathing in intertidal fishes.*

Martin et al. search for the cause of decreased anemone populations along the Southern California coastline. They find marked decrease in populations near storm sewer exits where salinity decreases markedly. The reading is an accessible study on the effects of human populations in an environment familiar to students and a professional model of an observational scientific report.

ABSTRACT

Coastal watersheds strongly impact the near-shore marine environment with freshwater inundation and runoff from the land. At Leo Carillo State Beach in Malibu, California, we have noticed marked effects of stormwater runoff on the local marine fauna. The aggregating sea anemone expels symbiotic algae under the influence of hyposaline stress, causing bleaching. The number and distribution of bleached sea anemones have increased dramatically from 1992 to 1995 at Leo Carillo State Beach under the influence of increased rainfall and the artificial broadening of the arroyo channel at its mouth.

On a gently sloping beach, many horizontal meters of marine habitat may be exposed to air during low tides. The area on rocks between the lowest low tide and the highest high tide, the rocky intertidal zone, is among the most productive habitats on earth, similar to a tropical rainforest or a coral reef (Leigh et al. 1987). Invertebrate animals living in the marine intertidal zone are hardy, generally well-adapted for the changing conditions of temperature, pH, oxygen, and carbon dioxide during tidal excursions (Truchot and Duhamel-Jouve 1980). However, because they are at the interface between the ocean and the land, they are more directly exposed to runoff than other marine organisms. If harmful conditions occur during low tides, any mitigating effects of dilution are not present and these organisms bear the full brunt of the exposure.

The intertidal sea anemone *Anthopleura elegantissima* normally maintains a symbiotic relationship with microscopic single-celled algae that live within its tissues. The dinoflagellate algae, or zooxanthellae, photosynthesize and provide a

From *Bulletin of the Southern California Academy of Science* 95 no. 1 (1996): 46–51.

97

substantial fraction of the host anemone's nutritional needs (Fitt et al. 1982). Sea anemones have millions of zooxanthellae for each gram of tissue. *A. elegantissima* is very tolerant, surviving coverage by sand, exposure to air, and starvation for extended periods. However, when exposed to prolonged darkness, high temperatures, cold shock, or excessive time in bright sunlight, some sea anemones react by expelling some of their zooxanthellae (Muscatine et al. 1991). This expulsion causes a reduction in the green-brown color of the anemone and is therefore called bleaching. Bleaching by expulsion of zooxanthellae is seen in many species of reef-building corals, and is considered a sign of stress (Jokiel and Coles 1990). Without their symbionts, anemones and corals have much less energy available for growth and reproduction, and they may die. The presence or absence of symbiotic zooxanthellae provides a simple and fairly reliable indicator of health of these hardy and adaptable intertidal animals, although some of their color may come from endogenous pigments (Buchsbaum 1969). We suggest that they may be used as an indicator species for hyposalinity of seawater in rocky intertidal zone.

Leo Carillo State Beach (LCSB) in Los Angeles County, California, has extensive rocky substrate and a gently sloping face that provides an excellent potential habitat for rocky intertidal animals and plants. During the drought of the late 1980's, the intertidal fauna here was lush and diverse, and the area was frequented by members of the public, school classes, and park rangers for educational and interpretive lessons. However, following the heavy rains of 1991–1992, we observed a drastic decrease in the numbers and diversity of the intertidal organisms. Of those animals still remaining, the sessile *A. elegantissima* appeared much paler than before, indicating that bleaching had occurred (Engebretson and Martin 1994).

We did a series of laboratory experiments that indicated that the loss of color in *A. elegantissima* in the field was the result of loss of zooxanthellae (Engebretson and Martin 1994). Bleached anemones taken from LCSB had significantly reduced numbers of zooxanthellae (Fig. 1). We hypothesized that the bleaching was caused by excessive exposure to freshwater runoff. Healthy anemones from another site were placed into several different dilutions of seawater for time periods ranging from several days to several weeks. These *A. elegantissima* lost their symbiotic zooxanthellae and bleached rapidly, proportional to the strength and duration of the hyposaline exposure (Fig. 2). The anemones remained closed and did not feed while in hyposaline water.

A line transect to measure the number of bleached *A. elegantissima* at LCSB was done parallel to shore at a tidal height of −0.15 m over a distance of 120 m in 1992 (Engebretson and Martin 1994). At that time the anemones that were bleached were located within a limited area of freshwater runoff, resulting from discharge of the Arroyo Sequit (Fig. 3). Anemones located at the same tidal height but on either side of this freshwater runoff area were apparently not affected. We returned to this site in 1995 and ran line transects at four different

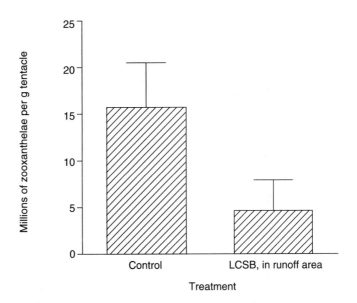

Figure 1 Zooxanthellae were counted from tentacles of *A. eleganissima* from a control site and from the freshwater influx area of LCSB. The numbers of zooxanthellae per gram of tissue were significantly lower in the LCSB anemones. Shown are means ± standard errors.

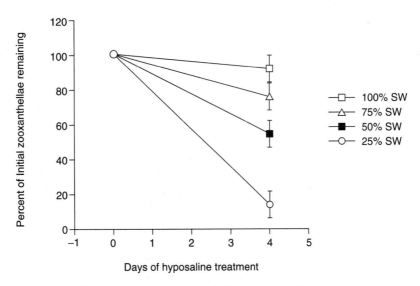

Figure 2 *A. elegantissima* expelled zooxanthellae in response to constant exposure to hyposaline water, at the levels stated (100% = 32 ppt, 75% = 24 ppt, 50% = 16 ppt, and 25% = 8 ppt). After 4 days, all treatments except the control (100% SW) showed significant losses of zooxanthellae. Shown are means ± standard errors.

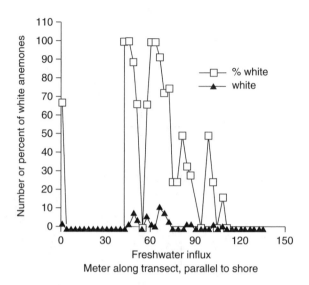

Figure 3   Line transect data from 1992, showing bleaching within the freshwater influx area. Very little bleaching is shown outside of the channel for runoff. Transects were taken at –0.15 m tidal height.

tidal heights, –0.3 m, –0.24 m,, –0.15 m, and –0.07 m, again parallel to shore over a distance of 132 m. These transect lines were separated by 3 m or more of horizontal distance. Line transects in 1995 indicated that anemones were bleached over a much greater area of the habitat, and at lower tidal heights, than in the previous transect (Fig. 4). We observed far less of the biological diversity that was so prevalent intertidally during the drought years in the intertidal zone at this site; all the sea urchins, snails, crabs, octopus, chitons, tidepool fish, and other marine organisms have apparently either died or moved into deeper water.

When anemones are exposed to short duration pulses of hyposaline water, similar to tidal exposure in tidepools during freshwater runoff, bleaching was even more pronounced and more rapid than bleaching in response to constant, long-term exposure to hyposaline conditions (Fig. 5). Thus, the field conditions of stormwater runoff during low tides over several days is potentially extremely detrimental and probably has caused the widespread bleaching of A. *elegantissima* seen in the transects at LCSB in 1995 (Lawson and Martin, unpublished), in addition to the profound loss of biodiversity in this habitat. Being sessile, A. *elegantissima* do not move away from harsh conditions. The hyposaline stress is likely to cause osmotic influx into cells and damage by rupture (Engebretson and Martin 1994; Gates et al. 1992).

Over the summer of 1995 we observed freshwater runoff from the arroyo on several occasions, covering a much greater area of the expanse of rocky inter-

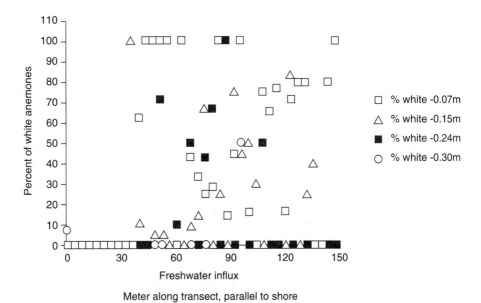

Figure 4   Line transect data from 1995, showing increased influence of freshwater runoff over a larger area of the beach. Transects were taken at four tidal heights, –0.07 m, –0.15 m, –0.24 m, and –0.3 m.

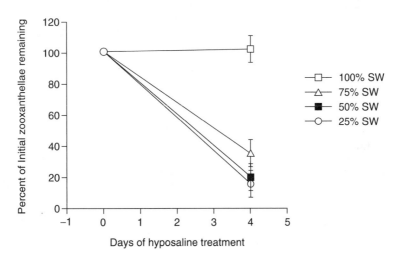

Figure 5   Percent of initial numbers of zooxanthellae remaining following 4 days of treatments in which anemones were held in 100% seawater except for one 3 h pulse of hyposalinity per day (100% = 32 ppt, 75% = 24 ppt, 50% = 16 ppt, and 25% = 8 ppt). Shown are means ± standard errors.

tidal habitat than the natural runoff channel. Heavy equipment had been used to bulldoze sand in order to direct the stormwater runoff much more broadly, rather than allowing it to continue to run in its natural, narrow channel. In addition, fresh water seeped farther across the beach by flow under the sand when the water was deep in the arroyo channel. From these studies it is not clear whether some other factors, such as pollutants, could also have contributed to the bleaching seen in the field. However, in the laboratory distilled water was used for all dilutions of artificial seawater in the experiments, and no contaminants were present. The hyposaline dilution alone is sufficient to cause the bleaching.

The increased area of LCSB containing bleached anemones in 1995 is cause for concern. Freshwater inundation is episodic but frequent at this site, and it is channeled artificially in a manner that causes direct effects in this near-shore marine environment. Particularly during low and minus tides, seawater dilution of stormwater runoff does not occur. We measured salinity in the field as low as 0 ppt, or freshwater, in the intertidal zone during a minus tide that occurred a few hours after a light rainfall. We are concerned that efforts to increase the speed and efficiency of stormwater runoff have taken precedence over efforts to preserve an important biological habitat that educates and is enjoyed by many people of the Los Angeles area.

ACKNOWLEDGMENTS

We thank J. G. Tallman and S. D. Davis for use of equipment, R. S. Darken and R. C. Van Winkle for assistance in the field, and S. Goode, V. Weis, and S. Yoder for valuable criticisms of the manuscript. This research was supported by a grant from the National Science Foundation Research Experience for Undergraduates program, BIR-9225034. Anemones were collected from Leo Carillo State Beach with permits issued by the California State Parks Service and from the control site with a permit from the California Department of Fish and Game (to KLMM).

LITERATURE CITED

Buchsbaum, V. M. 1968. Behavioral and physiological responses to light by the sea anemone *Anthopleura elegantissima* as related to its algal symbionts. Ph.D. diss., Stanford University, Stanford, California.

Engebretson, H., and K. L. M. Martin. 1994. Effects of decreased salinity on expulsion of zooxanthellae in the symbiotic sea anemone *Anthopleura elegantissima*. Pacific Sci., 48:446–456.

Fitt, W. K., R. L. Pardy, and M. M. Littler. 1982. Photosynthesis, respiration, and contribution to community productivity of the symbiotic sea anemone *Anthopleura elegantissima* (Brandt, 1835). J. Exp. Mar. Biol. Ecol., 61:213–232.

Gates, R. D., G. Baghdasarian, and L. Muscatine. 1992. Temperature stress causes host cell detachment in symbiotic cnidarians: implications for coral bleaching. Biol. Bull. (Woods Hole), 182:324–332.

Jokiel, P. L., and S. L. Coles. 1990. Response of Hawaiian and other Indo-Pacific reef corals to elevated temperatures. Coral Reefs, 8:155–162.

Leigh, E. G., Jr., R. T. Paine, J. F. Quinn, and T. H. Suchanek. 1987. Wave energy and intertidal productivity. Proc. Natl. Acad. Sci., 84:1314–1318.

Muscatine, L., D. Grossman, and J. Doino. 1991. Release of symbiotic algae by tropical anemones and corals after cold shock. Mar. Ecol. Prog. Ser., 77:233–243.

Truchot, J. P., and A. Duhamel-Jouve. 1980. Oxygen and carbon dioxide in the marine intertidal environment: diurnal and tidal changes in rockpools. Respir. Physiol., 39:241–254. ☙

QUESTIONS FOR THOUGHT AND STUDY

1. Restate the first two paragraphs of the study in your own words. What does the final sentence in paragraph two mean?

2. What is the hypothesis of the experiments?

3. What do Martin, Lawson and Engebretson measure to test their hypothesis?

4. What relationships are Figures 2–5 showing?

5. What inferences do Martin, Lawson, and Engebretson draw from the results of the experiments?

6. Insert the appropriate section headings into this article (Introduction, Methods and Materials, Results, Discussion).

7. Are there other things that might have caused the findings? What are they?

STUDENT PAPER FOR REVISION WORKSHOP

This observational study of foxes on a university campus provides a strong example of how personal curiosity about the natural world can be productively pursued through formal scientific method. The writer uses scientific report format and the trimodal observation method effectively to record direct empirical observation, to include connections to previous knowledge through review of the literature, and to comment upon larger issues of ecological ethics. How might further revision provide some opportunities to strengthen objective focus, to develop some of the findings sections more fully, and to apply sentence revisions skills explored in this chapter for increased specificity and clarity?

"Observing the Red Fox (*Vulpes vulpes*) on the UCSB Campus"

Student A

Abstract

This paper is a scientific inquiry into the foxes that live here at UCSB. Its purpose is to understand their relationship to the environment as well as to the home community. The observational results show that the foxes are of the species *Vulpes vulpes* or commonly known as the red fox. They are shown to have a complex relationship to the local ecosystem, serving as a top predator. The role of this animal is beneficial to the human community in terms of rodent control. In general, even though they thrive on campus, we must consider total encroachment onto their natural habitat as a breech of ecological ethics.

Introduction

Since the beginning of my freshman year I have been intrigued by the elusive and beautiful fox that makes its home here on the UCSB campus. Walking around late at night, I would often spot its sleek profile stalking through the shadows or trotting across a field or parking lot. Always I would stop and try to keep an eye on the regal creature for as long as possible before it disappeared into the night. However, it never seemed as though it stayed visible long enough to satisfy my curiosity for the animal. Yet as chance would have it, later that year I stumbled upon the location of a large den. This gave me the fortunate opportunity to do some considerable observation on these animals. This year when I returned to the same spot, I found them still living there, carrying on as usual. The purpose of this paper is to carry over my leisurely observations of these local predators into a more scientific arena. I am curious to know exactly what type of foxes are living here at UCSB, what their characteristics and habits are, and how they factor into our local ecosystem. Further, I am interested in our relationship to these small creatures. Ecologically speaking are we harming or helping them? It is my belief that the human development of their natural habitat is jeopardizing their future.

Tentatively, I believe that the foxes here at UCSB are red foxes. According to Burt (1976) this is the largest variety of fox. It has a head and body between 22 and 25 inches and a tail measuring 14 to 16 inches. Generally it weighs in around 10 to 15 pounds. They have a dense soft pelage on the upper body that is generally reddish yellow, with the darkest fur on the back. Black fur is characteristic of the ears and feet. The tail is white tipped and bushy and used for balance and for keeping the face warm while sleeping. The underbelly and chin are white, as well. The red fox is possibly the most adaptable carnivore on this planet (Macdonald, 1984). The researchers Samuel and Nelson (1982) explain that red foxes prefer diverse habitats consisting of intermixed cropland, pastures, brush, mixed hardwood, and edges of open areas that provide suitable hunting grounds. They may also inhabit suburban and even entirely urban areas. The "urban foxes" of London, England, for example, are no longer familiar with forests or meadows (Zimen, 1990).

Foxes are most active late evening night, and in the early morning (Burt, 1976). Their food consists of available animals ranging in size from insects to large hares. They will often round out their diet with berries and other fruits. Research shows that if given the choice they prefer mice (Macdonald, 1984). Even though foxes are considered social animals, they hunt alone (Zimen, 1990). They have one litter of pups per year, usually during March or April. Two to seven pups are usually born. Pups remain in the den for three to four weeks, then come to the entrance to play and feed (Burt, 1976). In much of its range the fox has a bounty on its head. Whether it is beneficial or harmful depends on the circumstances. If it kills pheasants, grouse, or rabbits, the hunter will consider it harmful, but if it kills hundreds of mice and rats the farmer might consider it beneficial. Actually many food studies show that because of the foxes' rodent control abilities, they actually do considerably more good than harm (Macdonald, 1984).

Method

I returned to observe the foxes at approximately 12 A.M. in early April 1999. The temperature was in the low sixties and the wind was negligible. The moon was nearly full, providing a rather well lit night for making observations. No attempt was made to camouflage myself or mask my scent. The den is located in the park behind Campus Point, directly across from the marine biology laboratory. The skulk has established itself beneath one of the portable class buildings on the edge of the lagoon. The park itself seems to be an excellent location for observing an animal like this for several reasons. First, it is quiet and somewhat secluded from any disturbing noises or commotion. Cars or people would not be an issue in terms of frightening off the wildlife. Next, because the park is situated next to a lagoon it is certainly prime feeding ground for the foxes. Finally, the open grassy spaces make it perfect for an unobstructed view of the animals. I positioned myself on one of the park benches next to the concrete pathway running through the park. This put me about 25 yards away from where the foxes would exit their burrow.

It was not long before the first fox came into view. For identification purposes I used this fox to record data concerning physical characteristics. Soon after many others came out behind it. I used the entire group for other data collection such as behavioral traits. I watched intently, scribbling anything I considered significant into the notebook I had brought with me. I used a trimodal observation format. This consists of separating the characteristics of the fox into static, dynamic, and systemic categories. Static description involves only the physical attributes of the foxes such as height or color. Dynamic description deals with the animal as existing at a certain point in time. An example of this type of description would be age. In systemic description one considers what kind of interactive role the animal plays within the environment it lives. This category considers things like behavior, food procurement, reproduction, etc. I recorded for about thirty-five minutes.

Results

Static

The fox used as the standard appeared to have a head and body length of about 18-24 inches and a tail that was approximately 12-14 inches long. It stood about 13-15 inches at the shoulders having front legs approximately 7 inches long. The back legs were slightly longer because of a joint that bowed out toward their posterior end giving them a boomerang-like appearance. The head was about 6 inches long and roughly triangular. The snout tapered down to a point where the nose and mouth were located. A series of whiskers protruded from an area on both sides of the muzzle directly behind the nose. They are 3 to 4 inches long. The eyes were positioned on either side of the ridge of the snout midway down the length of the head. The ears were located on the top of the head and were approximately 3 to 4 inches long. They were triangular and black. The length and color of the animal's pelage varied in relation to location on the body. The hair was short (1/2 cm) and red on the face. Short black hair covered the ears and feet. It became longer (1-2 cm) on the body of the animal and was black along the ridge of the back and red along the sides. The tail was relatively bushy with fur about 2-3 cm long. Here the fur was mostly red but faded to white as it approached the tip. White fur of basically the same length as the body was on the underbelly.

Dynamic

In all, 9 foxes were observed. Many different sizes of foxes were observed. They had head and body lengths ranging from 6 to 30 inches. The smaller foxes had thin and silky coats of fur. The larger foxes had thicker and coarser pelage.

Systemic

Overall, these animals retain many of the characteristics anal mannerisms of other small canines. An example of this is how they trotted briskly through the park with their nose to the ground sniffing everything in the vicinity. They traveled around the park individually, as well as in groups of 2 to 5. Generally the smaller foxes were accompanied at all times by the larger foxes. The behavior of the larger animals generally consisted of sniffing around the area and inspecting the bushes and shrubbery along the periphery of the park. The smaller foxes were observed to do two things: First, mimic the sniffing behavior of the larger foxes they followed; second, preoccupy themselves with small little leaps into the air. Finally, little barks and yelps were heard periodically throughout the observation.

Discussion

The foxes observed here at UCSB are most likely a hybrid subspecies of the red fox (*Vulpes vulpes*). This is indicated from the coloring of their pelt. Generally, the red fox can be distinguished from other species by the white fur at the end of its tail (Samuel & Nelson, 1982). The fact that the species living here has white at the end of its tail indicates that it is indeed a red fox. However, the black along the ridge of the back suggests that at one point it might have interbred with a variety of the gray fox. This variation is apparently not uncommon. Samuel and Nelson state, "Several color phases of red foxes are found, especially in cold regions: black, silver, cross (dark cross on shoulders and bluish gray" (p. 476). The size is also consistent with that of the red fox. In another field guide it gave the head and body length of this species of fox at 22 to 25 inches long, which is approximately the same size as the ones I observed (Burt, 1976).

The ages of the animals observed are obviously related to their size. The smallest of the foxes were probably just born in the past month. This is consistent with the March through April timeline for pups to be born (Samuel & Nelson, 1982). This also explains why their coats were less developed. Because of my untrained eye and the distance from which I was observing, I could not distinguish between the ages of the adult foxes. Yet, they are all probably between 6 months (when full growth is attained) and 5 years of age. Apparently, longevity for foxes living in the wild is not much beyond that (Samuel & Nelson, 1982).

The area where the foxes were observed is consistent with habitat research on the animals. In fact, this part of the UCSB campus is ideal for the foxes for several reasons. First, it is most certainly an area abundant with food foxes like to eat. The lagoon and the extensive networks of brush around it are teaming with insects, rodents, and rabbits. Second, hunting and heavy traffic will never be an issue for the survival of these animals. This is significant because the two leading causes of death for the red fox are in fact hunting and highways (Zimen, 1994). The relatively small area of land that the foxes have to live in, coupled with the likely low mortality rates, would explain why I saw such an uncommonly large number of foxes. I saw 9. Usually the maximum number of foxes that live together is five (Burt, 1976).

The behaviors of the foxes that I recorded during my observations all basically break down to food procurement. First, when the foxes trotted around the park with their noses to the ground they were searching for food. Red foxes hunt by scent (Macdonald, 1984). On a side note, the fact that the red fox hunts by scent is probably one of the main reasons why we observe it here at UCSB in the first place. The red fox is not indigenous to this area. Initially only the gray fox could be found here. When red foxes were released from fur farms they began to displace the gray fox. The fact that they hunt by scent gives them a distinct advantage finding prey. This is because local animals have coevolved with the gray fox who hunts by sight (Samuel & Nelson, 1982). Next, the little pounces the baby foxes were observed doing are actually trial "*moues* leaps.*" They are practicing springing off the ground and diving front paws first, onto prey. This aerial descent may be a device literally to squash the vertical jump used by some mice to escape predators (Macdonald, 1984).

The hunting attributes and techniques I have just outlined contribute to making the red fox one of the carnivorous predators in our local ecosystem. As stated in the beginning, they play a crucial role in keeping the bird and rodent population in check (Macdonald, 1984). This is an obvious advantage to us as residents of UCSB and Isle Vista. The fact that there are so many people living and working on this tiny area of land provides tons of food (in terms of waste) for a rodent population to subsist on. Without predators like the fox, the mouse population could undoubtedly grow significantly larger. An exploding mouse population is the last thing that over populated Isla Vista [student residential area] needs. Thus, a mutually beneficial relationship between us and the red fox is apparent. We provide it with local protection and attract a large amount of prey, and they keep the prey from overrunning Isla Vista.

Conclusion

My initial question of whether human development helps or hurts the red fox is still quite a debatable issue. On one hand, as I said before, the red fox is possibly the most adaptable carnivore on this planet. It can thrive everywhere from the arctic circle to downtown London. Thus, some have argued that human development has actually helped the species, for foxes have followed the abundant food sources provided by humans as we have advanced westward (Macdonald, 1984). On the other hand, foxes have paid a heavy toll for living so close to man. Traffic has killed many thousands of foxes. Also, there is or has been a bounty on the head of foxes in nearly every state. Additionally, many populations of foxes have been severely depleted through trapping due to an increase in the value of their pelts (Zimen, 1990). Tampering with the delicate equilibrium within the food web is not only risky business (rodent population explosion) but a matter of ethics, as well. This is discussed in *The Environmental Predicament* in an article written by Aldo Leopold called "Toward a Land Ethic." He professes a "land ethic" that sees man as merely a part of a community of interdependent parts. Every part relies on the others for quality existence of all. We must not exploit and develop every part of the land just because we can. For as Leopold (1981) states, "Land is not merely soil; it is a fountain of energy flowing through a circuit of soil, plants, and animals" (p. 6). Looking at the complex interactions the red fox has with the local ecosystem and how they in turn effect us truly gives credence to this concept. We must respect this dynamic and interdependent fountain of energy, for it is our life blood. This, we must refrain from ever reaching a point where all foxes are city or campus foxes.

References

Burt, H. (1976). *A field guide to the mammals*. Boston: Houghton Mifflin Co.

Leopold, A. (1981). Toward a land ethic. In C. Verbung (Ed.), *The Environmental Predicament* (pp. 4-12). Boston: Bedford Books of St. Martins Press.

Macdonald, D. (Ed.). (1984). *The encyclopedia of mammals*. London: George Allen & Unwin.

Nelson, B. & Samuel, D. (1982). *Vulpes vulpes* and allies. In J. Chapman (Ed.), *Wild Mammals of North America* (pp. 475-487). Baltimore: Johns Hopkins Press.

Zimen, E. (1990). True foxes. In W. Keienburg (Ed.), *Grizmek's Encyclopedia of Animals* (pp. 118-129). New York: McGraw-Hill Inc.

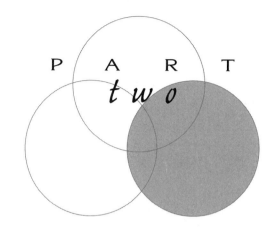

P A R T

two

The Social Sciences

three

Inquiry and Writing
in the Social Sciences

Who are those people?
Why are they behaving that way?
Do I belong here?
What will I become?

GOALS AND PURPOSES

The questions of social science are questions about humans, their identity, their behavior, and their social systems. Though the focus of inquiry shifts from physical systems to human behavior, the basic questions social science researchers ask remain much the same as those asked in the physical sciences: What is it? How does it develop and change? How does it function and interact? The "it" may refer to behaviors of individuals, groups, political systems, or cultures. For our purpose we have focused on the importance and function of human groups, both social and political. Humans are both systems in their own right and members of multiple larger systems simultaneously, and, as we saw in the science chapters, researchers today focus on systems. If we invited social scientists to gather around you as you stood in the middle of the campus on your first day, they would (as the researchers of the university-at-large did in the Introduction) identify and analyze you from the perspectives of their disciplines. You might be labeled "man/woman," "student," "citizen," "American," or "Caucasian/Afro-American/Latino/Asian," depending on the system under study. If you were identified as new to the university, you would, in addition, be noted as a person in the midst of change, moving from one system to another, adapting to a new environment. In other words the dynamics of change and adaptation

111

are as basic to social science study as they were in science. The psychologists will ask questions about the emotional and cognitive impacts of the new environment and new human relationships upon you and about the reaction of your system to those changes. The sociologists will focus their questions on the ways you become a member of new groups, move between groups, move between new systems and your home system. They will study the ways your attitudes change as a result of those interactions. The political scientists will study your sense of yourself as a citizen of a powerful nation or of the student government of your university, whereas the anthropologists will watch the rituals you establish as a member of student cultures as well as your interactions with other cultures. All, from their differing perspectives, will give different answers to the questions at the head of the chapter.

The goal of the social sciences, then, is similar to that of the natural, or physical sciences: to discover how systems work—human systems. The underlying assumption here, as in science, is that to change those systems or to understand our relationships to them, we must first understand how the systems work and interact with each other. Along with the goals, questions, and assumptions of the sciences, social science also shares the principles of systematic inquiry, principles basic to all academic argument diagrammed in Figure 5.

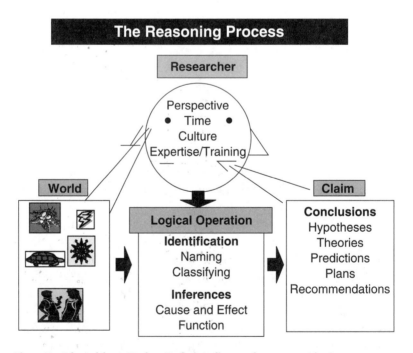

Figure 5   Adapted from Stephen Toulmin's diagram for argument in *An Introduction to Reasoning*, New York: Macmillan, 1979

"Good" thinking and "good" writing in the social sciences, therefore, are based on "good" process and "good" here means logically sound. To develop a sound sense of logic, remember these insights into critical thinking:

- Careful observation makes us aware of the distinction between data and inference.
- Forms in both inquiry and writing help us focus and systemize our observations.
- Taking multiple perspectives gives us a more complete view.
- Research tests inferences and prior knowledge.
- Claims about the way the world works rest on research, on the testing of inferences from data.
- Writing in the social sciences reflects the inquiry process of the field.

Finally, remember that methodical, critical thinking increases our knowledge and understanding of systems—the patterns and regularities scientists look for in nature and which social scientists seek in the behaviors of individuals and societies. This need to understand systems guides our study of the social sciences as we focus on the role of method and theory in the inquiry process.

METHOD IN THE SOCIAL SCIENCES

Social sciences, like natural and physical sciences, have roots in the classical philosophy of Aristotle and Plato and share a common history through the Middle Ages and the Enlightenment; however, unlike the natural and physical sciences, the experiment-based scientific method did not universally replace philosophers' methods of inquiry in the social sciences. Many social systems, such as governments, cultures, and events in the past, cannot be studied in a laboratory; thus in the social sciences, subject matter often dictates more appropriate methods of inquiry. Many social scientists hold to Aristotle's advice: "it is a mark of the trained mind never to expect more precision in the treatment of any subject than the nature of that subject permits" (65). Inquiry 3.1 will help you understand the inquiry issues and methods of inquiry in the social sciences. This in turn will help you understand the variations in writing forms.

We begin, as we did in science, with observation and with the core theme of identity, development (or change), and function of humans as members of multiple social and physical systems. You may focus as a class on social, political, cultural, or global systems, or the focus for research may be left to individual choice. In any case you will need to choose some category of human behavior discussed in the readings for study, such as the ones listed on the next page.

Examples

- Signs of group membership, solidarity, or isolation in the student body
- Signs of separation or integration of groups
- Evidence of differences in group power
- Signs of intergroup dating or lack thereof
- Evidence of the value of groups
- Signs of political activity and participation

INQUIRY 3.1: THE SCIENTIFIC METHOD IN THE SOCIAL SCIENCES

Step 1

Go to a spot where you can observe the behavior(s) you or your class has chosen for study in this unit, then observe and describe examples of the behavior(s), as you would naturally.

Give your descriptions to a classmate, and ask him or her to underline in red all words that hint at your own attitudes toward your subject, in blue all words or statements that require prior knowledge of the person, place, situation or culture, in black all words or statements that suggest judgment, and finally, in green all inferences made about internal states from external cues.

What did you have left after your partner highlighted these "nonobjective" elements? Probably not a lot. Does this mean that your description was "wrong"? Not at all. The multiple colors used in underlining should illustrate the multiple and complex abstraction processes you use in making sense of the world—in constructing meaning from sensory information. The same processes may also lead to distortion, however—as Bacon pointed out—and these exercises should help make you aware of both the processes and their capacity for error.

Step 2

Now try rewriting your description "scientifically," following the rules for static dynamic, and systemic descriptions from the science section; in other words treat your subjects as though you had just come upon them in a tide pool or imagine you are exploring an undiscovered country or planet and are recording your observations. Ask, What is it (the behavior)? Try to describe the visible physical characteristics without using prior knowledge or inferences about motivation, intent, mood, and so on. Next look at the behavior as a phenomenon that changes. What changes do you see? Now see the activity as a survival mechanism, adaptive to the environment. Observe and describe all interactions with the environment.

What did you see that you hadn't seen before? Did your descriptions open new possible explanations for the behavior(s) you were watching? Raise new questions about human behavior? Jot these down as possible questions for research. You also probably discovered that observation cannot answer some questions about human behavior. In the first place, social science is interested not only in what humans do, but also in why they do it. Behavior always suggests motivation, and motivation is simply not observable. We infer people's moods from expressions on their faces, from their laughs, their frowns, and the tones of their voices, but we cannot observe their moods themselves, and if we ask people about their motives, we may not hear the truth. People may not know or be honest about what makes them tick. Furthermore we detach our "affections" far more easily from the external world, even from the molecules of our own bodies, than we do from our reactions to fellow members of the species. Inquiry 3.2 will help increase awareness of these "subjective" forces.

INQUIRY 3.2: EXPLORING SUBJECTIVITY

Answer the following questions in your log:

- Why did you choose that group of subjects (in the previous inquiry)?
- Did you describe everything you saw or make selections?
- What behavioral cues did you focus on? Did you ignore others?

If you apply Bacon's idols to your descriptions, you can begin to understand how difficult objectivity is to obtain in the social sciences.

- Did you choose the subject(s) because you felt a personal affinity or animosity toward the type of person or group you believed he/she/they represented? Because they stuck out? Were different?
- Did you describe the behavior you witnessed in terms that fit your prior opinion?
- Did you, however, unconsciously, use words that were not neutral?

The preceding inquiry above demonstrates, we hope, the reasons why arguments about method have shaped various branches of the social sciences, and why theories, because they cannot be tested by uniform, universally accepted methods, are not easily accepted. Method debate in the social sciences focuses on several issues:

1. The influence of researchers on their data.

   (You may, in the inquiry above, have observed without attracting attention to yourself, but you could not have retained that anonymity while observing the Yanomamo of Brazil or the Pueblo of New Mexico.)

2. The indirect nature of evidence.

   (You cannot directly observe emotions, attitudes, motives, and other internal states.)

3. The inability to establish laboratory conditions and therefore to control variables.

   (It is impossible to establish experimental governments or cultures and ethics restricts experiments on humans where it is possible.)

4. The problem of removing cultural bias on the part of the researcher.

   (Social scientists generally accept Bacon's statement that our belief systems distort both our perception and our interpretations of data; the question, however, is whether such distortion can be avoided.)

5. Ethical restrictions on human subject research.

   (Subjects' rights and free choice must not be abused, and they must not be subjected to risk.)

To a large extent, social science researchers, faced with the complexity and number of human systems, have developed methods that combine both qualitative and quantitative approaches. Indeed methods of inquiry in social sciences range across the spectrum from the methods of philosophers to the methods of scientists (as shown in Figure 6). Our purpose here is not to study all these methods in detail, but rather to give you a sense of the range and variety of appropriate social science methods, so that you can better understand differences between those at the scientific end of the spectrum, which value quantification, and those at the philosophical end, which focus more on interpretive skills. The readings represent this range of methodologies. Political scholar and leader James Madison exemplifies the philosophical or interpretive approach; political scientist Judith Shklar combines political theory with empirical study. Political scientist Stephen Bennett exemplifies the scientific or quantitative approach, as does sociologist Carol Markstrom-Adams. Others, such as political scientist Craig Rimmerman, use interview and ethnographic methods that represent intermediate forms of social science research methods. Finally the Du Bois reading reflects the personal experience of a political leader and educator. By providing this range, we hope both to make you sensitive to the role

---

Methods in the Social Sciences

SCIENTISTS   **PHILOSOPHERS**

Quantitative/Experimental
Experimental Psychology/Communication

Quantitative: Field Observation
Sociology/Anthropology

Quantitative: Content Analysis
Communication

Quantitative: Field Study–Surveys
Sociology/Social Psychology/Political Science

Qualitative: Interview
Sociology/Political Science/Anthropology

Qualitative: Case Study, Policy Study
Clinical Psychology, Political Science, Sociology

Qualitative: Primary Source Analysis
History, Political Science

Qualitative: Ethnography/Participant Observation
Sociology/Anthropology

Qualitative: Interpretive Argument
History/Political Theory

Figure 6   Methods in the Social Sciences

method plays in social science and appreciative of the complexity of knowledge-making in these fields.

To understand the close relationship between questions and methods in the social sciences, complete the following Inquiry 3.3 as a warm-up for your own research activities.

INQUIRY 3.3: QUESTIONS AND METHODS

Think of ways you might study each of the research questions below using (1) observation, (2) a survey, and (3) in-depth interviews. After each research design, describe the kind of information the study would give and the kind it would not.

1. You want to test Gordon Allport's theory by finding out the extent to which college students feel uncomfortable outside their (a) in-group, (b) social class, or (c) ethnic group.

2. You want to test Craig Rimmerman's claims about our political attitudes by finding out about students' attitudes toward government leaders.

3. You want to test Judith Shklar's theory by finding out the amount of obligation or loyalty various ethnic group members feel toward their (a) organization, (b) school, (c) community, or (d) nation.

4. You want to test David Orr's claims about our perspective on the environment by finding out whether students believe in the importance of recycling.

5. Again testing David Orr's claims, you want to find out whether students would respect barricades to protect wooded areas on campus.

As you engage in these activities, you will undoubtedly discover that each method has both value and limitation. What more scientific methods gain in certainty may be countered by limitations on the kinds of questions that can be studied that way. A survey on Question A, for example, may not pick up differences in the kind of discomfort students feel outside their in-groups or whether that discomfort has positive or negative consequences. Even if you asked questions designed to tap all of these differences, you will still have to wonder whether people told the truth. How well, for example, would survey questions tap the mixture of fear and excitement you felt the first night in the dorm among strangers or the first night in a foreign country? Would you have confessed to being afraid? How many students, for example, would confess to violating their consciences to remain members of particular groups? How many would accuse their own groups of prejudice?

In-depth interviews generate more candor because they allow people to frame issues in their own way. In an in-depth interview, for example, a new student might say, "Being afraid is half the thrill!" or "Sure, but I was living for the day I got to leave my hometown." An older returning student might feel very out of place, but at the same time delight in his or her status in the class or in discovering how much wisdom a little living has given. Such individual variation is sacrificed in surveys precisely because it cannot be generalized, and the goal of the scientific method is to find those characteristics that are universal.

Many researchers use multiple methods to gain the advantages of each: qualitative methods, for example, may be employed early in the study of an issue when variables or forces in operation are not clear. Few in the West, for example, were clear on what political forces were operating in Eastern European countries after the dissolution of the Soviet bloc in 1989; we had had too little information for too long and the political science thinking, even of the experts, had been shaped by the Cold War. Case studies, therefore, seemed the most logical choice of method if we were to begin to understand the confusion of events that were upon us. Later, if the social and political forces become clearer and narrower, more quantitatively measurable questions can be asked. Thus different methods may be appropriate at different stages of research.

The final and perhaps most important reason for writers to understand differences in inquiry methods is that those differences have important consequences for writing. As we have said, writing comes out of and expresses inquiry processes, and forms of writing vary with research methods. Writing about research based on quantitative methods uses forms very similar to those of the natural and physical sciences and generally follows the scientific report form you practiced in the last unit. However, as we move toward the qualitative research methods—such as reporting ethnographic studies, case studies, or in-depth interviews—we find the subjects' responses and the researchers' analyses blended, rather than rigorously separated as in the science report; the form thus seems to deny the hard fast line between data and interpretation, acknowledging the role of interpretation. If we move further toward theoretical debate, the form approaches the essay, the common form of the humanities. In such debate the logical progression of ideas, rather than the data, takes the forefront, but solid argument still rests on data for support. We have included writing assignments from a range of methods and debate activity so that you can begin to practice these forms and understand them as marking places in the inquiry process.

THE ROLE OF THEORY

Despite their differences, the goal of social science research remains, as in science, to understand how systems work in order to predict, plan, and change their operations. All social science methods, therefore, depend on—and are tested against—some kind of data. The readings selected for this section demonstrate the differences between arguments or debates about method and theory and the kinds of argument essays you may have written on social problems, essays where you were asked to take a position or propose a solution. In those papers you were generally asked to defend a position or to argue the morality of some behavior or social action. Social science research writing, however, seeks explanations and debate centers on the reliability or validity of explanations. For example, Gordon Allport, in "The Formation of In-Groups," engages in a debate on the nature of prejudice, not on whether any given act is or is not prejudiced. He questions an accepted theory of prejudice, which is very different from arguing about whether we are or should be prejudiced or what to do about it if we are. In short these readings argue about the nature of things, about how systems work: they argue theory. James Madison, in *Federalist #10*, demonstrates the relationship between theory and action. He first gives his theory about how groups (factions) operate in the political sphere, then outlines the consequent hazards to the political system, and finally proposes that a federal constitution offers the best way to control the destructive effects of factions. His argument for action (signing the Constitution) thus follows from his theory of human political behavior. In *Ecological Literacy* David Orr theorizes about the influence of education on our worldview or our sense of our relationship to the environment. Analysis of the nature of behavior, then, is the hallmark of social science research.

As a result of debates about methodology, social science theories have not gained the universal acceptance accorded theories in the natural sciences. Though each field has a base of long-accepted general principles and assumptions, these are very broad: humans are social animals (they do not thrive in isolation); humans create institutional and cultural systems (none live without them), and so on. Within those broad parameters, however, theories undergo continuous testing and debate, but without the widely accepted standards of validity of the quantitative sciences. The Darwinian theory of human behavior competes with many others in the social realm. Understanding the vital role debate about theory plays in social science writing is therefore key to reading, understanding assignments, and writing, for theoretical debate is a major writing activity in many if not most social science courses.

As we said in our Introduction, theories are generalizations about how a system works to be tested and revised through research. In everyday life our theories about how systems work form the basis of our predictions and plans, and we test those theories through the lived results of our predictions. Your predictions about what college professors will expect (which usually take the form of what they will ask on the exam) draw upon your prior experience in educational systems. If you carry on a debate with another student about what a teacher will ask, you may discover your theories and the reasons behind them differ. One student may argue that teachers are sticklers for details. Why? "They want to know you've read the book." Another may insist that teachers care more about students' own ideas, and don't want them to just spit back the textbook. Why? "They don't believe recitation is real learning." As the debate continues, students compare previous experiences with teachers of different types and the evidence that the present teacher belongs in one or the other category. Furthermore each student will base his or her study strategies on his or her theory. The exam is the test, their grades the result.

The difference between personal and academic theory is, as with the close analysis of the thinking system in the science unit, that the soundness of generalization is tested continuously. In the university the tests and revisions are simply more thorough and systematic (though not necessarily less painful). In academia statements about what teachers are like become untested hypotheses, not yet reliable bases for action.

To conclude, then, theorizing is a critical human thinking activity, but like all human thinking activity, it may be also a source of error:

- Theories explain
- Theories form the basis of our predictions and plans
- Theories are the source of debate

The theories of the social sciences differ from everyday theories in that they are tested systematically through inquiry, but they are still theories and subject to debate.

Reading Theory as Argument

If you see your reading as an ongoing part of a debate, you will begin to look for the elements of argument as you read rather than simply absorbing the article as information, as you may be in the habit of doing if you have read mostly text-books. The readings of this chapter involve debates about theory between the authors and other researchers in the same field who are already familiar with the issues; therefore, if you are not familiar with the field, you may have to look carefully for the signals of debate. Madison's article, for example, was written as one of *The Federalist Papers,* a part of the public debate between political leaders on the need for a constitution. Do you know who his opponents were? Unlike textbooks such articles are written to other social scientists or experts, not to students, so to understand what is going on in an article, treat yourself as a novice social scientist. Imagine the article as a conversation going on in a room you have just entered. You will naturally search for the clues about the issue and the parties in the debate in order to join in the conversation. Taking that attitude restudy the readings you have read for this unit, making reading logs on each, according to the directions in Inquiry 3.4a and 4b.

INQUIRY 3.4A: READING LOGS

Go through the theory you are reading for this unit, and, in your informal writing notebook, create a reading log with headings as follows:

1. **Rhetorical Context.** First, write about where this theory discussion is coming from. Who is the author? What is his or her expertise? When was it written? To whom? Why?
2. **Issue and Parties.** Read the article for the issue under debate, not the topic. You are not gathering information; you are looking for the argument. See if

you can tell whom the author is debating. The authors may be debating other social scientists or accepted theory, and their position may become evident in any one of a number of ways.

Example: What is Allport's position relative to the Norm Theory of prejudice? What is Rimmerman's position vis-à-vis the two theories of political participation he discusses?

Who is David Orr arguing with in *Ecological Literacy?*

Once you have determined the parties, highlight the words in the text that signaled the shift in point of view, suggested the other party, or otherwise was a clue that there is more than one point of view in the article—that the article is not simply information but is an argument.

3. **Thesis.** Now that you have determined that there is a debate going on, find the author's thesis and the central points in his or her argument. See if you can state the thesis in a way that makes the parties in the argument clear.

   Example: Allport argues that the Norm Theory of prejudice is inadequate because . . .

   Rimmerman holds that the Participatory Democracy theory is superior because . . .

Writing it this way keeps your mind focused on the debate, so that you will not inadvertently revert to the information-gathering mode of reading.

4. **Argument Summary.** Find and list the points of the argument, the reasons given in support of the thesis. Once you see the text as an argument and realize that arguments must be supported, you may realize that much of what you took to be "wordiness" is necessary support. When students ask, "Why doesn't he just say it?" they indicate they are reading to pick up certainties to absorb, rather than argument points to be supported.

5. **Response.** Relate the issue under discussion to your own experience and free-write about whether you think the offered explanation fits. We will develop this part of the log further in Inquiry 4b.

Once you have practiced a few times, you will begin to see the debate and argument very quickly, which will, in turn, greatly speed up your reading and comprehension. You will discover that debate can take place anywhere in the inquiry process; use the diagram of the Reasoning Process (Figure 5) to help you identify which of the aspects of the reasoning below are being questioned:

- Perspective or biases of the researcher
- Identification of the issue or definition of the behavior itself
- Faulty cause-effect relationships
- Inclusion of factors not accounted for
- Generalizability of the claims

The structure of argument will become more familiar as you work with the readings, and that, in turn, will greatly aid in building your own structures.

Most students would not assume that the attitudes attributed to teachers in the earlier example apply to all human behaviors. They have experienced adult behavior in many contexts and realize that the behavior observed relates to the educational system, not the family or the courtroom. Students, then, are aware of multiple systems and that contexts influence behavior. They are not so aware, perhaps, of the way those systems shape perception and knowledge. Witness students' surprise when they spy a teacher laden with children and groceries in the supermarket parking lot. Did they really think teachers ceased to exist outside the classroom? Of course not, but a teacher's appearance in a different system still produced a shock of surprise. Such is the power of systems.

Theory also develops within systems in the university, and the difference, once again, lies in making the thinking activities systematic. As we saw in the science unit, you can study an object—whether a leaf, rock, snail, path, or radio—as a system in itself, as a part of its immediate environment (the tide pool, rock ledge, valley, dorm room, campus, etc.), as a part of a climatic zone, an economic system, or as a part of the global ecology. In the social sciences, methodical observation of social interaction leads to systematic identification and categorizing of the different systems that influence human behavior. The investigators from the disciplines who we invited you to study at the beginning of this book will study your interactions with (1) your own internal dynamics, if a psychologist; (2) other groups, if a sociologist; (3) the rituals of student life, if an anthropologist; (4) institutions of authority or power groups, if a political scientist. If you move to join a group of students crossing the mall toward the dining commons, a social psychologist may view your action as joining an in-group, a political scientist as a move to gain power, an anthropologist as joining the communal eating ritual, a biopsychologist as a survival move in a new environment. These approaches are not contradictory; they are different. However, the predictions each investigator makes about your interactions will come from the theories of the discipline, and, as you raise your fists to the first group member that turns, they will name your behavior "challenge," "play," or greeting," according to the theories of their disciplinary communities.

More important, theories tell researchers what to look for, what is important to notice, and they provide an interpretation. In everyday life people rarely understand the power theory wields in perception, opinion, prediction, and action. Though most professors stress disciplinary features as most important when describing their assignments, students typically don't think about such features at all. Instead students believe variation in assignments results from the topic and personality of the teacher. Students are undoubtedly applying their prior knowledge to the new situation, but in addition, they are applying a theory developed in one system—high school—to another—college.

Applying a theory developed in one system to another is a risky business. To interpret assignments intended to develop disciplinary thinking as based on personality preferences is not to understand the assignment at all. Nevertheless students, in our experience, behave much as the above suggests; furthermore they attribute poor grades to a misreading of the professor's personal values and continue to interpret evidence in personality terms. If, for example, a professor puts a time-line chart of events on the board or uses overheads to stress the meanings of words, he or she is a stickler for details. Their tenacity demonstrates the importance of our theories to our stability. As Bacon claimed we would far rather reshape the world to fit our systems than suffer the confusion and instability of change.

Students would greatly reduce their confusion if they realized that they have changed systems and that instead of asking what the professor is like (personality questions), they should ask what the field is like (discipline questions). Once they make this shift, they will recognize the time-line of events in a political science course overhead as evidence for an argument about the cause of revolutions, in an engineering course as stages in the evolution of a technology, in an anthropology course as moments of collision with other cultures, in a history class as tracing change through time. Thus the same physical object, the time-line, is interpreted differently depending on its context. In none of these is the time-line a list of dates to be memorized for its own sake simply because the professor is a stickler for details or wants to test students' attentiveness.

It is vital, therefore, that we understand not only what the nature of theory is, but also how it influences our interpretation of evidence, our planning, and our actions. Clearly their theories about the nature of writing assignments above will influence the way students write, and their grades on the papers will either confirm these theories or cause consternation. To see how heavily we depend on working theories (Bacon's "idol of the theatre"), look around at the distress of many students when teachers return their first papers. Listen to their explanations, their defenses, their revisions, and their tactics for coping; take note of the anxiety and distress, even hostility and despair that accompanies the failure of predictions. Your stress in the same situation will lessen considerably if you realize these additional characteristics of theory we have considered above:

- Theories predict safely only within their own systems.
- Theories shape the questions we ask, the evidence we look for, and the way we interpret what we see.
- Theory must be revised continuously in the light of new evidence.

These principles apply to both personal and academic theories.

Participating in Theoretical Debate

Professors want students to understand and eventually participate in the ongoing debates taking place in assigned readings, both in class and in their writing. There are undoubtedly exceptions to this as there are to any categorical statement; nevertheless the writing problem we hear about most frequently from professors across the university is thesis statements that (1) repeat back the course material, or (2) express opinions unrelated to the course material. The student samples below illustrate these two misfires.

Sample 1

Gordon Allport, in his essay "The Formation of In-Groups," tells the way people prefer the familiar, which means their own family, community, nationality, or race. We are all born as members of groups, the closest of which are our families. As we grow up and leave the family and join other groups, we seek those which are most like ourselves. According to Allport's Norm Theory of prejudice, this preference for people like ourselves is the cause of prejudice. For every "in-group" there is an "out-group" and we create our identities as much by "who we are not" as by who we are. For example, the "druggies" at my high school all wore black to show they were members of that "in-group" and were hostile to everyone else. Allport says we gain security by "circling the wagons" this way.

Sample 2

In high school, being in the "in-group" is all important to most students. Students imitate the way this elite group dresses, talks, and walks. It seems that very few high school students have enough nerve to be their own person; instead of wanting to be their own person, most want to "be somebody," and it seems the students in this high-status group are the "big men on campus," and their girls. Hopefully it will be different in college where there don't seem to be such definite in-groups. Maybe we will all become strong enough to exercise our individuality now, rather than needing the protection of a group around us all of the time.

Sample 3

Groups are very important; they give us power. But the groups we happen to be born into aren't necessarily the groups we feel most comfortable with. I know college students who couldn't wait to get away from home and from the kids at their high school. It also isn't true that the groups we get born into necessarily give us support. One reason those friends of mine were so eager to get away is that they were badly treated by others for being different. They were birth-members of that community, but they had to escape it to college to find people who valued what they did and would support them. It seems to me that those people back home who ridiculed my friends were prejudiced against members of their own in-group because they were different, but different doesn't mean they were part of a different "in-group."

The student in Sample 1 is still responding to the question, "Do you understand Allport?" Consequently she does not understand that she should make her own evaluation and take her own position; in addition she has not read the theory as argument, and therefore has not realized that there are multiple viewpoints in the chapter. The student in Sample 2 uses the word "in-group" as a jumping off place for his personal opinion, translating Gordon Allport's ingroup into the more familiar (but different) use of the term among high school students. The student in Sample 3, in fact, responds to Allport's argument, but doesn't mention him. All relate to the readings, but none bring personal experience into dialogue with the academic theory.

This is usually treated as a writing problem and perhaps it is; however, our discussion above suggests that students may be using a theory developed in a previous system where the expectation was either to show understanding of the readings or develop an opinion. They can develop a thesis in either case and have done so with great success; it is difficult to discard a theory that has always worked in the past. However, interaction within academia means participating in current debates about the state of knowledge. The key difference between this kind of interaction and the development of personal opinion is that your opinion must relate not only to the topic but also to the theory under discussion. The questions at the end of the readings should help you form such opinions by inviting you to apply the readings to your own lives, and Inquiry 3.4b will help further that development. These responses will also produce the questions for your field research, library research, and formal papers.

INQUIRY 3.4B: DEVELOPING RESPONSES

Return to part 5 of your previous reading logs and to the responses to the questions at the end of the readings.

6. **Response.** Write freely on your response to the article. Such response should include any concepts or logic you don't understand, and continue applying the statements made about function, need, cause, the types of behavior defined, to your own experience as indicated in your question responses. Do this for each individual point, not just the thesis. In doing so note where the theory doesn't quite fit, where it leaves out factors, or simply where the explanation doesn't satisfy you. Write out your dissatisfaction. This is the way you will find your interest, your questions, and the place where your own interests join the academic quest. Student Sample 3 above (on being uncomfortable in one's in-group) would be very appropriate as a reading log response, for it would be read, in that context, as a conversation with Allport. Response logs give you an opportunity to explore freely as this student does.

Examples

- For Allport, ask yourself whether you feel less strongly about groups more distant from you than those close (your identity as citizen compared with your identity as son or daughter) or whether your reasons for joining reference groups match Allport's.

- In responding to Rimmerman or Madison, name several political interest groups. Ask yourself what kinds of groups you are calling "interest groups," and whether power is balanced between different kinds. Ask whether, as Madison argues, regional differences keep one group or another from becoming dominant, from interfering too much with the "public good." How would you define the "public good?" How would you distinguish "public good" from "self-interest"?

- Responding to Judith Shklar, ask under what conditions your national identity would be stronger than your ethnic group identity, religious identity, or vice versa, and so on. Ask your friends the same question.

- For environment readings, ask yourself what relationship to the physical world was stressed in your own education, giving specific examples.

Your class may, of course, come up with many of its own questions in the course of discussion.

The response section of the reading log helps you to connect your academic and personal experiences in order to discover that you do indeed have something of value to say. We should point out, of course, that when you move into this stage of participation and genuinely open yourself to change you will undoubtedly face data that do not support your personal theories, and you therefore must either revise your views or ignore the data. The choice, though it seems self-evident, is not easy; as in the theories about teacher expectations described earlier, transformation causes anxiety and confusion. One group of first-year female students, for example, decided to study whether women are socialized to protect themselves against rape. As they developed their questions, a male classmate remarked that they seemed to concentrate on rape by strangers, whereas the research data shows that 80 percent of rapes are committed by men known to the women victims. "We aren't studying that," the women insisted. When the class prevailed upon them to include questions on date rape in the survey, the women uniformly ignored the data from those questions—data that indicated women are *not* socialized to protect themselves against date rape—in their reports. Thus do we avoid (as Bacon predicted) what we do not wish to deal with and restrict ourselves to the world of the familiar—and at such potential cost!

On the other hand, if you keep your personal view locked safely away in a cabinet to be pulled out only when asked to write a personal experience essay, your education will have achieved little and probably will have bored you in the process. When you connect the issues raised in readings to your life and discover their potential implications for your future, you will become genuinely interested in theory. Most students know very well, by the time they come to the university, that they cannot write well when they are not interested in a topic. Now we are telling you that half of the job of becoming interested, the application of abstract theories to your lives—is yours.

In addition to fostering engagement, the form of the log helps you keep your opinion separate from the authors'; doing so also prevents reverting to information-absorption mode and mistaking theory for fact. Keep the image of joining an ongoing conversation in your mind, and you will keep voices distinct, particularly your own. The student in Sample 3 *is* engaged, but treats ideas as free-floating, without regard to their origin. This is all right so long as the response is attached to the article itself; however, it is critical to keep ideas attached to their originators in formal writing. Losing track is to lose track of the fact that this is a debate and that debate, particularly debating the results of research, is the way knowledge is formed in the social sciences. Worse, students who absorb the ideas of others are not developing their own, a real source of frustration for many professors. They do not realize that they have a great deal to bring to a debate. Last but not least, losing track of the origin of ideas is seen in this community as expressing the ideas of others *as* your own, which is considered dishonest—plagiarism. To prevent committing this offense inadvertently, learn to write in voices.

Writing in Voices

To begin, let us make our point once again: neither your opinion nor your life experiences are irrelevant to engaged academic work. As we ask you to participate as a reader and a researcher in this unit, we will repeatedly ask you to apply concepts and logic of theories from your reading to your own life and times as well as to prior theories in order to create a critical dialogue between theory and experience. Personal engagement, when integrated with analysis of the reading, actually meets most professors' expectations; too often students who challenge their "B" grades because they have followed directions and performed all of the steps miss this critical aspect of "A" work. Professors are looking for a paragraph that reads more like this:

Sample 4

Groups, as social psychologist Gordon Allport claims, are an important part of our identity and self-esteem, but we do not automatically gain these qualities from the families we are born into as he suggests. Allport, in *The Nature of Prejudice,* argues that "the familiar provides the indispensable basis of our existence. Since existence is good, its accompanying groundwork seems good and desirable" (29). However, existence is not necessarily good; some children don't "fit in" their own families or early school groups. A boy, for example, may be ridiculed as a "wimp" by his own father, if he prefers books to sports, or a girl if she prefers sports to dolls. Allport cites cases where a person, usually a minority, wishes to identify with groups other than his own ascribed birth group, and says "he develops a condition that Kurt Lewin has called "self-hate"; if he repudiates his birth group (87). Where does that leave the child above who, because he or she is treated as an outsider, develops self-hate within the birth group? Allport seems to argue that only people outside the in-group are treated with hostility; a visit to Christmas dinner at a lot of homes would produce evidence that this isn't true. The one child who is different is alone in his or her room while the rest of the cousins play, the aunts prepare dinner, the uncles trade jokes in the living room. The family "misfits" at these dinners may have to wait for college to find groups that give them the kind of identity Allport says we receive from group membership. They do not get the security Allport correctly says we get from our original families (29); does that mean, as his theory suggests, that they can never gain that security even though they find groups later that suit their needs and personalities? Allport's theory seems right on the importance of groups, but membership is more complicated than his theory allows for.

Allport, Gordon. (1954). *The Nature of Prejudice.* Cambridge, MA: Addison-Wesley.

By actively bringing Allport's theories into dialogue, rather than simply absorbing them, and by clearly identifying whose ideas he is dealing with, this student can now develop his own questions for research. Once you have reached this stage, the next step is to express your opinion effectively and as a part of the community of researchers. Social theory, like scientific theory, is the product of many minds; it is therefore critical that you stay in dialogue with the reading.

In the science chapter, we integrated our thinking objectively and logically with sentence structure and word choice to demonstrate the relationship between thinking and writing in different disciplines. Below, we use paragraph structure and development to aid in the development of dialogue between you and the authors of the readings.

Structural Emphasis: Taking Charge in Topic Sentences

You have probably learned already that the topic sentence of a paragraph makes a point, the function of the rest of the paragraph is to develop that point with specific evidence or illustration, and the function of separating your work into paragraphs is to separate the points from each other, thus helping the reader follow your argument. If you now use those topic sentences largely to make your own points rather than to repeat the ideas of others, you will go a long way toward taking charge of your paper; the function of the topic sentence in the paragraph gives your own ideas the lead position in the debate.

Developing the Debate: Using Quotes and Paraphrases

As you develop a debate in your paper, you will need to begin by giving a full sense of the argument you are debating. Simply pulling quotes that appeal to you and citing them out of context may reinforce your own point of view, but this strategy does not develop sound argument. We say more about techniques for summarizing arguments in the paper assignment section when we talk about structuring whole papers. Here we only want to stress that summarizing the argument at hand is a necessary first step. Once you have given the full sense of the argument, your individual paragraphs should take up specific points and examine them thoroughly. Don't simply drop in a quotation then proceed with your own argument. Tell the reader how the quoted statement relates to your point or how it relates to the rest of the author's argument and use examples or evidence to illustrate and/or support your reasons for taking it up.

Citation as Identification of Voices

Frequently students learn the rules of citation without learning their function. In Sample 4, note that the citation devices (identification of authors in the sentences and reference page numbers in parentheses) make it clear whose ideas are whose. Without such identification readers become confused about the point of the debate itself. Finally, if all of the ideas in a paragraph need citing, it is a signal that you haven't responded to those ideas or expressed any opinions of your own. Thus citation can tell you a great deal about how successful you are at debating the author's theory. If you think of a paragraph as a part of a debate, you will find such identification comes naturally rather than as a cumbersome, tedious bunch of rules imposed by convention (or English teachers) alone. Indeed we have placed the details of reference style of citation and punctuation in the Appendix in order to stress only the pertinent function and principles here.

- The function of citation is to identify the source of material, facts or opinion, other than your own unless it is "common knowledge."
- "Common knowledge" is defined as facts known and accepted (not a topic of debate) by the audience. It may, therefore, vary from audience to audience.
- Sources are identified in the text by both name and page number.
- Facts may be cited by putting both author and page number in the parentheses. Authors of ideas, opinions, or interpretations of facts must be identified in the sentence itself using signal phrases ("according to," "X argues," "X reports," etc.).
- Further information necessary for readers to find the source itself is given in a list at the end of the work.

Note that in the discussion above, we stress "authors," not "titles." Though a great deal of information does come to us from seemingly authorless entities, such as newspaper articles, the Bureau of Census, or the National Aeronautic & Space Agency, to say nothing of the Internet, *use authors' names if they are available.* Keeping the authors' identities in mind serves to remind you that *people* generate information and knowledge, not computers. Identifying the authors of ideas *in the sentence* (not merely in the parentheses) keeps you constantly aware of the distinction between fact and interpretation. That distinction, as we stressed in the science unit, is critical in academic argument.

Finally the conventions of courtesy in social conversation hold in written conversation as well. When you first introduce authors, give their full names and describe their particular expertise. How often have you been introduced as "Joe" and left on your own to explain your identity, relationship to the introducer, and presence? In the same vein, it is useful to readers, though not mandatory, to give the title of the authors' texts at first reference also. Once these amenities have been taken care of, you may subsequently refer to the authors by last names only (not first name as in social situations). A number of complications, such as authors quoted by other authors, multiple authorship, and so on, will surely arise as you write. For the conventions covering such situations, see the appendix. This appendix also covers correct form, punctuation, and the variations of this system found in different disciplines. Here we seek only to highlight the guiding principles.

INQUIRY 3.5: PARAGRAPH AND CITATION PRACTICE

Practice the skills outlined above by writing three paragraphs, each of which begins with a point you would like to make on the issue under study. If you like, use Sample 4 as a model. After writing the topic sentences, develop your paragraphs by comparing or contrasting your point of view with that of at least one of your readings; you may discuss either a specific idea made by the author or a general attitude. Be sure to give at least one piece of specific evidence of your point. Finally make at least one of these paragraphs about a point of the author's you agree with, bringing in specific evidence of the way his or her point fits your own experience or knowledge. Developing your own view is often more difficult when you agree with the author than when you disagree; remember, you agree for a reason—maybe several. Find those reasons in your own experience.

Integrate at least two quotations or a quotation and a paraphrase from the reading you are debating into your paragraph using these five elements:

- A "signal phrase" introduction of the quotation (i.e., "Allport claims," "according to James Madison," "in Judith Shklar's view," "David Orr, on the other hand, believes," etc.)
- At least one additional piece of information about the source (title, expertise of author, publication date, etc.)
- Appropriate in-text parenthetical citation, including source page number and essential author, title, and/or date information not already included in the "signal phrase" introduction of the quotation (see Appendix A for further information on citation in the social sciences)
- A paraphrase of the quotation and reference to the context in which it was made.
- An application of the quotation to the development of your argument

End the paragraph with your own evaluation of the state of knowledge on the subject. Be sure to make clear whose opinion is whose by identifying all opinions that aren't yours and include the page number in parentheses at the end.

The Language of Argument

As you write paragraphs in response to readings, you may find you have more difficulty than usual in fitting all aspects of your idea into your sentences. The need to cite authors' names itself adds complexity to your sentences, to say nothing of the need to compare complex ideas, make distinctions, or modify claims. In first draft writing, we usually add information and qualifications as they occur to us without worrying overly much about grammar. We have therefore held most discussion of managing complexity for the "Revising for Clarity" section at the end of the chapter. At this point we only review the principles of sentence focus we presented in the science chapter, for this skill will help clarify your own thinking as you develop your argument.

Making complex thoughts clear depends heavily on focusing on your central meaning and relating additional information accurately. The subject and verb, we remind you, anchor the sentence; they are the bridge stanchions, the core—use whatever metaphor will help you keep their all-important structural function in mind. Choose them carefully. In the following compound sentence, the subjects and verbs are in bold print; the central meaning is italicized:

> **Example: It is** true, as social psychologist Gordon Allport claims, that *groups* **are**, an *important* part of our identity and *self-esteem*, but **it isn't** true that we *automatically* **gain** these qualities *from the families* we are born into as he suggests.

"It is" and "there are," known as "dummy subjects" because they convey no information whatever, are probably the most common causes of blurry sentences; they cautiously bury their real meaning in a "that" clause, hiding it successfully behind a cloud of words. Rewritten so that the central meaning and grammatical subject are one and the same, the sentence above becomes:

> **Example: Groups are,** as social psychologist Gordon Allport claims, an ***important*** part of our identity and self-esteem, but ***we don't*** automatically ***gain*** these qualities from the families we are born into as he suggests.

Whenever "which," or "that" clauses or prepositional phrases begin to multiply as you write a sentence, you should start again, follow the procedure below to find your core meaning, and rebuild:

- Highlight the three words that express the core, or central meaning of the paragraph as well as the sentence.
- Make sure those words are contained in the subject→verb→object string, or base clause.
- In the following example, the subject→verb→object are in bold, the central meaning italicized:

> **Example:** Original: The **quest** for *scientific knowledge* **has** always **been** an *elusive* **thing.**
> Revised: ***Scientific knowledge has*** always ***eluded*** the ***quest.***

If you work a few of these through, you will also see that clarifying the grammatical focus also serves to clarify the thinking—the relationships between the parts. To illustrate look at the information imparted by the bolded words (subject/complement) in the following example:

> **Example:** <u>Original</u>: **Scientific knowledge is** one type of **knowledge,** separate from methods such as philosophical knowledge, which embody subjective thought.

If we then *italicize* what we believe is the central meaning (always tricky with someone else's writing), it becomes:

> **Example:** <u>Original</u>: ***Scientific knowledge is*** one type of **knowledge,** *separate* from *methods* such as *philosophical knowledge,* which embody *subjective* thought.

To revise, the author will have to do more than simply rearrange words. He or she will have to ask what the relationship between the italicized words is and start over. The result might be something like this:

> **Example:** <u>Revised</u>: ***Knowledge*** gained from scientific methods ***is objective*** and therefore ***distinct*** from knowledge gained through the methods of philosophy, which include subjective elements.

Revision, in other words, clarifies relationships, an act that may require adding and changing—it is not simply rearranging the same words. The advantage of beginning with the bare bones of the sentence is that you will develop an ear for that central core and that you will only add words to clarify or emphasize meaning. Thus the practice guards against academia's most contagious disease—wordiness.

INQUIRY 3.6: SENTENCE FOCUS

Step 1

Follow the steps given above to restructure these wordy sentences:

1. David Orr, who is a professor of Environmental Studies, wrote a book entitled *Ecological Literacy* in which he argues that our relationship to the environment must be studied in the United States if environmental problems are to be understood.

2. *The New Citizenship*, which is a book by Craig Rimmerman, stresses the point that for the United States to gain better participation by its citizens in its government requires that we develop a new kind of citizenship.

3. Judith Skhlar's interviews with survivors of Japanese-American internment camps, which she reports in her article "Obligation, Loyalty, Exile," show evidence of her claim that national loyalty can survive mistreatment by the government.

Step 2

Add necessary information by converting phrases into single words (adjectives or adverbs) where possible, using the principles of compression and efficiency practiced in the science chapter.

> **Example:** "In the opinion of Gordon Allport who was a social psychologist who wrote in the 50s . . ." becomes, "Social psychologist Gordon Allport wrote, in the 50s, that. . . ."

Step 3

Add modifying clauses and phrases as necessary and only as necessary, again using the principles practiced in the science chapter. All words in a sentence should be doing work.

We do further work on modification and complexity in the "Revision for Clarity" section, but performing the above inquiry on your topic sentences as you write will help you keep your focus and sense of direction.

FORMAL PAPERS IN THE SOCIAL SCIENCES

Formal writing assignments may arise at many points in the inquiry process, and as we move into them now, remember the important features of social science inquiry and debate:

- Theories explain
- Hypotheses come out of theories
- Thesis statements come out of research; they are not formed prior to research and are different from hypotheses
- Research consists of testing theory against data
- Arguments are therefore data driven—thesis statements are based on data

You will need the reading and writing principles and techniques described in the previous sections for all of the formal papers you will write in the social sciences. For some assignments you will also use the observation and logic inquiries and/or the library research techniques outlined in the science chapter. The assignments below arise, as they did in the science chapter, from different locations in the inquiry process, but this time we begin with theory, because theory is, in fact, the starting place of most university research in all disciplines.

Experience-Based Theory Critique Essay

The first step in critiquing theory, and the one you will be asked to perform most frequently in your social science courses, is to apply a theory from your readings to your own experience or to the world around you to see how well it explains social behaviors. Writing such an essay involves little more than formalizing and refining issues raised in your reading logs and writing inquiries you have already performed earlier in this chapter. Reread your logs and inquiry exercises and review class discussions of the theories for topics. You might, for example, apply any of the research questions you discussed in Inquiry 3.3 to your own experience.

Sample Topics
- What characteristics do you and your friends look for in choosing groups to join? How do your choices reflect Allport's theory?
- Are college students, in your experience apathetic about politics, as Rimmerman claims and for the same reasons?
- Examine your own or others' experiences with divided loyalty. Do people indeed retain loyalty in the face of unfair treatment or abuse?
- Review your education, both at home and at school. What attitude toward the environment did it develop?
- As a test of Allport's theory that group membership doesn't require negative attitudes toward the "out group," can you tell by the language a people use whether they are members of a group or not and their attitude toward that group?

Global Features

Following are the overall features of the critique essay:

Purpose
The purpose of critiquing a theory is to test its explanation of behavior in order to raise questions for further research.

Audience
The audience is other social science researchers studying the same behaviors.

Form

This paper is an essay, so it uses no headings. Like all essays it moves from introduction to body to conclusion and may take many forms.

Local Features

The overall order of the theoretical critique essay is given by the argument rather than the research method, so it is much less defined than the science report; however, readers need to know and social scientists expect the features below to be present.

Introduction

The introduction should state the issue under study and its importance. It should also give the name(s) of the theoretician(s) being examined, give the author's(s') thesis(es), and indicate the part of the theory under debate in your paper.

Thesis

As stated above. The thesis may express your total satisfaction, partial satisfaction, or total dissatisfaction with the explanation, but should also specify the reason for your position. This thesis differs from many you may have written on position essays in that it must refer to the theory, not simply to the position—to Allport's theory of prejudice, not simply to prejudice itself.

Theory Summary

Your audience needs an overview of the theoretician's argument in order to put your critique into context. To avoid the bad habit of simply pulling quotes that sound good, be sure to give the full argument here, not just the points you wish to discuss.

Application

Describe a situation from life, giving the theoretician's probable explanation for that behavior. Use his or her key terms to name behaviors and relationships, taking care to use his or her definition of those terms (i.e., don't, as the student in the Sample 1 did, translate Allport's "in-group" into a more familiar definition).

Critique

First establish the common ground, the accepted knowledge not under debate. Then discuss where you find the theoretical explanation satisfactory and where it raises questions. Be sure to explore other possible causes of the behavior and for behaviors the theory does not explain. This discussion may be several paragraphs long. Make sure each paragraph satisfies the following requirements of good argument (and well-developed paragraphs):

- Topic sentences should state your point or your position about the author's point rather than simply reiterating the theory (as practiced in Inquiry 3.5).
- Most paragraphs should contain a specific point of the theoretician's, correctly cited, plus your interpretation of that point and its relevance to your point (Inquiry 3.5).
- Most paragraphs should contain concrete evidence from your application.
- Most paragraphs should conclude with a question for further research.

Conclusion

From your critique, give both the areas where the theory seems to work well and the areas where further research is needed. Your conclusion, in other words should point toward research rather than claiming final truth.

References

Attach a reference page, using correct APA citation (Appendix).

Surface Features

The principles of elegance used in science writing apply in the social sciences as well. Use the focus and emphasis principles practiced in this chapter and the last to help structure your sentences for elegance. Don't confuse technical language with jargon or complexity with wordiness.

The Literature Review

Rather than asking you to apply the theory of a single reading, a literature review asks you to synthesize material from several readings on the same question. These readings may be provided by your instructor or you may be asked to find them in the library, but your resulting paper, in either case, will follow the guidelines below.

Sample Topics

- Review the Allport, Markstrom, and Du Bois articles on in-group formation to determine areas of agreement, questions raised, and areas for further research.
- Find two current articles on in-group formation in the library to assess the extent theory has changed or developed since Allport's day or the extent it is still held. Raise questions for further research.
- Review the Madison, Rimmerman, and Bennett articles on political participation to determine areas of agreement, differences in focus, and areas in need of further research.
- Find articles on political factions to determine whether power is held by a few, as Rimmerman argues, or balanced, as Madison argues.

- Find two additional articles on current political factions, holders of power, or apathy and compare their studies to any one or all of the political participation articles to assess areas of agreement, differences, and areas in need of further research.
- Find and review two articles on multiculturalism and compare their views to Shklar's on the subject of loyalty, raising questions for further research.
- Find and review two articles on environmental attitudes to see whether they confirm or contradict Orr's claims about the American perspective on the environment. Raise questions for further attitude research.

Global Features

The overall features of the literature review are as described below; distinguish carefully between this essay and an essay where you take a position on the issue itself:

Purpose

The purpose of the social science literature review is, as it was in the science chapter, to assess the state of existing knowledge and to raise questions for further research. Because we stress the theoretical basis for knowledge in the social sciences, you may, and probably will, find yourself comparing and assessing theories.

Audience

As in science, your audience is fellow researchers studying the same topic. You may be asked to compare theories within a single discipline or from different disciplines (sociology and political science, for example), depending on the breadth of audience you are asked to consider.

Form

As in the science chapter, the literature review may either be a paper in its own right, in which case it will be an essay, or a part of a field study, in which case it is a part of the Introduction. In either case it should be organized around issues or questions. If several authors talk about an issue, their comments and views should be collected. *Sequential summaries of articles do not constitute a literature review.* In the science unit, we asked you to organize the literature review according to the three basic issues: identity, development or change, and systemic function. You may find it more difficult to find organizing principles that will synthesize your social science readings, so we have provided the following inquiry to help.

INQUIRY 3.7: TWO METHODS FOR SYNTHESIZING AND ORGANIZING A CRITIQUE PAPER

Method 1: Free-Written Draft

Step 1: Writing Reading Logs

Write full reading logs on each of your readings, following the instructions in Inquiry 3.4.

Step 2: Freewrite

Write your impressions of the way the readings work together. Describe areas of agreement, your degree of satisfaction, anything that comes to mind. Be sure to include all of the readings, but do not try to write the same amount on each; if you find yourself simply summarizing a reading, reiterating the author's ideas rather than discussing them, stop and start again, asking yourself, "What do I want to say about X?" If you find yourself agreeing with the theorist, ask yourself why you agree—what experiences support the explanation given. When you have finished, wrap it all up in a "nutshell" statement of what it all amounts to.

Step 3: Outline

Use your nutshell statement as a trial thesis, then go through your free-written draft and highlight the important points, either your own or points of your authors that you want to discuss. Pull these sentences out and make an outline with them.

Step 4: Development

Develop each point in your outline with discussion, bringing in the authors' views, your response to them, and evidence supporting your response.

Method 2: Structured

Step 1: Writing Reading Logs

Write full readings logs on each of your readings, following the instructions in Inquiry 3.4.

Step 2: Finding the Bases of Comparison

Examine each of your logs for similarities and differences in the following:

Point of View: Were the authors writing in the same environment (time, place, culture)? Do (or did) they come from the same discipline? How might the similarities or differences in their environment or expertise influence their research or their conclusions?

> **Example:** Sociologists studying "collective action" may be studying a broader range of activities than political scientists studying "political action groups."

Definition of Terms: Have all authors defined the issue under study in the same way? How might the definition of key terms change in different times, different disciplines, different cultures?

> **Example:** Madison's "factions" and contemporary "interest groups" may or may not be the same thing.

Common Ground: What do the authors seem to accept as common knowledge between them—aspects of the subject not under debate?

> **Example:** Most social scientists in the readings included here seem to accept that when groups with differing background and interests come into contact, tension results. They don't necessarily agree on whether that tension is a positive or negative social force.

Factors Studies: Most social scientists will include several variables in their research but focus on the effects of one or two. List the primary (independent) and secondary (dependent) variables for each.

> **Example:** Madison focuses on the hazards of tyranny (one group dominating the interests of weaker groups), while Rimmerman focuses on representation (attaining a voice).

Issues That Divide: List the points of agreement and disagreement among your authors.

You may or may not find significant differences on all of these dimensions. Eliminate any that proved unimportant, then organize those that clarified the similarities and differences between theories or conclusions.

Step 3: Organizing the Bases

Put your bases of comparison in logical order, using the principles below to help:

Primary/Secondary. Where differences on one dimension lead to differences on others, the primary difference should come first.

Example: If differences in the time or place of the theory seems to greatly influence the concerns of the thinkers, point of view should come first, so that you can show how it influences other aspects.

Level of Abstractness. If one author makes distinctions that another does not make, the contrasting levels and their significance in interpreting results provide an organizing principle.

Example: Allport makes no distinctions as to race or culture; Du Bois claims this omission is significant.

Causation and Correlation. Causation is always complex and usually social scientists are cautious about using the word at all. They do, however, study correlation as a way of approaching causation. If causation or correlation seems the central issue in your studies, one of the following schematics may help organize your paper.

Agreed Effect $\Rightarrow$ $\Rightarrow$ Multiple Cause

Agreed Cause $\Rightarrow$ $\Rightarrow$ Multiple Effects

Step 4: Full Sentence Outlining

Use your bases of comparison to construct an outline for your paper, using a full sentence to describe the significance or effect of the similarity or difference, rather than single word.

Example: I. Differing definitions of Social Distance: Allport, unlike Du Bois, does not treat race as a kind of social distance qualitatively different from social class.

Du Bois's distinction between racial and other kinds of in-groups open new questions on the validity of Allport's theory.

NOT

Social Distance

Allport

Du Bois

Outlining in full sentences has a threefold advantage: (1) it forces your own evaluation and argument into the foreground—forces you to take control of the paper and develop your own voice, (2) it gives you a clear view of the logic of your paper, and (3) makes clear that development means bringing in evidence for each claim made.

Thesis

If you are writing a freestanding essay, your thesis will express your assessment of the state of knowledge on the issue: the areas of agreement, disagreement, the completeness, omissions, and so on. If you are writing the literature review as a part of the introduction to a field study, however, you will not introduce a thesis here. Instead, as in the scientific report, your discussion of the literature will lead to the need for future research and to a description of your own study. Instead of a thesis, your paper, because it is the report of a study, will have a *hypothesis* or a description of the issues under study. See the study report paper option for further detail.

Local Features

Introduction

Whether a freestanding essay or a study report, the Introduction states the issue under study and the main theorists under debate.

Literature Review

The paragraphs are organized according to the issues rather than the authors, so that development means synthesizing what each author has to say on that issue, whether similar or different, and concluding with the implications or importance of that similarity or difference for further research. Use Inquiry 3.5 on structural emphasis to focus on the authors (if that is the main contrast you wish to make) or on the issue, and bring in paraphrases or quotes from their texts as evidence of their positions. Follow the paragraph inquiry (3.5) in constructing these paragraphs, and be sure to cite correctly, according to the APA style discussed in the Appendix.

Surface Features

Follow the same guidelines for clear, precise prose that have been discussed earlier for your rough draft. Further revision for the final draft will be discussed in the Revision for Clarity section.

Field Studies and Reports

Once you have reviewed and analyzed the literature on a social issue or behavior, you are ready to embark on field research. This is not a book on research methods nor is it intended to substitute for a methods course; the guidelines below give only the basic principles that underlie field research and the resulting reports. The first, and perhaps most important, constraint on social science research is ethics. Research on human subjects requires the approval of ethics committees in order to protect the rights of subjects. Your instructor will explain the guidelines and approval procedures for your institution; in general ethics require protection of your subjects' identity in survey and observation studies, and rigorously restrict research involving subjects under 18 years of age. Experiments, however, require more elaborate review well beyond the scope of composition courses; for that reason we have not included experiments among the options in the next section. In short be sure you know the ethical guidelines for observation, survey, and interview studies, and do not design experiments on human subjects without the explicit permission and guidance of your professor.

Participant Observation Study

Participant observation is appropriate when you wish to study interactions such as conversation with a minimal amount of researcher interference.

Choosing a Question

From your readings choose a behavior you can study through observation of a group where you can mingle freely and listen as an insider. You might choose a question discussed in Inquiry 3.3 or develop a question such as the ones below.

- Do students who hang out together share common characteristics in appearance or behavior? To research this question, you might observe specific characteristics of dress and behavior in a restaurant where particular groups hang out or in a dormitory cafeteria.
- Do college students take preserving the environment seriously as judged by their actions rather than their words? You might observe your own refuse disposal behavior and that of your roommates or family. You might record the reactions of your family or friends when you suggest turning to a nature program on the television.
- What are students' attitudes toward political activists? To investigate this question, you might observe the reaction of passing students to campus activists at the spot where such people pass out flyers, give speeches, and so on or study attendance at a series of campus meetings, political lectures, speechs, etc.

The goal in all of these is not to influence normal behavior by your presence and to be very sensitive to the effect of your presence on your study subjects. Identify clearly the aspect you wish to study.

Developing a Hypothesis

Some qualitative studies do not begin with hypotheses. Instead of predicting results, the focus is on gathering information on the topics identified in the research question. The following inquiry will help you focus your particular study.

INQUIRY 3.8: DESIGNING A PARTICIPANT OBSERVATION STUDY

Step 1

Research Question. Write your research question and identify the theory you are studying and the rationale for your question. Name the aspects of behavior on which you will focus.

Hypothesis. If either the theory or previous research predict what you will find and you wish to either confirm or counter it, write the prediction as a hypothesis, and give the reasons for your statement. Think of alternative explanations and give reasons why you think yours is the more likely. If you simply wish to observe behavior or attitudes without making predictions, use the research question as the focus rather than a hypothesis.

Define Key Terms. List key technical terms from the theory for the behaviors or attitudes you are studying, distinguishing them clearly from other behaviors. For example, distinguish Allport's "in-group" from the use of that term in ordinary conversation, distinguish Rimmerman's "alienation" from "apathy," and distinguish "necessary" from "unnecessary" disposal. In all definitions avoid value-loaded terms, such as "snobbish," "lazy," "wasteful," "careless," and so on.

Define Study Behaviors. Describe the behaviors and/or attitudes you intend to observe and record, distinguishing those behaviors clearly from similar ones. How, for example, will you distinguish food disposed of because it is spoiled from food left because it is surplus? How will you determine whether a group sits together out of choice? How will you distinguish "ignorance" of issues from "disinterest"?

Method. Describe the population you intend to study, what you plan to do, where, when, and for how long you plan to do it.

Measurement. This may seem irrelevant to quantitative studies, but describe how you will record behaviors and conversations so that you can retrieve them later. If you must depend on memory, say so. Take care that your field notes, whether taken at the time or later, are descriptive only (as practiced in the Science unit). Do not make judgments and interpretations.

The Participant Observation Study Report

The report of a participant observation study may take various forms, as described below, but retains the basic characteristics of the scientific study report.

Global Features

Following are the overall or conceptual features of the report.

Purpose

The purpose of a participant observation study and report is to test existing theory by applying it to groups you are a part of or can become part of and report your findings to other social scientists as either confirming or raising questions about the theory.

Audience

The audience for your report will be other social scientists in the same field—sociologists who are probably familiar with the theory but who will need to know the context within which you are raising your questions.

Form

Readers of studies will want to examine your interpretation of the theory, your hypotheses, your method, your results, and your interpretation as thoroughly as readers of science reports. The forms of study reports for participant observation studies, however, are more variable, as indicated below. All of the elements of the science report, however, must be present.

> Title Page
> Abstract
> Introduction
> Methods (may be a descriptive paragraph)
> Results (may be combined with Discussion)
> Discussion (may be combined with Results)
> Conclusion
> References (APA form)

Ethical Constraints

Research ethics forbids revealing the identity of your subjects. Create fictitious names for organizations and people.

You may, in the course of your studies, find studies where headings are not used or where results are discussed as they are presented rather than in a separate section. They may, in fact, look more like essays. However, until you are practiced at distinguishing findings from interpretation of those findings, the headings can aid in making the necessary critical distinctions.

Local Features

As methods move from quantitative toward qualitative, you will find more variation in the content and even the order of various sections. Therefore, the headings below should be taken as guides to the work each section needs to perform for the reader, rather than as rules for ordering the content.

Title Page

Titles of social science studies should be (as in science) descriptive rather than rhetorical.

> **Example:** "Peer pressure and attitude change in college freshmen."
>
> ***Not***
> "Monkey See Monkey Do."

Abstract

As in the science unit, the abstract gives a quick overview of your report: describing your research question, hypothesis, method, results, and the significance of those results in less than 100 words. Once again, you will find it easier to write when you have finished a draft of the paper.

Introduction

The introduction sets your study into a context. It informs the reader of the issue under study, the theoretical background, including other research done on the issue, and arrives at the question under study in your report. If you derive your research question from theoretical readings, summarize aspects relevant to your study; if you have also researched the literature, your literature review belongs in this section. This discussion should lead to the question you are researching and to your hypothesis, if you are using one. If you are simply exploring the role of specific factors, describe the factors and the questions you are trying to answer.

Methods

In some qualitative reports, this section is included in the introduction, but all reports will require some description of your research methods. Describe the procedures you plan to follow and the reasons behind your choices. Precision and clarity matter as much in social science as they do in science; though your study is qualitative (i.e., requiring a great deal of interpretation and judgment), take care in selecting your population, deciding on the degree of participation you will engage in, the site, the time, and the issues or behaviors on which you will focus. The care and clarity with which you define these elements will determine the quality of your interpretations later. This section, whether under its own heading or part of the introduction, is evidence of your care in planning and will be read as such.

Results

Again, this section, in a qualitative report, may not be under a separate heading and in some reports the authors may discuss the results as they go along. We separate them here to stress the need for careful distinction between data and interpretation. Alternative organizations may be equally acceptable, but this is not a chronological or verbatim account. As with any description, you will be clearest if you begin with an overview, a summary of the activities during the study period. Following that, study your field notes, underlining behaviors relevant to your research question and hypothesis. Underlining different behaviors in different colors will help you spot patterns of interaction, frequency of occurrence, absence of some features, and changes over time.

> **Example:** You watched a group of college students viewing television for indications of interest in politics. You may note, in reviewing your notes, that interest, or comments about politics, occur more during some kinds of news shows than others, on some topics more than others, that they occur but are shut off by other members of the group.

> **Example:** You observed traffic patterns through and around that patch of woods on campus before and after a barrier was placed at the entrance to the path. You notice, on reviewing your notes, that more people went around the barrier and used the path at certain times of day, that males went through it more than females, or that a substantial number cut a new path.

Remember, as E. O. Wilson said in the science chapter, you are looking for patterns. Patterns will disappear if you simply list frequencies of behaviors or fail to consider their contexts. The patterns you discover should determine your organizational system. It is possible to organize the section by the features or topics that were your focus, but it is also possible, if one feature occurred much more often than any other, that such an organization will distort the image. You are writing a *portrait* of the study scene; your goal is to communicate to your reader as clear an image of the scene as you can. What were the dominant features, the major shifts or changes in expression, the absent qualities? These should determine the order and topic sentences of your paragraphs. Remember, as in science, absence of expected features is as important as presence—negative results are still results.

Within the paragraphs your task is to make the scene come alive quickly, without long verbatim accounts. You will have to generalize behaviors in order to accomplish this, but do so with care; counter the tendency to overgeneralize with liberal use of quotations, choosing quotes that are typical (i.e., they share characteristics with others you are leaving out). Avoid making your reader look through you and your interpretations; where you have set an interaction going through active participation, you clearly belong in the description. If you are commenting on your findings as you go along rather than writing a separate Discussion section, as described below, be careful not to let your interpretation substitute for a clear picture of the scene itself.

The purpose of this section, as when writing the science report, is to give your readers a clear view of the data so that they may see where their interpretation confirms yours, as you discuss its significance, or differs. Distinguish clearly between what happened and your interpretation, whether or not you include it in the same paragraph.

Discussion

In a participant observation study, the contents of this section may be interwoven with the results rather than given in a separate section. The point of the discussion, however, remains the same in either case; it is, as it was in the science report, to discuss the quality of your data and relate it back to the readings.

If you are doing this in a separate section, begin with a statement of the overall fit of your results to the theory or theories you were testing, and then discuss similarities and differences in detail, remembering to cite all sources carefully as practiced earlier in the chapter. As you do so, you should discuss probable explanations for the differences, critiquing both your own study and the theory. Remember you are discussing degrees of certainty and possible causes of difference; avoid overstating your claims. You may speculate on causes and explanations, and should, but remember that your generalizations must be supported by, and stay close to, the data. This is not the time to write a personal opinion essay on your topic. Instead you should revise your own opinion in light of the data, as well as revising the theory, if need be, and in either case, your discussion leads, not to a finale, but to further questions for research. As in the science report, the overall purpose of the social science report is to contribute to knowledge in the field by applying theory and to lead to the next research project, whether by you or by others. Your study is part of a community endeavor.

Surface Features

Elegance in this paper depends both on the smooth interaction between your work and the readings and on the clarity of your logic. The sentence complexity inquiries earlier in the chapter gave some practice in this, and the "Revision for Clarity" section will give further techniques for managing the complexity of your thoughts without giving in to a flood of prepositional phrases or passive voice constructions. Academic writing requires caution—not saying more than your data will support; however, you need to distinguish the language of caution from sheer wordiness—words to sound sophisticated, words to fill space.

> **Example:** Overstatement: Time of day determined the behavior of students. Cautious: Time of day appeared to influence defiance of the barrier. Wordy: The incidence of time of day appeared to be a factor in barrier removal by students.

The Survey Study

The survey method is appropriate when your research question is specific enough to be measurable, or quantifiable.

Choosing a Question

If the questions arising from your reading and discussion have to do with people's attitudes and beliefs, a survey may be the most appropriate method for your research. Review the questions discussed in Inquiry 3.3 for ideas.

Sample Questions
- Do students, as Rimmerman claims, feel they have no voice in their government?
- Do students see themselves as future political leaders (or as members of the elite to use Rimmerman's terms)?
- Do students' choice of in-groups on campus reflect the groups they hope to belong to in the future (i.e., their reference groups in Allport's terms)?
- How important is the environment to students compared with other events and issues of the day?

Remember the research question identifies what you are trying to find out, not what you will ask your subjects.

Developing a Hypothesis and Rationale

Write a statement on what you think your results will show and clearly state your thinking—the reasoning behind your hypothesis.

Collaborating in a research group with others who have similar interests and questions greatly improves the quality of the data and interpretation. Members of the group need not have the same hypothesis and probably will be asked to write different papers, but many heads produce better questions, sounder logic, and more data. Inquiry 3.9 is designed for groups to use in developing a single survey.

INQUIRY 3.9: STUDY DESIGN WORKSHEET FOR SURVEYS

Step 1. Developing a Hypothesis

Questions. List the question(s) you would like to study (from above) and relate them to the theories read in the unit.

Hypotheses. State the hypotheses you have developed above, relating them to the theories read.

> **Example:** Student participation in national politics will be less than with Rimmerman's 1970s subjects, suggesting that students no longer believe in social change through politics.

Alternative Hypotheses. What other answers (or explanations) might there be? Try to come up with at least two.

> **Example:** (1) Student attitudes toward national politics are different from the attitudes expressed by Rimmerman's student subjects, supporting his hypothesis that individualism reduces social participation. (2) Student attitudes toward national politics fit Rimmerman's expectations, but the cause of their disaffection is different.

Rationale. Why do you think your hypothesis provides the best answer to the research question?

> **Example.** Because I think the kind of apathy Rimmerman's subjects expressed is more widespread today—not confined to middle class adults.

Step 2. Defining Concepts

Underline all of the important terms in the hypothesis, and define each of them here. Use either the definition of one of the authors or call his/her definition into question and say how you define the word.

> **Example:** "Students": College students at West College, Fall '97; "Participation": voting, passing petitions, working for a candidate, attending rallies and meetings, writing letters.

Step 3. The Study Design

Population. Who or What will you study? Individuals? Groups? Organizations? Products (including books, music, etc.)? Media?

Example: West College students who pass through the Student Center between 12 and 1P on Friday, October 24, 1997. Equal number of males and females, random ethnic groups.

Study Partners should help to define these terms clearly (all groups? size? age? gender? etc.).

Site. Where will you conduct the survey? At a particular place? On a particular occasion or time of day? In a particular environment? Give reasons for your decisions.

Identify Variables: What Are You Measuring? Write a very specific statement of what you are measuring.

Example: Level of political interest as measured by voting, participation in social action groups, and participation in political campaigns.

Identify all the factors that may influence the way a person answers your questions: gender, race, parental attitudes, religion, time of day, and so on. Get information that will identify these factors so that you can measure whether there are significant differences due to these factors.

Design Survey Questions. What will you ask and what do the answers to your questions mean? Principle: you do not ask your research question directly. You need to determine what activities or behaviors indicate the attitudes you are looking for and direct your questions toward those. Your definitions, above, should help here.

Example: (1) A question asking what a subject would do if none of his/her friends were in the dorm cafeteria might indicate closeness or dependence on in-group. (2) A person's participation in campus groups may be an indication of interest in civic activities (though not necessarily political).

Survey questions range from open-ended prompts that ask subjects to write narrative answers to closed-ended queries that ask subjects to check boxes and give definitive, quantifiable answers. There are appropriate uses for both, but because the data from closed-ended questions are far easier to handle and interpret, this section is written with closed-ended questions in mind.

Tips for Constructing Questions. Questions that suggest, however indirectly, what the researcher wants to hear (leading questions) tend to elicit that response, regardless of the real attitude of the subject.

Example: "Do you think political participation is important in a democracy?"

Vague questions produce vague answers.

Example: "Do you think people are more apathetic today?" (More than when? What people? Apathetic measured how?)

Responses to questions on nonapproved attitudes are notoriously unreliable (rarely will someone admit to prejudice, etc.).

Example: "How does your group talk about homosexuals?"

Questions that allow a breadth of answers will produce more useable information.

Examples: Questions to measure the degree of interest in politics.
Too broad: Are you interested in politics? Answer: I dunno. Sometimes. (likely to produce ambiguous responses)
Too narrow: Are you registered to vote? Answer: Yes. (does not necessarily indicate interest and certainly not degree)
Revised: Please indicate how often you have engaged in the following:

Voting
_Always, _Frequently, _Sometimes, _Rarely, _Never

Signing Petitions
_Always, _Frequently, _Sometimes, _Rarely, _Never

Writing letters to elected representatives
_Always, _Frequently, _Sometimes, _Rarely, _Never

Etc.

Limit the number of questions to the number that can be comfortably answered in three minutes or less.

Try the questions on a class member not in the group. Then ask whether the subject could guess what answers you wanted.

Procedure. How will you measure? Give details.

Example: (1) Pencil and paper survey forms will ask subjects to identify their degree of interest by using a range grid (Strongly Dislike, Neutral, Somewhat, Very Interested) or frequency grid (above). (2) Surveys will be distributed anonymously to students' mailboxes with instructions to return to a designated location (also anonymous).

Relationship of Evidence to Hypothesis. For each question, give the reasons the responses will answer your research question.

Example: (Question above) Interest in politics is indicated by a variety of activities in addition to voting.

Study partners should test the respondent's reliability. Are there other explanations for the behavior? Will the generalization hold under all conditions? What might affect the response?

The Survey Study Report

As in the science unit, the form of the social science study report expresses and reflects the process of the study itself. The sections of the quantitative survey report, therefore, look very much like sections of a natural science report, though important differences are noted below.

Global Features

Purpose
The purpose of the survey study report is to test existing theory by applying it to similar or different populations to confirm or raise questions about the theory.

Audience
The audience for the report is other social scientists in the same field, social scientists who are probably familiar with the theory, but who need to know your interpretation of it and the reasons behind your questions.

Form
The social scientist readers will want to examine your interpretation of the theory, your methods, results, and interpretations as thoroughly as readers of science reports. Though the form of the report may vary according to the type of survey conducted, the underlying form remains that of the scientific study report.

Title Page
Abstract
Introduction
Methods
Results
Discussion/Conclusion
References (APA form)

Ethical Constraints

Research ethics forbids revealing the identity of your subjects. Create fictitious names for organizations and people.

Local Features

As in the science study report, each section has a specific function, representing the steps of the inquiry process.

Title Page

Titles in the sciences and social sciences are descriptive and informative rather than rhetorical. That is, their intent is to inform the reader of the issue under study and the population studied: attention getting or effect are secondary.

> **Example:** "Political participation among college students," *not* "Kennedy? Who's That?"

Abstract

An abstract is a very brief summary of your study, giving the type of study, the behavior under study, the type and size of the study population, the procedure and the results. Conclude with a statement of the significance of the results and indications for further study. These statements must be very brief, frequently 150 words or less, and often appear in indexes separate from the study itself. They must therefore stand alone—not as prefaces to the study report itself. You will find that, though they appear first, right after the title page, they are easier to write after you have completed the report.

Introduction

The introduction to your social science report will be longer than in either your science paper or in most standard essays you have written. Because your research questions arose out of theoretical debate, you must review that debate here sufficiently to make clear where your research questions came from and why you believe they require further study. Thus, your introduction may run two to three pages, for it must contain the following:

- A statement of the problem, issue, or behavior under study and its importance.
- A literature review, which summarizes the theoretical debate, providing a context for your study.
- A one- or two-sentence description of your study, stating the hypothesis your study will test.

Methods

Describe your research procedures in detail, using the subcategories (Population, Site, Questions, etc.) from your Study Design Worksheet (Inquiry 3.9) as subheadings. The purpose of this section, as in science, is to be clear enough so that other researchers can both critique and replicate your method. Summarize the questions asked (if a survey) and include a blank copy of your questionnaire as an Appendix. If your instructor wishes you to avoid the first-person, this section may be written legitimately in the passive voice.

Results

As in science, your social science results must be kept scrupulously separate from your interpretation of them (below). What your subjects said (survey) or did (observation) belongs in this section; what you interpret those answers or behaviors to mean belongs in the Discussion section below. Open this section with a statement of whether the results supported your hypothesis totally, in part, or not at all. Proceed, then, to a narrative account of your chief findings. You will discover, however, that writing about numbers and percentages clearly is difficult if not impossible without visual aids. Therefore, also present your complete findings (answers to all questions), in both numbers and percents, in tabular form, and your significant findings, those you will discuss in your Discussion section, in chart or graphic form.

The interaction between graphics and text is a subject in itself and more complex than we have time for here. However, the ability to use graphics is an essential part of quantitative research approaches, so we will introduce a few basic principles:

- Bar charts compare answers among groups,
- Pie charts show how a population is divided,
- Graphs show change over time or compare groups over time.

These brief definitions will at least allow you to think about your choices and try out appropriate forms for their effectiveness.

Discussion

In this section you discuss the meaning of your results and relate them to the theory you reviewed in the Introduction. You should focus on your hypothesis first, accounting, if you can, for unexpected divergence from your expectations. Then go on to discuss interesting and perhaps unexpected patterns that emerge in your data. You must bring your chief authors back into this discussion, discussing the relationship of your findings to their theories. You should raise questions for further research as you go along. Finally you should discuss the limitations of your study and the value of negative findings. Describe what you might do the next time to prevent defects or ambiguities, and to explore new patterns.

Conclusion

Sum up the discussion, relating your study to larger principles (from the debate), and raise questions for further research.

References

Use APA citations throughout and APA form for the Reference List (see Appendix).

Surface Features

Elegance in this paper depends both on the smooth interaction between your work and the readings and on the clarity and thoroughness of your logic. The sentence complexity inquiries earlier in the chapter gave some practice in this, and made clear the relationship between complex thinking and complex writing. The Revision for Clarity section later in the chapter will help you express complex relationships more clearly. You will need to modify statements carefully to avoid generalizing beyond what your data will support. Once you supply the words needed for this, you will find that you cannot afford words that do no work; they muddy the waters. This is the key difference between academic writing and sheer wordiness. Many academic writers *are* wordy, which makes their prose almost impenetrable. Don't add your name to that list.

> **Example:**
> Vague Overstatement: People voted far less often in local than in national elections.
> Precise Statement: UCSB students, in this 1999 study, were twice as likely to vote in national elections (85 percent) than in local races (42 percent).
> Wordy Statement: The incidence of voting in national elections among student respondents was twice that of the corresponding incidence of voting in local elections.

Theoretical Debate Essay

The observation and survey research reports above are forms used to report research to others in the field. Reporting research, however, is not the only writing activity of professionals in the social sciences. More often than not, they also move on, with the evidence gained in their own research, to argue theoretical issues within and beyond the boundaries of their disciplines. As potential participants in such theoretical debates, you will frequently be asked to compare and contrast theories, to evaluate them, to arrive at your own positions on them.

It is far easier to enter such debates successfully if you have been through the research process so that you know how to argue from research data rather than from personal experience alone. Writing such essays brings home key differences between personal opinion and theory, between experience based positions and databased positions, between essays in the social sciences (based on field research) and the humanities (based on analysis of texts).

For the above reasons, this assignment asks you to begin by doing one of the field research projects above, and to write up your field results according to appropriate study report form. You may do this in rough draft form only, and though you will need to explain how your hypothesis is related to the theory you are testing, you don't need to write a full review of the literature. Your results and your analysis of those results in the Discussion section provide the necessary first steps toward entering a theoretical debate.

Global Features

Purpose
To enter an ongoing debate on particular social phenomena or issue.

Audience
Other parties in the debate and/or other professionals interested in the issue. You can assume a general familiarity with the issue and the theory, though not necessarily with the debate itself.

Form
The form of the theory debate is an essay; it uses no headings, but follows the familiar essay form:

> Introduction
> Thesis
> Argument
> Conclusion

It is organized by the logic of the argument as expressed in the thesis. As we point out below, however, there are some important differences between this essay and the more familiar personal opinion essay.

Local Features

Introduction
Your introduction, as in all of the papers in this section, should state the issue and its importance. You should also give the names of the theorists you are debating.

Thesis

After comparing your results with the theories under discussion in Inquiries 3.4 and 5, what would you say about the validity of those theories, or of the specific claims you were testing? Write a statement that sums this up. This is your thesis, and it differs from the thesis of a personal opinion essay in that it takes a position relative to a theorist's—not simply on the topic—and is based on your study data. Correctly written your thesis should also serve to remind you of these features:

- You are debating the issue, not writing a report of your study.
- Your position is on the theory, not simply about the issue.
- Your personal opinion as it comes out of evaluating the theory gives form to this essay.

Example: Rimmerman argues that preoccupation with private life is the chief cause of apathy, and while this proved true of University of X students, lack of knowledge was also a contributor to nonparticipation in the political process.

Not

This study hypothesizes that lack of knowledge is the chief cause of nonparticipation in the political process for University of X students.

or

Americans today don't feel sufficiently informed to participate in the political process.

The most common difficulty students encounter in moving from the study report to the debate essay form is the tendency to give an account of their studies rather than to debate the issue. The chart on p. 160 (Figure 7) diagrams the difference in the forms.

Theoretical Overview and Definition of Concepts

Readers find it difficult to follow a debate if they don't have a map of the playing field in their minds first. Therefore give an overview, laying out the common ground and the terms of debate; for guidance review those elements in the theoretical debates you read for this unit. Those readings should give you a sense of the variety of ways of providing readers a context for the coming debate. You may need to define terms, or you may need to report the lack of consistent definition. If the latter you may need to give more space to distinguish between definitions and to establish which definition you will use and why. You will need to give brief summaries of the theories, so that readers have a view of the whole before you begin discussing the parts. A paragraph, or perhaps a paragraph for each theorist, should be enough for this task.

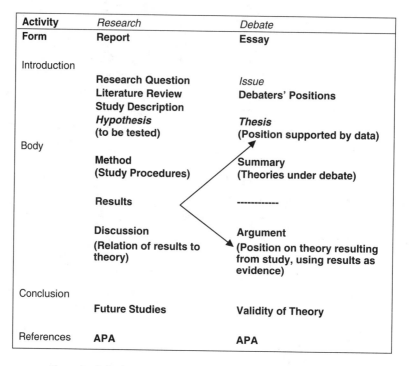

Activity	*Research*	*Debate*
Form	**Report**	**Essay**
Introduction		
	Research Question	*Issue*
	Literature Review	**Debaters' Positions**
	Study Description	
	Hypothesis	*Thesis*
	(to be tested)	**(Position supported by data)**
Body		
	Method	**Summary**
	(Study Procedures)	**(Theories under debate)**
	Results	------------
	Discussion	**Argument**
	(Relation of results to theory)	**(Position on theory resulting from study, using results as evidence)**
Conclusion		
	Future Studies	**Validity of Theory**
References	**APA**	**APA**

Figure 7   Science Report and Theoretical Debate Essay Differences

Argument

Now you will need a clearly developed argument, specifying which of the author's claims you are challenging, using evidence from your study to develop both your agreement and disagreement with the theorists. You may use anecdotal evidence (individual cases of an event) in addition to your study evidence, but this should be by the way of illustrating a point or suggesting avenues for further study. You cannot generalize from anecdotal evidence alone.

- *Control.* Be careful not to simply present the theory. The essay should be organized around your *evaluation* of the theorist's claims. You should be in charge.
- *Organization.* To achieve the above, write a list of sentences stating your position on each of the chief points of the theory, from major premise to conclusion. Put these into logical order, and they become your outline. Each point you wish to make about the theory becomes a paragraph lead so that each paragraph begins with your position. This prevents the essay from becoming a report on the meaning of the theory (as in Student Sample 1 earlier in the chapter).
- *Development.* As in the paragraph practices (Inquiry 3.5), follow your statement of your point with the theorist's position, a sentence saying how that position relates to your findings, and the specific findings that support your point. Then discuss the agreement, discrepancy, or whatever point you are making, concluding

with the relationship of this point to the next. You will later become far more flexible and innovative in the ways you relate to theorists, but this procedure will help you to form the habit of interacting actively with the theorists rather than returning to old habits of referring only to personal opinion.

Citation
Cite all ideas not your own to the author(s) using APA style, as practiced in Inquiry 3.5, and include a Reference page at the end.

Surface Features

Write in a style as close to your natural style as possible for your first draft; look at your own reading logs for a model. As you draft your essay, practice the paragraph development and sentence complexity inquiries from this chapter to aid in keeping track of your argument and staying in control. When you have drafted your argument, go on to the revision section for additional work on your language.

REVISING FOR CLARITY

Complex ideas require complex sentences: the more qualifications you need to add to an idea, the greater the strain on the architecture of your sentences— and your thinking will increase in complexity very rapidly during your college years. You need, therefore, to be an increasingly skillful architect to cope with this growth. Revision, however, requires not only that we recognize when we have overtaxed a sentence, but that we possess tools to fix it. *Sentence revision is also thought revision—reseeing our words and ideas.* Thought revision does not stop, even at the editing stage. In the inquiries below, we move beyond the principles of focus and efficiency developed so far to precision of relationships, modification, and emphasis as tools for managing complexity and further development of thought.

Focusing Paragraphs

We apply the same principle used to focus sentences on paragraphs, so that you can see clearly whether the topic and content of your paragraphs correlate well.

INQUIRY 3.10: FOCUSING PARAGRAPHS

Practice on the sentences below, then take the topic sentence of each paragraph in your essay and check its focus, using the steps practiced earlier for sentence focusing in Inquiry 3.6. Highlight the three words that express the core, or central meaning of the paragraph as well as the sentence. Make sure those words are contained in the Subject→Verb→Object string, or base clause.

1. In the survey conducted at North College, we found that students vote more often in national elections than they do in local ones. (Paragraph on reasons for voting in national elections.)

2. Gordon Allport wrote a book called *Prejudice* in which he examined the behavior of groups and found that people prefer the familiar. (Paragraph on preference for those we know.)

3. College students are in an institution to learn and expand their knowledge about their surroundings, making them more aware of the environmental truths of today, and the fact that reducing is the answer. (Paragraph on environmental knowledge.)

4. The industry can be changed through their income status, which is altered by the public's demands due to an increased amount of information. (Paragraph on influencing industry.)

5. The information to the public needs to be more influential and more specific because the ambiguous and general solutions lack motivation, which causes a loss in participation. (Paragraph on influencing the public.)

In some cases, such as 2 above, you have a choice. You may focus on the author or the concept, as follows:

Examples: Craig Rimmerman argues that the Founders didn't design government for full participation of the people.

The **Founders,** according to Craig Rimmerman, **didn't design the government** for full participation of the people.

Full participation of the people, **was not,** according to Craig Rimmerman, **the intent** of the Founders when they designed the government.

To decide between these options, ask yourself whether the paragraph focuses on the debaters or the issue.

Examples: Craig Rimmerman argues that the Founders didn't design government for full participation of the people, but **James Madison argues** otherwise. (Point of the paragraph is to give conflicting opinions.)

The structure of our government **prevents full participation** of the people, according to Craig Rimmerman, by confining membership in the legislature to an elite. (Point of the paragraph is that the structure is to blame for lack of citizen participation.)

Once again the act of focusing helps in reviewing and sharpening the thinking of the essay. In this case, it helps to sharpen the point being made in the paragraph.

Modification

Once your sentences are in focus, decide what modifying words or phrases are needed to present your claims accurately and prevent overgeneralization.

> **Example:** Students   vote   elections
> surveyed at North College   in national more often than local

The grammar and punctuation rules for modification are many and complex, but the central principle is not: keep modifiers near the words they modify. Failure to do so produces sentences like these:

> **Examples:**
> **1.** The patient has chest pain if she lies on her left side for over a year.
> **2.** Without a doubt, I knew that people would consider that unnatural oil spills were the main motivation for abolishing the oilrigs, over superficial reasons.

Frequently sentences like these occur because we develop ideas as we write when we are drafting. The sentence below illustrates the way ideas flow onto a page through free association as much as through logical connection:

> **Example:**
> Allport's theory of group behavior seems right on when we think about how important it was to belong and not be considered "weird" back in high school. But in college we are supposed to be developing our individuality so that we can find out what we want to do for the rest of our lives not letting a group decide for us, not just fitting in as Allport says. If we continue to let groups be that important so we won't be considered odd, we are likely not to choose some profession we aren't good at or don't like so Allport's less right about this.

If the student were asked to put the idea that came out of that writing into a nutshell, he or she might say:

> **Example:** Fitting in with a group is more important in high school than in college.

That kind of condensing and reframing is far more valuable in clarifying meaning than tinkering with first draft sentences. Once that clear framework is in place, detail can be added through modification:

> **Example:** Fitting in with a group is *far* more important in high school, *where the penalty for difference is banishment* than *it is* in college, *where the prize for individuality is admiration.*

Adding modifications in this way, to recapture or add texture, emphasis, and detail is to use the language for everything it can give. The content of the freewrite, for example, justifies a further sentence on the consequences of behavior.

> **Example:** Fitting in with a group is far more important in high school, where the penalty for difference is banishment than it is in college, where individuality is admired. To attend college because everyone else does is one thing, to become a lawyer because everyone else is is quite another.

The point here is that editing is not necessarily the elimination of words; it is making words effective.

Modification also allows you to add necessary information without destroying the flow of your ideas. In the sentences above, for example, Allport's name has dropped out, though we are still talking about his ideas. To correct this oversight, we can embed a clause and make minor revisions to adjust for the addition:

> **Example:** *The need to fit* in with a group, *which Allport claims is primal for humans,* seems far more important in high school, where the penalty for difference is banishment than it is in college, where individuality is admired. To attend college because everyone else does is one thing, to become a lawyer because everyone else is is quite another.

The embedding also serves as a reminder that we are supposed to be debating Allport and that the argument we have introduced needs to be further developed.

> **Example:** The need to fit in with a group, which Allport claims is primal for humans, seems far more important in high school, where the penalty for difference is banishment than it is in college, where individuality is admired. *Thus it seems that this dependence on groups is, in our culture, treated as something to be outgrown; in high school, we are urged not to go along with the group no matter what they are doing. By college, overdependence is frowned upon all the more.* To attend college because everyone else does is one thing, to become a lawyer because everyone else is is quite another. *In this culture, at any rate, we are supposed to work against our need for groups, a point Allport doesn't seem to take into consideration.*

Thus does embedding lead us back to the debate, which in turn further develops our thought.

Coordination and Subordination

Coordination and subordination are grammatical tools for creating hierarchies of importance. Without help, readers cannot create relationships between ideas, cannot see what is important, what secondary, particularly when the information and ideas are complex. Both principles begin with the base sentence, S→V, S→V→O, or S→C, which we will now simply name *independent clauses.*

Coordination

Coordination joins two independent clauses and makes them equally important:

> ### *Example*
>
> | **S→V→O** | **+** | **S→V→O** |
> |---|---|---|
> | John hit Joe, | and | Joe hit the telephone pole. |
> | Allport focuses on needs, | ; | Rimmerman stresses obligations. |
> | Allport says we need groups, | but | we need to resist that need. |
> | You need to attend this class, | if | you want to pass this course. |
> | Sue didn't call John | so | he didn't show up. |

The words in the column under the + sign are coordinating conjunctions, the only words used for this construction. Note that the semicolon serves the same purpose. Mark the joint with a comma plus a coordinating conjunction unless you are using the semicolon. Coordinate to emphasize equal value or bring ideas into equivalence. Here is John Steinbeck's opening line in *The Grapes of Wrath*: "The houses stood vacant upon the land, and the land was vacant because of this" (1).

Subordination

Subordination, as the name suggests, subordinates one idea or piece of information to another. This can be done in two ways:

1. By introducing the independent clause with a subordinating conjunction:

> **Example**
> *Though* hit by John, Joe managed not to hit the telephone pole.
> Allport focuses on needs, whereas Rimmerman only stresses obligations.
> *Though* Allport says we need groups, we need to resist that need.
> *Despite* your regular attendance, you aren't passing this course.
> *Because* Sue didn't call John, he didn't show up.

2. By removing the subject of the less important clause, thus making it a *dependent clause,* a clause that cannot stand alone.

> **Example**
> *Though* wounded, Joe managed not to hit the telephone pole.
> Allport focuses on needs, *not* obligations, as Rimmerman does.
> We need to resist the groups *that* Allport says we need.
> *Despite* regular attendance, you aren't passing this course.
> *Because* he wasn't called, John didn't show up at Sue's.

Lists of coordinating conjunctions can be found in any handbook; each expresses a slightly different relationship to the main clause, so use them with care. Punctuate the joints with commas.

Whether the above constructions are correct or effective depends, once again, on your intended focus. When reading the sentences in 2 above, for example, the reader expects "Joe," "Allport," "we," "you," and "John" to be the subjects under discussion. If they are not, the sentences need revising.

INQUIRY 3.11: PRACTICING COMPLEX STRUCTURES

Step 1

Write the lead sentence of each of your paragraphs in three different ways:

1. Using a separate sentence for each piece of information. **Example:** John hit Joe. Joe hit the telephone pole.
2. Using coordination.
3. Using subordination.

Select the one you think most clearly represents your intended point. Now review the paragraph to see whether it does indeed develop that point or needs revision to do so.

Step 2

Embed an additional piece of information or a citation phrase into the sentence and revise to fit. Review the paragraph to be sure the reason for embedding the information is developed in the paragraph itself.

Punctuation, Rhythm, and Beat

We have noted the punctuation as we went along above, because punctuation is not a separate topic from construction; it is a way of marking joints. If you read music, think of punctuation as marking the beat, or the pauses, and indicating the length of those pauses. Indeed the best way to get an underlying sense of punctuation is to remember that it is sound transcribed to paper. Like music, it needs to be marked properly to be translated back into sound. We group words into phrases for meaning the way music does as demonstrated in Inquiry 3.12.

INQUIRY 3.12: PUNCTUATING BY RHYTHM

Step 1

Read the following sentence aloud, inserting musical phrase lines to mark its natural rhythm:

> **Example:** After the party when everyone was talked out danced out eaten and drunk out Roberta who was always thinking ahead suggested we go for a swim before going home.

Now replace the phrase lines with commas and put a full stop, a period at the end; your sentence is punctuated. Thus the comma becomes a quarter beat rest, the semicolon a half beat rest, the period a full beat rest.

Step 2

1. Locate and mark the subject, verb, and object.
2. Locate any coordinating and subordinating conjunctions.
3. Look at the relationship between the punctuation marks and the base clause elements.

This should demonstrate that punctuation is essentially a way of marking the construction and rhythm of a sentence, so that the reader groups words and phrases in the way that the author intended. To demonstrate the use of the different markers, take the same thought and mark it differently.

> **Example:** After the party, everyone was worn out. We had talked, danced, eaten, and drunk ourselves into exhaustion. Roberta was always thinking ahead; she suggested we go for a swim before going home.

Note that you must change the dependent clauses to independent if you want to make separate sentences; thus punctuation, construction, and rhythm are interrelated and inseparable.

The purpose of these revision inquiries is to convince you of the power of revision. Too often people treat the revision stage as a final error-catching inquiry, that is, editing or proofreading, not revising. Taken seriously revision brings out the best in your ideas and the best in the language. Students frequently complain that academic writing is dry, flat, and wordy—tedious to read. Part of the reason for this undoubtedly lies in the nature of the subject matter; theories are abstract and inquiry stresses objectivity. Much of the problem can be cured, however, if you understand the capacity of language to give texture, emphasis, and rhythm—and if you take the time to work with your language once it is on the page.

MOVING ON

The social science unit has moved from the model of logical thinking provided by science to the study of theory, a very long way indeed. Learning the inquiry process of the social science disciplines has changed the way you read, the way you interact with readings, the way you look at your world, the way you construct arguments. You have, in short, moved into the heart of academic thinking. Your writing skills have had to grow along with your thinking skills, developing mastery of more and more complex forms, from formats to sentences.

As you applied theories to your own experience and then debated differing perspectives, whether between disciplines or theories, you have undoubtedly become more and more aware of how much research depends on the kind of question asked and how much the kind of question asked depends, in turn, on the way theory shapes perception and interpretation. Theories are, after all, human constructs; they differ from personal opinion in that they are tested against the world more rigorously and revised more conscientiously in light of the data. However, the concepts formed from the data are ideas, abstracted from the world. The human capacity to create ideas, to create the systems of ideas called theories, to say nothing of the ability to create imaginative forms, to create art, is in itself a fascinating area of study. We now move from theory to the study of theory-making, the study of the ways humans create meaning in science, philosophy, religion and the arts.

four

Readings in the Social Sciences

INTRODUCTION

The readings in social science all address questions of identity, interdependence (community), and change from the point of view of the social sciences. Sociologists Allport and Markstrom-Adams deal with the human need for groups, the role of groups in forming identity, and in-group formation as a cause of intergroup conflict and prejudice. Afro-American leader W. E. B. Du Bois speaks to the problem of divided identity from the point of view of an excluded minority and discusses his and Booker T. Washington's opposing solutions to this problem. Judith Shklar studies the same problem of conflicting loyalties on the part of those excluded from or mistreated by majority groups from the point of view of a contemporary political scientist. James Madison, in *Federalist #10,* presents the classical political theory on abuse of power by factions, the position on which the Constitution is based. Bennett and Rimmerman, both political scientists, discuss apathy and nonparticipation in the American political process and its causes. Finally Orr critiques the value system of individual domination and argues for a view that stresses our interdependence with the physical environment.

Thus any two or three readings may be combined to produce complete units with slightly different themes:

- Individual and group identity formation
- Identity and conflicting group loyalties
- Group domination and political equality
- Group loyalty and political change
- Individual and group from the different disciplinary perspectives

- Conflicting loyalties and obligations: personal and disciplinary perspectives
- The double face of group loyalty: solidarity and exclusion
- Domination and interdependence: the environment view

Together the readings provide professional examples of writing across the range of social science genre—from the scientific report (Markstrom-Adams) to philosophical essay (Madison)—and to a variety of audiences. The student papers selected for revision workshop demonstrate successful synthesis of the theory, method, and the students' own interests. They provide examples of both the scientific study report form and the theoretical debate essay. Both papers provide opportunities for global, local, and sentence level revision.

The Formation of In-Groups

Gordon Allport

Biography: Gordon Allport (1897–1967) was one of the founding fathers of the field of social-psychology. Head of Harvard University's Department of Psychology, he formulated theories of personality and prejudice. His theories set the definitions of key terms for the field, and he was one of the first to define prejudice as an historical and cultural phenomenon important to study.

A classical theory of the relationship of our need for in-groups and prejudice. Allport argues that groups are integral to the formation of identity and that we identify our birth groups as good. He takes issue with the "Group-Norm Theory of Prejudice" which postulates that for every in-group, there must be an out-group, arguing that negative attitudes toward other groups, though it increases group solidarity, is not necessary. As a textbook chapter, this reading provides an example of an explanation of theory to a non-professional audience.

CHAPTER 3

The proverb *familiarity breeds contempt* contains considerably less than a half-truth. While we sometimes do become bored with our daily routine of living and with some of our customary companions, yet the very values that sustain our lives depend for their force upon their familiarity. What is more, what is familiar tends to *become* a value. We come to like the style of cooking, the customs, the people, we have grown up with.

From *The Nature of Prejudice*, Ch. 3. Cambridge: Addison Wesley, 1954: pp. 29–47.

Psychologically, the crux of the matter is that the familiar provides the indispensable basis of our existence. Since existence is good, its accompanying groundwork seems good and desirable. A child's parents, neighborhood, region, nation are given to him—so too his religion, race, and social traditions. To him all these affiliations are taken for granted. Since he is part of them, and they are part of him, they are *good*.

As early as the age of five, a child is capable of understanding that he is a member of various groups. He is capable, for example, of a sense of ethnic identification. Until he is nine or ten he will not be able to understand just what his membership signifies—how, for example, Jews differ from gentiles, or Quakers from Methodists, but he does not wait for this understanding before he develops fierce in-group loyalties.

Some psychologists say that the child is "rewarded" by virtue of his memberships, and that this reward creates the loyalty. That is to say, his family feeds and cares for him, he obtains pleasure from the gifts and attentions received from neighbors and compatriots. Hence he learns to love them. His loyalties are acquired on the basis of such rewards. We may doubt that this explanation is sufficient. A colored child is seldom or never rewarded for being a Negro—usually just the opposite, and yet he normally grows up with a loyalty to his racial group. Thoughts of Indiana arouse a glow in the breast of a native Hoosier—not necessarily because he passed a happy childhood there, but simply because he *came* from there. It is still, in part, the ground of his existence.

Rewards may, of course, help the process. A child who has plenty of fun at a family reunion may be more attached thereafter to his own clan because of the experience. But normally he would be attached to his clan anyway, simply because it is an inescapable part of his life.

Happiness (i.e., "reward") is not then the only reason for our loyalties. Few of our group memberships seem to be sustained by the pleasures they provide—an exception perhaps being our recreational memberships. And it takes a major unhappiness, a prolonged and bitter experience, to drive us away from loyalties once formed. And sometimes no amount of punishment can make us repudiate our loyalty.

This principle of the *ground* in human learning is important. We do not need to postulate a "gregarious instinct" to explain why people like to be with people: they have simply found people lock-stitched into the very fabric of their existence. Since they affirm their own existence as good, they will affirm social living as good. Nor do we need to postulate a "consciousness of kind" to explain why people adhere to their own families, clans, ethnic groups. The self could not be itself without them.

Scarcely anyone ever wants to be anybody else. However handicapped or unhappy he feels himself, he would not change places with other more fortunate mortals. He grumbles over his misfortunes and wants his lot improved; but it is *his* lot and *his* personality that he wants bettered. This attachment to one's own being is basic to human life. I may say that I envy *you*. But I do not want to *be* you; I only want to have for myself some of your attributes or possessions. And along with this beloved self go all of the person's basic memberships. Since he cannot alter his family stock, its traditions, his nationality, or his native language, he does well to accept them. Their accent dwells in the heart as well as on the tongue.

Oddly enough, it is not necessary for the individual to have direct acquaintance with all his in-groups. To be sure, he usually knows the members of his immediate family. (An orphan, however, may be passionately attached to parents he has never seen.) Some groups, such as clubs, schools, neighborhoods, are known through personal contacts. But others depend largely on symbols or hearsay. No one can have direct acquaintance with his race as a whole, nor with all his lodge brothers or co-religionists. The young child may sit enthralled while he hears of the exploits of the great-grandfather whose role as a sea-captain, a frontiersman, or nobleman sets a tradition with which the child identifies himself. The words he hears provide him just as authentic a ground for his life as do his daily experiences. By symbols one learns family traditions, patriotism, and racial pride. Thus in-groups that are only verbally defined may be nonetheless firmly knit.

WHAT IS AN IN-GROUP?

In a static society it would be fairly easy to predict just what loyalties the individual will form—to what region, to what phratry, or to what social class. In such a static society kinship, status, even place of residence, may be rigidly prescribed.

> In ancient China at one time residential arrangements actually coincided with social distance. Where one lived indicated all of one's memberships. The inner circle of a region was the Tribute Holding where government officials only were permitted to reside. A second circle contained the nobility. Beyond this an outer but defended area, known as the Peaceful Tenures, contained literary workers and other citizens of repute. Farther out lay the Prohibited territory divided between foreigners and transported convicts. Finally came the Unstrained territory, where only barbarians and ostracized felons were allowed to dwell.[1]

In a more mobile, technological society such as ours no such rigidity exists.

There is one law—universal in all human societies—that assists us in making an important prediction. *In every society on earth the child is regarded as a member of his parents' groups.* He belongs to the same race, stock, family tradition, religion, caste, and occupational status. To be sure, in our society, he may when he grows older escape certain of these memberships, but not all. The child is ordinarily expected to acquire his parents' loyalties and prejudices; and if the parent because of his group-membership is an object of prejudice, the child too is automatically victimized.

Although this rule holds in our society, it is less infallible than in more "familistic" regions of the world. While the American child normally acquires a strong sense of family membership and a certain loyalty to his parents' country of origin, race, and religion, he has considerable latitude respecting his attachments. Each individual pattern will be somewhat different. An American child is free to accept some of his parents' memberships and to reject others.

It is difficult to define an in-group precisely. Perhaps the best that can be done is to say that members of an in-group all use the term *we* with the same essential significance. Members of a family do so, likewise schoolmates, members of a lodge, labor union, club, city, state, nation. In a vaguer way members of international bodies may do the same. Some we organizations are transitory (e.g., an evening party), some are permanent (e.g., a family or clan).

Sam, a middle-aged man of only average sociability, listed his own in-group memberships as follows:

> his paternal relatives
> his maternal relatives
> family of orientation (in which he grew up)
> family of procreation (his wife and children)
> his boyhood circle (now a dim memory)
> his grammar school (in memory only)
> his high school (in memory only)
> his college as a whole (sometimes revisited)
> his college class (reinforced by reunions)
> his present church membership (shifted when he was 20)
> his profession (strongly organized and firmly knit)
> his firm (but especially the department in which he works)
> a "bunch" (group of four couples who take a good deal of recreation together)
> surviving members of a World War I company of infantry (growing dim)
> state where he was born (a fairly trivial membership)
> town where he now lives (a lively civic spirit)
> New England (a regional loyalty)
> United States (an average amount of patriotism)
> United Nations (in principle firmly believed in but psychologically loose because he is not clear concerning the "we" in this case)
> Scotch-Irish stock (a vague feeling of kinship with others who have this lineage)
> Republican party (he registers Republican in the primaries but has little additional sense of belonging)

Sam's list is probably not complete—but from it we can reconstruct fairly well the membership ground on which he lives.

In his list Sam referred to a boyhood circle. He recalls that at one time this in-group was of desperate importance to him. When he moved to a new neighborhood at the age of 10 he had no one of his own age to pal with, and he much desired companionship. The other boys were curious and suspicious. Would they admit him? Was Sam's style compatible with the gang's style? There was the usual ordeal by fistfight, set in motion at some slight pretext. This ritual—as is customary in boys' gangs—is designed to provide a swift and acceptable test of the stranger's manners and morale. Will he keep within the limits set by the gang, and show just enough boldness, toughness, and self-control to suit the other boys? Sam was fortunate in this ordeal, and was forthwith admitted to the coveted in-group. Probably he was lucky that he had no additional handicaps in terms of his racial, religious, or status memberships. Otherwise the probation would have been longer and the tests more exacting; and perhaps the gang would have excluded him forever.

Thus some in-group memberships have to be fought for. But many are conferred automatically by birth and by family tradition. In terms of modern social science the former memberships reflect *achieved* status; the latter, *ascribed* status.

SEX AS AN IN-GROUP

Sam did not mention his membership (ascribed status) in the male sex. Probably at one time it was consciously important to him—and may still be so.

The in-group of sex makes an interesting case study. A child of two normally makes no distinction in his companionships: a little girl or a little boy is all the same to him. Even in the first grade the awareness of sex-groups is relatively slight. Asked whom they would choose to play with, first-grade children on the average choose opposite-sexed children at least a quarter of the time. By the time the fourth grade is reached these cross-sexed choices virtually disappear: only two percent of the children want to play with someone of the opposite sex. When the eighth grade is reached friendships between boys and girls begin to re-emerge, but even then only eight percent extend their choices across the sex boundary.[2]

For some people—misogynists among them—the sex-grouping remains important throughout their lives. Women are viewed as a wholly different species from men, usually an inferior species. Such primary and secondary sex differences as exist are greatly exaggerated and are inflated into imaginary distinctions that justify discrimination. With half of mankind (his own sex) the male may feel an in-group solidarity, with the other half, an irreconcilable conflict.

Lord Chesterfield, who in his letters often admonished his son to guide his life by reason rather than by prejudice, nevertheless has this to say about women:

"Women, then, are only children of a larger growth; they have an entertaining tattle, and sometimes wit; but for solid reasoning, good sense, I never knew in my life one that had it, or who reasoned or acted consequentially for four and twenty hours together. . . .

"A man of sense only trifles with them, plays with them, humors and flatters them, as he does a sprightly, forward child; but he neither consults them about, nor trusts them with serious matters; though he often makes them believe that he does both; which is the thing in the world that they are most proud of. . . .[3]

"Women are much more like each other than men; they have in truth but two passions, vanity and love: these are their universal characteristics."[4]

Schopenhauer's views were much like Chesterfield's. Women, he wrote, are big children all their life long. A fundamental fault of the female character is that it has no sense of justice. This is mainly due to the fact, Schopenhauer insisted, that women are defective in the powers of reasoning and deliberation.[5]

Such antifeminism reflects the two basic ingredients of prejudice—denigration and gross overgeneralization. Neither of these famous men of intellect allows for individual differences among women, nor asks whether their alleged attributes are in fact more common in the female than in the male sex.

What is instructive about this antifeminism is the fact that it implies security and contentment with one's own sex-membership. To Chesterfield and to Schopenhauer the cleavage between male and female was a cleavage between accepted in-group and rejected out-group. But for many people this "war of the sexes" seems totally unreal. They do not find in it a ground for prejudice.

THE SHIFTING NATURE OF IN-GROUPS

Although each individual has his own conception of in-groups important to himself, he is not unaffected by the temper of the times. During the past century, national and racial memberships have risen in importance, while family and religious memberships have declined (though they are still exceedingly prominent). The fierce loyalties and rivalries between Scottish clans is almost a thing of the past—but the conception of a "master race" has grown to threatening proportions. The fact that women in Western countries have assumed roles once reserved for men makes the antifeminism of Chesterfield and Schopenhauer seem old-fashioned indeed.

A change in the conception of the national in-group is seen in the shifting American attitude toward immigration. The Native American nowadays seldom takes an idealistic view of immigration. He does not feel it a duty and privilege to offer a home to oppressed people—to include them in his in-group. The legend on the Statue of Liberty, engraved eighty years ago, already seems out of date:

Give me your tired, your poor,
Your huddled masses yearning to breathe free,
The wretched refuse of your teeming shore.
Send these, the homeless, the tempest-tost to me.
I lift my lamp beside the golden door.

The lamp was virtually extinguished by the anti-immigration laws passed in the period 1918–1924. The lingering sentiment was not strong enough to relax the bars appreciably following the Second World War when there were more homeless and tempest-tost than ever before crying for admission. From the standpoint of both economics and humanitarianism there were strong arguments for relaxing the restrictions; but people had grown fearful. Many conservatives feared the importation of radical ideas; many Protestants felt their own precarious majority might be further reduced; some Catholics dreaded the arrival of Communists; anti-Semites wanted no more Jews; some labor-union members feared that jobs would not be created to absorb the newcomers and that their own security would suffer.

During the 124 years for which data are available, approximately 40,000,000 immigrants came to America, as many as 1,000,000 in a single year. Of the total immigration 85 percent came from Europe. Until a generation ago, few objections were heard. But today nearly all applicants are refused admission, and few champions of "displaced persons" are heard. Times have changed, and whenever they change for the worse, as they have, in-group boundaries tend to tighten. The stranger is suspect and excluded.

Not only do the strength and definition of in-groups change over the years in a given culture, but a single individual, too, may have occasion at one time to affirm one group-loyalty and at a different time another. The following amusing passage from H. G. Well's *A Modern Utopia* illustrates this elasticity. The passage depicts a snob—a person whose group loyalties are narrow. But even a snob, it appears, must have a certain flexibility, for he finds it convenient to identify himself sometimes with one in-group and sometimes with another.

The passage illustrates an important point: in-group memberships are not permanently fixed. For certain purposes an individual may affirm one category of membership, for other purposes a slightly larger category. It depends on his need for self-enhancement.

Wells is describing the loyalties of a certain botanist:

He has a strong feeling for systematic botanists as against plant physiologists, whom he regards as lewd and evil scoundrels in this relation; but he has a strong feeling for all botanists and indeed all biologists, as against physicists, and those who profess the exact sciences, all of whom he regards as dull, mechanical, ugly-minded scoundrels in this relation; but he has a strong feeling for all who profess what he calls Science, as against psychologists, sociologists, philosophers, and literary men, whom he regards as wild, foolish, immoral scoundrels in this re-lation; but he has a strong feeling for all educated men as against the working man, whom he regards as a cheating, lying, loafing, drunken, thievish, dirty scoundrel in this relation; but as soon as the working man is comprehended to-gether with these others, as *Englishmen* . . . he holds them superior to all sorts of Europeans, whom he regards.[6]

Thus the sense of belonging is a highly personal matter. Even two mem-bers of the same actual in-group may view its composition in widely divergent ways. Take, for instance, the definition that two Americans might give to their own national in-group.

The narrowed perception of Individual A is the product of an arbitrary categorization, one that he finds convenient (functionally significant) to hold. The larger range of perception on the part of Individual B creates a wholly dif-ferent conception of the national in-group. It is misleading to say that both be-long to the same in-group. Psychologically, they do not.

Each individual tends to see in his in-group the precise pattern of security that he himself requires. An instructive example comes from a recent resolution of the convention of the Democratic Party in South Carolina. To the gentlemen assembled the Party was an important in-group. But the definition of Party (as stated in its national platform) was unacceptable. Hence in order to re-fence the in-group so that each member could feel secure, the category "Democrat" was redefined to "include those who believe in local self-government as against the idea of a strong centralized, paternalistic government; and exclude those whose ideas or leadership are inspired by foreign influences, Communism, Naxism, Fascism, statism, totalitarianism, or the Fair Employment Practices Commission."

Thus in-groups are often recreated to fit the needs of individuals, and when the needs are strongly aggressive—as in this case—the redefinition of the in-group may be primarily in terms of the hated out-groups.

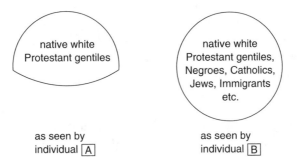

Figure 1   The national in-group as perceived by two Americans.

IN-GROUPS AND REFERENCE GROUPS

We have broadly defined an in-group as any cluster of people who can use the term "we" with the same significance. But the reader has noted that individuals may hold all manner of views concerning their membership in in-groups. A first-generation American may regard his Italian background and culture as more important than do his children, who are second-generation Italian-Americans. Adolescents may view their neighborhood gang as a far more important in-group than their school. In some instances an individual may actively repudiate an in-group, even though he cannot escape membership in it.

In order to clarify this situation, modern social science has introduced the concept of reference group. Sherif and Sherif have defined reference groups as "those groups to which the individual relates himself as a part, or to which he aspires to relate himself psychologically."[7] Thus a reference group is an in-group that is warmly accepted, or a group in which the individual wishes to be included.

Now usually an in-group is also a reference group, but not always. A Negro may wish to relate himself to the white majority in his community. He would like to partake of the privileges of this majority, and be considered one of its members. He may feel so intensely about the matter that he repudiates his own in-group. He develops a condition that Kurt Lewin has called "self-hate" (i.e., hatred for his own in-group). Yet the customs of the community force him to live with, work with, and be classified with the Negro group. In such a case his in-group membership is not the same as his reference group.

Or take the case of a clergyman of Armenian descent ministering in a small New England town. His name is foreign. Townsmen classify him as an Armenian. Yet he himself seldom thinks of his ancestry, though he does not actively reject his background. His reference groups (his main interests) are his church, his family, and the community in which he lives. Unfortunately for him, his fellow townsmen persist in regarding him as an Armenian; they regard this ethnic in-group as far more important than he himself does.

The Negro and the Armenian cleric occupy *marginal* roles in the community. They have difficulty relating themselves to their reference groups because the pressures of the community force them always to tie to in-groups of small psychological importance to them.

To a considerable degree all minority groups suffer from the same state of marginality, with its haunting consequences of insecurity, conflict, and irritation. Every minority group finds itself in a larger society where many customs, many values, many practices are prescribed. The minority group member is thus to some degree forced to make the dominant majority his reference group in respect to language, manners, morals, and law. He may be entirely loyal to his minority in-group, but he is at the same time always under the necessity of relating himself to the standards and expectations of the majority. The situation is particularly clear in the case of the Negro. Negro culture is almost entirely the same as white American culture. The Negro must relate himself to it. Yet whenever he tries to achieve this relatedness he is likely to suffer rebuff. Hence there is in his case an almost inevitable conflict between his biologically defined in-group and his culturally defined reference group. If we follow this line of thinking we see why all minority groups, to some degree, occupy a marginal position in society with its unhappy consequents of apprehension and resentment.

The concepts of in-group and reference group help us to distinguish two levels of belongingness. The former indicates the sheer fact of membership; the latter tells us whether the individual prizes that membership or whether he seeks to relate himself with another group. In many cases, as we have said, there is a virtual identity between in-groups and reference groups; but it is not always so. Some individuals, through necessity or by choice, continually compare themselves with groups which for them are not in-groups.

SOCIAL DISTANCE

The distinction between in-group and reference group is well brought out in studies of social distance. This familiar technique, invented by E. S. Bogardus, asks respondents to indicate to which steps on the following scale they would admit members of various ethnic and national groups:

1. to close kinship by marriage
2. to my club as personal chums
3. to my street as neighbors
4. to employment in my occupation
5. to citizenship in my country
6. as visitors only to my country
7. would exclude from my country

Now the most striking finding from this procedure is that a similar pattern of preference is found across the country, varying little with income, region, education, occupation, or even with ethnic group. Most people, whoever they are, find the English and Canadians acceptable as citizens, as neighbors, as social equals, and as kinsmen. These ethnic stocks have the least social distance. At the other extreme come Hindus, Turks, Negroes. The ordering—with a few minor shifts—stays substantially constant.[8]

While members of the unfavored groups tend to put their own groups high in the list, yet in all other respects they choose the prevailing order of acceptability. In one study of Jewish children, for example, it was found that the standard pattern of social distance existed excepting only that most Jewish children place Jews high in acceptability.[9] In similar investigations it turns out that on the average the Negro places the Jew at about the same distance as does the white gentile; and the Jew ordinarily places the Negro low on his list.

From such results we are forced to conclude that the member of an ethnic minority tends to fashion his attitudes as does the dominant majority. In other words, the dominant majority is for him a *reference group*. It exerts a strong pull upon him, forcing attitudinal conformity. The conformity, however, rarely extends to the point of repudiating his own in-group. A Negro, or Jew, or Mexican will ordinarily assert the acceptability of his own in-group, but in other respects he will decide as does his larger reference group. Thus, both in-group and reference group are important in the formation of attitudes.

THE GROUP-NORM THEORY OF PREJUDICE

We are now in a position to understand and appreciate a major theory of prejudice. It holds that all groups (whether in-groups or reference groups) develop a way of living with characteristic codes and beliefs, standards and "enemies" to suit their own adaptive needs. The theory holds also that both gross and subtle pressures keep every individual member in line. The in-group's preferences must be his preference, its enemies his enemies. The Sherifs, who advance this theory, write:

> Ordinarily the factors leading individuals to form attitudes of prejudice are not piecemeal. Rather, their formation is functionally related to becoming a group member—to adopting the group and its values (norms) as the main anchorage in regulating experience and behavior.[10]

A strong argument in favor of this view is the relative ineffectiveness of attempts to change attitudes through influencing individuals. Suppose the child attends a lesson in intercultural education in the classroom. The chances are this lesson will be smothered by the more embracing norms of his family, gang, or neighborhood. To change the child's attitudes it would be necessary to alter the cultural equilibrium of these, to him, more important groups. It would be necessary for the family, the gang, or the neighborhood to sanction tolerance before he as an individual could practice it.

This line of thought has led to the dictum, "It is easier to change group attitudes than individual attitudes." Recent research lends some support to the view. In certain studies whole communities, whole housing projects, whole factories, or whole school systems have been made the target of change. By involving the leaders, the policies, the rank and file, new norms are created, and when this is accomplished, it is found that individual attitudes tend to conform to the new group norm.[11]

While we cannot doubt the results, there is something unnecessarily "collectivistic" about the theory. Prejudice is by no means exclusively a mass phenomenon. Let the reader ask himself whether his own social attitudes do in fact conform closely to those of his family, social class, occupational group, or church associates. Perhaps the answer is yes; but more likely the reader may reply that the prevailing prejudices of his various reference groups are so contradictory that he cannot, and does not, "share" them all. He may also decide that his pattern of prejudice is unique, conforming to none of his membership groups.

Realizing this individual play of attitudes, the proponents of the theory speak of a "range of tolerable behavior," admitting thereby that only approximate conformity is demanded within any system of group norms. People may deviate in their attitudes to some extent, but not too much.

As soon as we allow, however, for a "range of tolerable behavior" we are moving toward a more individualistic point of view. We do not need to deny the existence of group norms and group pressure in order to insist that each person is uniquely organized. Some of us are avid conformists to what we believe the group requirement to be. Others of us are passive conformists. Still others are nonconformists. Such conformism as we show is the product of individual learning, individual needs, and individual style of life.

In dealing with problems of attitude formation it is always difficult to strike a proper balance between the collective approach and the individual approach. This volume maintains that prejudice is ultimately a problem of personality formation and development; no two cases of prejudice are precisely the same. No individual would mirror his group's attitude unless he had a personal need, or personal habit, that leads him to do so. But it likewise maintains that one of the frequent sources, perhaps the most frequent source, of prejudice lies in the needs and habits that reflect the influence of in-group memberships upon the development of the individual personality. It is possible to hold the individualistic type of theory without denying that the major influences upon the individual may be collective.

CAN THERE BE AN IN-GROUP WITHOUT AN OUT-GROUP?

Every line, fence, or boundary marks off an inside from an outside. Therefore, in strict logic, an in-group always implies the existence of some corresponding out-group. But this logical statement by itself is of little significance. What we need to know is whether one's loyalty to the in-group automatically implies disloyalty, or hostility, or other forms of negativism, toward out-groups.

The French biologist, Felix le Dantec, insisted that every social unit from the family to the nation could exist only by virtue of having some "common enemy." The family unit fights many threatening forces that menace each person who belongs to the unit. The exclusive club, the American Legion, the nation itself, exists to defeat the common enemies of its members. In favor of Le Dantec's view is the well-known Machiavellian trick of creating a common enemy in order to cement an in-group. Hitler created the Jewish menace not so much to demolish the Jews as to cement the Nazi hold over Germany. At the turn of the century the Workingmen's Party in California whipped up an anti-Oriental sentiment to consolidate its own ranks which, without a common enemy, were indifferent and wavering. School spirit is never so strong as when the time for an athletic contest with the traditional "enemy" approaches. Instances are so numerous that one is tempted to accept the doctrine. Studying the effect of strangers entering a group of nursery school children, Susan Isaacs reports, "The existence of an outsider is in the beginning an essential condition of any warmth or togetherness within the group."[12]

So deeply was William James impressed by the fact that social cohesiveness seems to require a common enemy that he wrote a famous essay on the subject. In *The Moral Equivalent for War* he recognized the adventuresomeness, the aggression, and the competitiveness that marked human relationships, especially among young people of military age. In order that they themselves might live at peace he recommended that they find an enemy that would not violate man's growing sense of loyalty to humanity. His advice was: fight nature, fight disease, fight poverty.

Now there is no denying that the presence of a threatening common enemy will cement the in-group sense of any organized aggregate of people. A family (if it is not already badly disrupted) will grow cohesive in the face of adversity, and a nation is never so unified as in time of war. But the psychological emphasis must be placed primarily on the desire for security, not on hostility itself.

One's own family is an in-group; and by definition all other families on the street are out-groups; but seldom do they clash. A hundred ethnic groups compose America, and while serious conflict occasionally occurs, the majority rub along in peace. One knows that one's lodge has distinctive characteristics that mark it off from all others, but one does not necessarily despise the others.

The situation, it seems, can best be stated as follows: although we could not perceive our own in-groups excepting as they contrast to out-groups, still the in-groups are psychologically primary. We live in them, by them, and, sometimes, for them. Hostility toward out-groups helps strengthen our sense of belonging, but it is not required.

Because of their basic importance to our own survival and self-esteem we tend to develop a partisanship and ethnocentricism in respect to our in-groups. Seven-year-old children in one town were asked, "Which are better, the children in this town or in Smithfield (a neighboring town)?" Almost all replied, "The children in this town." When asked why, the children usually replied, "I don't know the kids in Smithfield." This incident puts the initial in-group and out-group situation in perspective. The familiar is *preferred*. What is alien is regarded as somehow inferior, less "good," but there is not necessarily hostility against it.

Thus while a certain amount of predilection is inevitable in all in-group memberships, the reciprocal attitude toward out-groups may range widely. At one extreme they may be viewed as a common enemy to be defeated in order to protect the in-group and strengthen its inner loyalties. At the other extreme the out-group may be appreciated, tolerated, even liked for its diversity. Commenting on this matter in his Encyclical entitled *Unity of the People*, Pope Pius XII recognized value in the existing variety of cultural groups. Let this diversity remain, he urged, but let it not be marked by hostility. The unity of people, he said, is a unity of attitude—of tolerance and love—not a unity of uniformity.

CAN HUMANITY CONSTITUTE AN IN-GROUP?

One's family ordinarily constitutes the smallest and the firmest of one's in-groups. It is probably for this reason that we usually think of in-groups growing weaker and weaker the larger their circle of inclusion. Figure 2 expresses the common feeling that the potency of the membership becomes less as the distance from personal contact grows larger. Only a few sample memberships are included in the diagram in order not to complicate the point at issue.

Such an image implies that a world-loyalty is the most difficult to achieve. In part the implication is correct. There seems to be special difficulty in fashioning an in-group out of an entity as embracing as mankind. Even the ardent believer in One World has trouble. Suppose a diplomat is dealing at a conference table with representatives of other countries whose language, manners, and ideology differ from his own. Even if this diplomat believes ardently in One

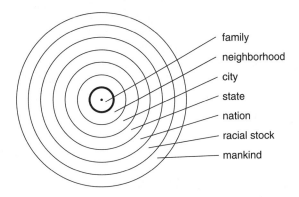

Figure 2   Hypothetical lessening of in-group potency as membership becomes more inclusive.

World, still he cannot escape a sense of strangeness in his encounters. His own model of propriety and rightness is his own culture. Other languages and customs inevitably seem outlandish and, if not inferior, at least slightly absurd and unnecessary.

Suppose the delegate is so broadminded that he can see many defects in his own nation, and suppose he sincerely wants to build an ideal society, where the good features of many cultures are blended. Even such an extreme idealism is likely to wring from him only minor concessions. With utmost sincerity he finds himself fighting for his own language, religion, ideology, law, forms of etiquette. After all, his nation's way of life is *his* way of life—and he cannot lightly abrogate the ground of his whole existence.

Such almost reflex preference for the familiar grips us all. To be sure, a well-traveled person, or one who is endowed with cosmopolitan tastes, is relatively more hospitable to other nations. He can see that differences in culture do not necessarily mean inferiority. But for persons neither imaginative nor well-traveled artificial props are needed. They require *symbols*—today almost lacking—in order to make the human in-group seem real. Nations have flags, parks, schools, capitol buildings, currency, newspapers, holidays, armies, historical documents. Only gradually and with small publicity are a few of these symbols of unity evolving on an international scale. They are greatly needed in order to provide mental anchorage points around which the idea of world-loyalty may develop.

There is no intrinsic reason why the outermost circle of membership needs to be the weakest. In fact, race itself has become the dominant loyalty among many people, especially among fanatic advocates of "Aryanism" and among certain members of oppressed races. It seems today that the clash between the idea of race and of One World (the two outermost circles) is shaping into an issue that may well be the most decisive in human history. The important question is, Can a loyalty to mankind be fashioned before interracial warfare breaks out?

Theoretically it can, for there is a saving psychological principle that may be invoked if we can learn how to do so in time. The principle states that *concentric loyalties need not clash*. To be devoted to a large circle does not imply the destruction of one's attachment to a smaller circle.[13] *The loyalties that clash are almost invariably those of identical scope.* A bigamist who has founded two families of procreation is in fatal trouble with himself and with society. A traitor who serves two nations (one nominally and one actually) is mentally a mess and socially a felon. Few people can acknowledge more than one alma mater, one religion, or one fraternity. On the other hand, a world-federalist can be a devoted family man, an ardent alumnus, and a sincere patriot. The fact that some fanatic nationalists would challenge the compatibility of world-loyalty with patriotism does not change the psychological law. Wendell Willkie and Franklin

Roosevelt were no less patriots because they envisioned a United Nations in One World.

Concentric loyalties take time to develop, and often, of course, they fail completely to do so. In an interesting study of Swiss children Piaget and Weil discovered the resistance of young children to the idea that one loyalty can be included within another. The following record of a seven-year-old is typical of that age:

> Have you heard of Switzerland? *Yes.* What is it? *A canton.* And what is Geneva? *A town.* Where is Geneva? *In Switzerland.* (But the child draws two circles side by side.) Are you Swiss? *No, I'm Genevese.*

At a later stage (eight to ten) children grasp the idea that Geneva is enclosed spatially in Switzerland and draw their relationship as one circle enclosing the other. But the idea of concentric loyalty is still elusive.

> What is your nationality? *I'm Swiss.* How is that? *Because I live in Switzerland.* You're Genevese too? *No, I can't be.* Why not? *I'm Swiss now and can't be Genevese as well.*

By the age of ten or eleven the child can straighten the matter out.

> What is your nationality? *I'm Swiss.* How is that? *Because my parents are Swiss.* Are you Genevese as well? *Naturally, because Geneva is in Switzerland.*

Likewise by the age of ten or eleven the child has an emotional evaluation of his national circle.

> *I like Switzerland because it's a free country.*
> *I like Switzerland because it's the Red Cross country.*
> *In Switzerland our neutrality makes us charitable.*

It is evident that these emotional valuations are learned from teachers and parents, and are adopted ready-made. The mode of teaching ordinarily stops the process of enlargement at this point. Beyond the borders of the native land there is only the domain of "foreigners"—not of fellow men. Michel, aged nine and one-half, answered the interviewer as follows:

> Have you ever heard of such people as foreigners? *Yes, the French, the Americans, the Russians, the English.* Quite right. Are there differences between all these people? *Oh yes, they don't speak the same language.* And what else? Try to tell me as much as possible. *The French are not very serious, they don't worry about anything, and it's dirty there.* And what do you think of the Americans? *They're ever so rich and clever. They've discovered the atom bomb.* And what do

you think of the Russians? *They're bad, they're always wanting to make war.* Now look, how did you come to know all you've told me? *I don't know . . . I've heard it . . . that's what people say.*

Most children never enlarge their sense of belonging beyond the ties of family, city, nation. The reason seems to be that those with whom the child lives, and whose judgment he mirrors, do not do so. Piaget and Weil write, "Everything suggests that, on discovering the values accepted in his immediate circle, the child feels bound to accept the circle's opinions of all other national groups."[14]

While the national orbit is the largest circle of loyalty that most children learn, there is no necessity for the process to stop there. In some children of twelve and thirteen years of age these investigators found a high sense of "reciprocity," i.e., a willingness to admit that all peoples have equal value and merit, although each prefers its own mode of life. When such a sense of reciprocity is firmly established, the way is prepared for the integrated conception of larger and larger units of mankind, to all of which the young person can be loyal without losing his earlier attachments. Until he learns this attitude of reciprocity, he is unlikely to accept other countries as lying within the orbit of his loyalty.

In summary, in-group memberships are vitally important to individual survival. These memberships constitute a web of habits. When we encounter an outsider who follows different customs we unconsciously say, "He breaks my habits." Habit-breaking is unpleasant. We prefer the familiar. We cannot help but feel a bit on guard when other people seem to threaten or even question our habits. Attitudes partial to the in-group, or to the reference group, do not necessarily require that attitudes toward other groups be antagonistic—even though hostility often helps to intensify the in-group cohesion. Narrow circles can, without conflict, be supplemented by larger circles of loyalty. This happy condition is not often achieved, but it remains from the psychological point of view a hopeful possibility.

NOTES AND REFERENCES

1. W. G. Old. *The Shu King, or the Chinese Historical Classic.* New York: J. Lane, 1904; 50–51. See also J. Legge (Transl.), Texts of Confucianism, in *The Sacred Books of the East.* Oxford: Clarendon Press, 1879, Vol. III, 75–76.

2. J. L. Moreno. *Who shall survive?* Washington: Nervous & Mental Disease Pub. Co., 1934, 24. These data are somewhat old. At the present time there are grounds for believing that the sex boundary is not so important among children as formerly.

3. C. Strachey (Ed.). *The Letters of the Earl of Chesterfield to his Son.* New York: G. P. Putnam's Sons, 1925, Vol. I, 261.

4. *Ibid.,* Vol. II, 5.

5. E. B. Bax (Ed.). *Selected Essays of Schopenhauer.* London: G. Bell & Sons, 1914, 340.

6. Reprinted by permission of Chapman & Hall, Ltd., from *A Modern Utopia.* London, 1905, 322.

7. M. and Carolyn W. Sherif. *Groups in Harmony and Tension.* New York: Harper, 1953, 161.

8. The order found by Bogardus in 1928 (E. S. Bogardus, *Immigration and Race Attitudes,* Boston: D. C. Heath, 1928) was found essentially unchanged by Hartley in 1946, and again by Spoerl in 1951. (Cf. E. L. Hartley, *Problems in Prejudice,* New York: Kings Crown Press, 1946; and Dorothy T. Spoerl, Some aspects of prejudice as affected by religion and education, *Journal of Social Psychology,* 1951, 33, 69–76.)

9. Rose Zelics. Racial attitudes of Jewish children. *Jewish Education,* 1937, 9, 148–152.

10. M. and Carolyn W. Sherif. *Op. cit.,* 218.

11. Among the studies of this type we may refer especially to: A. Morrow and J. French, Changing a stereotype in industry, *Journal of Social Issues,* 1945, 1, 33–37; R. Lippitt, *Training in Community Relations,* New York: Harper, 1949; Margot H. Wormser and Claire Selltiz, *How to Conduct a Community Self-survey of Civil Rights,* New York: Association Press, 1951; K. Lewin, Group decision and social change in T. M. Newcomb and E. L. Hartley (Eds.), *Readings in Social Psychology,* New York: Holt, 1947.

12. Susan Isaacs. *Social Development in Young Children.* New York: Harcourt, Brace, 1933, 250.

13. This spatial metaphor has its limitations. The reader may ask, What really is the innermost circle of loyalty? It is by no means always the family, as Fig. 2 implies. May not the core be the primordial self-love we discussed in Chapter 2? If we regard self as the central circle, then the broadening loyalties are, psychologically speaking, simply extensions of the self. But as the self widens, it may also *re-center* itself, so that what is at first an outer circle may become psychologically the focus. Thus a religious person, for example, may believe that man is made in God's image: therefore his own love of God and man may, for him, lie in the innermost circle. Both loyalties and prejudices are features of personality organization, and in the last analysis each organization is unique. While this criticism is entirely valid, still for our present purposes Fig. 2 can stand as an approximate representation of the fact that for many people the larger the social system the less easily do they encompass it in their span of understanding and affection.

14. J. Piaget and Anne-Marie Weil. The development in children of the idea of the homeland and of relations with other countries. *International Social Science Bulletin,* 1951, 3, 570. 🐾

QUESTIONS FOR THOUGHT AND STUDY

1. What is an in-group? List the in-groups to which you belong in order of their importance to you.

2. Does Allport believe people acquire loyalty to their in-groups by being rewarded for membership? What affects your loyalty to the in-groups on your list (question 1)?

3. Divide the list you made in question 1 into "acquired" and "ascribed" groups. Do the values of one category ever conflict with the values of the other?

4. What is the relationship between an "in-group" and a "reference group"? Mark the in-groups on your original list that are also reference groups and add reference groups you hope to become part of in the future.

5. Which of the in-groups you have listed defines itself in part by its difference from another group? Describe that "other" (or "out") group.

6. What is the Group Norm Theory of prejudice? Is this Allport's theory? Why or why not?

7. Do the members of the in-groups you feel closest to feel equally strongly about group membership? What is the evidence of the importance of the group to others?

Attitudes on Dating, Courtship, and Marriage: Perspectives on In-Group Versus Out-Group Relationships by Religious Minority and Majority Adolescents

Carol Markstrom-Adams

Biography: *Carol Markstrom-Adams is a faculty member in the Department of Family Studies, University of Guelf, in Ontario, Canada.*

Markstrom-Adams's in-depth interviews with Mormon and non-Mormon high school students explore felt barriers to dating out of the in-group, and whether members of the majority religion have different attitudes than the religious majority. Her findings confirm Allport's theory to some extent, but explore the reasons for group barriers in more detail. This article provides an example of a scientific report testing Allport's theory.

In this study, 47 non-Mormon, religious minority high school students and 36 Mormon, religious majority high school students were asked to identify perceived barriers in dating Mormons (if they were non-Mormon) or in dating non-Mormons (if they were Mormon). They also were asked if they advised dating between members of both groups. More barriers in dating were identified by Mormons, in contrast to non-Mormons. Further, the Mormon adolescents expressed greater reluctance in advising dating between Mormons and non-Mormons. Based on these findings, theoretical implications, questions for future research on the topic, and implications for youth and religious workers dealing with either religious minority or majority youths are given.

The subject of this article is attitudes pertaining to dating held by members of a religious majority group and members of religious minority groups from the same community. Practitioners, such as religious leaders and youth workers, as well as research scientists should find this article worthwhile. While the topic of interfaith dating has generalizability to similar minority-majority configurations throughout the broader societal context, the populations targeted in the present investigation are Mormon and non-Mormon adolescents

From *Family Relations* (January 1991): pp. 40, 91–96.

living in a predominantly Mormon community. It is this point that furnishes a unique perspective to the study. That is, the majority group examined in this study (i.e., Mormon) is generally a minority in geographical locations outside of the state of Utah. In contrast, the Catholic and Protestant minority adolescents in this study are members of larger groups that often are segments of religiously plural communities or reside in religious majority circumstances.

A qualitative methodology was employed to interview adolescents concerning their attitudes on dating outside of their religious minority or majority groups. It is important to note that while respondents were only asked questions pertaining to this topic, dating has been identified in the literature as constituting an early stage of courtship (Duck & Miell, 1983; Kieren, Henton, & Marotz, 1975). Similarly, Skipper and Nass (1966) identify the functions of dating as recreation, socialization, status and achievement, and mate selection or courtship. Several authors, in their various models of mate selection (e.g., Kerckhoff & Davis, 1962; Lewis, 1972; Reiss, 1960; Winch, 1958) have identified religion as a filtering factor in screening potential marital partners at the level of the dating relationship. It will become apparent in this article that mate selection, as a function of dating, was given greater adherence to by both majority and minority adolescents than what otherwise might be expected. Thus, a discussion of this function of dating is warranted.

LITERATURE REVIEW

While the literature on interfaith dating is fairly scant, there is a body of literature on the role of religion in courtship and marriage that is pertinent to the present article. Existing evidence suggests that interfaith marriage was given stronger adherence to in earlier decades of this century (Young, 1989), and prior to the 1920s, the sole purpose of dating was mate selection (Santrock, 1990). Strauss (1946) reported that 41.6% of men and 42.5% of women, in a sample of 373 individuals, indicated that a potential mate of a different faith was an eliminating factor in mate selection. More recent research demonstrates that religion still operates as a filter in mate selection for many people. For instance, Davis-Brown, Salamon, and Surra (1987) examined the occurrence of mixed ethnoreligious marriages in one community over a 50-year period. They found that, among other characteristics, those with strong religious ties were more careful in selecting marital choices.

More specific to the sample in this study, Young (1989) found, that among six religious groups, Latter-Day Saints (Mormons) were significantly more likely than other groups to indicate diminished marital worth of someone of a different faith, someone of no formal religion, and someone not religious. Markstrom-Adams (1989) interviewed Presbyterian adolescents concerning their perceptions of being religious minorities in a predominantly Mormon community. Concerns about dating Mormon males were raised by the young women in the sample, and they observed problems that might beset marriages between Mormons and non-Mormons. Dacey (1986) reported that with religious pluralism, dogmatism is diminished and religious tolerance is enhanced. Thus, since the Mormon subjects in Markstrom-Adams's (1989) and Young's (1989) studies were not living in religiously plural environments, greater resistance to interfaith dating is not an unlikely outcome.

Given the facts that: (a) mate selection is one function of dating; (b) religion still plays a role in mate selection; and (c) Mormons have been found, in prior research, to be resistant to interfaith marriages, it was expected that the Mormon adolescents would identify more barriers to interfaith dating than the non-Mormon adolescents in the present study. It also was anticipated that mate selection, as one function of dating, would be highly significant to both Mormon and non-Mormon respondents.

METHODS

Sample

Participants of the study included 47 non-Mormon (18 male and 29 female) and 36 Mormon (15 male and 21 female) high school students. The 47 non-Mormon participants were from Episcopal, Lutheran, Presbyterian, Roman Catholic, and Southern Baptist religious backgrounds. All of the non-Mormon participants were of religious minority status. Both Mormon and non-Mormon participants were from middle-class backgrounds. They lived in the same valley with a population of 57,176 (Census of Population and Housing, 1982). According to the most recent statistics available from 1971 when the population of the region was 43,000, the religious demographics were 90% Mormon, 1% Presbyterian, 1% Roman Catholic; and Lutheran, Episcopal, and Southern Baptist were each less than 1% of the population (Wahlquist, 1981). The population of the region has increased since that time, and it is believed that the non-Mormon population has increased correspondingly.

Research Design

The topic of this study is relatively unique and has not been as explicitly addressed in previous research as it is in the present study. Given such an observation and taking into account the distinctive nature of the sample, the research design in this study should be regarded as exploratory in nature. Exploratory research is less structured and allows for an examination of phenomena in which prior investigations have proved insufficient or in which new perspectives or insights are required (Adams & Schvaneveldt, 1985). A further benefit to utilizing an exploratory research design is related to a heuristic function. That is, theoretical implications and questions for future research on the study of dating and religious minority and majority statuses should be generated from the findings.

The utilization of qualitative research methods is well suited for carrying out an exploratory research design. Specifically, this study may be classified as primarily qualitative (LaRossa & Wolf, 1985). In-depth interviewing is one method of data collection employed in qualitative research (Reichardt & Cook, 1979) and was adopted for use in the present study. Subjects in this study were regarded as informants who provided first-hand accounts of their attitudes pertaining to dating, courtship, and marriage between the religious minority and majority groups represented in their community.

Procedures

In selecting both the Mormon and non-Mormon sample, leaders from the religious groups represented supplied the investigator with the names and addresses of high school students in their wards or congregations. Potential participants and their parents were sent a letter from the investigator that described the study and requested adolescents' participation. A phone call was then made to the home, and if both the adolescent and his/her parent agreed to allow the adolescent to participate in the study, an interview date was set.

Trained interviewers met individually with adolescent participants for approximately 2 hours in the adolescents' homes. A private room was requested for the use by the interviewer and the respondent. Approximately ½ to 1 hour was spent in administering the Religious Experience Survey. In addition, participants completed instrumentation related to religious identity formation and religious beliefs and attitudes.

The Religious Experience Survey is a semistructured interview devised by the investigator to tap issues related to being either a religious minority or religious majority teenager. Thus, there are two versions of the survey. The basis for the questions in the Religious Experience Survey were drawn from an earlier study in which a group of Presbyterian adolescents were asked to give their perceptions of being religious minorities (Markstrom-Adams, 1989).

Each respondent was asked the same questions from either the Mormon or the non-Mormon version of the Religious Experience Survey. Depending on a particular subject's response, follow-up probes were used to encourage responsiveness and provide clarity to answers. The interviews were audiotaped and then transcribed. There are two questions from the Religious Experience Survey that pertain to the findings presented in this study. The first question reads: Do you feel any barriers in dating Mormons? (If so, what are these barriers?) The counterpart of this question that was posed to Mormon participants reads: Do you feel any barriers in dating non-Mormons? (If so, what are these barriers?) The second question posed both to non-Mormons and Mormons asks: Do you advise dating between Mormons and non-Mormons? (Why or why not?)

RESULTS AND DISCUSSION

A cross-case analysis (Patton, 1990) was utilized in the organization and presentation of respondents' answers. In essence, this approach involves grouping together common answers of respondents in order to facilitate content analysis of the data. In relation to the question posed to respondents as to their perceptions of barriers in dating due to religious differences, overall, 63% of the respondents said that there were identifiable barriers to Mormon and non-Mormon dating. Of that number, more Mormons (83%) than non-Mormons (47%) perceived barriers in dating someone of the opposite group. Specific barriers to dating identified by 83% of the Mormon subjects ($n = 30$) and 47% of the non-Mormon subjects ($n = 22$) are given in Table 1, as well as the frequency each barrier was cited. The percentages in parentheses are linked to the number of Mormons (or non-Mormons) who specified particular barriers. Some respondents cited more than one barrier and multiple responses are reflected in the frequencies and percentages. It is apparent in Table 1, that some barriers were cited only by Mormons (Barriers 1, 3, 5, and 8); and other barriers were given only by non-Mormons (Barriers 6, 7, 10, 11, 12, and 13).

It was not possible to tabulate strict "yes" or "no" responses to the second question posed to respondents, "Do you advise dating between Mormons and non-Mormons?," as respondents provided many qualifiers to their answers. Nonetheless, it was possible to categorize the qualifiers given in response to this question (see Table 2). Percentages reflect the number of Mormon (or non-Mormon) subjects who gave the particular response. Similar to Table 1, since many adolescents gave more than one answer to this question, several of their responses applied to more than one category. In general, it is evident that more non-Mormons than Mormons would advise dating between the two groups and that more Mormons than non-Mormons would not advise dating between the two groups.

In analyzing qualitative data, it is useful to identify salient themes to aid in the organization and discussion of the results. Utilizing tools of content analysis and inductive reasoning in respect to the data, three themes are recognized for discussion purposes. A major theme that is recognized is that, clearly, religion was perceived as a greater barrier in interfaith dating by the Mormon adolescents than by the non-Mormon adolescents. A second and related theme is that while the Mormon adolescents were in a majority position, their attitudes toward dating non-Mormons resembled defensive posturing that might be expected from a minority group. A third apparent theme from these data is that, for many of the respondents, dating was viewed as a precursor to marriage.

Further elaborations will be provided on these three themes, but before this occurs it is important to discuss their reliability.

The frequently unaddressed issue of reliability in qualitative research revolves around a question of repeatability (Denzin, 1977; Kirk & Miller, 1986). This is not a simple issue to address, however, as Patton (1990) noted: "There are no ways of perfectly replicating the researcher's analytical thought processes. There are no straightforward tests for reliability and validity" (p. 372). Nonetheless, once themes or patterns from the data have been recognized it is possible to test their credibility by exploring rival or alternative themes (Patton, 1990). A rival theme to the first two themes is that the non-Mormon adolescents were as reluctant or more reluctant than the Mormon adolescents to date outside of their group. The evidence does not appear to support such a statement in that fewer non-Mormons (47%) than Mormons (83%) were able to offer barriers to dating those of the other group. As shown in Table 1, 42% of the Mormon subjects thought that unacceptable beliefs,

Table 1. *Responses and Frequencies and Percentages of Responses to Question: "Do You Feel Any Barriers in Dating Mormons (Non-Mormons)?"*

	Frequency of Responses by:			
	Mormons (n = 30)		Non-Mormons (n = 22)	
Response	Number	Percent	Number	Percent
Unacceptable beliefs, values, standards, and moral conduct of non-Mormons.	15	42	0	
Not willing to engage in serious dating with a non-Mormon (Mormon).	7	19	7	15
Many Mormons desire to marry within their faith	13	36	0	
The perception that Mormon parents do not approve of their children dating non-Mormons.	4	11	8	17
Church teachings directing Mormon adolescents to not date non-Mormons.	6	17	0	
Barriers to dating strict Mormons and Mormons who desire a temple wedding.	0		6	13
Refusal of some Mormons to date non-Mormons.	0		5	11
Not being able to engage in Mormon church activities with non-Mormon dates.	5	14	0	
The perception that non-Mormon parents do not approve of their children dating Mormons.	2	6	2	4
Mormons cannot date until they are 16, while many non-Mormons can date at younger ages.	0		3	6
Religious conflicts and communication problems in dating relationships with Mormons	0		3	6
Not liking the way Mormon men treat women.	0		2	4
Limited opportunities to socially interact with Mormon peers.	0		1	2

values, standards, and moral conduct of non-Mormon adolescents were barriers to dating. None of the non-Mormon adolescents raised such concerns in respect to the Mormon adolescents. Further, more Mormons (31%) than non-Mormons (6%) would not advise any dating between members of the two groups and more non-Mormons (45%) than Mormons (22%) would advise dating between the two groups.

It also is difficult to argue a rival theme to the third theme that has been identified, that is, many of the respondents viewed dating as a precursor to marriage. Barriers 2, 3, 5, and 6 found in Table 1 provide either direct or indirect evidence for this theme. Respondents had many comments to make in this respect and some are given later in the article for illustrative purposes.

It is important to consider if there are additional salient themes to be found in the data that have not been recognized. One point that can be made is that many non-Mormons and a smaller number of Mormons did not perceive problems in dating between the two groups. While the present data do not allow for an examination of this theme, future investigations might utilize further probing with respondents who do not find interfaith dating problematic in order to acquire an understanding of what factors might account for their comfort with interfaith dating.

There are several subthemes that can be recognized in an examination of Tables 1 and 2. Distinctions made between casual and serious dating and the role of parents in adolescents' decision making about interfaith dating

Table 2 *Responses and Frequencies and Percentages of Responses to Question: "Do You Advise Dating Between Mormons and Non-Mormons?"*

| | Frequency of Responses by: | | | |
| | Mormons (n = 36) | | Non-Mormons (n = 47) | |
Response	Number	Percent	Number	Percent
Would advise dating between Mormons and non-Mormons. It is an individual choice.	8	22	21	45
Would advise casual dating, but not serious dating.	11	31	13	28
Would not advise dating between Mormons and non-Mormons.	11	31	3	6
Dating non-Mormons is all right as long as you maintain your standards and/or you try to convert your date.	8	22	0	
Would not advise dating a strict Mormon or a Mormon from a strong religious family.	0		6	13
Would advise dating between Mormons and non-Mormons because there is a lack of potential non-Mormon dating partners.	0		6	13
No opinion or didn't understand question.	1	3	2	4

are examples of smaller themes. These points are recognized in the present study and are discussed in relation to the larger themes. For organization purposes, however, it is the opinion of the author that the three themes highlighted best encompass the many issues raised by the subjects in respect to interfaith dating.

Theme 1: Mormon Adolescents Reticence toward Interfaith Dating

To aid in interpreting this first theme, a microanalytic examination of the peculiarities of the sample is warranted. There are certain aspects of Mormon theology that endorse an endogamous marital system. For example, in order to participate in the highly valued ceremony of marrying in a Mormon temple, one must marry a Mormon. Many Mormon adolescents expressed concerns of this nature when considering the question of dating non-Mormons. The following statement from a 15-year-old Mormon female is illustrative of comments made by others:

> Everyone I date I want to think, "Could I marry him? Could I be married with him eternally?" I don't want to be with a non-Mormon, I can't be with him eternally. I probably wouldn't want to date a non-Mormon, just because he wouldn't be who I would want to marry.

Another explanation for Mormons' reluctance to date non-Mormons is that the Mormon adolescents, as opposed to the non-Mormon adolescents, more often reported that they were given explicit messages from their church leaders to not date out of their religion. Several adolescents had statements to make in this regard. One 17-year-old male explained: "We're taught in the Mormon church that it is best to stay with the Mormon religion when you're dating. Supposedly it (dating non-Mormons) will pull you down or pull you away from your religion."

Some adolescents also reported that their parents affirmed the church's teachings on the topic. In this regard, an 18-year-old Mormon female had this remark to say: "My parents wouldn't be happy because they want me to marry and raise a Mormon family." Statements such as this one are overt messages that reinforce the norm of religious endogamy in marriage.

Juxtaposed against the previous statements, however, is the finding that more non-Mormons than Mormons perceived that Mormon parents did not want their children dating non-Mormons (see Table 1). The reason for such a finding is unclear; however, Davis-Brown et al.'s (1987) study may shed some light on the matter. They reported that parents influence their children in mate selection utilizing subtle socialization techniques, rather than exerting strong authoritarian control. Thus, it is reasonable to speculate that the Mormon parents of the participants in this study may not have explicitly restricted their children from dating non-Mormons, but may have used more subtle forms of influence to socialize their children to not date (and/or subsequently marry) non-Mormons. The non-Mormon adolescents may have perceived such indirect influence and legitimately felt uncomfortable in the presence of their Mormon dates' parents.

As a majority, the Mormon subjects were at a distinct advantage that allowed them to be selective concerning their choices of dating partners. When a majority group member holds an endogamous marital aspiration, his/her field of desirables (Kerckhoff, 1974) is greater than that of the minority group member. One has the luxury to be selective and limit dating choices to one's own group. However, minority adolescents are at distinct disadvantages in such situations and often feel the effects of such discrimination. A 17-year-old non-Mormon male had this instance to relate in this regard:

> It was my first date, which made it especially bad. She was a really good friend. Initially she said yes, that she would go with me. I don't know if her parents found out and didn't want her to go or she just changed her mind or what. Anyway, she gave me a letter that explained her religion taught that she would marry those whom she dated, and she just felt like she couldn't date me. I was really hurt and angry by that. All I wanted to do was go and have some fun. Sometimes I feel a little nervous asking some of the stricter, more religious types out because they might have that problem.

If the minority individual also values marital endogamy, he/she is placed at an even greater disadvantage in the dating arena. In order to date, some individuals may consciously rationalize that they can date someone without viewing that person as a potential marital partner. This point will be discussed in more detail in relation to Theme 3.

In summary, while it is possible to understand Mormons greater reluctance to date non-Mormons from the perspective of Mormon church teachings, there are other reasons for this particular finding that have more to do with the nature of majority and minority groups than the peculiarities of this sample. For example, majority group members have a wider pool of potential dating partners than do minority group members.

Theme 2: Similarity of Mormons' Attitudes to Those of Other Minorities

It is interesting to note that the attitudes toward dating held by the Mormon subjects appeared similar to those that might be expected from minority group members, in general. For instance, it might be expected that a member of a minority group would have greater concern about the consequences of interacting with those of a majority group, than to the contrary. Yet, the Mormon adolescents, as majorities in this study, appeared highly defensive and protective when the issue of dating non-Mormons was raised. For example, as shown in Table 1, 42% of the Mormons thought that a barrier in dating non-Mormons was the unacceptable beliefs, values, standards, and moral conduct of non-Mormons. The following quote from a 15-year-old Mormon reflects her inner conflict in this regard:

> They just don't believe what I do. They just don't have the same standards I do. I am afraid that they might push me into something. I guess it is hard to say because it is not like Mormons won't.

This comment and others like it seem out of context coming from majority group members who have a large contingency of like-minded individuals to offer reinforcement for their group's beliefs. Yet, some of the Mormon adolescents in this study imparted a feeling of fear that they could be led astray by someone of the non-Mormon minority.

It could be argued that, in the context of the larger society, Mormons are a minority group. Only in certain areas of the Rocky Mountain West are Mormons in the majority. In this light, then, it makes sense that even when Mormon adolescents are a majority in the local culture, that there is an awareness that they still are a minority and it is important to maintain affiliation with one's group.

Such defensive posturing on the part of the Mormon adolescents in this study may not be an isolated occurrence. For example, Jewish adolescents also hold a minority status in the broader society, and some of these youths live in majority situations in their immediate environment. Holding an awareness that one is a minority in the broader society and having a history of religious persecution (characteristics shared by both Mormon and Jewish groups) are factors that may contribute to greater reticence toward interfaith dating on the part of these minority youths. There also may be an awareness (conscious or unconscious) that for the survival of one's group, group coherence must be upheld.

Theme 3: The Perception That Dating Is a Precursor to Marriage

Comments made by both Mormon and non-Mormon subjects indicated that they viewed dating as a precursor to marriage. This was evident by the fact that in their interviews respondents were only asked about dating and not about marriage, yet they imposed linkages between the two. The fact that respondents regarded dating as leading to marriage led to a perceived barrier in dating between the two groups. The following quote from a 17-year-old non-Mormon female illustrates this point: "I couldn't date someone who was going to tell me:

'Well, we have to get married in the temple.'" A 15-year-old non-Mormon male had this to say on the topic: "There are problems when you get married. Both of you will believe that unless the other converts, they'll go to hell."

Even though respondents linked dating and marriage and many thought marriage was not acceptable outside of their groups, many Mormon and non-Mormon adolescents did date outside of their religious groups. In such cases, the adolescents (both Mormon and non-Mormon) provided rationalizations for why they thought dating could be acceptable, even though marriage was not. For example, the respondents were careful to make distinctions between casual dating and serious dating and indicated that they thought casual dating between members of both groups was acceptable. Respondents identified several potential problems that might beset more serious dating, particularly if the relationship led to marriage. In this regard, a 17-year-old non-Mormon female noted:

> When I'm serious with someone then I want to tell them a lot about myself and, of course, religion is a big, major part of my life. So I already know that I'm not going to marry a Mormon.

Such statements like this one reflect a great deal of realism on the part of these adolescents. Both groups of adolescents understood how important a temple marriage is to Mormons. Further, some of the respondents observed interfaith marriages between Mormons and non-Mormons and noted corresponding difficulties.

Some Mormon adolescents rationalized dating non-Mormons if the motive was to convert their dates. For example, a 17-year-old Mormon male stated that dating non-Mormons was okay as long as you: "try to convert them while you're still dating."

It appeared from many comments given that the non-Mormon adolescents seemed better equipped to separate dating from marriage than were the Mormons, as the following comment from a 15-year-old non-Mormon female illustrates:

> My parents want me to marry a Catholic boy. I've never gone out with a Catholic boy because there just aren't many. So I don't see anything wrong with it (dating Mormons). Even if you strictly want to marry a Catholic, somebody you date doesn't mean that you're going to marry them anyway.

One non-Mormon young woman noted that her mother did not want her dating Mormons. In response to her mother she said: "What are you talking about, look around where I live. There are probably 30 guys in my school that are non-Mormon. And half of them you consider jerks, and that limits it a lot." This comment and the previous one indicate both young women's awareness of the few dating options inside of their group.

In summary, the perception that dating is a precursor to marriage is found among many groups in society, not just those represented in the present study. Many groups hold endogamous marital preferences and encourage their young people to date exclusively within their group. While some individuals may choose not to heed such advice, they may make a distinction between those whom they date for social recreational reasons and those whom they date for courtship purposes.

THEORETICAL IMPLICATIONS

As Glaser and Strauss (1967) have pointed out, qualitative research is well suited in the development of grounded theory. An attempt is made in this article to give summations that can contribute to theory development on the topic of interfaith dating, courtship, and marriage. Based on the findings of this study and related studies, the following conclusions are given.

1. In communities characterized as having large religious majorities, religion becomes a major consideration in the selection of dating partners among adolescents.

2. Whether a religious majority group will be more selective of dating partners depends on the nature of the majority group in the broader society. That is, if the majority group is generally a minority group in the broader society, they may be prone to greater selectivity of dating partners.

3. Individuals, who otherwise might be selective of their dating partners, may be less selective in a minority context due to the small number of potential dating partners of their religious faith. In such situations, potential dates may be regarded as acceptable for casual dating, but unacceptable for serious dating.

4. When a particular religious community strongly endorses endogamy, dating among adolescents is more likely to be viewed as a precursor to marriage as opposed to the consideration of other functions of dating (e.g., recreation, socialization, status and achievement, Skipper & Nass, 1966).

TOPICS FOR FUTURE RESEARCH

A qualitative analysis of the data from this study has given rise to questions that might be addressed in future research projects. An interesting comparison might involve replicating this study where Mormon adolescents are in the minority context. Further, in order to make a fair comparison to the present study it would be important to find a social context where another religious group is clearly in the majority. Questions to ask in this regard include, are the Mormons more willing to date non-Mormons given limited dating options, or are they resistant toward interfaith dating as were the Mormon respondents in the present study? It also might be useful to examine the Mormon adolescents' attitudes toward dating in contexts where there is greater religious plurality and where one religion does not predominate. In such cases, more interfaith dating may occur and less defensiveness toward interfaith dating might be expected given that there is not an overwhelming religious majority present. Another question to ask is, in religiously plural environments, do the Mormon adolescents consider themselves as one religious group among many or do they continue to hold the perception of being a minority? The latter is a strong possibility in that the Mormon faith has developed in more recent history and incidences of religious matyrdom have occurred as recent as the last century.

It also is important to explore attitudes on interfaith dating with groups other than Mormons who may be similar to Mormons in that they often are in minority contexts. For example, Jewish adolescents would be an interesting comparison group. In a developmental sense, an examination of how attitudes toward interfaith dating changes with age would be useful. It would be expected that, with age, individuals would become less resistant and more open to dating outside of their group.

IMPLICATIONS FOR YOUTH AND RELIGIOUS WORKERS

Based on the findings of this study, there are several applied implications for youth and religious workers of both religious minority and majority groups to take into account. Further, these implications may be generalized beyond the specific religious minority and majority adolescents investigated in this study.

It is not appropriate in this discussion to suggest that certain religious organizations should discard the norm of religious endogamy and encourage interfaith dating and marriage. Nor is it appropriate to assert that the norm of religious endogamy should be maintained. Such statements involve value judgments that require assessment on the part of the individual and/or individuals in conjunction with their religious groups. Nonetheless, given the reality of the norm of religious endogamy in many communities, recommendations can be given to aid those working with both religious minority and majority adolescents.

In contrast to religious majority youths, the minority youths are at a disadvantage in the formation of heterosexual relationships. The religious communities of minority youths need to be attuned to this fact and make efforts to offset associated negative effects. There are several strategies religious communities and youth workers may adopt to aid their young people.

Forums can be provided for adolescents to discuss their experiences and related frustrations of being religious minorities. However, discussions should not be allowed to turn into a defamation of the majority group. Sensitive adults, possessing strong group leadership skills, are needed to direct discussions into productive, problem-solving directions. It would be advantageous to engage the adolescents in perspective-taking tasks to allow them to understand the beliefs and practices of the religious majority group. Adolescents should be encouraged to explore their own feelings concerning interfaith dating and whether or not they regard dating as purely social recreation or as a preliminary step in the courtship process. Without denigrating other religious groups, the position of the minority adolescents' religious organization toward such practices should be clarified. Adolescents also can be reminded that circumstances are likely to change when they graduate from high school and go on to college, and that their options for dating are likely to expand.

If, as in the present study, the religious minority youths live in a community where religious endogamy is promoted among the majority group, it is important to teach the minority adolescents coping strategies. In order to combat feelings of rejection, adolescents need to learn not to personalize decisions by members of the majority group not to date those outside of their group. One proactive strategy religious organizations can take is to provide settings where their young people can meet and interact with one another. This may involve organizing weekly social gatherings for the religious minority youths. In some situations activities at regional and/or state levels may need to be organized periodically for larger gatherings for youths. Such activities, on a larger scale, can impart a feeling to minority youths that there are many others, of similar religious traditions, in circumstances much like themselves.

Even when efforts are taken such as these, the reality for religious minority high school students may be that they will experience delays in the establishment of more committed heterosexual relationships. College may be the entry point into a wide array of dating experiences for many young people. Indeed, irrespective of religion, many young people do not form serious relationships with members of the opposite sex until they are in college or in the early phases of their career development.

There are implications in this discussion pertinent to youth leaders of religious majority adolescents, as well. Religious leaders can engage their young people in perspective-taking tasks that promote understanding in respect to feelings and perceptions of religious minorities. Attitudes of prejudice toward minority groups must be minimized, and tolerance must be encouraged. If a majority religious group does not endorse dating outside of its group, then religious leaders need to teach their young people how to diplomatically and sensitively disengage from invitations for dates they might receive from those outside of their group.

REFERENCES

Adams, G. R., & Schvaneveldt, J. D. (1985). *Understanding research methods.* New York: Longman.

Census of Population and Housing. (1982). *Summary characteristics for governmental units and standard metropolitan statistical areas.* Washington, DC: U.S. Government Printing Office.

Dacey, J. S. (1986). *Adolescents today* (3rd ed.). Glenview, IL: Scott, Foresman and Company.

Davis-Brown, K., Salamon, S., & Surra, C. A. (1987). Economic and social factors in mate selection. An ethnographic analysis of an agricultural community. *Journal of Marriage and the Family, 49,* 41–55.

Denzin, N. K. (1977). *Childhood socialization.* San Francisco: Jossey Bass.

Duck, S., & Miell, D. (1983). Mate choice in humans as an interpersonal process. In P. Bateson (Ed.), *Mate choice* (pp. 377–386). Cambridge: Cambridge University Press.

Glaser, B. G., & Strauss, A. L. (1967). *The discovery of grounded theory: Strategies for qualitative research.* Chicago: Aldine.

Kerckhoff, A. C. (1974). The social context of interpersonal attraction. In T. L. Huston (Ed.), *Foundations of interpersonal attraction* (pp. 61–78). New York: Academic Press.

Kerckhoff, A., & Davis, K. (1962). Value consensus and need complementarity in mate selection. *American Sociological Review, 27,* 295–303.

Kieren, D., Henton, J., & Marotz, R. (1975). *Hers and his.* Hinsdale, IL: The Dryden Press.

Kirk, J., & Miller, M. L. (1986). *Reliability and validity in qualitative research: Qualitative Research Methods* (Vol. 1). Beverly Hills: Sage Publications.

LaRossa, R., & Wolf, J. H. (1985). On qualitative family research. *Journal of Marriage and the Family, 47,* 531–541.

Lewis, R. A. (1972). A developmental framework for the analysis of premarital dyadic formation. *Family Process, 35,* 16–25.

Markstrom-Adams, C. (1989). A qualitative analysis of the impressions and experiences of religious minority adolescents. *Religious Education, 84,* 417–427.

Patton, M. Q. (1990). *Qualitative evaluation and research methods* (2nd ed.). Newbury Park, CA: Sage.

Reichardt, C. S., & Cook, T. D. (1979). Beyond qualitative versus quantitative methods. In T. D. Cook & C. S. Reichardt (Eds.), *Qualitative and quantitative methods in evaluation research* (pp. 7–32). Newbury Park, CA: Sage.

Reiss, I. L. (1960). Toward a sociology of the heterosexual love relationship. *Marriage and Family Living, 22,* 139–145.

Santrock, J. W. (1990). *Adolescence* (4th ed.). Dubuque, IA: Wm. C. Brown.

Skipper, J. K., & Nass, G. (1966). Dating behavior: A framework for analysis and an illustration. *Journal of Marriage and the Family, 28,* 412–420.

Strauss, A. (1946). The ideal and chosen mate. *American Journal of Sociology, 52,* 204–208.

Wahlquist, W. L. (1981). *Atlas of Utah.* Provo, UT: Brigham Young University Press.

Winch, R. F. (1958). *Mate selection: A study of complementary needs.* New York: Harper.

Young, M. H. (1989). *Mate selection in contemporary America: An exchange theory perspective.* Unpublished master's thesis, Utah State University, Logan.

QUESTIONS FOR THOUGHT AND STUDY

1. What is Markstrom-Adams's hypothesis? What is the logic behind the hypothesis (the rationale)?

2. Would Allport support Markstrom-Adams's hypothesis? Why? What would his logic be?

3. Why would Markstrom-Adams select a population from a single socioeconomic class and geographic location for her study?

4. Why does Markstrom-Adams choose the qualitative method of in-depth interviewing for her study?

5. What does "heuristic" mean? Can you get its meaning from the context?

6. Can you use Allport's language to explain Markstrom-Adams's findings?

7. What is the relationship between the hesitation felt by the Mormon adolescents to date non-Mormons (or vice versa) and intergroup conflict? Prejudice?

8. Describe a situation where you have felt similar barriers to those felt by the majority Mormons to socializing with or dating other groups. What are the felt rules and what is the cost of defying them?

9. Why does Markstrom-Adams urge more nondating contact between groups? How much contact do the in-groups you are part of have with groups whose values are different?

Of Our Spiritual Strivings

W. E. B. Du Bois

Biography: *William Edward Burghardt Du Bois (1868–1963), an eminent African-American historian, sociologist, and equal rights campaigner, studied at Fisk, Harvard, and Berlin Universities. His writings explore the lives of African-Americans. He campaigned for full equality, opposing Booker T. Washington, cofounder of the National Association for the Advancement of Colored People (NAACP), who argued that African-Americans should accept their separate status.*

In this classic essay on the problem of being Black and American, Du Bois works through the difficulties of double identity (or "split consciousness"), conflicting loyalties, and compares his position to Booker T. Washington's on the way to achieve political power and inclusion for Black Americans. The essay is an example of a political leader writing in the public domain.

Between me and the other world there is ever an unasked question: unasked by some through feelings of delicacy; by others through the difficulty of rightly framing it. All, nevertheless, flutter round it. They approach me in a half-hesitant sort of way, eye me curiously or compassionately, and then, instead of saying directly, How does it feel to be a problem? they say, I know an excellent colored man in my town; or, I fought at Mechanicsville; or, Do not these Southern outrages make your blood boil? At these I smile, or am

From *The Souls of Black Folk.* (1903). "Introduction," Ch. 1, pp. 86–103. New York: A. C. McClurg.

interested, or reduce the boiling to a simmer, as the occasion may require. To the real question, How does it feel to be a problem? I answer seldom a word.

And yet, being a problem is a strange experience,—peculiar even for one who has never been anything else, save perhaps in babyhood and in Europe. It is in the early days of rollicking boyhood that the revelation first bursts upon one, all in a day, as it were. I remember well when the shadow swept across me. I was a little thing, away up in the hills of New England, where the dark Housatonic winds between Hoosac and Taghkanic to the sea. In a wee wooden schoolhouse, something put it into the boys' and girls' heads to buy gorgeous visiting-cards—ten cents a package—and exchange. The exchange was merry, till one girl, a tall newcomer, refused my card,—refused it peremptorily, with a glance. Then it dawned upon me with a certain suddenness that I was different from the others; or like, mayhap, in heart and life and longing, but shut out from their world by a vast veil. I had thereafter no desire to tear down that veil, to creep through; I held all beyond it in common contempt, and lived above it in a region of blue sky and great wandering shadows. That sky was bluest when I could beat my mates at examination-time, or beat them at a foot-race, or even beat their stringy heads. Alas, with the years all this fine contempt began to fade; for the worlds I longed for, and all their dazzling opportunities, were theirs, not mine. But they should not keep these prizes, I said; some, all, I would wrest from them. Just how I would do it I could never decide: by reading law, by healing the sick, by telling the wonderful tales that swam in my head,—some way. With other black boys the strife was not so fiercely sunny: their youth shrunk into tasteless sycophancy, or into silent hatred of the pale world about them and mocking distrust of everything white; or wasted itself in a bitter cry, Why did God make me an outcast and a stranger in mine own house? The shades of the prison-house closed round about us all: walls strait and stubborn to the whitest, but relentlessly narrow, tall, and unscalable to sons of night who must plod darkly on in resignation, or beat unavailing palms against the stone, or steadily, half hopelessly, watch the streak of blue above.

After the Egyptian and Indian, the Greek and Roman, the Teuton and Mongolian, the Negro is a sort of seventh son, born with a veil, and gifted with second-sight in this American world,—a world which yields him no true self-consciousness, but only lets him see himself through the revelation of the other world. It is a peculiar sensation, this double-consciousness, this sense of always looking at one's self through the eyes of others, of measuring one's soul by the tape of a world that looks on in amused contempt and pity. One ever feels his two-ness,—an American, a Negro; two souls, two thoughts, two unreconciled strivings; two warring ideals in one dark body, whose dogged strength alone keeps it from being torn asunder.

The history of the American Negro is the history of this strife,—this longing to attain self-conscious manhood, to merge his double self into a better and truer self. In this merging he wishes neither of the older selves to be lost. He would not Africanize America, for America has too much to teach the world and Africa. He would not bleach his Negro soul in a flood of white American-ism, for he knows that Negro blood has a message for the world. He simply wishes to make it possible for a man to be both a Negro and an American, with-out being cursed and spit upon by his fellows, without having the doors of Op-portunity closed roughly in his face.

This, then, is the end of his striving: to be a co-worker in the kingdom of culture, to escape both death and isolation, to husband and use his best powers and his latent genius. These powers of body and mind have in the past been strangely wasted, dispersed, or forgotten. The shadow of a mighty Negro past flits through the tale of Ethiopia the Shadowy and of Egypt the Sphinx. Throughout history, the powers of single black men flash here and there like falling stars, and die sometimes before the world has rightly gauged their brightness. Here in America, in the few days since Emancipation, the black man's turning hither and thither in hesitant and doubtful striving has often made his very strength to lose effectiveness, to seem like absence of power, like weakness. And yet it is not weakness,—it is the contradiction of double aims. The double-aimed struggle of the black artisan—on the one hand to escape white contempt for a nation of mere hewers of wood and drawers of water, and on the other hand to plough and nail and dig for a poverty-stricken horde— could only result in making him a poor craftsman, for he had but half a heart in either cause. By the poverty and ignorance of his people, the Negro minister or doctor was tempted toward quackery and demagogy; and by the criticism of the other world, toward ideals that made him ashamed of his lowly tasks. The would-be black *savant* was confronted by the paradox that the knowledge his people needed was a twice-told tale to his white neighbors, while the knowl-edge which would teach the white world was Greek to his own flesh and blood. The innate love of harmony and beauty that set the ruder souls of his people a-dancing and a-singing raised but confusion and doubt in the soul of the black artist; for the beauty revealed to him was the soul-beauty of a race which his larger audience despised, and he could not articulate the message of another people. This waste of double aims, this seeking to satisfy two unreconciled ideals, has wrought sad havoc with the courage and faith and deeds of ten thou-sand thousand people,—has sent them often wooing false gods and invoking false means of salvation, and at times has even seemed about to make them ashamed of themselves.

Away back in the days of bondage they thought to see in one divine event the end of all doubt and disappointment; few men ever worshipped Freedom with half such unquestioning faith as did the American Negro for two centuries. To him, so far as he thought and dreamed, slavery was indeed the sum of all vil-lainies, the cause of all sorrow, the root of all prejudice; Emancipation was the key to a promised land of sweeter beauty than ever stretched before the eyes of wearied Israelites. In song and exhortation swelled one refrain—Liberty; in his tears and curses the God he implored had Freedom in his right hand. At last it came,—suddenly, fearfully, like a dream. With one wild carnival of blood and passion came the message in his own plaintive cadences:—

> Shout, O children!
> Shout, you're free!
> For God has bought your liberty!

Years have passed away since then,—ten, twenty, forty; forty years of national life, forty years of renewal and development, and yet the swarthy spectre sits in its accustomed seat at the Nation's feast. In vain do we cry to this our vastest social problem:—

> Take any shape but that, and my firm nerves
> Shall never tremble!

The Nation has not yet found peace from its sins; the freedman has not yet found in freedom his promised land. Whatever of good may have come in these years of change, the shadow of a deep disappointment rests upon the Negro people,—a disappointment all the more bitter because the unattained ideal was unbounded save by the simple ignorance of a lowly people.

The first decade was merely a prolongation of the vain search for freedom, the boon that seemed ever barely to elude their grasp,—like a tantalizing will-o'-the-wisp, maddening and misleading the headless host. The holocaust of war, the terrors of the Ku-Klux Klan, the lies of carpet-baggers, the disorganization of industry, and the contradictory advice of friends and foes, left the bewildered serf with no new watch-word beyond the old cry for freedom. As the time flew, however, he began to grasp a new idea. The ideal of liberty demanded for its attainment powerful means, and these the Fifteenth Amendment gave him. The ballot, which before he had looked upon as a visible sign of freedom, he now regarded as the chief means of gaining and perfecting the liberty with which war had partially endowed him. And why not? Had not votes made war and emancipated millions? Had not votes enfranchised the freedmen? Was anything impossible to a power that had done all this? A million black men started with renewed zeal to vote themselves into the kingdom. So the decade flew away, the revolution of 1876 came, and left the half-free serf weary, wondering, but still inspired. Slowly but steadily, in the following years, a new vision began gradually to replace the dream of political power,—a powerful movement, the rise of another ideal to guide the unguided, another pillar of fire by night after a clouded day. It was the ideal of "book-learning"; the curiosity, born of compulsory ignorance, to know and test the power of the cabalistic letters of the white man, the longing to know. Here at last seemed to have been discovered the mountain path to Canaan; longer than the highway of Emancipation and law, steep and rugged, but straight, leading to heights high enough to overlook life.

Up the new path the advance guard toiled, slowly, heavily, doggedly; only those who have watched and guided the faltering feet, the misty minds, the dull understandings, of the dark pupils of these schools know how faithfully, how piteously, this people strove to learn. It was weary work. The cold statistician wrote down the inches of progress here and there, noted also where here and there a foot had slipped or some one had fallen. To the tired climbers, the horizon was ever dark, the mists were often cold, the Canaan was always dim and far away. If, however, the vistas disclosed as yet no goal, no resting-place, little but flattery and criticism, the journey at least gave leisure for reflection and self-examination; it changed the child of Emancipation to the youth with dawning self-consciousness, self-realization, self-respect. In those sombre forests of his striving his own soul rose before him, and he saw himself,—darkly as through a veil; and yet he saw in himself some faint revelation of his power, of his mission. He began to have a dim feeling that, to attain his place in the world, he must be himself, and not another. For the first time he sought to analyze the burden he bore upon his back, that dead-weight of social degradation partially masked behind a half-named Negro problem. He felt his poverty; without a cent, without a home, without land, tools, or savings, he had entered into competition with rich, landed, skilled neighbors. To be a poor man is hard, but to be a poor race in a land of dollars is the very bottom of hardships. He felt the weight of his ignorance,—not simply of letters, but of life, of business, of the humanities; the accumulated sloth and shirking and awkwardness of decades and centuries shackled his hands and feet. Nor was his burden all poverty and ignorance. The red stain of bastardy, which two centuries of systematic legal defilement of Negro women had stamped upon his race, meant not only the loss of ancient African chastity, but also the hereditary weight of a mass of corruption from white adulterers, threatening almost the obliteration of the Negro home.

A people thus handicapped ought not to be asked to race with the world, but rather allowed to give all its time and thought to its own social problems. But alas! while sociologists gleefully count his bastards and his prostitutes, the very soul of the toiling, sweating black man is darkened by the shadow of a vast despair. Men call the shadow prejudice, and learnedly explain it as the natural defence of culture against barbarism, learning against ignorance, purity against crime, the "higher" against the "lower" races. To which the Negro cries Amen! and swears that to so much of this strange prejudice as is founded on just homage to civilization, culture, righteousness, and progress, he humbly bows and meekly does obeisance. But before that nameless prejudice that leaps beyond all this he stands helpless, dismayed, and well-nigh speechless; before that personal disrespect and mockery, the ridicule and systematic humiliation, the distortion of fact and wanton license of fancy, the cynical ignoring of the better and the boisterous welcoming of the worse, the all-pervading desire to inculcate disdain for everything black, from Toussaint to the devil,—before this there rises a sickening despair that would disarm and discourage any nation save that black host to whom "discouragement" is an unwritten word.

But the facing of so vast a prejudice could not but bring the inevitable self-questioning, self-disparagement, and lowering of ideals which ever accompany repression and breed in an atmosphere of contempt and hate. Whisperings and portents came borne upon the four winds: Lo! we are diseased and dying, cried the dark hosts; we cannot write, our voting is vain; what need of education, since we must always cook and serve? And the Nation echoed and enforced this self-criticism, saying: Be content to be servants, and nothing more; what need of higher culture for half-men? Away with the black man's ballot, by force or fraud,—and behold the suicide of a race! Nevertheless, out of the evil came something of good,—the more careful adjustment of education to real life, the clearer perception of the Negroes' social responsibilities, and the sobering realization of the meaning of progress.

So dawned the time of *Sturm und Drang:* storm and stress to-day rocks our little boat on the mad waters of the world-sea; there is within and without the sound of conflict, the burning of body and rending of soul; inspiration strives with doubt, and faith with vain questionings. The bright ideals of the past,—physical freedom, political power, the training of brains and the training of hands,—all these in turn have waxed and waned, until even the last grows dim and overcast. Are they all wrong,—all false? No, not that, but each alone was over-simple and incomplete,—the dreams of a credulous race-childhood, or the fond imaginings of the other world which does not know and does not want to know our power. To be really true, all these ideals must be melted and welded into one. The training of the schools we need to-day more than ever,— the training of deft hands, quick eyes and ears, and above all the broader, deeper, higher culture of gifted minds and pure hearts. The power of the ballot we need in sheer self-defence,—else what shall save us from a second slavery? Freedom, too, the long-sought, we still seek,—the freedom of life and limb, the freedom to work and think, the freedom to love and aspire. Work, culture, liberty,—all these we need, not singly but together, not successively but together, each growing and aiding each, and all striving toward that vaster ideal that swims before the Negro people, the ideal of human brotherhood, gained through the unifying ideal of Race; the ideal of fostering and developing the traits and talents of the Negro, not in opposition to or contempt for other races, but rather in large conformity to the greater ideals of the American Republic, in order that some day on American soil two world-races may give each to each those characteristics both so sadly lack. We the darker ones come even now not altogether empty-handed: there are to-day no truer exponents of the pure human spirit of the Declaration of Independence than the American Negroes; there is no true American music but the wild sweet melodies of the Negro slave; the American fairy tales and folklore are Indian and African; and, all in all, we black men seem the sole oasis of simple faith and reverence in a dusty desert of dollars and smartness. Will America be poorer if she replace her brutal dyspeptic blundering with light-hearted but determined Negro humility? or her coarse and cruel wit with loving jovial good-humor? or her vulgar music with the soul of the Sorrow Songs?

Merely a concrete test of the underlying principles of the great republic is the Negro Problem, and the spiritual striving of the freedmen's sons is the travail of souls whose burden is almost beyond the measure of their strength, but who bear it in the name of an historic race, in the name of this the land of their fathers' fathers, and in the name of human opportunity. ✖

Of Mr. Booker T. Washington and Others

W. E. B. Du Bois

Easily the most striking thing in the history of the American Negro since 1876 is the ascendancy of Mr. Booker T. Washington. It began at the time when war memories and ideals were rapidly passing; a day of astonishing commercial development was dawning; a sense of doubt and hesitation overtook the freedmen's sons,—then it was that his leading began. Mr. Washington came, with a simple definite programme, at the psychological moment when the nation was a little ashamed of having bestowed so much sentiment on Negroes, and was concentrating its energies on Dollars. His programme of industrial education, conciliation of the South, and submission and silence as to civil and political rights, was not wholly original; the Free Negroes from 1830 up to war-time had striven to build industrial schools, and the American Missionary Association had from the first taught various trades; and Price and others had sought a way of honorable alliance with the best of the Southerners. But Mr. Washington first indissolubly linked these things; he put enthusiasm, unlimited energy, and perfect faith into this programme, and changed it from a by-path into a veritable Way of Life. And the tale of the methods by which he did this is a fascinating study of human life.

From *The Souls of Black Folk* by W. E. B. Du Bois, ch. 3. Published by A. C. McClurg & C., 1903.

It startled the nation to hear a Negro advocating such a programme after many decades of bitter complaint; it startled and won the applause of the South, it interested and won the admiration of the North; and after a confused murmur of protest, it silenced if it did not convert the Negroes themselves.

To gain the sympathy and cooperation of the various elements comprising the white South was Mr. Washington's first task; and this, at the time Tuskegee was founded, seemed, for a black man, well-nigh impossible. And yet ten years later it was done in the word spoken at Atlanta: "In all things purely social we can be as separate as the five fingers, and yet one as the hand in all things essential to mutual progress:" This "Atlanta Compromise" is by all odds the most notable thing in Mr. Washington's career. The South interpreted it in different ways: the radicals received it as a complete surrender of the demand for civil and political equality; the conservatives, as a generously conceived working basis for mutual understanding. So both approved it, and to-day its author is certainly the most distinguished Southerner since Jefferson Davis, and the one with the largest personal following.

Next to this achievement comes Mr. Washington's work in gaining place and consideration in the North. Others less shrewd and tactful had formerly essayed to sit on these two stools and had fallen between them; but as Mr. Washington knew the heart of the South from birth and training, so by singular insight he intuitively grasped the spirit of the age which was dominating the North. And so thoroughly did he learn the speech and thought of triumphant commercialism, and the ideals of material prosperity, that the picture of a lone black boy poring over a French grammar amid the weeds and dirt of a neglected home soon seemed to him the acme of absurdities. One wonders what Socrates and St. Francis of Assisi would say to this.

And yet this very singleness of vision and thorough oneness with his age is a mark of the successful man. It is as though Nature must needs make men narrow in order to give them force. So Mr. Washington's cult has gained unquestioning followers, his work has wonderfully prospered, his friends are legion, and his enemies are confounded, To-day he stands as the one recognized spokesman of his ten million fellows, and one of the most notable figures in a nation of seventy millions. One hesitates, therefore, to criticise a life which, beginning with so little, has done so much. And yet the time is come when one may speak in all sincerity and utter courtesy of the mistakes and shortcomings of Mr. Washington's career, as well as of his triumphs, without being thought captious or envious, and without forgetting that it is easier to do ill than well in the world.

The criticism that has hitherto met Mr. Washington has not always been of this broad character. In the South especially has he had to walk warily to avoid the harshest judgments,—and naturally so, for he is dealing with the one subject of deepest sensitiveness to that section. Twice—once when at the

Chicago celebration of the Spanish-American War he alluded to the color-prejudice that is "eating away the vitals of the South," and once when he dined with President Roosevelt—has the resulting Southern criticism been violent enough to threaten seriously his popularity. In the North the feeling has several times forced itself into words, that Mr. Washington's counsels of submission overlooked certain elements of true manhood, and that his educational pro-gramme was unnecessarily narrow. Usually, however, such criticism has not found open expression, although, too, the spiritual sons of the Abolitionists have not been prepared to acknowledge that the schools founded before Tuskegee, by men of broad ideals and self-sacrificing spirit, were wholly failures or worthy of ridicule. While, then, criticism has not failed to follow Mr. Washington, yet the prevailing public opinion of the land has been but too willing to deliver the solution of a wearisome problem into his hands, and say, "If that is all you and your race ask, take it."

Among his own people, however, Mr. Washington has encountered the strongest and most lasting opposition, amounting at times to bitterness, and even to-day continuing strong and insistent even though largely silenced in out-ward expression by the public opinion of the nation. Some of this opposition is, of course, mere envy; the disappointment of displaced demagogues and the spite of narrow minds. But aside from this, there is among educated and thoughtful colored men in all parts of the land a feeling of deep regret, sorrow, and apprehension at the wide currency and ascendancy which some of Mr. Washington's theories have gained. These same men admire his sincerity of purpose, and are willing to forgive much to honest endeavor which is doing something worth the doing. They cooperate with Mr. Washington as far as they conscientiously can; and, indeed, it is no ordinary tribute to this man's tact and power that, steering as he must between so many diverse interests and opin-ions, he so largely retains the respect of all.

But the hushing of the criticism of honest opponents is a dangerous thing. It leads some of the best of the critics to unfortunate silence and paralysis of ef-fort, and others to burst into speech so passionately and intemperately as to lose listeners. Honest and earnest criticism from those whose interests are most nearly touched,—criticism of writers by readers, of government by those gov-erned, of leaders by those led,—this is the soul of democracy and the safeguard of modern society. If the best of the American Negroes receive by outer pres-sure a leader whom they had not recognized before, manifestly there is here a certain palpable gain. Yet there is also irreparable loss,—a loss of that peculiarly valuable education which a group receives when by search and criticism it finds and commissions its own leaders. The way in which this is done is at once the most elementary and the nicest problem of social growth. History is but the record of such group-leadership; and yet how infinitely changeful is its type and character! And of all types and kinds, what can be more instructive than the leadership of a group within a group?—that curious double movement where real progress may be negative and actual advance be relative retrogression. All this is the social student's inspiration and despair.

Now in the past the American Negro has had instructive experience in the choosing of group leaders, founding thus a peculiar dynasty which in the light of present conditions is worth while studying. When sticks and stones and beasts form the sole environment of a people, their attitude is largely one of determined opposition to and conquest of natural forces. But when to earth and brute is added an environment of men and ideas, then the attitude of the imprisoned group may take three main forms,—a feeling of revolt and revenge; an attempt to adjust all thought and action to the will of the greater group; or, finally, a determined effort at self-realization and self-development despite environing opinion. The influence of all of these attitudes at various times can be traced in the history of the American Negro, and in the evolution of his successive leaders.

Before 1750, while the fire of African freedom still burned in the veins of the slaves, there was in all leadership or attempted leadership but the one motive of revolt and revenge,—typified in the terrible Maroons, the Danish blacks, and Cato of Stono, and veiling all the Americas in fear of insurrection. The liberalizing tendencies of the latter half of the eighteenth century brought, along with kindlier relations between black and white, thoughts of ultimate adjustment and assimilation. Such aspiration was especially voiced in the earnest songs of Phyllis, in the martyrdom of Attucks, the fighting of Salem and Poor, the intellectual accomplishments of Banneker and Derham, and the political demands of the Cuffes.

Stern financial and social stress after the war cooled much of the previous humanitarian ardor. The disappointment and impatience of the Negroes at the persistence of slavery and serfdom voiced itself in two movements. The slaves in the South, aroused undoubtedly by vague rumors of the Haytian revolt, made three fierce attempts at insurrection,—in 1800 under Gabriel in Virginia, in 1822 under Vesey in Carolina, and in 1831 again in Virginia under the terrible Nat Turner. In the Free States, on the other hand, a new and curious attempt at self-development was made. In Philadelphia and New York color-prescription led to a withdrawal of Negro communicants from white churches and the formation of a peculiar socio-religious institution among the Negroes known as the African Church,—an organization still living and controlling in its various branches over a million of men.

Walker's wild appeal against the trend of the times showed how the world was changing after the coming of the cotton-gin. By 1830 slavery seemed hopelessly fastened on the South, and the slaves thoroughly cowed into submission. The free Negroes of the North, inspired by the mulatto immigrants from the West Indies, began to change the basis of their demands; they recognized the slavery of slaves, but insisted that they themselves were freemen, and sought as-similation and amalgamation with the nation on the same terms with other men. Thus, Forten and Purvis of Philadelphia, Shad of Wilmington, Du Bois of New Haven, Barbadoes of Boston, and others, strove singly and together as men, they said, not as slaves; as "people of color," not as "Negroes." The trend of the times, however, refused them recognition save in individual and excep-tional cases, considered them as one with all the despised blacks, and they soon found themselves striving to keep even the rights they formerly had of voting and working and moving as freemen. Schemes of migration and colonization arose among them; but these they refused to entertain, and they eventually turned to the Abolition movement as a final refuge.

Here, led by Remond, Nell, Wells-Brown, and Douglass, a new period of self-assertion and self-development dawned. To be sure, ultimate freedom and assimilation was the ideal before the leaders, but the assertion of the manhood rights of the Negro by himself was the main reliance, and John Brown's raid was the extreme of its logic. After the war and emancipation, the great form of Frederick Douglass, the greatest of American Negro leaders, still led the host. Self-assertion, especially in political lines, was the main programme, and be-hind Douglass came Elliot, Bruce, and Langston, and the Reconstruction politi-cians, and, less conspicuous but of greater social significance(,) Alexander Crummell and Bishop Daniel Payne.

Then came the Revolution of 1876, the suppression of the Negro votes, the changing and shifting of ideals, and the seeking of new lights in the great night. Douglass, in his old age, still bravely stood for the ideals of his early man-hood,—ultimate assimilation *through* self-assertion, and on no other terms. For a time Price arose as a new leader, destined, it seemed, not to give up, but to re-state the old ideals in a form less repugnant to the white South. But he passed away in his prime. Then came the new leader. Nearly all the former ones had become leaders by the silent suffrage of their fellows, had sought to lead their own people alone, and were usually, save Douglass, little known out-side their race. But Booker T. Washington arose as essentially the leader not of one race but of two,—a compromiser between the South, the North, and the Negro. Naturally the Negroes resented, at first bitterly, signs of compromise which surrendered their civil and political rights, even though this was to be ex-changed for larger chances of economic development. The rich and dominating North, however, was not only weary of the race problem, but was investing largely in Southern enterprises, and welcomed any method of peaceful cooper-ation. Thus, by national opinion, the Negroes began to recognize Mr. Washing-ton's leadership; and the voice of criticism was hushed.

Mr. Washington represents in Negro thought the old attitude of adjust-ment and submission; but adjustment at such a peculiar time as to make his programme unique. This is an age of unusual economic development, and Mr.

Washington's programme naturally takes an economic cast, becoming a gospel of Work and Money to such an extent as apparently almost completely to overshadow the higher aims of life. Moreover, this is an age when the more advanced races are coming in closer contact with the less developed races, and the race-feeling is therefore intensified; and Mr. Washington's programme practically accepts the alleged inferiority of the Negro races. Again, in our own land, the reaction from the sentiment of war time has given impetus to race-prejudice against Negroes, and Mr. Washington withdraws many of the high demands of Negroes as men and American citizens. In other periods of intensified prejudice all the Negro's tendency to self-assertion has been called forth; at this period a policy of submission is advocated. In the history of nearly all other races and peoples the doctrine preached at such crises has been that manly self-respect is worth more than lands and houses, and that a people who voluntarily surrender such respect, or cease striving for it, are not worth civilizing.

In answer to this, it has been claimed that the Negro can survive only through submission. Mr. Washington distinctly asks that black people give up, at least for the present, three things,—

> First, political power,
> Second, insistence on civil rights,
> Third, higher education of Negro youth,—

and concentrate all their energies on industrial education, the accumulation of wealth, and the conciliation of the South. This policy has been courageously and insistently advocated for over fifteen years, and has been triumphant for perhaps ten years. As a result of this tender of the palm-branch, what has been the return? In these years there have occurred:

1. The disfranchisement of the Negro.
2. The legal creation of a distinct status of civil inferiority for the Negro.
3. The steady withdrawal of aid from institutions for the higher training of the Negro.

These movements are not, to be sure, direct results of Mr. Washington's teachings; but his propaganda has, without a shadow of doubt, helped their speedier accomplishment. The question then comes: Is it possible, and probable, that nine millions of men can make effective progress in economic lines if they are deprived of political rights, made a servile caste, and allowed only the most meager chance for developing their exceptional men? If history and reason give any distinct answer to these questions, it is an emphatic *No.* And Mr. Washington thus faces the triple paradox of his career:

1. He is striving nobly to make Negro artisans business men and property-owners; but it is utterly impossible, under modern competitive methods, for

workingmen and property-owners to defend their rights and exist without the right of suffrage.

2. He insists on thrift and self-respect, but at the same time counsels a silent submission to civic inferiority such as is bound to sap the manhood of any race in the long run.

3. He advocates common-school and industrial training, and depreciates institutions of higher learning; but neither the Negro common-schools, nor Tuskegee itself, could remain open a day were it not for teachers trained in Negro colleges, or trained by their graduates.

This triple paradox in Mr. Washington's position is the object of criticism by two classes of colored Americans. One class is spiritually descended from Toussaint the Savior, through Gabriel, Vesey, and Turner, and they represent the attitude of revolt and revenge; they hate the white South blindly and distrust the white race generally, and so far as they agree on definite action, think that the Negro's only hope lies in emigration beyond the borders of the United States. And yet, by the irony of fate, nothing has more effectually made this programme seem hopeless than the recent course of the United States toward weaker and darker peoples in the West Indies, Hawaii, and the Philippines,—for where in the world may we go and be safe from lying and brute force?

The other class of Negroes who cannot agree with Mr. Washington has hitherto said little aloud. They deprecate the sight of scattered counsels, of internal disagreement; and especially they dislike making their just criticism of a useful and earnest man an excuse for a general discharge of venom from small-minded opponents. Nevertheless, the questions involved are so fundamental and serious that it is difficult to see how men like the Grimkes, Kelly Miller, J. W. E. Bowen, and other representatives of this group, can much longer be silent. Such men feel in conscience bound to ask of this nation three things:

1. The right to vote.
2. Civic equality.
3. The education of youth according to ability.

They acknowledge Mr. Washington's invaluable service in counselling patience and courtesy in such demands; they do not ask that ignorant black men vote when ignorant whites are debarred, or that any reasonable restrictions in the suffrage should not be applied; they know that the low social level of the mass of the race is responsible for much discrimination against it, but they also know, and the nation knows, that relentless color-prejudice is more often a cause than a result of the Negro's degradation; they seek the abatement of this relic of barbarism, and not its systematic encouragement and pampering by all agencies of social power from the Associated Press to the Church of Christ. They advocate, with Mr. Washington, a broad system of Negro common schools supplemented by thorough industrial training; but they are surprised that a man of Mr. Washington's insight cannot see that no such educational system ever has rested or can rest on any other basis than that of the well-equipped college and university, and they insist that there is a demand for a few such institutions throughout the South to train the best of the Negro youth as teachers, professional men, and leaders.

This group of men honor Mr. Washington for his attitude of conciliation toward the white South; they accept the "Atlanta Compromise" in its broadest interpretation; they recognize, with him, many signs of promise, many men of high purpose and fair judgment, in this section; they know that no easy task has been laid upon a region already tottering under heavy burdens. But, nevertheless, they insist that the way to truth and right lies in straightforward honesty, not in indiscriminate flattery; in praising those of the South who do well and criticising uncompromisingly those who do ill; in taking advantage of the opportunities at hand and urging their fellows to do the same, but at the same time in remembering that only a firm adherence to their higher ideals and aspirations will ever keep those ideals within the realm of possibility. They do not expect that the free right to vote, to enjoy civic rights, and to be educated, will come in a moment; they do not expect to see the bias and prejudices of years disappear at the blast of a trumpet; but they are absolutely certain that the way for a people to gain their reasonable rights is not by voluntarily throwing them away and insisting that they do not want them; that the way for a people to gain respect is not by continually belittling and ridiculing themselves; that, on the contrary, Negroes must insist continually, in season and out of season, that voting is necessary to modern manhood, that color discrimination is barbarism, and that black boys need education as well as white boys.

In failing thus to state plainly and unequivocally the legitimate demands of their people, even at the cost of opposing an honored leader, the thinking classes of American Negroes would shirk a heavy responsibility,—a responsibility to themselves, a responsibility to the struggling masses, a responsibility to the darker races of men whose future depends so largely on this American experiment, but especially a responsibility to this nation,—this common Fatherland. It is wrong to encourage a man or a people in evil-doing; it is wrong to aid and abet a national crime simply because it is unpopular not to do so. The growing spirit of kindliness and reconciliation between the North and South after the frightful differences of a generation ago ought to be a source of deep congratulation to all, and especially to those whose mistreatment caused the war; but if that reconciliation is to be marked by the industrial slavery and civic death of those same black men, with permanent legislation into a position of inferiority, then those black men, if they are really men, are called upon by every consideration of patriotism and loyalty to oppose such a course by all civilized methods, even though such opposition involves disagreement with Mr. Booker

T. Washington. We have no right to sit silently by while the inevitable seeds are sown for a harvest of disaster to our children, black and white.

First, it is the duty of black men to judge the South discriminatingly. The present generation of Southerners are not responsible for the past, and they should not be blindly hated or blamed for it. Furthermore, to no class is the indiscriminate endorsement of the recent course of the South toward Negroes more nauseating than to the best thought of the South. The South is not "solid"; it is a land in the ferment of social change, wherein forces of all kinds are fighting for supremacy; and to praise the ill the South is to-day perpetrating is just as wrong as to condemn the good. Discriminating and broad-minded criticism is what the South needs,—needs it for the sake of her own white sons and daughters, and for the insurance of robust, healthy mental and moral development.

To-day even the attitude of the Southern whites toward the blacks is not, as so many assume, in all cases the same; the ignorant Southerner hates the Negro, the workingmen fear his competition, the money-makers wish to use him as a laborer, some of the educated see a menace in his upward development, while others—usually the sons of the masters—wish to help him to rise. National opinion has enabled this last class to maintain the Negro common schools, and to protect the Negro partially in property, life, and limb. Through the pressure of the money-makers, the Negro is in danger of being reduced to semi-slavery, especially in the country districts; the workingmen, and those of the educated who fear the Negro, have united to disfranchise him, and some have urged his deportation; while the passions of the ignorant are easily aroused to lynch and abuse any black man. To praise this intricate whirl of thought and prejudice is nonsense; to inveigh indiscriminately against "the South" is unjust; but to use the same breath in praising Governor Aycock, exposing Senator Morgan, arguing with Mr. Thomas Nelson Page, and denouncing Senator Ben Tillman, is not only sane, but the imperative duty of thinking black men.

It would be unjust to Mr. Washington not to acknowledge that in several instances he has opposed movements in the South which were unjust to the Negro; he sent memorials to the Louisiana and Alabama constitutional conventions, he has spoken against lynching, and in other ways has openly or silently set his influence against sinister schemes and unfortunate happenings. Not withstanding this, it is equally true to assert that on the whole the distinct impression left by Mr. Washington's propaganda is, first, that the South is justified in its present attitude toward the Negro because of the Negro's degradation; secondly, that the prime cause of the Negro's failure to rise more quickly is his wrong education in the past; and, thirdly, that his future rise depends primarily on his own efforts. Each of these propositions is a dangerous half-truth. The supplementary truths must never be lost sight of: first, slavery and race-prejudice are potent if not sufficient causes of the Negro's position; second, industrial and common-school training were necessarily slow in planting because they had to await the black teachers trained by higher institutions,—it being extremely doubtful if any essentially different development was possible, and certainly a Tuskegee was unthinkable before 1880; and, third, while it is a great truth to say that the Negro must strive and strive mightily to help himself, it is equally true that unless his striving be not simply seconded, but rather aroused and encouraged, by the initiative of the richer and wiser environing group, he cannot hope for great success.

In his failure to realize and impress this last point, Mr. Washington is especially to be criticised. His doctrine has tended to make the whites, North and South, shift the burden of the Negro problem to the Negro's shoulders and stand aside as critical and rather pessimistic spectators; when in fact the burden belongs to the nation, and the hands of none of us are clean if we bend not our energies to righting these great wrongs.

The South ought to be led, by candid and honest criticism, to assert her better self and do her full duty to the race she has cruelly wronged and is still wronging. The North—her co-partner in guilt—cannot salve her conscience by plastering it with gold. We cannot settle this problem by diplomacy and suaveness, by "policy" alone. If worse come to worst, can the moral fibre of this country survive the slow throttling and murder of nine millions of men?

The black men of America have a duty to perform, a duty stern and delicate,—a forward movement to oppose a part of the work of their greatest leader. So far as Mr. Washington preaches Thrift, Patience, and Industrial Training for the masses, we must hold up his hands and strive with him, rejoicing in his honors and glorying in the strength of this Joshua called of God and of man to lead the headless host. But so far as Mr. Washington apologizes for injustice, North or South, does not rightly value the privilege and duty of voting, belittles the emasculating effects of caste distinctions, and opposes the higher training and ambition of our brighter minds,—so far as he, the South, or the Nation, does this,—we must unceasingly and firmly oppose them. By every civilized and peaceful method we must strive for the rights which the world accords to men, clinging unwaveringly to those great words which the sons of the Fathers would fain forget: "We hold these truths to be self-evident: That all men are created equal; that they are endowed by their Creator with certain unalienable rights; that among these are life, liberty, and the pursuit of happiness." ✲

QUESTIONS FOR THOUGHT AND STUDY

1. Compare the personal experience of being an African-American man with Allport's account of that experience. Where do they agree and disagree? Does Allport's theory explain this experience adequately?

2. What is the African-American dilemma, according to Du Bois? How ought African-Americans deal with it?

3. Booker T. Washington, as Du Bois said, proposed that black and white could "in all things social be as separate as the five fingers, and yet as one as the hand in all things essential to mutual progress." Can you describe such a relationship in terms of Allport's social distance? Does Allport's theory express it satisfactorily? Why and why not?

4. Does Du Bois agree with Washington's position? Describe the differences between them.

5. Compare the split consciousness described by Du Bois with Judith Shklar's account of divided loyalty.

6. Describe a situation where you have felt the conflict between adapting to a group, despite their prejudice, and confronting them.

The Federalist #10

James Madison

Biography: *James Madison (1751–1836), the fourth president of the United States (1809–1817), was educated at Princeton. Sometimes called "the father of the Constitution," he played a major role in the Constitutional Convention of 1787. He then collaborated with other leaders, under the name of "Publius" in writing* The Federalist Papers, *public essays arguing for the acceptance of the Constitution by state assemblies. He was later founder of the Jeffersonian Republican Party and served as secretary of state under Thomas Jefferson before becoming president.*

This is a classic essay in political theory. Madison, arguing the need of a Federal Constitution, discusses the power of factions and the tendency of powerful groups to oppress others, thus undermining the common good. Factions, he argues, cannot be prevented without destroying the democracy but the larger the state, the more varied the factions, thus the less chance that one will dominate others.

"TO BREAK AND CONTROL THE VIOLENCE OF FACTION"

TO THE PEOPLE OF THE STATE OF NEW-YORK.

Among the numerous advantages promised by a well constructed Union, none deserves to be more accurately developed than its tendency to break and control the violence of faction. The friend of popular governments, never finds himself so much alarmed for their character and fate, as when he contemplates

From *The Debate on the Constitution*, (1787) Part 1 pp. 404–411, Library of America Series. New York: Library Classics of the United States, Inc.

their propensity to this dangerous vice. He will not fail therefore to set a due value on any plan which, without violating the principles to which he is attached, provides a proper cure for it. The instability, injustice and confusion introduced into the public councils, have in truth been the mortal diseases under which popular governments have every where perished; as they continue to be the favorite and fruitful topics from which the adversaries to liberty derive their most specious declamations. The valuable improvements made by the American Constitutions on the popular models, both ancient and modern, cannot certainly be too much admired; but it would be an unwarrantable partiality, to contend that they have as effectually obviated the danger on this side as was wished and expected. Complaints are every where heard from our most considerate and virtuous citizens, equally the friends of public and private faith, and of public and personal liberty; that our governments are too unstable; that the public good is disregarded in the conflicts of rival parties; and that measures are too often decided, not according to the rules of justice, and the rights of the minor party; but by the superior force of an interested and over-bearing majority. However anxiously we may wish that these complaints had no foundation, the evidence of known facts will not permit us to deny that they are in some degree true. It will be found indeed, on a candid review of our situation, that some of the distresses under which we labor, have been erroneously charged on the operation of our governments; but it will be found, at the same time, that other causes will not alone account for many of our heaviest misfortunes; and particularly, for that prevailing and increasing distrust of public engagements, and alarm for private rights, which are echoed from one end of the continent to the other. These must be chiefly, if not wholly, effects of the unsteadiness and injustice, with which a factious spirit has tainted our public administration.

By a faction I understand a number of citizens, whether amounting to a majority or minority of the whole, who are united and actuated by some common impulse of passion, or of interest, adverse to the rights of other citizens, or to the permanent and aggregate interests of the community.

There are two methods of curing the mischiefs of faction: the one, by removing its causes; the other, by controlling its effects.

There are again two methods of removing the causes of faction: the one by destroying the liberty which is essential to its existence; the other, by giving to every citizen the same opinions, the same passions, and the same interests.

It could never be more truly said than of the first remedy, that it is worse than the disease. Liberty is to faction, what air is to fire, an aliment without which it instantly expires. But it could not be a less folly to abolish liberty, which is essential to political life, because it nourishes faction, than it would be to wish the annihilation of air, which is essential to animal life, because it imparts to fire its destructive agency.

The second expedient is as impracticable, as the first would be unwise. As long as the reason of man continues fallible, and he is at liberty to exercise it, different opinions will be formed. As long as the connection subsists between his reason and his self-love, his opinions and his passions will have a reciprocal influence on each other; and the former will be objects to which the latter will attach themselves. The diversity in the faculties of men from which the rights of property originate, is not less an insuperable obstacle to a uniformity of interests. The protection of these faculties is the first object of Government. From the protection of different and unequal faculties of acquiring property, the possession of different degrees and kinds of property immediately results: and from the influence of these on the sentiments and views of the respective proprietors, ensues a division of the society into different interests and parties.

The latent causes of faction are thus sown in the nature of man; and we see them every where brought into different degrees of activity, according to the different circumstances of civil society. A zeal for different opinions concerning religion, concerning Government, and many other points, as well of speculation as of practice; an attachment to different leaders ambitiously contending for pre-eminence and power; or to persons of other descriptions whose fortunes have been interesting to the human passions, have in turn divided mankind into parties, inflamed them with mutual animosity, and rendered them much more disposed to vex and oppress each other, than to co-operate for their common good. So strong is this propensity of mankind to fall into mutual animosities, that where no substantial occasion presents itself, the most frivolous and fanciful distinctions have been sufficient to kindle their unfriendly passions, and excite their most violent conflicts. But the most common and durable source of factions, has been the various and unequal distribution of property. Those who hold, and those who are without property, have ever formed distinct interests in society. Those who are creditors, and those who are debtors, fall under a like discrimination. A landed interest, a manufacturing interest, a mercantile interest, a monied interest, with many lesser interests, grow up of necessity in civilized nations, and divide them into different classes, actuated by different sentiments and views. The regulation of these various and interfering interests forms the principal task of modern Legislation, and involves the spirit of party and faction in the necessary and ordinary operations of Government.

No man is allowed to be a judge in his own cause; because his interest would certainly bias his judgment, and, not improbably, corrupt his integrity. With equal, nay with greater reason, a body of men, are unfit to be both judges and parties, at the same time; yet, what are many of the most important acts of legislation, but so many judicial determinations, not indeed concerning the rights of single persons, but concerning the rights of large bodies of citizens; and what are the different classes of legislators, but advocates and parties to the causes which they determine? Is a law proposed concerning private debts? It is a question to which the creditors are parties on one side, and the debtors on the other. Justice ought to hold the balance between them. Yet the parties are and must be themselves the judges; and the most numerous party, or, in other words, the most powerful faction must be expected to prevail. Shall domestic manufactures be encouraged, and in what degree, by restrictions on foreign manufactures? are questions which would be differently decided by the landed and the manufacturing classes; and probably by neither, with a sole regard to justice and the public good. The apportionment of taxes on the various descriptions of property, is an act which seems to require the most exact impartiality; yet there is perhaps no legislative act in which greater opportunity and temptation are given to a predominant party, to trample on the rules of justice. Every shilling with which they over-burden the inferior number, is a shilling saved to their own pockets.

It is in vain to say, that enlightened statesmen will be able to adjust these clashing interests, and render them all subservient to the public good. Enlightened statesmen will not always be at the helm: Nor, in many cases, can such an adjustment be made at all, without taking into view indirect and remote considerations, which will rarely prevail over the immediate interest which one party may find in disregarding the rights of another, or the good of the whole.

The inference to which we are brought, is, that the *causes* of faction cannot be removed; and that relief is only to be sought in the means of controlling its *effects*.

If a faction consists of less than a majority, relief is supplied by the republican principle, which enables the majority to defeat its sinister views by regular vote: It may clog the administration, it may convulse the society; but it will be unable to execute and mask its violence under the forms of the Constitution. When a majority is included in a faction, the form of popular government on the other hand enables it to sacrifice to its ruling passion or interest, both the public good and the rights of other citizens. To secure the public good, and private rights, against the danger of such a faction, and at the same time to preserve the spirit and the form of popular government, is then the great object to which our enquiries are directed: Let me add that it is the great desideratum, by which alone this form of government can be rescued from the opprobrium under which it has so long labored, and be recommended to the esteem and adoption of mankind.

By what means is this object attainable? Evidently by one of two only. Either the existence of the same passion or interest in a majority at the same time, must be prevented; or the majority, having such co-existent passion or interest, must be rendered, by their number and local situation, unable to concert and carry into effect schemes of oppression. If the impulse and the opportunity be suffered to coincide, we well know that neither moral nor religious motives can be relied on as an adequate control. They are not found to be such on the injustice and violence of individuals, and lose their efficacy in proportion to the number combined together; that is, in proportion as their efficacy becomes needful.

From this view of the subject, it may be concluded, that a pure Democracy, by which I mean, a Society, consisting of a small number of citizens, who assemble and administer the Government in person, can admit of no cure for the mischiefs of faction. A common passion or interest will, in almost every case, be felt by a majority of the whole; a communication and concert results from the form of Government itself; and there is nothing to check the inducements to sacrifice the weaker party, or an obnoxious individual. Hence it is, that such Democracies have ever been spectacles of turbulence and contention; have ever been found incompatible with personal security, or the rights of property; and have in general been as short in their lives, as they have been violent in their deaths. Theoretic politicians, who have patronized this species of Government, have erroneously supposed, that by reducing mankind to a perfect equality in their political rights, they would, at the same time, be perfectly equalized and assimilated in their possessions, their opinions, and their passions.

A Republic, by which I mean a Government in which the scheme of representation takes place, opens a different prospect, and promises the cure for which we are seeking. Let us examine the points in which it varies from pure Democracy, and we shall comprehend both the nature of the cure, and the efficacy which it must derive from the Union.

The two great points of difference between a Democracy and a Republic are, first, the delegation of the Government, in the latter, to a small number of citizens elected by the rest: secondly, the greater number of citizens, and greater sphere of country, over which the latter may be extended.

The effect of the first difference is, on the one hand to refine and enlarge the public views, by passing them through the medium of a chosen body of citizens, whose wisdom may best discern the true interest of their country, and whose patriotism and love of justice, will be least likely to sacrifice it to temporary or partial considerations. Under such a regulation, it may well happen that the public voice pronounced by the representatives of the people, will be more consonant to the public good, than if pronounced by the people themselves convened for the purpose. On the other hand, the effect may be inverted. Men of factious tempers, of local prejudices, or of sinister designs, may by intrigue, by corruption or by other means, first obtain the suffrages, and then betray the interests of the people. The question resulting is, whether small or extensive Republics are most favorable to the election of proper guardians of the public weal; and it is clearly decided in favor of the latter by two obvious considerations.

In the first place it is to be remarked that however small the Republic may be, the Representatives must be raised to a certain number, in order to guard against the cabals of a few; and that however large it may be, they must be limited to a certain number, in order to guard against the confusion of a multitude. Hence the number of Representatives in the two cases, not being in proportion to that of the Constituents, and being proportionally greatest in the small Republic, it follows, that if the proportion of fit characters, be not less, in the large than in the small Republic, the former will present a greater option, and consequently a greater probability of a fit choice.

In the next place, as each Representative will be chosen by a greater number of citizens in the large than in the small Republic, it will be more difficult for unworthy candidates to practise with success the vicious arts, by which elections are too often carried; and the suffrages of the people being more free, will be more likely to centre on men who possess the most attractive merit, and the most diffusive and established characters.

It must be confessed, that in this, as in most other cases, there is a mean, on both sides of which inconveniences will be found to lie. By enlarging too much the number of electors, you render the representative too little acquainted with all their local circumstances and lesser interests; as by reducing it too much, you render him unduly attached to these, and too little fit to comprehend and pursue great and national objects. The Federal Constitution forms a happy combination in this respect; the great and aggregate interests being referred to the national, the local and particular, to the state legislatures.

The other point of difference is, the greater number of citizens and extent of territory which may be brought within the compass of Republican, than of Democratic Government; and it is this circumstance principally which renders factious combinations less to be dreaded in the former, than in the latter. The smaller the society, the fewer probably will be the distinct parties and interests composing it; the fewer the distinct parties and interests, the more frequently will a majority be found of the same party; and the smaller the number of individuals composing a majority, and the smaller the compass within which they are placed, the more easily will they concert and execute their plans of oppression. Extend the sphere, and you take in a greater variety of parties and interests; you make it less probable that a majority of the whole will have a common motive to invade the rights of other citizens; or if such a common motive exists, it will be more difficult for all who feel it to discover their own strength, and to act in unison with each other. Besides other impediments, it may be remarked, that where there is a consciousness of unjust or dishonorable purposes, communication is always checked by distrust, in proportion to the number whose concurrence is necessary.

Hence it clearly appears, that the same advantage, which a Republic has over a Democracy, in controlling the effects of faction, is enjoyed by a large over a small Republic—is enjoyed by the Union over the States composing it. Does this advantage consist in the substitution of Representatives, whose enlightened views and virtuous sentiments render them superior to local prejudices, and to schemes of injustice? It will not be denied, that the Representation of the Union will be most likely to possess these requisite endowments. Does it consist in the greater security afforded by a greater variety of parties, against the event of any one party being able to outnumber and oppress the rest? In an equal degree does the increased variety of parties, comprised within the Union, encrease this security. Does it, in fine, consist in the greater obstacles opposed to the concert and accomplishment of the secret wishes of an unjust and interested majority? Here, again, the extent of the Union gives it the most palpable advantage.

The influence of factious leaders may kindle a flame within their particular States, but will be unable to spread a general conflagration through the other States: a religious sect, may degenerate into a political faction in a part of the Confederacy; but the variety of sects dispersed over the entire face of it, must secure the national Councils against any danger from that source: a rage for paper money, for an abolition of debts, for an equal division of property, or for any other improper or wicked project, will be less apt to pervade the whole body of the Union, than a particular member of it; in the same proportion as such a malady is more likely to taint a particular county or district, than an entire State.

In the extent and proper structure of the Union, therefore, we behold a Republican remedy for the diseases most incident to Republican Government. And according to the degree of pleasure and pride, we feel in being Republicans, ought to be our zeal in cherishing the spirit, and supporting the character of Federalists. ☙

QUESTIONS FOR THOUGHT AND STUDY

1. What is Madison's thesis?
2. Who are Madison's opponents and what do they believe?
3. What are "factions"? Are they the same as "interest groups"? How do they compare to Allport's groups? Make a list of the qualities that divide people, according to Madison, and give a contemporary example of each. What is the problem with factions, according to Madison?
4. Identify the factions within some large group you are familiar with (church, school, town, etc.). Do they behave as Madison describes?

5. Do you agree that the republican, or representative, form of democracy best controls the effects of factions, or does it give a few elected officials (an "elite") too much power? To answer consider the student government of your high school, the governing board of your church, fraternity/sorority, or other organization.

6. Have our representative governments (of city, state, or nation) successfully controlled the bad effects of factions? Do "ordinary citizens" have sufficient voice in government today? Give cases.

Apathy in Political Theory and Political Behavior

Stephen Earl Bennett

Biography: Stephen E. Bennett, Professor of Political Science at the University of Cincinnati, received his Ph.D. at the University of Illinois; his fields of interest cover methodology, American government, political psychology, political behavior, and public opinion. He began his career studying mass belief systems then shifted, in the 1950s and 1960s, to the question of why some people pay more attention to public affairs and some less.

A study of political apathy in the United States, the chapters review both historical and quantitative research. Chapter 2 reviews theories of apathy and the problem in defining the term. It discusses the many different attitudes included in the word. Chapter 3 reports on current quantitative study and is a useful historical and quantitative base for discussing Americans' sense of inclusion, power, and obligation to the state. The reading illustrates theoretical debate, focusing both on the definition of terms, previous research in the field, and quantitative study; it provides an excellent example of a dialogue among researchers as well as of quantitative research reporting.

PREFACE

I wonder how many authors should admit that, "this is not the book I set out to write." Certainly such is the case here. When, a few years ago, after almost a decade of laboring in the increasingly muddied fields of mass belief systems research, I decided to take up the study of another facet of American political behavior, I initially wanted to do a more general analysis of changes in ordinary citizens' basic political orientations since the halcyon days of the late 1950s and early 1960s.

From Preface, Ch. 2. *Apathy in America, 1960–1984: Causes and Consequences of Citizen Political Indifference*, Dobbs Ferry, NY: Transnational Publishers, 1986.

Two factors dissuaded me from that effort. The first was the appearance of several studies with a similar thrust: Paul Abramson's *Political Attitudes in America* (1983), David Hill and Norman Luttbeg's *Trends in American Electoral Behavior* (1983), and especially Seymour Martin Lipset and William Schneider's *The Confidence Gap* (1983). Not only did these books plow some of the same ground I had wanted to till, they had probably borne a richer harvest than the work I had in mind.

The second factor was more personal. At about the same time I was doing background work for the original work, a young lady who was in her late teens uttered two wonderful lines. First, she admitted she had no idea of what Skylab was. It was about to fall out of the sky. Later, she asked: "Who's Ted Kennedy, anyway?" At the time the senior senator from Massachusetts was a possible contender for his party's nomination to the highest elective office in the land.

The young lady in question was then a very bright, outgoing college undergraduate who was doing well in her classes. (She has since graduated and gone on to a professional career.) Her remarks started me to thinking about why some people pay more, and some less, and a few, none at all, attention to government and public affairs. From that beginning, the present effort has evolved. I wonder if she remembers how she indirectly caused me finally to write a book.

It is said that scholarship is a lonely enterprise, and work on this book has been no exception. Nonetheless, I find that in the process I have acquired a substantial number of debts, acknowledgement of which cannot begin to repay. To the following, then, my heartfelt thanks. Roger Stuebing, of the University of Cincinnati's Institute for Policy Research. He gave much counsel on statistical analysis techniques which I have haltingly tried to follow. Professor Seymour Martin Lipset of Stanford University. He critique an article which became the basis of this work. At the time I did not accept all his suggestions, but later I came to see he was probably right. Samuel Long, editor of *Micropolitics*, who published that paper, and encouraged me to expand it. Professor Abraham H. Miller, my colleague in the Political Science Department at the University of Cincinnati. He stepped in at a critical moment with very good advice. Ms. Heike Fenton, publisher of Transnational Publishers, Inc. She encouraged me to set a deadline which, lo and behold, I beat, . . . barely. Ms. Donna Scheeler, assistant editor at Transnational, who gave encouragement.

Finally, I come to the one person without whom I literally could not have done this book: my wife, Professor Linda L. M. Bennett of Wittenberg University's Political Science Department. "She who must be obeyed!" She is at once my best friend, confidant, coauthor, and . . . well, . . . you know. Without her sometimes gentle, *sometimes not so gentle,* prodding, I could not have done it. Thanks, "Emma."

Xenia, Ohio
September 20, 1985

CHAPTER 2 APATHY IN POLITICAL THEORY AND POLITICAL BEHAVIOR

Introduction

In his rendition of Pericles' famous "funeral oration," Thucydides (1972: 147) has the Athenian statesman say this about grassroots psychological involvement in the politics of his city:

> Here each individual is interested not only in his own affairs but in the affairs of the state as well: even those who are mostly occupied with their own business are extremely well-informed on general politics—this is a peculiarity of ours: we do not say that a man who takes no interest in politics is a man who minds his own business; we say that he has no business here at all.

It is a nice historical question whether Pericles' description of the highly involved Athenians was accurate or merely a fifth-century B.C. example of "Fourth of July" hyperbole. While historians have long debated the issue, the conclusion of W. G. Forrest (1969: 143) seems balanced and fair: "The Athenians were probably more alive politically than any people has been since but it would still be strange if the normal pattern of political interest did not roughly repeat itself there." As M. I Finley recently noted (1983: 72–73), if the objections against participation by ordinary citizens raised by contemporary aristocrats have any "evidentiary value," they argue in favor of widespread popular involvement.

In any event, Pericles' point about widespread grassroots political interest has been a central theme of popular government over the centuries. Many philosophers have staked the future of democratic politics upon the responsibility and the capability of the typical citizen to maintain an active interest in the public affairs. Three decades ago, Bernard Berelson (1952) catalogued the "requirements" he claimed traditional philosophers had made of ordinary citizens in democracies (see also Berelson, Lazarsfeld, and McPhee, 1954: chap. 14). One of these Berelson (1952: 316) called *"the factor of interest and participation"*:

> Political democracy requires a fairly strong and fairly continuous level of interest from a minority, and from a larger body of the citizenry a moderate-to-mild and discontinuous interest but with stable readiness to respond in critical political situations. Political distinterest or apathy is not permitted, or at least not approved.

An illustration of the requirement is found near the beginning of Rousseau's *The Social Contract* (1968: 49): "Born as I was the citizen of a free state and a member of its sovereign body, the very right to vote imposes on me the duty to instruct myself in public affairs, however little influence my voice may have in them." Of course, Rousseau was one of the most radical theorists of the eighteenth century, and has been called "the theorist *par excellence* of [political] participation . . ." (Pateman, 1970: 22; see also Miller, 1985; Shklar, 1985). It is not surprising, therefore, that someone with his orientation would expect widespread citizen attention to the public affairs.

It is startling, however, to discover that the conservative British statesman, Edmund Burke (1959: 119), could write to his Bristol constituents that, "In a free country every man thinks he has a concern in all public matters; that he has a right to form and a right to deliver an opinion upon them. They sift, examine, and discuss them. They are curious, eager, attentive, and jealous. . . ."

Indeed, most proponents of democratic government assumed that an essential ingredient to its successful operation was a vigorous and watchful citizenry. In his seminal work on *Modern Democracies* (1921, 1: 47–49), Viscount James Bryce opens his description of "an Ideal Democracy" thusly: "In it the average citizen will give close and constant attention to public affairs, recognizing that this is his interest as well as his duty."

Of the multitude of reasons given for paying attention to politics, two stand out. First, it is a matter of civic duty, of fulfilling one's "public spiritedness" (Bryce, 1913: 2). Also, by following politics one could become a better informed, wiser, and possibly a more rational citizen participant. Therefore, one could better protect one's self-interests, which has been the second main justification for attending to the political process. Those who did not keep a weather eye on politics ran the risk of being victimized by political elites. As Thomas Jefferson warned in 1787, "If once . . . [the people] become inattentive to the public affairs, you, I, and Congress, and the Assemblies, judges and governors, shall all become wolves" (1977: 415).

Of course, it is one thing to hold up the ideal of the attentive, involved citizen. Practice is often quite another matter. How well have ordinary Americans lived up to the expectation by democratic theorists that they will pay heed to what goes on in politics and government?

Citizen Political Interest in the American Past

Immediately the topic of past grassroots political behavior is raised we confront one fundamental problem: absence of hard information upon which to base judgments about the relative incidence of a political disposition among ordinary people in the American past (Benson, 1967–1968; Kann, 1968). The problem is complicated when the focus is on a widespread cultural desideratum, such as the expectation of citizen political interest, where there is a tendency, in the absence of hard evidence to the contrary, to assume the equivalence of hope and habit.

The most obvious source of the problem is the unavailability prior to the late 1930s of nationwide scientific public opinion polls. Until a historical survey reaches that late date, then, all that one can use is impressionistic evidence picked up from a variety of sources: comments by political practitioners and politicians that have come down to the present in one form or another, observations by a succession of (mostly) foreign travellers who have written about the American scene, documents (mostly letters) produced by ordinary citizens, and the reconstruction of the past by contemporary American historians. Admittedly, none of these is entirely satisfactory, and even when—as in the 1830s with de Tocqueville, the 1880s with Bryce, or the 1920s with the Lynds—one is given a tantalizing tidbit of evidence to consider, it must be recognized how partial and inadequate such is. Still, even in the face of the very great odds against the enterprise, a brief historical survey of grassroots political interest is warranted in order to set contemporary data in proper chronological relief.

Someone who has studied the electoral process and voting behavior in early American history is Robert J. Dinkin. He has written two monographs (1977, 1982) on voting during the colonial period and during the revolution and confederal era. If Dinkin is correct, the expectation that the colonist had a duty to keep abreast of politics and government was a part of the American political culture even before the breach with the mother country (1977: 188). However, Dinkin also presents evidence that there must have been many who were inattentive, for there were "[m]any writers" who commented on "the 'criminal indifference' to who was elected, and the profound feeling of general apathy toward the electoral process." Nor were apathetic colonists necessarily apologetic. As Dinkin notes, "it was not uncommon" to hear, as a justification for political indifference, expressions such as: "'What can one man do against a Torrent? It is not our Business, let those who are upon the Watch look out.'" Dinkin wryly notes that such sentiments are hauntingly familiar in our own time.

Given the conditions of colonial society and politics—the primitive means of transportation and communication, fairly severe limitations on the franchise, and the control of politics in many of the colonies by a relatively narrow elite—it is perhaps not surprising to find significant numbers of the people indifferent to the public affairs. However, one would certainly expect greater citizen political involvement during the revolutionary war and in the first decade or so of national independence. In all likelihood, such was the case. Yet there also must have been many who still remained indifferent to politics, for Dinkin (1982: 137) writes there were "[s]everal contemporaries [who] complained of voter apathy and of the people's 'fatal omission of their duty.'" Lack of political interest during the revolution and immediate post-war period also must have contributed to substantial political ignorance among the electorate, for it was alleged that many people cast ballots innocent of anything save "'who was in last. . . .'"

As noted above, in eighteenth century America, the belief was widely held that the citizen had a duty to maintain an interest in government and politics. That duty, evidently, was not only to protect one's self-interest, but also to posterity. In an oft-quoted letter to his wife Abigail, written in 1780, John Adams declared that,

> I must study politics and war that my sons may have liberty to study mathematics and philosophy. My sons ought to study mathematics and philosophy, geography, natural history, naval architecture, navigation, commerce, and agriculture, in order to give their children a right to study painting, poetry, music, architecture, statuary, tapestry, and porcelain.

In short, the purpose of the revolutionary generation's attention to public affairs was less because of some intrinsic value thereto, than because, if successful, the fruits of their concern would leave their offspring free to attend to more personally rewarding subjects.

Once the revolution was fought, the problems associated with the Articles of Confederation withstood, and the new Constitution in place,[1] what became of citizen political interest in the first decades of the American Republic? If political scientist James Young's study of *The Washington Community* during the first three decades of the nineteenth century (1966) is any indication, the public was characterized more by apathy than interest, at least where national affairs were concerned. Young points out that the attempt to launch the new capital city—begun during the administration of George Washington in the early 1790s—nearly foundered on a sea of citizen apathy (1966: 17–23). As Young notes, to some degree the problems encountered in securing widespread popular backing in creation of the new seat for the national government were due to the location of the city in a pestilential swamp and to poor communication facilities and inept management of the enterprise (1966: 26–27). But there was a more fundamental reason: public indifference to the national government itself.

Why was that? According to Young, the primary source of widespread citizen indifference to national politics during the Jeffersonian era and thereafter was the limited role of the federal government in American politics. Government was simply too limited an affair to be of much significance to ordinary people's personal lives. As Young puts it (1966: 30–32):

> What government business there was was not, most of it, of a sort to attract any widespread, sustained citizen interest. . . . Almost all of the things that republican governments do which affect the everyday lives and fortunes of their citizens, and

---

[1]Certainly it would be reasonable to have expected an unusually high grassroots involvement during the war itself, while the Constitution was being framed at Philadelphia during that hot, muggy summer of 1787, and during the period when its ratification was under debate.

therefore engage their interest, were in Jeffersonian times *not* done by the national government. . . . An institution whose involvement in the internal life of the nation was limited largely to the collection and delivery of letters could hardly have expected to be much in the citizens' consciousness. . . .

This widespread citizen apathy toward the national government also must have influenced the tenor and tempo of politics during the first three decades of the nineteenth century. According to Young (1966: 34). "The comparatively low 'temperature' of national politics and its relative decorum before the Jacksonian era may have testified not so much to the skill of a ruling Republican oligarchy as to a generalized or residual indifference among citizens toward national government itself."

Perhaps. But if Alexis de Tocqueville's comments on the importance of attention to public affairs among the Americans during the early 1830s are correct, things changed, and quickly, with "Old Hickory" in the White House. Based on his travels about the country during the Jacksonian Era, the young French aristocrat concluded that (1966: 243),

> It is hard to explain the place filled by the political concerns in the life of an American. To take a hand in the government of society and to talk about it is his most important business and, so to say, the only pleasure he knows. That is obvious even in the most trivial habits of his life; even the women often go to public meetings and forget household cares while they listen to political speeches.

Moreover, "if an American should be reduced to occupying himself with his own affairs, at that moment half his existence would be snatched from him; he would feel it as a vast void in his life and would become incredibly unhappy." If Tocqueville's characterization of the intense politicization of the people during the 1830s is correct, Pericles would have felt right at home in Andy Jackson's America.

It is not hard to account for the intense interest shown by ordinary people in the politics of the time. While the election of Andrew Jackson in 1828 did not immediately herald "the rise of the common man," it did "provide the ordinary citizen—who had been 'rising' for decades—with an elaborate party machine through which he could more effectively control the operation of government and shape public policy" (Remini, 1963: 203). The successes of Jackson's party—"the Democracy"—were brought about by a new type of politician who created a "new style" of electioneering, one which engaged the emotions of the ordinary people much more fervently than hitherto (Hofstadter, 1970: chap. 6). According to Richard McCormick (1973: 350),

> Politics in this era took on a dramatic function. It enabled voters throughout the nation to experience the thrill of participating in what amounted to a great demo-

cratic festival that seemed to perceptive foreign observers to be remarkably akin to the religious festivals of Catholic Europe.

McCormick also makes another important point. Since there were so few alternative forms of popular entertainment, people viewed the political process as a dramatic spectacle. Small wonder, then, that Tocqueville and other European travellers found such high levels of political interest in the 1830s (see, *e.g.,* Grund, 1959).

The extensive grassroots interest and participation in elections and politics generally that had begun with the election of 1828 continued throughout the next three decades. Certainly turnout in national elections surged ahead, although at an uneven pace, throughout the 1830s and 1840s (Chambers and Davis, 1978). Nor was the intense politicization of the citizenry simply confined to election time. According to Chambers and Davis (1978: 196), "Once voters were politically socialized to a pattern of political involvement, at least at the polls, they were likely to continue their concern for and excitement over political issues, parties, and campaigns."

Between 1848 and 1861, a series of political events, issues, and personalities marched across the American scene, all joined by the growing sectional crisis which would eventually produce what one historian dubbed *The Disruption of American Democracy* (Nichols, 1967; see also Potter, 1976). While historians have long debated the "causes" of the civil war, for present purposes Nichols focuses on the "hyperemotionalism" of the people by 1860 (1967: chap. 27). Not only did the people of that era fail to comprehend the cultural differences underlying sectional rivalries (Nichols, 1967: 503–504),

> This lack of understanding was accompanied by a deep-seated enjoyment of political activity by Americans which proved dangerous. They gave themselves so many opportunities to gratify their desire for this sport. There were so many elections and such constant agitation. . . . A great disruptive fact was the baneful influence of elections almost continuously in progress, of campaigns never over, and of political uproar endlessly arousing emotions.

The endless campaigning, fought out by virtually independent party organizations in each of the states, gave demagogues of every political stripe in all regions multiple opportunities to whip public interest into such an emotional fervor that compromise became impossible, and the Union was torn asunder (Nichols, 1967: 504–507).

Nichols' contention that an excess of public spirit and popular involvement in public affairs played a determinative role on the onset of civil war may be correct. However, according to Converse (1964: 251), letters written by ordinary Ohioans during the 1850s and 1860s reveal a growing awareness of and interest in the crisis on the eve of secession and war, but "later than is customarily assumed."

Whatever its causes, the sectional crisis of the 1850s and the Civil War ushered in a new era of grassroots political participation that was characterized by exceptionally high rates of turnout (Burnham, 1965; Kleppner, 1979, 1982b). While there is general agreement that voting in national elections was quite high (however, see Shortridge, 1981b), scholars are at loggerheads over the factors responsible. According to some, "The second half of the nineteenth century was an era of strong partisanship, high levels of political enthusiasm and involvement, and a more fully mobilized electorate than this country had ever before, or ever since, witnessed" (Kleppner, 1982b: 28; see also Burnham, 1965: 22). Other researchers demur, contending that a variety of technical factors associated with electoral administration in the thirty years after 1865 accounted for what only seem to be atypically high levels of voter participation (Rusk, 1970; Converse, 1972). Given the low levels of formal schooling and large portions of the electorate living in rural isolation, these scholars argue it is highly unlikely that the late nineteenth-century electorate was especially politically aware of interested (Converse, 1972: 271–276). Converse also warns that evidence from contemporary third-world countries reveals "how risky it is to draw simple equations between turnout levels and public involvement or alienation from the affairs of state" (1972: 287).

Not surprisingly, the question of how politically engaged and sophisticated the late nineteenth century electorate was has generated a lively intellectual debate (in addition to the citations above, see Burnham, 1971, 1974; Converse, 1974; Rusk, 1971, 1974; Kleppner and Baker, 1980; Shortridge, 1980, 1981a; Claggett, 1981). For the most part, this scholarly controversy is beyond the present volume's scope.

Suffice it to say that both quantitative and qualitative historical evidence support the proposition that, between 1865 and 1896, Americans maintained a fairly high level of interest in public affairs. First, as Kleppner has shown (1970, 1979, 1982b), the type of partisan divisions of the era which, especially in the northeast and upper midwest, were rooted in ethnoreligious identifications, produced a "quasi-confessionalism" in virtually all strata of society (see also, Jensen, 1971). Partly because they were closely linked with such basic social identifications as ethnoreligious group membership, the partisan struggles of the period were especially intense (Kleppner, 1982b: 46). Consequently, as Kleppner notes (1982b: 47),

> In that earlier society, politics occupied a greater share of the individual's life-space [than today]. Political matters were not complex, intangible, and remote, but simple, concrete, and directly related to the concerns of daily life. Because ethnoreligious and political communications reinforced each other, it placed no severe cognitive burden on most citizens to perceive the relationship.

In short, not only was the citizen of the late nineteenth century under a fairly strong goad to follow what was happening in political life, the psychological "costs" associated with political involvement were less than today.

Jensen (1971: 2–4) points to another factor behind the relatively greater citizen political involvement of the late nineteenth century: "Perhaps people who lacked electronic amusement and commercialized sports sought entertainment from the political arena." As he notes, there was a sufficiency of "spellbinders, oddballs, cranks, and demagogues" to more than meet the demand. Partly because they wanted entertainment, partly because political attachments were imbued with an intensity akin to religious affiliation (Jensen, 1971: 3), people not only voted at higher rates, but also were much more likely to take part in more demanding activities than is true today.

> The electorate followed political developments, recognized politicians, and understood the issues. They sat through hours of speeches without a break, not only to display their support of favorite candidates but also to soak up the details and the minute points of the tariff, the money question, educational policies, prohibition laws, and the myriad of minor issues that erupted from time to time.

Not only did they read "a good many pamphlets," the people also avidly consumed the strongly partisan newspapers of the time (Jensen, 1971: 4–6). While Jensen's account deals with the Midwest, it is unlikely that things were much different in other regions.

Even though it appears that political interest and concern were fairly high during the last third of the nineteenth century, there were observers who worried about signs of public apathy. One such was James Bryce (1891, II: chap. 84), who wrote of what he called "the fatalism of the multitude." By this he meant the tendency for even well-educated Americans to believe that the majority must be right and ought to prevail, and therefore "to acquiesce in the dominant opinion, to submit thought as well as action to the encompassing power of numbers" (1891, II: 331). While it is difficult to know how prevalent this tendency was in the 1880s, Bryce believed that, "there are in the United States signs of such a fatalistic temper" (1891, II: 333), and that it was rooted in certain cultural beliefs and practices: among them were "the unbounded freedom of discussion" and "the intense faith which the Americans have in the soundness of their institutions, and in the future of their country." Both work to "dispose . . . a man to acquiescence and submission" (II: 334).

Although it is likely that Bryce's concerns about political fatalism were in a minority among observers of the American scene in the 1880s, within a couple of decades or so many had become worried about apathy. Several factors account for this. First, beginning in 1896, turnout in national elections began to decline. This turn-down in turnout would continue unabated throughout the 1920s (Kleppner, 1982b). While some have blamed the admission of women into the electorate in 1920 for most of the turnout decline, Kleppner (1982a) has shown that it began much earlier and affected men's voting participation as well.

There is a good deal of controversy about why voting fell after 1896. Some, such as Burnham (1965, 1971, 1974) believe that the causes are primarily the result of the domination of the post-1896 party system by politico-economic elites determined to insulate themselves from the vagaries of a completely democratic electoral process. As Burnham puts it (1965: 26), "Confronted with a narrowed scope of effective democratic options, an increasingly large proportion of the eligible adult population either left, failed to enter or—as was the case with Southern Negroes after the completion of the 1890–1904 disenfranchisement movement in the old Confederacy—was systematically excluded from the American voting universe." Other scholars point to changes in the administration of the electoral process, most notably the institution of voter registration and residency requirements—in order to clean up fraudulent voting practices in urban areas—as the primary factors in the decline of voting (Converse, 1972, 1974; Rusk, 1974). Still other researchers believe that the partisan realignment after 1896, which replaced a generally competitive party system rooted in ethnoreligious group memberships with a largely uncompetitive system based primarily on regional cleavages (Kleppner, 1982b; see also Burnham, 1981). The resulting "politics as usual" could not attract the interests nor integrate large segments of the population, particularly younger persons, into the active citizenry (Kleppner and Baker, 1980; Kleppner, 1982b).

Had the decline in voting been the only factor of grassroots political behavior between 1896 and 1930, it would be difficult to characterize the period as one of growing citizen indifference to politics. However, there are other indications of widespread disengagement from public affairs by ordinary Americans. Fortunately, some have been documented by classics in social science research. Two are particularly relevant to present purposes: Merriam and Gosnell's *Non-Voting* (1924) and the Lynds' *Middletown* (1929).

The former deals with abstention from Chicago's mayorality election of 1923, and is based on in-person interviews with 6,000 nonvoters in that contest. As such, the monograph was based on the first sample survey recorded in the annals of American political science (Bennett and Bennett, 1986). While several factors accounted for the decision not to vote, the most important one was what Merriam and Gosnell (1924: 159) call "general [political] indifference." Depending upon how it is conceived, somewhere between one-quarter and two-fifths of the nonvoters did not take part in selection of the city's mayor because they were politically apathetic (Merriam and Gosnell, 1924: 158). While most prevalent among older women of foreign stock, no section of Chicago's society was completely free of political indifference at the time (Merriam and Gosnell, 1924: chap. 7).

The final chapter of the book deals with "methods for controlling non-voting." Although they had some ideas for dealing with the problem (1924: 235–238), Merriam and Gosnell admit that (235), "It is in the area designated as 'general indifference,' 'inertia,' or 'disbelief' [in women's suffrage] that the most serious difficulties are encountered in the effort to obtain a 100 per cent vote."

Another classic social science work that permits some insights into political apathy during the 1920s is Robert and Helen Lynd's analysis of "Middletown" (actually, Muncie, Indiana). In their chapter on the "machinery of government" (24), the Lynds distinguish the prevailing apathy toward politics and elections of the 1920s from the much greater citizen politicization of the 1880s and 1890s. Not only were "Middletowners" less likely to vote in local and national elections than had the previous generation, they were also less prone to be politically engaged in other ways. For example, they were less likely to go hear political stump speeches, and less likely even to care who won. Moreover, local newspapers devoted much less space to coverage of the electoral process.

The Lynds attribute the greater apathy of contemporary (*i.e.,* 1920s) residents to two factors: (1) "new inventions [especially radio] offering a variety of alternative interests are pressing upon politics as upon lodges, unions, and churches;" and (2) "in the minds of many citizens, politics is identified with fraud" (1929: 416, 420). There were two main consequences of citizen indifference: (1) fewer of the "best citizens" sought public office (1929: 421), and (2) ordinary citizens, unless their personal interests were directly engaged, did not concern themselves with what happens in politics but felt much more critical of anything that happened (422–424). Finally, as apathy more and more pervaded "Middletown," politics and government was increasingly left to the influence of what a later generation of political observers would call "special interests" (Lynd and Lynd, 1929: 425–427).

Granted, both the monograph by Merriam and Gosnell and the Lynds' book dealt with local affairs. However, there was also ample commentary during the 1920s on a pervasive public indifference to national politics as well (see, *e.g.,* Monroe, 1928; Wilson, 1930). A particularly interesting example was Walter Lippmann's essay on "The Causes of Political Indifference To-day" (1927). According to Lippmann, there were three primary factors behind the political apathy of the 1920s. First, unlike the case when Theodore Roosevelt or Woodrow Wilson were on the scene, "There are no parties, there are no leaders, there are no issues" (1927: 18). Second, there had been a deliberate effort by President Calvin Coolidge to dampen down "popular interest in popular government," mainly in order not "to distract business" (1927: 21). The third reason is more basic: so ample were opportunities to make money during the 1920s that "it was a waste of time to think about politics" (1927: 23). Given both the economic boom of the decade and the more enlightened policies of corporate leadership, the major causes for "political agitation" had been removed. With economic conflict, which is always the prime mover in politics, alleviated by prosperity, the issues that remained—prohibition, nativism, xenophobia, and fundamentalism—were orthogonal to the traditional issues that had historically divided the major political parties. Since both the Republicans and Democrats were internally divided over the "new" issues, they had become essentially irrelevant to large segments of the public, and the result was political indifference. Worse, there was no leadership prepared to bring either party to grips with the current "realities of American life" (1927: 34).

While Lippmann's conclusions were basically pessimistic, the one major factor he did not reckon with was a quick return of economic conflict as a primary source of political discord, and interest. Within a few years of the appearance of his essay, such and more had happened. The onset of the Great Depression, the emergence of a new generation of political leaders attuned to contemporary issues, and the rise of Nazism, Fascism, Communism, and Japanese expanionism had, by the end of the 1930s, combined to effect a resurgence of citizen political interest and electoral participation (Kleppner, 1982b: chap. 5). However, at least in terms of citizen turnout, the 1930s saw only an incomplete remobilization of the electorate.

Fortunately, the 1930s also witnessed the emergence of both nationwide scientific surveys of public opinion. Unhappily, another decade would pass before there was serious concern by quantitatively oriented social scientists in the problem of political apathy. It is to those early attempts by scholars to deal with citizen indifference that we now turn.

Political Apathy and Social Scientists

With the advent of nationwide public opinion polling in the 1930s, political scientists had for the first time the chance to plumb systematically how interested people were in public affairs, and to determine which segments of the population were politically engaged and which were apathetic. It is surprising, therefore, that students of American politics were relatively slow to take advantage of the opportunity. In large measure, of course, this was because the dominant research paradigms in the discipline at the time eschewed quantitative studies (Somit and Tanenhaus, 1967: chap. 9). Other than the famed "Chicago school," of which *Non-Voting* was a prime example, most political scientists' work was little different from that of historians, philosophers, and legal scholars. As a result, most of the early work on apathy was done by either sociology or social psychology scholars.

Many of the early social scientists who studied the phenomenon tended to equate apathy with nonvoting (Connelly with Field, 1944; Knupfer, 1947; see Chapter 3). One important exception was the study of grassroots voting behavior during the 1940 election by Lazarsfeld, Berelson, and Gaudet (1968: chap. 5). At that, however, the approach taken by the authors of *The People's Choice* toward conceptualization and measurement of their respondents' interest was narrowly focused; they plumbed only interest in the election campaign (1968: 40–41). Nonetheless, self-reported campaign interest gave Lazarsfeld and his colleagues very useful purchase on other forms of political involvement and participation. People who were highly interested were more likely to have opinions on a wider range of issues, were more likely to expose themselves to communications about the Roosevelt-Wilkie campaign, and were more likely to take part in campaign activities (1968: 41–42). In their efforts to pin down who was more likely to be politically interested Lazarsfeld, Berelson, and Gaudet (1968: 45) discovered that, "the person most interested in the election is more to be found in urban areas among men on higher levels of education, with better socio-economic status, and among older age groups." As will be seen in Chapter 4, their finding is, with few alterations, still relevant today.

While Lazarsfield and his associates conceptualized political interest in fairly simplistic terms, social scientists gradually came to view apathy as "a fairly complex psychological orientation" (Riesman and Glazer, 1950: 531). Reisman and Glazer conceive of apathy as a product of two distinct but closely related dimensions: "affect" and "competence" (1950: 536–547). "Affect" refers to the individual's investment of genuine but "appropriate" feelings of involvement and concern with the political arena. The adjective "appropriate" serves to warn against including the excessive feelings of those with psychopathological orientations "who look for opportunities of releasing indignation onto politics" (1950: 539). "Competence" means the mastery of political terminology and skills that are suitable to the individual's station in life.

By combining the components of affect and competence, Riesman and Glazer claim to be able to identify three different variants of apathetic orientations toward politics in the twentieth century[2] (1950: 537): (1) the "indifferents," who are low on both dimensions; (2) the "indignants," who are high in affect but low in competence; and (3) the "inside-dopesters," who are affectless but high in competence (see also Reisman, with Glazer and Denney, 1961: 180–187). Unfortunately, despite the theoretically rich discussion they provide, Riesman and Glazer are forced to concede that their efforts to provide empirical indicators of key concepts were not particularly successful (1950: 544–547).

More recently, as political scientists have focused on apathy, one approach has been to concentrate on the links between political indifference and alienation. For example, Gilmour and Lamb (1975: 111) create a typology of the

---

[2]Riesman and Glazer believe that, although absolute levels of apathy did not change much from the nineteenth to the twentieth centuries, the bases and manifestations in each were considerably different (1950: 506–530).

different ways people can respond to American politics by superimposing an indicator of "extreme political alienation" upon an indicant of apathy. Despite some technical questions about the underlying measures (see 1975: 160–165), Gilmour and Lamb's scheme has the advantage of having been constructed from at least reasonably direct empirical measurements of key concepts.[3]

Gilmour and Lamb differentiate four separate variants of apathetic orientations to American politics in 1972. The largest bloc of apathetics is labelled the "Indifferents;" this grouping made up 46 percent of all apathetics. These were people who, because they were disillusioned with contemporary American politics, did not participate. The second largest group of apathetics—39 percent of the total—were the "Withdrawn." These were persons who were extremely "alienated" from politics, and did not take part in what they believed was a hopelessly spoiled political system. Making up 11 percent of all apathetics, the "Disgruntled" were people who were either severely disillusioned or even outright "alienated" from American politics. In some ways, this variant of apathy is the most interesting of all, for, although politically indifferent, they tended to engage in political participation, usually to spew their bile. When given the chance these people vote, usually against incumbents. They are the "agin," or "crank" voters. (This points to a fact worth remembering: some persons low in interest may still vote, either out of a sense of duty or, more likely, to "get even.") Finally, there was a small group of apathetics that Gilmour and Lamb call the "Contenteds." Making up only four percent of all apathetics, they were both disinterested and inactive because they were basically satisfied with things as they were. (This grouping reminds one of Arthur Hadley's [1978: 68] "positive apathetics," who did not vote in the 1976 election "because at present their lives are too full for the act of voting to seem important.")

Gilmour and Lamb's approach to the analysis of apathy can be criticized on conceptual grounds (see Chapter 3). However, it is important because it points indirectly to some of the factors social scientists have alleged to be responsible for political indifference. One of the more interesting efforts to identify the major factors that influence apathy is by Morris Rosenberg (1954–1955). Based on an admittedly non-random sample of 70 individuals in the early 1950s, he identifies three main factors that contribute to political indifference and inactivity. Some people are apathetic because they view political involvement as threatening. Politics, after all, often involves conflict, and many view such as potentially detrimental to business interests, friendships, and even, on occasion, family relationships. Other individuals fear that political involvement could result in serious blows to already fragile egos. (In this connection,

---

[3]Gilmour and Lamb utilize the Center for Political Studies' 1972 national election study as their database.

one is reminded of Abraham Lincoln's famous dictum that it is better to remain quiet and be thought a fool than to speak out, thereby removing any possible doubts about it.)

Another factor responsible for apathy is the perception that political activity is ultimately futile. Man may not be a completely rational political actor, but people do like to think there would be at least the possibility of a successful payoff to their involvement. When the likely results of engagement are seen as dismal at best, it is small wonder that people lose interest. According to Rosenberg, the belief that political activity would be futile has two components. Some individuals focus on their own incompetence as political actors; politics is a complicated business, involving the actions of many far more powerful actors than a single individual. Hence, it would be foolish to expect much to happen as a result of one's measly endeavors. The second component focuses on the relative political impotence of the ordinary citizen. Many people subscribe to the traditional American belief about the domination of our political system by powerful, well-organized forces (A. Miller, 1974a; Citrin, 1974; Gilmour and Lamb, 1975; Sniderman, 1981; Abramson, 1983; Lipset and Schneider, 1983a). They are thus likely to disparage the clout of the "little man." The "system" is also seen as unresponsive to grassroots attempts at influence. Since they feel powerless, they withdraw from political attention and involvement. (It should be noted that Rosenberg's two components of the sense of political futility are similar to the two dimensions scholars have found in the Survey Research Center's concept of political efficacy [Balch, 1974; Abramson, 1938]).

Rosenberg labels the third factor "absence of spurs to action." By this he means that many people find the subject matter of government and politics to be dull and boring, that there are seldom direct, palpable satisfactions to be gained from political involvement, and that people are much more likely to be concerned with direct, immediate, and concrete personal needs. Moreover, some people are indifferent simply because they have never been asked to take a personal hand in public affairs.

Rosenberg also points out that other factors also affect one's psychological involvement in public affairs. Those who are basically satisfied with how things are going may be under no goad to pay heed to politics. Others are indifferent because they see no basic differences between the major political parties. Still others lack any firm convictions about politics. Finally, others may be subjected to social pressures against political involvement.

Rosenberg's work reminds us that a variety of factors shape the individual's usual level of political interest or indifference. However, he was unable to determine how much interest/apathy there was at the grassroots level in the early 1950s. Someone who could was Bernard Berelson (1952), and it is to his work we return.

Apathy in Theories of Democracy

According to Berelson (1954: 316), public opinion surveys of the time indicated that, "Less than one-third of the electorate is 'really interested' in politics, and that group is by no means a cross-section of the total electorate." The discovery that citizens remained basically uninterested in politics led Berelson and other scholars (Parsons, 1959; Lipset, 1981; Dahl, 1961; Almond and Verba, 1963; Milbrath, 1965) to attempt reformulations of democratic philosophy to bring theory more into line with practice. In the new version, rather than being detrimental to democracy as older notions had held (Bryce, 1913), a sizable bloc of apathetic persons became an advantage, for it provided a "cushion" for elites against the actions of highly interested, intense partisans. Apathy gave political decision-makers leeway to bargain and compromise. Berelson believed that if everyone were intensely interested, the political system ran a serious risk of political immobilism (see also Berelson, Lazarsfeld, and McPhee, 1954: chap. 14; Dahl, 1961; Almond and Verba, 1963). He concluded that democracy might be better suited if most people maintained a lukewarm interest in political life, and elites had to secure their approval or acquiescence. Later (Berelson, Lazarsfeld, and McPhee, 1954: 315), he added: "Some people are and should be highly interested in politics, but not everyone is or needs to be" (see Chapter 3).

Attempts to create an "empirical theory" of democracy elicited criticism by scholars who believed the reformulated versions had denuded traditional democratic theory of its radical thrust (Duncan and Lukes, 1963; Davis, 1964; Walker, 1966; Bachrach, 1967; Pateman, 1970; Thompson, 1970). To its critics the reconstituted version of democratic theory was more "elitist" than "democratic." According to Thompson (1970: 25), "Elitist democratic theory reinforces the potent historical forces toward centralized, bureaucratic power that make citizens feel remote from politics and that discourage citizenship."

Critics of empirical democratic theory especially rejected its notions about citizen apathy. In Jack Walker's view (1966: 289),

> The most unsatisfactory element in the theory is its concept of the passive, apolitical common man who pays allegiance to his governors and to the sideshow of politics while remaining primarily concerned with his private life, evenings of television with his family, or the demands of his job.

In the main, however, even Berelson's critics had to agree that most citizens were politically indifferent. The bones of contention centered on whether apathy dampened the fires of political cleavage and provided room for elites to maneuver in the quest for political solutions, as Berelson (1952) and Almond and Verba (1963) contended, or insulated them from grassroots political influence, as critics of the "elitist" theory of democracy believed.

Another element in the "debate" about apathy was the diversity of conceptualizations of the concept. There were many, often-conflicting, ways of defining what apathy meant. In addition, the "debate" over apathy took place in the absence of satisfactory operationalizations of the term. Because they conceived it and measured it differently, scholars very often talked "past," rather than "at," one another. Until this conceptual and operational disarray is resolved, it is unlikely that the "debate" can be resolved. Chapter 3 seeks to address each of these problems.

CHAPTER 3 THE CONCEPTUALIZATION AND MEASUREMENT OF APATHY

Introduction

This chapter has two parts. The first is a reconsideration of the concept of political apathy as it has been presented in the literature on political behavior. Previous analyses have either misconceived the concept or added several conceptual dimensions that tend to obfuscate, rather than clarify, its meaning. Some are drawn from social psychological research on attitudes and personality traits. Some come from studies of other basic political orientations such as political efficacy and cynicism. These extraneous attributes are not integral to apathy, and must be stripped from conceptual treatments of the concept.

The second part of the chapter reviews previous measurements of political interest, and develops an operational definition of the concept, based on the Survey Research Center/Center for Political Studies' data that are available for over-time research. At this point, the technical aspects of the new measure are explored.

Conceptions of Political Apathy in the Literature

Given the volume of research on political participation, it is not surprising that a number of scholars have studied interest in politics (Milbrath and Goel, 1977: 35–42, 46–49). However, a sizable portion of this work deals with interest or involvement in specific election campaigns (Lazarsfeld, Berelson, and Gaudet, 1968: 40–45; Berelson, Lazarsfeld, and McPhee, 1954: 24–28; Campbell, Gurin, and Miller, 1954: 33–35; and Campbell, Converse, Miller, and Stokes, 1960: 101–103). While the two are related, interest in a particular campaign is a narrower construct than is the notion of political apathy.

Another tendency has been for many students of political behavior to equate apathy with the absence of participation (Rosenberg, 1954–1955; Kornhauser, 1959: 46–47; Lane, 1965: 108, 116–118; DiPalma, 1970: 2; Verba and Nie, 1972: 28, 33; Milbrath and Goel, 1977: 11; and Hadley, 1978: 39–40,

68–74). This is unfortunate, as there are several good reasons for making a conceptual distinction between apathy and nonparticipation.

For one thing, people may not take part in politics for a variety of reasons, some having nothing to do with apathy. Riesman and Glazer (1950: 535) point out that it is possible to be genuinely interested in politics but to remain passive because no appropriate mode of activity is presently at hand. Also, people may be interested in politics but abstain from acts such as voting because they believe politicians to be insincere, corrupt, or even incompetent (Johnson, 1980: 122–123). Also, some persons—such as southern blacks prior to passage of the 1965 Voting Rights Act—may dearly wish to take part in politics, by voting, for example, but avoid doing so because they fear harassment, intimidation, or even outright violence (Salamon and Van Evera, 1973; but see also Kernell, 1973). Finally, a more tendentious point is made by those who regard nonparticipation, especially by the most disadvantaged segments of society, as "a justifiable reaction to a politics that is meaningless in its electoral content and disappointing in its policy results" (Parenti, 1977: 208).

On a different note, Riesman and Glazer (1950: 518–520) contend that, increasingly in this century, as the nature of politics and the relation of citizens to the political process have changed, some people have engaged in various forms of participation for what are "apolitical," possibly even "apathetic," reasons. This happens when politics is not used for its own sake, but instead to conform to group pressures, or as a form of personal reaction, or even for the displacement of individual psychopathology. According to some, projection of psychopathological tendencies has been an especially compelling motivation for engagement in politics during the twentieth century (Lasswell, 1960, 1962; Neumann, 1957: chap. 11; Hofstadter, 1965). It should be noted in passing that most of the studies in which psychopathological dispositions figure heavily as goads to political participation have focused on engagement in right-wing social protest (see, for example, Adorno, *et al.*, 1950; the essays in Bell, ed., 1963; and Lipset and Raab, 1977), although some have also looked at various forms of leftist extremism (Almond, 1954; Liebert, 1971).

For these reasons, and because apathy originally meant "without feeling," it seems more appropriate for the concept to signify a particular type of political disposition rather than a pattern of (in)action. Among those who have used apathy to mean a particular political orientation, most seem to have had in mind some notion of "indifference," or similar terms such as "disinterest," "withdrawal," "passivity," or "lack of motivation" (Bryce, 1913: 2–3; Lippman, 1927: 18–34; Reisman and Glazer, 1950: 531–547; Berelson, 1952: 316; Dean, 1960: 187; Lipset, 1981: 226; Riesman, Glazer, and Denney, 1961: 165–171; Campbell, 1962: 9; McClosky, 1968: 252; Pranger, 1968: 27–28, 51; and Gilmour and Lamb, 1975: 21, 91–111). As Gilmour and Lamb (1975: 96) put it, apathy is "simply a matter of [lack of] political interest."

However, in most previous analyses of apathy, the concept has seldom been so narrowly conceived. Rather, the term has usually been made to carry a heavy load of normative and/or empirical freight. It was typical for earlier generations of political observers to castigate the disinterested for their "failure" to abide by the norms of "good citizenship" (Bryce, 1913; Connelly, with Field, 1944). The indifferent citizen was informed, nay, lectured, about his "slackness," "indolence," or "laziness," which was believed to be harmful to democracy.

Especially during the early decades of the twentieth century, a legion of what Roelofs (1957: 3) would later call the "professional preachers of good citizenship" travelled about the country, appearing at Chataqua meetings, lecturing before learned foundations, and writing pamphlets, monographs, and textbooks, reminding the ordinary citizenry of the responsibility to maintain an active interest in the public affairs. To some degree, these sentiments were a carry over of sentiments expressed even before independence from Great Britain was achieved (Dinkin, 1977: 188; see also Dinkin, 1982: 137). It was also common among politicians of the progressive era to threaten the political indifferent with loss of their political liberties (Roosevelt, 1958: 73).

Occasionally, someone tried to justify, if not excuse, grass-roots disinterest (Lippmann, 1925: 16–39, 1927: 18–34; Dewey, 1927: 134–135). Far more common, however, was the expression of disdain, and even outright hostility toward those who, in the pursuit of private business or pleasure, neglected their civic responsibilities (see esp. Bryce, 1913).

Even though later generations of social scientists would jettison much of the hyperbole and excess normative baggage, they would continue to conceptualize apathy in multifaceted terms. One approach has been to link apathy with basic personality traits, so that discussion of the concept became almost an exegesis on political psychopathology (Knupfer, 1947; Riesman and Glazer, 1950: 536–546; Lipset, 1981: 103–104, 115–116; Campbell, 1962: 10–13). The apathetic citizen, especially if from the lower social orders, was found to suffer from enervating personality maladies (such as low self-esteem), and to manifest a variety of sociopathic attitudes (including xenophobia, racial and ethnic bigotry, and authoritarianism).

Another multifaceted approach has been to conceptualize apathy in conjunction with such basic political orientations as trust, cynicism, and alienation (Dean, 1960; Campbell, 1962; Gilmour and Lamb, 1975). A particularly interesting study is Campbell's "The Passive Citizen." Although quick to recognize that some people are apathetic simply out of detachment, he also claims that there are many whose orientation to politics is one "of suspicion, distrust, hostility, and cynicism" (1962: 14). As Campbell puts it, "It would appear that some part of political apathy is more than simple passivity. With some individuals an active rejection of political matters is involved" (1962: 14).

Another perspective on the multiple meanings that have been attached to apathy comes from the scholars who have focused on the consequences of indifference for the future of democracy. Reacting to the breakdown of democratic regimes, especially the case of Weimar Germany, several analysts have worried about the implications for democracy should substantial proportions of the previously apathetic become suddenly mobilized. Based on findings from early studies of participation, special attention was drawn to the tendency for the chronically apathetic to come disproportionately from the same population elements, namely those that were least socialized into the norms of democratic politics. It was felt that such previously disinterested groups could, especially if a severe economic or social crisis were to arise, comprise a potentially mobilizable public on behalf of an anti-democratic demagogue or mass movement (Kornhauser, 1959: 46–47; Lipset, 1981: 226–227). The sudden emergence into the political arena of the chronically apathetic, who would bring their sociopathic attitudes along, would constitute a grave threat to the democratic order.

There has been a consistent worry among students of political participation that the sudden irruption of the previously apathetic—whether defined attitudinally in terms of indifference or behaviorally with regard to abstention from voting—into the political arena would drastically alter the political process. An obvious question has been what the entry of chronic nonvoters into the electoral process would portend. Some analysts fret over the potential for realignment of the political agenda and/or the balance of power among contending political parties. As E. E. Schattschneider (1960: 103) put it a quarter-century ago. "Anyone who finds out how to involve the forty million [nonvoters] in American politics will run the country for a generation." Other students of political behavior are concerned about the potential for transformation of the political system itself. According to Arthur Hadley (1978: 17, 126),

> The [apathetic] nonvoters tamp our political system with an explosive mass, waiting for some trigger to change the course of history. . . . As there is a critical mass of nuclear material necessary to trigger an atomic explosion, so there appears to be a critical percentage of nonvoters necessary to produce rapid social change. Historically that percentage has been close to the 50 percent we now approach. They sit out there, . . . disconnected from the process of democracy, but able at any moment to dominate our future. . . . To start them back now as voters is important. Not because our country will necessarily be governed better if they return, but because their growing presence menaces any government.

Whether one's concern is as profound as the impact of the previously apathetic on the character of the regime or as mundane as their consequence for the alignment of political forces, evidence from studies of nonvoters indicates the problem may have been overblown. Not only are nonvoters essentially indistinguishable from voters in their ideological proclivities and policy opinions (Wolfinger and Rosenstone, 1980; Shaffer, 1982), it is unlikely that the sudden entry of the previously passive into the voting booth would alter the balance of power between the major political parties (De Nardo, 1980; however, see also Perry, 1973).

While studies of the likely consequences of the addition of chronic non-voters into the political process are important, they do not indicate what might happen should the indifferent suddenly become mobilized. That query is addressed in Chapter 6.

Some scholars view political apathy from a different angle. They are not especially troubled by the presence of substantial numbers of disinterested citizens. According to this view, rather than being detrimental to democracy, a sizable bloc of apathetic persons becomes an advantage, for it provides a "cushion" for elites against the actions of highly interested, intense partisans. Apathy thus gives political decision-makers leeway to bargain and compromise. As Bernard Berelson (1952: 317) puts it, "If everyone in the community were highly interested, the possibilities of compromise and gradual solution of political problems might well be lessened to the point of danger" [see also Berelson, Lazarsfeld, and McPhee, 1954; Dahl, 1961; Almond and Verba, 1963). Berelson concludes that, "Perhaps what . . . [democracy] really requires is a body of moderately and discontinuously interested citizens within and across social classes, whose approval of or at least acquiescence in political policies must be secured." In a similar vein, Almond and Verba (1963: 478–479) contend that to maintain the delicate balance between governmental power and responsiveness, "the democratic citizen is called on to pursue contradictory goals; he must be active, yet passive; involved, yet not too involved; influential, yet deferential." (Needless to say, the argument that apathy is beneficial to democracy has not gone unchallenged [see, *e.g.*, Duncan and Lukes, 1963; Davis, 1964; Walker, 1966; Pateman, 1970; Thompson, 1970]).

Regarding either the contention that apathy constitutes a potential threat or that it is a blessing to democracy, one sees a superimposition onto political indifference of extra conceptual dimensions. On the one hand, there is the blending of disinterest with sociopathic dispositions such as bigotry, authoritarianism, and anti-civil libertarianism. On the other hand, there is an admixture of political ignorance and acquiescence to elite policy decisions. In either case, political indifference has lost its pristine conceptual status and, in the end, becomes important only in terms of its real or imagined consequences for the functioning of democratic politics.

This partial review of research on apathy reveals that some conceptual reworking of the concept is in order. It is necessary to prune the concept, to strip away the extra baggage that has been added over the years.

Apathy Reconsidered

The concept of political apathy refers to the varying degrees to which people are or are not interested in and attentive to politics and public affairs. It is similar to Almond and Verba's (1963: 88) idea of "civic cognition" and to Verba and his associates' (Verba, Nie, and Kim, 1978: 47–48, 70–73) notion of "general psychological involvement in politics and public affairs."

To describe levels of political interest across a large population, imagine a continuum of awareness, interest, and attention. At the one end is the individual who is so engrossed with his own psychological needs, or the affairs of his family, his work, or even his entertainment and recreational activities, that he has little or no psychic energy left for interest in public affairs. When such an individual declares that he "hardly thinks about politics at all," or does not "follow public affairs much at all," he can be classified as politically disinterested, or apathetic. At the opposite end of the continuum is the person who says he follows public affairs "very closely," or thinks about politics "most of the time."[1] This person can be considered to be psychologically involved in governmental affairs.

The concept of political apathy serves a dual utility in the study of political behavior. First, it is an important indicator of an individual's potential for political activity. Political behavior research has repeatedly found that those who are highly interested in politics are considerably more likely to be active than those who are not (Milbrath and Goel, 1977: 46–47).

However, it would be mistaken too readily to accept the proposition that high levels of psychological involvement necessarily result in participation. As Dahl (1961: 280) has pointed out, it is considerably easier to be "merely" interested, which demands only "passive participation," than it is to be actually active Interest "costs" but little in terms of psychic and physic energy and time; activity demands much more of each. Moreover, Dahl argues, "mere" political interest can even be a form of "escape" (see also Riesman and Glazer, 1950: 510–518). Without leaving a favorite easy chair or missing a TV soap opera, "interest" allows the expression of a range of emotions, from admiration to abhorrence. Or the person can daydream about the easy achievement of miraculous solutions to today's vexing problems, while denigrating the "measly" accomplishments of those who actually grapple with them in the mundane world of reality. "Interest" also permits Riesman's "inside dopster" (Riesman, with Glazer and Denney, 1961: 180–186) to use any information gleaned thereby to impress his peers with his "savvy," without having to sully himself through

---

[1]I have deliberately shortened the continuum somewhat to exclude the political activists, who constitute the shock-troops of political campaigns, causes, organizations, and movements. Their activities provide American politics with much of its driving verve. Much good research has been done on them recently (Rosenau, 1974; Kirkpatrick, 1976; Broder, 1980; Lamb, 1982); there is little I can add to this literature.

actual participation in the political fray. Finally, on a more prosaic level, the expression of "interest" in public affairs may offer partial absolution of the guilt that accompanies real or imagined failure to live up to culturally ingrained expectations of a high level of political participation (Lane, 1973: 286).

Nevertheless, the concept of political apathy remains useful as a device for estimating the degree to which citizens are psychologically "engaged" in the political process. As Almond and Verba (1963: 88) put it, "We may assume that if people follow political and governmental affairs, they are in some sense involved in the process by which decisions are made." They are aware, of course, that this may be a minimal involvement. Yet, someone with even a minuscule level of political interest has at least a dim and hazy awareness that he is a member of a polity and that the governmental process does, however, marginally, affect his daily life. In this sense, he is, however slightly, more involved than the individual Almond and Verba (1963: 17–18) call a "parochial." The latter is virtually without any awareness of the commonwealth, and does not see government as encroaching in any significant way upon his existence (1963: 79–83).

Of course, as noted above, it is possible to be aware that governmental decisions affect one's life, but to be politically disinterested nonetheless.[2] But those who do admit to even a minimal degree of political interest have made some small investment of psychological involvement in the political system. *Citizens who claim interest in public affairs may not yet have crossed the border into the realm of political participation, but they have made a substantial down payment on the keys to the kingdom.*

Considered as either an indicator for potential for participation or an estimate of psychological engagement in the governmental process—the two are, of course, related—the concept of political apathy is clearly a very important one for grassroots political behavior. However, before empirical assessments can be made, a workable operationalization of the concept is needed.

QUESTIONS FOR THOUGHT AND STUDY

1. What is Bennett's purpose—his research question?
2. What is the purpose of the section on history in the first section?
3. What for Bennett is the chief problem in studying apathy?

[2]The Five Nation Study and the Comparative State Election Project included the same question on perceptions of the central government's impact on the individual's daily life (Almond and Verba, 1963: 529; Black, Kovenock, and Reynolds, 1974: 182). Each study also had a measure of general political interest (Almond and Verba, 1963: 527; Black, Kovenock and Reynolds, 1974: 180). Despite the fact that the interest questions were worded differently, it is instructive that, in each survey, people who saw the national government as having a great effect on their lives were more than twice as likely to be highly interested than were those who did not think their lives were affected by government.

4. Make a list of any friends and relatives with whom you have discussed politics. Match up their attitude toward politics with the different attitudes Bennett describes. How well do they match up? Are there attitudes among them not described by Bennett?

5. Do most of your friends and relatives feel they ought to vote? Ought to listen to political debates at election time? Ought to read up on issues? Ought to go to public meetings? Ought to belong to a political party or to groups working for social cause? Ought to work for a candidate for political office? Ought to run for office? Judging from your answers, to what extent do the people around you (whether American citizens or not) feel obligated to participate in the political process today? How does that compare with the historical accounts cited by Bennett?

6. Describe your own attitude toward political involvement, relating it to attitudes Bennett describes and adding more if needed.

Theoretical Perspectives on the New Citizenship

Craig A. Rimmerman

Biography: *Craig Rimmerman is a Professor of Political Science at Hobart & William Smith College in Geneva, New York. He received his Ph.D from Ohio State University in 1984, specializing in American government and public policy.*

Rimmerman considers two theories on role of citizens in American democracy: elitism and participatory democracy. Rimmerman argues that the founders structured the government for minimal participation, that the representative system privileges the few (the elite), and creates barriers to participation. He claims the elitism, radical individualism, and materialism are the cause of political cynicism and lack of civic virtue (a sense of obligation to the community). Chapter 3 explores causes of civic indifference and includes analysis of indifference of youth. Blames the system and the nature of contemporary politics for apathy of youth. The reading provides an example of theoretical debate and combines theory and ethnographic research.

CHAPTER 2

The theory of participatory democracy is built round the central assertion that individuals and their institutions cannot be considered in isolation from one another.... The major function of participation in the theory of participatory democracy is therefore an educative one, educative in the very widest sense, in-

From Ch. 2 and Ch. 3, *The New Citizenship*. San Francisco, CA: Westview, 1997.

cluding both the psychological aspect and the gaining of practice in democratic skills and procedures.

—Carole Pateman, *Participation and Democratic Theory*

What role should the citizenry play in the American political system? This normative question lies at the heart of debates over issues of democracy, citizenship, and participation. To be sure, democracy is and has been a contested idea throughout history and in political theory. As we will see, the framers of the Constitution devoted considerable attention to the precise role that citizens should play in the newly created political system. There is a link between the framers' efforts and existing barriers to achieving a more participatory form of citizenship. In retrospect, one can see that the framers' constitutional design helped to foster relative system stability. Can this stability be maintained in the future?

In this chapter I will identify the various ways that balance and stability are maintained while citizens are engaging in political activities. I will examine two traditions in democratic political theory: participatory democracy and the democratic theory of elitism. Underlying this analysis are two additional questions: (1) What does it mean to be a "citizen"? and (2) What do we mean by "democracy"? My goal in this chapter is to provide the appropriate theoretical framework for understanding civic indifference and participation and balance and stability in contemporary American politics, and also to show relevant connections to the New Citizenship. But first, I must outline some of the practical barriers facing those who call for a more expansive democratic vision and a new conception of citizenship. One such obstacle is the structure of the government designed by the constitutional framers. A second is the hero worship attached to the framers' efforts and reinforced by the political socialization process. It is to these barriers that we now turn.

The Constitutional Context for Citizen Participation

To the constitutional framers, the stability of the political system was of great concern (Rimmerman, 1993). The delegates to the Constitutional Convention confronted two major questions: (1) How can a political system be created that allows the individual the freedom and equality of opportunity (Lipset, 1979) needed to acquire private property? In modern terms, what kind of political system will allow capitalism to survive? (2) Can a stable political and economic system be created when human beings are inherently bad?

Many of the men who gathered in Philadelphia in 1786–1787 had a Hobbesian, or negative, conception of human nature. Alexander Hamilton argued in the "Federalist No. 6" that "men are ambitious, vindictive, and rapacious." Edmund Randolph warned that the stability of the political system would be threatened due to "the turbulence and follies of our constitutions."

This argument led Elbridge Gerry to conclude that democracy was "the worst of all political evils," whereas Roger Sherman argued that "the people (should) have as little to do as may be about the government" and William Livingston said that "the people have been and ever will be unfit to retain the exercise of power in their own hands" (Hofstadter, 1986, p. 63). Madison himself argued in the "Federalist No. 51" that "if men were angels, no government would be necessary. If men were to govern men, neither external or internal controls on government would be necessary."

The framers' worst fears had been confirmed in fall 1786, when Daniel Shays, a former Continental Army officer, led a group of western Massachusetts farmers in protesting mortgage foreclosures. The response to Shays's Rebellion illustrates how perceived threats to system stability influenced the framers as they prepared for the Constitutional Convention in Philadelphia. Madison and the other framers recognized that for the republic to survive, the increasing political pressure generated by small propertied interests would have to be controlled. These interests challenged the existing distribution of property, and the framers fully expected such challenges to resurface time and again. The framers feared that system stability was at stake. Responding to Shays's Rebellion, George Washington expressed many of the framers' concerns in a letter to James Madison: "What gracious god, is man! That there should be such inconsistency and perfidiousness in his conduct? It is but the other day, that we were shedding our blood to obtain the state constitutions of our own choice and making; and now we are unsheathing the sword to overturn them" (Burns, 1984, pp. 105–106). Washington wrote further that if the newly created government could not control these disorders, "what security has a man for life, liberty, or property?" (p. 106). It is no surprise, then, that the constitutional framers devised a Madisonian system that attempted to insulate the governmental process from the exigencies of public opinion.

Concern for stability is also expressed in Madison's brilliant "Federalist No. 10," which serves as a compelling defense of republican government. He begins with a negative conception of human nature and argues that "the latent causes of faction are sown in the nature of man." In addition, he contends that "the most common and durable source of factions has been the various and unequal distribution of property." John Diggins argues that Madison's negative view of human nature is connected directly to his vision of government:

> Madison trusted neither the people nor their representatives because he believed that no faction or individual could act disinterestedly. Madison traced the problem of man's invirtuous conduct to the origin of factions in unequal property relations, the "natural" conditions that led man to be envious, interested, passionate, and aggressive. Convinced that the human condition was unalterable, Madison advised Americans that the Constitution's "auxiliary" precautions were essential,

that the Republic would be preserved by the "machinery of government," not the morality of man. (Diggins, 1984, p. 53)

Given these assumptions, the problem, according to Madison, was how to control the factional struggles that came from inequalities in wealth. Writing well before Marx, Madison recognized that inequalities in the distribution of property could lead to the instability of the political system. Because the causes of faction were inherent in man, it would be unrealistic to try to remove them. Instead, the government devised by the framers would try to control the effects of factions. Thus the framers adopted majority rule, established a system of separate institutions that shared powers and that had checks and balances, created federalism, and allowed for only limited participation by the citizenry in periodic elections. Women and slaves were excluded from the franchise; only property holders could vote for members of the House of Representatives. Until the Seventeenth Amendment was adopted in 1913, U.S. senators were elected by state legislatures. The cumbersome Electoral College reflects the framers' distrust of human nature and their desire to limit popular participation by the masses.

The framers understood that the republican principle would grant legitimacy and stability to their newly created political system. They recognized that it would be unwise and impractical to extend democracy too broadly. To the framers, the representative was to play two key roles: to represent sectional and other interests in the national decisionmaking process by mediating competing claims, and to mediate and moderate the passions of the mob. Accountability would be provided for by establishing a system of periodic elections where qualified citizens could choose their representatives. Benjamin Barber concludes that representative government promised the possibility of system stability by emphasizing "popular control and wise government, self-government, accountability, and centripetal efficiency" (Barber, 1986, p. 48).

In the end, the government was created "to guard against what were thought to be the weaknesses of popular democracy" (Mathews, 1994, p. 51). The goal of the framers was to "permit political participation but prevent democracy in the United States" (Manley and Dolbeare, 1987, p. x). Indeed, much of the current criticism voiced by participatory democrats is rooted in their frustration that the framers provided too limited a role for the citizenry in the political system. This view was represented over two hundred years ago by the Anti-federalists, who warned that a governmental apparatus was being devised wherein "the bulk of the people can have nothing to say to [the government]" (Main, 1961, p. 52).

It is not just the structure of the framers' government that is a source of concern for those who embrace the participatory democratic tradition. They are also concerned about the radical notion of individualism embraced by the framers. This notion, which came to be known as classical liberalism and which serves as the basis for liberal democracy, grew out of the writings of theorists John Locke, J.S. Mill, and Adam Smith. Radical individualism, which Tocqueville ultimately believed would undermine community and "the habits of the heart," has been a part of the American creed for more than two centuries. In addition to individualism, the American creed includes a fervent belief in equality of opportunity, liberty and freedom, the rule of law, and limited government (Herson, 1984).

This set of values is noteworthy in that it does not include "community" or "participation in politics." To be sure, the United States was born a political economy, stressing the right of individuals to pursue private property and their individualistic impulses in the private economic sphere. In *Habits of the Heart,* Robert Bellah and his coauthors underscore the connection between American individualism and the free market: "Hence, the liberal individualist idealizing of the free market is understandable, given this cultural context, since, in theory, the economic position of each person is believed to derive from his or her own competitive effort in an open market" (Bellah et al., 1985, p. 204). The authors conclude that "the rules of the competitive market, not the practices of the town meeting or the fellowship of the church, are the real arbiters of living" (p. 294). Bellah and like-minded scholars follow Tocqueville's analysis and lament the negative consequences of the American radical individualistic impulse. The central concern articulated by these social commentators is that as the people pursue "the American dream" as personified by the acquisition of private property and other material pleasures, they fail to devote the time and energy to engaging in the kind of public politics required by advocates of the participatory democratic vision. In this sense, the basic elements of liberal democracy are inimical to the fundamental values associated with participatory democracy, values that we will discuss later in this chapter. Indeed, Sheldon Wolin accurately points out that students of democratic theory and practice must devote considerable attention to examining the republican form, with the ultimate goal of evaluating "the tensions between republicanism, with its strong historical attraction to elitism, and democracy" (Wolin, 1989, p. 5). As it is, the emphases on acquiring private property and on voting in periodic elections are the central elements of American democracy and are also crucial tenets of the democratic theory of elitism. This perspective continues to be reinforced at all levels of society. Seymour Martin Lipset echoed the concerns of the framers and embraced the central elements of the democratic theory of elitism when he wrote that it was still necessary to "sustain the separation of the political system from the excesses inherent in the populist assumptions of democracy" (Lipset, 1979, p. 208). As we will soon see, it is this view, rather than the participatory democratic perspective, that forms the basis of the political socialization process. The political socialization process in America, then, is a central barrier to developing the kind of critical citizenry that is at the core of the New Citizenship and the participatory democratic tradition. I will next explore that political socialization process.

Political Socialization and Citizenship in American Politics

Political socialization is the process by which citizens acquire their attitudes and beliefs regarding the political system in which they live and their roles within that system. Political scientists have identified several key agents of political socialization—the family, schools, peers, the media, religious institutions, and the workplace.

From the vantage point of participatory democrats, the political socialization process impedes meaningful and effective participation because citizens are socialized to embrace the values of privatism and radical individualism that are rooted in liberal democracy. Indeed, participatory democrats claim that the thrust of political socialization in America reinforces the underlying tenets of the democratic theory of elitism, tenets that highlight the passivity of the citizenry and that allow elites in power to make the crucial decisions that affect the quality and direction of the people's lives. From this vantage point, citizens are to be involved in politics only in ways that might hold elites accountable—voting, joining an interest group, working within a political party, or working for a specific candidate. In this way, then, citizens abdicate any meaningful responsibility for what happens in the public sphere to a small group of elite decision-makers who will supposedly make decisions in the larger public interest. According to the elitist view, citizens do not have the time, energy, or education to make informed decisions about the direction of American public policy at all levels of government.

It should come as no surprise, then, that a recent People for the American Way study, "Democracy's Next Generation," states that many young people have an incomplete definition of politics, though they bear little responsibility for their limited conception of what it means to be a citizen. The report concludes that the "institutions with the best opportunity to teach young people citizenship—family, school, and government—have let them down" (Morse, 1992, p. 3). This conclusion surely would not surprise others who have found that the American political socialization process reinforces a limited conception of citizenship, one that lauds participation in the private rather than the public sphere. For example, in their study of the conflict between individualism and community in American life, the authors of *Habits of the Heart* conclude:

> What would probably perplex and disturb Tocqueville most today is the fact that the family is no longer an integral part of a larger moral ecology tying the individual to community, church, and nation. The family is the core of the private sphere, whose aim is not to link individuals to the public world but to avoid it as

far as possible. In our commercial culture, consumerism, with its temptations, and television, with its examples augment that tendency. (Bellah et al., 1985, p. 112)

In his analysis of what motivates people to avoid participation in politics, sociologist Richard Flacks devotes considerable attention to political socialization. He argues that "Americans do not simply avoid politics; their avoidance tends to be a feature of their political consciousness. People on the average believe that they are politically inactive, that history is being made by actors other than themselves; and they are prone to accept and even welcome this situation" (Flacks, 1988, p. 51). Many citizens embrace this situation because they are merely trying to live their daily lives, which means maintaining their jobs, putting food on their tables, and providing the basic necessities of life for themselves and their families.

It is indeed the case that Americans are socialized to "equate democracy with our own constitutional structure" (Hudson, 1995, p. 31). Americans revere the Constitution and the principles underlying the document without having a basic understanding of their full meaning and the consequences of those principles for their daily lives (Kammen, 1986). This hero worship of the framers and the Constitution has contributed to overall system stability through the years, has reinforced the underlying tenets of the democratic theory of elitism, and has served as a major barrier to the development of participatory democracy on a widespread scale in the United States.

The Participatory Democratic Tradition

The participatory democratic model came to the fore during the political turmoil of the 1960s, though many of its underlying ideas grow out of the classical works of Rousseau and John Stuart Mill and have been seen in New England town meetings for almost two centuries. Indeed, the New England town meeting is a model of the participatory democratic tradition. Tocqueville recognized that when he concluded that New England small towns were ideal settings for participatory democracy, because it was in those settings that citizens "take part in every occurrence" pertaining to government (Tocqueville, 1956, p. 61).

Student political activists in the 1960s embraced participatory democratic principles when they created organizations such as the Students for a Democratic Society (SDS) and the Student Nonviolent Coordinating Committee (SNCC). In 1962, core SDS members gathered in Port Huron, Michigan, and wrote a set of principles that came to be known as the "Port Huron Statement," "which included a call for 'a democracy of individual participation'" (Hudson, 1995, p. 19).

The problem of defining what is meant by meaningful and effective citizen participation pervades the literature of participatory democracy (Rimmerman,

1993, esp. pp. 126–132) and was a central concern of those who wrote the Port Huron Statement (see Box 2.1). A thorough examination of participatory democratic arguments reveals that three elements must be present if meaningful and effective citizen participation is to be achieved: (1) a sense of community identity; (2) education and the development of citizenship; and (3) self-determination by those participating (Pateman, 1970; Macpherson, 1976; Mason, 1982).

Proponents of participatory democracy argue that increased citizen participation in community and workplace decisionmaking is important if people are to recognize their roles and responsibilities as citizens within the larger community. Community meetings, for example, afford citizens knowledge regarding other citizens' needs. In a true participatory setting, citizens do not merely act as autonomous individuals pursuing their own interests, but instead, through a process of decision, debate, and compromise, they ultimately link their concerns with the needs of the community.

The arguments for participatory democracy are based on two additional tenets: (1) a belief that increased citizen participation will contribute both to the development of the individual and to the individual's realization of citizenship; and (2) a belief that individuals should participate in community and workplace decisions that will affect the quality and direction of their lives. Each of these tenets is grounded in a positive conception of liberty (Berlin, 1969).

Proponents of participatory democracy extend the Rousseauian notion that citizen participation in decisionmaking has a favorable psychological effect on those participating. Carole Pateman argues that through participation in political decisionmaking, the individual learns to be a public as well as a private citizen (Pateman, 1970).

Besides developing the individual's creative capacities, participation in decisionmaking encourages the individual to become more informed about the political process. Citizen participation theorists such as Benjamin Barber emphasize the beneficial learning process that is afforded to all those who participate with and talk to one another in community decisionmaking (Barber, 1984). From this perspective, the political education, rather than the socialization, of the individual will be benefited wherever increased citizen participation is encouraged.

From the vantage point of participatory democrats, citizens "have to become a public in order to sustain a democracy." What will enable citizens to become a public? According to David Mathews, president of the Kettering Foundation, a nonprofit organization dedicated to infusing participatory democratic principles into all levels of society, the central means for turning a collection of people into a public is through deliberation. Mathews defines deliberation in the following way: "To deliberate means to weigh carefully both the consequences of various options for action and the views of others" (Mathews, 1994, p. 111). To Mathews, deliberation is at the core of the participatory

BOX 2.1   THE PARTICIPATORY DEMOCRATIC IDEAL

We would replace power rooted in possession, privilege, or circumstance by power and uniqueness rooted in love, reflectiveness, reason, and creativity. As a social system we seek the establishment of a democracy of individual participation, governed by two central aims: that the individual share in those social decisions determining the quality and direction of his life; that society be organized to encourage independence in men and provide the media for their common participation.

In a participatory democracy, the political life would be based in several root principles:

that decision-making of basic social consequence be carried on by public groupings;

that politics be seen positively, as the art of collectively creating an acceptable pattern of social relations;

that politics has the function of bringing people out of isolation and into community, thus being a necessary, though not sufficient, means of finding meaning in personal life;

that the political order should serve to clarify problems in a way instrumental to their solution; it should provide outlets for the expression of personal grievance and aspiration; opposing views should be organized so as to illuminate choices and facilitate the attainment of goals; channels should be commonly available to relate men to knowledge and to power so that private problems—from bad recreation facilities to personal alienation—are formulated as general issues.

The economic sphere would have as its basis the principles:

that work should involve incentives worthier than money or survival. It should be educative, not stultifying; creative, not mechanical; self-directed, not manipulated, encouraging independence, a respect for others, a sense of dignity, and a willingness to accept social responsibility, since it is this experience that has crucial influence on habits, perceptions, and individual ethics;

that the economic experience is so personally decisive that the individual must share in its full determination;

that the economy itself is of such social importance that its major resources and means of production should be open to democratic participation and subject to democratic social regulation.

Source: "The Port Huron Statement," as reprinted in James Miller, *Democracy Is in the Streets: From Port Huron to the Siege of Chicago* (New York: Simon and Schuster, 1987), p. 333.

democratic tradition because "without becoming public citizens capable of giving common direction to government, people are capable of being little more than consumers of government services" (p. 112).

This third component of the participatory democratic model is based on the notion that individuals from all classes in society must share in the decisions that determine the quality and direction of their lives. From this vantage point, important community decisions should not be made solely by bureaucrats and elected officials. Participatory democrats are particularly concerned that "so many socially and politically relevant decisions are in the hands of people who are not democratically accountable" (Hudson, 1995, p. 20). That is certainly true of corporate officials who have the unilateral power to close a factory, a decision that has negative consequences for the workers and the surrounding community. Indeed, participatory democrats contend that citizens should participate more vigorously in their workplaces, where they spend many hours of their day.

Participatory democracy proponents also believe that if the multiple perspectives of those involved are to be consulted, the group decision process is essential (see Box 2.2). Individuals who participate in the local decisionmaking process will be afforded a sense of participation and commitment that is nonexistent in a system where elites rule the policymakers and implementation process. Participatory democracy, besides contributing to the self-development of individuals and giving them practice in citizenship, ideally wrests the policy implementation process away from the elite and allows citizens to have a say in the decisions affecting their lives. In so doing, participatory democracy challenges the fundamental assumptions of leadership and followership associated with the political system.

Participatory democrats have identified several forces that drive individuals to participate more actively in decisions that affect the quality and direction

---

BOX 2.2   THREE TYPES OF PARTICIPATORY SITUATIONS

Full Participation: Each member of a decisionmaking body has equal power to determine the outcome of decisions.

Partial Participation: The worker does not have equal power to decide the outcome of decisions but can only influence them.

Pseudo Participation: A situation where no participation in decision-making takes place (e.g., where the supervisor, instead of telling the employees of a decision, allows them to question her/him about it and discuss it).

Source: Adapted from Carole Pateman, *Participation and Democratic Theory* (Cambridge: Cambridge University Press, 1970), pp. 68–71.

of their lives. One such force "is the desire for greater control over an uncertain future" (Mathews, 1994, p. 125). A second is the individuals' desire to improve public policy decisionmaking and make the world and their communities better places in which to live. The third force is the citizens' recognition of the importance of addressing deteriorating civic relationships and the wish to develop the means and ability to work together more effectively (pp. 125–126).

In the end, a participatory citizen politics can be distinguished from conventional politics in a number of different ways. Whereas "conventional politics concentrates more on getting to solutions quickly, citizens politics concentrates on carefully defining and, if need be, redefining problems before moving to solutions." At the heart of conventional politics is a belief that leaders who will create solutions are needed, whereas at its core, "citizen politics stresses the importance of citizens claiming their own responsibility and becoming solutions themselves." Those who support a new kind of participatory citizen politics emphasize "creating new forms of power at all levels of a community," whereas conventional politics proponents advocate "using existing power wisely and empowering the powerless." The resources associated with conventional politics are generally more financial and legislative; "citizen politics uses public will as its primary political capital." Conventional politics devotes considerable time to assessing people's needs, whereas citizen politics focuses its attention on assessing their capacities. The language associated with conventional politics is rooted in "advocacy and winning," whereas citizen politics embraces a "language of practical problem solving and relationship building." A central goal of conventional politics is to attain more diversity, whereas citizen politics uses diversity to get diverse groups to work together. For conventional politics advocates, the public is a source of accountability, whereas citizen politics advocates look "to the public for direction." Conventional politics attempts to teach "the skills of effective public action." The creation of public events is crucial to conventional politics, whereas citizen politics emphasizes the creation of public space (Mathews, 1994, pp. 136–137).

This book will examine the kind of citizen politics associated with participatory democracy and the New Citizenship in considerable detail. But before we do so, we must look at the democratic theory of elitism as a basis for understanding conventional politics.

The Democratic Theory of Elitism Critique

What role should the citizenry play in the American political system? According to those who subscribe to the democratic theory of elitism, it should be a limited one. Critics of participatory democracy base their arguments on five key beliefs: (1) the role expected of the citizen in a participatory setting is unrealistic; (2) widespread citizen participation in decisionmaking is not feasible given problems of implementing it in a society of more than 250 million people; (3) studies confirm that participatory democrats have an unrealistic conception of the capability of ordinary citizens to participate actively in politics both in their communities and in the workplace; (4) too much participation will contribute to the instability of the political and economic system; and (5) increased citizen participation replaces clear legislative goals and fosters fragmentation throughout the policymaking and implementation process.

Those who subscribe to the democratic theory of elitism attack the notion of individual self-development through citizen participation because "to continue to advocate such a theory in today's world is bound to foster cynicism toward democracy as it becomes evident that the gap between the reality and the ideal cannot be closed" (Bachrach, 1971, p. 8). Other political scientists agree that participatory democracy is based on a utopian conception of human nature. One opponent contends that most individuals will not be able to transcend their own private interests and consider the concerns of the larger community in a participatory setting. Daniel Kramer, in his analysis of the failure of works councils and the War on Poverty, concludes that citizens "are more interested in their own advancement than in aiding their constituents" (Kramer, 1972, p. 128).

A second set of criticisms of the call for increased citizen participation emanates from the tenet that participatory democracy is too cumbersome and cannot be achieved in a country of more than 250 million people. Martin Oppenheimer challenges proponents of increased participation with this difficult question: "In a large-scale society, how much decentralization will be possible and necessary to promote real democracy? The concrete problem of where to draw the line has still to be faced" (Oppenheimer, 1971, p. 281).

In *Beyond Adversary Democracy,* Jane Mansbridge responds that democracies as large as the modern nation-state must be primarily adversary in nature. To those calling for increased citizen participation, that is clearly a depressing conclusion. Yet Mansbridge also points out that "preserving unitary virtues requires a mixed polity—part adversary, part unitary—in which citizens understand their interests well enough to participate effectively in both forms at once? (Mansbridge, 1980, p. 302). Mansbridge's conclusions are based on her empirical study of citizen participation in a New England town meeting (Selby, Vermont) and an urban crisis center (Helpline). Her analyses of Selby and Helpline reveal that "face-to-face meetings of the whole encourage members to identify with one another and with the group as a whole" in developing common interests (p. 100). She finds that certain individuals—the educated, the wealthy, and middle class—are more likely to participate in the town meetings because they feel less inhibited to express their views than the uneducated. With its concentration on procedure, or form, rather than outcome, citizen participation might only serve to preserve the status quo. To be sure, the participation process does not ensure equality of results. Citizen participation might be a ritual that merely stabilizes and legitimizes "the prevailing political and economic order" (Smith, 1979, p. 263).

Critics of participatory democracy are quick to point to the existing gap between what might be called "the democratic ideal" and the reality of citizen participation in America (Hudson, 1995, p. 15). In addition, they argue that for participatory democracy to occur on a widespread scale, an inordinate time commitment on the part of those participating would be required. Empirical evidence for these views is found in a 1954 book, *Voting*, by Bernard Berelson, Paul Lazarsfeld, and William McPhee. The authors conducted a survey of citizens in Elmira, New York, during the 1948 presidential election and found that "the behavior of Elmira's citizens differed significantly from the democratic ideal" that had been espoused by those committed to participatory democratic principles (Hudson, 1995, p. 16). Citizens interviewed had little basic knowledge of the election. In addition, they differed in their attitudes toward participation, as some respondents were quite interested and involved, others were only mildly interested, and some were profoundly apathetic. For Berelson, Lazarsfeld, and McPhee, this evidence supports their view that civic indifference contributes to system stability in a democracy:

> How could mass democracy work if all the people were involved in politics? Lack of interest by some people is not without its benefits, too. . . . Extreme interest goes with extreme partisanship and might culminate in rigid fanaticism that could destroy democratic processes if generalized throughout the community. Low affect toward the election . . . underlies the resolution of many political problems; votes can be resolved into a two party split instead of fragmented into many parties. . . . Low interest provides maneuvering room for political shifts necessary for a complex society. . . . Some people are and should be highly interested in politics, but not everyone is or needs to be. (Berelson, Lazarsfeld, and McPhee, 1954, p. 314)

The concern for system stability and fear of instability leads to a fourth set of arguments of those opposed to the participatory democratic vision. The concern for stability runs through much of the literature supporting the notion that democracy should be a political method or mechanism for choosing elite leaders. Writing in the 1940s, Joseph Schumpeter offered his conception of democracy, one that lies at the core of conventional politics and the democratic theory of elitism: "The democratic method is that institutional arrangement for arriving at political decisions in which individuals acquire the power to decide by means of a competitive struggle for the people's vote" (Schumpeter, 1950, p. 269). Schumpeter warns that the masses were capable of an electoral stampede that might threaten the stability of the political and economic system. More recent theorists have extended Schumpeter's arguments. Reflecting on the tumult of the 1960s, Samuel Huntington laments the "democratic distemper" that threatened "the governability of democracy" in the United States. To Huntington, the excesses of democracy "overloaded" the system from all sides and through a variety of competing interests in ways that made it increasingly difficult for the American policy process to respond effectively. As a result, Huntington concludes by calling for "a greater degree of moderation in democracy" (Huntington, 1975, p. 113). Like others who subscribe to the democratic theory of elitism, Huntington has serious problems with the participatory democratic vision.

A final set of arguments raised by those opposed to increased citizen participation in community decisionmaking and participatory democracy is expressed forcefully by Theodore Lowi in *The End of Liberalism.* Lowi laments the lack of goal clarity in federal legislation that accompanies the delegation of power and argues that the new bureaucratic fiefdoms are even more powerful than the old urban machines. These functional feudalities garner much of their power from the discretion they are afforded in implementing federal programs at the local level. Lowi rejects citizen participation as a solution for bureaucratic accountability because "the requirement of standards has been replaced by the requirement of participation" (Lowi, 1979, p. 56) and this participation leads to increased fragmentation throughout the policymaking and implementation process. Lowi calls instead for legislation that issues "clear orders along with powers" to ensure bureaucratic accountability (pp. 311–312).

My book is a response to those who contend that the citizenry has little interest in American politics and in participating in decisions that affect the quality and direction of their lives. I will next explore the connection between the New Citizenship and overall system stability.

The Theoretical Basis for the New Citizenship

In many ways, the New Citizenship is an extension of participatory democratic ideas that arose in the 1960s. For example, many of the core values associated with the New Citizenship are also central to participatory democratic theory. These values include civic engagement, political equality, solidarity, trust, and tolerance for diverse views and people, and encouragement of civic organizations and associations (Putnam, 1993, pp. 87–91). If conflict occurs among citizens, it occurs within the broader context of these agreed-upon values, all of which indicate support for a larger community interest rooted in participation and the development of citizenship. The goal of the New Citizenship is to reengage political theory with practical politics. The conception of citizenship that emerges is an active, engaged, and informed citizenry, one that embraces a positive conception of liberty (Berlin, 1969).

Proponents of the New Citizenship also address some of the concerns of the democratic theory of elitism. For example, the proponents tend to eschew protest politics in favor of creating structures that will enable diverse people with often competing interests to come together and, through spirited debate and discussion, to understand one another's perspectives and to identify sources for common ground. In this way, by avoiding factionalized conflicts of the kind that concerned the constitutional framers, proponents of the New Citizenship foster overall system stability. However, New Citizenship theorists also recognize that protest politics is necessary and invaluable for promoting change, especially for those who have been structurally excluded from the political decisionmaking process at all levels of government. As we will see in Chapter 4, there are many useful connections that can be made between the African American Civil Rights movement of the 1950s and 1960s, and the New Citizenship of today. The ultimate goal of the New Citizenship is for citizens to bridge the gap between the public and the private through active participation in politics and/or community service. Then citizens will help shape a culture of civic engagement, one where they are central participants in promoting political and social change.

Conclusion

This book is designed to provide readers with a more expansive and comprehensive conception of democracy and citizenship than the constitutional framers embraced. One way that the traditional political socialization process and the democratic theory of elitism can surely be challenged is through education. Yet much of education at all levels of society has failed to play this role. David Mathews has particularly harsh words for college education: "Unfortunately, most campuses seem to reinforce, perhaps unwittingly and certainly not alone, society's worst attitudes about politics" (Mathews, 1994, p. 114). In Chapter 6 I will devote considerable attention to educational models for creating more actively engaged and involved citizens in the public sphere. But before we can explore the important connection between education and citizenship, we need to examine the empirical evidence on democracy, participation, and civic indifference. ✸

Civic Indifference in Contemporary American Politics

Craig A. Rimmerman

The steady decline in voting is the most visible evidence that something is wrong. Elections are the most direct link to governing power—the collective lever that is meant to make citizens sovereign and officeholders accountable to them. So why don't people use it, especially when they are so unhappy with government?

—William Greider, *Who Will Tell the People?*

CHAPTER 3

It is indeed ironic that at the very moment that Eastern Europe is celebrating a transition to a Western-style liberal democracy, we in the United States are becoming increasingly critical of our own. Two recent books, William Greider's *Who Will Tell the People?* and E. J. Dionne's *Why Americans Hate Politics*, examine what Greider calls the betrayal of American democracy, albeit from different perspectives. Written by popular journalists, these books are important not only because of the substance of their arguments but also because of the attention they have received in the press. Dionne laments the polarization of elections around highly charged social issues such as abortion, school prayer, and affirmative action. A focus on these issues presents the electorate a set of "false choices" that fail to connect with practical problems faced by the citizenry. This polarization fosters an environment where citizens distrust politicians, "hate politics," and fail to vote in elections (Dionne, 1991). In sum, they display the civic indifference or civic disengagement that is a central characteristic of American politics.

Greider's analysis focuses more on structural explanations for the betrayal of American democracy. To Greider, the explanations for civic indifference largely emanate from "the politics of governing, not the politics of winning elections" (Greider, 1992, p. 13). Citizens fail to participate in the electoral arena because they do not see the link between their vote and the decisions made by those who hold power in the American policy process. Yet Greider accurately points out that although many Americans eschew voting, they participate in politics through a variety of alternative channels, such as town meetings and protest politics. It is the latter that potentially threatens overall system stability and raises the question germane to the core dilemma of this book: How does a polity strike a balance between the varieties of political participation engaged in by its citizens and residents?

One answer to that question is that if people had a greater chance to participate in meaningful ways, then perhaps they would not turn to the alternative forms of political participation that threaten to disrupt overall system stability. Another possible response is offered by the democratic theory of elitism, which we examined in Chapter 2: Civic indifference is functional for overall system stability to the extent that citizens do not participate at all in the American political system. This chapter will examine the implications of these two explanations within the broader context of the empirical literature on political participation.

The chapter also explores the empirical evidence for the claim that Americans are increasingly displaying civic indifference. I will evaluate both individual and structural explanations for that civic indifference, largely measured by the decline of voting in presidential and off-year elections. At the same time, I will provide alternative explanations for civic indifference by considering the explosion of citizen activism that has occurred in the United States in recent years. After exploring how civic indifference is manifested, I examine college students' attitudes toward politics and their political behavior as measured by various studies. Political participation in America cannot possibly be adequately explained by merely focusing on the individual characteristics of the participants and nonparticipants. The analysis must be broad enough to encompass many structural and individual explanations, as we attempt to explain the decline in voting at the same time as there is an increase in citizen activism.

Measuring Civic Indifference

The most traditional means for measuring civic indifference is voter turnout in elections. Fortunately, however, voting in elections is not the only criterion for measuring the health of a democratic society. If it were, the United States would be in big trouble, given voting-turnout rates in presidential and off-year elections (Hudson, 1995, p. 112). The United States ranks last among industrial democracies in average voter turnout in recent elections (see Table 3.1). Participation in even low in U.S. presidential elections, despite the fact that they generate the most attention and excitement among the voting public. Only 49 percent of all eligible voters actually turned out to vote in the 1996 election. This meager figure represented the lowest voter turnout since the 1924 presidential election (p.112). As Table 3.2 indicates, there was a gradual decline in presidential election turnout between 1960 and 1988, with a small increase in the 1984 presidential election between Ronald Reagan and Walter Mondale. In 1992 there was a fairly substantial increase in voter turnout, though the turnout rate of 55.2 percent was still considerably lower than the average voter turnout in other industrial democracies. Some analysts have suggested that we can expect continued improvement in voting-turnout figures in presidential

Table 3.1 *Voter Participation Rates in Selected Democracies*

	Percent
Australia (1993)	90
Austria (1986)	87
Canada (1988)	75
East Germany (1990)	93
France (1988)	81
Hungary (1990)	64
Italy (1991)	85
Japan (1993)	75
South Korea (1992)	79
Switzerland (1987)	46
United States (1992)	55

Source: Bruce Miroff, Raymond Seidelman, Todd Swanstrom, *The Democratic Debate* (Boston: Houghton Mifflin, 1995), p. 120.

Table 3.2 *Voting Turnout in U.S. Presidential Elections, 1932–1996 (in percentages)*

1932	52.4
1936	56.0
1940	58.9
1944	56.0
1948	51.1
1952	61.6
1956	59.3
1960	62.8
1964	61.9
1968	60.9
1972	55.2
1976	53.5
1980	52.6
1984	53.1
1988	50.1
1992	55.2
1996	49.0

Sources: 1932–1992 data from U.S. Department of Commerce, Bureau of Census, *Statistical Abstract of the United States* (Washington, D.C.: Government Printing Office, 1993), p. 284. 1996 data estimated by the Committee for the Study of the American Electorate.

elections. But before we get too excited about these improved figures, we should remember that nearly one-half of the eligible voting electorate chose to stay home rather than cast their ballots in the 1992 presidential election. In addition, we should also "remember that President Clinton's 44 percent plurality of the voters translates into an endorsement by only 24 percent of the citizenry" (Mathews, 1994, p. 29).

Voter turnout in midterm elections is even lower. As Table 3.3 indicates, voter participation in statewide midterm elections reached a high of 48.4 percent in 1966 before declining. Even in 1974, the first time that eighteen-to-twenty-year-olds participated in an off-year election, turnout in statewide elections was only 38.3. After 1974, turnout continued falling slowly, declining from the 1974 percentage in every year but 1982. In 1990, just over one-third of the eligible voting electorate voted in statewide elections (Rosenstone and Hansen, 1993, p. 58). In sum, if we use voter turnout as an indicator of citizen participation and citizen interest in American politics, then these figures reveal a detached and apathetic citizenry, one that displays a remarkable amount of civic indifference.

What factors account for this low voter turnout in presidential and off-year elections? In answering this question, we are indeed constrained by the kinds of information that pollsters and social scientists have gathered over the past forty years (Rosenstone and Hansen, 1993, pp. 4–5). Political scientists have offered both individual and structural explanations.

At the individual level, a number of explanations have been suggested. All emanate from the belief that "the key to the puzzle of why so many people do

Table 3.3 *Voting Turnout in Off-Year Elections, 1962–1994*

	U.S. Total[a]
1962	47.5
1966	48.4
1970	46.8
1974	38.3
1978	37.3
1982	40.5
1986	36.3
1990	36.4
1994	38.8

[a]Average of state turnout percentages in statewide or congressional elections.
Source: Compiled from Ruy Teixeira. *The Disappearing American Voter* (Washington, D.C.: Brookings Institution, 1992), p. 6 and *New York Times.*

not vote lies in one or another of their attitudes and preferences, or their lack of necessary resources" (Piven and Cloward, 1988, p. 113). One explanation is that people fail to vote because of a sense of political ineffectiveness, which is measured by a decline in political efficacy. Political efficacy refers to "both a sense of personal competence in one's ability to understand politics and to participate in politics, as well as a sense that one's political activities can influence what the government actually does" (Rosenstone and Hansen, 1993, p. 15). A second explanation is that people lack the required sense of civic obligation. The decline in political parties and the concomitant decrease in partisan attachment, a strong relationship to political parties, is a third explanation. The lack of educational resources provides a fourth reason for the decline in voting turnout. Those who are more highly educated are more likely to vote in elections because "education imparts information about politics and cognate fields and about a variety of skills, some of which facilitate political learning. . . . Schooling increases one's capacity for understanding and working with complex, abstract and intangible subjects, that is, subjects like politics" (p. 14). Political mobilization by elites can also enhance voting turnout. Some scholars contend that in recent years we have seen a decline in political mobilization, fostering lower voter turnout in elections (p. 229). Perhaps the most important factor is the socioeconomic status (SES) of individual voters. Individuals with high SES, which is generally measured by education level, occupational status, and income, are more likely to vote than those with lower SES. Finally, political scientists claim that the electorate exhibits some combination of the above factors that prevents them from participating in elections (Piven and Cloward, 1988, p. 113).

Voting-turnout rates, however, cannot be explained entirely by the characteristics or beliefs of individual citizens. A number of political, institutional, and structural factors deserve serious consideration as well. For example, scholars contend that legal and administrative barriers to voting depress voting-turnout rates. These legal and administrative barriers, such as complicated voter registration forms, are important because they impede the well-off and well-educated much less than they do the poor and the undereducated (Piven and Cloward, 1988, p. 119). Therefore, there is a bias that favors more highly educated and wealthy voters. Historically, the political parties in power have supported antiquated voter registration procedures as a way to protect incumbent members of their own parties. Voter registration laws supported by the Democratic and Republican parties do impede challengers who would seek the support of voters whose views are perceived to be unrepresented in the American policy process. This obstruction occurs at all levels of government. In 1983 a number of political activists formed Human Serve as a way to reform voter registration laws in the United States. The goal was to "enlist public and private nonprofit agencies to register their clients to vote." Under the Human Serve plan, citizens would be able to register to vote at hospitals and public health centers, motor vehicle bureaus and departments of taxation, unemployment and welfare offices, senior citizen centers and agencies for the disabled, day-care centers and family planning clinics, settlement houses and family service agencies, housing projects and agricultural extension offices, and libraries and municipal recreation programs. With the program, the founders of Human Serve hoped to make access to voter registration virtually universal (p. 209). Despite the political and legal obstacles, Human Serve claims to have registered a considerable number of previously unregistered voters, many of whom have little education, have never participated before in elections, and are living in or near poverty. In 1993, with the support of President Bill Clinton, Democrats in Congress were able to pass the "Motor Voter" bill, despite strenuous Republican party opposition. This legislation enables potential voters to register as they stand in line to get their driver's licenses. The Motor Voter legislation requires all states to simplify their procedures for voter registration, requires states to allow potential voters to register when they renew or apply for licenses at State Departments of Motor Vehicles offices, permits voters to register at military recruitment, social service, and other public agencies, and allows voters to register by mail (Dreier, 1994, p. 490). Piven and Cloward's analysis suggests that since the National Voter Registration Act went into effect in January 1995, "people have been registering or updating their voting addresses at the rate of nearly one million per month in 42 states." Early estimates were that the voter registration rolls would increase by twenty million before the 1996 election and twenty million more by the 1998 midterm election (Piven and Cloward, 1996, p. 39).

In sum, the attributes most likely to be associated with a willingness on the part of individuals to vote—"from education to positive feelings about politics—are more likely to be present among the more affluent" (Hudson, 1995, p. 121). For these reasons, then, the electorate is hardly representative of all citizens.

Political scientist Robert Putnam addressed the broader implications of civic indifference for the quality of American public life and overall system stability. To Putnam, the vitality of civil society—networks of civic associations and social trust that contribute to high levels of voluntary cooperation and participation—in the United States has declined considerably over the past twenty-five years or so. In his analysis, Putnam incorporates the work of the French diplomat, Alexis de Tocqueville, who visited the United States in the 1830s and reported that Americans' participation in civic associations was a central element of their democratic experience. In *Democracy in America,* Tocqueville wrote:

> Americans of all ages, all stations in life, and all types of disposition are forever forming associations. There are not only commercial and industrial associations in which all take part, but others of a thousand different types—religious, moral, serious, futile, very general and very limited, immensely large and very minute. . . .

Nothing in my view, deserves more attention than the intellectual and moral associations in America. (Putnam, 1995b, p. 66)

Putnam suggests that over the past two decades Americans have witnessed a decline in civic engagement. The metaphor that he employs to describe this trend toward greater isolation is that more Americans are "bowling alone." Reports that millions of Americans have withdrawn from community affairs support Putnam's claim that there has been a decline in civic engagement. Additional factors include the decline in voter turnout, a reduction in the number of Americans working for political parties, and a decline in the number of Americans attending a political rally or speech. To Putnam, these trends are disturbing because they lead to a decline in what he calls "social capital—networks, norms, and trust—that enable participants to act together more effectively to pursue shared objectives" (Putnam, 1996, p. 34). In the end, Putnam believes that technological developments, such as television and computers, have contributed considerably to the decline in civic engagement. He worries that television and the computer revolution have served to isolate individuals from their communities to the point where technology might be "driving a wedge between our individual interests and our collective interests" (Putnam, 1995b, p. 75). These technological developments have had particularly deleterious consequences for the typical college-aged student of today, who most likely has spent a considerable amount of time watching television and interacting with computers in virtual isolation from others. Putnam warns that "high on America's agenda should be the question of how to reverse these adverse trends in social connectedness, thus restoring civic engagement and civic trust." How this might be accomplished is a central theme of the present book. But any attempt to restore civic engagement and civic trust must also be placed within the broader dilemma of this book: how to foster a more meaningful and participatory democracy, one that also promotes overall civility.

And what do recent qualitative surveys of voters' attitudes concerning politics and political participation suggest regarding civic indifference? One such study conducted by the Kettering Foundation in 1990–1991 found empirical support for David Mathews's claim that people think that "the political arena today is too large and distant for individual actions to have an impact" (Mathews, 1994, p. 34). The Kettering study, entitled *Citizens and Politics: A View from Main Street America,* gathered citizen groups in ten different cities in an effort to understand what Americans think about their roles as citizens in the political system at large. For many of the participants in these focus group discussions, a sense of powerlessness and exclusion from government decisions translated into a feeling that they had a limited role in the political system. The Kettering study also identified the usual "popular dissatisfaction with government and politicians" (Mathews, 1994, p. 11). It found that participants believed that they were "pushed out" of a political process dominated by special-interest lobbyists and politicians and that negative attacks and sound bites dominated public discourse in ways that turned citizens off from politics. People felt that debate on the issues of the day offered little opportunity for citizen participation and was generally remote from their concerns. One participant concluded, "I'm never aware of an opportunity to go somewhere and express my opinion and have someone hear what I have to say" (Hudson, 1995, p. 131).

At the same time, many of the citizens in the focus groups were far from apathetic or too interested in their own private matters to be concerned about politics. Indeed, they had a clear sense of their civic responsibilities and wished to have more-meaningful opportunities to participate in the political system (Harwood Group, 1991). But at the same time, they displayed frustration, anger, cynicism, and alienation toward politics in America. They were particularly worried about passing on their cynicism and alienation to their children. To these Americans, a professional political class of incumbent politicians, powerful lobbyists, the media elite, and campaign managers all hindered their ability from participating in the broader political system in a meaningful way. People in the study perceived that the system was dominated by money and that voting in elections simply would not make a difference because the overall system is closed to the average citizen (Mathews, 1994, p. 12).

There are additional signs of this citizen anger toward politics besides low voter turnout. As political scientist Susan Tolchin suggests in her recent book *The Angry American,* "political leaders from both parties worry about the absence of civility, the decline of intelligent dialogue, and the rising decibels of hate" (Tolchin, 1996, pp. 4–5). In recent years there has been an increase in the number of incumbents who have chosen to leave office voluntarily for fear of losing their seats. The loss would stem from the votes of a citizenry increasingly frustrated with professional politicians. Some of these same politicians have decided to leave office because they are increasingly concerned about the rise of incivility increasingly characterizing American politics. For example, Senators Bill Bradley (D-New Jersey), Hank Brown (R-Colorado), James Exxon (D-Nebraska), Nancy Landon Kassebaum (R-Kansas), and Tim Wirth (D-Colorado) have all declined to seek reelection at the height of their political careers. In addition, laws to limit terms at all levels of government have been passed by large margins in various states.

Citizens have also embraced the initiative and referendum as vehicles for addressing the problems that the political system at large has neglected. Through the initiative and referendum, citizens enact or reject laws directly rather than relying on elected officials to solve problems. An initiative, a proposed new law initiated by citizens, is placed on the ballot through a petition signed by a specified number of voters. Through a referendum, a law approved by elected officials is referred to the ballot either by the officials or by citizen petition (Isaac, 1992, p. 171). The initiative and referendum process most approximates direct democracy in the United States. California's Proposition 13, which was ratified in the late 1970s, ushered in an era in which the referendum has been increasingly used. For example, in Long Beach, California, citizens called for a referendum on zoning ordinances. In Olympia, Washington, citizens decided state legislators' salaries by referendum. In Chicago, citizens proposed a referendum to limit school taxing power. Citizens in California's San Gabriel Valley attempted to block a controversial redevelopment project through the use of the referendum. The message of all these referendum efforts is that representative government has failed to tackle the policy issues under question, thus contributing to a more angry, alienated, and frustrated citizenry, one that will bypass the normal policy process in order to achieve its goals (Mathews, 1994, p. 12).

Ross Perot clearly capitalized on the citizenry's frustration with "politics as usual" in his quixotic 1992 campaign for the White House. Perot, running on the Independent party ticket, presented himself as an antipolitician, an outsider who truly understood the frustrations of mainstream America, one who could provide the leadership required to pass timely and meaningful public policies in response to the major issues of the day. To Perot, lobbyists, political action committees, and the elected officials who serve them are at the heart of what is wrong with the American political system. Perot was most effective in attacking the nation's political elites and rallying his supporters around the populist banner of "United We Stand." As one commentator pointed out, "Far more than most leading Democrats and Republicans, Perot has a feel for how millions of ordinary people actually experience life in contemporary America, and he expresses that understanding keenly" (Wilentz, 1993, p. 33). As a result, he was able to rally supporters who were concerned about undemocratic abuses of power at the same time that they wished to have more meaningful involvement in the political system. To his most avid supporters, many of whom had become angry and frustrated with American politics, it did not seem to matter that Perot increasingly appeared to critics as "an egomaniac with a clever sales pitch and a fortune to spend" (p. 29). In the end, both Democrats and Republicans recognized that the Perot phenomenon would not quickly disappear. In July 1993 the Democratic Leadership Council (DLC), a group of elected officials who wanted to overhaul the party's liberal image and move the party to the center of the ideological spectrum, especially on social issues, published a document designed to provide Democrats with the building blocks for a leadership, policy, and electoral strategy to persuade Perot supporters to support the Democrats in future elections. It concluded, in part:

> The Perot bloc is for real and has considerable staying-power. Perot voters remain committed to the 1992 vote and, for the moment, want to stick with Perot in

1996—even if he were to run as a Republican. That is a measure of their independence and alienation which will remain important in our future national elections. (Greenberg, From, and Marshall, 1993, p. II–2)

Perot's ability to win 19 percent of the popular vote in the 1992 presidential election provides more empirical evidence for the claim that many Americans are increasingly disheartened with "politics as usual." However, his disappointing showing in the 1996 presidential election is a reminder of the barriers that third parties face at the national level.

Citizen alienation and frustration has also manifested itself in the increased popularity of television and radio call-in talk shows, which are often devoted to discussions of politics. *Newsweek* devoted a February 1993 cover story to the popularity of the talk-show format and reported that call-in shows were growing so fast that they numbered nearly 1,000 of the nation's 10,000 radio shows. At that time, *Larry King Live* was the highest-rated show broadcast on CNN (Fineman, 1993, p. 25). Rush Limbaugh has emerged as such an unrelenting critic of the Clinton presidency that the president saw fit to unleash a barrage of public criticism against the conservative talk-show host in June 1994. The president recognized that he could not let Limbaugh's attacks go unanswered any longer.

What is the broader significance of all of this "noise" across the airwaves? At one level, it surely signifies that a portion of the American electorate continues to be frustrated by the normal operation of American politics and desires more meaningful opportunities to participate in decisions that affect the quality and direction of their lives. At the same time, politicians who wince because of what they hear on television or radio talk shows are surely overreacting. To be sure, only the most outraged, motivated, and devoted listeners call in. They constitute only about 2 or 3 percent of the total audience (Fineman, 1993, p. 27). As a result, the angry voices often heard in the talk-show format are hardly representative of the larger public. What they do signify, however, is that attention is being paid to citizen disaffection at a time when both scholars and average citizens are discussing issues of democracy, citizenship, and accountability. This is certainly true of the amount of recent attention devoted to young people's beliefs and values regarding politics, which I will discuss next.

American Youth and Civic Indifference

Many studies through the years have provided considerable evidence to support the conclusion that young people are largely apathetic, uninterested, indifferent, and disengaged when it comes to politics. Indeed, recent studies of the political lives of today's youth provide additional support for this claim. Yet these studies also "reflect two contradictory stereotypes: that of an apathetic

Me Generation and that of a college population motivated by idealism" (Morse, 1992, p. 2). It is the tension between these two stereotypes that warrants further examination. In addition, we need to explore the reasons why many young people appear to be indifferent toward politics.

When eighteen-to-twenty year-olds were given the right to vote in 1971, it was thought that the extension of the franchise would do much to address youth alienation. Since that time, however, there has been a steady decline in young voters' interest and participation in the political process. This lack of interest in voting culminated in the 1990 off-year elections when just one in five eighteen-to-twenty year-olds bothered to vote (Morin and Balz, 1992). We have already seen that many citizens think that voting has little meaningful impact on important policy decisions. Apparently, America's youth share this view, although there was an upturn in voter turnout among eighteen-to-twenty year-olds in the 1992 presidential election. In 1988 only 36 percent of members of that age group voted in the presidential election, but 45 percent of eligible voters aged eighteen to twenty voted in 1992 (Mathews's introduction to Kettering study [Harwood Group, 1993, p. iii]). It remains to be seen whether this increase in voter turnout among the young can be maintained in future elections.

Indeed, recent studies of college students conducted by the UCLA/American Council on Education, "The American Freshman," and the annual "Roper College Track" report found that college freshmen matriculating during the 1994–1995 academic year were "more disengaged from politics than any previous entering class; only 31.9 percent of the fall 1994 freshmen—lowest in the history of the survey—say that 'keeping up with political affairs' is an important goal in life, compared to 42.4 percent in 1990, and 57.8 percent in 1966." The authors of the report concluded that "considering that the figure from 1993—a nonelection year—was 37.6 percent, the sharp drop in the fall 1994 election year survey is all the more unexpected." The UCLA findings provide more evidence of disengagement from politics. The percentage of "freshmen who say they frequently 'discuss politics' reached its lowest point ever in the fall 1994 survey: 16.0 percent, compared to 18.8 percent the previous year and 24.6 percent in 1992 (the highest point of 29.9 percent was recorded during the 1968 election year) (Higher Education Research Institute, [1995], p. 1).

The UCLA data for the fall 1995 entering class suggest an even grimmer picture regarding college students' interest in political affairs. The study found that "students' commitment to 'keeping up to date with political affairs' as an important life goal dropped for the third straight year to an all-time low of 28.5 percent, compared with 42.4 percent in 1990 and 57.8 percent in 1966." The percent who discuss politics frequently also continued its downward slide to an all-time low of 14.8 percent (down from 24.6 percent in 1992 and 29.9 in 1968). Finally, reinforcing these trends is the conclusion that more and more students feel that "an individual can do little to change society." Indeed, this finding reached a ten-hear high of 33.6 percent (Higher Education Research Institute, [1996], p. 1).

One explanation for college students' disengagement from politics is that they did not have a chance to confront their potential roles as citizens prior to college. Since the UCLA study measured the attitudes only of entering first-year college students, it did not address the attitudes of upper-division students who might have developed an interest in politics and public life as a result of their college educational experiences. To be sure, a college education reinforces the notion that one has a duty to participate, if only through voting in periodic elections.

There is another explanation, however, for young people's apparent civic disengagement. One political scientist believes that many young Americans have virtually no sense of civic duty or societal obligation. They "regard themselves solely as the clientele of government" (Markus, 1992a) and demand rights without responsibilities. It is this view that has led some to call this generation of youth the "Me generation."

Indeed, several recent studies provide support for this grim conclusion. For example, a 1989 People for the American Way study conducted by Peter D. Hart Research Associates found:

1. Young people cherish America's freedoms without understanding what it takes to preserve them;
2. This generation is—by its own admission and in the eyes of teachers—markedly less involved and less interested in public life than previous generations;
3. Institutions with the best opportunity to teach young people citizenship—family, school and government—have let them down (People for the American Way, 1989, pp. 12–13).

A 1990 Times Mirror Study found that "today's young Americans, aged eighteen to thirty, know less and care less about news and public affairs than any other generation of Americans in the past fifty years." The authors of this study labeled this generation of youth as "the age of indifference" (Times Mirror Center for the People and the Press, 1990, p. 1 [press release]).

Previous generations of young people have surely been preoccupied with personal concerns such as individual happiness and career success. Indeed, these two goals are often linked by the importance of making enough money to provide for one's family and to pursue a variety of materialistic pleasures. But there is a sense that the present generation of youth is more preoccupied with career goals and making money than previous generations. It may well be that today's students perceive that they face numerous pressures stimulated by a changing and more unfriendly economy, changes that could mean that the young may not be able to achieve the kind of material well-being of their parents and grandparents. The headlines of the early 1990s reminded students of the difficult job market: "Economic Trend for the 90s: Fear"; "Middle-Class and Jobless, They Share Sorrows"; "Graduates March Down Aisle into Job Nightmare"; and "Pay of College Graduates Is Outpaced by Inflation" (Sidel, 1994, p. 52). As a result of these economic pressures, much of America's youth embraces the kind of radical individualism discussed in Chapter 2.

The most exhaustive recent study of college students' views was conducted in 1992–1993 by the Harwood Group for the Kettering Foundation. First-year and upper-division students on ten college campuses from across the country were brought together in ten discussion focus groups and asked to explore the following questions:

1. What do college students believe it means to be a citizen?
2. How do college students view politics today?
3. How have college students come to learn what they know about politics and citizenship?
4. How would college students like to see politics practiced?
5. What opportunities do college students see for learning politics at the university? (Harwood Group, 1993, p. xvi)

The strength of this study is that it goes far beyond merely reporting what students think about politics, but instead explores *why* they hold certain political views and *how* they think about politics.

In addressing these broader issues, the Kettering study offered three main findings. The first was that "many students have concluded that politics is irrelevant" (Harwood Group, 1993, p. 2). Students in this study held a narrow conception of politics and identified three basic ways that they might participate in the American political system—all rooted in individual action. Students perceived that they could participate by voting and signing petitions, by joining interest groups or by protesting, though they saw little value in any of these three forms. In light of this evidence, the researchers concluded that "the politics of pessimism" best captures the mood of students today.

A second and more hopeful conclusion was that "students can imagine a different politics." For many of the students interviewed, this different politics would be rooted in bringing people together at the community level to "find ways to talk and act on problems." In this way, politics would be more engaging to the average citizen. But students also recognize that the way U.S. politics was practiced today did not correspond to this alternative vision.

Finally, the study found that "students say that they are not learning to practice politics." They offered a specific indictment of political education at the collage level because campus conversations reinforced "everything that they believe to be wrong with politics." More specifically, campus discussions of politics tended to be far too polarized (Harwood Group, 1993, p. 2). A Wake Forest student provided evidence to support this claim: "People are very opinionated in my classes. There is no moderation at all and [the discussion] gets totally out of bounds." A related problem is that when people take such strident positions both inside and outside the classroom, it is difficult to discuss possible solutions to the problems at hand. As a result, these heated arguments have little relevance for addressing major policy concerns. One Morgan State student concluded: "There are no solutions discussed; it is all rhetoric" (p. vii).

In sum, this study revealed that many students were alienated from politics and not particularly hopeful about the future. It is little wonder, then, that despite the increase in voter turnout among college-age youth in the 1992 presidential election, voter turnout among the young falls far below the national average. The students' views echoed the attitudes of the citizens interviewed for *Citizens and Politics: A View from Main Street America,* a study prepared by the Harwood Group (1991) for the Kettering Foundation and discussed earlier in this chapter. At the same time, however, there are some key differences between the two studies.

The first is that whereas "citizens are frustrated, students feel resigned." The 1991 study found that Americans were angry abut politics because they perceived that they had been "pushed out" of the political process. Students, in contrast, "seem resigned to the conclusion that politics is what it is, that politics always has been this way, and that it may always be something that has little relevance to their lives" (Harwood Group, 1993, p. 3).

A second key difference is that whereas "citizens are seeking to reengage in politics, students see little purpose in ever becoming engaged." At least citizens claimed that they desperately wanted to be more involved in meaningful ways in the political process, but they could not find the appropriate place to participate. College students were so convinced that politics did not solve real problems that they saw no real reason to participate (Harwood Group, 1993, p. 3).

The respective studies also pointed out that whereas "citizens argue that politics should be different, students seem to be missing a context for thinking about politics." It is interesting that citizens recognized that the current conditions that shaped the political process should be different, but students accepted them as the norm. It was "only when they are given the opportunity to imagine a new set of political practices do they see possibilities for change" (Harwood Group, 1993, p. 3).

Finally, whereas "citizens have a strong sense of civic duty, students see primarily entitlement." Citizens believed that for the political process to work effectively, they had to participate. In this sense, they perceived that they were a key part of the political process. Students, however, conceptualized citizenship "almost exclusively in terms of individual rights." They saw little connection, then, between citizenship and politics.

It is indeed disturbing that young people today appear to be so indifferent toward and alienated from politics. But if the Kettering study of college students reveals anything hopeful for the future it is this:

> This study suggests college students will engage in politics, but only if it is a different kind of politics—one that challenges them to learn new political skills and provides opportunities to put those skills to use. More "politics as usual" will only deepen their sense of the irrelevance of the political process (Harwood Group, 1993, p. 53).

It is also worth emphasizing that college students perceived that the educational process failed to provide them with meaningful and alternative ways to conceive of politics and to become involved in decisions of import on their campuses and in the larger society. Chapter 6 will devote considerable attention to exploring alternative models for conceptualizing how colleges and universities might restructure their general curricula to take into account the concerns that college students identified in the Kettering study. In the meantime, we need to discuss in greater detail the evidence for the rise in citizen activism.

Sources of Citizen Activism

The study *Main Street America* (Harwood Group, 1991) found that the key to citizen participation by those who actually participated was the possibility of change, not the certainty of success. If this study is at all accurate, then Americans can overcome participation obstacles if they perceive that their participation may have a meaningful effect—"that there is some opportunity to create and witness change." One woman offered this realistic observation: "You just keep trying. That doesn't mean that you will win all the time." The possibility of change thus becomes an important force for actually reconnecting citizens and politics (Mathews, 1994, p. 36).

Those who subscribe to the democratic theory of elitism believe that citizens have little interest in politics, have minimal knowledge of what is happening politically, and fail to participate because they perceive that the system is working well enough as it is. But those who embrace the more participatory democratic perspective challenge the civic-indifference notion by identifying various ways that citizens have attempted to become more meaningfully involved politically in their respective communities. Citizens do care and they struggle in all sorts of ways to find opportunities to have their voices heard in decisions at all levels of government that impinge on their lives.

The *Main Street America* study revealed that citizens wanted more meaningful public dialogue around key public policy concerns. Citizens identified three specific problems with politics as usual: "the way the political agenda is set, the way policy issues are framed, and the limited opportunities for public deliberation." Citizens were particularly vocal about the way that the public agenda was set in American politics. A woman from Texas said, "The issues that policymakers jump, on the bandwagon and carry on about aren't really the issues that deal with mainstream people" (Mathews, 1994, p. 43). What citizens want to avoid is the kind of polarization of emotional issues in public discourse, such as abortion and school prayer, that E. J. Dionne contends is a major factor in why so many Americans hate politics.

The study found that many of the citizens who expressed helplessness about the political process participated in their communities "in many ways and with great intensity of purpose." Their involvement takes a number of different forms—membership in neighborhood organizations, crime-watch groups, school committees, and ad hoc bodies that have been formed to address specific problems in the community. At the same time that voter turnout has been in decline, we have witnessed an explosion of citizen activism. During the past three decades, more Americans have become involved in an array of grass-roots citizen groups such as ACORN (Association of Community Organizations for Reform Now), OPIC (Ohio Public Interest Campaign), and Clean Water Action. These organizations are increasingly playing a more active role in local policy debates and decisions. *Main Street America* concluded that citizens were involved in these ways because they believed that their participation could make a difference and that there was a direct connection between their actions and possible policy solutions (Harwood Group, 1991). As we will discuss later in this book, participation in these citizen organizations is one element of the New Citizenship.

College students, too, have shown renewed attention to broader community concerns and issues of social justice. A wider variety of community service programs and student literacy programs have spread across college campuses as students yearn for the opportunity to make a connection between what goes on in the classroom and the larger communities in which they live. A number of campuses, such as Colby College, LeMoyne College, the University of Minnesota, Providence College, Rutgers University, Stanford University, Syracuse University, and Hobart and William Smith Colleges, have begun to offer specific courses that require some form of community service. We will devote considerable attention to these course offerings and their connection to broader issues of democracy, citizenship, and difference in Chapter 6.

Like their counterparts in the 1960s, today's progressive students protest acts of social injustice around issues of racial, gender, and sexual discrimination. When President Bush built up American troops in the Middle East during the summer and fall of 1990 as a prelude to the Persian Gulf War, college students organized antiwar protests. Indeed, my own campus, Hobart and William Smith Colleges, had one of the first college antiwar rallies in November 1990.

To be sure, what separates this generation of college students from their 1960s peers is the presence of outspoken conservative voices on many campuses and in the classroom who attack their more progressive colleagues and college faculty supporters as kowtowing to "political correctness." This often contributes to the polarized climate and discourse in the classroom and in the broader college community that students lamented in the Harwood study. At the same time, the rise of community service programs and discussion of highly charged political issues such as race, gender, class, and sexuality concerns on college campuses indicate an interest on the part of students who wish to link their courses of study with public policy solutions to current issues. This, too, is a central element of the New Citizenship and a source of optimism as we consider the ways citizens can be more meaningfully connected to the American political system.

Conclusion

This chapter has emphasized the importance of conceptualizing political participation far more broadly than mere participation in periodic elections. The right to vote may well be the central element of any democracy, but if that is the case, American voting-turnout rates suggest that the nation is characterized by civic indifference. Indeed, those who do vote in elections are overwhelmingly from the upper and middle classes, thus reinforcing the class bias in American politics.

Several studies of the electorate point out that many citizens are apathetic and uninterested in "politics as usual," which they perceive is dominated by special interests and closed to meaningful participation by the average citizen. At the same time, these studies suggest that Americans wish to have more meaningful opportunities to participate in the political system.

America's youth mirror and reinforce the political indifference of the larger society. If anything, the young are less well informed and less inclined to participate in mainstream electoral politics. College students, however, appear to be more likely to vote than American youth as a whole. These same students report that they are increasingly disgusted by the popularized discourse in the larger society and on college campuses as well.

There is reason for optimism, however. At all levels of society, citizens wish to expand their sense of civic responsibility. In other words, citizens wish to go beyond voting and participate meaningfully in decisions that will affect the quality and direction of their lives in both their communities and their workplaces.

It is this desire for public participation that is at the core of the New Citizenship. For us to fully understand the elements of the New Citizenship, we must place our discussion in its proper historical context by looking at the political movements and community organizations of the 1960s that were rooted in a broader vision of citizenship associated with the participatory democratic tradition. After examining the legacy of these movements, particularly the Civil Rights movement, one can more meaningfully discuss and evaluate contemporary proposals for increasing citizen involvement in public life. It is not enough, however, merely to discuss the political movements growing out of the 1960s. Indeed, if the central dilemma of this book is how can a polity strike a balance between the varieties of political participation engaged in by its citizens, then I must also address contemporary organizations of both the Left and the Right whose approach to politics potentially threatens overall system stability.

QUESTIONS FOR THOUGHT AND STUDY

1. What does "normative" mean?
2. Rimmerman compares two theories of democracy: "participatory democracy" and "elitism." Define each and describe the difference.
3. Which theory (from question 2) does Rimmerman hold superior? Who are the chief proponents of the other theory?
4. From your discussion of your friends' and relatives' attitudes toward politics, which you examined in the Bennett reading, would you agree with Rimmerman that Americans feel they have little effective voice in their government?
5. Does the system Madison describes in the *Federalist 10* control the evil effects of factions (the oppression of one group by another) or limit participation to the few? Both?
6. Judging from your exploration of your friends' and family's attitudes in the Bennett reading, would you say, as Rimmerman does, that American values of individualism do not include obligation to the community or require participation in politics? Give examples.
7. How have you heard the political activism of the 1960s described by family, friends, and teachers?
8. What is the difference between conventional politics and participatory politics?
9. What examples of participatory democracy do you see around you, both on campus and off? Is this evidence for or against Rimmerman's claim about the attitudes of the citizens today, and the young people in particular?
10. Can you describe differences in political involvement (or sense of obligation) in terms of Allport's theory? Use the concepts of reference group and social distance to help.

Obligation, Loyalty, Exile

Judith N. Shklar

Biography: *Judith N. Shklar (1928–1992), Professor of Government at Harvard University, gave this text as a lecture in March 1992, shortly before her death. The daughter of a German-speaking Jewish family living in Latvia, Shklar fled Hitler with her parents in 1939 through Sweden to Russia to Japan, through the United States and finally to Canada. Stanley Hoffman, Harvard colleague and author of the "In Memoriam" preface to the article, quotes Shklar as claiming, "there are two kinds of political scientists—those who study power because they like to exert it, and those who study it because they fear it" (p. 172). She spent her professional life studying, according to Hoffman, "the dialectic of inclusion and exclusion," focusing on humans as social beings, citizens and decision makers rather than as private persons (p. 174).*

Shklar studies the attitudes of exiles in order to explore the effect of discrimination and abuse on loyalty, sense of obligation to nation, and identity. Studies historical cases: Jim Crow victims and the internment of Japanese Americans. An empirical application of political theory, but also a philosophical essay on civil disobedience, obligation, and the limits of political loyalty. A political scientist's view of inclusion, exclusion, and their relationship to justice. The essay provides an excellent example of the way personal experience drives research interests and of the integration of theory, empirical study, and the perpetually unfinished nature or research on difficult questions.

This is a work in progress. Not even a respectable title.

I began work on political obligation and loyalty with a view to getting away from my preoccupation with political evil, but I soon found out better. It began harmlessly enough as a project to figure out the differences between political obligation and political loyalty. I turned to exiles only thanks to a chance conversation, which made me recognize that exiles because their situation is so extreme constitute a perfect limiting case for illustrating the nuances and implications of all the notions related to both obligation and loyalty. That is how I got to the topic.

To be sure, I have long been interested in betrayal, and exiles are often created by governments that betray their own citizens. Governments also frequently abuse residents under their jurisdiction by denying them membership in the polity and other rights, not as a matter of legal punishment but because they belong to a group that is thought to be inherently unfit for inclusion. These people are also exiles. In fact, the more one thinks about them, the more numerous the forms of exile turn out to be. Exile itself is but a part of a larger social category, ranging from the forcibly excluded to people who exile themselves without moving by escaping into themselves, as it were, because

From *Political Theory*, Vol. 21, no. 2:181–197 (1993).

their world is so politically evil. I came to look all the way from coerced exiles to inner emigrants.

In spite of the difficulties and scope of the topic, I remain certain that exiles not only offer us a concrete way of examining the meaning of obligation and loyalty but also a chance to rethink some of the arguments made on behalf of the obligation to obey or disobey the laws and specifically the diverging claims of personal conscience and of group loyalty.

To that end I must first fit the special condition of exiles into the more general topic of the relations between obligation and loyalty. Let me begin with the current state of the literature on the subject, as I see it. The two dominant ways of discussing obligation and loyalty at present deal with benign ways of thought. Currently the discussion is often deeply apolitical as it tries to demonstrate the differences between universalistic morality and local, inherited and more partial attachments. Occasionally this is a spin-off from the communitarian debate, but by no means always. Indeed the discussion often begins with a rejection of political obligation in favor of some form of anarchism, possibly Godwin's or odd versions of Kant. So while moral obligation and personal attachments are certainly set apart there is little effort to put either one of them in specific political contexts.

The second and more political form of discussion is only too deeply tied to recent events and disappeared with them. It arose out of the civil rights movement in the USA and later out of the protests against the Vietnam War and it died as soon as these conflicts ceased to dominate the front page and the TV screen. It was not a great literature. Given its deeply American setting it never really rose above the particular character of the American legal system, or the American Dilemma, our greatest and enduring moral and social burden, black slavery and its legacy. The brief protest against the war in Vietnam soon got bogged down in the issues of conscientious objection and just war theory. The result is that very little remains that is not tied to specific events. What is left is a rather tepid debate about whether one has or has not a prima facie duty to obey the law of a relatively just state. Little follows from this, since no one argues for unconditional obedience in response. It has been noted that one of Hitler's services to political theory has been to do away with theories of unconditional obedience to all and any ruler. Among his disservices is that he haunts every discussion of the subject.

If the discussion of obligation is tethered to events, so is the debate about loyalty. It usually comes up in the USA when there is an effort to extract test oaths from people suspected of subversion and a general anxiety about foreigners, dangerous radicals and the like. This is now known as McCarthyism, but there have been far worse episodes of enforced loyalty in our history, especially during the First World War, of which Senator McCarthy's rampage was the last outburst. In any case when McCarthyism died down so did the volume of published material on loyalty.

As a rule these two discussions of obligation and loyalty have had little to do with one another. But in ordinary talk the two words loyalty and obligation are generally used interchangeably as if they were identical. What then is their relation and are there significant differences between loyalty and obligation? It will be my argument that it is important not only to keep them apart but to go on to make clear the distinctions between obligation, commitment, loyalty, allegiance, and fidelity. I shall say nothing about piety, the devotion that it is felt by religious persons for their deity, for my subject is politics, in which loyalty to a church is very relevant, but which is not directly affected by inward faith.

By obligation I mean rule-governed conduct, and political obligation specifically refers to laws and lawlike demands, made by public agencies. This comes out very clearly in most of our obligation talk. We are called to obey because it is right to do so according to natural law and reason, or utility or the historical mission of the modern state. The reasons for accepting or rejecting political obligations in liberal democracies are said to derive from consent, explicit or tacit, while the modern state that merely enforces the rule of law is legitimated by the security and fairness that it gives its citizens. The very word legitimacy reminds us of the law-bound character of political obligation. And whatever else tyrannies are and have been, they are always lawless regimes that we may resist.

I do not need to choose between these grounds for political obligation here, for I merely want to underline their rational rule-related character. We are told that we have a duty to comply with the rules of the political society in which we live because it is rational to do so, even though the definition of rationality may be disputed. It is rational to follow or reject rules because it is prudent to do so when all consequences to oneself and others are considered. It is rational to obey or not because there is a universal moral law we recognize when we consider impartially and impersonally what duty as such or justice imply. It is rational to obey because we have in some sense promised to do so and promises must be kept for reasons of coherence, or because that is what promising *means*, or because promise breaking is to lie and lying is against the universal law. These are all examples of rational, rule immersed thinking. Natural law, utilitarianism, deontology: all agree there are rational rules to guide us. They may not agree about the meaning of rationality, but they do know that obligation is a matter of rational rules and based on rule guided grounds. That is what defines it.

We do not, however, talk only about political obligations. Even if we limit ourselves to politics, which I do, we hear terms like commitment, fidelity, and most of all loyalty. Commitment seems to be the broadest term and it refers to chosen obligations. The term implies a voluntary engagement to do something in the future. It seems a lot looser than a promise and it can cover a vast range of actions. What is stable in its usage is that it is an engagement made voluntarily and is fully accepted by the person who is said to be committed to doing something. Political commitments usually imply the intention to support a party, a political agent, a public cause, or a political ideology. At that point feelings of loyalty may, but need not, be involved. The reasons for commitment may indeed be crassly self-interested and calculating. The dictionary speaks of pledges, and that seems right.

Commitment is my broadest category, but it has its limits. Commitments are meant to be enduring, and they imply choice. That would be as true of nonpolitical cases, such as commitment to the Society for the Prevention of Cruelty to Animals, or to a political cause, such as Amnesty International. I use these examples to show that not all our commitments are directly political or need have a direct bearing on human affairs, hence the broadness of the notion. I would suggest that both political obligation and loyalty are more specific than just any commitment and, above all, they may be less than voluntary.

What distinguishes loyalty is that it is deeply affective and not primarily rational. For the sake of clarity we should take loyalty to be an attachment to a social group. Membership may or may not be chosen. Belonging to an ascriptive group to which one has been brought up, and taught to feel loyal to it, since one's earliest infancy is scarcely a matter of choice. And when it comes to race, ethnicity, caste, and class, choice is not obvious. The emotional character of loyalty also sets it apart from obligation. If obligation is rule driven, loyalty is motivated by the entire personality of an agent. Political loyalty is evoked by nations, ethnic groups, churches, parties, and by doctrines, causes, ideologies, or faiths that form and identify associations. When it is a result of choice loyalty is a commitment that is affective in character and generated by a great deal more of our personality than calculation or moral reasoning. It is all of one that tends to be loyal.

If loyalty is given to groups, individuals may and do receive our fidelity. We remain true to them and to ourselves. We think of fidelity to our friends and this must include spouses and lovers. Causes, be they moral, political, or aesthetic, demand loyalty, friendship calls for fidelity. Of the two, fidelity is the most personal of all, the most expressive of our personality and emotional life. We are faithful to our spouses and to our friends; we are committed to these relationships in which there is, at least in principle, an element of choice. Once chosen we expect fidelity. That is why one can speak of a commitment to fidelity, as in marriage vows.

Fidelity does play a part in politics. Political leaders often expect and receive fidelity and are expected to show it to their followers. Harry Truman was renowned for both the fidelity he inspired and showed his supporters. Loyalty is the word used, but it seems wrong, because personal dynamics persist in all political systems. There are, I believe, good Freudian reasons for this. But in any event, leadership for better or worse involves fidelity.

Loyalty to groups, as I noted, is not, and often is not meant to be, a matter of choice. Very often we have no choice at all whether we belong to a group or not. Most of the memberships people have in groups are taken out at birth. You do not choose to be black, you do not fully chose to be Jewish, and you certainly do not choose your parents. And whether or not you choose your nationality is a very conditional and tricky question, but you are stuck with your race. And the language in which you learn to talk at all at two has a different bearing upon you than all the others you may master in later years. Now you have a choice to be either loyal or disloyal to these groups, but you do not have the choice of being neither. That is a pretty severe limitation. Fidelity can come to a stop: two people cease to care for each other, and there's an end to it. In a free society your commitments to parties and causes are expected to alter over a life span. But we characteristically demand loyalty to groups where the assumption of limited choice prevails. Selling out is the great crime of persons who have gone over to the "other side" but who by some definition still belong to the group.

In the days when a lot of people were interested in class politics there was always the distinction between workers, who had no choice about who they were as part of a class, and intellectuals who had made a choice. The reason for distrusting the latter was obvious: they could not give full and unselective loyalty, only a chosen commitment.

When we look at politics there is yet another bond: allegiance, a relationship that I think is clearly derived from feudal bonds. If you too have been deeply influenced by Bloch's *Feudal Society,* then you will recognize that in the anarchy after the collapse of Charlemagne's empire, the only way to reestablish political cohesion among armed men was to bind them through personal bonds, in which the inferior becomes "the man" of his superior, his vassal in due course. Eventually as oaths became an additional means of gluing the baronage together a religious element entered the bond as well. It was a very significant ritual that has not entirely disappeared. Not only do promises play a great role in creating political obligations, but, in spite of Hume's efforts, it has been very difficult to get God out of them. An oath is not an interpersonal bond, but in the first instance a promise to obey God. It is a covenant as much as a contract and entails both personal fidelity and social loyalty. So allegiance stands between fidelity and loyalty. The totally irrational habit of extracting oaths to which the USA is addicted has its roots in these rituals, and they are assumed to retain some of their ancient meaning, at least to the extent that they are not test oaths designed to entrap people into perjuring themselves.

I think I have now drawn a shaky intellectual map. It is meant less to be accurate than to throw a lurid light upon the difficulties of my project. One thing ties all of these notions together: They all invite conflict; trouble is their middle name. Conflicts are common between obligations, commitments, loyalties, fidelities, and allegiances. Moreover, each of these has to endure internal conflicts as well. Loyalties clash and so do obligations. However sincere we may be in our commitments, however rational our sense of political obligation, however devoted to our country, cause, and spouse, we will have diverse claims on our feelings and calculations. Probably the most severe tensions are between fidelity and all the others, but both fidelity and loyalty are most likely to collide with political obligation because they are different in kind not just in extent and intensity. They are not rule-bound imperatives. Personal fidelity and group loyalties have always put political obligation into question. Literature, especially the tragic drama, is a storehouse of examples of individuals torn between their obligations as public figures and their personal feelings for family and friends. Creon (backed by Hegel) had a rational point when he said to Antigone that authority saves lives. From Agamemnon to Cinna we have the clash of public roles and personal fidelity to child, sweetheart, and parents. The defenders of obligation, like Socrates, have told their friends to go away, while those who clung to them could look forward to anything from martyrdom to accusations of irrationality. At one time there was a flourishing literature about the conflict between fidelity to persons and loyalty to the Communist party when its line changed. "Dirty hands" was a serious problem. That may seem a long time ago, but it is not.

Because groups are the sites of most political action they are also the locus of conflict, and part of their language of combat is about loyalty, especially now. For the age of ideology has left us with only one survivor able to make claims upon primary loyalties: nationalism. It is all the more powerful because it has no serious rivals. That nationalism can and does conflict with personal fidelity is painfully clear. Think of all those wretched couples in Croatia, one of whom is Serb and the other Croat! Not to mention much that is closer to home. As for loyalty and obligation it is evident that nationality and state structures must conflict, because there is no single territorial state, except perhaps Iceland, that is not multiethnic and multinational or could ever be or have been.

Of course, this brief list certainly does not exhaust the possibilities. There are conflicts also within each form of attachment, such as conflicts of fidelity, say, to two friends who are at odds with one another, as when couples divorce. Then there are genuine conflicts of loyalty, say, between one's church and one's political party, such as many socialist Catholics faced in America in the Thirties. More recently, members of the democratic political organizations have had to give up their membership in exclusive golf clubs. And most important of all are conflicts of obligation, as when two constitutional rights conflict, for example, the right to free press and the right to a fair trial, which has long been a sore point in American constitutional law. And then there is the perennial conflict in constitutional states between the demands of military security and the obligation to the laws, which presidents since Jefferson have bent, to say the least.

Illegality, disloyalty, and infidelity are sometimes unavoidable, and they are witness to the conflict between our incompatible attachments.

I do not wish to imply that conflict between loyalty and obligation is inherent and inevitable, though it is very likely. Loyalty can and does sustain obligation, often. If state and nationality coincide, national loyalty will do much to reinforce obligation to the state and its laws. The *ancien régime* owed much to caste ties and interests. And party loyalty is necessary to maintain representative public institutions. When Max Weber claimed, quaintly it now seems, that devotion to a cause gave politics its ethical substance he was pointing to the dependence of loyalty and obligation on one another. Unreflective citizenship is often habitual and not really an expression of obligation. Once the question of whether one should or should not obey is asked, however, the difference between loyalty and obligation emerges. Then we cannot ignore the difference and the ways in which loyalty can both sustain and undermine public rules.

Having recognized that conflict is only part of the story, I do now want to return to it. In the conflicts between obligation, loyalty, and fidelity a decision one way or another will be a betrayal of the loser. While conflicts between loyalties and fidelities are particularly likely to induce a deep sense of betrayal among individuals, personal relationships are not the only ones that invite betrayal. States and groups also betray each other and states may betray some of their individual members by treating them unjustly and illegally, in some cases by exiling them. One advantage of looking closely at such exiles is that they help one to illustrate how obligation, loyalty, and fidelity support and undermine each other. The second interest of exiles is that they have been viewed very differently at various times and these differences reveal changes in attitudes to obligation and loyalty, especially in classical as contrasted with modern political theory, but also by different modern political theorists. Lastly, I think that exile can throw some light on the justifications we offer for our choices, specifically the claims of personal conscience.

What is an exile? I despair of ever completing my list. An exile is someone who involuntarily leaves the country of which he or she is a citizen. Usually it is thanks to political force, but extreme poverty may be regarded as a form of coercive expulsion. I will stick to the classic exile, involuntary emigrées who leave under threat of harm to themselves and to their family. I put aside ordinary criminals who are on the run and limit myself to persons who have good grounds to claim that the state has treated them unjustly by excluding them from its borders. They are the injured party. What are their political duties now? Consider a pair of famous ancient exiles, Themistocles and Aristides, who both appear in Plutarch and the former memorably in Thucydides.

Themistocles was ostracized because he had become too powerful and because he was not trusted. Ostracism was not a punishment. It was a public policy designed to prevent a too powerful individual from threatening democratic rule. There was no guilt or shame involved. Themistocles certainly felt neither; he just went over to the Persians, became an adviser to their king, dressed in Persian styles, and never seems to have given Athens a second thought. Thucydides who tells us of his career has nothing but admiration for this man. He was intelligent, prudent, and adaptable, a perfect survivor who never threatened the internal peace of either Athens or Persia. He served each state capably and did well for himself as well. If you think, as Thucydides did, that civil war is the most horrible thing that can happen, that civilization is very thin ice and that savagery and murderous rage are just below the surface of society, then loyalty and obligation are not to be regarded as nearly as important as adaptability, moderation, and prudence. And so Thucydides tells us that Themistocles was the most admirable politician he had known. Of him it could be said that he scrupulously met his political obligations and had no loyalties at all.

In his lack of effective political attachment Themistocles was quite unusual. Loyalty to the city was intense among the Athenian people at least, though perhaps not among the aristocrats. The practice of ostracism did nothing to make the latter more tractable and eventually the practice was dropped. In terms of Aristotelian notions of justice ostracism was certainly unjust, although Aristotle accepted its necessity under certain circumstances: as a matter of political prudence, not justice. Even some exiles seem to have taken that view, for, there were great men who did not behave like Themistocles, nor was he universally admired in antiquity. Plutarch did not think much of him and praised the Roman Camillus in contrast, who, although banished and then recalled by most of the citizens, would not return until his sentence had been legally revoked. And then, even more notoriously, there was Aristides, who was Themistocles' contemporary and constant rival. He also was ostracized, but at no time did he contemplate going over to the enemy and in due course he was invited to come back. When he did, he did nothing to revenge himself on his enemies. He was in due course universally known as "the just." Clearly, this was a man who met all his obligations, no less than Themistocles, but there must have been an element of loyalty as well. We do not know.

It is not insignificant that Aristides in order to meet his obligations had no political friends, and he avoided all those actions and preferences which could disturb the frail civil peace of Athens. In this he was unlike Coriolanus, my third character out of Plutarch. Here is a story of personal fidelity triumphing over both loyalty and obligation. Coriolanus was noble, brave, and a great general. What was unique about him was that having lost his father as a child he was intensely devoted to his mother with whom he lived even after his marriage. In politics, out of aristocratic arrogance he did everything he could to insult the people and in this, gained the support of many young men from families like his own. Everything he did was designed to bring about a civil war until he finally left the city after losing a trial. He went right over to Rome's worst enemies to help them to destroy the city. So the women of Rome implored his mother to plead with him, which she did successfully. What Plutarch found so utterly objectionable in Coriolanus was not that Coriolanus had betrayed Rome but that first he threatened it with civil war and then returned out of love for his mother, a private and personal fidelity, not a political or military act. Plutarch was, in fact, following a long line of thinking about the political implications of personal friendship. As far as he was concerned, personal fidelity was a threat to the republic because it concentrates on particular individuals not on the city as a whole. And so, to top it all off, Plutarch compares him unfavorably to Alcibiades, after having painted a truly horrible portrait of the latter, because at least he did not bring Athens to the brink of civil war. He was consistently egotistic.

I mention these examples from classical political theory because they present a view of political obligation and loyalty that is gone. Even when, like Plutarch, treason is regarded as a crime and the fact that it is particularly excoriated by the people is recognized, serious political theory does not make much of an ado about it. The obligations and loyalties of the individual agent are entirely subordinated to the necessity of avoiding civil war. The single most important political aim is to avoid the carnage of internal war. That is the supreme evil. Everything is destroyed when that happens. It is the political equivalent of the bubonic plague. What else is Aristotle's *Politics* about? There is bound to be tension between justice and political prudence and that is a practical difficulty, rendered dangerous by the impetuosity of unruly aristocrats and an edgy people. It is wholly a question of policy. That is in fact what is meant by the priority of the city over its individual members. If biblical religiosity had been compatible with this view, my story would be over, but it is not so. It is also not the way modern political theory has thought of exiles and other excluded people. In fact it has not said as much as it should about the rights and obligations of exiles.

For modern exiles illuminate loyalty and obligation no less than their very different ancient counterparts. If we stick to relatively just regimes as Athens and Rome had been, the most interesting cases occur when fundamental public principles are disregarded and the legally defined and protected rights are violated, by subjecting an individual or a group to exile or by excluding them from citizenship. What happens when legally created expectations, based on a public and published system of rights and duties, are cast aside in this way? The excuse is usually that these regrettable measures were a matter of dire necessity. In fact, they rarely are. In retrospect there are few cases of governmental criminality that can be justified on grounds of unavoidable necessity. Moreover, governmental illegality is not a disregard for casual understandings, such as exist in many private quasi-contracts, but a disruption of the law as it stands and is known. It violates trust in a way that renders the very basis of public life unreliable and vitiates the chief reasons for our obligation to obey the law. Political loyalty may survive, but not obligation to obey the law. That is why I assume that exiles have no obligations to the country that expels them illegally and unconstitutionally.

Official illegality may also create a nonterritorial form of exile, internal exclusion from citizenship, which afflicts slaves, unwelcome immigrants and ethnic groups, and morally upright people trapped within the borders of tyrannical states. The excluded, or internal exiles as they have sometimes been called, even sometimes appear in constitutional regimes on those occasions when these engage in exceptionally unjust and immoral policies. The morally isolated individual may be reduced to living in accordance with no rule other than his private conscience, and I shall try to say something about the arguments that such people make, as part of my review of the obligations and loyalties of politically excluded persons.

Given that legality is the core of the legitimacy of the modern state, unjust exile evokes responses quite unlike those of the classical political scientists with their concern about civil war. Exile is subject to judgments based on the claims of the individual. The rights of and the wrongs suffered by the victims are therefore of primary interest. Take the case of Captain Dreyfus. He was accused and found guilty in 1894 of having passed secret French Army documents to the Germans. He was palpably innocent, but he was a natural suspect because he was a Jew. Even when his innocence was perfectly clear no court would clear him and the Army argued that the innocence of the individual was less important than the honor of the Army, which could therefore never admit that many of its officers had perjured themselves. The Army officers felt that their primary obligation was to the Army and to France as they saw it, not to the French republic, that is, to the political order that they were supposed to serve. Moreover, they managed to successfully persecute anyone who published evidence proving the innocence of Dreyfus, now on Devil's Island. They in effect ostracized the man because they thought it best for the state as a whole. Finally, to be sure, the government was forced to pardon him, and only in 1906 did an appeals court finally quash his sentence.

When war broke out in 1914 Dreyfus immediately rejoined the Army and served with distinction. At no time did he ever cease to be anything but a superpatriotic, loyal French citizen. He merely wanted his honor as a loyal officer reestablished. It never seems to have occurred to him that he was living in a corrupt society and serving in a criminal officer corps. His sense of loyalty to the Army and to France was theirs in fact. Here is an example of loyalty sustaining an obligation he may not even have owed to a state that had rejected and betrayed him. Certainly here, loyalty overcame injustice.

It is an interesting case because the victim's sense of obligation was greater than that of the official authorities of the state. The point may be that he was not an exile from a systematically oppressive regime or an imposed one like those of Eastern Europe during the Cold War. Does that, as it were, render his loyalty to France and his enduring sense of obligation to its institutions justifiable or even meritorious?

One might suppose that at the very least Dreyfus might have led a political campaign against the way the French Army conducted itself or he could have emigrated to the USA. Dreyfus's obligations to the state clearly were terminated when it exiled him and betrayed him. He however defended only his own conduct, remained loyal to France and to its army, and thus sustained his sense of obligation. I think he was crazy, but many people admire him, because they think that loyalty to one's nation is the highest political virtue. I do not think he was just a victim identifying with the oppressor; he did look at himself as they did. Far from admitting that he was unfit to serve, he regarded himself as a model officer. He was one of them, and the victim of an error. At the least what this case demonstrates is the way in which loyalty can sustain obligation.

Dreyfus's case is not unique. No one was ever exiled more completely than the Americans of Japanese ancestry who were interned after Pearl Harbor. In 1943, after all that had been done to them, it became mandatory to declare themselves loyal or disloyal to the U.S. That was because the War Relocations Authority wanted for various reasons to empty the camps as much as possible. Not least there was a manpower shortage and the military wanted to draft the young men, some of whom had fathers who had fought in Europe in the First World War. The exiles were asked to swear allegiance to the USA and to renounce any loyalty to Japan. Three-quarters of them chose to do so and others said they would have done so had it not been for the internment. It was in any event clear that among those who refused to swear there was a deep and justifiable sense of betrayal. Not they but their country had betrayed them. Why should you not act as an enemy alien if you are treated as one?

The parents of the young men were especially bitter at the demand that their sons now fight for the U.S. For them, family values, always important among Japanese people, now seemed all that was left. The more Americanized the individuals were, the more likely they were to swear allegiance to the U.S. and also feel the most outraged by what they knew to be a violation of their rights.

As one of the internees put it,

> I felt that the Constitution had failed me. Actually, it wasn't the Constitution that failed me; the Supreme Court failed me, and the other people who were entrusted with the upholding of the Constitution failed me. . . . They failed because the will of the people wasn't behind upholding the Constitution.

One of the most important points in this awful story is a human one. Each one of these people had to make a personal choice involving a family and one's own future. For many, a return to Japan was unthinkable, so they really had no choice. In the event, a Japanese-American regiment fought with great distinction in Italy. Segregated, of course. Here there is both conflict between obligation and loyalty as well as a reconciliation between the two, but at the expense of the exiles. Recently the federal government has apologized to the internees, but the principles which made these official acts possible remain intact.

No such relatively easy denouement is possible in the case of radically unjust states. Willy Brandt returned to Germany after years of forced exile in Norway and said that he had kept faith with the real Germany, the true Germany. He cannot have meant the majority of his people, only their better possibilities, to which he remained loyal. He even returned to Germany to see his friends secretly. At no time did he lose faith in the German labor movement. But he certainly supported the Norwegians in the war against Germany. His obligations to Germany had evidently lapsed and been transferred. He acquired Norwegian citizenship and worked for the Norwegian government briefly after the war. From the first he emphasized and publicized the difference between criminal and other Germans. And ultimately he resumed his citizenship, becoming first mayor of Berlin and then chancellor of West Germany.

The German Jews, however, could retain no conceivable obligations to Germany even after the destruction of the Nazi state, and only a handful returned. They also had no grounds for loyalty, since their erstwhile fellow citizens had abandoned them with such alacrity. One can look at their condition in Lockean terms. Both contracts had been broken, the first between members of society as well as the second between citizens and the state. They were betrayed at both levels, excluded from civil no less than from political society. Personal ties of fidelity remained occasionally and so did nostalgia. "How shall I sing the Lord's song in a strange land?" sang an exile in the saddest of Old Testament Psalms. And for many of them that is what exile came down to. What am I trying to show is that the extent of the rejection determines whether there is, even after the elimination of any obligation, any possibility of retaining some loyalty to the native land. It makes all the difference to the exile and it is an issue that may also create problems for the host state to which the exiles are now obliged.

For enduring loyalty can often cause some real damage to new political obligations. If exiles retain ties of loyalty to the country that expelled them, they may be less than either loyal or obedient to the laws of the host state. Brandt only remained loyal to an idea of Germany and the Jews not even that, but often new political obligations are rendered murky by the volatility of loyalty. Diasporas can be unreliable, if they do not feel wholly alienated from the state that exiled them or from ideologies that were acquired there. Nevertheless, it is surprising how few American traitors were actually foreign born.

It might be argued that the problems of exiles are not so special but, rather, just like those of everyone else faced with having to decide whether to obey the law or not, and trying to assess the degree of evil in the government that has provoked the question in the first place. They have to ask themselves whether the government that betrayed them is a tyranny or whether just some of its policies are manifestly unjust, but capable of being altered. Clearly, Dreyfus and the Japanese Americans unlike Willy Brandt and the German Jews had to deal with a reasonably just state, not Hitler. How do their questions differ from those of a Southern black student in the 1960s in the USA? I think that there is a difference in the degree of exclusion between exiles and other victims of public injustice. Refugees who have been expelled beyond all hope of return have no political obligations at all to their former state. After such an expulsion there is no point in trying to reclaim one's rights as Dreyfus and the Japanese Americans did, and ultimately did successfully. That is, however, not the only consideration. Most exiles today simply have nowhere to go, whatever they might wish to do. The dreadful reality of our world is that no one wants to accept this huge exiled population. What they need is a place to go to, and these are increasingly hard to find. It is at least a tolerable solution for ethnic groups to emigrate en masse if they have a welcoming home country, such as the *pieds noirs* from North Africa who went to France or Jews who can go to Israel. But these are exceptions. Most people do not merely fear foreign exile; many of them will be exiles in pure limbo.

The dwellers in refugee camps can best be compared to America's African slaves. And as we all look on helplessly at the ever-growing numbers of human refuse heaps, we might perhaps listen to the voice of conscience. At the very least we might reexamine anew the claims that are made for and against the call of conscience in the face of group loyalty. That is why a look at the secular abolitionists may not be irrelevant. An injustice as great as slavery, especially in an otherwise reasonably just state, is bound to create moral outrage. And some of the Americans who were determined to end slavery found themselves in a very curious situation. Those among them who felt that the entire Constitution, not only specific laws, was a slave document could have no obligation to obey the laws at all. For some, religious loyalty was the only significant bond left. These were the majority of abolitionists who were members of radical Protestant congregations or abolitionist societies, most of which were religious as well. But what of the secular abolitionist, like Thoreau, for example? I should like to undertake a defense of his position in an essentially psychological way, by suggesting that he had little choice but to base himself in his conscience and nothing else, to make what one might call a "pure conscience" argument. I do not propose to examine its ultimate validity, but to see it in the context within which it emerges.

What we get here is personal isolation of the most extreme sort. Now Thoreau's argument for disobedience relies exclusively on his conscience in refusing to obey to pay his taxes. *No* government that rules over slaves is good enough to rule him, and while he is perfectly ready to leave the running of many insignificant public matters to the lawyers in state houses, the evil on his mind is not trivial. So he refuses to recognize his obligations. If he had a friend or a group who shared his cause we do not hear of it. He was not choosing between loyalty and laws. Not at all. He was asserting the unconditional primacy of conscience in the face of what he regarded as absolute evil. The moral "empire of me" was created because there was no other.

The situation of an American abolitionist was wholly different from that of European radical vintage 1848. It was more like the condition of the opponents of Nazism who remained in Germany cut off from their exiled friends by war, and utterly alone among their Nazified countrymen. Abolitionists lived not in the midst of ideological struggles but in a moral vacuum and their agony was being implicated in an evil they abhorred. Every time they put on a shirt they were abetting the slavery of the blacks who had picked the cotton. But in no way could they identify with the slaves, be part of their society, or become blacks.

A Thoreau had neither the camaraderie of the revolutionary, nor a shared identity with the slaves. There was no "we." They were alone to the point of self-exclusion. The "Inner Civil War" as it is called could only be ended by the real war. They could not resort to loyalty because they had no local support. It was to be sure a social cause, but there was no community, the object was too remote. Although, unlike most abolitionists he was not a racist, as far as we know, Thoreau certainly could not join the blacks. Nor could he be expected to do so. He was protesting on their behalf, but abolitionism did not require him to take the slightest interest in the actual life and future of the enslaved population. There is often nothing *there* when one protests against abstract and absolute evil, and it is exceptionally isolating.

I want to consider this example of exclusion because I think that the pure conscience argument has often been misunderstood, at least as it appears in America. The general *fons et origo* of the case against conscience as the sole ground for either disobedience or disloyalty has been Hegel and I won't repeat all of his argument, but it comes down to identifying conscience with a sort of moral egotism and shiftiness. I would suggest that if we evaluate conscience claims in politics in terms of their setting, we will recognize the voice of men and women who have been so completely isolated by the injustice they perceive around them that ties of loyalty and fidelity may be eroded along with political obligation. It is this situation that has in our century been called "internal exile," and it is expressed in the pure conscience argument and justifies it. It is also a very rare occurrence. In the USA it receives its relevance soley from a single, though searing, experience of enduring injustice to one group in an otherwise constitutionally respectable polity. It was repeated in Europe in our century, under circumstances which Hegel did not foresee.

In spite of these considerations, loyalty to groups, to causes, to a class, a caste, a party, or any association has long had a far better press than the dissociated insubstantial conscience. None have done better than ethnic solidarity and nationalism which inspire the most intense political loyalty, especially in their most xenophobic aspects. The approval of group-based loyalty and arguments for and against political obligation based on such loyalty tends, however, to mute, indeed to forget, that exclusion is an unavoidable and essential feature of such loyalty. This is the case even when exclusion is not a given group's primary purpose and hostility to outsiders is not encouraged. In the political world of the present, political loyalty is however often very exclusive, especially nationalism, which has done much to create the current refugee population and certainly ensures their and their children's continued exile. Who can these people be expected to trust, especially if they are dumped into states which refuse to grant citizenship to anyone who is not a member of their nation? Would they be bad citizens? The experience of Canada and the United States denies it. Diaspora groups in countries that permit naturalization are usually quite law abiding and as bound by obligation as the native in paying their taxes and following public health rules. Here I need only mention again Japanese Americans who are one of the least crime- or spy-ridden communities in the country.

Even if in open immigrant societies the lot of the refugee is at first a difficult one, their troubles do abate. We need not forget the endless efforts to shoeborn citizens into Anglo-Saxon conformity which began with the mass immigration of the 1880s from Eastern and Southern Europe and which have not entirely ended yet. But these hurdles are as nothing compared to those of permanent refugee groups, guest workers, camp dwellers bereft of every civic tie and hope, surviving as best they can in countries that will never grant citizenship to anyone but their own nationals. This is the consequence of making political obligation dependent on group membership and loyalty both national and ethnic. Religious sects once had such policies as well and in some countries this is still the case, but it is the national and ethnic loyalty that undermines legality and the principles of political obligation. By excluding people who would obey the law, but might speak a foreign language, the actual consequences of communal cohesion, so often praised as the only valid ground for either political resistance or obedience, reveals its primary and insuperable defect. It is the path of injustice. Great as the gratifications and privileges of membership may be and natural as their desperate cohesion in a world of endless migrations and civil wars is, the plight of the dispersed and excluded is unbearable.

This suggests that human rights may have much to do with the way these conflicts evolve. If citizenship in *some* country is, as Hannah Arendt argued, the one necessary human right of our century because all others depend on it, then offering citizenship to exiles may prove the most significant means of taming political loyalty. The evidence is clear that when political obligations are assumed they are not lightly shaken off, and when they are, it is usually because there is real and reasonably perceived injustice, as in the various cases of exclusion that I have recounted. In short it might be a good idea to discuss issues raised by legal and political obligation not as issues of individual autonomy and legal doctrine, but more politically in terms of the prevailing policies of states as they affect excluded groups.

I am not good at conclusions. The desire to arrive at them strikes me, frankly, as slightly childish. A need for an "and they lived happily ever after" ending does not seem to me to fit a type of discourse that is unending. However, in order to remain reasonably conventional, I would suggest that injustice not only cancels obligations and undermines loyalties, however resilient the latter may seem; it also engenders the conflicts between obligation and the affective ties that bind us. The hatred that injustice perceived and real, and most perceived injustice *is* real, creates stirs up most of the trouble. It is, I fear, vain to hope that the simple effort to establish just institutions can create a modus vivendi, let alone build a shared sense of political right, once these conflicts have emerged. Nevertheless, the less injustice there is, the less likely it is that refugees will populate the world and bring with them their terrible misery and mischief. ⊛

QUESTIONS FOR THOUGHT AND STUDY

1. What might Shklar mean by "my preoccupation with political evil"? Think of examples of governments betraying their people or the kinds of political acts Shklar cites in her second paragraph.

2. How does Shklar distinguish between obligation, commitment, loyalty, allegiance, and fidelity? Make a list of three groups that are important to you, or, if the Allport article is part of your assignment, choose the three most important groups from your Allport list. For each group, see if you can distinguish your obligations from your commitment, from your loyalty, using Shklar's definitions.

3. Civil disobedience such as Thoreau's is the rejection of obligation—what justifies such defiance, in Shklar's opinion? What instances of civil disobedience do you know of? Were they justifiable? Why or why not?

4. Shklar states that group loyalty has always received better press than personal conscience. Do you agree? Think of examples. Have you ever felt that you ought to leave a group because you didn't approve of their beliefs or actions? What was or would have been the cost of leaving the group? Of denouncing them? Would the cost be rational (arrest, penalty), emotional (isolation) or both?

5. Does Shklar believe loyalty to be good? Totally good? Why or why not? How important is group solidarity to groups you belong to? Why? Would speaking up against the group be criticized? Tolerated?

6. Compare Shklar's theory with Allport's. What common ground and what differences do you find? Compare it with Du Bois's. What similarities and differences do you find there?

7. What is Shklar's thesis? Where in the article is it stated?

Ecological Literacy

EDUCATION AND THE TRANSITION TO A POSTMODERN WORLD

David W. Orr

Biography: David W. Orr is a Professor of Environmental Studies at Oberlin College and cofounder of the Meadowcreek Project, a nonprofit environmental education organization. He is coauthor of The Global Predicament *and coeditor of the SUNY Press series,* Environmental Public Policy. *The book from which this chapter is drawn seeks a worldview beyond the modern, a view based on individual achievement and the infinite creation of wants—a view that Orr and others believe will soon carry us beyond the earth's capacity to sustain us. The book asks what people need to know about the limited capacity of the earth and how they should learn it.*

Orr argues that our education reflects attitudes grounded in an age of economic dominance and specialization, and that we fail, therefore to teach ecological literacy—an appreciation of the interrelation of our social and physical environments. Ecological literacy requires knowledge of several fields and of the interaction of those fields plus a renewal of our aesthetic sense, our sense of wonder, our sense of being an integral and interdependent part of the universe. An interdisciplinary article that shares features with science, social science, and the humanities. The chapter presents a strong philosophical position, thus providing an example of a writing at the intersection of social science and the humanities.

L iteracy is the ability to read. Numeracy is the ability to count. Ecological literacy, according to Garrett Hardin, is the ability to ask "What then?" Considerable attention is properly being given to our shortcomings in teaching the young to read, count, and compute, but not nearly enough to ecological literacy. Reading, after all, is an ancient skill. And for most of the twentieth century we have been busy adding, subtracting, multiplying, dividing, and now computing. But "What then?" questions have not come easy for us despite all of our formidable advances in other areas. Napoleon did not ask the question, I gather, until

From Ch. V: *Ecological Literacy: Education and the Transition to a Postmodern World*. Albany: State University of New York Press, (1992).

he had reached the outskirts of Moscow, by which time no one could give a good answer except "Let's go back home." If Custer asked the question, we have no record of it. His last known words at Little Big Horn were, "Hurrah, boys, now we have them," a stirring if dubious pronouncement. And economists, who are certainly both numerate and numerous, have not asked the question often enough. Asking "What then?" on the west side of the Niemen River, or at Fort Laramie, would have saved a lot of trouble. For the same reason, "What then?" is also an appropriate question to ask before the last rain forests disappear, before the growth economy consumes itself into oblivion, and before we have warmed the planet intolerably.

The failure to develop ecological literacy is a sin of omission and of commission. Not only are we failing to teach the basics about the earth and how it works, but we are in fact teaching a large amount of stuff that is simply wrong. By failing to include ecological perspectives in any number of subjects, students are taught that ecology is unimportant for history, politics, economics, society, and so forth. And through television they learn that the earth is theirs for the taking. The result is a generation of ecological yahoos without a clue why the color of the water in their rivers is related to their food supply, or why storms are becoming more severe as the planet warms. The same persons as adults will create businesses, vote, have families, and above all, consume. If they come to reflect on the discrepancy between the splendor of their private lives in a hotter, more toxic and violent world, as ecological illiterates they will have roughly the same success as one trying to balance a checkbook without knowing arithmetic.

FORMATION OF ATTITUDES

To become ecologically literate one must certainly be able to read and, I think, even like to read. Ecological literacy also presumes an ability to use numbers, and the ability to know what is countable and what is not, which is to say the limits of numbers. But these are indoor skills. Ecological literacy also requires the more demanding capacity to observe nature with insight, a merger of landscape and mindscape. "The interior landscape," in Barry Lopez's words, "responds to the character and subtlety of an exterior landscape; the shape of the individual mind is affected by land as it is by genes."[1] The quality of thought is related to the ability to relate to "where on this earth one goes, what one touches, the patterns one observes in nature—the intricate history of one's life in the land, even a life in the city, where wind, the chirp of birds, the line of a falling leaf, are known." The fact that this kind of intimate knowledge of our landscapes is rapidly disappearing can only impoverish our mental landscapes as well. People who do not know the ground on which they stand miss one of the elements of good thinking which is the capacity to distinguish between health and disease in natural systems and their relation to health and disease in human ones.

If literacy is driven by the search for knowledge, ecological literacy is driven by the sense of wonder, the sheer delight in being alive in a beautiful, mysterious, bountiful world. The darkness and disorder that we have brought to that world give ecological literacy an urgency it lacked a century ago. We can now look over the abyss and see the end of it all. Ecological literacy begins in childhood. "To keep alive his inborn sense of wonder," a child, in Rachel Carson's words, "needs the companionship of at least one adult who can share it, rediscovering with him the joy, excitement and mystery of the world we live in."[2] The sense of wonder is rooted in the emotions or what E. O. Wilson has called "biophilia," which is simply the affinity for the living world.[3] The nourishment of that affinity is the beginning point for the sense of kinship with life, without which literacy of any sort will not help much. This is to say that even a thorough knowledge of the facts of life and of the threats to it will not save us in the absence of the feeling of kinship with life of the sort that cannot entirely be put into words.

There are, I think, several reasons why ecological literacy has been so difficult for Western culture. First, it implies the ability to think broadly, to know something of what is hitched to what. This ability is being lost in an age of specialization. Scientists of the quality of Rachel Carson or Aldo Leopold are rarities who must buck the pressures toward narrowness and also endure a great deal of professional rejection and hostility. By inquiring into the relationship between chlorinated hydrocarbon pesticides and bird populations, Rachel Carson was asking an ecolate question. Many others failed to ask, not because they did not like birds, but because they had not, for whatever reasons, thought beyond the conventional categories. To do so would have required that they relate their food system to the decline in the number of birds in their neighborhood. This means that they would have had some direct knowledge of farms and farming practices, as well as a comprehension of ornithology. To think in ecolate fashion presumes a breadth of experience with healthy natural systems, both of which are increasingly rare. It also presumes that the persons be willing and able to "think at right angles" to their particular specializations, as Leopold put it.

Ecological literacy is difficult, second, because we have come to believe that education is solely an indoor activity. A good part of it, of necessity, must be, but there is a price. William Morton Wheeler once compared the naturalist with the professional biologist in these words: "[The naturalist] is primarily an observer and fond of outdoor life, a collector, a classifier, a describer, deeply impressed by the overwhelming intricacy of natural phenomena and revelling in their very complexity." The biologist, on the other hand, "is oriented toward and dominated by ideas, and rather terrified or oppressed by the intricate hurly-burly of concrete, sensuous reality. . . . he is a denizen of the laboratory. His besetting sin is oversimplification and the tendency to undue isolation of the organisms he studies from their natural environment."[4] Since Wheeler wrote, ecology has become increasingly specialized and, one suspects, remote from its subject matter. Ecology, like most learning worthy of the effort, is an applied subject. Its goal is not just a comprehension of how the world works, but, in the light of that knowledge, a life lived accordingly. The same is true of theology, sociology, political science, and most other subjects that grace the conventional curriculum.

The decline in the capacity for aesthetic appreciation is a third factor working against ecological literacy. We have become comfortable with all kinds of ugliness and seem incapable of effective protest against its purveyors: urban developers, businessmen, government officials, television executives, timber and mining companies, utilities, and advertisers. Rene Dubos once stated that our greatest disservice to our children was to give them the belief that ugliness was somehow normal. But disordered landscapes are not just an aesthetic problem. Ugliness signifies a more fundamental disharmony between people and between people and the land. Ugliness is, I think, the surest sign of disease, or what is now being called "unsustainability." Show me the hamburger stands, neon ticky-tacky strips leading toward every city in America, and the shopping malls, and I'll show you devastated rain forests, a decaying countryside, a politically dependent population, and toxic waste dumps. It is all of a fabric.

And this is the heart of the matter. To see things in their wholeness is politically threatening. To understand that our manner of living, so comfortable for some, is linked to cancer rates in migrant laborers in California, the disappearance of tropical rain forests, fifty thousand toxic dumps across the U.S.A., and the depletion of the ozone layer is to see the need for a change in our way of life. To see things whole is to see both the wounds we have inflicted on the natural world in the name of mastery and those we have inflicted on ourselves and on our children for no good reason, whatever our stated intentions. Real ecological literacy is radicalizing in that it forces us to reckon with the roots of our ailments, not just with their symptoms. For this reason, I think it leads to a revitalization and broadening of the concept of citizenship to include membership in a planetwide community of humans and living things.

And how does this striving for community come into being? I doubt that there is a single path, but there are certain common elements. First, in the lives of most if not all people who define themselves as environmentalists, there is experience in the natural world at an early age. Leopold came to know birds and wildlife in the marshes and fields around his home in Burlington, Iowa before his teens. David Brower, as a young boy on long walks over the Berkeley hills, learned to describe the flora to his nearly blind mother. Second, and not surprisingly, there is often an older teacher or mentor as a role model: a grandfather, a neighbor, an older brother, a parent, or teacher. Third, there are seminal books that explain, heighten, and say what we have felt deeply, but not said so well. In my own life, Rene Dubos and Loren Eiseley served this function of helping to bring feelings to articulate consciousness.

Ecological literacy is becoming more difficult, I believe, not because there are fewer books about nature, but because there is less opportunity for the direct experience of it. Fewer people grow up on farms or in rural areas where access is easy and where it is easy to learn a degree of competence and self-confidence toward the natural world. Where the ratio between the human-created environment to the purely natural world exceeds some point, the sense of place can only be a sense of habitat. One finds the habitat familiar and/or likeable but without any real sense of belonging in the natural world. A sense of place requires more direct contact with the natural aspects of a place, with soils, landscape, and wildlife. This sense is lost as we move down the continuum toward the totalized urban environment where nature exists in tiny, isolated fragments by permission only. Said differently, this is an argument for more urban parks, summer camps, green belts, wilderness areas, public seashores. If we must live in an increasingly urban world, let's make it one of well-designed compact green cities that include trees, river parks, meandering green belts, and urban farms where people can see, touch, and experience nature in a variety of ways. In fact, no other cities will be sustainable in a greenhouse world.

ECOLOGICAL LITERACY AND FORMAL EDUCATION

The goal of ecological literacy as I have described it has striking implications for that part of education that must occur in classrooms, libraries, and laboratories. To the extent that most educators have noticed the environment, they have regarded it as a set of problems which are: (1) solvable (unlike dilemmas, which are not) by (2) the analytic tools and methods of reductionist science which (3) create value-neutral, technological remedies that will not create even worse side effects. Solutions, therefore, originate at the top of society, from governments and corporations, and are passed down to a passive citizenry in the form of laws, policies, and technologies. The results, it is assumed, will be socially, ethically, politically, and humanly desirable, and the will to live and to sustain a humane culture can be preserved in a technocratic society. In other words, business can go on as usual. Since there is no particular need for an ecologically literate and ecologically competent public, environmental education is most often regarded as an extra in the curriculum, not as a core requirement or as an aspect pervading the entire educational process.

Clearly, some parts of the crisis can be accurately described as problems. Some of these can be solved by technology, particularly those that require increased resource efficiency. It is a mistake, however, to think that all we need is better technology, not an ecologically literate and caring public willing to help reduce the scale of problems by reducing its demands on the environment and to accept (even demand) public policies that require sacrifices. It all comes down to whether the public understands the relation between its well-being and the health of the natural systems.

For this to occur, we must rethink both the substance and the process of education at all levels. What does it mean to educate people to live sustainably, going, in Aldo Leopold's words, from "conqueror of the land community to plain member and citizen of it"?[5] However it is applied in practice, the answer will rest on six foundations.

The first is the recognition that *all education is environmental education.* By what is included or excluded, emphasized or ignored, students learn that they are a part of or apart from the natural world. Through all education we inculcate the ideas of careful stewardship or carelessness. Conventional education, by and large, has been a celebration of all that is human to the exclusion of our dependence on nature. As a result, students frequently resemble what Wendell Berry has called "itinerant professional vandals," persons devoid of any sense of place or stewardship, or inkling of why these are important.[6]

Second, *environmental issues are complex and cannot be understood through a single discipline or department.* Despite a decade or more of discussion and experimentation, interdisciplinary education remains an unfulfilled promise. The failure occurred, I submit, because it was tried within discipline-centric institutions. A more promising approach is to reshape institutions to function as transdisciplinary laboratories that include components such as agriculture, solar technologies, forestry, land management, wildlife, waste cycling, architectural design, and economics.[7] Part of the task, then, of Earth-centered education is the study of interactions across the boundaries of conventional knowledge and experience.

Third, *for inhabitants, education occurs in part as a dialogue with a place and has the characteristics of good conversation.* Formal education happens mostly as a monologue of human interest, desires, and accomplishments that drowns out all other sounds. It is the logical outcome of the belief that we are alone in a dead world of inanimate matter, energy flows, and biogeochemical cycles. But true conversation can occur only if we acknowledge the existence and interests of the other. In conversation, we define ourselves, but in relation to another. The quality of conversation does not rest on the brilliance of one or the other person. It is more like a dance in which the artistry is mutual.

In good conversation, words represent reality faithfully. And words have power. They can enliven or deaden, elevate or degrade, but they are never neutral, because they affect our perception and ultimately our behavior. The use of words such as "resources," "manage," "channelize," "engineer," and "produce" makes our relation to nature a monologue rather than a conversation. The language of nature includes the sounds of animals, whales, birds, insects, wind, and water—a language more ancient and basic than human speech. Its books are the etchings of life on the face of the land. To hear this language requires patient, disciplined study of the natural world. But it is a language for which we have an affinity.

Good conversation is unhurried. It has its own rhythm and pace. Dialogue with nature cannot be rushed. It will be governed by cycles of day and night, the season, the pace of procreation, and by the larger rhythm of evolutionary and geologic time. Human sense of time is increasingly frenetic, driven by clocks, computers, and revolutions in transportation and communication.

Good conversation has form, structure, and purpose. Conversation with nature has the purpose of establishing, in Wendell Berry's words: "What is here? What will nature permit here? What will nature help us do here?"[8] The form and structure of any conversation with the natural world is that of the discipline of ecology as a restorative process and healing art.

Fourth, it follows that *the way education occurs is as important as its content.* Students taught environmental awareness in a setting that does not alter their relationship to basic life-support systems learn that it is sufficient to intellectualize, emote, or posture about such things without having to live differently. Environmental education ought to change the way people live, not just how they talk. This understanding of education is drawn from the writings of John Dewey, Alfred North Whitehead, J. Glenn Gray, Paulo Friere, Ivan Illich, and Eliot Wigginton. Learning in this view best occurs in response to real needs and the life situation of the learner. The radical distinctions typically drawn between teacher and student, between the school and the community, and those between areas of knowledge, are dissolved. Real learning is participatory and experiential, not just didactic. The flow can be two ways between teachers, who best function as facilitators, and students who are expected to be active agents in defining what is learned and how.

Fifth, *experience in the natural world is both an essential part of understanding the environment, and conducive to good thinking.* Experience, properly conceived, trains the intellect to observe the land carefully and to distinguish between health and its opposite. Direct experience is an antidote to indoor, abstract learning. It is also a wellspring of good thinking. Understanding nature demands a disciplined and observant intellect. But nature, in Emerson's words, is also "the vehicle of thought" as a source of language, metaphor, and symbol. Natural diversity may well be the source of much of human creativity and intelligence. If so, the simplification and homogenization of ecosystems can only result in a lowering of human intelligence.

Sixth, *education relevant to the challenge of building a sustainable society will enhance the learner's competence with natural systems.* For reasons once explained by Whitehead and Dewey, practical competence is an indispensable source of good thinking. Good thinking proceeds from the friction between reflective thought and real problems. Aside from its effects on thinking, practical competence will be essential if sustainability requires, as I think it does, that people must take an active part in rebuilding their homes, businesses, neighborhoods, communities, and towns. Shortening supply lines for food, energy, water, and materials—while recycling waste locally—implies a high degree of competence not necessary in a society dependent on central vendors and experts.

THE AIM: ECOLOGICAL LITERACY

If these can be taken as the foundations of Earth-centered education, what can be said of its larger purpose? In a phrase, it is that quality of mind that seeks out connections. It is the opposite of the specialization and narrowness characteristic of most education. The ecologically literate person has the knowledge necessary to comprehend interrelatedness, and an attitude of care or stewardship. Such a person would also have the practical competence required to act on the basis of knowledge and feeling. Competence can only be derived from the experience of doing and the mastery of what Alasdair MacIntyre describes as a "practice."[9] Knowing, caring, and practical competence constitute the basis of ecological literacy.

Ecological literacy, further, implies a broad understanding of how people and societies relate to each other and to natural systems, and how they might do so sustainably. It presumes both an awareness of the interrelatedness of life and knowledge of how the world works as a physical system. To ask, let alone answer, "What then?" questions presumes an understanding of concepts such as carrying capacity, overshoot, Liebig's Law of the minimum, thermodynamics, trophic levels, energetics, and succession. Ecological literacy presumes that we understand our place in the story of evolution. It is to know that our health, well-being, and ultimately our survival depend on working with, not against, natural forces. The basis for ecological literacy, then, is the comprehension of the interrelatedness of life grounded in the study of natural history, ecology, and thermodynamics. It is to understand that "There ain't no such thing as a free lunch"; "You can never throw anything away"; and "The first law of intelligent tinkering is to keep all of the pieces." It is also to understand, with Leopold, that we live in a world of wounds senselessly inflicted on nature and on ourselves.

A second stage in ecological literacy is to know something of the speed of the crisis that is upon us. It is to know magnitudes, rates, and trends of population growth, species extinction, soil loss, deforestation, desertification, climate change, ozone depletion, resource exhaustion, air and water pollution, toxic and radioactive contamination, resource and energy use—in short, the vital signs of the planet and its ecosystems. Becoming ecologically literate is to understand the human enterprise for what it is: a sudden eruption in the enormity of evolutionary time.

Ecological literacy requires a comprehension of the dynamics of the modern world. The best starting place is to read the original rationale for the domination of nature found in the writings of Bacon, Descartes, and Galileo. Here one finds the justification for the union of science with power and the case for separating ourselves from nature in order to control it more fully. To comprehend the idea of controlling nature, one must fathom the sources of the urge to power and the paradox of rational means harnessed to insane ends portrayed in Marlow's *Doctor Faustus,* Mary Shelley's *Frankenstein,* Melville's *Moby-Dick,* and Dostoevsky's "Legend of the Grand Inquisitor."

Ecological literacy, then, requires a thorough understanding of the ways in which people and whole societies have become destructive. The ecologically literate person will appreciate something of how social structures, religion, science, politics, technology, patriarchy, culture, agriculture, and human cussedness combine as causes of our predicament.

The diagnosis of the causes of our plight is only half of the issue. But before we can address solutions there are several issues that demand clarification. "Nature," for example, is variously portrayed as "red in tooth and claw," or, like the film "Bambi," full of sweet little critters. Economists see nature as natural resources to be used; the backpacker as a wellspring of transcendent values. We are no longer clear about our own nature, whether we are made in the image of God, or are merely a machine or computer, or animal. These are not trivial, academic issues. Unless we can make reasonable distinctions between what is natural and what is not, and why that difference is important, we are liable to be at the mercy of the engineers who want to remake all of nature, including our own.

Environmental literacy also requires a broad familiarity with the development of ecological consciousness. The best history of the concept of ecology is Donald Worster's *Nature Economy.*[10] It is unclear whether the science of ecology will be "the last of the old sciences, or the first of the new." As the former, ecology is the science of efficient resource management. As the first of the new sciences, ecology is the basis for a broader search for pattern and meaning. As such it cannot avoid issues of values, and the ethical questions raised most succinctly in Leopold's "The Land Ethic."

The study of environmental problems is an exercise in despair unless it is regarded as only a preface to the study, design, and implementation of solutions. The concept of sustainability implies a radical change in the institutions and patterns that we have come to accept as normal. It begins with ecology as the basis for the redesign of technology, cities, farms, and educational institutions, and with a change in metaphors from mechanical to organic, industrial to biological. As part of the change we will need alternative measures of well-being such as those proposed by Amory Lovins (least-cost end-use analysis),[11] H. T. Odum (energy accounting),[12] and John Cobb (index of sustainable welfare).[13] Sustainability also implies a different approach to technolgy, one that gives greater priority to those that are smaller in scale, less environmentally destructive, and rely on the free services of natural systems. Not infrequently, technologies with these characteristics are also highly cost-effective, especially when subsidies for competing technologies are leveled out.

If sustainability represents a minority tradition, it is nonetheless a long one dating back at least to Jefferson. Students should not be considered ecologically literate until they have read Thoreau, Kropotkin, Muir, Albert Howard, Alfred North Whitehead, Gandhi, Schweitzer, Aldo Leopold, Lewis Mumford, Rachel Carson, E. F. Schumacher, and Wendell Berry. There are alternatives to the present patterns that have remained dormant or isolated, not because they did not work, were poorly thought out, or were impractical, but because they were not tried. In contrast to the directions of modern society, this tradition emphasizes democratic participation, the extension of ethical obligations to the land community, careful ecological design, simplicity, widespread competence with natural systems, the sense of place, holism, decentralization of whatever can best be decentralized, and human-scaled technologies and communities. It is a tradition dedicated to the search for patterns, unity, connections between people of all ages, races, nationalities, and generations, and between people and the natural world. This is a tradition grounded in the belief that life is sacred and not to be carelessly expended on the ephemeral. It is a tradition that challenges militarism, injustice, ecological destruction, and authoritarianism, while supporting all of those actions that lead to real peace, fairness, sustainability, and people's right to participate in those decisions that affect their lives. Ultimately, it is a tradition built on a view of ourselves as finite and fallible creatures living in a world limited by natural laws. The contrasting Promethean view, given force by the success of technology, holds that we should remove all limits, whether imposed by nature, human nature, or morality. Its slogan is found emblazoned on the advertisements of the age: "You can have it all" (Michelob Beer), or "Your world should know no limits" (Merrill Lynch). The ecologically literate citizen will recognize these immediately for what they are: the stuff of epitaphs. Ecological literacy leads in other, and more durable, directions toward prudence, stewardship, and the celebration of the Creation.

NOTES

1. Barry Lopez, *Crossing Open Ground* (New York: Vintage, 1989), 65.
2. Rachel Carson, *The Sense of Wonder* (New York: Harper and Row, 1984), 45.
3. E. O. Wilson, *Biophilia* (Cambridge: Harvard University Press, 1984).

4. In Charles P. Curtis, Jr. and Ferris Greenslet, eds., *The Practical Cogitator*, 3rd ed. (Boston: Houghton Mifflin Co., 1962), 226–29.

5. Aldo Leopold, *A Sand County Almanac* (New York: Ballantine, 1966), 240.

6. Wendell Berry, *Home Economics* (San Francisco: North Point Press, 1987), 50.

7. On the structure of environmental education, see Lynton K. Caldwell, "Environmental Studies: Discipline or Metadiscipline," *The Environmental Professional* (1983): 247–59.

8. Wendell Berry, *Home Economics* (San Francisco: North Point Press, 1987), 146.

9. Alasdair MacIntyre, *After Virtue* (South Bend: Notre Dame University Press, 1981), 169–89.

10. Donald Worster, *Nature's Economy* (San Francisco: Sierra Club Books, 1977; reissued by Cambridge University PRess, 1985).

11. Amory Lovins, *Soft Energy Paths* (Cambridge: Ballinger, 1977).

12. For the best discussion of energy accounting, see Charles Hall et al, *Energy and Resource Quality* (New York: Wiley and Sons, 1986) 3–151.

13. In Herman Daily and John Cobb, *For the Common Good* (Boston: Beacon Press, 1990), 405–55. ☁

QUESTIONS FOR THOUGHT AND STUDY

1. What do Orr and Harding mean by asking "What then?" What is "ecological literacy"?

2. Do you feel a kinship with any parts of the physical world? What parts and why? Can you find evidence of E. O. Wilson's kinship with that world in "Storm over the Amazon?"

3. What does Orr mean when he says education has become an "indoor activity"? How does such study differ from Orr's ideal? What, for Orr, are the consequences of such an education?

4. To help determine the legitimacy of Orr's case against contemporary education, test the italicized characteristics of ecological education against your own education in the sciences, in the social sciences, and in history, and in literature, philosophy, or religion.

5. Does Orr's perspective on the nature of "truth" seem most similar to the static, dynamic, or system perspectives studied in the science unit?

6. Is this a social science article? Why or why not? How does it differ from other articles in the section? Is it a science article? A humanities article? What characteristics does it share with those disciplines?

STUDENT PAPERS FOR REVISION WORKSHOP

This study of student water-uses synthesizes environmental theory, social science research methods, and firsthand experience in order to recommend solutions to a local resource problem. Revision would provide opportunity to compare the strengths and weaknesses of the students' creative section titles with the conventional titles of the sections. Though the writing is confident, it might well be reviewed for sentence level revisions.

Sober Up with a Cold Shower ... Or Maybe a Coin Operated One

Student B

Just a Cup Please

In California, water is a precious commodity that we cannot afford to waste. To explain why students at UCSB consume present water quantities and to uncover the value of water to students, a selected group of 60 dorm residents were surveyed about their water consumption during showers. The results did not support the belief that a lack of education is a probable cause for their values of water. Further research and tests of new methods including coin operated showers are needed to determine what would be the most efficient recommendation for reducing student shower water consumption in the residence halls.

The Reservoir

In California today, water is not a luxury, not a prize, and not an extravagance; it is expected, used in excess and wasted. Despite the numerous internal battle Californians fought regarding water rights, from Hetch Hetchy to Mono Lake, citizens still seem to treat water as if it were a commodity that had no environmental price tag and no limits. During, and for a few years following, the drought (1987-1992), water began to receive the respect it deserved. Water conservation became the trend in the late eighties. "Please conserve water" reminder stickers were found in the newspaper, lawns were spray painted green, car washes used recycled water, families had buckets in the shower, citizens used tanks to catch the small amounts of rainwater off the roof and the government stepped in to support low-flow toilets. It looked as though water conservation was here to stay. Yet, as the nineties come and go, old wasteful habits seem to be reappearing. Unfortunately, the quantity of fresh water available is not growing in accordance with this level of consumption. In fact, demands for water are growing rapidly due to three main factors that the Water Education Foundation, in its pamphlet *To Quench a Thirst* (1995), identifies:

1. Booming population growth
2. Increasing demands for more water to benefit fish and wildlife
3. No significant water development in the past 20 years.

When compared with most Americans, individual students are not responsible for large amounts of water consumption. Collectively, however, students can greatly determine the amount of water used in a small suburb like Goleta, California. According to the brochure called *The Water of Santa Barbara County* (1997), showers only account for 17 percent of the total amount of water used in a residential home. Because the majority of students do not have yards, which accounts for 48 percent of a residential home's water use (The Water of SB County 1997), the largest and most common use of water within the students population is for showers.

Growing up as an active member of the eighties and now nineties environmental movement, I have seen firsthand the change in attitudes about water. Before the drought, I never thought about the length of showers, or turning off the water when I brushed my teeth or rinsed the dishes. The strong push for water conservation from environmental organizations as well as from the local government made me, along with the rest of California's population, realize the values and importance of our water. Now that the drought has ended, high-flow shower heads and toilets remain taboo, but observations lead me to believe that because water conservation is no longer a pressing issue in the media and not widely taught in general education classes at every level, it is longer in the forefront of citizen concern.

Numerous attempts have been made to develop plans to impress water conservation as a vital issue in the minds of citizens. According to *The Layperson's Guide to Water Conservation* (1992), "To be effective, a conservation program should be tailored to meet the needs and specific opportunities in each community. A successful formula to permanently reduce per capita demand might include a mix of consumer education, water saving technologies, economic incentives, metering and other regulations." To aim for a higher success rate, the following ideas need to be clearly understood before any recommendations are made:

1. The values that the subjects place on water

2. How they did and did not attain those values

3. How those values relate to the amount of water consumed

Without knowing the answers to these questions, researchers will be unable to make effective recommendations.

Commonly, social science research looks at the facts and not the values that society holds for different environmental goods. David Orr, an environmental educator and social science researcher, comments in his essay entitled "What Good Is a Rigorous Research Agenda if You Don't Have a Decent Planet to Put it On?" (1992) that "environmental issues do not fit neatly into indoor paradigms . . . they are issues of values as much as of fact" (165). Understanding the above ideas provide an insight to the value of water held by students.

In an attempt to attain this insight, we surveyed almost 60 students living in the residence halls located in Goleta. The quantitative responses to a survey on water consumption (see the appendix) began to uncover these values. However, as with most social science research, our survey has weak links and cannot with complete accuracy, determine the value that student population places on water. Despite complications, it did expose some values that could in turn be used to make effective recommendations for solving inefficient water consumption problems in college towns.

The Key to the Dam

To begin to unlock underlying causes of a populations' values regarding water, we decided to survey select groups of students living in residence halls both on and off campus. Almost 60 students filled out the survey during the weekend of October 25th to 26th, 1997, half of whom live in Santa Cruz residence hall on the UCSB campus, and the rest in Francisco Torres' residence hall in Goleta. The students selected in Santa Cruz and FT were friends or acquaintances of GC and AA, respectively. This sample population, although not random, is a fair representation of both on and off campus students.

The survey was written with the intent of providing both quantitative and qualitative data (for a copy of the actual survey see the appendix). Both types of data, we hoped, would provide an overview of student values as well as allow students to give specific responses regarding the rationale (if any) supporting the amount of water they use in the shower, the amount and quality of the education they have received in school on water issues, and their solutions to help students shorten shower time. In addition, a list of questions, intended more to make the students think about the amount of water they use in the shower rather than to provide useful information for this research, were included followed in two informational paragraphs explaining the amount of water that flows through the shower head per minute (an average shower head releases 2.5 gallons/minute according "To Quench a Thirst" [1995]), and what food could be produced with that water instead.

Thirst

The results showed that the average shower time per student per day was 10.6 minutes. 23 percent of the students surveyed claimed they have no conscious awareness of the amount of time they spend in the shower, while 74 percent said they did.

This data show that although two-thirds of the study population claims that they are aware of their shower time, they still spend over 10 minutes a day in the shower, sometime showering up to three times a day. The data, when analyzed per students, do not appear to have significant consequence on water consumption. If multiplied out by dorm room, floor, building, campus and community, it is easy to see that massive amounts of water are consumed by student showers alone.

The survey asked if the students would change their shower time based on the presented information. 39 percent said they would shorten their shower time, 46 percent said they would not, and 15 percent were indecisive. The responses to the question "Do you feel you have received enough education in school regarding water and conservation?" were split down the middle, telling us that half of them fell well educated about the critical water problems facing the state, and yet they still consciously continue to take longer showers.

Students offered creative suggestions on how to make people shorten their shower time including the following: charge more for water, provide more facts on water use, only have cold showers, provide a timer, and make showers coin operated. One student simply replied, "A lot."

Situation

Social science research has to deal with many obstacles. Henry Bauer, author of *Scientific Literacy and the Myth of the Scientific Method*, compares quantitative and qualitative science as "hard' and "soft," respectively. It can be argued that these descriptions of the two types of sciences are misleading and inaccurate. Though the quantitative research may not provide statistical data, qualitative data can provide explanations for "yes and no" answers. Without explanation of their figures, scientists are left with some numbers, but no real answers.

One of many problems we faced in our research was the unclear intent of questions. The question about consciousness of time spent in the shower, I fear is inherently, but not intentionally, misleading. Of course students are aware of the time spent; they have schedules and they know when they turn the water on and when they turn it off. The intention of the question was to ask whether, while in the shower, they think, "Gosh, I have use over 20 gallons of water in my ten minute shower today!" Writing the questions so that they are not misinterpreted and understood completely by the subjects of the study is a difficult task in itself.

Another problem that occurs in social science research surveys, including ours, is the reliability of answers provided by the subject population. One student, who identified herself as "Ms. Piggy," claims she takes a 40-minute shower every day. In an interview, a researcher can analyze the tone of voice as well as the rhetorical context of other comments within the interview. On paper, as was demonstrated by a few students, not just "Ms. Piggy," subjects have and take the liberty to be dishonest and not put the required effort into the research to provide accurate, comprehensive results.

Future research for this project, to overcome some of these obstacles, might include interviewing the students rather just surveying, providing students with stop watches and charts so they may keep accurate count of shower times, and testing possible questions for clarity and purpose before large scale interviewing.

Aqueduct

A large percentage of the students surveyed said they are conscious that on average they spend over ten minutes in the shower a day. The education they have received, that is considered sufficient by over half of the study, has not influenced them to take significantly shorter showers. If the assumption is made that they interpreted the unclear question correctly, these data show a great deal about the value they place on water, despite it being a quantitative question. It shows that the marginal utility gained from the ten-minute average shower is greater than the marginal environmental cost of the water consumed for the surveyed student population. As economic theory proves, the price and the quantity demanded are determined where the marginal cost and marginal demand curves meet. This concept does not necessarily apply to students living in residential halls; many never see a rent or food bill, let alone a water bill. To these students, all the water they want is included in the bill that they never see. How do we then make the economic and ecological cost apparent to this type of student? The surveyed students offered several suggestions, but only one holds water (pun intended):

1. Charge more for water. This option has already been discussed; the students using the water do not directly pay for it.

2.Offer facts on water use. Half of the students questioned believed they have received enough water education, and yet they still consciously take long showers. This might be a good start, but alone it is not a sufficient way to get students to cut back.

3.Provide only cold water showers. Though this very well may work, not many will warm to the idea.

4.Use a timer. This might work, but because it does not teach any long-term lessons about water conservation, students will be frustrated with being forced to take shorter showers rather than understanding the reasons behind it, plus, you can always reset a timer.

5."A lot." Yet another example of a student putting quality effort into the survey.

6.Make showers coin operated. By far the best solution offered by a student surveyed, and also my recommendation.

According to Economist and UCSB Professor Charles Kolstad in the reader for his class in Environmental Economics (1997), the best way to study the economic implications of environmental values is through a hedonic praise approach. "In the very hedonic approach, the goal is to see how the price of a conventional good [e.g., rent] varies as the amount of a closely related environmental good changes [e.g., the quantity of water available for consumption]" (Environmental Economics Reader, 1997). Rather than charging more for water and watching how pricing affects the demand curve (it won't be accurate because many students don't pay for their water), a possible option might be to designate specific quantities of water to each dorm in the form of tokens (each token could be worth 12.5 gallons equivalent to a five-minute shower). A coin operated shower system is similar in theory to the pollution allotments granted by the EPA. If each dorm on campus is allowed a certain number of coins to distribute to students for the quarter, all affected students will learn several lessons. The most important lesson, as far as water conservation is concerned, that water is not finite and it comes with a price tag, will be learned when each student is only allowed a specific number of showers per time period. Students will also learn about economic efficiency when they begin trading, buying and selling their water allotments. A woman with long hair could trade her note-taking services to a man who only showers three times a week and would never use all of the water tokens. An infinite number of possible trades could be made. The student population in the dorm would begin to act as an economic market and, after much trading and selling, would eventually reach an equilibrium. Students would learn to ask why and how to conserve water as well as some fundamental economic principles.

Before conducting this research, I would have assumed that students consume more water than they need because they do not receive adequate education about water conservation issues. The research does not support this hypothesis, though it does not completely refute it either. Further studies would need to be done, including testing the coin theory on one dorm, surveying students about their reactions to the idea, interviewing students, and even asking for written reports from those who feel strongly for or against the idea.

Teaching water conservation practices to all college students would result in much less water use in dorms, and it would also have significant long-term effects as those students graduate and have families of their own. Our water cannot supply the growing population at current consumption standards. Many changes must occur before water use becomes sustainable, and making changes at the college level may be an effective way to start.

Works Cited

Bauer, Henry. (1994). *Scientific literacy and the myth of the scientific method.* Chicago: University of Illinois.

City of Santa Barbara. (1997). *The water of Santa Barbara County.* Santa Barbara, CA: Water Conservation Office.

Kolstad, Charles. (1997). *Environmental economics.* Santa Barbara: Author.

Orr, David. (1992). *Ecological literacy: Education and the transition to a postmodern world.* New York: State University.

Water Education Foundation. (1992). *Layperson's guide to water conservation.* Sacramento, CA: Author.

Water Education Foundation. (1995). *To quench a thirst.* Sacramento, CA: Author.

Appendix

Water, Use Questionnaire

Name (optional): _____

Sex: _____

Place of Residence: _____

How long is your average shower? _____

How many times a day do you shower? _____

On average, how many showers do you take in a week? _____

Do you shave in the shower? _____

If so, do you let the water run while you shave? _____

Do you use the shower for other purposes (i.e., rinsing wet suits), and if so what? _____

Do you wash your hair every time you shower? _____

If not, how frequently do you wash your hair? _____

Do you shower in the morning or evening? _____

Do you notice a difference in shower time between morning and evening showers, and if so, what is the difference? _____

The average shower head allows 2.5 gallons of water per minute to flow. If you take a 10-minute shower, you have used 25 gallons of water. If everyone on your floor (approx. 60 people) takes a 10-minute shower every day, 1,500 gallons of water are used per day. In a week that is 10,500 gallons. Imagine the impact that students could have on water consumption if they reduced their shower time.

This paper succeeds in synthesizing the issues discussed in the readings with the results of field study into a theoretical debate essay that engages the student's own interest in historical and national affairs. It also demonstrates the challenges of such synthesis. How might the student clarify the relationship between the theorist's proposed causes of apathy and the results of her own campus survey? How would clarification of that relationship strengthen her thesis? How would a strengthened thesis guide the organization of the paper more efficiently? How might the structural clarifications suggested above lead to more precise word choice and effective transitions between sentences?

Political Apathy: Is America Becoming Indifferent?

Student C

As citizens of the United States, we are reminded, year after year, of what makes our country function the way it does. Annual elections bring on political awareness and the evening news generally mentions something about the president or a politician. Every day, in newspaper and other media, Americans hear about decisions that are being made regarding running a nation. Why, then, are so many U.S. citizens so unconcerned about the American political system? Is this an indication that America is becoming increasingly indifferent? Kenneth Weiss, an editor of the *Los Angeles Times*, believes that a survey given to college freshmen shows evidence that a "disengaged generation" is developing (*L.A. Times*, January 12, 1998). However, Stephen Bennett states in *Apathy in America* that levels of political apathy have fluctuated over the centuries depending on the current national issues (1986).

At the college student level, several factors can encourage political apathy. Indifference and simply being uninformed are very common reasons today. However, the time period also plays a large role in whether an individual becomes involved or not. During periods when national crises directly impact the American people, the citizens, students in particular, are more likely to participate in political groups and vote, than at a time when national issues do not involve the average citizen. In addition, peer and parental influence help to determine whether or not a student votes and participates in political groups even though the student may not recognize this influence. These are just a few of the many influences on political apathy at the student level.

Bennett claims there are many factors that earn importance in explaining political nonparticipation. However, a survey taken at the University of California, Santa Barbara in February 1998, indicated that indifference seems the dominant reason why many U.S. college students do not participate in politics. Weiss's theory from surveys of incoming college freshmen is that Americans are evolving into being more apathetic (*L.A. Times*).

Many people define political nonparticipation and political apathy as synonymous. However, the concept of apathy signifies a lack of interest in political issues, as well as a lack of participation.

When political issues at a national and a local level directly affect citizens of the United States, more individuals are likely to become involved in activist groups and vote than at a time when their lives are not touched by political issues. There are always issues at hand, but when the country is not at war and the government and economy are relatively stable, the majority of U.S. citizens often feel the issues do not affect them directly. This results in them not becoming involved in political activist groups and not voting in elections. Statistics taken from a 1998 college students survey indicated that more people watched the State of the Union this year than last year, because it involved Clinton's sex scandal. This issue interested many U.S. citizens because it involved their president. Statistics showed that 43 percent watched the State of the Union this year, while only 35 percent watched it last year. Many were curious as to how the issue would turn out, causing an increase in the number who watched the State of the Union. Clinton's sex scandal is an example of an issue that did not directly affect the citizens, but was merely an issue that stimulated public interest. Today, there are no political events that directly affect most U.S. citizens. In addition, U.S. citizens feel content with the status of their country. Thus, some say the political interest of U.S. citizens as a whole is currently declining. This decline in political interest is bringing about what some call the "disengaged generation" (*L.A. Times*, 1998). The *L.A. Times* reported recent statistics taken according to an annual survey which gathered responses from 252,082 college freshmen:

> As it has done throughout the 1990s, the number who said it is important to keep abreast of politics dropped, with only 26.7% listing that as a priority. Political interest among freshmen reached a high in 1966, when 57.8% of students tuned in to current affairs.

These statistics are not the evidence of a "disengaged generation," but merely a generation at ease. The situation was entirely different in 1966. At the peak of the Vietnam war, students, and citizens in general, were very active in political activist groups, protesting against the war. The war was directly affecting the lives of many United States citizens, particularly students, whose age group was being drafted into the war. Either the students themselves or their peers were being drafted. Many American lives were being lost for reasons that many citizens believed were not worth dying for, causing the majority of the nation to fight for what was, in fact, their own lives. The Vietnam war era is an example of a time when the national issues of the time period caused many citizens to become active in politics. Americans were uncomfortable with the status of the country and how its status could affect their lives, and therefore became involved in politics because of their fears.

The Great Depression was also a time of increased citizen involvement. Bennett mentions the Great Depression as a time when national economic conflict was the primary source that brought about the return of political interest: "The onset of the Great Depression, the emergence of a new generation of political leaders attended to the contemporary issues . . . combined to effect a resurgence of citizen political interest and electoral participation" (Bennett, 1986). At this time, the economic status of the country was unstable, forcing nationwide job losses and anxiety.

During the presidential elections every four years, more people become involved in politics than at other times. People want the best president possible to make their country run smoothly, and this desire causes them to become more politically active. For the 1998 congressional election, only 31 percent of the students who were surveyed voted, whereas for the 1996 presidential election, 54% students voted.

The recent study taken at UCSB shows that the main explanation for political apathy among college students is indifference and being politically uninformed. Of the 52 percent of the students who did not vote in the November 1998 congressional elections, 50 percent responded that they did not vote because they were either indifferent or uninformed. At the local level, many students do not sacrifice time to participate in community groups or become involved in community issues because they feel their living place is not permanent, and their vote and their participation will not affect them while they are at the university. Thus, they do not feel their time and effort would be worthwhile. The current national politics do not interest the individual enough to break away from their busy schedule and vote or become involved in active political groups. As Bennett puts it:

> The individual who is so engrossed with his own psychological needs, or the keeping up with the flow of political issues is a time-consuming activity. Unless a student is majoring in political science and is very interested in the politics of the country, most students do not spend time keeping up-to-date on politics. Affairs of his family, his work, or even his entertainment and recreational activities . . . has little or no psychic energy left for interest in public affairs. (37)

This example demonstrates that students tend to find the events making up their personal life more important than the events of the political world.

Recent surveys have also found that students who come from families whose parents are active in politics and vote regularly are more likely to be active in politics themselves. Students from nonvoting parents generally do not vote or become involved in politics. Another poll taken at UCSB in early February 1998 found that 71 percent of the students with voting parents did vote, and 20 percent of the students from nonvoting families did vote. This strong correlation indicates that parents' political habits have powerful influences on their children. Those students who come from nonparticipating families tend to be apathetic. Since their parents did not vote, voting is not a top priority for them either.

Peers may also influence a student's choice of whether to be politically involved even though recent surveys did not indicate any such correlation. The 1998 statistics showed that only 16 percent of the people surveyed would attend a political group if friends were going. However, these results must be questioned as this is usually not the case in real life. These results may be faulty because many students do not want to admit, or do not recognize the influences on them by their peers. When a student has friends who are politically involved and vote regularly, that same student is more inclined to become involved, too. With politically involved friends, a student is often exposed to political issues that are brought up during conversations. This leads to political awareness, so that, when it comes time to vote, the student is more likely to vote because he or she is informed and because the student's friends vote. If a student has friends who do not participate in political groups, the student does not become exposed to political issues and is more likely to become involved in things other than politics. When this is the case, voting in an election is not a top priority.

Levels of political apathy change over the years depending on the number of citizens affected by current political issues. At a time like the present, when no major national events are taking place and the nation is calm, levels of apathy, as discussed earlier, are increasing. However, at a time when the majority of the population is impacted by a political issue and the country is unstable, levels of political apathy tend to be much less. In addition, political indifference can be the result of lack of time and/or interest and, therefore, being uninformed. Indifference can also be influenced by parents and peers. Political indifference among Americans does not indicate an uncaring, unfeeling nation, it merely represents a tranquil nation. It is primarily at times when American citizens are unsatisfied and uncomfortable with government decisions that they feel the need to express their heartfelt opinions.

References

Bennett, Stephen Earl. (1986). *Apathy in America, 1960-1984: Causes and consequences of citizen political indifference.* Dobbs Ferry, NY: Transitional Publishers.

Weiss, Kenneth R. (1998, January 12). Freshmen get high marks-in apathy. *The Los Angeles Times,* pp. A1.

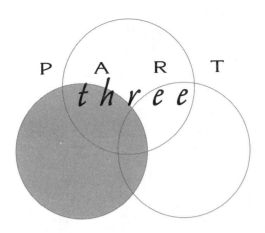

PART

three

The Humanities

C H A P T E R

five

Inquiry and Writing
in the Humanities

Is graffiti art?
Are hip hop lyrics poetry?
Does the First Amendment protect Internet pornography?
Is human cloning ethical?
Who won the space race?

GOALS AND PURPOSES

We have seen that writing in the natural and social sciences shapes, and is shaped by, processes of inquiry that lead to naming, analysis, and explanation of objects and events in our physical and social worlds. Knowledge generated by these processes enables us to understand how things, phenomena, and people acquire their particular features and characters. We have seen how such understanding of the nature of things in both our physical and social worlds allows us to make and to test theories about what causes them to behave as they do. We have also seen how testing our theories about the causes of past and present behaviors enables us both to revise them and to better predict outcomes of future phenomena and events. To further knowledge of the nature of things, we see how processes of scientific inquiry that enable us to name, to explain, and to predict things also allow us to test the validity of our predictions and to refine them for further reliability. We have also seen how methodical inquiry is a refinement of thinking skills we use in everyday life.

These processes of scientific inquiry have become invaluable tools in the advancement of human life and at times they may seem to be almost limitless in their power to solve myriad mysteries and problems of our existence. Only tools used by skillful tool-users for their appropriate tasks, however, can produce fully satisfying results. How do we decide which problems to solve? In what order? For whose benefit? At whose expense? Inquiry and writing in the humanities evaluates choices and results in terms of the values they may ultimately bring to our lives. In addition to questions asked by all disciplines of objects and phenomena—What is it? How does it change over time? How does it interact within systems?—the humanities also ask several sorts of "so what" questions: So what does it matter? So what is it worth? So what good does it do? So what do we do about it? In essence these questions add up to the central question asked by the humanities: So, in the largest possible sense, what does it mean?

- So what does it mean if we won the space race?
- So what difference does it make if graffiti is art?
- So what does it mean to limit some kinds of speech?
- So what does it mean to impose ethical limitations upon scientific research?

We have seen how thesis statements in the sciences and social sciences (more properly called *hypo*theses) are statements to be tested for their ability to explain objects and phenomena and/or to predict outcomes of events. Ongoing research may further affirm or challenge such statements. A thesis such as "Successful cloning of laboratory animals may provide the key to human cloning" is a statement that may be supported or challenged by emerging research in molecular biology. Its truth value or falsity relies upon analyses of further research results available to scientific observers. When we address such a statement with a "so what" question, we enter the realm of humanities argumentation: So what differences might cloning make in human identity? In families? In societies? In religions? So what effects of cloning do we find desirable? What effects do we fear? So what should we do to accelerate the production of human clones? What should we do to prevent it? So what does human cloning mean to the quality of human existence, to the worth of the individual, to the survivability of the species? Our arguments over our answers to such questions will involve our personal, collective, and subjective conceptions of the good (ethics) and the beautiful (aesthetics) as much as they do any objective truth. As we will see in this chapter, arguments supporting thesis statements such as "human cloning is immoral and must be prevented at all costs" or "human cloning may be the best thing since sliced bread" will require very different types of evidence and organizational structures than those we have examined so far.

INQUIRY 5.1: WRITING THESIS STATEMENTS IN THE HUMANITIES

1. On your own, consider the following statements and practice responding to them with "so what" questions. Make note of how your questions invite different kinds of research and argument:

   A. Many of the most famous works of classic American literature—including James Fennimore Cooper's *The Last of the Mohicans*, Henry David Thoreau's *Walden*, Herman Melville's *Moby Dick*, and Mark Twain's *Huckleberry Finn*—feature solitary male characters seeking escape from civilization into the frontier wilderness.

   B. The framers of the U.S. Constitution could not have foreseen the development of Internet communication technologies when they wrote the first amendment.

   C. A significantly higher proportion of males than females entering college still declare majors in math, the sciences, or engineering.

   D. The physiques of high fashion models do not represent attainable ideals of healthy bodies for most people.

   E. Scholars have reported that human slave traffic still exists in Mauritania and Sudan today.

   F. Though technicolor technology was already available, most World War II films made in the 1950s were still produced in black and white.

   G. Many forms of mainstream popular music—including jazz, rhythm and blues, rock and roll, rap, and hip hop—were first explored by African Americans.

   H. The mysterious species *Pfiesteria piscicida*, a microbe responsible for massive die-offs in many of the world's fisheries and for neurological disorders in fishermen and researchers, was first identified by science in the late 1980s.

2. With a group of classmates, select three of the statements above to develop as potential thesis statements for humanities papers. First generate at least three "so what" questions for each of the selected statements. Then brainstorm as many possible tentative answers as you can for each of your questions. Finally select three tentative answers to the "so what" questions that your group finds most worth researching.

3. Present your potential thesis statements in class with explanations of how they have interpreted initial statements of "fact" as issues of value and meaning worthy of continued consideration and inquiry.

Some issues raised by sample statements in Inquiry 5.1 seem to obviously concern humanities disciplines such as literature, music, and film studies. Others clearly involving matters of law, ecology, and social policy may, at least at first blush, seem like strange ground to cover from humanities perspectives. To gain an understanding of the various types of objects and phenomena studied in the humanities, you may want to develop a clearer sense of what academic disciplines make up this branch of the university and consider further how their goals and purposes may be distinguished from, and be complementary to, objects and methods of study in the sciences and social sciences. Remember how we explained in the introduction to this book that different disciplines might focus on the same object of study by asking different questions of it? We indicated that while a scientist studying you, for instance, might ask questions concerning your biological functions, a social scientist might address questions concerning your psychological conceptions of "self" or your participation in group behaviors. A philosopher, on the other hand, might ask questions that concern even more abstract and less observable aspects of your identity such as those concerning your individual rights, freedoms, or moral obligations.

As we have seen, interpreting data gained by observation and experimentation is a critical element of research in science and social science disciplines; however, the quest for meaning in humanities disciplines frequently involves interpreting data not necessarily generated by scientific methods. While the more abstract inquiries of the humanities may not generate scientific truths or proofs, even the value of "scientific proofs" as a human production may become an object of inquiry in humanities disciplines. In fact, any and all artifacts and events produced by human individuals, societies, and cultures—including those of science—may potentially become objects of study in various humanities disciplines. The productions and performances of artists, musicians, poets, architects, and dancers as well as those of political leaders, legislators, military personnel, social activists, molecular biologists, and religious communities may all be subject to humanistic inquiry. Notice, for instance how Stephen Mallioux's essay titled "Interpretation" included in the readings for this chapter applies the same interpretive theories to poems by Emily Dickinson and to international nuclear test-ban treaties. Such a range of possible areas of inquiry will also require a wide range of methods of study and give rise to even larger questions and debates about interpretive theory itself.

INQUIRY 5.2: DISCIPLINES AND KNOWLEDGE IN THE HUMANITIES

1. Strengthen your familiarity with humanities disciplines by listing departments and programs at your college you think might be included in the humanities. Have you included the fine and performing arts—music, drama, dance, film

studies? What about English literature, comparative literature, foreign language departments, classics? Why are these disciplines commonly associated with the humanities? Did you include history, philosophy, or religious studies? Why? Why not? What about interdisciplinary programs such as Environmental Studies, Women's Studies, Chicano/a Studies? How does humanistic inquiry complement scientific and social science research in these disciplines?

2. Compare your brainstormed list of humanities disciplines with some of your classmates' and explain how different disciplines confront significant questions of meaning and human experience.

3. Compare your list and your classmates' lists with humanities departments listed in your college catalogue. Study descriptions of some of the departments and programs. Look closely at descriptions of some courses they offer. How extensive is the range of objects and phenomena studied by them? How widely do their methods of inquiry vary?

4. Group the departments according to their common features. Compare your grouping with that of other groups and arrive at a consensus, if you can, on the features that distinguish the groups. Imagine you and your group of classmates are planning to attend an interdisciplinary conference to address an issue of global concern. As a group select a particular humanities discipline and write a proposal for funding that explains how you as scholars in that field would approach one of the following issues:

   • Human population growth
   • Computer technologies and distance-learning in higher education
   • Deforestation and species extinction in the Amazon
   • Toxic waste disposal and issues of social justice
   • International trade treaties

5. What kinds of questions would members of your selected discipline ask? What kinds of data could you gather? What kinds of claims might you make? What form might your presentation take? How might your findings complement or challenge knowledge generated by your colleagues from the sciences and social sciences?

6. Present your proposal in class and respond to questions from your classmates and instructor.

ROLE OF ASSUMPTIONS IN THE HUMANITIES

Questions of meaning are complex and usually resist single, absolute answers. The same thing—a fact about the feeding behaviors of mollusks, an historic example of racial prejudice, or a poem by a famous author—may mean different things in different cultures and to different individuals within a culture. It may even mean different things to the same person at different times or in different situations. The meanings we find in facts, situations, and expressions are products of our interpretations and they may change as we change. Every interpretation of a thing is in some way only a part of the larger picture, a part perceived from a particular perspective. This is not to suggest, therefore, that all interpretations are equally valid or satisfactory or that "since it's all relative" anything goes. Even some partial and perspectival interpretations may work better than others for particular purposes or occasions. However, in order to develop the fullest possible sense of the meanings of things and their relevance to broader spectrums of history and human experience, we must learn to broaden our interpretive skills to include the fullest range of perspectives possible. Just as social science researchers benefit from combining complementary research methods incorporating both quantitative and qualitative analyses, interpreters in the humanities strengthen their views by looking at things from a variety of angles. Broadening our awareness and skills of interpretation—and thus expanding and enriching our understanding of our place in the broader human experience—is a primary pursuit of inquiry in the humanities.

We believe that the more you develop multiple interpretive skills and perspectives, the more fully you may consider and "know" various possible meanings of things. We also believe that developing multiple interpretive skills and perspectives will productively enhance your awareness of practical scopes, applications, and limits of various kinds of knowledge. As a knowledgeable interpreter with such increased awareness, you may also serve a critical function for others by translating your special knowledge into terms more readily understood by wider audiences. You may, for example, be able to explain to others why whaling has become such a painful issue between Japanese, Inuit, and American cultures. Or you may be able to explain why printed texts deserve to be preserved in libraries in an age of electronic communications. To be a knowledgeable interpreter and translator, you must become skillful with specialized vocabularies, the particular terms that represent various perspectives on things. An interpreter of film, for instance, must know the terms that filmmakers use to refer to particular types of camera shots—"establishing shot," "two-shot," and "close-up"—*and* the terms audiences use to describe and evaluate sensory and emotional responses to various scenes produced by those shots—"intense," "spectacular," "cathartic." To facilitate translations of your interpretations of things from more specialized to more general vocabularies, you must also develop knowledge of another critical vocabulary: the terminology of interpretive theories and methods. The following inquiry should help you see how interpretive skills you employ in daily life can be developed and applied for academic purposes.

INQUIRY 5.3: EXPLORING INTERPRETIVE PERSPECTIVES

1. On your own first consider the photographic examples of graffiti (at the bottom of this page and the top of the next page) and then write quick responses to the following questions: How would you judge the images as territorial markings? As art? As vandalism? How do perceptions of graffiti as social communication, individual expression, or destruction of property depend upon interpretive perspectives? You may also wish to consider other examples of graffiti found in your community, on your campus, or in your classroom as you think about the questions above.

2. Select the image that intrigues you most and write interpretations of it as communication, as art, and/or as vandalism. Describe the image's particular features and overall effects in as much detail as you can and comment upon its meaning or value. You may use particular aspects of the image and its effects to elaborate upon your responses to the more general questions above. How many perspectives have you addressed? How have you considered the point of view of the graffitist? Of the graffitist's peers? Of the building's owner? Of passersby? How have you accounted for the image as a reflection of the graffitist's inner world? Of the graffitist's outer world? How have you accounted for

Eye Six and Mac, "SPA (and Banshee)" Railyards

Voodoo, "THE SHADOW" Railyards

its various effects upon others? Feel free to develop your interpretation further in response to these questions.

3. Get together with a small group (3–5) of your classmates who have selected the same image and share your commentaries. (It may be helpful to have photocopies or extra printouts to distribute.) Develop a list of various justifications mentioned by your group members for interpreting the graffiti as art and/or vandalism. Synthesize carefully selected portions of your various commentaries into a two or three paragraph miniessay addressing the question: "Graffiti: Art or Vandalism."

4. Read your miniessay aloud in class as a "position statement" in a larger discussion regarding the interpretation of graffiti. Be prepared to question the position statements of other groups and to respond to questions asked of your group by classmates.

ROLES OF THEORY AND METHOD IN THE HUMANITIES

Theory and method in the humanities are closely tied to various perspectives used to interpret artifacts of human expressions. Whether we interpret movies, poems, historical events, legal documents, or the social significance of scientific findings, approaches used to describe, to explain, and to evaluate human events and artifacts reveal much about our theories of how things come to have meaning. Your interpretations and your classmates' interpretations of graffiti in Inquiry 5.3 probably agreed and varied to significant extents according to theoretical assumptions each of you brought to the inquiry, theoretical assumptions about the purposes of art, about the creativity of individuals, about the rights of others. The evaluatory claims you made and the types of evidence you used to support them probably owed much to your fundamental conceptions of what is good, true, and beautiful. These theoretical assumptions and fundamental conceptions profoundly influenced the similar and divergent angles of approach, the interpretive perspectives, you and your classmates used to describe and evaluate the images.

As you responded to the questions and claims of others, your arguments involved something significantly more than the accuracy of various interpretations under discussion, they also involved defenses and challenges of the relative validity of various interpretive perspectives. Just as we saw that much writing in the social sciences involves debate about theories and methods, much humanities writing involves debate over interpretive theory. As you become more involved in supporting your interpretive arguments, you will find it helpful to have a vocabulary for identifying and classifying the interpretive theories and perspectives you and others bring to the discussion. We hope also that developing such a vocabulary will help you to broaden and enrich the approaches—to deepen the knowledge, appreciation, and responses—you bring to your experiences and interpretations of events and things encountered in your world. Begin this vocabulary development with the word "assumption" itself. Inquiry 5.4 will help you identify the assumptions you used in the positions you took in Inquiry 5.3.

INQUIRY 5.4: IDENTIFYING ASSUMPTIONS

After each of the claims and positions you took in the previous inquiry, add the word "because" and freewrite. Every time you identify a reason for your belief, ask "because" again and write again until you reach a statement about the basic nature of things—of humans, of society, of art, and so on. These unstated principles underlie all of your positions and are your *assumptions*.

In his *Orientation of Critical Theories* (1954), M. H. Abrams developed a classification system and terminology to explain how approaches toward interpretations of things may be aligned loosely with one or more of four basic theoretical perspectives (p. 4):

1. An understanding of artifacts as representations or imitations of things in the universe
2. An understanding of artifacts through their effects upon their audiences
3. An understanding of artifacts as expressions of their makers
4. An understanding of artifacts as simply what they are as objects in and of themselves

Abrams' diagram (Figure 5.1) provides a rough map of these interpretive perspectives as related coordinates and introduces theoretical terms that will be defined more fully below and developed even more fully in the readings following this chapter:

If you evaluated graffiti images in terms of how well they realistically or even satirically portrayed objects or events in the world—faces, human figures, images of death, or more "legitimate" or "conventional" forms of written communication—you applied what Abrams terms a *mimetic* perspective. The series of activities in Inquiry 5.5 is designed to help you identify and catalog the presence of this and other perspectives outlined in Abrams' orientation to critical theory in your own efforts at interpretation.

INQUIRY 5.5A: IDENTIFYING *MIMETIC* ELEMENTS

Identify the mimetic elements in your interpretations and mark them "M." You might do so by asking yourself the importance of being able to tell what the drawing represents or what the words say. How important were these elements to the meaning you derived?

This perspective was perhaps most fully articulated during the classical period by the philosopher Plato who argued in his *Republic* that even objects of furniture such as a bed in fact imitated an idea held in the human mind of an

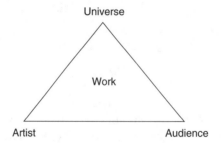

Figure 5.1   Element of Interpretation
Based on Abrams, M. H.

ideal bed. According to Plato the carpenter building a bed imitated this ideal, whereas the artist painting a bed imitated, in a third-order regress, the work of the carpenter. According to this *mimetic* perspective, the meanings or worth of artistic creations are derived from their *representational* values, from their realistic depictions of the truths of things. In fact Plato argued that because poets distorted or created their own fictitious meanings of things they should therefore be exiled from his ideal republic.

During the Renaissance humanist critics took issue with Plato's intolerant view of poets and began to argue that both imitation and fiction in poetry and art served loftier purposes. The *pragmatic* function of artistic works, they argued, was to delight and to teach—to elevate—their audiences. From this perspective the meaning or worth of poetry or art is derived from its power to move audiences to noble sentiments and actions and to enlighten their human sensibilities. Well into the eighteenth century, this *pragmatic* approach to interpretation emphasized a focus upon matters of taste, decorum, and moral appropriateness communicated by artistic creations. Interpretative evaluations of graffiti as social communication and the effects it might have upon the graffitist's peers, property owners, or passersby—either as territorial marking or as social commentary or protest—would be aligned significantly, though perhaps not entirely, with *pragmatic* perspectives. From this perspective inquiry into the function of graffiti could even be seen as similar to questions that have long surrounded anthropologists' study of the ancient cave paintings at Laxcaux.

INQUIRY 5.5B: IDENTIFYING *PRAGMATIC* ELEMENTS

Identify the *pragmatic* elements in your interpretation and mark them "P." You can do this by asking yourself the extent to which you viewed the graffiti as a comment on society, whether your view of that commentary was positive or negative. Expand this inquiry by identifying the conditions of the world of the graffitist is commenting on. How much of the meaning you arrived at depends on your knowledge of that world?

Messages, as we know, have senders as well as receivers and your interpretations of graffiti as social or even personal communication would also be aligned with another of Abrams' critical interpretive perspectives. During the nineteenth century, Romantic critics shifted their focus from artistic creations alone to embrace a concern for the unique creativity of the artist. They argued that artistic works should be understood as expressions of the genius of individual creators. From this perspective, interpretation involved appreciating artists' intentions and might even require critical understanding of their personal lives, social situations, and psychological desires. *Intentionalist* and *expressivist* approaches to interpretation continue to occupy much critical attention. Interpretation of graffiti images as representations of the graffitist's inner-world, even apart from communicative intentions, would also be aligned with this *expressivist* perspective.

INQUIRY 5.5C: IDENTIFYING *INTENTIONALIST/EXPRESSIVIST* ELEMENTS

Identify the *intentionalist/expressivist* elements in your interpretations and mark them "E." These comments will concern the individual artistic or emotional qualities of the piece. Ask yourself how much of the meaning you arrived at depends on these qualities.

Perhaps your responses to the graffiti examples in Inquiry 5.3 did not concern representations of things in the world, social communication, effects on viewers, or the artists' intentions as much as they focused upon the shapes, colors, and juxtapositions contained in the images as images. Throughout the twentieth century, emphasis upon representational value, social worth, and even individual subjectivity has been increasingly challenged, especially by more object-centered approaches to artifacts themselves. Under the "art for art's sake" motto of aestheticism, late nineteenth- and twentieth-century *formalist* interpreters argued that the value of an artistic creation comes solely from itself with no necessary dependence upon, or relevance to, the universe, the audience, or the artist. Though such an interpretive approach may satisfy our need to understand and appreciate artistic works, it may not finally satisfy our need to understand other human artifacts such as contracts, treaties, or laws.

Still *objectivist* interpreters of these types of socially binding documents may argue that their meaning is nonetheless contained within themselves. *Objectivist, literalist,* and *formalist* critics insist that texts may be best understood through literal readings, that texts mean what they say. If a difficult text does not make its literal meaning obvious, the objectivist interpreter may study its form more closely to explain the relations of its parts to its whole. Still, according to this theoretical orientation, nothing outside the text determines its ultimate meaning.

INQUIRY 5.5D: IDENTIFYING *FORMALIST* ELEMENTS

1. Identify the extent your interpretation depends on the formal elements of the graffiti—the colors, shapes, placement, and so on. When you have done so, ask yourself how much of the meaning you derived depended on these elements alone.
2. Try explaining the difference between graffiti and cave art.

According to the formalist perspective, if the language of a text is too removed technically or historically for various audiences, the role of the interpreter is simply to translate it for them. You probably found, in the last inquiry, that you included other interpretive perspectives into your explanation in 2. Even decoding unfamiliar calligraphic figures such as highly stylized letters or numbers in graffiti, no matter how focused it is on the stylizations themselves, begins to integrate perspectives involving representation, communication, and expression.

Though Abrams' diagram continues to provide useful orientation to distinguish interpretive theories, contemporary interpreters of art, culture, law, and history often develop more sophisticated explanations and evaluations of their objects of study by consciously combining perspectives associated with two or more of the orientations mapped above. In our exploration of inquiry and writing in the social sciences, we saw that thorough researchers applied varieties of quantitative and qualitative methods to gain fuller perspectives on their research subjects. Similarly you will want to take some account of perspectives offered by all four of the theoretical orientations presented here as you approach your objects of study in the humanities. Indeed you may have already discovered the importance of each in Inquiry 5.5.

For practical purposes, you might well begin developing your interpretation with consideration of the objects and events themselves and ask the same initial question we have asked of things in the sciences and of behaviors in the social sciences: What is it? To answer this question about various human artifacts studied in humanities disciplines—from literary works to legal documents, to political revolutions, or from classical symphonies to popular music to television "sit-coms" to the architecture of public buildings—we may first begin with the same methodical process of observation and description used in both the sciences and social sciences. Let us take, for instance, what may be one of the shortest examples of a complete poem in the English language:

I
Why?

Our first task in our effort to answer the question "What is it?" must be to consider how or why we might even begin to identify or classify this particular two-word sequence as a poem at all. As you will see in one of the readings included in this unit, "How to Recognize a Poem When You See One" by Stanley Fish, even this seemingly straightforward task may have very sophisticated interpretive implications. For our present purposes, however, we may approach this question of identity with an already familiar method. Using the same process of trimodal observation and description we employed in the sciences and social sciences, we can begin the task of identification and classification by considering the static features or attributes of the textual object. Does it contain the elements of poetry? Does it have poetic form? By addressing the "What is it?" question, we emphasize a *formalist* or *objectivist* orientation toward the text. In this case we might argue that these two single-syllable words do make a poem because, like much poetry, they are separated into individual lines linked together by rhyme. Following this orientation further, we might also argue that the text is a poem because we need no further information about the world outside the text or about its author's intentions in order to experience poetic effect as the simple juxtaposition of these two words stimulates our curiosity, reflection, and imagination. By considering the text's effects upon us as readers, however, we have already begun to combine our formalist orientation with more audience-centered pragmatist orientations.

From the pragmatist orientation, our further study of "I/Why?" involves observation and description of its functions and brings us to the second of our initial questions: How does it change over time? To address this question we might record the sequence of our various personal responses to the question it raises. For instance, upon different readings at different times in your life, you might first respond with different questions such as Why not? or Who cares? or Who wants to know? or Why do you ask? In addition to your own responses to the poem, you might attempt to survey and document its reception by others. You might ask, for instance, Are some types of readers more or less appreciative of the work than others? or How much do the interpretations of different readers agree or disagree with one another? As you develop a wider range of speculative responses to questions you might ask of the poem from a *pragmatist* or *reader response* interpretive orientation, you may also begin to ask, But what did the author originally intend to say?

The *intentionalist* or *expressivist* orientation also considers the ways texts change through time. To discover original meanings, we must work back through time, as though peeling away layers of an onion in search of its center, to strip away interpretations we and others before us might have added to them. In a sense, we may even try to peel away the actual texts themselves so we may see what their authors may have intended to express. To address the Why do you ask? question with relation to our "I/Why?" poem, for instance, we might wish to know something particular about the author's biography: Perhaps the writer composed the poem to celebrate a moment of youth when life's possibilities seemed various and rich; or, perhaps, the author composed the poem near death when life had felt futile. In addition to biographical perspective, we may also wish to know something about the historical context surrounding both the author's life and the poem's composition: Perhaps the author lived during a time when questions about the purpose of identity and existence were considered blasphemous and socially unacceptable, or perhaps the author lived during a time when such questions were considered quite banal and commonplace. Certainly knowledge about biographical and historical conditions that influenced the author can enhance our appreciation of the poem's function and value. By reaching back through the poem to its historical influences, however, we also open our interpretive perspectives beyond an author's intentions themselves to consideration of the psychological and social worlds the poem may represent and evoke.

Our consideration of *representational* perspectives here, however, involves much more than Plato's concept of *mimesis* with which we began our orientation toward interpretive theories. Our "I/Why?" poem does not simply imitate an object in an ideal or a physical realm. In order to understand the poem as an imitation or representation at all, we must ask our third guiding question: Of what systems is it a part, and how does it interact with those systems? Each orientation we have explored in our consideration of the poem so far provides some partial answer to this question. From the *objectivist* perspective, the poem is viewed primarily as part of a formal linguistic system where particular sounds and the letters that represent them as written words acquire meaning through their similarities and differences to one another. From *pragmatist* and *intentionalist* perspectives, we have seen how this formal linguistic system participates in communication systems that connect poets and readers meaningfully to one another and to their separate worlds even across thresholds of time and space. Perhaps we might say, finally, that as poems participate in complex and interrelated systems of meaning-making, a single poem imitates or represents an attempt to make meaning itself. Further from the text of our particular "I/Why?" poem, we might conclude that such efforts to discover identity and to make knowledge from changing conditions of our existence represent an essential part of what it "means" to be human. From this perspective, what may initially seem to be a glib little quip may be situated in a very ancient system of inquiry which is known in Sanskrit as the meditation upon *sat nam*—the contemplation of the question of true (*sat*) identity (*nam*).

Communication of meaning through artistic creations ultimately depends upon our knowledge of how representation works, our knowledge of how more concrete things may stand—as allusions, metaphors, or allegories—for more abstract things. Consider Francis Bacon's interpretation of the riddle of the

Sphinx (which you will find in the readings chapter) as an example translation of a particular story's concrete, surface features as allusions, metaphors, and allegories for deeper, abstract, and more universal meanings.

INQUIRY 5.6: RESPONDING TO INTERPRETATIONS

1. Bacon's particular interpretive translation, or "reading," of this well-known tale certainly seems to put a new spin on an old story. Consider your initial reactions to Bacon's reading of the tale of the Sphinx by discussing the following questions with a partner. Keep notes of your responses:
   - How plausible is Bacon's interpretation?
   - How valuable are the insights he generates from it?
   - How might other valid interpretations question or challenge Bacon's reading of the tale?

2. In order to move beyond our initial reactions to evaluate translations of particular allusions, metaphors, or allegories more fully and critically, we may draw upon our awareness of various theoretical orientations and interpretive perspectives that may be taken toward texts. Discuss the following questions with your partner to consider how some of the theoretical approaches explored earlier in this chapter might strengthen or challenge some of your responses to the questions above. Remember to keep notes of your discussion:
   - In what ways does Bacon, as a Renaissance philosopher of science, rely solely upon mimetic and objectivist orientations to identify deeper meanings beyond the surface features of this classical story?
   - How might insight into the effects of the tale upon audiences of the classical period suggest that its author had intentions not recognized by Bacon's reading?
   - How might Bacon's experience of *his* relatively more modern historical situation and *his* intentions as a writer add to or distort the story's more original meanings?
   - In what ways might Bacon's interpretation of the Sphinx's tale become a text requiring further translation and interpretation itself for readers sharing our present historical situation?
   - How might your previous familiarity with Bacon's "Four Idols" influence your own interpretations of his reading of the Sphinx's tale?

3. On your own write a paragraph or two about how your discussion of the questions above has challenged your initial understanding of the complications and stakes of interpretation. List further questions you now have about the processes and functions of interpretation and about the various interpretive perspectives outlined in this chapter.

The questions raised in Inquiry 5.6 illustrate several complexities of both representation and interpretation. In order to approach these types of questions with productive sophistication, you will want to know more about the theoretical issues and stakes involved. Readings from several theorists included in this section explore challenges, advantages, limitations, and consequences of the various orientations toward interpretation mapped by Abrams' diagram and discussed above. They will help you to see how various interpretations of a text raise questions not only about the text in question but about the nature of interpretation itself.

Stephen Mallioux's essay, "Interpretation," for instance, could help you give further consideration to the questions about intentions and historical context raised above and give you critical vocabulary to discuss Bacon's allegorizing. Stanley Fish's essay, "How to Recognize a Poem When You See One," could help you to see and more fully explain Bacon's reading of the tale as a product of his own interpretation rather than as a property of its formal features. Susan Sontag's essay, "Against Interpretation," might help you to argue that by burdening the tale with so much content, that by reading into it his own fascination with science, Bacon actually impoverishes the story for other readers. By broadening your awareness of the complexities and issues at stake in interpretations of all types of texts, these readings invite you to bring aspects of several interpretive perspectives together as you use your personal experiences and research to translate your insights and appreciation for others.

THE CLOSE READING

As we have seen, scientific interpretation of objects and phenomena strives ideally toward a convergence type of knowledge, toward a consensus of understanding and toward a regularity of explanation. On the other hand, humanities interpretation must always contend with divergent types of knowledge, with debates about meanings derived from multiple perspectives. In science, the strength of arguments comes from the objectivity, consistency, and universality of their conclusions. In the humanities, on the other hand, strong arguments may owe much to the subjectivity, idiosyncrasy, and uniqueness of their singular insights. Where inquiry and writing in the sciences tends to subordinate the role of the observer to the things observed, inquiry and writing in the humanities often acknowledges and sometimes even celebrates influences of the observer's personality and particular points of view. Nonetheless, convincing humanities arguments, like convincing interpretations of data in the sciences, generally begin with methodical observation and accurate description of the object of study. With a little adaptation, the trimodal tools of static, dynamic, and systematic description you developed for writing in the sciences can provide a firm foundation for writing in the humanities as well. Before moving on to more complex and relative questions or arguments about what a text may ultimately mean, effective humanities writers usually start with some description and analysis of the properties, functions, and relationships of its constituent parts from a more or less formalist or objectivist orientation. Literary scholars have called this method *close reading*.

As you approach any of the assignment options below, we suggest that prior to developing your own interpretive analysis or argument, you first write a detailed and descriptive close reading of your selected texts. What are the key elements and formal features of the text—terms, premises, metaphors? How are its elements and features arranged to construct a narrative, a chain of logic or an emotional affect? How does the text identify itself or function as part of a larger class or genre of related texts? Much of the material you produce in your close reading may later be integrated as support for particular evaluative and argumentative claims you may make in your fuller interpretation. In fact many of your most interesting interpretive insights will probably result from your careful consideration of your text's form and content through close reading. Further, as you develop your own interpretations more fully, you will want to provide your readers with a clear depiction of the texts as *you* have viewed it. By providing a complete description of your most objective perception of the text—which they may then compare with their own close reading of it—you give your readers a fairer and more complete basis for evaluation and appreciation of your interpretive claims.

While much of the discussion of humanities-based interpretation presented in this chapter has been drawn from theories and terms of literary study, these concepts—including the concept of close reading—can be applied to objects of study from across the disciplines if you approach them metaphorically. Whether they be dramatic or musical performances, DNA codes, or the architecture of a building, view them as "texts" with meanings worthy of translation and of critical assessment for your readers. Essays included in the readings for this unit can help to broaden your appreciation of the range of texts available for interpretation. Jack Solomon's "Masters of Desire: The Culture of American Advertising" reveal, for instance, how images that saturate our popular culture to the point of seeming nearly meaningless may have very critical social and even political implications. Stephen Mallioux's essay shows how interpretation itself is almost always political and how political texts are always subject to interpretation.

The first of the assignment options below provides you opportunity to consider how the most familiar debates within our political system, for example, surround arguments about "correct" interpretations of constitutionality with regard to such issues as free speech, gun control, abortion, or flag burning. Should the Constitution and the Bill of Rights be understood as a rendering of our political belief system without reference to its authors' times and intentions, or should it be understood as a rendering of the beliefs of particular men in a particular historical period? If the latter, then how should it be understood as a reflection of those times? How should such understanding bear upon our applications of its text to present-day issues? Abrams' triangle provides a valuable tool for exploring such questions.

If you work with this assignment option, you'll want to pay particular attention to how Stephen Mailloux's essay applies terms outlined in our consideration of Abrams' triangle so you can use them in your own interpretive efforts. Mallioux first applies concepts articulating various interpretive perspectives to familiar objects of literary study, including a story by Mark Twain and a poem by Emily Dickinson. After exploring complexities of interpretation resulting from encounters with these conventional objects of interpretation, Mailloux turns his attention to a contemporary historical debate surrounding interpretations and applications of an intercontinental antiballistic missile treaty to consider the enormous political implications issues of interpretation may have in very real and practical concerns. In approaching these issues and concerns, Mallioux shows how even interpretive perspectives themselves may be political in nature.

WRITING INTERPRETIVE ESSAYS IN THE HUMANITIES

The assignment options suggested below invite you to consider a range of interpretive activities across the disciplines, from evaluating creative and expressive values of popular and fine arts, to assessing social impacts of mass media, to determining legal policies of governance. The topics suggested here, and in previous inquiries in this chapter, provide just a sampling of issues that may involve data and concepts drawn from the sciences, social sciences, and arts for humanities-based interpretation of various "texts." With the direction and approval of your instructor, select one of the assignment options and topics provided to write an interpretive essay, or use the suggestions below as models to develop a topic and approach that more directly addresses your and your classmates' particular interests and concerns. You may well want to incorporate quotations from readings in this unit to support the particular interpretive perspectives you develop. Remember to cite your sources!

Compare and Contrast Two Policy Interpretations of a Text

Compare and contrast two interpretations of a text intended to direct legal policy on a critical social issue current in public debate. The first Ten Amendments to the United States Constitution, known as the "Bill of Rights," provide some obvious and interesting opportunities for interpretive debate in relation to contemporary social issues and emergent technologies. For instance you might consider any one of the following interpretive questions current in contemporary American political debate:

1. How do First Amendment guarantees of "free speech" apply to efforts to ban flag burning or to governmental regulation of Internet communications with regard to commercial distribution of pornography?

2. How do Second Amendment protections of the "right to bear arms" apply to citizens' possession and use of automatic weapons or to their freedom to form paramilitary organizations?

3. How do Fourth Amendment protections against "unreasonable searches and seizures" apply to automobile passengers in traffic stops, to practices of "racial profiling" by law enforcement agencies, or to seizures of property to finance operations of drug enforcement agencies?

4. How do Fifth Amendment protections against self-incrimination apply to the confidentiality of an individual's medical or mental health records or to emergent procedures of blood and DNA testing?

All of these questions have been debated vigorously in the press and popular media in recent years, and most have been raised in cases and suits addressed by the Supreme Court. As you select and enter a debate as a scholarly researcher, remember that the primary purpose of your inquiry is to increase understanding of the issue and of complex matters of interpretation, not simply to rehearse current opinions or to align yourself with already polarized opinions. Your scholarly function is to translate the terms of the debate, the issues involved, and the interpretive challenges presented by a particular text. Your interpretive efforts should contribute to more informed and judicious consideration of the controversy by other reasonable thinkers who will ultimately be reasonable for arriving at their own positions on the issues. The thesis of your paper should make a statement about the importance of studying the document in this way and make some claims about what your investigation can contribute to understanding the work.

Therefore, before you even begin to determine your own ultimate position on the issue—and before you even actually draft the body of your paper—you should complete the following preliminary writing steps:

1. Locate two sources in a library or Internet search that use constitutional arguments to develop their differing positions on one of the issues above.

2. Refer back to Abrams' orientation to critical theories and Mailloux's essay and remember the skills you developed in Inquiry 5.5 to identify and catalog the types of interpretive strategies used by your sources.

3. Write a tentative introductory passage explaining the significance of the debate and problems inherent in its resolution by constitutional interpretation. Also

describe the varying interpretations that led to debate, the persons and parties involved, the conflicts of values at stake, and the potential positive and negative consequences—including the potentials for establishing problematic precedents—of possible policy decisions.

4. Conduct your own close reading of the amendment subjected to interpretive debate.

5. Explain how features of the text and/or various other historical social and political forces have created controversy over its ultimate meaning in terms of the issue debated.

6. Conduct a close reading of the interpretive sources you have selected for comparison.

7. Develop a table of comparison that contrasts your sources' respective positions on each of the key points central to the debated issue.

8. Develop a tentative conclusion that explores your responses to both the arguments developed by your sources *and* to the interpretive and rhetorical methods they have used to make their arguments. As in your conclusions to research writing in the sciences and social sciences, you should also raise and address some questions here regarding the limitations of your study of the issue so far and suggest some avenues for further inquiry.

As you draft the body of your paper, you may select one of two standard comparison and contrast arrangement strategies: You may choose to describe the argument and critically examine the interpretive strategies of each source as a whole, or you may wish to dissect each of the arguments to compare point by point. The trimodal observation and description skills you have developed through previous inquiries and assignments should be helpful here. Either strategy will require appropriate transitional passages to guide your readers from point to point and from position to position while maintaining their focus upon the larger social policy issues, as well as their focus upon the critical interpretive issues, you are exploring. After drafting the body of your paper, you may well want to rethink and to revise your tentative introductory and conclusion passages to acknowledge more of the interpretive complexities and subtle insights you have discovered in your analysis.

Optional Approach

If you and your instructor decide it is appropriate to pursue a stronger personal position version of this assignment option, you may consider comparing and contrasting your own personally developed interpretation of the primary text with one or more interpretive sources. Remember that even in this version of the assignment your scholarly purpose is to generate knowledge about other positions and to discover insights about challenges of interpretation itself—not to produce pure polemic or one-sided argumentative prose. At least one of your interpretive sources should therefore represent a valid perspective differing from your own.

Either version of this assignment option may be readily adapted to address other legislative acts and laws that direct social and legal policy: How, for instance, should the Endangered Species Act be interpreted to affect the activities of private property owners? How should patent law be applied to emergent biotechnology? How should immigration law affect the educational and social services provided to the children of "illegal aliens"? Issues and debates addressed in some of your other course work may provide even more topics you might wish to address with your instructor's approval. In any case the procedures and guidelines provided above should serve you well in your efforts to understand the interpretive complexities involved in determining policies with regard to pressing social issues.

Compare and Contrast Two Creative Texts

Compare and contrast two creative texts from the fine arts or from popular media for their abilities to instruct, to move, or to delight audiences. The possibilities for selected objects of study in this assignment option are as broad as your imagination allows and will be narrowed by the kinds of questions you wish to explore about the functions of art and the influences various media, genre, historical periods, subjects, and audience appeal have on the meanings and values we ascribe to various texts. The suggestions provided here are intended only as some possible points of departure to begin focusing your own interests and thinking.

For instance, if you are interested in the effectiveness of mass media in influencing personal and social behaviors, you might choose to evaluate television ads or billboard signs from two public information campaigns related to the same or similar issues such as recycling and energy conservation, or to anti-smoking and drug prevention, or to family planning and child abuse. If your interest is in contrasting effects of popular media, you might choose to study different treatments of a single story such as the contrasting appeals of the original text and a movie version of a Shakespearean play, or of a classic novel by Jane Austen, or of a best-seller by Stephen King. If your interest is in the more traditional fine arts, you might select any two poems addressing a similar theme, or two Renaissance paintings depicting the same episode from the Bible or from classical mythology, or any two pieces of music from composers of the same historical period, and so forth. As you can see, almost any pairing of creative texts can provide the basis for interpretive essays, but all must be driven by a clear statement of purpose. Comparison without purpose is an empty exercise.

Choose art forms, subjects, and issues of creative expression you already know—and wish to know more—about. Your procedure here will be twofold:

First you'll translate or interpret possible meanings of your selected texts for your readers; then, through comparison, you'll evaluate their significance in terms of critical criteria you develop. As explained at the beginning of this chapter, you will need to use two vocabularies to accomplish these tasks: the appropriate terms and concepts associated with processes of production and with specific features of the artistic media selected for study to explain the works themselves; *and* the terminology of interpretive theories and methods to develop your larger claims about the meaning and value of your texts. Our discussion of Abrams' orientation to critical theories introduced useful terms and criteria for this assessment. You may find that the arguments of Mailloux, Fish, or Sontag in the readings included in this unit either lend support to or conflict with your own; either may be food for further thought about your interpretation, in which case you may want to include their ideas (properly quoted or paraphrased and cited) in your essay.

As you enter into interpretive evaluation as a scholarly researcher, remember that your primary purpose is to contribute to the discussions of artistic value and upon complex matters of interpretation, not to identify the one and only "true" meaning and ultimate worth of your selected texts. Your scholarly function is to translate unfamiliar elements of the texts to enhance your readers' appreciation of them and to explore how their value may be understood in terms of particular artistic functions. Your interpretive efforts should contribute to an enhanced understanding of the texts as creative expressions that may—depending upon the particular theoretical perspectives you wish to explore—more or less effectively delight, instruct, or move their audiences.

Therefore, before you even begin to determine your own final assessments of the text—and before you even actually draft the body of your paper—you should complete the following preliminary writing steps:

1. Select two creative texts as suggested above for comparative analysis.
2. Remember the skills you developed in Inquiry 5.5 and refer back to Abrams' orientation to critical theories and to assigned theoretical essays for terms and quotations to define the critical perspectives you have taken and explored above.
3. Write a tentative introductory passage that raises questions of artistic meaning and value you wish to address. Describe the competing critical perspectives that may suggest different approaches and answers to these questions with relation to your texts. Explore various consequences different understandings of artistic functions may have for appreciation of your selected texts and for the entertainment and education of their audiences.
4. Write a position statement identifying your preferred critical perspectives.
5. Conduct a trimodal description, or close reading, of your selected texts, using terminologies associated with their processes of production and with specific features of their artistic media.

6. Explain how features of the respective texts function or fail to fulfill the expectations of your critical perspectives in terms of their entertainment and educational impacts upon their audiences. Support your statements here by incorporating and citing quotations from one or more of the readings included in this unit.

7. Explain how features of the respective texts might function or fail to meet expectations of other critical perspectives you explored above.

8. Draft a tentative conclusion that explores your fuller appreciation of your selected texts *and* of the complexities of interpretive evaluation you have encountered. You may also wish to suggest how the challenges and insights you have encountered in your study might be applied to the appreciation and evaluation of other types of creative expression and artistic media.

As you draft the body of your paper, you may follow one of two standard comparison and contrast arrangement strategies: You may choose to describe, interpret, and evaluate each text entirely separately, or you may wish to describe, interpret, comparable elements of both text item by item against your evaluative criteria. Either strategy will require appropriate transitional passages to guide your readers through your description and analysis while maintaining their focus upon the larger interpretive issues you are exploring. After drafting the body of your paper, you may well want to rethink and to revise your tentative introductory and conclusion passages to acknowledge more of the interpretive complexities and subtle insights you have discovered in your analysis.

Optional Approach

If you and your instructor decide it is appropriate to pursue a more personally creative version of this assignment option, you may consider comparing and contrasting a creative text—poem, poster, piece of music—of your own creation with another selected for study. In this version of the assignment, you may have a much stronger sense of the intended function or purpose of your own creative effort, but remember to give careful consideration to the impacts or effects your work may have on potential audiences that do not share this knowledge.

This version of the assignment is particularly well suited to considering possible improvements of public information campaigns where the desired effects of the creative texts may be assessed in terms of actual personal and social behaviors. In this case, you may think of your creative effort as an attempt to improve upon an important message for a particular audience or purpose. For instance you may notice that a poster campaign intended to encourage students on campus to sort and recycle plastic and glass bottles does seem to result in a significant reduction of these materials in trash containers. How might your knowledge of student interests and motivations enable you to design catchier posters that would really work? In this case your essay would become a critique of the existing public information campaign and an explanation of design innovations you have incorporated into your own poster with a clear and practical purpose.

Compare and Contrast Two Interpretations of Artistic Texts

Compare and contrast two critical interpretations of a single artistic text or medium. Your approach to this assignment might be as direct as comparing two reviews of the same new-release motion picture, book, play, or CD. Or you might join debates about the merit of whole genres or media of expression and communication as we did earlier in this chapter in our discussion of graffiti art. The social impacts of commercial advertising have recently been the subject of such debate. The relative merits of different popular musical forms—from swing to rhythm and blues, to rock and roll, to disco, to rap and hip hop—have often been the subject of debate between generations of listeners. Remember that all campaigns for censorship or for public sponsorship of any particular piece or form of artistic expression are essential interpretive arguments and may, therefore, provide engaging topics for this assignment option. Consider some of the following interpretive claims:

- Television violence contributes to increased violent behavior in our nation's youth.
- Commercial ads featuring high fashion contribute to unhealthy ideals of female beauty and eating disorders among young women.
- Digitally synthesized musical sounds are superior (or inferior) to those produced by acoustic instruments.
- Graphic birth control information about human reproductivity may be considered "obscene" under certain proposed antipornography legislation for Internet regulation.
- Rod Stewart's remakes of popular songs by other artists are always superior (inferior) to the originals.
- The book is always better than the movie.
- Rap music advocating violence against the police should be banned.

All these statements have been made and countered in interpretive debate. As you enter such debates as a scholarly researcher, remember that your primary purpose is to contribute to the understanding of the artistic and social values at stake and on complex matters of interpretation, not simply to adjudicate the issue through your own personal taste. Your scholarly function is to translate the terms of the debate to reveal the various theoretical and cultural assumptions upon which particular claims are made. Your interpretive efforts should contribute to an enhanced understanding of larger social consequences and logical difficulties inherent in making and in resolving differences in critical interpretations and judgments of artistic expression.

Therefore before you even begin to determine your own judgments—and before you even actually begin to draft the body of your own paper—you should complete the following preliminary writing steps:

1. Select and study two reviews or critical interpretations focused on the same pieces or medium of artistic expression as suggested above.

2. Conduct your own close reading or trimodal description of the pieces or media of artistic expression being critiqued.

3. Remember the skills you developed in Inquiry 5.5 and refer back to Abrams' orientation to critical theories and to assigned essays for terms and quotations to define critical perspectives you have identified.

4. Write a tentative introductory passage that explores questions of artistic meaning and value you wish to address. Describe the competing perspectives and theoretical and cultural assumptions that contribute to the divergent critical interpretations of artistic expression under study. Consider the conflicts of values at stake and the larger potential social and cultural consequences that may be associated with these critical interpretations. Remember the "so what" question at the heart of humanities inquiry and make certain to develop a clear thesis statement.

5. Conduct a close reading of the critical interpretations and describe their premises, chains of logic, claims to authority, and relations to other interpretive arguments.

6. List questions you have about the value of the pieces or media of artistic expression that are unanswered by the interpretive debate.

7. Draft a tentative conclusion that explores your fuller appreciation of the complexities of interpretive debate and of the social and cultural significance of artistic expression.

As you draft the body of your paper, you may follow one of two standard comparison and contrast arrangement strategies: You may choose to describe and evaluate each critical interpretation separately, or you may wish to contrast their arguments point by point. Either strategy will require appropriate transitional passages to guide your readers through your analysis while maintaining their focus upon the larger interpretive, social, cultural, and artistic issues you are exploring. After drafting the body of your paper, you may well want to rethink and to revise your tentative introductory and conclusion passages to acknowledge more of the insights you have gained into the complexities and stakes of interpretive debates.

Optional Approach

If you and your instructor decide it is appropriate to pursue a stronger personal position version of this assignment option, you may consider comparing your own critical interpretation of the artistic expression under study with those of one or more reviewers or critics. Use quotations from readings included in this unit to support your perspective. Remember that even in this version of the assignment your scholarly purpose is to generate greater knowledge about other critical perspectives and to discover insights into the larger complexities and stakes of interpretation itself—not simply to render the final "right" judgment. You should be able to acknowledge at least some validity in the critical interpretations you have chosen to debate. Establish your own credibility as a critic by showing that you can bring something additional—overlooked by others—to the debate and remember the old Latin phrase *De gustibus non est disputandum*: "there is no arguing about taste." You need to bring more than subjective preferences to your interpretive debates.

REVISING AND REWRITING ESSAYS IN THE HUMANITIES

As you drafted your descriptions, interpretations and critiques of various texts for the assignment options above, you undoubtedly encountered some global level challenges in designing the structure and arrangement of your essay that you had perhaps not met—at least to the same degree—in your writing for the sciences or social sciences. You also may have encountered more local level questions about how to develop support for your interpretive claims without the clearly defined types of data you had worked with in the other disciplines. Further, as you engaged more of your subjective responses to texts in this essay, you may have had some surface level questions about the appropriateness of different types of syntax and diction. Finally, as you shifted from using the APA to the MLA standards for citation and documentation, you may have been curious about reasons for the subtle but significant differences between the two systems. As we try to provide helpful suggestions for strengthening and polishing your writing for the humanities, we'll attempt to provide some answers and explanations for some of these writing issues that can help you to revise your essay with a clearer sense of the functions and purposes of writing in the humanities. Understanding these functions and purposes should help you become a better editor of your present work and help you to develop more effective initial drafts in the future. Finally, the Appendix will address issues in citation and documentation.

Global Organization and Logical Progression

As we have seen in earlier chapters, organization in writing for sciences and social sciences is largely governed by the logical progression of the academic inquiry process. The logical progression of inquiry in these disciplines has become fairly formalized in the standard structure and subheadings of the scientific report formats strongly associated with scientific method. The absence of formally prescribed subheadings in humanities writing may seem to suggest that no clear structure exists to govern the logical progression of inquiry in this field. Certainly it is true that the wide range of objects available for study in the humanities, and the even wider range of interpretive perspectives available, require greater latitude and flexibility in organizational structures for inquiry and writing. Nonetheless, regardless of the presence or absence of subheadings, the basic components of inquiry processes we have investigated in science and social science writing are also integral in writing for the humanities and can provide a basic organizational structure for your interpretive essays.

In its most elemental form, this structure has the following basic components:

1. The importance of a particular issue is acknowledged and critical questions are asked.
2. A research plan for addressing these questions is mapped.
3. Textual data and contextual information relevant to the questions is compiled and presented.
4. The textual data are interpreted in terms of the insight they provide with respect to the critical questions asked.
5. The whole preceding inquiry process is evaluated, and new questions and investigations are suggested.

In the formal scientific research report, these components are clearly labeled with subheadings and follow a set order determined by the scientific method of inquiry: Introduction, Methods, Findings, Discussion, Conclusion. In writing for humanities, order is determined by the logic of your interpretation and method by the interpretive theories (or plan) you are using. Your descriptive findings will be included to illustrate and support your interpretive claims as you proceed, rather than being confined to a separate section. Thus all of the components of inquiry are present, but the interrelationship of ideas rather than the method controls the order. To guide your readers through the logic of your organizational variations of the inquiry process, you will need carefully crafted transitional passages that highlight the relationships between interpretive method and meaning (result) that you are using and to emphasize the function of your inquiry.

INQUIRY 5.7: PLANNING GLOBAL REVISIONS

You may apply the following global revision techniques to your own paper, or work with a partner to practice your editorial skills on one another's paper. For an even more complete view of your work, you might do both! Print out two copies of your paper, one to work over on your own and one to exchange. Compare your own assessments with those of your peer-respondent to develop your final revision plan.

Develop a working description of what your draft accomplishes so far by writing an abstract of your draft. As described in the science unit, an abstract should provide a concise statement of the *purpose, method,* and *results* of your study. Read your draft over quickly and then try to boil the gist of it down to one or two statements for each of these elements. Such a distillation of your work should prove invaluable in guiding your rewriting for clarity and directness of purpose. If you are unable to generate such a concise abstract identifying your purpose, method, and results, it may be that your essay lacks some essential aspect of true inquiry and needs more drafting before you can proceed with further revision for organizational structure. Pay close attention to your partner's abstract of your work. Whether your partner's reading concurs with your intentions or not, reveals much about your success in conveying your attentions and you will certainly want to revise accordingly.

After you have drafted necessary additions or changes to your work and have produced an accurate abstract that meets your goals for the essay, go through the piece paragraph by paragraph and use the subheads from the formal research report format to identify the work of each paragraph in pursuing your inquiry: Where are you establishing your purpose and questions for investigation? Where are you presenting evidence? Interpreting? Drawing conclusions? Write the terms *introduction, methods, findings, discussion,* and *conclusion* in the margins next to corresponding paragraphs. As noted in the assignment options above, different arrangement strategies exist for comparison and contrast, and there is no one correct order in which these terms will necessarily appear. By clearly labeling the places where your writing is doing these different kinds of intellectual work, you can begin to look for balances and imbalances in your analyses. You can also consider alternative possibilities for more effective arrangements.

Another procedure you may use in place of—or in conjunction with—this functional labeling of each paragraph is to give each paragraph its own working subtitle which gives some clue about the topics it covers and the intellectual work that it does. Transcribe these paragraph titles as a list on separate sheet of paper, and you have a topical outline which you can also use to consider alternate organizational strategies. Simply rearrange the titles into a more effective order and you have a global revision plan. If you are working with a peer-respondent, it should be interesting to see how close your outline of your draft is to your partner's description of it and to consider their suggestions for possible reorganizations.

Once you are satisfied with the logical progression of your essay from paragraph to paragraph, you can use the functional labeling and working subtitles of paragraphs to begin to develop transitional words or passages that will help your readers navigate their ways through your inquiry. Transitions provide readers with two kinds of assistance. Effective transitions show how a new paragraph relates to the previous paragraph either by further developing a concept or topic introduced there, or by announcing a necessary shift in focus. They also indicate how the new paragraph relates to the overall governing question or thesis statement that establishes the purpose of your inquiry in your essay's introduction. In many cases, transitional sentences will also be *topic sentences* because they declare a paragraph's subject, but remember that providing your readers with a map of your logical progression also means showing relation— how one subject leads to another and to the larger goals of your inquiry. Key transitional passages in your essay not only will link the subjects of succeeding paragraphs to one another but also they will link the progression of your thought back to your initial question or hypothesis.

Developing Well-Integrated Quotations

Though humanities inquiry may not necessarily appear to be as clearly data-driven as inquiry in the sciences and social sciences, effective academic writing in the humanities—as in any other discipline—ultimately relies on clear presentation of accurate and relevant evidence to support a writer's analysis and conclusions. The various kinds of "data" that drive inquiry in the humanities may consist of particular aspects of the actual texts under study, facts regarding historical and sociological conditions of their production and reception, as well as critical differences and similarities in interpretive responses they have generated. While collected data in the sciences may sometimes be presented most clearly in graphic tables and charts, the data of inquiry in the humanities will most often be incorporated into your text in the form of quotations. Therefore, in order to develop support for your interpretive claims, you will want to understand features of— and strategies for developing—well-integrated quotations into your essays.

Well-integrated quotations generally possess most or all of four important features:

- A clear signal phrase
- Appropriately selected, edited, and cited text
- An accurate paraphrase of the quoted material
- Clear application of the quoted material to the analysis and inquiry at hand.

Signal phrases do more than simply indicate shifts from your own words to another's words in your text. A signal phrase is an important feature of writer etiquette analogous to making polite introduction of a friend or acquaintance you wish to bring into a conversation already underway. By incorporating quotations into your text, you are introducing new speakers, and your polite introduction should obviously include the speaker's name at the very least. A more complete introduction would also acknowledge the new speaker's background and familiarity with the subject at hand. Imagine you are having a conversation about recent movies or a new music CD with a group of fellow students in the hall after your writing class. Somebody you know from another class walks up and seems interested. Of course you'd say something like, "Hey, everybody. This is Robert" or "Meghan," or whatever. If you really wanted to include them in the conversation, though, you'd also say something about them relevant to the topic such as "Robert writes movie reviews for the school newspaper" or "Meghan has all of Pearl Jam's CDs." Your fuller introduction would provide some context and help bring more credibility to whatever your friend might have to say.

In the case of academic writing, some mention in a signal phrase of the essay or book from which a statement is drawn can provide helpful context; some acknowledgment of your quoted or cited speaker's stature or recognition in a field, or some mention of their historical period or life accomplishments, can bring credibility to their ideas. In general you should use signal phrases to give readers some sense of your purpose for incorporating a particular quotation or citation into your text and some sense of why they should pay particular attention to the words of the speaker you're introducing.

Your own sense of your purpose for incorporating a particular speaker into your text should also guide your attention to careful selection and editing of the particular words you chose to quote or cite. Your first issue in selection is whether to actually quote at all or whether a paraphrase or simple citation will suffice. Academic writing is like an ongoing conversation, and readers familiar with a subject or topic will likely be familiar with speakers who have already contributed significantly. Less familiar readers will appreciate gaining some sense of how the conversation has been shaped by key contributors and of how various positions are represented by particular speakers. In either case you will serve your readers well by citing the sources of terms, concepts, and arguments that are not necessarily your own or that are associated with the scholarship of others. Think back to our earlier example of a hallway conversation. Whether you are agreeing with a position someone has already stated, conventions of etiquette, as well as dynamics of convincing argument, would encourage you to acknowledge that speaker in direct association with their name. You might say, for instance, something like, "I think Robert's right when he says movies aren't responsible for the violent behaviors of audiences," or "Well, unlike Meghan, I like the newest Pearl Jam best of all." That's the idea of citation, to provide attribution for the source of an idea, whether you quote the speaker verbatim or simply paraphrase their words.

To decide whether to paraphrase or to quote directly, you should consider the particular strengths of a source's actual statements to decide how you will select from them and edit them into your own text. If Robert had actually said something catchy like, "Movies are made to entertain, not to influence," you might want to repeat, or quote, his actual phrase to give more force to your agreement. In this case you'll still need to edit his complete statement to work his words into the grammar and sense of your own sentence. You might, for instance, wind up with something like, "Robert's right, a movie's point is 'to entertain, not to influence.'" If Meghan had said, "Pearl Jam's newest CD seems suspiciously self-derivative," you might want to disagree by saying something like, "What's wrong with being 'self-derivative' when you're the best?" In this case you would have edited down her initial statement to her single term for a key concept you wish to debate. The point here is that though citation recognizes the sources of concepts, your decision to paraphrase or to quote should be based on the originality or effectiveness a speaker's particular articulation. The purpose of quotation is not to let another speaker make statements for you, but to share their memorable formulations of statements with your readers.

Even when you quote another speaker directly, you should consider also paraphrasing their statements into your own words to show readers exactly how you are understanding their ideas. You might also wish to paraphrase in order to be clear about how you wish your audience to understand particular statements and terms in different contexts. In the case of Robert's phrase, you might want to translate the statement for a more academic context into terms of interpretive theory such as those we explored earlier in this chapter. After quoting him directly, you might, for instance, go on to say something like, "The art of film has an *aesthetic*, rather than a *pragmatic* function." If you wanted to bring Meghan's statement down to more familiar terms for a less formal audience, and to give it your own spin, you might say something like, "being 'self-derivative' is just following your own success and not being a copy-cat like everyone else." Of course as you restate and reinterpret the words of others, you also begin to show how you are applying their ideas expressed in quotations to the development of your own inquiry and thought.

In many ways application of a source's statements to your own purpose is the most critical feature of a well-integrated quotation. The ability to apply quoted material to your own purpose characterizes a crucial distinction between critical thinking and mere reporting. Because thorough application of quotations represents the difference between just using the words of others and doing your own thinking, we believe it is among the most essential skills of effective and successful academic writing. As we've already said, some of your purpose in incorporating a particular quotation may be made clear in your introductory signal phrase and in your paraphrase of it. Often, however, additional discussion of key terms and concepts introduced in quoted material may be necessary for fully developed application and integration of it to the purpose at hand. One rule of thumb to determine whether you have worked in sufficient application and integration of quotations as you revise your essays is to simply count the number of lines on the page occupied by quotation. Then count the lines occupied by your signal phrase, paraphrase, and further discussion. If the quotation is longer than your integration of it, you may be letting your source do too much of your own intellectual work for you. Some critical readers might even suggest that your integrative material should be at least twice as developed as the quotation itself. At any rate almost any local development you can incorporate in fuller integration of quotations is likely to greatly enhance the clarity of your overall purpose and the development of local support for your interpretive claims. In many cases your instructors will already be quite familiar with what your primary sources think. A well-integrated quotation not only shows that you also have this familiarity, but also that you have and can support thinking of your own worthy of their consideration.

As you proofread and revise your essay, see the Appendix on citation systems for more information and understanding of the specific features of MLA formats for citation and documentation. To sharpen your editorial sense of well-integrated quotations, complete the following suggested inquiry activities.

INQUIRY 5.8: ASSESSING INTEGRATED QUOTATIONS

1. Quickly reread one of the sources you read in preparing to write your humanities essay to consider another writer's integration of quotations. Write a number in the margin next to each use of quotation by the writer. Mark the integration of quotations by drawing vertical lines in the margins of the page next to all of the material incorporating the quoted material, including signal phrases, quotations themselves, paraphrases, and additional applications. Draw an additional vertical line in the margin next to the quoted passages themselves. In the text draw a single horizontal line beneath signal phrases and double horizontal lines beneath paraphrasings and applications of the quotations. A quick scanning of your numbering, marking, and underlining should reveal much about the frequency, distribution, and extent of the writer's reliance upon quotation and allow you to make some evaluation of the writer's purposeful incorporation of quoted material into the essay.

2. Describe and evaluate amount, character, and value of the writer's incorporation and integration of quotations in a few sentences, and be prepared to discuss your assessment with your peer-respondent.

3. Exchange papers with a partner and follow the steps outlined above to assess and discuss the incorporation and integration of quotations in your peer-respondent's essay.

4. Make notes on your peer-respondent's assessment of the integration of quotations in your draft to incorporate into the revision of your essay.

Surface Clarity: Maintaining Coherence through Transitions

As we stated in the section on global organization, transitional passages in humanities writing are essential to helping your readers navigate through the logical progression of your essay. Transitional passages between significant sections of your inquiry may consist of several sentences to show how each section relates to one another *and* to the overall purpose of your inquiry. In this section, however, we specifically discuss uses of single transitional sentences to link individual paragraphs to one another. The concepts detailed here can, of course, be expanded on a larger scale to develop critical linkages between more significant shifts in your topic focus. Our purpose here is to demonstrate how clarity of syntax in single sentences relates directly to much larger matters of coherence. In some cases transitional sentences will also be *topic sentences* because they announce a paragraph's subject, but remember that providing your readers with a map of your logical progression also means showing relation, how one paragraph leads to another and to the larger goals of your inquiry.

Sentences can establish relations within themselves, as well as between one another. In the two grammatical types of English sentences, a verb generally relates a subject to some effect upon an object or to some fuller explanation of itself. That is, as we saw in the section on sentence clarity from our chapter on writing in the sciences, active sentences connect their subjects with *direct objects*, and passive sentences connect their subjects to *complements*. In the section on sentence focus in the chapter on social sciences, we saw that clear sentences position the topic—what the sentence is basically about—as the grammatical subject. Further, scholars of style have shown that grammatical subjects are clearest and most concise when expressed near the beginning of sentences as characters, as concrete entities capable of executing the action or of receiving the complement of the verb. Consider, for instance, the following sets of sentences: Which do you find clearest and most effective? What features give it particular expressive force? Start by using the same techniques discussed in the previous chapter (and illustrated below) for identifying and tightening sentence focus.

Example

1. It is usually regarded as the function of interpretation in the humanities to clarify the meanings of and to assess values in cultural productions.
2. The function of interpretation in the humanities is generally regarded as the clarification of meanings and the assessment of values in cultural productions.
3. Interpretation in the humanities, as generally regarded, functions to clarify meanings and assess values in cultural productions.
4. Interpreters in the humanities generally clarify meanings and assess values in cultural productions.

Perhaps you agreed with us that sentence 4 communicates best; certainly it is the shortest of the set. But can you explain other features that also contribute to its clarity? In this sentence the subject *interpreters* is not just an abstract noun like *interpretation*, nor an even more abstract noun phrase like *the function of interpretation*, nor, we believe worst of all, the completely abstract pronoun *it* which even lacks clear referent. All these sentences say more or less the same thing about the topic of interpretation. Sentence 1, however, pushes the topic from the front of the sentence and demotes it to the grammatical position of an object with an unnecessary substitute for an actual subject. Though the next two sentences do at least move their topics into grammatical subject positions at their beginnings, only the last sentence has the concreteness of human agency actually capable of *clarifying* and *assessing* cultural productions. Though such concreteness is not always possible to achieve with many academic topics, we believe it is preferable whenever possible.

Having considered how the concreteness and position of a sentence's topic as its grammatical subject contributes to its clarity within sentences, we may now consider how relations between sentences can contribute to the coherence of your writing. When several sentences form a unified paragraph with a shared topic, their subjects may have significant similarities. Notice how many of the sentences in the previous paragraph have the words *sentence* or *sentences* in or very near the subject position. Such repetition, with some variation, of a familiar topic as clear subjects of subsequent sentences gives a paragraph considerable coherence as it is clear how all its sentences relate to one another. Notice, however, that the paragraph does not begin, nor does it end, with the topic of *sentences* in subject positions. The opening and closing sentences of the paragraph serve to transition into and out of this particular topic. The first two sentences continue with the implied subject *you* from the instructions at the end of the earlier paragraph leading into the sample sentences we asked you to consider. In these sentences, the concept of a specific, presumably superior, *sentence* is the object of the verbs. In the transition of the paragraph from or our consideration of clarity to specific features of various sentences, the concept of *sentences* moves from the object to the subject positions in the body of the paragraph.

Notice another transition toward the end of this same paragraph. The second to last sentence introduces a new concept, *concreteness of human agency*, as its direct object. In the next and final sentence of the paragraph, this concept becomes the new topic focus as the term *concreteness* moves into the subject position. A clear transition in related topics between sentences has been accomplished through careful grammatical shifting. The older, familiar, concise, and concrete subject of *sentence* at the beginning of a sentence introduced a newer, longer, and less concrete concept at the end. In the last sentence, this concept becomes more familiar and takes more concise expression in the opening subject position. It is almost as though the idea has been set up as a grammatical loop in the object position of one sentence to be hooked and crocheted as a topic in the subject position of the next. If all this analysis of sentences and their grammatical relations in one paragraph has seemed excessive or confusing, just remember the following points:

- In clear sentences the topic is also generally the grammatical subject.
- Clear subjects are expressed as concise and concrete nouns placed near the beginnings of sentences.
- Clear subjects are already familiar to readers.
- New topics can be introduced coherently as the objects or complements of sentences with already familiar subjects.
- Once introduced in object or complement positions, these now familiar topics can coherently become subjects of subsequent sentences.

Once you've grasped the basics of using clear internal relations within sentences as a basis for developing coherent relations between sentences and to guide transitions between topics within paragraphs, you are ready to apply the idea of grammatical looping and hooking to crochet careful transitional sentences between paragraphs. Furthermore you can use these same techniques for shifting and relating topic focus between paragraphs to articulate and relate phases of your inquiry as you move between larger sections of your essay. Here are the main points:

- To craft a careful transition between paragraphs, knit a subject at the beginning of the first sentence of a new paragraph from a concept or topic introduced at the end of the last sentence or sentences of the preceding paragraph.
- To develop transitional passages between significant sections of your essay, write a sentence or two summarizing how a preceding section has both advanced your inquiry and introduced new materials for consideration. Then write another sentence or two to map how a following section will further advance your inquiry by examining the newly introduced material.

In short transitions at all levels of your prose simply provide your readers with connections between the old and familiar to the new. They are coordinating points that allow your readers to navigate the logical progression of your inquiry.

INQUIRY 5.9: ASSESSING AND REVISING TRANSITIONS

Quickly reread one of the sources you read in preparing to write your humanities essay to consider another writer's uses of transitions between paragraphs and sections. Mark the transitions you find as follows:

- Write a number in the margin next to each use of effective transitional passages by the writer.
- Mark the transitional sentences and passages by drawing vertical lines in the margins of the page next to them.
- In the text, draw a single horizontal line beneath familiar topics developed earlier in the paragraph or section.
- Draw double horizontal lines beneath newly introduced materials.
- Circle key transitional words and phrases that signal significant phases in the inquiry such as *in comparison, on the other hand, to summarize,* or *in conclusion.*

A quick scanning of your numbering, marking, and underlining, and circling should reveal much about the frequency, distribution, and extent of the writer's use of effective transitions and allow you to pick up some tips on how to incorporate transitional passages into your own essay.

1. Describe and evaluate amount, character, and value of the writer's use of effective transitions in a few sentences, and be prepared to discuss your assessment with your peer-respondent.
2. Exchange papers with a partner, and follow the steps outlined above to assess and discuss the use of transitional sentences and passages in your peer-respondent's essay.
3. Make notes on your peer-respondent's assessment of effective transitions in your draft to incorporate into the revision of your essay.

MOVING ON

Moving on from our considerations of inquiry and writing in the humanities, we complete our introductory survey of the major disciplinary areas—the sciences, social sciences, and humanities—and our exploration of their aims and methods in the production and communication of knowledge. As in many aspects of life, such a completion can only have meaning as a new beginning. We begin to reconsider the products of knowledge anew each time we are called upon to apply them to any new situation. In the next unit on critical applications, we ask you to bring your developing understanding of disciplinary processes of inquiry and writing to bear upon complex questions with very practical purposes and consequences—questions that involve making evaluations and assessments, making decisions, and taking actions. The types of judgments involved in such questions will require you to exercise the skills of interpretation we have explored in this humanities unit as you attempt to give academic knowledge fuller meaning by applying it to very real human situations.

As we have seen in this unit, developing the fullest possible sense of the meanings of things and their relevance to human experience requires that we broaden the range of interpretive perspectives we bring to bear in our inquiries. Our survey of the disciplines has shown how major disciplinary areas function as interpretive perspectives upon the world, as different ways of seeing defined and guided by particular ways of identifying and regarding objects of study, as distinctive worldviews communicated through discursive expectations and conventions shaped by those particular methods of study. To apply disciplinary knowledge meaningfully in the world, we must finally create forums for the disciplines to communicate with one another, to share their interpretations of the world in ways that can inform and inspire our continued efforts to respond to the actual and ever-changing conditions of life. Ultimately, to have practical application to the real world, we must develop *interdisciplinary* approaches to the production and communication of knowledge.

Interdisciplinarity involves the critical thinking skills of synthesis, the ability to draw together different types of knowledge, to identify their productive contributions to the understanding and solution of a problem, and to discover from them an approach that takes into account the realities of how *things work*, of how *people act*, and, finally, of what values *make us human*. As you engage the critical application assignments in the next unit, we hope you will take with you the writing skills that have helped you to make deeper inquiry into the nature of things, people, and values. Among these skills we include precision of accurate description; scholarly integration of and response to theories, concepts, and words of other inquirers; and the organizational principles of logical progression. Most important, we hope you will take with you the skills of *revision*—literally of *reseeing*. Revision means seeing again, trying on new perspectives to gain fuller vision. It means rethinking and deepening inquiry by bringing together a synthesis of different kinds of knowledge. Revision is the interdisciplinary synthesis of writing processes. It means bringing together our most productive understanding of how words and texts work as things, of how people act through them, and how, finally, we find value in them through our practical applications of them to the critical problems we face.

s i x

Readings in the Humanities

INTRODUCTION

The readings in the humanities section introduce students to the key terms, skills, and critical stakes of interpretation, a central activity in the humanities. Bacon's tale introduces science, metaphor, and interpretation simultaneously, making an excellent arena for exploring the interaction of these domains. Stanley Fish stresses the role of the reader (or viewer) and the reader's prior knowledge in interpretation, whereas Mailloux organizes interpretive theories in both literature and law, giving students theoretical language for talking about our interpretive activity. Sontag then counters the intellectual/analytical focus of the previous readings by stressing the role of impact in art and literature. Thus the readings give a multidimensional view of interpretation, cover interpretation in science and law as well as art and literature, and introduce students to the debates surrounding methods of interpretation. The final reading, by Solomon, puts the interpretive tools to work on popular culture. Though this reading refers to one specific kind of cultural creation, the interpretive tools discussed in the core group of readings can be applied texts from across the arts and sciences.

The student paper selected for revision workshop illustrates the generative effect of close reading and interpretation from multiple theoretical perspectives. The paper provides opportunity for revision to establish clearer statement of purpose, guidance, and cohesion through work on thesis and transitions.

Tale of the Sphinx

Francis Bacon

Biography: See entry in the science unit for fuller biographic information. In the selection included here, we can see how during Bacon's age science and philosophy largely overlapped.

Sir Francis Bacon's essay interprets the ancient tale of the sphinx who waylaid travelers with riddles, then dispatched them if they could not solve them. Bacon argues that the sphinx represents science, which presents man with riddles on the nature of man and the nature of things. He argues that Oedipus solved the riddle because he did not hurry (being lame) and therefore deliberated carefully. We hope this piece provides an example of both the possibilities and problems of interpretation by allegory.

XXVIII.—SPHINX, OR SCIENCE.

Explained of the Sciences.

They relate that Sphinx was a monster, variously formed, having the face and voice of a virgin, the wings of a bird, and the talons of a griffin. She resided on the top of a mountain, near the city Thebes, and also beset the highways. Her manner was to lie in ambush and seize the travelers, and having them in her power, to propose to them certain dark and perplexed riddles, which it was thought she received from the Muses, and if her wretched captives could not solve and interpret these riddles, she with great cruelty fell upon them, in their hesitation and confusion, and tore them to pieces. This plague, having reigned a long time, the Thebans at length offered their kingdom to the man who could interpret her riddles, there being no other way to subdue her. (Œdipus, a penetrating and prudent man, though lame in his feet, excited by so great a reward, accepted the condition, and with a good assurance of mind, cheerfully presented himself before the monster, who directly asked him, "What creature that was, which being born four-footed, afterward became two-footed, then three-footed, and lastly four-footed again?" (Œdipus, with presence of mind, replied it was man, who, upon his first birth and infant state, crawled upon all fours in endeavoring to walk; but not long after went upright upon his two natural feet; again, in old age walked three-footed, with a stick; and at last, growing decrepit, lay four-footed confined to his bed; and having by this exact solution obtained the victory, he slew the monster, and, laying the carcass upon an ass, led her away in triumph; and upon this he was, according to the agreement, made king of Thebes.

From "Wisdom of the Ancients: A Series of Mythological Fables," *Bacon's Essays.* New York: A. L. Burt Co., 1883, pp. 360–363.

Explanation.   This is an elegant, instructive fable, and seems invented to represent science, especially as joined with practice. For science may, without absurdity, be called a monster, being strangely gazed at and admired by the ignorant and unskillful. Her figure and form is various, by reason of the vast variety of subjects that science considers; her voice and countenance are represented female, by reason of her gay appearance and volubility of speech; wings are added, because the sciences and their inventions run and fly about in a moment, for knowledge, like light communicated from one torch to another, is presently caught and copiously diffused; sharp and hooked talons are elegantly attributed to her, because the axioms and arguments of science enter the mind, lay hold of it, fix it down, and keep it from moving or slipping away. This the sacred philosopher observed, when he said, "The words of the wise are like goads or nails driven far in."[*] Again, all science seems placed on high, as it were on the tops of mountains that are hard to climb; for science is justly imagined a sublime and lofty thing, looking down upon ignorance from an eminence, and at the same time taking an extensive view on all sides, as is usual on the tops of mountains. Science is said to beset the highways, because through all the journey and peregrination of human life there is matter and occasion offered of contemplation.

Sphinx is said to propose various difficult questions and riddles to men, which she received from the Muses; and these questions, so long as they remain with the Muses, may very well be unaccompanied with severity, for while there is no other end of contemplation and inquiry but that of knowledge alone, the understanding is not oppressed, or driven to straits and difficulties, but expatiates and ranges at large, and even receives a degree of pleasure from doubt and variety; but after the Muses have given over their riddles to Sphinx, that is, to practice, which urges and impels to action, choice, and determination, then it is that they become torturing, severe, and trying, and, unless solved and interpreted, strangely perplex and harass the human mind, rend it every way, and perfectly tear it to pieces. All the riddles of Sphinx, therefore, have two conditions annexed, viz., dilaceration to those who do not solve them, and empire to those that do. For he who understands the thing proposed obtains his end, and every artificer rules over his work.[†]

Sphinx has no more than two kinds of riddles, one relating to the nature of things, the other to the nature of man; and correspondent to these, the prizes of the solution are two kinds of empire—the empire over nature, and the empire over man. For the true and ultimate end of natural philosophy is dominion over

---

[*]Eccles. xii. 11.

[†]This is what the author so frequently inculcates in the *Novum Organum*, viz., that knowledge and power are reciprocal; so that to improve in knowledge is to improve in the power of commanding nature, by introducing new arts, and producing works and effects.

natural things, natural bodies, remedies, machines, and numberless other particulars, though the schools, contented with what spontaneously offers, and
swollen with their own discourses, neglect, and in a manner despise, both
things and works.

But the riddle proposed to (Œdipus, the solution whereof acquired him
the Theban kingdom, regarded the nature of man; for he who has thoroughly
looked into and examined human nature, may in a manner command his own
fortune, and seems born to acquire dominion and rule. Accordingly, Virgil
properly makes the arts of government to be the arts of the Romans.[†] It was,
therefore, extremely apposite in Augustus Cæsar to use the image of Sphinx in
his signet, whether this happened by accident or by design; for he of all men
was deeply versed in politics, and through the course of his life very happily
solved abundance of new riddles with regard to the nature of man; and unless
he had done this with great dexterity and ready address, he would frequently
have been involved in imminent danger, if not destruction.

It is with the utmost elegance added in the fable, that when Sphinx was
conquered, her carcass was laid upon an ass; for there is nothing so subtile and
abstruse, but after being once made plain, intelligible, and common, it may be
received by the slowest capacity.

We must not omit that Sphinx was conquered by a lame man, and impo-
tent in his feet; for men usually make too much haste to the solution of Sphinx's
riddles; whence it happens, that she prevailing, their minds are rather racked
and torn by disputes, than invested with command by works and effects. ∞

[†]"Tu regere imperio populos, Romane, memento: Hæ tibi erunt artes."—Æn. vi. 851.

How to Recognize a Poem When You See One

Stanley Fish

Biography: *Stanley Fish, Professor of English and Criminal Justice at the University of Illinois, Chicago, grew up in a working-class urban family, and his interests and opinions challenge traditional boundaries. His works span the distance from English Renaissance to law (and its relation to literature), from linguistics to psychoanalysis, and from philosophy to political correctness, affirmative action, and free speech.*

Fish uses a classroom experience with poetry to demonstrate that interpretation is culturally situated. The interpretation poetry students give a list of random names illustrates that recognition and interpretation are taught, and that meaning resides as much in the reader as in the poem—meaning is created, not found, and it is embedded in institutions. This essay invites students to explore the strengths and limitations of knowledge and experience they bring to their own interpretations.

In the summer of 1971 I was teaching two courses under the joint auspices of the Linguistic Institute of America and the English Department of the State University of New York at Buffalo. I taught these courses in the morning and in the same room. At 9:30 I would meet a group of students who were interested in the relationship between linguistics and literary criticism. Our nominal subject was stylistics but our concerns were finally theoretical and extended to the presuppositions and assumptions which underlie both linguistic and literary practice. At 11:00 these students were replaced by another group whose concerns were exclusively literary and were in fact confined to English religious poetry of the seventeenth century. These students had been learning how to identify Christian symbols and how to recognize typological patterns and how to move from the observation of these symbols and patterns to the specification of a poetic intention that was usually didactic or homiletic. On the day I am thinking about, the only connection between the two classes was an assignment given to the first which was still on the blackboard at the beginning of the second. It read:

Jacobs–Rosenbaum
Levin
Thorne
Hayes
Ohman (?)

I am sure that many of you will have already recognized the names on this list, but for the sake of the record, allow me to identify them. Roderick Jacobs

From *Is There a Text in This Class?* Cambridge, MA: Harvard University Press, 1980.

and Peter Rosenbaum are two linguists who have coauthored a number of textbooks and coedited a number of anthologies. Samual Levin is a linguist who was
one of the first to apply the operations of transformational grammar to literary
texts. J. P. Thorne is a linguist at Edinburgh who, like Levin, was attempting to
extend the rules of transformational grammar to the notorious irregularities of
poetic language. Curtis Hayes is a linguist who was then using transformational
grammar in order to establish an objective basis for his intuitive impression that
the language of Gibbon's *Rise and Fall of the Roman Empire* is more complex
than the language of Hemingway's novels. And Richard Ohmann is the literary
critic who, more than any other, was responsible for introducing the vocabulary
of transformational grammar to the literary community. Ohmann's name was
spelled as you see it here because I could not remember whether it contained
one or two n's. In other words, the question mark in parenthesis signified nothing more than a faulty memory and a desire on my part to appear scrupulous.
The fact that the names appeared in a list that was arranged vertically, and that
Levin, Thorne, and Hayes formed a column that was more or less centered in
relation to the paired names of Jacobs and Rosenbaum, was similarly accidental
and was evidence only of a certain compulsiveness if, indeed, it was evidence of
anything at all.

In the time between the two classes I made only one change. I drew a
frame around the assignment and wrote on the top of that frame "p. 43." When
the members of the second class filed in I told them that what they saw on the
blackboard was a religious poem of the kind they had been studying and I asked
them to interpret it. Immediately they began to perform in a manner that, for
reasons which will become clear, was more or less predictable. The first student
to speak pointed out that the poem was probably a hieroglyph, although he was
not sure whether it was in the shape of a cross or an altar. This question was set
aside as the other students, following his lead, began to concentrate on individual words, interrupting each other with suggestions that came so quickly that
they seemed spontaneous. The first line of the poem (the very order of events
assumed the already constituted status of the object) received the most attention: Jacobs was explicated as a reference to Jacob's ladder, traditionally allegorized as a figure for the Christian ascent to heaven. In this poem, however, or so
my students told me, the means of ascent is not a ladder but a tree, a rose tree
or rosenbaum. This was seen to be an obvious reference to the Virgin Mary who
was often characterized as a rose without thorns, itself an emblem of the im-
maculate conception. At this point the poem appeared to the students to be operating in the familiar manner of an iconographic riddle. It at once posed the
question, "How is it that a man can climb to heaven by means of a rose tree?"
and directed the reader to the inevitable answer: by the fruit of that tree, the
fruit of Mary's womb, Jesus. Once this interpretation was established it received support from, and conferred significance on, the word "thorne," which

could only be an allusion to the crown of thorns, a symbol of the trial suffered by Jesus and of the price he paid to save us all. It was only a short step (really no step at all) from this insight to the recognition of Levin as a double reference, first to the tribe of Levi, of whose priestly function Christ was the fulfillment, and second to the unleavened bread carried by the children of Israel on their exodus from Egypt, the place of sin, and in response to the call of Moses, perhaps the most familiar of the old testament types of Christ. The final word of the poem was given at least three complementary readings: it could be "omen," especially since so much of the poem is concerned with foreshadowing and prophecy; it could be Oh Man, since it is man's story as it intersects with the divine plan that is the poem's subject; and it could, of course, be simply "amen," the proper conclusion to a poem celebrating the love and mercy shown by a God who gave his only begotten son so that we may live.

In addition to specifying significances for the words of the poem and relating those significances to one another, the students began to discern larger structural patterns. It was noted that of the six names, in the poem three—Jacobs, Rosenbaum, and Levin—are Hebrew, two—Thorne and Hayes—are Christian, and one—Ohman—is ambiguous, the ambiguity being marked in the poem itself (as the phrase goes) by the question mark in parentheses. This division was seen as a reflection of the basic distinction between the old dispensation and the new, the law of sin and the law of love. That distinction, however, is blurred and finally dissolved by the typological perspective which invests the old testament events and heroes with new testament meanings. The structure of the poem, my students concluded, is therefore a double one, establishing and undermining its basic pattern (Hebrew vs. Christian) at the same time. In this context there is finally no pressure to resolve the ambiguity of Ohman since the two possible readings—the name is Hebrew, the name is Christian—are both authorized by the reconciling presence in the poem of Jesus Christ. Finally, I must report that one student took to counting letters and found, to no one's surprise, that the most prominent letters in the poem were S, O, N.

Some of you will have noticed that I have not yet said anything about Hayes. This is because of all the words in the poem it proved the most recalcitrant to interpretation, a fact not without consequence, but one which I will set aside for the moment since I am less interested in the details of the exercise than in the ability of my students to perform it. What is the source of that ability? How is it that they were able to do what they did? What is it that they did? These questions are important because they bear directly on a question often asked in literary theory, What are the distinguishing features of literary language? Or, to put the matter more colloquially, How do you recognize a poem when you see one? The commonsense answer, to which many literary critics and linguists are committed, is that the act of recognition is triggered by the observable presence of distinguishing features. That is, you know a poem when you see one because its language displays the characteristics that you know to be proper to poems. This, however, is a model that quite obviously does not fit the present example. My students did not proceed from the noting of distinguishing features to the recognition that they were confronted by a poem; rather, it was the act of recognition that came first—they knew in advance that they were dealing with a poem—and the distinguishing features then followed.

In other words, acts of recognition, rather than being triggered by formal characteristics, are their source. It is not that the presence of poetic qualities compels a certain kind of attention but that the paying of a certain kind of attention results in the emergence of poetic qualities. As soon as my students were aware that it was poetry they were seeking, they began to look with poetry-seeing eyes, that is, with eyes that saw everything in relation to the properties they knew poems to possess. They knew, for example (because they were told by their teachers), that poems are (or are supposed to be) more densely and intricately organized than ordinary communications; and that knowledge translated itself into a willingness—one might even say a determination—to see connections between one word and another and between every word and the poem's central insight. Moreover, the assumption that there *is* a central insight is itself poetry-specific, and presided over its own realization. Having assumed that the collection of words before them was unified by an informing purpose (because unifying purposes are what poems have), my students proceeded to find one and to formulate it. It was in the light of that purpose (now assumed) that significances for the individual words began to suggest themselves, significances which then fleshed out the assumption that had generated them in the first place. Thus the meanings of the words and the interpretation in which those words were seen to be embedded emerged together, as a consequence of the operations my students began to perform once they were told that this was a poem.

It was almost as if they were following a recipe—if it's a poem do this, if it's a poem, see it that way—and indeed definitions of poetry *are* recipes, for by directing readers as to what to look for in a poem, they instruct them in ways of looking that will produce what they expect to see. If your definition of poetry tells you that the language of poetry is complex, you will scrutinize the language of something identified as a poem in such a way as to bring out the complexity you know to be "there." You will, for example, be on the look-out for latent ambiguities; you will attend to the presence of alliterative and consonantal patterns (there will always be some), and you will try to make something of them (you will always succeed); you will search for meanings that subvert, or exit in a tension with the meanings that first present themselves; and if these operations fail to produce the anticipated complexity, you will even propose a significance for the words that are *not* there, because, as everyone knows, everything about a poem, including its omissions, is significant. Nor, as you do these things, will you have any sense of performing in a willful manner, for you will only be doing what you learned to do in the course of becoming a skilled reader of poetry. Skilled reading is usually thought to be a matter of discerning what is there, but if the example of my students can be generalized, it is a matter of knowing how to *produce* what can thereafter be said to be there. Interpretation is not the art of construing but the art of constructing. Interpretations do not decode poems; they make them.

To many, this will be a distressing conclusion, and there are a number of arguments that could be mounted in order to forestall it. One might point out that the circumstances of my students' performance were special. After all, they had been concerned exclusively with religious poetry for some weeks, and therefore would be uniquely vulnerable to the deception I had practiced on them and uniquely equipped to impose religious themes and patterns on words innocent of either. I must report, however, that I have duplicated this experiment any number of times at nine or ten universities in three countries, and the results are always the same, even when the participants know from the beginning that what they are looking at was originally an assignment. Of course this very fact could itself be turned into an objection: doesn't the reproducibility of the exercise prove that there is something about these words that leads everyone to perform in the same way? Isn't it just a happy accident that names like Thorne and Jacobs have counterparts or near counterparts in biblical names and symbols? And wouldn't my students have been unable to do what they did if the assignment I gave to the first class had been made up of different names? The answer to all of these questions is no. Given a firm belief that they were confronted by a religious poem, my students would have been able to turn any list of names into the kind of poem we have before us now, because they would have read the names within the assumption that they were informed with Christian significances. (This is nothing more than a literary analogue to Augustine's rule of faith.) You can test this assertion by replacing Jacobs-Rosenbaum, Levin, Thorne, Hayes, and Ohman with names drawn from the faculty of Kenyon College—Temple, Jordan, Seymour, Daniels, Star, Church. I will not exhaust my time or your patience by performing a full-dress analysis, which would involve, of course, the relation between those who saw the River Jordan and those who saw *more* by seeing the Star of Bethlehem, thus fulfilling the prophecy by which the temple of Jerusalem was replaced by the inner temple or church built up in the heart of every Christian. Suffice it to say that it could easily be done (you can take the poem home and do it yourself) and that the shape of its doing would be constrained not by the names but by the interpretive assumptions that gave them a significance even before they were seen. This would be true even if there were no names on the list, if the paper or blackboard were blank; the blankness would present no problem to the interpreter, who would immediately see in it the void out of which God created the earth, or the abyss into which unregenerate sinners fall, or, in the best of all possible poems, both.

Even so, one might reply, all you've done is demonstrate how an interpretation, if it is prosecuted with sufficient vigor, can impose itself on material which has its own proper shape. Basically, at the ground level, in the first place, when all is said and done, "Jacobs-Rosenbaum Levin Thorne Hayes Ohman(?)" is an assignment; it is only a trick that allows you to transform it into a poem, and when the effects of the trick have worn off, it will return to its natural form and be seen as an assignment once again. This is a powerful argument because it seems at once to give interpretation its due (as an act of the will) and to maintain the independence of that on which interpretation works. It allows us, in short, to preserve our commonsense intuition that interpretation must be interpretation of *something*. Unfortunately, the argument will not hold because the assignment we all see is no less the product of interpretation than the poem into which it was turned. That is, it requires just as much work, and work of the same kind, to see this as an assignment as it does to see it as a poem. If this seems counterintuitive, it is only because the work required to see it as an assignment is work we have already done, in the course of acquiring the huge amount of background knowledge that enables you and me to function in the academic world. In order to know what an assignment is, that is, in order to know what to do with something identified as an assignment, you must first know what a class is (know that it isn't an economic grouping) and know that classes meet at specified times for so many weeks, and that one's performance in a class is largely a matter of performing between classes.

Think for a moment of how you would explain this last to someone who did not already know it. "Well," you might say, "a class is a group situation in which a number of people are instructed by an informed person in a particular subject." (Of course the notion of "subject" will itself require explication.) "An assignment is something you do when you're not in class." "Oh, I see," your interlocutor might respond, "an assignment is something you do to take your mind off what you've been doing in class." "No, an assignment is a part of a class." "But how can that be if you only do it when the class is not meeting?" Now it would be possible, finally, to answer that question, but only by enlarging the horizons of your explanation to include the very concept of a university, what it is one might be doing there, why one might be doing it instead of doing a thousand other things, and so on. For most of us these matters do not require explanation, and indeed, it is hard for us to imagine someone for whom they do; but that is because our tacit knowledge of what it means to move around in academic life was acquired so gradually and so long ago that it doesn't seem like knowledge at all (and therefore something someone else might *not* know) but a part of the world. You might think that when you're on campus (a phrase that itself requires volumes) that you are simply walking around on the two legs God gave you; but your walking is informed by an internalized awareness of institutional goals and practices, of norms of behavior, of lists of do's and don'ts, of invisible lines and the dangers of crossing them; and, as a result, you see everything as *already* organized in relation to those same goals and practices. It would never occur to you, for example, to wonder if the people pouring out of that building are fleeing from a fire; you *know* that they are exiting from a class (what could be more obvious?) and you know that because your perception of their action occurs within a knowledge of what people in a university could possibly be doing and the reasons they could have for doing it (going to the next class, going back to the dorm, meeting someone in the student union). It is within that same knowledge that an assignment becomes intelligible so that it appears to you immediately as an obligation, as a set of directions, as something with parts, some of which may be more significant than others. That is, it is a proper question to ask of an assignment whether some of its parts might be omitted or slighted, whereas readers of poetry know that no part of a poem can be slighted (the rule is "everything counts") and they do not rest until every part has been given a significance.

In a way this amounts to no more than saying what everyone already knows: poems and assignments are different, but my point is that the differences are a result of the different interpretive operations we perform and not of something inherent in one or the other. An assignment no more compels its own recognition than does a poem; rather, as in the case of a poem, the shape of an assignment emerges when someone looks at something identified as one with assignment-seeing eyes, that is, with eyes which are capable of seeing the words as already embedded within the institutional structure that makes it possible for assignments to have a sense. The ability to see, and therefore to make, an assignment is no less a learned ability than the ability to see, and therefore to make, a poem. Both are constructed artifacts, the products and not the producers of interpretation, and while the differences between them are real, they are interpretive and do not have their source in some bedrock level of objectivity.

Of course one might want to argue that there is a bedrock level at which these names constitute neither an assignment nor a poem but are merely a list. But that argument too fails because a list is no more a natural object—one that wears its meaning on its face and can be recognized by anyone—than an assignment or a poem. In order to see a list, one must already be equipped with the concepts of seriality, hierarchy, subordination, and so on, and while these are by no mean esoteric concepts and seem available to almost everyone, they are nonetheless learned, and if there were someone who had not learned them, he or she would not be able to see a list. The next recourse is to descend still lower (in the direction of atoms) and to claim objectivity for letters, paper, graphite, black marks on white spaces, and so on; but these entities too have palpability and shape only because of the assumption of some or other system of intelligibility, and they are therefore just as available to a deconstructive dissolution as are poems, assignments, and lists.

The conclusion, therefore, is that all objects are made and not found, and that they are made by the interpretive strategies we set in motion. This does not, however, commit me to subjectivity because the means by which they are made are social and conventional. That is, the "you" who does the interpretive work that puts poems and assignments and lists into the world is a communal you and not an isolated individual. No one of us wakes up in the morning and (in French fashion) reinvents poetry or thinks up a new educational system or decides to reject seriality in favor of some other, wholly original, form of organization. We do not do these things because we could not do them, because the mental operations we can perform are limited by the institutions in which we are *already* embedded. These institutions precede us, and it is only by inhabiting them, or being inhabited by them, that we have access to the public and conventional senses they make. Thus while it is true to say that we create poetry (and assignments and lists), we create it through interpretive strategies that are finally not our own but have their source in a publicly available system of intelligibility. Insofar as the system (in this case a literary system) constrains us, it also fashions us, furnishing us with categories of understanding, with which we in turn fashion the entities to which we can then point. In short, to the list of made or constructed objects we must add ourselves, for we no less than the poems and assignments we see are the products of social and cultural patterns of thought.

To put the matter in this way is to see that the opposition between objectivity and subjectivity is a false one because neither exists in the pure form that would give the opposition its point. This is precisely illustrated by my anecdote in which we do *not* have free-standing readers in a relationship of perpetual adequacy or inadequacy to an equally free-standing text. Rather, we have readers whose consciousness is constituted by a set of conventional notions which when put into operation constitute in turn a conventional, and conventionally seen, object. My students could do what they did, and do it in unison, because as members of a literary community they knew what a poem was (their knowledge was public), and that knowledge led them to look in such a way as to populate the landscape with what they knew to be poems.

Of course poems are not the only objects that are constituted in unison by shared ways of seeing. Every object or event that becomes available within an institutional setting can be so characterized. I am thinking, for example, of something that happened in my classroom just the other day. While I was in the course of vigorously making a point, one of my students, William Newlin by name, was just as vigorously waving his hand. When I asked the other members of the class what it was that Mr. Newlin was doing, they all answered that he was seeking permission to speak. I then asked them how they knew that. The immediate reply was that it was obvious; what else could he be thought to be doing? The meaning of his gesture, in other words, was right there on its surface, available for reading by anyone who had the eyes to see. That meaning, however, would not have been available to someone without any knowledge of what was involved in being a student. Such a person might have thought that Mr. Newlin was pointing to the fluorescent lights hanging from the ceiling, or calling our attention to some object that was about to fall ("the sky is falling," "the sky is falling"). And if the someone in question were a child of elementary or middle-school age, Mr. Newlin might well have been seen as seeking permission not to speak but to go to the bathroom, an interpretation or reading that would never occur to a student at Johns Hopkins or any other institution of "higher learning" (and how would we explain to the uninitiated the meaning of *that* phrase).

The point is the one I have made so many times before: it is neither the case that the significance of Mr. Newlin's gesture is imprinted on its surface where it need only be read off, or that the construction put on the gesture by everyone in the room was individual and idiosyncratic. Rather, the source of our interpretive unanimity was a structure of interest and understood goals, a structure whose categories so filled our individual consciousness that they were rendered as one, immediately investing phenomena with the significance they *must* have, given the already-in-place assumptions about what someone could possibly be intending (by word or gesture) in a classroom. By seeing Mr. Newlin's raised hand with a single shaping eye, we were demonstrating what Harvey Sacks has characterized as "the fine power of a culture. It does not, so to speak, merely fill brains in roughly the same way, it fills them so that they are alike in fine detail."[1] The occasion of Sacks's observation was the ability of his hearers to understand a sequence of two sentences—"The baby cried. The mommy picked it up."—exactly as he did (assuming, for example that "the 'mommy' who picks up the 'baby' is the mommy of that baby"), despite the fact that alternative ways of understanding were demonstrably possible. That is, the mommy of the second sentence could well have been the mommy of some other baby, and it need not even have been a baby that this "floating" mommy was picking up. One is tempted to say that in the absence of a specific context we are authorized to take the words literally, which is what Sacks's hearers do; but as Sacks observes, it is within the assumption of a context—one so deeply assumed that we are unaware of it—that the words acquire what seems to be their literal meaning. There is nothing *in the words* that tells Sacks and his hearers how to relate the mommy and the baby of this story, just as there is nothing *in the form* of Mr. Newlin's gesture that tells his fellow students how to determine its significance. In both cases the determination (of relation and significance) is the work of categories of organization—the family, being a student—that are from the very first giving shape and value to what is heard and seen.

Indeed, these categories are the very shape of seeing itself, in that we are not to imagine a perceptual ground more basic than the one they afford. That is, we are not to imagine a moment when my students "simply see" a physical configuration of atoms and *then* assign that configuration a significance, according to the situation they happen to be in. To be in the situation (this or any other) is to "see" with the eyes of its interests, its goals, its understood practices, values, and norms, and so to be conferring significance *by* seeing, not after it. The categories of my students' vision are the categories by which they understand themselves to be functioning as students (what Sacks might term "doing studenting"), and objects will appear to them in forms related to that way of functioning rather than in some objective or preinterpretive form. (This is true even when an object is seen as not related, since nonrelation is not a pure but a differential category—the specification of something by enumerating what it is not; in short, nonrelation is merely one form of relation, and its perception is always situation-specific.)

Of course, if someone who was not functioning as a student was to walk into my classroom, he might very well see Mr. Newlin's raised hand (and "raised hand" is already an interpretation-laden description) in some other way, as evidence of a disease, as the salute of a political follower, as a muscle-improving exercise, as an attempt to kill flies; but he would always see it in *some* way, and never as purely physical data waiting for his interpretation. And, moreover, the way of seeing, whatever it was, would never be individual or idiosyncratic, since its source would always be the institutional structure of which the "see-er" was an extending agent. This is what Sacks means when he says that a culture fills brains "so that they are alike in fine detail"; it fills them so that no one's interpretive acts are exclusively his own but fall to him by virtue of his position in some socially organized environment and therefore always shared and public. It follows, then, that the fear of solipsism, of the imposition by the unconstrained self of its own prejudices, is unfounded because the self does not exist apart from the communal or conventional categories of thought that enable its operations (of thinking, seeing, reading). Once one realizes that the conceptions that fill consciousness, including any conception of its own status, are culturally derived, the very notion of an unconstrained self, of a consciousness wholly and dangerously free, becomes incomprehensible.

But without the notion of the unconstrained self, the arguments of Hirsch, Abrams, and the other proponents of objective interpretation are deprived of their urgency. They are afraid that in the absence of the controls afforded by a normative system of meanings, the self will simply substitute its own meanings for the meanings (usually identified with the intentions of the author) that texts bring with them, the meanings that texts *"have"*; however, if the self is conceived of not as an independent entity but as a social construct whose operations are delimited by the systems of intelligibility that inform it, then the meanings it confers on texts are not its own but have their source in the inter-pretive community (or communities) of which it is a function. Moreover, these meanings will be neither subjective nor objective, at least in the terms assumed by those who argue within the traditional framework: they will not be objective because they will always have been the product of a point of view rather than having been simply "read off"; and they will not be subjective because that point of view will always be social or institutional. Or by the same reasoning one could say that they are *both* subjective and objective: they are subjective be-cause they inhere in a particular point of view and are therefore not universal; and they are objective because the point of view that delivers them is public and conventional rather than individual or unique.

To put the matter in either way is to see how unhelpful the terms "subjec-tive" and "objective" finally are. Rather than facilitating inquiry, they close it down, by deciding in advance what shape inquiry can possibly take. Specifically, they assume, without being aware that it is an assumption and therefore open to challenge, the very distinction I have been putting into question, the distinction between interpreters and the objects they interpret. That distinction in turn as-sumes that interpreters and their objects are two different kinds of *a*contextual entities, and within these twin assumptions the issue can only be one of control: will texts be allowed to constrain their own interpretation or will irresponsible interpreters be allowed to obscure and overwhelm texts. In the spectacle that ensues, the spectacle of Anglo-American critical controversy, texts and selves fight it out in the persons or their respective champions, Abrams, Hirsch, Reichert, Graff on the one hand, Holland, Bleich, Slatoff, and (in some charac-terizations of him) Barthes° on the other. But if selves are constituted by the ways of thinking and seeing that inhere in social organizations, and if these con-stituted selves in turn constitute texts according to these same ways, then there can be no adversary relationship between text and self because they are the necessarily related products of the same cognitive possibilities. A text cannot be overwhelmed by an irresponsible reader and one need not worry about protect-ing the purity of a text from a reader's idiosyncrasies. It is only the distinction between subject and object that gives rise to these urgencies, and once the dis-tinction is blurred they simply fall away. One can respond with a cheerful yes to the question "Do readers make meanings?" and commit oneself to very little because it would be equally true to say that meanings, in the form of culturally derived interpretive categories, make readers.

Indeed, many things look rather different once the subject-object di-chotomy is eliminated as the assumed framework within which critical discus-sion occurs. Problems disappear, not because they have been solved but

°**Abrams, Hirsch, Reichert, Graff . . . , Holland, Bleich, Slatoff, and . . . Barthes**   Central fig-ures in the critical controversy over whether meanings should properly be said to reside in texts or in readers.

because they are shown never to have been problems in the first place. Abrams, for example, wonders how, in the absence of a normative system of stable meanings, two people could ever agree on the interpretation of a work or even a sentence; but the difficulty is only a difficulty if the two (or more) people are thought of as isolated individuals whose agreement must be compelled by something external to them. (There is something of the police state in Abrams's vision, complete with posted rules and boundaries, watchdogs to enforce them, procedures for identifying their violators as criminals.) But if the understandings of the people in question are informed by the same notions of what counts as a fact, of what is central, peripheral, and worthy of being noticed—in short, by the same interpretive principles—then agreement between them will be assured, and its source will not be a text that enforces its own perception but a way of perceiving that results in the emergence to those who share it (or those whom it shares) of the same text. That text might be a poem, as it was in the case of those who first "saw" "Jabcobs-Rosenbaum Levin Thorne Hayes Ohman(?)," or a hand, as it is every day in a thousand classrooms; but whatever it is, the shape and meaning it appears immediately to have will be the "ongoing accomplishment"[2] of those who agree to produce it.

NOTES

1. "On the Analysability of Stories by Children," in *Ethnomethodology*, ed. Roy Turner (Baltimore: Penguin, 1974), p. 218.

2. A phrase used by the ethnomethodologists to characterize the interpretive activities that create and maintain the features of everyday life. See, for example, Don H. Zimmerman, "Fact as a Practical Accomplishment," in *Ethnomethodology*, pp. 128–143.

QUESTIONS FOR THOUGHT AND STUDY

1. How does Fish's approach to poetry agree with or challenge the way you were taught poetry in high school (or previously in college)?

2. Which of Abrams' orientations to critical theory is emphasized by Fish's concept of "poetry seeing eyes"?

3. Fish argues that "the fear of solipsism, of the imposition by the unconstrained self of its own prejudices, is unfounded because the self does not exist apart from the communal or conventional categories of thought that enable its operations (of thinking, seeing, reading)." Translate this statement into your own language. Do you agree?

4. How would a sociologist or anthropologist describe and interpret systems of power and interpretive rituals occurring in Fish's classroom?

5. Fish argues that the statement "all objects are made and not found" does not commit him to subjectivity. What cultural constraints, according to him, limit the range of interpretation?

6. Fish argues that eliminating the subject/object dichotomy opens rich possibilities for interpretation. What examples of interpretive activity from daily life support this claim? What examples challenge it?

Interpretation

Stephen Mailloux

Biography: *Stephen Mailloux is a Professor of English at Syracuse University. He is editor of* Rhetoric, Sophistry, and Pragmatism *(1995) and author of* Rhetorical Power *(1989), a book that explores theories of literary criticism.*

Mailloux provides a thorough definition of the concept of interpretation as translation, then illustrates through example the different interpretive orientations typical of the humanities. Though his original examples are from poetry (Dickinson), he then applies the same perspectives to an antiballistic missile treaty. He thus brings home the consequences of interpretation in all spheres and concludes his own argument that interpretation is always political and open to question. This challenging but useful reading expands upon terms introduced in Abrams's orientation to critical theory and provides both a fuller interpretive vocabulary and a map of debates about interpretive methods. Its application to issues beyond literature gives coherence to the interpretive activities of the rest of the course.

> *When I think back on all the crap I learned*
> *in high school,*
> *It's a wonder I can think at all.*
> *The lack of education hasn't hurt me none.*
> *I can read the writing on the wall.*
>
> —Paul Simon, "Kodachrome"

Reading words on walls. Explicating poems in classrooms. Making sense of treaties in Congress. Reading, explicating, making sense: these are three names given to the activity of "interpretation," the topic of this essay. We can begin to explore this topic by looking briefly at the word's etymology.

In English, "interpret" has most often meant, according to the *Oxford English Dictionary*, "to expound the meaning of (something abstruse or mysterious); to render (words, writings, and author) clear or explicit; to elucidate; to

From *Critical Terms for Literary Study*. Ed. Frank Lentricchia. Chicago: University of Chicago Press, 1990, pp. 121–134.

explain." But an earlier sense of the verb was "to translate," and so "interpretation" is also "the act of translating; a translation or rendering of a book, word, etc." *(OED)*. The word "interpretation" itself derives from the Latin, *interpretatio,* meaning not only "the action of expounding, explaining" but also "a translation, a rendering." In Latin rhetoric, *interpretatio* referred to "the explanation of one word by another, the use of synonyms." *Interpretatio* was formed on *interpres:* "an intermediary, agent, go-between" and "an interpreter of foreign languages, a translator" (Glare 1982, 947). In its etymology, then, "interpretation" conveys the sense of translation pointed in two directions simultaneously: *toward* a text to be interpreted and *for* an audience in need of the interpretation. That is, the interpreter mediates between the translated text and its new rendering *and* between the translated text and the audience desiring the translation.

It is the heritage of these two etymological senses—translation *of* a text and translation *for* an audience—that we might try to capture in a working definition: "interpretation" is "acceptable and approximating translation." Each term here provokes additional questions: (1) Approximating *what?* (2) Translating *how?* and (3) Acceptable *to whom?* For the next few pages, we can use these questions to organize our discussion of "interpretation."

1. APPROXIMATING *WHAT?*

Translating is always an approximation, which is to say that interpretation is always directed. It is always an approximation of something; it is always directed *toward* something: situations, actions, gestures, graffiti, poems, treaties, novels, and so forth. Such objects of interpretation we can call "texts." Ultimately, anything can be viewed as a text, anything can be interpreted. Our focus here will be on written texts, like this poem by Emily Dickinson:

> Belshazzar had a letter—
> He never had but one—
> Belshazzar's Correspondent
> Concluded and begun
> In that Immortal Copy
> The Conscience of us all
> Can read without its Glasses
> On Revelation's Wall—

If we think of interpreting as the translation of texts, then this is clearly a text requiring translation. In fact, here we have two texts in need of interpreting: Dickinson's poem and the "letter . . . on Revelation's Wall" to which the poem refers. Just as the words of the "letter" are missing, so too are some of the usual textual markers in the poem, like traditional punctuation. Dickinson's idiosyncratic dashes do give us some guidance but not much.

The poem itself translates a biblical story. In chapter 5 of the Book of Daniel, Belshazzar, king of the Chaldeans, holds a feast using sacred vessels taken from the Jewish temple at Jerusalem. During the feast, a hand appears and writes on the wall the words "Mene, Mene, Tekel, Upharsin." The king cannot interpret the writing, nor can any of his advisors. The problem of reading, making sense of texts, thus becomes foregrounded in the story. Daniel is summoned for help, and he ends up interpreting the "letter" from the "Correspondent," God:

> This is the interpretation of the thing: Mene: God hath numbered thy kingdom, and finished it. Tekel: Thou art weighed in the balances, and art found wanting. Peres: Thy kingdom is divided, and given to the Medes and Persians.

The three words written on the wall refer literally to three measures of weight: a mina, a shekel, and two half-minas. Daniel interprets the message by punning off these words: the first resembles a Hebraic verb meaning "numbered"; the second, "weighed"; and the third, "to divide." He uses these verbal puns to interpret the message as an accusation and a prophecy. And in the chapter's final lines the prophecy of punishment is indeed fulfilled: "In that night was Belshazzar the king of the Chaldeans slain. And Darius the Mede took the kingdom . . ." Here we have an interpretation made in the context of political oppression and presented as a consequence of the oppressor's moral iniquity: Israel had been conquered, the Jews enslaved, and now their religious vessels were desecrated. The reading of the wall-writing both advertises the king's crime and announces his punishment (see Buttrick 1952, 418–33).

It is possible that Dickinson meant her poem to serve as a similar announcement. Adding the inscription, "Suggested by our Neighbor," she sent it to her brother probably after the 1879 Lothrop scandal in Amherst. This local incident involved newspaper reports of a father's physical cruelty to his daughter and resulted in a libel suit filed against the *Springfield Republican* by Reverend C. D. Lothrop, the accused father. The court found against Lothrop on 15 April, and Dickinson may have been commemorating the occasion with this poem. From this biographical perspective, the poem refers to the judgment made by the court, which found Lothrop guilty of patriarchal oppression (see Johnson 1955, 1008–9; Leyda 1960, 245–50, 257–59).

More generally, Dickinson's poem takes the biblical tale and makes it into an allegory for the conscience "of us all," through which God points out and warns us about our sins, giving each of us our own private "letter." This allegorizing of the poem translates the literary text, which itself translates a biblical story into a poem. Just as the poem approximates—is directed toward—the biblical story, so too does my interpretation approximate the poem.

Now, there are various ways to take the question, What does interpretation approximate? and develop it into a *theory* of interpretation, a general account of how readers make sense of texts. For example, we could say that the words of my reading approximately translate those of the poem and that Daniel's words approximately translate those on the wall. Such a *formalist* theory could go on to claim that what determines our interpretations is what they approximate, the words on the page. A different theoretical approach argues that what is approximately translated—for example, by Dickinson's reader and by Daniel—is, ultimately, the author's intention. Such an *intentionalist* theory could go on to claim that interpretations are constrained by the intention behind or in the words. Dickinson in the poem and God in the letter intended a meaning that the interpreter must decipher to read the text correctly. Both formalist and intentionalist theories attempt to provide a foundation for constraining the interpretive relationship between reader and text. Often, such theories not only claim to *describe* how interpretation takes place but to *prescribe* how it should take place. These *foundationalist* theories present themselves as both general accounts of making sense and specific guides to correct interpretations. Later we will take up the issue of whether such theoretical guarantees work in actual interpretive practice.

2. TRANSLATING *HOW?*

Our second question moves away from the *object* of interpretation—the text and its sense—to the *activity* of interpreting—the process of sense-making. In reading the Dickinson poem above, I provided two kinds of interpretive approaches, both grounded in a theory of the author's intention: historicizing and allegorizing. In the former approach, I suggested that Dickinson intended to refer specifically to Rev. Lothrop getting a well-deserved public humiliation. In the latter, I suggested that Dickinson intended a more universal message about the conscience of us all. It is not necessary to choose between these two complementary meanings, but it is important to recognize the contrasting *methods* used to arrive at these different interpretations. In historicizing I used a strategy of placing the text in the historical context of its production. In allegorizing I followed a strategy that assumes poetry can refer to a second, more universal level of meaning beyond its particular historical reference. These reading strategies or *interpretive conventions* provide a way of describing the process of interpretation rather than its textual object. They are ways of characterizing how interpretive translation takes place. They emphasize what the reader contributes to interpretation rather than what the text gives the reader to interpret.

We have now seen displayed several different strategies for interpreting texts. For example, Daniel uses puns or verbal resemblances to read the writing on the king's wall, and I earlier used etymologies to explore meanings for "interpretation" itself. Methods or strategies of making sense are associated with various theories of how interpretation does or should take place. Above, I connected historicizing and allegorizing a text's meaning with intentionalist theories of interpretation. Punning and etymologizing are as often associated with formalist theories of interpretation as they are with intentionalist approaches. All these strategies—historicizing, allegorizing, punning, and using etymologies—can be restated as rules for correct interpretation. That is, certain interpretive conventions become in certain contexts the privileged way of making sense of texts. Identifying puns may be acceptable for interpreting ancient and contemporary graffiti but not for reading constitutions. Allegorizing may be appropriate for poetry and scripture but not for international treaties. For these supposedly more straightforward legal texts, theories of *neutral principles* are often proposed as ways to guarantee that interpreters resist more literary methods of making sense. Theories of neutral principles posit rules for guaranteeing correct interpretations, e.g., formalist rules for looking at "the words on the page" or intentionalist rules for respecting authorial purposes. These rules or interpretive principles are presented as neutral in the sense that they are viewed as capable of being applied in a disinterested manner safe from personal idiosyncrasy or political bias. We will return below to questions about whether treaties are in fact inherently more straightforward than literary texts and whether interpretive theories can actually constrain readings or avoid political entanglements. But for now let us turn to our third question.

3. ACCEPTABLE *TO WHOM?*

We can begin with an episode from the *Adventures of Huckleberry Finn:* In chapter 15 of Mark Twain's novel, Huck, the boy narrator, and Jim, the runaway slave, are separated in the fog while traveling down the Mississippi River. In despair after a night-long search, Jim gives Huck up for dead and, exhausted, falls into a troubled sleep. Meanwhile, Huck finds his way back to the raft, and, after Jim awakes, Huck plays a rather insensitive trick on his companion, convincing him that the pain and horrors of the night before never really happened. It was all just a dream. Jim then says "he must start in and 'terpret' it, because it was sent as a warning." After Jim presents a wild translation of the dream that wasn't a dream, Huck tries to clinch the joke by responding: "Oh, well, that's all interpreted well enough, as far as it goes, Jim . . . but what does *these* things stand for?" as he points to the leaves, rubbish, and smashed oar, all evidence of the previous night's catastrophe. Now one way to view Jim's dream interpretation is to see it as a rather laughable misreading. This is Huck's view and the view he wants his readers to share so that they get the joke on Jim.

But Huck's request for another interpretation, not of the dream but of the proof that there was no dream, produces a more serious response that makes Huck's joke backfire.

> Jim looked at the trash, and then looked at me, and back at the trash . . . [H]e looked at me steady, without ever smiling, and says:
> "What do dey stan' for? I's gwyne to tell you. When I got all wore out wid work, en wid de callin' for you, en went to sleep, my heart wuz mos' broke bekase you wuz los', en I didn' k'yer no mo' what become er me en de raf'. En when I wake up en fine you back agin, all safe en soun', de tears come en I could a got down on my knees en kiss' yo' foot I's so thankful. En all you wuz thinking 'bout wuz how you could make a fool uv ole Jim wid a lie. Dat truck dah is *trash;* en trash is what people is dat puts dirt on de head er dey fren's en makes 'em ashamed."

If we saw Jim's dream interpretation as a misreading, we certainly see nothing wrong with his allegorical reading of the trash. We get the point and so does Huck, as he writes that Jim then "got up slow, and walked to the wigwam, and went in there, without saying anything but that. But that was enough. It made me feel so mean I could almost kissed *his* foot to get him to take it back." Twain turns the incident into another episode in Huck's struggle with his racist upbringing when he has the boy write further: "It was fifteen minutes before I could work myself up to go and humble myself to a nigger—but I done it, and I warn't ever sorry for it afterwards, neither." Interpreting this passage, readers recognize how Huck's apology undercuts his continuing racial prejudice, how his respect and affection for Jim work to undermine his society's ideology of white supremacy.

If you agree that Jim misread the "dream" but convincingly interpreted the "trash," if you agree with my reading of these readings and with my interpretation of the final passage, then we are agreeing on what to count as a *correct interpretation* for these various texts. Correct interpretations are those that are considered accurate, valid, acceptable. But acceptable to whom? One answer is suggested by another Dickinson poem:

> Much Madness is divinest Sense—
> To a discerning Eye—
> Much Sense—the starkest Madness—
> 'Tis the Majority
> In this, as All, prevail—
> Assent—and you are sane—
> Demur—you're straightway dangerous—
> And handled with a Chain—

This poem is about how correct interpretations are established, how sensemaking is defined as right or wrong, sense or nonsense, sanity or madness. Read literally, it simply states that sense or meaning is in the eye of the beholder, rather than in the object beheld. The poem suggests further that the majority of interpreters determine what counts as sense. Of course, the point of the poem does not end there. Dickinson is not simply describing the conditions of "correct" interpreting—majority rules—but is sarcastically protesting against the fact. Thus the poem rewrites the question—To whom are correct interpretations acceptable?—as a problem about the politics of interpretation, about a reading's status within the power relations of a historical community. These questions point us away from the exchange between interpreter and text and toward that between interpreter and interpreter—that is, from the hermeneutic question of how text and reader interact to the *rhetorical* question of how interpreters interact with other interpreters in trying to argue for or against different meanings.

4. THE POLITICS OF INTERPRETATION

As we move from foundationalist theories about reading texts to the rhetorical politics of interpretive disputes, we will not completely abandon the questions dealt with in the first three sections. In one sense, we will simply be broadening our area of concern. When we focus only on the text, an author's intention, or a reader's interpretive conventions, as we did in the first two sections, there is a strong tendency to view interpretation as a private reading experience involving only an independent text (and author) and an individual reader. Many foundationalist theories give in to this temptation and compound the mistake by completely ignoring the sociopolitical context in which interpretation takes place. By focusing now on interpretive rhetoric, we will see how interpretation is always a politically-interested act of persuasion.

In the cases of reading discussed earlier, I hinted at this politics of interpretation whenever I noted how an interpretive act took place within the context of power relations in a historical community. For example in section 1, we saw how Daniel's reading of the wall-writing functioned within a national situation of political oppression and then how Dickinson's poem translated this biblical story into a new context involving the politics of family and gender. In section 3, Jim's dream interpretation and Huck's reactions play a part in Mark Twain's commentary on the politics of race in nineteenth-century America. In each of these cases, interpretation takes place in a political context and each interpretive act relates directly to the power relations (whether of nation, family, gender, class, or race) involved in that context.

However, what is not quite as clear in these example is how interpretation itself can be politically interested, how claims for a reading are always direct attempts to affect power relations through coercion or persuasion. These effects can be subtle and microscopic, as in cases where students ask a teacher to explain a line of poetry and she convinces them to accept a particular reading. The effects become more obvious when there are radical disagreements over interpretations, when the correct reading is in actual dispute. At such times, the least persuasive interpretation loses out. Indeed, in some extreme cases of interpretive controversy, Dickinson seems to be right:

> 'Tis the Majority
> In this, as All, prevail—
> Assent—and you are sane—
> Demur—you're straightway dangerous—
> And handled with a Chain—

Most situations involving interpretive disagreement do not result in such blatant suppression of dissent. However, a poem protesting a majority's tyranny over an individual dissenter does foreground what is always the case: any interpretive dispute involves political interests and consequences.

In my final example of reading a text, I will focus on a treaty debated in Congress, but the interpretive rhetoric used by the disputants here relates directly to that used by interpreters in an academic classroom or a religious meetinghouse. In different ways, reading treaties, explicating poems, and interpreting scripture all involve arguments over such topics as textual meaning, authorial intention, past readings, historical contexts, and interpretive methods. All involve the rhetorical politics of interpretation.

The following rhetorical analysis will refer back to issues discussed earlier and deliver on various promissory notes. We will see, for example, how some of the interpretive theories described above work in actual disputes over meaning. What I hope to demonstrate is that theories of interpretation function not so much as constraints on reading as resources for arguing. That is, formalist, intentionalist, and objectivist theories do not provide guarantees of correct interpretation or algorithms for resolving interpretive disputes. They simply make available to the disputants some additional rhetorical tactics for continuing the arguments over meaning.

In 1972 the United States Senate ratified the Anti-Ballistic Missile Treaty with the Soviet Union. This treaty contained a crucial provision as Article V (1): "Each Party undertakes not to develop, test, or deploy ABM systems or components which are sea-based, air-based, space-based, or mobile land-based." For thirteen years, through three administrations, this short text was interpreted not only as outlawing the militarization of space but as prohibiting even the *development and testing* of space-based ABM systems.

On March 23, 1983, President Ronald Reagan announced his Strategic Defense Initiative, a research and development program leading to a space-based, anti-ballistic missile system using laser technology. The president promised that this program would be "consistent with our obligations" under the ABM Treaty, but it soon became clear that at some future date development of "Star Wars" would bump up against the explicit constraints of the treaty. Nevertheless, the Reagan administration continued to uphold the traditional interpretation of Article V (1). For example, its *Fiscal Year 1985 Arms Control Impact Statements* (1984, 252) declared: "The ABM Treaty prohibition on development, testing, and deployment of space-based ABM systems, or components for such systems, applies to directed energy technology (or any other technology) used for this purpose. Thus, when such directed energy programs enter the field testing phase they become constrained by these ABM Treaty obligations."

This interpretation held throughout 1984 and most of 1985. Then on October 6, National Security Advisor Robert McFarlane offered a new reading of Article V (1). On "Meet the Press," McFarlane claimed that the treaty "approved and authorized" development and testing of space-based ABM systems "involving new physical concepts" including lasers or directed energy. Such a radical reinterpretation provoked immediate controversy. As one newspaper put it: "This startling pronouncement by a high official, almost a 180-degree reversal of the longstanding U.S. position on the treaty, was a shock to the ABM Treaty's negotiators and other arms control advocates, to U.S. allies in Europe and arms control minded members of Congress" (Oberdorfer 1985, A10).

Eight days later, Secretary of State George Shultz took up this new interpretation in a speech to the North Atlantic Assembly, a speech which clearly set out to create an opening for the revised reading: "The treaty can be variously interpreted as to what kinds of development and testing are permitted, particularly with respect to future systems and components based on new physical principles." The traditional interpretation, once so obvious, was thus declared problematic, and room was immediately established for a new, less restrictive interpretation that allowed what had previously been prohibited: "It is our view, based on a careful analysis of the treaty text and the negotiating record, that a broader interpretation of our authority is fully justified." Out-of-laboratory testing of SDI technology would now fall outside the constraints of the ABM Treaty. Having asserted the validity of this new interpretation, Shultz then attempted to distance its consequences from actual policy: That the "broader interpretation" is "fully justified" is "however, a moot point" because "our SDI research program has been structured and, as the President has reaffirmed last Friday, will continue to be conducted in accordance with a restrictive interpretation of the treaty's obligations" (Shultz 1985, 23).

This attempt to depoliticize the new interpretation, to separate simply reading the text from political policy-making, did not satisfy the critics. On October 22 the House Subcommittee on Arms Control, International Security, and Science convened to discuss the "ABM Treaty Interpretation Dispute." The record of this hearing provides a useful context for analyzing the arguments supporting the old and new, the "restrictive" and "broader" interpretations of Article V (1) of the ABM Treaty and thus for "explaining" its reinterpretation. Only when such a rhetorical analysis is done within the historical narrative I have outlined can the hermeneutics of the argument become clear. We will see how appeals to foundationalist theory fail to resolve the dispute and how theoretical appeals function rhetorically within a specific political controversy.

The most outspoken administration representative at the hearing was Abraham Sofaer, legal advisor to the secretary of state. Following the rhetorical strategy of his boss, Sofaer began by questioning the obviousness of the traditional interpretation: "My study of the [ABM] treaty led me to conclude that its language is ambiguous and can more reasonably be read to support a broader interpretation" (*AM Treaty* 1986, 5). Noting that the "restrictive interpretation rests on the premise that article V (1) is clear on its face," Sofaer suggested that such a view ignores the document's ambiguities and proceeded to argue that a broader interpretation was just as plausible and in fact more reasonable (*ABM Treaty* 1986, 5). To establish good reasons for the broader interpretations, Sofaer appealed to several hermeneutic criteria: the language of the document, the intentions of the negotiators, relevant canons of construction, and, surprisingly, the postnegotiation tradition of interpreting the treaty.

The rhetorical effectiveness of these appeals depends upon the acceptability of the relevant hermeneutic theories that constitute these sources as guides for correct interpreting. Thus, a formalist theory undergirds the appeal to the language in the text; an intentionalist theory supports the study of the negotiator's mental purposes; and a theory of neutral principles provides a rationale for legal canons of construction. Although these theories are often developed as foundationalist accounts of interpreting, here we will see how they are best viewed as rhetorical resources rather than hermeneutic foundations in debates over interpretation.

Sofaer began his arguments with a formalist appeal, but it was not only the advocates of the broad reinterpretation who pointed directly to the text. So did the advocates of the restrictive interpretation: John Rhinelander, former legal advisor to the ABM Treaty negotiators, stated emphatically that *"the prohibitions are clear from the text of the Treaty,* particularly Article V (1)" (*ABM Treaty* 1986, 58); and similarly Leonard Meeker and Peter Didisheim, both of the Union of Concerned Scientists, claimed in a statement submitted to the subcommittee: "The ordinary meaning of the treaty's terms are [sic] self-evident. The Administration's argument that the treaty permits the development and field testing of [space-based] ABM weapons and components based on new physical principles cannot qualify as an interpretation 'in good faith'"

(*ABM Treaty* 1986, 117). In contrast, Sofaer rejected any clear or self-evident meaning in the language and in his formalist argument produced ambiguity by reading various parts of the text against each other. Thus, he claimed that Agreed Statement D (negotiated at the time of the original treaty) suggests that Article II (1)'s definition of "ABM system" refers only to technology current in 1972, and therefore the prohibitions in Article V (1) do not constrain development and testing of systems based on future technology, such as that involved in SDI. Congressman Henry Hyde found this formalist appeal persuasive, declaring that "the plain intent of those English words leaps out at you" and noting, "There isn't much of a conflict as I see it here between the English language and the interpretation [Sofaer] found that fits within the four corners of this document" (*ABM Treaty* 1986, 25, 43).

Others, of course, were not so easily convinced, and the rhetorical ground soon shifted from formalist claims about the text to intentionalist arguments about the negotiating history. Sofaer announced this shift early in his interpretive argument: "Under international law, as under U.S. domestic law, once an agreement has been found ambiguous, one must seek guidance in the circumstances surrounding the drafting of the agreement. Thus, in the present situation, once we concluded that the treaty is ambiguous, we turned to the negotiating record to see which of the possible constructions most accurately reflects the parties' intentions" (*ABM Treaty* 1986, 7). This move toward the broader interpretation was questioned in two ways by the advocates of the restrictive reading. First, the rule invoked for guidance in interpretation immediately became the new occasion for interpretive controversy: Rhinelander declared that Sofaer's interpretation rested "on a new canon of construction, never before heard of, that the *unambiguous* text of a treaty should be distorted to give an agreed interpretation [Agreed Statement D] an independent and amendatory role" *ABM Treaty* 1986, 173). Second, when Sofaer began filling in the intention behind the text, the new source for guidance marked out still another area of interpretive controversy: even if the negotiator's past intentions do have priority over the present words on the page, it still remains an issue what those intentions actually were.

The argument over the negotiators' original intentions becomes especially interesting when the negotiators themselves turn up on both sides of the dispute. Gerard Smith, former chief of the U.S. delegation to the ABM negotiations, criticized the administration's revisionism and remembered the negotiators' intentions as supporting the restrictive interpretation of Article V (1). In contrast, Paul Nitze, also a member of the original negotiating team and President Reagan's special advisor on arms control, strongly endorsed the administration's new, broader interpretation. Certainly an appeal to a ground of intention fails to resolve the interpretive dispute when the appeal ends up supporting both sides of the argument. The thoroughly rhetorical nature of the intentionalist "ground" became even more obvious in an exchange between Nitze and Congressman Lee Hamilton at the hearing:

> *Mr. Hamilton:*   Ambassador Nitze, I am curious about your interpretation of this treaty through this 13-year period. If I understood you correctly a moment ago, and I may not have, you suggested that you have been persuaded by recent legal interpretation that the agreement says something that you didn't think it said at the time you participated in the crafting of the treaty; is that correct?
>
> *Mr. Nitze:*   That is approximately correct. I think the facts of the matter are that it is hard to recollect exactly what one thought at the time 13 years ago. I know that some time thereafter I was asked a question about the treaty which differs from what I now understand to be the negotiating record.
>
> *Mr. Hamilton:*   Well, what then comes through to me is that for 13 years you at least, by your silence on this important point, have given us all the impression that this treaty is to be interpreted restrictively, but now you say that the lawyers have persuaded you that you reached an agreement that you didn't know you reached? (*ABM Treaty* 1986, 41).

This exchange demonstrates how establishing past intention, like construing present meaning, can depend crucially on specific acts of persuasion. The example seems so striking because the person persuaded to a different view of the past is the same person whose original intention is at issue!

But if the rhetoric of interpretation cannot be permanently grounded in the text, intention, or interpretive rules, perhaps the history of interpretations will serve. Ralph Earle, former director of the U.S. Arms Control and Disarmament Agency, suggested just this option at the hearing in defense of the traditional, restrictive interpretation: "It would be a unique episode in international negotiations to have a completely unambiguous record, especially in a bargaining process requiring 2½ years. But be that as it may, the 13-year record for the parties holding the original version [the restrictive interpretation] should carry far greater weight than some statements reportedly inconsistent with the final language of the Treaty" (*ABM Treaty* 1986, 23). Rhinelander developed this reception argument further by citing still another guiding principle: "the Vienna Convention on the Law of Treaties and the A[merican] L[aw] I[nstitute] Restatement of the Foreign Relations Law of the United States . . . stress the importance of subsequent *practice* in interpreting a treaty," and "[s]ubsequent practice, including statements, of *both* the US and the Soviets *reinforce* the historic [restrictive] interpretation of the ABM Treaty" (*ABM Treaty* 1986, 173). The turn to interpretive history, then, would seem to decide the matter: The restrictive interpretation has been the traditionally accepted (and thus privileged) reading of the treaty. After all, isn't there at least agreement that the administration's interpretation is in fact a new one?

Not so, says Sofaer: "We do not accept the premise that this administration is departing from a consistent record of 13 years of statements of the restrictive view" (*ABM Treaty* 1986, 40). In fact, the broader interpretation was not new but old, and the administration's view was not so much a reinterpretation as the remembering of a forgotten tradition. Indeed, Sofaer concluded his lengthy narrative of the treaty's past readings with this moral: "[T]he 'broad' view of the Treaty has as strong a basis as the 'restrictive' view for being called 'traditional' or accepted" (*ABM Treaty* 1986, 212). Rhinelander provided a detailed critique of Sofaer's interpretive history, but this leaves untouched the fact that Sofaer was still able to make that history an effective part of his case (for Rhinelander's critique, see *ABM Treaty* 1986, 186–99).

After all the rhetorical exchanges, the congressional hearing ended somewhere close to where it began: in radical disagreement over the interpretation of the ABM Treaty. The text is clear, one side claims; no it's not, replies the other. If the text is ambiguous, both rhetorical lines of reasoning suggest, then we can turn to the negotiating record. Still no resolution. Since this record of intentions is ambiguous, we can turn to the treaty's thirteen-year interpretive history. But even here both sides are able to appeal to that "same" history to support their antagonistic cases. No appeal to theories or principles resolves the dispute, for the theories themselves become the new sources of controversy, either because of their theoretical claims or their practical applications. Which theories are relevant to the interpretive dispute? How should a relevant theory's principles be interpreted before being applied? Once interpreted, how should the principles be applied to govern this case? If the relevant theory is apparent (say, intentionalism), if its principles are clear (discover the negotiators' original intentions), if the principles can then be applied (ask the negotiators and check the negotiating record), we are still left with the problem of interpreting and arguing over texts, recollections, histories.

It is in this sense that I want to claim that interpretive theories are not foundational but rhetorical, establishing no permanent grounding or guiding principles guaranteeing correct interpretation but certainly providing much rhetorical substance for interpretive debate. That this debate is political through and through is perhaps too obvious to require further mention, but the "ABM Treaty Interpretation Dispute" does thematize its politics more emphatically than most interpretive arguments. In defending the Reagan administration's reinterpretation of the treaty, Congressman Hyde accused the critics of mixing politics with simply reading the text: "You are seeing a lot of people who have little use for the SDI, and they are going to assert an interpretation of the ABM Treaty which obstructs development of that system" (*ABM Treaty* 1986, 43). One of these "obstructionists," Gerard Smith, raised similar questions from the other side, asking: "Why did the administration decide to float this new treaty version just 6 weeks before a summit at which the ABM Treaty was expected to be an important part? Was it an exercise in playing hard ball? A gesture of machismo? ... Or was it a bargaining ploy looking to a summit accommodation somewhere between the Soviet presummit position of no research at all and the Reagan new version of no limits on strategic defense development?" (*ABM Treaty* 1986, 22). It has been the argument of this final section that textual interpretation and rhetorical politics can *never* be separated. Indeed, the failure of foundationalist theory is just another instance of how interpretions can have no grounding outside of rhetorical exchanges taking place within institutional and cultural politics. The Reagan administration's emphasis on a clear "distinction between a legal interpretation and a [governmental] policy" (*ABM Treaty* 1986, 19) is another example of a theoretical attempt to separate a textual interpretation from its context of rhetorical power. In this case, it is not only bad hermeneutics; it is also dangerous politics.

   I want, if I can, to avoid one possible misunderstanding of my argument here. I am certainly *not* saying that it is impossible to disagree effectively with the Reagan administration's absurd reinterpretation of the ABM treaty. One does not, however, have to become a foundationalist theorist in order to do so. Instead, one simply and rigorously argues a counterinterpretation making such rhetorical moves as pointing to the text, citing the authors' intentions, noting the traditional reading, and invoking the consensus—just as the supporters of the restrictive interpretation did at the congressional hearing. However, such moves are just as politically interested as those of the State Department in that they are interested attempts to persuade an audience to interpret the ABM Treaty in an antimilitaristic way. And the resulting interpretation is just as contingent and open to further debate as the militaristic reading. To admit this contingency, to recognize the rhetorical politics of every interpretation, is not to avoid taking a position. Taking a position, making an interpretation, cannot be avoided. Moreover, such historical contingency does not disable interpretive argument, because it is truly the only ground it can have. We are always arguing at particular moments in specific places to certain audiences. Our beliefs and commitments are no less real because they are historical, and the same holds for our interpretations. If no foundationalist theory will resolve disagreements over poems or treaties, we must always argue our cases. In fact, that is all we can ever do.

SUGGESTED READINGS

Levinson, Sanford, and Steven Mailloux, eds. 1988. *Interpreting Law and Literature: A Hermeneutic Reader.*

Mailloux, Steven. 1982. *Interpretive Conventions: The Reader in the Study of American Fiction.*

Mitchell, W. J. T., ed. 1983. *The Politics of Interpretation.*

———. 1985. *Against Theory: Literary Studies and the New Pragmatism.*
Palmer, Richard E. 1969. *Hermeneutics: Interpretation Theory in Schleiermacher, Dilthey, Hei-degger, and Gadamer.*
Rabinow, Paul, and William M. Sullivan, eds. 1979. *Interpretive Social Science: A Reader.*
Tompkins, Jane P., ed. 1980. *Reader-Response Criticism: From Formalism to Post-Structuralism.*

QUESTIONS FOR THOUGHT AND STUDY

1. According to Mailloux, what are the two directions of translation? What are the implications of this split for interpretation?
2. How does Mailloux expand on Abrams's vocabulary of critical terms?
3. How would Mailloux respond to Sontag's claim that "in place of a hermeneutics we need an erotics of art"?
4. Mailloux states that "translation is always an approximation, which is to say that interpretation is always directed." What examples of interpretive activity from your daily life support or challenge this statement?
5. Would Mailloux agree with Fish that the subject/object dichotomy can be eliminated?
6. What practical criteria does Mailloux provide for evaluating interpretive perspectives?

Against Interpretation

Susan Sontag

Biography: *Susan Sontag (1933–), author and critic, is a graduate of the University of Chicago and Harvard University. She has written both fiction and nonfiction, but is best known for her innovative essays on literature and interpretation in general. Labeled "new intellectual," her most influential works include* Styles of Radical Will *(1969),* On Photography *(1977),* Illness as Metaphor *(1978), and* AIDS and Its Metaphors *(1989).*

Tracing the history of art interpretation from Plato forward, Sontag attacks contemporary critics for overintellectualizing art to the point where interpretation has replaced the art itself. She calls for a return to the experience of art, the transparence, "the luminousness of the thing itself." This valuable reading validates the experience of art in other than intellectual terms and provides support for the appreciation of art for art's sake.

From *Against Interpretation and Other Essays.* New York: Farrar, Straus, & Giroux, 1966, pp. 3–14.

Content is a glimpse of something, an encounter like a flash. It's very tiny—very tiny, content.

—WILLEM DE KOONING,[a] in an interview

It is only shallow people who do not judge by appearances. The mystery of the world is the visible, not the invisible.

—OSCAR WILDE, in a letter

I

The earliest experience of art must have been that it was incantatory, magical; art was an instrument of ritual (cf. the paintings in the caves at Lascaux, Altamira, Niaux, La Pasiega, etc.). The earliest *theory* of art, that of the Greek philosophers, proposed that art was mimesis, imitation of reality.

It is at this point that the peculiar question of the *value* of art arose. For the mimetic theory, by its very terms, challenges art to justify itself.

Plato, who proposed the theory, seems to have done so in order to rule that the value of art is dubious. Since he considered ordinary material things as themselves mimetic objects, imitations of transcendent forms or structures, even the best painting of a bed would be only an 'imitation of an imitation'. For Plato, art is neither particularly useful (the painting of a bed is no good to sleep on), nor, in the strict sense, true. And Aristotle's arguments in defence of art do not really challenge Plato's view that all art is an elaborate *trompe l'oeil*, and therefore a lie. But he does dispute Plato's idea that art is useless. Lie or no, art has a certain value according to Aristotle because it is a form of therapy, Art is useful, after all, Aristotle counters, medicinally useful in that it arouses and purges dangerous emotions.

In Plato and Aristotle, the mimetic theory of art goes hand in hand with the assumption that art is always figurative. But advocates of the mimetic theory need not close their eyes to decorative and abstract art. The fallacy that art is necessarily a 'realism' can be modified or scrapped without ever moving outside the problems delimited by the mimetic theory.

The fact is, all Western consciousness of and reflection upon art have remained within the confines staked out by the Greek theory of art as mimesis or representation. It is through this theory that art as such—above and beyond given works of art—becomes problematic, in need of defence. And it is the defence of art which gives birth to the odd vision by which something we have learned to call 'form' is separated off from something we have learned to call

---

[a]American abstract expressionist painter.

'content', and to the well-intentioned move which makes content essential and form accessory.

Even in modern times, when most artists and critics have discarded the theory of art as representation of an outer reality in favour of the theory of art as subjective expression, the main feature of the mimetic theory persists. Whether we conceive of the work of art on the model of a picture (art as a picture of reality) or on the model of a statement (art as the statement of the artist), content still comes first. The content may have changed. It may now be less figurative, less lucidly realistic. But it is still assumed that a work of art is its content. Or, as it's usually put today, that a work of art by definition *says* something. ('What X is saying is . . .', 'What X is trying to say is . . .', 'What X said is . . .' etc., etc.)

II

None of us can ever retrieve that innocence before all theory when art knew no need to justify itself, when one did not ask of a work of art what it *said* because one knew (or thought one knew) what it *did*. From now on to the end of consciousness, we are stuck with the task of defending art. We can only quarrel with one or another means of defence. Indeed, we have an obligation to overthrow any means of defending and justifying art which becomes particularly obtuse or onerous or insensitive to contemporary needs and practice.

This is the case, today, with the very idea of content itself. Whatever it may have been in the past, the idea of content is today mainly a hindrance, a nuisance, a subtle or not so subtle philistinism.

Though the actual developments in many arts may seem to be leading us away from the idea that a work of art is primarily its content, the idea still exerts an extraordinary hegemony. I want to suggest that this is because the idea is now perpetuated in the guise of a certain way of encountering works of art thoroughly ingrained among most people who take any of the arts seriously. What the overemphasis on the idea of content entails is the perennial, never consummated project of *interpretation*. And, conversely, it is the habit of approaching works of art in order to *interpret* them that sustains the fancy that there is such a thing as the content of a work of art.

III

Of course, I don't mean interpretation in the broadest sense, the sense in which Nietzsche (rightly) says, 'There are no facts, only interpretations'. By interpretation, I mean here a conscious act of the mind which illustrates a certain code, certain 'rules' of interpretation.

Directed to art, interpretation means plucking a set of elements (the X, the Y, the Z, and so forth) from the whole work. The task of interpretation is virtually one of translation. The interpreter says, Look, don't you see that X is really—or, really means—A? That Y is really B? That Z is really C?

What situation could prompt this curious project for transforming a text? History gives us the materials for an answer. Interpretation first appears in the culture of late classical antiquity, when the power and credibility of myth had been broken by the 'realistic' view of the world introduced by scientific enlightenment. Once the question that haunts post-mythic consciousness—that of the *seemliness* of religious symbols—had been asked, the ancient texts were, in their pristine form, no longer acceptable. Then interpretation was summoned, to reconcile the ancient texts to 'modern' demands. Thus, the Stoics, to accord with their view that the gods had to be moral, allegorized away the rule features of Zeus and his boisterous clan in Homer's epics. What Homer really designated by the adultery of Zeus with Leto, they explained, was the union between power and wisdom. In the same vein, Philo of Alexandria interpreted the literal historical narratives of the Hebrew Bible as spiritual paradigms. The story of the exodus from Egypt, the wandering in the desert for forty years, and the entry into the promised land, said Philo, was really an allegory of the individual soul's emancipation, tribulations, and final deliverance. Interpretation thus presupposes a discrepancy between the clear meaning of the text and the demands of (later) readers. It seeks to resolve that discrepancy. The situation is that for some reason a text has become unacceptable; yet it cannot be discarded. Interpretation is a radical strategy for conserving an old text, which is thought too precious to repudiate, by revamping it. The interpreter, without actually erasing or rewriting the text, is altering it. But he can't admit to doing this. He claims to be only making it intelligible, by disclosing its true meaning. However far the interpreters alter the text (another notorious example is the Rabbinic and Christian 'spiritual' interpretations of the clearly erotic Song of Songs), they must claim to be reading off a sense that is already there.

Interpretation in our own time, however, is even more complex. For the contemporary zeal for the project of interpretation is often prompted not by piety towards the troublesome text (which may conceal an aggression), but by an open aggressiveness, an overt contempt for appearances. The old style of interpretation was insistent, but respectful; it erected another meaning on top of the literal one. The modern style of interpretation excavates, and as it excavates, destroys; it digs 'behind' the text, to find a sub-text which is the true one. The most celebrated and influential modern doctrines, those of Marx and Freud, actually amount to elaborate systems of hermeneutics[a], aggressive and impious theories of interpretation. All observable phenomena are bracketed, in Freud's phrase, as *manifest content*. This manifest content must be probed and pushed aside to find the true meaning—the *latent content*—beneath. For Marx, social

---

[a]The art or science of interpretation, especially of scripture.

events like revolutions and wars; for Freud, the events of individual lives (like neurotic symptoms and slips of the tongue) as well as texts (like a dream or a work of art)—all are treated as occasions for interpretation. According to Marx and Freud, these events only *seem* to be intelligible. Actually, they have no meaning without interpretation. To understand *is* to interpret. And to interpret is to restate the phenomenon, in effect to find an equivalent for it.

Thus, interpretation is not (as most people assume) an absolute value, a gesture of mind situated in some timeless realm of capabilities. Interpretation must itself be evaluated, with a historical view of human consciousness. In some cultural contexts, interpretation is a liberating act. It is a means of revising, of transvaluing, of escaping the dead past. In other cultural contexts, it is reactionary, impertinent, cowardly, stifling.

IV

Today is such a time, when the project of interpretation is largely reactionary, stifling. Like the fumes of the automobile and of heavy industry which befoul the urban atmosphere, the effusion of interpretations of art today poisons our sensibilities. In a culture whose already classical dilemma is the hypertrophy of the intellect at the expense of energy and sensual capability, interpretation is the revenge of the intellect upon art.

Even more. It is the revenge of the intellect upon the world. To interpret is to impoverish, to deplete the world—in order to set up a shadow world of 'meanings'. It is to turn *the* world into *this* world. ('This world'! As if there were any other.)

The world, our world, is depleted, impoverished enough. Away with all duplicates of it, until we again experience more immediately what we have.

V

In most modern instances, interpretation amounts to the philistine refusal to leave the work of art alone. Real art has the capacity to make us nervous. By reducing the work of art to its content and then interpreting *that*, one tames the work of art. Interpretation makes art manageable, comfortable.

This philistinism of interpretation is more rife in literature than in any other art. For decades now, literary critics have understood it to be their task to translate the elements of the poem or play or novel or story into something else. Sometimes a writer will be so uneasy before the naked power of his art that he will install within the work itself—albeit with a little shyness, a touch of the good taste of irony—the clear and explicit interpretation of it. Thomas Mann is an example of such an over-co-operative author. In the case of more stubborn authors, the critic is only too happy to perform the job.

The work of Kafka, for example, has been subjected to a mass ravishment by no less than three armies of interpreters. Those who read Kafka as a social allegory see case studies of the frustrations and insanity of modern bureaucracy and its ultimate issuance in the totalitarian state. Those who read Kafka as a psycho-analytic allegory see desperate revelations of Kafka's fear of his father, his castration anxieties, his sense of his own impotence, his thraldom to his dreams. Those who read Kafka as a religious allegory explain that K. in *The Castle* is trying to gain access to heaven, that Joseph K. in *The Trial* is being judged by the inexorable and mysterious justice of God. . . . Another *oeuvre* that has attracted interpreters like leeches is that of Samuel Beckett. Beckett's delicate dramas of the withdrawn consciousness—pared down to essentials, cut off, often represented as physically immobilized—are read as a statement about man's alienation from meaning or from God, or as an allegory of psychopathology.

Proust, Joyce, Faulkner, Rilke, Lawrence, Gide . . . one could go on citing author after author; the list is endless of those around whom thick encrustations of interpretation have taken hold. But it should be noted that interpretation is not simply the compliment that mediocrity pays to genius. It is, indeed, *the* modern way of understanding something, and is applied to works of every quality. Thus, in the notes that Elia Kazan published on his production of *A Streetcar Named Desire*, it becomes clear that, in order to direct the play, Kazan had to discover that Stanley Kowalski represented the sensual and vengeful barbarism that was engulfing our culture, while Blanche Du Bois was Western civilization, poetry, delicate apparel, dim lighting, refined feelings and all, though a little the worse for wear to be sure. Tennessee Williams's forceful psychological melodrama now became intelligible: it was *about* something, about the decline of Western civilization. Apparently, were it to go on being a play about a handsome brute named Stanley Kowalski and a faded mangy belle named Blanche Du Bois, it would not be manageable.

VI

It doesn't matter whether artists intend, or don't intend, for their work to be interpreted. Perhaps Tennessee Williams thinks *Streetcar* is about what Kazan thinks it to be about. It may be that Cocteau in *The Blood of a Poet* and in *Orpheus* wanted the elaborate readings which have been given these films, in terms of Freudian symbolism and social critique. But the merit of these works certainly lies elsewhere than in their 'meanings'. Indeed, it is precisely to the extent that Williams's plays and Cocteau's films do suggest these portentous meanings that they are defective, false, contrived, lacking in conviction.

From interviews, it appears that Resnais and Robbe-Grillet consciously designed *Last Year at Marienbad* to accommodate a multiplicity of equally plausible interpretations. But the temptation to interpret *Marienbad* should be resisted. What matters in *Marienbad* is the pure, untranslatable, sensuous immediacy of some of its images, and its rigorous if narrow solutions to certain problems of cinematic form.

Again, Ingmar Bergman may have meant the tank rumbling down the empty night street in *The Silence* as a phallic symbol. But if he did, it was a foolish thought. ('Never trust the teller, trust the tale,' said Lawrence.)[a] Taken as a brute object, as an immediate sensory equivalent for the mysterious abrupt armoured happenings going on inside the hotel, that sequence with the tank is the most striking moment in the film. Those who reach for a Freudian interpretation of the tank are only expressing their lack of response to what is there on the screen.

It is always the case that interpretation of this type indicates a dissatisfaction (conscious or unconscious) with the work, a wish to replace it by something else.

Interpretation, based on the highly dubious theory that a work of art is composed of items of content, violates art. It makes art into an article for use, for arrangement into a mental scheme of categories.

VII

Interpretation does not, of course, always prevail. In fact, a great deal of today's art may be understood as motivated by a flight from interpretation. To avoid interpretation, art may become parody. Or it may become abstract. Or it may become ('merely') decorative. Or it may become non-art.

The flight from interpretation seems particularly a feature of modern painting. Abstract painting is the attempt to have, in the ordinary sense, no content; since there is no content, there can be no interpretation. Pop Art works by the opposite means to the same result; using a content so blatant, so 'what it is', it, too, ends by being uninterpretable.

A good deal of modern poetry as well, starting from the great experiments of French poetry (including the movement that is misleadingly called Symbolism) to put silence into poems and to reinstate the *magic* of the word, has escaped from the rough grip of interpretation. The most recent revolution in contemporary taste in poetry—the revolution that has deposed Eliot and elevated Pound—represents a turning away from content in poetry in the old sense, an impatience with what made modern poetry prey to the zeal of interpreters.

I am speaking mainly of the situation in America, of course. Interpretation runs rampant here in those arts with a feeble and negligible avant-garde: fiction and the drama. Most American novelists and playwrights are really either journalists or gentlemen sociologists and psychologists. They are writing the literary equivalent of programme music. And so rudimentary, uninspired, and stagnant has been the sense of what might be done with *form* in fiction and drama that even when the content isn't simply information, news, it is still peculiarly visible, handier, more exposed. To the extent that novels and plays (in America),

[a]Lawrence actually said: 'Never trust the *artist*.'

unlike poetry and painting and music, don't reflect any interesting concern with changes in their form, these arts remain prone to assault by interpretation.

But programmatic avant-gardism—which has meant, mostly, experiments with form at the expense of content—is not the only defence against the infestation of art by interpretations. At least, I hope not. For this would be to commit art to being perpetually on the run. (It also perpetuates the very distinction between form and content which is, ultimately, an illusion.) Ideally, it is possible to elude the interpreters in another way, by making works of art whose surface is so unified and clean, whose momentum is so rapid, whose address is so direct that the work can be . . . just what it is. Is this possible now? It does happen in films, I believe. This is why cinema is the most alive, the most exciting, the most important of all art forms right now. Perhaps the way one tells how alive a particular art form is, is by the latitude it gives for making mistakes in it, and still being good. For example, a few of the films of Bergman—though crammed with lame messages about the modern spirit, thereby inviting interpretations—still triumph over the pretentious intentions of their director. In *Winter Light* and *The Silence*, the beauty and visual sophistication of the images subvert before our eyes the callow pseudo-intellectuality of the story and some of the dialogue. (The most remarkable instance of this sort of discrepancy is the work of D. W. Griffith.) In good films, there is always a directness that entirely frees us from the itch to interpret. Many old Hollywood films, like those of Cukor, Walsh, Hawks, and countless other directors, have this liberating antisymbolic quality, no less than the best work of the new European directors, like Truffaut's *Shoot the Piano Player* and *Jules and Jim,* Godard's *Breathless* and *Vivre Sa Vie,* Antonioni's *L'Avventura,* and Olmi's *The Fiancés.*

The fact that films have not been overrun by interpreters is in part due simply to the newness of cinema as an art. It also owes to the happy accident that films for such a long time were just movies; in other words, that they were understood to be part of mass, as opposed to high, culture, and were left alone by most people with minds. Then, too, there is always something other than content in the cinema to grab hold of, for those who want to analyze. For the cinema, unlike the novel, possesses a vocabulary of forms—the explicit, complex, and discussable technology of camera movements, cutting, and composition of the frame that goes into the making of a film.

VIII

What kind of criticism, of commentary on the arts, is desirable today? For I am not saying that works of art are ineffable, that they cannot be described or paraphrased. They can be. The question is how. What would criticism look like that would serve the work of art, not usurp its place?

What is needed, first, is more attention to form in art. If excessive stress on *content* provokes the arrogance of interpretation, more extended and more thorough descriptions of *form* would silence. What is needed is a vocabulary—a descriptive, rather than prescriptive, vocabulary—for forms.[1] The best criticism, and it is uncommon, is of this sort that dissolves considerations of content into those of form. On film, drama, and painting respectively, I can think of Erwin Panofsky's essay, 'Style and Medium in the Motion Pictures', Northrop Frye's essay, 'A Conspectus of Dramatic Genres', Pierre Francastel's essay, 'The Destruction of a Plastic Space'. Roland Barthes's book *On Racine* and his two essays on Robbe-Grillet are examples of formal analysis applied to the work of a single author. (The best essays in Erich Auerbach's *Mimesis*, like 'The Scar of Odysseus', are also of this type.) An example of formal analysis applied simultaneously to genre and author is Walter Benjamin's essay, 'The Story Teller: reflections on the works of Nicolai Leskov'.

Equally valuable would be acts of criticism which would supply a really accurate, sharp, loving description of the appearance of a work of art. This seems even harder to do than formal analysis. Some of Manny Farber's film criticism, Dorothy Van Ghent's essay, 'The Dickens World: a view from Todgers' ', Randall Jarrell's essay on Walt Whitman are among the rare examples of what I mean. These are essays which reveal the sensuous surface of art without mucking about in it.

IX

Transparence is the highest, most liberating value in art—and in criticism— today. Transparence means experiencing the luminousness of the thing in itself, of things being what they are. This is the greatness of, for example, the films of Bresson and Ozu and Renoir's *The Rules of the Game.*

Once upon a time (say, for Dante), it must have been a revolutionary and creative move to design works of art so that they might be experienced on several levels. Now it is not. It reinforces the principle of redundancy that is the principal affliction of modern life.

Once upon a time (a time when high art was scarce), it must have been a revolutionary and creative move to interpret works of art. Now it is not. What we decidedly do not need now is further to assimilate Art into Thought, or (worse yet) Art into Culture.

Interpretation takes the sensory experience of the work of art for granted, and proceeds from there. This cannot be taken for granted, now. Think of the sheer multiplication of works of art available, to every one of us, superadded to the conflicting tastes and odours and the sights of the urban environment that bombard our senses. Ours is a culture based on excess, on overproduction; the result is a steady loss of sharpness in our sensory experience. All the conditions of modern life—its material plentitude, its sheer crowdedness—conjoin to dull our sensory faculties. And it is in the light of the condition of our senses, our capabilities (rather than those of another age), that the task of the critic must be assessed.

What is important now is to recover our senses. We must learn to *see* more, to *hear* more, to *feel* more.

Our task is not to find the maximum amount of content in a work of art, much less to squeeze more content out of the work than is already there. Our task is to cut back content so that we can *see* the thing at all.

The aim of all commentary on art now should be to make works of art—and, by analogy, our own experience—more, rather than less, real to us. The function of criticism should be to show *how it is what it is*, even *that it is what it is*, rather than to show *what it means*.

In place of a hermeneutics we need an erotics of art.

NOTES

1. One of the difficulties is that our idea of form is spatial (the Greek metaphors for form are all derived from notions of space). This is why we have a more ready vocabulary of forms for the spatial than for the temporal arts. The exception among the temporal arts, of course, is the drama; perhaps this is because the drama is a narrative (i.e. temporal) form that extends itself visually and pictorially, upon a stage. . . . What we don't have yet is a poetics of the novel, any clear notion of the forms of narration. Perhaps film criticism will be the occasion of a breakthrough here, since films are primarily a visual form, yet they are also a subdivision of literature. ⊗

QUESTIONS FOR THOUGHT AND STUDY

1. According to Sontag, what interests does interpretation serve?
2. How would Sontag respond to Mailloux's claim that interpretation is always politically interested?
3. How useful is Sontag's interpretive position for resolving Constitutional debates?
4. How does Sontag expand on Abrams's vocabulary of critical terms?
5. How would you relate Sontag's argument in Abrams's triangle?
6. Sontag argues that much innovation in art is motivated by a "flight from interpretation." Can you give examples of this "flight" from popular culture and media?
7. How would Sontag respond to Fish's suggestion that the subject/object dichotomy can be eliminated in interpretation?

Masters of Desire: The Culture of American Advertising

Jack Solomon

Biography: *Jack Solomon is a Professor of English at University of California, Los Angeles and a semiotician—a student of the meaning of signs and symbols. He believes that only if we understand the meaning of the signs and symbols that inundate us from the media, can we control their influence (and the influence of their creators) on our lives.*

Solomon uses semiology, the study of signs, to analyze the role of advertising in American culture. He argues that advertising exploits the needs and fears produced by the American dream and satisfies our need for status, belonging, and so forth. Though intellectually we may dismiss the claims of ads, Solomon explains that they work at an unconscious level more than we admit. This essay provides an analytical rubric for critical interpretation of commercial advertising and other popular culture productions.

> *Amongst democratic nations, men easily attain a certain equality of condition; but they can never attain as much as they desire.*
>
> —ALEXIS DE TOCQUEVILLE

On May 10, 1831, a young French aristocrat named Alexis de Tocqueville arrived in New York City at the start of what would become one of the most famous visits to America in our history. He had come to observe firsthand the institutions of the freest, most egalitarian society of the age, but what he found was a paradox. For behind America's mythic promise of equal opportunity, Tocqueville discovered a desire for *unequal* social rewards, a ferocious competition for privilege and distinction. As he wrote in his monumental study, *Democracy in America:*

> When all privileges of birth and fortune are abolished, when all professions are accessible to all, and a man's own energies may place him at the top of any one of them, an easy and unbounded career seems open to his ambition . . . But this is an erroneous notion, which is corrected by daily experience. [For when] men are nearly alike, and all follow the same track, it is very difficult for any one individual to walk quick and cleave a way through the same throng which surrounds and presses him.

From *The Signs of Our Times.* The Putnam Publishing Group, 1988.

Yet walking quick and cleaving a way is precisely what Americans dream of. We Americans dream of rising above the crowd, of attaining a social summit beyond the reach of ordinary citizens. And therein lies the paradox.

The American dream, in other words, has two faces: the one communally egalitarian and the other competitively elitist. This contradiction is no accident; it is fundamental to the structure of American society. Even as America's great myth of equality celebrates the virtues of mom, apple pie, and the girl or boy next door, it also lures us to achieve social distinction, to rise above the crowd and bask alone in the glory. This land is your land and this land is my land, Woody Guthrie's populist anthem tells us, but we keep trying to increase the "my" at the expense of the "your." Rather than fostering contentment, the American dream breeds desire, a longing for a greater share of the pie. It is as if our society were a vast high-school football game, with the bulk of the participants noisily rooting in the stands while, deep down, each of them is wishing he or she could be the star quarterback or head cheerleader.

For the semiotician, the contradictory nature of the American myth of equality is nowhere written so clearly as in the signs that American advertisers use to manipulate us into buying their wares. "Manipulate" is the word here, not "persuade"; for advertising campaigns are not sources of product information, they are exercises in behavior modification. Appealing to our subconscious emotions rather than to our conscious intellects, advertisements are designed to exploit the discontentments fostered by the American dream, the constant desire for social success and the material rewards that accompany it. America's consumer economy runs on desire, and advertising stokes the engines by transforming common objects—from peanut butter to political candidates—into signs of all the things that Americans covet most.

But by semiotically reading the signs that advertising agencies manufacture to stimulate consumption, we can plot the precise state of desire in the audiences to which they are addressed. Let's look at a representative sample of ads and what they say about the emotional climate of the country and the fast-changing trends of American life. Because ours is a highly diverse, pluralistic society, various advertisements may say different things depending on their intended audiences, but in every case they say something about America, about the status of our hopes, fears, desires, and beliefs.

We'll begin with two ad campaigns conducted by the same company that bear out Alexis de Tocqueville's observations about the contradictory nature of American society: General Motors' campaigns for its Cadillac and Chevrolet lines. First, consider an early magazine ad for the Cadillac Allanté. Appearing as a full-color, four-page insert in *Time,* the ad seems to say "I'm special—and so is this car" even before we've begun to read it. Rather than being printed on the ordinary, flimsy pages of the magazine, the Allanté spread appears on glossy coated stock. The unwritten message here is that an extraordinary car deserves an extraordinary advertisement, and that both car and ad are aimed at an extraordinary consumer, or at least one who wishes to appear extraordinary compared to his more ordinary fellow citizens.

Ads of this kind work by creating symbolic associations between their product and what is most coveted by the consumers to whom they are addressed. It is significant, then, that this ad insists that the Allanté is virtually an Italian rather than an American car, an automobile, as its copy runs, "Conceived and Commissioned by America's Luxury Car Leader—Cadillac" but "Designed and Handcrafted by Europe's Renowned Design Leader—Pininfarina, SpA, of Turin, Italy." This is not simply a piece of product information, it's a sign of the prestige that European luxury cars enjoy in today's automotive marketplace. Once the luxury car of choice for America's status drivers, Cadillac has fallen far behind its European competitors in the race for the prestige market. So the Allanté essentially represents Cadillac's decision, after years of resisting the trend toward European cars, to introduce its own European import—whose high cost is clearly printed on the last page of the ad. Although $54,700 is a lot of money to pay for a Cadillac, it's about what you'd expect to pay for a top-of-the-line Mercedes-Benz. That's precisely the point the ad is trying to make: the Allanté is no mere car. It's a potent status symbol you can associate with the other major status symbols of the 1980s.

American companies manufacture status symbols because American consumers want them. As Alexis de Tocqueville recognized a century and a half ago, the competitive nature of democratic societies breeds a desire for social distinction, a yearning to rise above the crowd. But given the fact that those who do make it to the top in socially mobile societies have often risen from the lower ranks, they still look like everyone else. In the socially immobile societies of aristocratic Europe, generations of fixed social conditions produced subtle class signals. The accent of one's voice, the shape of one's nose, or even the set of one's chin, immediately communicated social status. Aside from the nasal bray and uptilted head of the Boston Brahmin, Americans do not have any native sets of personal status signals. If it weren't for his Mercedes-Benz and Manhattan townhouse, the parvenu Wall Street millionaire often couldn't be distinguished from the man who tailors his suits. Hence, the demand for status symbols, for the objects that mark one off as a social success, is particularly strong in democratic nations—stronger even than in aristocratic societies, where the aristocrat so often looks and sounds different from everyone else.

Status symbols, then, are signs that identify their possessors' place in a social hierarchy, markers of rank and prestige. We can all think of any number of status symbols—Rolls-Royces, Beverly Hills mansions, even Shar Pei puppies (whose rareness and expense has rocketed them beyond Russian wolfhounds as status pets and has even inspired whole lines of wrinkle-faced stuffed toys)— but how do we know that something *is* a status symbol? The explanation is quite simple: when an object (or puppy!) either costs a lot of money or requires influential connections to possess, anyone who possesses it must also possess the necessary means and influence to acquire it. The object itself really doesn't matter, since it ultimately disappears behind the presumed social potency of its owner. Semiotically, what matters is the signal it sends, its value as a sign of power. One traditional sign of social distinction is owning a country estate and enjoying the peace and privacy that attend it. Advertisements for Mercedes-Benz, Jaguar, and Audi automobiles thus frequently feature drivers motoring quietly along a country road, presumably on their way to or from their country houses.

Advertisers have been quick to exploit the status signals that belong to body language as well. As Hegel observed in the early nineteenth century, it is an ancient aristocrat prerogative to be seen by the lower orders without having to look at them in return. Tilting his chin high in the air gazing down at the world under hooded eyelids, the aristocrat invites observation while refusing to look back. We can find such a pose exploited in an advertisement for Cadillac Seville in which we see an elegantly dressed woman out for a drive with her husband in their new Cadillac. If we look closely at the woman's body language, we can see her glance inwardly with a satisfied smile on her face but not outward toward the camera that represents our gaze. She is glad to be seen by us in her Seville, but she isn't interested in looking at *us!*

Ads that are aimed at a broader market take the opposite approach. If the American dream encourages the desire to "arrive," to vault above the mass, it also fosters a desire to be popular, to "belong." Populist commercials accordingly transform products into signs of belonging, utilizing such common icons as country music, small-town life, family picnics, and farmyards. All of these icons are incorporated in GM's "Heartbeat of America" campaign for its Chevrolet line. Unlike the Seville commercial, the faces in the Chevy ads look straight at us and smile. Dress is casual; the mood upbeat. Quick camera cuts take us from rustic to suburban to urban scenes, creating an American montage filmed from sea to shining sea. We all "belong" in a Chevy.

Where price alone doesn't determine the market for a product, advertisers can go either way. Both Johnnie Walker and Jack Daniel's are better-grade whiskies, but where a Johnnie Walker ad appeals to the buyer who wants a mark of aristocratic distinction in his liquor, a Jack Daniel's ad emphasizes the down-home, egalitarian folksiness of its product. Johnnie Walker associates itself with such conventional status symbols as sable coats, Rolls-Royces, and black gold; Jack Daniel's gives us a Good Ol' Boy in overalls. In fact, Jack Daniel's Good Ol' Boy is an icon of backwoods independence, recalling the days of the moonshiner and the Whisky Rebellion of 1794. Evoking emotions quite at odds with those stimulated in Johnnie Walker ads, the advertisers of Jack Daniel's have chosen to transform their product into a sign of America's populist tradition. The fact that both ads successfully sell whisky is itself a sign of the dual nature of the American dream.

Beer is also pitched on two levels. Consider the difference between the ways Budweiser and Michelob market their light beers. Bud Light and Michelob Light cost and taste about the same, but Budweiser tends to target the working class while Michelob has gone after the upscale market. Bud commercials are set in working-class bars that contrast with the sophisticated nightclubs and yuppie watering holes of the Michelob campaign. "You're one of the guys," Budweiser assures the assembly-line worker and the truck driver, "this Bud's for you." Michelob, on the other hand, makes no such appeal to the democratic instinct of sharing and belonging. You don't share, you take, grabbing what you can in a competitive dash to "have it all."

Populist advertising is particularly effective in the face of foreign competition. When Americans feel threatened from the outside, they tend to circle the wagons and temporarily forget their class differences. In the face of the Japanese automotive "invasion," Chrysler runs populist commercials in which Lee Iacocca joins the simple folk who buy his cars as the jingle "Born in America" blares in the background. Seeking to capitalize on the popularity of Bruce Springsteen's *Born in the USA* album, these ads gloss over Springsteen's ironic lyrics in a vast display of flag-waving. Chevrolet's "Heartbeat of America" campaign attempts to woo American motorists away from Japanese automobiles by appealing to their patriotic sentiments.

The patriotic iconography of these campaigns also reflects the general cultural mood of the early- to mid-1980s. After a period of national anguish in the wake of the Vietnam War and the Iran hostage crisis, America went on a patriotic binge. American athletic triumphs in the Lake Placid and Los Angeles Olympics introduced a sporting tone into the national celebration, often making international affairs appear like one great Olympiad in which America was always going for the gold. In response, advertisers began to do their own flag-waving.

The mood of advertising during this period was definitely upbeat. Even deodorant commercials, which traditionally work on our self-doubts and fears of social rejection, jumped on the bandwagon. In the guilty sixties, we had ads like the "Ice Blue Secret" campaign with its connotations of guilt and shame. In the feel-good Reagan eighties, "Sure" deodorant commercials featured images of triumphant Americans throwing up their arms in victory to reveal—no wet marks! Deodorant commercials once had the moral echo of Nathaniel Hawthorne's guiltridden *The Scarlet Letter;* in the early eighties they had all the moral subtlety of *Rocky IV*, reflecting the emotions of a Vietnam-weary nation eager to embrace the imagery of America Triumphant.

The commercials for Worlds of Wonder's Lazer Tag game featured the futuristic finals of some Soviet-American Lazer Tag shootout ("Practice hard,

America!") and carried the emotions of patriotism into an even more aggressive arena. Exploiting the hoopla that surrounded the victory over the Soviets in the hockey finals of the 1980 Olympics, the Lazer Tag ads pandered to an American desire for the sort of clear-cut nationalistic triumphs that the nuclear age has rendered almost impossible. Creating a fantasy setting where patriotic dreams are substituted for complicated realities, the Lazer Tag commercials sought to capture the imaginations of children caught up in the patriotic fervor of the early 1980s.

LIVE THE FANTASY

By reading the signs of American advertising, we can conclude that America is a nation of fantasizers, often preferring the sign to the substance and easily enthralled by a veritable Fantasy Island of commercial illusions. Critics of Madison Avenue often complain that advertisers create consumer desire, but semioticians don't think the situation is that simple. Advertisers may give shape to consumer fantasies, but they need raw material to work with, the subconscious dreams and desires of the marketplace. As long as these desires remain unconscious, advertisers will be able to exploit them. But by bringing the fantasies to the surface, you can free yourself from advertising's often hypnotic grasp.

I can think of no company that has more successfully seized upon the subconscious fantasies of the American marketplace—indeed the world marketplace—than McDonald's. By no means the first nor the only hamburger chain in the United States, McDonald's emerged victorious in the "burger wars" by transforming hamburgers into signs of all that was desirable in American life. Other chains like Wendy's, Burger King, and Jack-In-The-Box continue to advertise and sell widely, but no company approaches McDonald's transformation of itself into a symbol of American culture.

McDonald's success can be traced to the precision of its advertising. Instead of broadcasting a single "one-size-fits-all" campaign at a time, McDonald's pitches its burgers simultaneously at different age groups, different classes, even different races (Budweiser beer, incidentally, has succeeded in the same way). For children, there is the Ronald McDonald campaign, which presents a fantasy world that has little to do with hamburgers in any rational sense but a great deal to do with the emotional desires of kids. Ronald McDonald and his friends are signs that recall the Muppets, "Sesame Street," the circus, toys, storybook illustrations, even *Alice in Wonderland.* Such signs do not signify hamburgers. Rather, they are displayed in order to prompt in the child's mind an automatic association of fantasy, fun, and McDonald's.

The same approach is taken in ads aimed at older audiences—teens, adults, and senior citizens. In the teen-oriented ads we may catch a fleeting glimpse of a hamburger or two, but what we are really shown is a teenage fantasy: groups of hip and happy adolescents singing, dancing, and cavorting together. Fearing loneliness more than anything else, adolescents quickly respond to the group appeal of such commercials. "Eat a Big Mac," these ads say, "and you won't be stuck home alone on Saturday night."

To appeal to an older and more sophisticated audience no longer so afraid of not belonging and more concerned with finding a place to go out to at night, McDonald's has designed the elaborate "Mac Tonight" commercials, which have for their backdrop a nightlit urban skyline and at their center a cabaret pianist with a moon-shaped head, a glad manner, and Blues Brothers shades. Such signs prompt an association of McDonald's with nightclubs and urban sophistication, persuading us that McDonald's is a place not only for breakfast or lunch but for dinner too, as if it were a popular off-Broadway nightspot, a place to see and be seen. Even the parody of Kurt Weill's "Mack the Knife" theme song that Mac the Pianist performs is a sign, a subtle signal to the sophisticated hamburger eater able to recognize the origin of the tune in Bertolt Brecht's *Threepenny Opera.*

For yet older customers, McDonald's has designed a commercial around the fact that it employs a large number of retirees and seniors. In one such ad, we see an elderly man leaving his pretty little cottage early in the morning to start work as "the new kid" at McDonald's, and then we watch him during his first day on the job. Of course he is a great success, outdoing everyone else with his energy and efficiency, and he returns home in the evening to a loving wife and a happy home. One would almost think that the ad was a kind of moving "help wanted" sign (indeed, McDonald's *was* hiring elderly employees at the time), but it's really just directed at consumers. Older viewers can see themselves wanted and appreciated in the ad—and perhaps be distracted from the rationally uncomfortable fact that many senior citizens take such jobs because of financial need and thus may be unlikely to own the sort of home that one sees in the commercial. But realism isn't the point here. This is fantasyland, a dream world promising instant gratification no matter what the facts of the matter may be.

Practically the only fantasy that McDonald's doesn't exploit is the fantasy of sex. This is understandable, given McDonald's desire to present itself as a family restaurant. But everywhere else, sexual fantasies, which have always had an important place in American advertising, are beginning to dominate the advertising scene. You expect sexual come-ons in ads for perfume or cosmetics or jewelry—after all, that's what they're selling—but for room deodorizers? In a magazine ad for Claire Burke home fragrances, for example, we see a well-dressed couple cavorting about their bedroom in what looks like a cheery preparation for sadomasochistic exercises. Jordache and Calvin Klein pitch blue jeans as props for teenage sexuality. The phallic appeal of automobiles, traditionally an implicit feature in automotive advertising, becomes quite explicit in a Dodge commercial that shifts back and forth from shots of a young man in an automobile to teasing glimpses of a woman—his date—as she dresses in her apartment.

The very language of today's advertisements is charged with sexuality. Products in the more innocent fifties were "new and improved," but everything in the eighties is "hot!"—as in "hot woman," or sexual heat. Cars are "hot." Movies are "hot." An ad for Valvoline pulses to the rhythm of a "heat wave, burning in my car." Sneakers get red hot in a magazine ad for Travel Fox athletic shoes in which we see male and female figures, clad only in Travel Fox shoes, apparently in the act of copulation—an ad that earned one of *Adweek*'s annual "badvertising" awards for shoddy advertising.

The sexual explicitness of contemporary advertising is a sign not so much of American sexual fantasies as of the lengths to which advertisers will go to get attention. Sex never fails as an attention-getter, and in a particularly competitive, and expensive, era for American marketing, advertisers like to bet on a sure thing. Ad people refer to the proliferation of TV, radio, newspaper, magazine, and billboard ads as "clutter," and nothing cuts through the clutter like sex.

By showing the flesh, advertisers work on the deepest, most coercive human emotions of all. Much sexual coercion in advertising, however, is a sign of a desperate need to make certain that clients are getting their money's worth. The appearance of advertisements that refer directly to the prefabricated fantasies of Hollywood is a sign of a different sort of desperation: a desperation for ideas. With the rapid turnover of advertising campaigns mandated by the need to cut through the "clutter," advertisers may be hard pressed for new ad concepts, and so they are more and more frequently turning to already-established models. In the early 1980s, for instance, Pepsi-Cola ran a series of ads broadly alluding to Steven Spielberg's *E.T.* In one such ad, we see a young boy, who, like the hero of *E.T.*, witnesses an extraterrestrial visit. The boy is led to a soft-drink machine where he pauses to drink a can of Pepsi as the spaceship he's spotted flies off into the universe. The relationship between the ad and the movie, accordingly, is a parasitical one, with the ad taking its life from the creative body of the film.

Pepsi did something similar in 1987 when it arranged with the producers of the movie *Top Gun* to promote the film's video release in Pepsi's television advertisements in exchange for the right to append a Pepsi ad to the video itself. This time, however, the parasitical relationship between ad and film was made explicit. Pepsi sales benefited from the video, and the video's sales benefited from Pepsi. It was marriage made in corporate heaven.

The fact that Pepsi believed that it could stimulate consumption by appealing to the militaristic fantasies dramatized in *Top Gun* reflects similar fantasies in the "Pepsi generation." Earlier generations saw Pepsi associated with high-school courtship rituals, with couples sipping sodas together at the corner drugstore. When the draft was on, young men fantasized about Peggy Sue, not Air Force Flight School. Military service was all too real a possibility to fantasize about. But in an era when military service is not a reality for most young Americans, Pepsi commercials featuring hotshot fly-boys drinking Pepsi while streaking about in their Air Force jets contribute to a youth culture that has forgotten what military service means. It all looks like such fun in the Pepsi ads, but what they conceal is the fact that military jets are weapons, not high-tech recreational vehicles.

For less militaristic dreamers, Madison Avenue has framed ad campaigns around the cultural prestige of high-tech machinery in its own right. This is especially the case with sports cars, whose high-tech appeal is so powerful that some people apparently fantasize about *being* sports cars. At least, this is the conclusion one might draw from a Porsche commercial that asked its audience, "If you were a car, what kind of car would you be?" As a candy-red Porsche speeds along a rain-slick forest road, the ad's voice-over describes all the specifications you'd want to have if you *were* a sports car. "If you were a car," the commercial concludes, "you'd be a Porsche."

In his essay "Car Commercials and 'Miami Vice,'" Todd Gitlin explains the semiotic appeal of such ads as those in the Porsche campaign. Aired at the height of what may be called America's "myth of the entrepreneur," these commercials were aimed at young corporate managers who imaginatively identified with the "lone wolf" image of a Porsche speeding through the woods. Gitlin points out that such images cater to the fantasies of faceless corporate men who dream of entrepreneurial glory, of striking out on their own like John DeLorean and telling the boss to take his job and shove it. But as DeLorean's spectacular failure demonstrates, the life of the entrepreneur can be extremely risky. So rather than having to go it alone and take the risks that accompany entrepreneurial independence, the young executive can substitute fantasy for reality by climbing into his Porsche—or at least that's what Porsche's advertisers wanted him to believe.

But there is more at work in the Porsche ads than the fantasies of corporate America. Ever since Arthur C. Clarke and Stanley Kubrick teamed up to present us with HAL 9000, the demented computer of *2001: A Space Odyssey*, the American imagination has been obsessed with the melding of man and machine. First there was television's "Six Million Dollar Man," and then movieland's *Star Wars*, *Blade Runner*, and *Robocop*, fantasy visions of a future dominated by machines. Androids haunt our imaginations as machines seize the initiative. *Time* magazine's "Man of the Year" for 1982 was a computer. Robot-built automobiles appeal to drivers who spend their days in front of computer screens—perhaps designing robots. When so much power and prestige is being given to high-tech machines, wouldn't you rather be a Porsche?

In short, the Porsche campaign is a sign of a new mythology that is emerging before our eyes, a myth of the machine, which is replacing the myth of the human. The iconic figure of the little tramp caught up in the cogs of industrial production in Charlie Chaplin's *Modern Times* signified a humanistic revulsion to the age of the machine. Human beings, such icons said, were superior to machines. Human values should come first in the moral order of things. But as Edith Milton suggests in her essay "The Track of the Mutant," we are now coming to believe that machines are superior to human beings, that mechanical nature is superior to human nature. Rather than being threatened by machines, we long to merge with them. "The Six Million Dollar Man" is one iconic figure in the new mythology; Harrison Ford's sexual coupling with an android is another. In such an age it should come as little wonder that computer-synthesized Max Headroom should be a commercial spokesman for Coca-Cola, or that Federal Express should design a series of TV ads featuring mechanical-looking human beings revolving around strange and powerful machines.

FEAR AND TREMBLING IN THE MARKETPLACE

While advertisers play on and reflect back at us our fantasies about everything from fighter pilots to robots, they also play on darker imaginings. If dream and desire can be exploited in the quest for sales, so can nightmare and fear.

The nightmare equivalent of America's populist desire to "belong," for example, is the fear of not belonging, of social rejection, of being different. Advertisements for dandruff shampoos, mouthwashes, deodorants, and laundry detergents ("Ring Around the Collar!") accordingly exploit such fears, bullying us into consumption. Although ads of this type are still around in the 1980s, they were particularly common in the fifties and early sixties, reflecting a society still reeling from the witch-hunts of the McCarthy years. When any sort of social eccentricity or difference could result in a public denunciation and the loss of one's job or even liberty, Americans were keen to conform and be like everyone else. No one wanted to be "guilty" of smelling bad or of having a dirty collar.

"Guilt" ads characteristically work by creating narrative situations in which someone is "accused" of some social "transgression," pronounced guilty, and then offered the sponsor's product as a means of returning to "innocence." Such ads, in essence, are parodies of ancient religious rituals of guilt and atonement, whereby sinning humanity is offered salvation through the agency of priest and church. In the world of advertising, a product takes the place of the priest, but the logic of the situation is quite similar.

In commercials for Wisk detergent, for example, we witness the drama of a hapless housewife and her husband as they are mocked by the jeering voices of children shouting "Ring Around the Collar!" "Oh, those dirty rings!" the housewife groans in despair. It's as if she and her husband were being stoned by an angry crowd. But there's hope, there's help, there's Wisk. Cleansing her soul of sin as well as her husband's, the housewife launders his shirts with Wisk, and behold, his collars are clean. Product salvation is only as far as the super-market.

The recent appearance of advertisements for hospitals treating drug and alcohol addiction has raised the old genre of the guilt ad to new heights (or lows, depending on your perspective). In such ads, we see wives on the verge of leaving their husbands if they don't do something about their drinking, and salesmen about to lose their jobs. The man is guilty; he has sinned; but he up-holds the ritual of guilt and atonement by "confessing" to his wife or boss and agreeing to go to the hospital the ad is pitching.

If guilt looks backward in time to past transgressions, fear, like desire, faces forward, trembling before the future. In the late 1980s, a new kind of fear commercial appeared, one whose narrative played on the worries of young cor-porate managers struggling up the ladder of success. Representing the night-mare equivalent of the elitist desire to "arrive," ads of this sort created images of failure, storylines of corporate defeat. In one ad for Apple computers, for ex-ample, a group of junior executives sits around a table with the boss as he asks each executive how long it will take his or her department to complete some publishing jobs. "Two or three days," answers one nervous executive. "A week, on overtime," a tight-lipped woman responds. But one young up-and-comer can have everything ready tomorrow, today, or yesterday, because his depart-ment uses a Macintosh desktop publishing system. Guess who'll get the next promotion?

Fear stalks an ad for AT&T computer systems too. A boss and four junior executives are dining in a posh restaurant. Icons of corporate power and pres-tige flood the screen—from the executives' formal evening wear to the fancy table setting—but there's tension in the air. It seems that the junior managers have chosen a computer system that's incompatible with the firm's sales and marketing departments. A whole new system will have to be purchased, but the tone of the meeting suggests that it will be handled by a new group of man-agers. These guys are on the way out. They no longer "belong." Indeed, it's probably no accident that the ad takes place in a restaurant, given the joke that went around in the aftermath of the 1987 market crash. "What do you call a yuppie stockbroker?" the joke ran. "Hey, waiter!" Is the ad trying subtly to sug-gest that junior executives who choose the wrong computer systems are doomed to suffer the same fate?

For other markets, there are other fears. If McDonald's presents senior citizens with bright fantasies of being useful and appreciated beyond retire-ment, companies like Secure Horizons dramatize senior citizens' fears of being caught short by a major illness. Running its ads in the wake of budgetary cuts in the Medicare system, Secure Horizons designed a series of commercials featuring a pleasant old man named Harry—who looks and sounds rather like Carroll O'Connor—who tells us the story of the scare he got during his wife's recent illness. Fearing that next time Medicare won't cover the bills, he has purchased supplemental health insurance from Secure Horizons and now securely tends his rooftop garden.

Among all the fears advertisers have exploited over the years, I find the fear of not having a posh enough burial site the most arresting. Advertisers usually avoid any mention of death—who wants to associate a product with the grave?—but mortuary advertisers haven't much choice. Generally, they solve their problems by framing cemeteries as timeless parks presided over by priestly morticians, appealing to our desires for dignity and comfort in the face of bereavement. But in one television commercial for Forest Lawn we find a different approach. In this ad we are presented with the ghost of an old man telling us how he might have found a much nicer resting place than the rundown cemetery in which we find him had his wife only known that Forest Lawn was so "affordable." I presume the ad was supposed to be funny, but it's been pulled off the air. There are some fears that just won't bear joking about, some nightmares too dark to dramatize.

THE FUTURE OF AN ILLUSION

There are some signs in the advertising world that Americans are getting fed up with fantasy advertisements and want to hear some straight talk. Weary of extravagant product claims and irrelevant associations, consumers trained by years of advertising to distrust what they hear seem to be developing an immunity to commercials. At least, this is the semiotic message I read in the "new realism" advertisements of the eighties, ads that attempt to convince you that what you're seeing is the real thing, that the ad is giving you the straight dope, not advertising hype.

You can recognize the "new realism" by its camera techniques. The lighting is usually subdued to give the ad the effect of being filmed without studio lighting or special filters. The scene looks gray, as if the blinds were drawn. The camera shots are jerky and off-angle, often zooming in for sudden and unflattering close-ups, as if the cameraman was an amateur with a home video recorder. In a "realistic" ad to AT&T, for example, we are treated to a monologue by a plump stockbroker—his plumpness intended as a sign that he's for real and not just another actor—who tells us about the problems he's had with his phone system (not AT&T's) as the camera jerks around, generally filming him from below as if the cameraman couldn't quite fit his equipment into the crammed office and had to film the scene on his knees. "This is no fancy advertisement," the ad tries to convince us, "this is sincere."

An ad for Miller draft beer tries the same approach, recreating the effect of an amateur videotape of a wedding celebration. Camera shots shift suddenly from group to group. The picture jumps. Bodies are poorly framed. The color is washed out. Like the beer it is pushing, the ad is supposed to strike us as being "as real as it gets."

Such ads reflect a desire for reality in the marketplace, a weariness with Madison Avenue illusions. But there's no illusion like the illusion of reality. Every special technique that advertisers use to create their "reality effects" is, in fact, more unrealistic than the techniques of "illusory" ads. The world, in reality, doesn't jump around when you look at it. It doesn't appear in subdued gray tones. Our eyes don't have zoom lenses, and we don't look at things with our heads cocked to one side. The irony of the "new realism" is that it is more unrealistic, more artificial, than the ordinary run of television advertising.

But don't expect any truly realistic ads in the future, because a realistic advertisement is a contradiction in terms. The logic of advertising is entirely semiotic: it substitutes signs for things, framed visions of consumer desire for the things itself. The success of modern advertising, its penetration into every corner of American life, reflects a culture that has itself chosen illusion over reality. At a time when political candidates all have professional image-makers attached to their staffs, and the President of the United States can be an actor who once sold shirt collars, all the cultural signs are pointing to more illusions in our lives rather than fewer—a fecund breeding ground for the world of the advertiser. ✇

QUESTIONS FOR THOUGHT AND STUDY

1. How could terms for Abrams's orientation to critical theories be used to paraphrase Solomon's claim that "advertising campaigns are not sources of project information; they are exercises in behavior modification"?

2. Draw quotations from Solomon's essay to develop a full definition of "semiotics," explaining its meaning as well as its purpose.

3. Give examples from your own daily life of the "two faces" of the American Dream.

4. How would Sontag respond to Solomon's close reading of advertising campaigns? How would Mailloux? How would Fish?

5. Comment on Solomon's statement that "there's no illusion like the illusion of reality"?

6. What use-value do status symbols have, according to Solomon? According to Allport?

STUDENT PAPER FOR REVISION WORKSHOP

This close reading of a popular—and controversial—cigarette ad campaign effectively uses perspectives from contrasting interpretive theories to generate lively insights. The introductory discussion and application of interpretive theory to the topic successfully sets up the writer's reading of the ad text, but does it clearly establish the essay's purpose? Can you follow the logical progression of the argument and clearly identify the writer's position as the essay shifts between applications of formalist and intentionalist perspectives? How could more carefully crafted transitions between some paragraphs—and the incorporation of some transitional passages keyed back to a clearly stated thesis—strengthen the essay's structural coherence?

Joe Camel

Student D

Joe Camel folds up the sleeves of his shirt, lights a CAMEL cigarette and puts it in the right side of his mouth. Before taking a pool cue, he turns his red hat backwards and puts on dark sunglasses. He reaches for the long cue and rubs the tip of it with a blue chalk. Suave, he holds the end of the cue with his right hand and the front with his left. Placing the tip of the cue right behind the white ball, he aims for the solid five, which is at the lower right-hand corner of the photograph. Now, he is ready for the picture to be taken. Finally, Joe's ad is published on a full page of *Sports Illustrated* magazine. It seems to me that he represents the "hipster" of the 90s with his strange figure.

A construction worker, after his long and tiresome day, steps into a grocery store to get some tobacco and to have a little break from his hard day. While waiting in line, he quickly browses through the magazines displayed on the shelf. A football star on the cover of *Sports Illustrated* attracts his attention. His curiosity in sports urges him to reach for the magazine and have a quick look at it before it is his turn to buy the tobacco. But before he grabs the magazine, he wipes the sweat from his forehead with his left arm of his blue denim shirt. Then he takes the magazine and searches for the article about his football hero. After spending a few minutes on it, he leafs through the pages to see if something else grabs his attention. Suddenly, this cartoon character on a full-length page stops his hand from turning more pages. He pauses a moment, laughs his heart out and says to the person who is standing before him, "Hey, man! Don't you think this is a cool picture of our pal Joe Camel? He had his cap backwards and is smoking a Camel cigarette while shooting pool at the same time. What a guy!" The person, who appears to be an average worker, too, shares the laugh with the construction worker. The construction worker continues, "Hey wait a minute! It looks like he's staring at me. Anyway this is a funny picture." He puts the magazine back on the shelf again and buys the cigarettes. As soon as he leaves the store he lights a Camel cigarette while smiling at Joe Camel's pose.

There are many ways of interpreting this ad. One way is that of the working class individual, who takes a quick look at Joe Camel's ad, finds the picture humorous. At first glance he sees that Joe's look suggests that he is a "hipster" and that it is great to be different from others. This suggests Susan Sontag's viewpoint, which is respecting an art just the way, it is without getting too analytical and thus lose the initial meaning of the text (131).

However, there are other angles that could be taken to make sense of the picture. For instance, for a closer analysis, Steven Mailloux's formalist and intentionalist ways of interpretation could be applied to identify signs and symbols that are all connected in one way or the other to smoking Camel cigarettes. As he mentions, intentionalists would look for the intention behind or in the text (117). Therefore, this method could be used in order to see the purpose behind this ad. In the meanwhile, the viewers could directly refer to the text and describe their opinions without even attempting to find the intention of the picture (117). This is what Mailloux calls the formalists' way of interpretation. In either case, as both authors agree, interpretation is a way of translating the text. But this translation, as Mailloux mentions, is always an approximation targeted toward something (116). Thus, interpretation does not guarantee a final answer toward anything; rather it offers ways to see the text in a different way (122).

The first question that would come across in intentionalists' viewpoint would be, why is an animated camel chosen to be the character for advertising the product since they would like to know the reason beyond the creation of the character? Aside from the fact that name of the cigarette is Camel, they may suggest that the animation of a camel implies escapism. Using history as a reference they would further explain a camel in reality is a desert animal. He works hard all day long while tolerating the dry and hot weather of the desert. When the camel is humanized, he escapes his own troublesome life. In this way he frees himself from his own real identity. Likewise, working class folks in real life are dealing with stress and depression almost everyday. Therefore the intentionalists would approximate that by smoking Camel cigarettes, working class men can forget their stressed moments just as a camel is freed from his depressing life. In other words, smoking a Camel can be a door open to peace of mind, which is one of the major desires of human beings. And this ad takes advantage of this typical reader's desire to be free from hardship, by creating a cartoon character named "Joe Camel." This and the following interpretations show that intentionalists look beyond the text and try to come up with such approximations to predict the artists' intention (117).

Furthermore, the camel's name Joe sounds like a common and a friendly name. Also because of the fact that Joe is wearing a blue denim shirt, turns his cap and wears sunglasses, we get the picture of the "average Joe" or the typical worker in our minds. Therefore the name "Joe," combined with average worker's outfit, is possibly intended to symbolize the working class guys of society.

The word "lights" and an orangish glow above Joe's head would suggest to formalists that he, the friendly fellow, or the Camel cigarette can enlighten the working class man's life since formalists use the content to feel things in the picture. They would say that the dark background behind Joe gives him a relaxing mood. Further, they would explain the fact that there is no one around this cartoon figure gives the impression to the viewer that the character wants to be in his own world of comfort. This is what Sontag defines as "transparent" which is experiencing things as the way they are (136). As seen in the above analysis, formalists did not get deep into the picture to find something that is not there. They described the mood that the picture tends to transform into the readers' minds.

The game of pool is selected cleverly out of all the other games for a particular purpose. Pool is not just any other game like playing cards, which would create a tense environment for the viewer because there is money involved. It is meant to target the working class men since pool is the most popular game among this group of people. This is another way to portray escapism and relaxation in the minds of the average working men.

In addition to the game chosen, there is also a reason behind Joe's targeting the solid ball. Once again, this concept could be related to the intentionalists since they search for a purpose behind what is already there. It seems that Joe's aim for solid five is accurate, and he is going to make the shot. The reason for this, as an intentionalist may say, is to show that his personality is as hard as the solid ball. Fortunately, this solid ball happens to be on the lower right-hand corner. But why? Because in this way the ad corners its viewers and implies that, "You better watch me make this shot!" The whole focus on the right side belittles the "Surgeon General's Warning" which is positioned in the lower left-hand corner. There could also be a psychological reason for placing the warning on the left side because it attracts less attention there. Since Joe Camel is the rebel and his viewers are entertained by what he does, he brings all the attention towards himself rather than to the warning. Another powerful logic behind Joe's cornering his viewers is that he has absolute control over whoever watches him. In this way he has the authority to influence the typical worker by showing that smoking is a complement to human's desire, just because he is the center of attention.

Now if close attention is paid to the four balls on the pool table, formalists could come up with interpretations of the way the balls are positioned and the relationships among them. They would use puns as a way of playing with the words in text (118), in this case numbers in the picture; the formalists might say that there are two solid balls, the four and the five, and two striped balls, the eleven and the twelve. They are chosen to be consecutive numbers and are placed in an increasing order. Number four is behind five, and eleven is behind twelve. Numbers four and eleven are next to each other like five and twelve but they are further apart. This is as far as formalists could get. It would take the intentionalists to get deeper and to give a reason for the coordination of such numbers. The intentionalists would probably say that the difference between solid and striped balls that are side by side is seven. They would conclude that the number seven could possibly symbolize leisure or a great time because according to the history of mankind the seventh day of the week is the day when working class men take some time off from their tiresome work to do anything they please. Because the balls are consecutively numbered and because their difference is constant, this may also suggest to them that every day of the typical worker's life could be as relaxing as the seventh day of the week if he spent time playing pool and smoking Camel cigarettes. Thus, the formalists would use punning to give the physical description of the numbers, but it would require intentionalists to take a further step and to approximate the intent beyond such numbers.

Even though the character in the ad is a cartoon figure and appears to be funny, it seems a little bizarre to see a camel smoking a Camel cigarette, or better yet, smoking himself. It looks like Michael Jordan advertising for his own shoe, the Air Jordan. This appears snobbish. It is like saying "Hey, look! I'm having my own product, and if it was not good, I would not bother even myself to use it at a first place." Maybe this arrogant figure of Joe with his sleeves rolled up and with masculine hairy arms gives him more power to make working class men follow what he does, in this case smoking Camel cigarettes.

Every little thing that appears in Joe's ad has messages to give about the product to the group of people who are in "average Joe's" category. Some of the messages could be pointed out just by a quick glance—like Joe Camel's "hipster" figure—but some others may take a little more time to analyze, such as the relationship among the pool balls. Even though taking every little thing and analyzing it may lead the viewer to see the picture in another way, these interpretations are valid since, as Sontag mentions, they come from "the conscious act of the mind, which illustrates a certain code of interpretation." Thus from these interpretations, Mailloux's intentionalist approach of sense making could suggest to the viewer that Joe Camel's ad has one goal and that is to target the average workers' needs and desires to escape and relax. This suggests that they can fulfill those desires by smoking Camel cigarettes.

Works Cited

Mailloux, Steven "Interpretation," Writing 2 Course Reader, Judith Kirscht, Spring 1994.
Sontag, Susan "Against Interpretation," Writing 2 Course Reader, Judith Kirscht, Spring 1994.

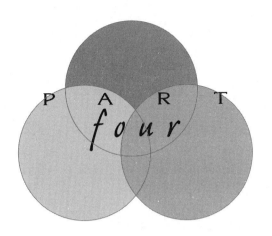

PART
four

Critical
Applications

C H A P T E R

seven

Critical Applications

Why did I only get a "C" on my Political Science paper?
Can I believe information I find on the World Wide Web?
How serious are environmental problems such as global warming?
What does academic inquiry have to do with "real life" decisions?

GOALS AND PURPOSES

So far, in this book, our goal has been to show you how academic inquiry can develop critical thinking and writing needed for college work in science, social science, and humanities. Throughout your work in each of these disciplines, you have also learned how methods of inquiry in each academic field contribute to human knowledge about things, events, behaviors, and our attitudes toward them. We have also stressed that by applying the theories of the fields to events and experiences from your everyday life, you can bring academic and personal spheres together, gain a better understanding of the theories, and discover that you have something to say. We have concentrated, thus far, on understanding, engagement, and dialogue as keys to good reading and writing in the academic setting. As we begin to apply inquiry to "real world" situations, however, we must draw on the kinds of knowledge produced by more than one discipline. Problems, as we encounter them in everyday life, are rarely purely scientific, social, or humanistic. Indeed interdisciplinary programs within the university emerge in response to complex human concerns of the times. Black Studies, Chicano Studies, Environmental Studies, and Women's Studies all draw on the knowledge produced by scientists, social scientists, and humanists to address twentieth-century social problems. Now we would like to show you how the methods of academic inquiry developed in each of the disciplines can contribute to a better understanding of complex issues that shape events in your everyday life. Further we would like to demonstrate how the principles of good critical thinking and "elegance" in writing can help draw together, or synthesize, different types of knowledge. Such interdisciplinary synthesis is critical to the resolution of "real world" situations.

In this unit we will explore ways to apply what you have learned in this book beyond the boundaries of the course itself. The inquiry and writing skills you have developed can, we believe, help you conduct your own inquiry into the issues that confront you, from the grade you received on a paper, to problems confronted on the job, to issues debated in the public sphere. The applications given here are only samples of many possible applications, but they cover a range of different inquiry skills:

- Recognizing and analyzing the values and expectations of particular rhetorical communities.
- Analyzing the kinds of claims being made and the appropriate evidence for each.
- Recognizing and evaluating the interdisciplinary interaction of different kinds of knowledge claims in many personal, professional. and public issues.
- Writing coherent, sound, well-written arguments appropriate to the issue under debate.

The assignments below provide you with further opportunities to strengthen your mastery of these critical thinking and writing skills by applying them in interdisciplinary contexts. They ask you to apply these "academic" skills in situations that have very real and practical value to you as a thinker, as a writer, and as a citizen of an increasingly complex world—a world characterized, in part, by virtual explosions in both the amount and the availability of information and "knowledge" in our daily lives. We hope that these further applications of skills here will help you realize that you have indeed acquired methods of critical thought and cogent expression inquiry that will continue to make you a more thoughtful, insightful, and productive member of the various communities you will occupy, from biology class, to staff meeting, to public hearing.

With your instructor's guidance and approval, you may select from among three critical application assignment options depending upon your personal interests and goals and upon the objectives of your writing class.

Assignment A
The Critical Paper Revision and Commentary provides an opportunity to apply your understanding of academic inquiry and your mastery of critical reading, thinking, and writing skills to an effective rethinking and rewriting of a paper

completed and graded in another of your general education courses. For a less-sophisticated version of this assignment, you may even select to rethink and rewrite a paper you have written and had graded in your writing course. The assignment asks you to both work systematically through a guided rethinking and rewriting of a previously written paper to produce an improved revision *and* to produce a reflective commentary that explains your reasons for making particular editorial and revision decisions.

Two essays included with this unit should help you to appreciate the intellectual growth and insight involved in the revision process. Inge Bell's essay, "Everybody Hates to Write," comes from an irreverent little book titled *This Book Is Not Required,* which offers very frank and realistic advice and survival strategies for new college students. Inge describes the challenges that confront all writers and outlines the pitfalls that too often lead to unsatisfactory written results. The essay goes on to provide some very practical advice as to how you may approach various steps in the process of revision and suggests that your own intellectual interests should provide your best motivations for writing *and* rewriting.

David Bartholomae's essay, "Inventing the University," is a classic essay among writing teachers. Bartholomae gives even more detailed description of what students new to college are up against when they write papers for their different teachers and courses. His explanation of academic disciplines as "discourse communities" informs and inspires much of the approach we have brought to the previous chapters of this book, as we have tried to help you to understand how various types of writing in the disciplines reflect various modes of inquiry. Further, as you approach your own reassessment of your work, Bartholomae's essay should give you a glimpse into how writing teachers think and talk with one another about their students' efforts. We hope that insights gained from these essays and from your reflection upon your practical experience with methodical revision will provide a firm foundation for improvement of your writing in all your future course work.

Assignment B
Disciplinary Analysis and Evaluation of Electronic Information Sources provides an opportunity to apply your understanding of academic inquiry and your mastery of critical reading and thinking skills by comparing two Web sites as research sources on a critical issue. The assignment asks you to consider how various types of knowledge from the sciences, social sciences, and humanities are presented as information *and* as rhetorical appeals to educate and to move readers toward particular positions on complex social issues. In particular this assignment asks you to consider how specific features of emerging information technologies create new horizons and challenges for critical thinking in public policy debate.

Like Bartholomae's "Reinventing the University," "Web Literacy: Challenges and Opportunities for Research in a New Medium" by Sorapure, Inglesby, and Yatchisin was also written for writing teachers. We think this essay will show you how much and how quickly emerging communications media are changing the environment in which academic research writing takes place. We think it will also show you how you may have as much or more expertise in this new environment as many of your instructors. At any rate the practical advice this essay offers for teachers should also be an invaluable guide for you, as you work through your comparison of Web sources. We hope that your practical experience in assessing Web sources will benefit you in all of your academic research and beyond, as you use the Web to research personal hobby, health, or professional issues

Assignment C
The Critical Analysis of Contemporary Issues provides an opportunity to apply your understanding of academic inquiry to develop interdisciplinary approaches to study complex social issues. The assignment asks you to select a compelling issue for further study and investigation and then to consider how methods of inquiry from each of the three major disciplinary fields might contribute to our understanding and resolution of it. This assignment invites you to evaluate the appropriateness of a wide range of research resources in addressing and informing particular public policy debates.

We have included three essays among the readings for this chapter which address public policy debates about human factors in global atmospheric and climate change—just one of the possible issues among many you might explore for this assignment. The range of opinions and the types of factual support developed in "The Greenhouse Effect" by Helen Caldicott, "Greenhouse Earth" by Dixie Lee Ray and Ray Guzzo, and "Gaia and Global Warming" by Isaac Azimov and Frederick Pohl should help you to see how information from the scientific domain alone may not be enough to resolve complex social issues. Whether or not you focus your paper on issues of global warming, these essays should alert you to the ways "pure" science may be used for various rhetorical purposes and suggest how social science and humanities perspectives must also be integrated into your critical thinking.

Whichever assignment option you and your instructor select for your work in this unit, we hope you will consider how the short descriptions of them in this introduction suggest an even wider range of possible applications for the critical reading, thinking, and writing skills developed throughout this textbook. More importantly, we hope you will consider how the applications here illustrate how crucial it is for thinkers, writers, and citizens to understand how the production and communication of knowledge from various fields of inquiry contribute and compete in complicated ways to define and to address issues and problems that face us all. Finally we hope that through the work you have done here you will feel better informed, equipped, and inspired to enter into the ongoing investigations and debates surrounding these issues and problems. We hope you will have found the skills, confidence, and courage to explore even more productive methods of inquiry and communication that may one day lead us to the knowledge required for their solutions.

FORMAL APPLICATIONS OF INQUIRY

The following assignment options provide three types of applications of the critical thinking skills described above; we hope they will suggest many others, both in other courses in the university and beyond.

The Methodical Paper Revision and Commentary

In this assignment, your methodical revision and rewrite of a paper written for and graded in another general education course provides an opportunity for inquiry into the processes of academic writing. Your "research" will begin by identifying areas for revision through analyses and assessments of the original assignment and your initial approach to it, the paper you initially produced, your instructor's response, and your overall impression of the work and the knowledge you produced. You will then apply your knowledge of disciplinary argument and develop more effective strategies to communicate your knowledge of a subject more fully. Your rewritten paper will then provide the "data" from which you will draw your "findings" as insights into processes of academic writing.

In your self-reflective commentary, you will introduce the aims of your revision project, outline the methods used for analyzing and rewriting your original paper, and describe the changes and improvements made in your revision. To finish your report of your research into academic writing processes, you will discuss the implications of revision methods used and of changes and improvements accomplished by your revision in terms of the aims and goals you had set out for rewriting the paper. In your conclusion you may suggest ways you might apply analytical skills and revision methods used to rewrite this particular paper—and the insights you have gained from reflecting upon the process of rewriting it—to assignments you will encounter, to research you will pursue, and to papers you will produce in your further academic course work across the disciplines.

When you submit your portfolio for this methodical revision project, your evaluation and reflective commentary will count most heavily. Your preliminary analyses of the original work and the revision you produce will provide the background data and illustrative support for claims you make in your commentary.

The following procedure will guide you through the rewriting process, development of your reflective commentary, and preparation of your portfolio for submission in more detail.

Selecting a Paper for Methodical Revision

Review the papers you have written in your various classes and consider your instructors' responses to them. With your writing instructor's approval and guidance, you may confine your review of previously written and graded work in your writing class. To select a paper for methodical revision, you will want to consider several key criteria:

- Your understanding of the assignment
- The grade you received on the paper
- The nature of your instructor's comments upon the paper
- Your own sense of your relative success or frustration in producing and communicating knowledge in the paper
- Your continuing interest and curiosity in the subject matter and inquiry of the paper
- The writing and revision skills you hope to strengthen in rewriting the paper

Though you may very well select a paper upon which you received a less than satisfying grade for this project, the criteria above should certainly suggest that an effort to "raise a grade" need not—and probably should not—be your primary motivation. Besides, the grade you earned on the initial writing of the assignment is already recorded history.

Your purpose in this assignment is to demonstrate mastery of critical writing and revision skills gained in this course combined with an opportunity to revisit an interesting subject you have already researched. As Inge Bell says, "Rewriting is perhaps the best way of increasing writing skills"(130). You might well think of this project as a sort of *final exam* for your writing course where you bring everything together to show you and your instructor what you have learned. A paper that initially earned a high grade and seemed perfectly satisfactory to you and to your instructor at the time may provide very good material for this project if you can see how skills developed through your work in this course could produce even better work *and* you still have sincere investment in the topic.

Preliminary Analyses

Before you actually begin to edit and to plan your revision of the selected paper, complete the following preliminary analyses:

Assignment Analysis

Review the specific instructions you received for the assignment. Circle key verbs in the assignment instructions that define specific things you *should have done* in researching and writing the paper. Underline phrases that define criteria your paper should have met. Now write an extended description of the assignment in your own words. Feel free to integrate knowledge relevant to the assignment that you may have gained through further course work, through your study of academic inquiry and writing in this course, or from further reflections upon the aims, methods, and objects of study in the discipline for which the paper was written. If you no longer have the original assignment, or if there never was a detailed written version, write your own description of it from what you remember and/or from the way it was presented in lecture.

Your developed description of the original assignment should identify criteria and requirements at the global, local, and surface levels of the text and explain how these requirements and criteria represent the disciplinary perspectives of that course—its objects of study, research topics, theoretical concepts, research methods, and presentation, formatting, syntax, and diction for communication in that field of study.

Evaluation Analysis

Review all the responses you received on the paper from your instructor, including overall comments, marginal notes, text-editing, and the grade. Perhaps your instructor read closely and commented generously, giving you plenty to work with as an editor or engaged colleague might. Perhaps the only response was a grade and a general note like "*very good*" or "*try harder,*" and you are left on your own to figure out what worked or what went wrong. In either case you can return to the initial assignment as a guide for writing your own evaluation of your instructor's evaluation of you. How do your instructor's evaluations of your work compare or contrast with your own assessments of it? You might even use this opportunity to make some evaluatory comments upon the initial assignment itself because this should have articulated the criteria upon which your work would be assessed.

Developing the Revision Plan

Begin to develop a directed plan for your revision by reviewing your assignment and evaluations analyses and then write a short statement of your motivations and objectives for rewriting this particular paper. Use this opportunity to explain your selection of this particular paper for this project and to discuss how your revisions and rewriting could result in new critical insight into the topic *and* in stronger written communication of your inquiry and conclusions.

Next follow the procedures introduced in the previous chapters to produce an abstract and topical outline of the original version of your paper. Your abstract and outline should provide a basis for planning revisions at the global level that use your understanding of inquiry in the field to rethink organizational structures governing the logical progression of your ideas. Use the abstract and outline of the original paper to produce a topical outline to follow as you rewrite.

Now you are ready to go through your paper carefully to mark particular passages for local and surface level revisions. Highlight each phrase, line, or block of text to be revised and give each highlighted passage a sequential number in the margin. Use copyediting marks to make revisions or make notes in the margins that will guide your revisions as you rewrite.

Finally write a short description of your revision plan which specifies how particular changes you will make at surface, local, and global levels of the text will accomplish the objectives you set out in your statement of purpose above.

Preparing the Rewrite for the Portfolio

After you have revised the paper following the revised outline, editing markings, and revision plan described above, complete the following steps to prepare to write your reflective commentary and to present your revisions in your portfolio:

a. Highlight revised passages in your rewrite and give each highlighted passage a number in the margin that keys to the corresponding highlighted and numbered passage in the original.

b. Inventory and describe your revisions in a list keyed by number to highlighted passages in your original and rewrite. Here you will want to emphasize specific revision skills you have demonstrated at surface, local, and global levels. Consider the following list for some suggestions:

Global

- Addressing the assignment more fully
- Strengthening of governing thesis statement
- Reorganizing material and paragraphs to strengthen the logical progression of your argument
- Providing clear transitions between paragraphs which also track development of the governing thesis through a logical progression of your argument

Local

- Improving paragraph structure by clarifying focus of topic sentence and unity of development
- Revising your claims to more closely match your evidence

- Providing more or more appropriate evidence for your claims
- Fully integrating and interpreting quotations

  ### Surface

- Focusing sentences
- Improving sentence structure: modification, embedding, subordination, and so on
- Editing to remove words that do no work
- Revising for active voice
- Checking for precise diction: its/it's, affect/effect, and so on
- Correcting punctuation, spelling, usage, and so on as needed
- Checking and editing citations

  c. Write an abstract for your rewritten paper.

Writing the Analytical Commentary

Consider the original and revised papers and abstracts you have produced through the preceding procedure as results generated in an inquiry into rewriting processes. How can you interpret these results? What hypotheses or claims do they support? Rework the material you developed in your preliminary writing for this project to tell the story of your revision process. Describe your motives and objectives. Outline your methods, the challenges you encountered, and your techniques for meeting them. You should make direct reference to corresponding highlighted passages in your original and in your rewrite to support very specific revision claims. Evaluate and discuss your rewrite both as an exploration of the paper's topical subject *and* as a demonstration of critical thinking and revising skills developed in this writing course. Finally conclude your commentary by considering how you may further apply insights into inquiry and writing processes you have gained in this project in your future course work and academic writing.

    Organize all the materials collated and generated in the preceding procedures in a portfolio in more or less reverse chronological order, so that your commentary appears first.

Disciplinary Analysis and Evaluation of Electronic Information Sources

Electronic communication media such as the Internet and the World Wide Web have created virtual explosions in the volume and availability of information related to almost any topic or issue. Though these dramatic increases in the quantity and ease of access to information have opened and greatly facilitated many types of research and inquiry, they also present new challenges to scholars and academic researchers who must rely upon the quality of information—its creditability, currency, and relevance—in their production of knowledge. In addition to knowing how they might apply new information to their research, scholars must be able to think critically about how information located on-line has been produced and communicated in order to assess its quality and worth as a reliable source of data and as evidence upon which they may build further questions and claims. They must ultimately consider how much a particular information source will contribute to—or detract from—the worth and creditability of their own scholarship.

The article included in the readings for this critical applications unit, "Web Literacy: Challenges and Opportunities for Research in a New Medium," was written for writing teachers to help their students develop the technological literacy required for critical evaluation of electronic information sources. We think you will find it provides both understanding and practical techniques for meeting challenges of the Internet: finding, selecting, and evaluating sources and information. Developing such skills should help you maximize opportunities presented by emerging electronic media. We also think you will find it interesting and useful to listen to the way instructors and scholars revise their approaches for evaluating sources as new technologies develop.

The authors of "Web Literacy" point out that many conventional strategies and criteria for evaluating library materials and other print sources can be transferred productively to electronic media. Nonetheless they also identify two key aspects of most Web sites not typically encountered in library research that further complicate the evaluation of on-line information sources for students.

The first challenge, they explain, is that "While library materials are organized and 'filtered' (by publishing houses, peer reviewers, faculty and librarians), the Web presents mostly 'unfiltered' material in an uncontextualized manner" (Sorapure, et al., 2). One of the most exciting and democratic features of the Web as an information source, the fact that anyone can post anything they wish, also makes it increasingly difficult to know who to trust or what to believe—especially when their presentations may easily seem professional and technologically sophisticated.

Presentational aspects of the Web lead to the second critical challenge addressed in "Web Literacy":

> The second challenge for student researchers, then, is to determine the effects of the medium on the message. For instance what information do images and graphic design convey? How does the associative logic of a hypertextual Web site affect its content? How does interactivity affect the site's credibility and the audience's response? (Sorapure, et al., 2)

The authors of "Web Literacy" suggest that as you develop vocabulary to discuss technological and presentational features more particular to electronic information sources, you may begin to draw analogies and parallels to print documents as you gain practical experience with skills of rhetorical analysis. They suggest that the critical insights you develop by learning to evaluate Web sites will also allow you "to [view] library sources with a keener eye and a wider range of questions to ask" (Sorapure et al., 2). In many ways, working with Web sites places you in a position much more like that of any scholar working with primary materials, and your mastery of the challenges encountered here will highlight and contribute greatly to your development of many of "the fundamental critical and intellectual skills necessary for good research writing" (Sorapure, et al., 12). We suggest you read "Web Literacy" closely and discuss the issues and suggestions it raises with your classmates before you begin the procedures for the assignment outlined below. You may even wish to integrate quotations from the article to address new concepts, as we have done here, as you write your final evaluations of the Web sites you assess.

Select Two Web Sites for Evaluation

To direct your attention toward assessment of the way information on an issue is presented—rather than toward a debate or resolution of the issue itself—this assignment asks you to compare and to contrast two Web sites addressing a single controversial topic. One effective way to focus a controversial topic is to raise a policy question, a question that involves making decisions about specific actions society should take to resolve an issue. Interesting policy questions frequently involve evidence and arguments from across the disciplines. For instance the following policy questions, if debated fully, should all invoke interdisciplinary consideration of scientific or technical data, social behavior, and cultural values and meaning:

- Should the United States limit carbon emissions from automobiles in order to slow global warming?
- Should developments in biotechnology be regulated by current patent law?
- Under what conditions should abortion be permitted or prohibited?
- When does an individual have the right to refuse medical life support?
- Should private property owners be subjected to constraints of the Endangered Species Act on their own lands?
- Should all gun owners be required to register their weapons?

Information and opinions addressing all of the issues listed above, and many more like them, may be easily located on several Web sites.

When you have chosen your issue, locate several relevant sites and then select two that represent very opposite positions on, or at least very different approaches to, the issue in question. Before you proceed to the next step of the assignment, complete the following short preliminary writings:

- A statement explaining your reasons for choosing your particular topic
- A description of your Web search and your criteria for selecting the two particular sites you have chosen for evaluation
- A trimodal description of each of the Web sites

Evaluating Web Sites—Disciplinary Analysis

As you evaluate the appropriateness of particular Web sites as information sources for academic inquiry, one critical consideration will be to assess types of disciplinary knowledge they contain and disciplinary conventions used to communicate that knowledge. As we suggested above, critical policy questions usually invoke knowledge produced by several disciplines. To what extents do each of your selected Web sites draw information, use conventions of communication, or make rhetorical appeals drawn from the sciences, social sciences, and humanities? Consider the example of the global warming debate discussed below.

The issue of global warming involves highly technical geochemical atmospheric science. Do either or both sites selected contain quantitative scientific data? Do they describe the methods used to obtain the data? Do they contain charts, graphs, or diagrams? A global warming site that built arguments about regulating automobile production solely upon concepts of rights or economic necessity would certainly commit critical oversights. A site that used text alone to convey scientific data would miss critical opportunities for effective communication. On the other hand, a site presenting scientific data in graphic form alone would probably lack sufficient interpretation to productively address the policy question at hand.

Despite the obvious scientific dimensions of the global warming debate, scientific facts describing global atmospheric changes—whether they establish automobile emissions as significant factors—still cannot answer the policy questions of what to do about the problem without consideration of national and global economic, political, and cultural dynamics of power, responsibility, and value. Furthermore these dynamics cannot be addressed without some incorporation of social theory, rhetorical premises, and figurative language such as analogy and metaphor. What claims do the texts of your sites make or assume about human nature and behavior as they build the logic of their arguments? What allegiances and values do they appeal to—personal freedom, national sov-

ereignty, international brotherhood? What images or symbols do they invoke—
God, the flag, Spaceship Earth, Mother Earth, progress, apocalypse?

Of course different sites addressing the same topic will have different purposes. No single site should be expected to necessarily provide a fair balance of
disciplinary approaches to the issue any more than a reasonable researcher
should expect to find all the information necessary to reach a resolution on an
issue from a single source. Sites addressing the topic of global warming sponsored by the Environmental Protection Agency, an association of automobile
manufacturers, the International Panel on Climate Change, and a group of
"Global Warming Skeptics" will all have very different motives, agendas, bud-
gets, and responsibilities to meet with the information they present. The point of
your disciplinary analyses of their sites should be first to use critical thinking
skills and the understanding of the processes of academic inquiry and communication you have developed to identify perspectives, and to assess its uses or
abuses of disciplinary knowledge to advance its purposes. Your next step is to assess the legitimate contributions a site makes to the debate and to identify its
distractions from—and distortions of—productive policy issue considerations.
Finally your function as a scholarly researcher is to suggest how the information
presented and the purposes advanced by different sites may be drawn together,
or synthesized, to provide useful insights in addressing complex policy questions.

Evaluating Web Sites—Rhetorical Analysis

Rhetorical analysis seeks to evaluate the way something is communicated, the
strategies and methods used to present information or to advance an argument.
Its focus, like yours in this project, is primarily upon the medium rather than
upon the message. Many of the elements of rhetorical analysis of texts described below will be embedded in the type of disciplinary analysis outlined
above. Further, as explained in the article "Web Literacies," your rhetorical
analysis will necessarily extend beyond consideration of your Web sites' text to
assessment of the influences presentational and technological features have
upon readers, as well. The following discussion of elements of rhetorical analysis is intended as an introduction to applications of the study of rhetoric and is
far from a comprehensive coverage of the subject. We think you will find, however, that critical thinking skills of rhetorical analysis outlined here simply make
systematic the "common sense" kind of skepticism you might bring to your consideration of any information or communication intended to influence you in an
important choice decision.

Remember that your task here is to go beyond describing the influences
of a text; your analysis is aimed at assessing *how* the text exerts its influences. As
you identify and describe the dynamics of each of the following five elements of

rhetorical analysis in both of your selected Web sites, remember to give careful attention to the specific features of the text below, as well as specific words, phrases, or images that generate particular effects.

Rhetorical Context

The "rhetorical context" of a communication is characterized by the occasion and circumstances in which it occurs. It is the *forum* for the communication, and it has critical implications for the relationships of knowledge, power, and influence between communicators and their audiences. Write brief responses to the following questions as you consider this element of rhetorical analysis in the texts of your selected Web sites:

- What are the relationships between the speaker, listeners, and the topic of discussion?
- Who is the speaker? How does the speaker establish identity, authority, and credibility?
- Who is the intended audience? How does the text identify and target a particular interest group for its message?
- Do the speaker and listeners share equal access/authority in relation to the topic of discussion? If not, what are the details and implications of the inequalities?
- How does the speaker create an in-group among listeners? How does the speaker create out-groups? Do the in-groups and out-groups created by the speaker accurately reflect the audience's interests in the topic?

Logic

The logic of an argument is the connection it builds from evidence to conclusions, the way it interprets data, the way it builds claims from demonstrated fact or from previously established claims. After you write brief responses to the following questions for each of your selected Web sites, see if you can diagram their logical connections as flowcharts:

- How does the speaker define the problem?
- What is the speaker's thesis?
- How appropriate are the kinds of data or evidence introduced to the inquiry or argument developed?
- What types of reasoning does the speaker use to draw conclusions from the evidence?

Premises/Assumptions

Not all steps in a chain of logic are necessarily stated explicitly. Some statements may be presented as self-evident, and some claims may be built from unstated assumptions rather than demonstrated fact or presented evidence. Such missing steps are called premises. Gaps you may have encountered as you attempted to draw flowcharts of your texts' logical connections in the preceding step may help you identify problematic premises. If you can, articulate the unstated assumptions of your texts and write brief responses to the following questions:

- How might the logic of the argument be strengthened or weakened by fuller articulation of its premises?
- Are there legitimate reasons for various audiences to reject the argument's premises?
- How does acceptance or rejection of the text's premises depend upon various aspects of an audience's relations to power, gender, race, history, nature, and so on?

Figurative Language

Figurative language—similes, metaphors, and analogies—works by drawing comparisons. We expect to find figurative language in poetry and usually think that more scientific and technical discourse will rely on direct and objective description. Even the most technical aspects of scientific discourse, however, often contain figurative comparisons. The term "greenhouse effect" found in discussions of global warming, for instance, compares the difficult-to-visualize trapping of solar radiation by the earth's protective atmosphere with the more familiar features of a type of shelter most of us have seen. Even graphics make implicit comparisons. A piechart, for instance, presents portions of a body of statistical data as "slices" of different proportions. Consider even the subtlest comparisons drawn in your selected Web sites as you write brief responses to the following questions:

- What are the strengths and weaknesses of metaphors and analogies used by the speaker?
- Do the speaker's metaphors involve unexamined premises or unstated assumptions?
- How do the speaker's choices of metaphors and analogies make strategic appeals or reveal particular motives or anxieties?

Appeals

Rhetorical appeals suggest the reasons and motives—both rational and extra-rational—for an audience's acceptance of an argument. They are the ultimate grounds upon which an argument builds its influence. At some level appeals generally boil down to a type of interest. What does the audience seek? What does the audience wish to avoid? Why? Educated audiences and critical thinkers like to believe that their responses to arguments rest solely upon logic and rea-son, but effective communicators know that even rational thought is driven by some kind of desire and that emotions are often stronger influences and moti-vators than pure reason. What aspects of human character do the texts of your selected Web sites appeal to?

- Reason?
- Fear (of loss, pain, death, alienation, or the "unknown")?
- Self-interest (preservation, kin, money, power, sex)?
- Enlightened self-interest (community, country, planet)?
- Justice
- Indulgent irrationality (revenge, hatred, pride, self-destruction)?

As you identify the appeals made by your texts, write a brief assessment of their relevance to the policy issue at hand and evaluate their likelihood of contribut-ing to sound policy decisions.

Evaluating Web Sites—Presentational Analysis

Finally, having developed disciplinary and rhetorical analyses of your selected Web sites, evaluate the influences of their extratextual elements upon audi-ences. How do their authorship, visual design, their technological sophistica-tion, their associations through links to other sites affect their credibility, message, and influences on audiences? How do they establish—or do they ob-scure—the creditability of their authorship? In this analysis, though you are considering a new medium, you may use interpretive skills like those developed in the humanities unit of this text. Though features presented in electronic in-formation sources are in many ways unlike those encountered in more conven-tional library research, the authors of "Web Literacy" will help you to draw some productive analogies to both library resources and to other more familiar print and communication media. We believe interpretive skills exercised here may build upon and further strengthen the kinds of visual, technological, and cultural literacies you must master in order to think critically about the deluge of informational, commercial, and political messages encountered every day from a wide range of media.

Writing the Disciplinary Analysis and Evaluation of Electronic Information Sources

As you prepare to write, you may consider this project as a kind of final exami-nation for your writing course, an opportunity to demonstrate mastery of the many skills developed through the preceding units. As we have suggested above, much of your Web site analysis can build upon your exploration of processes of inquiry and communication in the primary disciplinary areas. As you bring together the preliminary writings generated through the preceding steps, remember the formats and organizational strategies suggested for developing comparisons and contrasts in the humanities unit. Use the suggestions made there as well to develop the logical progression of your essay with clear transitions and well-integrated quotations. Use the suggestions for revision to rethink and rewrite your drafts.

Finally remember that this project, like your previous assignments in this course, emphasizes inquiry. Though you began with a particular policy issue question, you are not ultimately trying to answer a question such as What should we do about global warming? Nor are you necessarily trying to answer a more limited question such as Which of these two Web sites gives us a better answer to the question of global warming? Instead you are demonstrating the critical thinking skills of an academic researcher evaluating sources that can further our understanding of an issue. Your final paper should address practical questions such as the following: What kinds of knowledge do these sources supply? How accurate, reliable, and relevant are they to the question at hand? Do they present information clearly or distort it in order to guide or manipulate our thinking about the question?

Basically you might imagine this assignment as an imaginary phase of a much larger research project you, or others, might someday undertake. Basically you are examining source materials and asking whether or not, and if so *how*, you should use them to draw and present your own conclusions on the topic. From this evaluation you may also wish to draw some larger conclusions relevant to processes of academic inquiry and communication. How, you might ask, using your comparative analysis of two selected Web sites as a case study, can students and scholars learn to better navigate and evaluate the seemingly overwhelming amounts of information made available by emerging technologies and media as they attempt to further the production of useful knowledge?

Interdisciplinary Analysis of Contemporary Issues

The evening news, television talk shows, and weekly news magazines provide a panorama of political, social, scientific, and artistic issues for public discussion. Sometimes a single event—the Columbine High School shootings, the Clinton impeachment hearings, the Los Angeles riots, the O.J. Simpson trial—monopolizes public attention for a long period of time because it is felt to be a social crisis. Other issues—abortion, violence on TV, pornography, racism, drug abuse—are perennial issues. Advances in technology present us daily with still another group of issues—cloning, priority for organ donation, euthanasia, privacy of records, Internet access for minors—to name just a few. Finally each of us sees as problematic features of contemporary life that others see as positive—loud music, divorce, working mothers, violent sports, graffiti, body piercing—and more. In short many see concrete events in our daily life or the life of our communities as symptoms of social, moral, or scientific problems; others see no cause for worry. We have chosen global warming, an issue of the last sort, as a model for this assignment; you may be asked to pursue this topic or to choose one of your own.

We caution against choosing one about which you already have strong feelings or convictions; remember this is a course in inquiry—in pursuing answers to the unknown. If you already "know" the answer, you will find opening yourself to inquiry difficult and will be very inclined to search for support rather than insight. As you recall we discussed in the Introduction and in our discussion of Bacon the human tendency to distort evidence in support of our existing beliefs. You will be better off choosing an issue that bewilders you or about which you have conflicting feelings or opinions. On such issues inquiry can be productive and rewarding. We also caution against choosing issues that are too broad, such as the disintegration of morals, the failure of education, and so forth. If you phrase the problem in that way, you have already made a judgment about what is going on based on existing convictions about what morals and education should produce; you are already interpreting the meaning of specific events from that belief system. Again you will find it very difficult, if not impossible, to put those convictions aside. Instead choose a specific event that is symptomatic, in your eyes, of larger social ills—a Supreme Court decision, statistics on divorce, the burning of synagogues—so that you have concrete, observable phenomena or trends to study.

Conducting Inquiry

Once you have chosen your event, begin your inquiry with the three guiding questions we have used throughout. If possible answer all three from the point of view of a scientist, social scientist, and humanist. Describe your chosen object of study using the trimodal system below; do so first as a scientist, then as a social scientist, and finally as a humanist. You may find that your object of study does not lie within the realm of study for one or another of the disciplines or that you need to take the perspective of specific subdisciplines to write the descriptions. Such discoveries are simply part of defining the issue and are legitimate differences.

Static View. What Is It?

Describe the event objectively from the point of view of at least one field within each disciplinary group, looking for the characteristics that discipline would focus on. As in the science unit, isolate the object from all surrounding elements and avoid inference and judgment insofar as possible.

Questions
- What would a scientist find of interest in this event or trend?
- How would a scientist in the field chosen define and classify the object of study?
- Would the researcher see the object as a part of a larger topic of study?
- If so, what topic or question?

> **Example:** Object: News article on possible effects of the thinning ozone layer.
> Science: Physics/Geology. Gaia hypothesis; geo-engineering technology.
> Social Science: *Economics, Law:* Responsibility of company for damage to ozone layer. *Political Science:* Interest group politics and public policy.
> Humanities: Ethics/Philosophy. Free enterprise versus responsibility to atmosphere.

Dynamic View. How Does It Change, Develop, or Vary over Time?

Describe observable evidence of change, life cycle stage, or variations between similar events, again from the point of view of at least one member of each disciplinary group. Again you will look for and describe the characteristics that discipline would look for. Mark your necessary inferences for further study.

Questions
- Why have you chosen those specific characteristics as evidence of change or development?
- What further study would be necessary to confirm your inferences?

> **Example:** Object: News article on possible effects of the thinning ozone layer.
> Science: Measured change in ozone layer over time—conflicting accounts.
> Social Science: *Political Science:* Change in political power of various interest groups over time.
> Humanities: *Cultural Studies:* Impact of science on ethics or cultural belief.

Systemic View. How Does It Function as a System and in Systems?

Describe the object's observed interaction with its environment, as a functioning part of systems appropriate for study in at least one member of each disciplinary group.

Questions
- Is the object a system in its own right?
- What kind(s)?

- Is the object part of more than one system?
- Which systems seem most important or relevant?
- How does the object's current behavior affect the most relevant system(s)?

> **Example:** Object: News article on possible effects of the thinning ozone layer.
> Science: *Atmospheric Science*. System 1: Interaction of earth and atmosphere. System 2: interaction of human emissions and atmosphere.
> Social Science: *Political Science*. System 1: Interaction of economics and politics. System 2: Interaction of science and politics. *Communication/Mass Media*. System 1: Media and public belief. System 2: Interaction of science and public belief. *Economics*. System 1: Influence of government policy on production. System 2: Interaction of science and economics.
> Humanities. *Ethics*. Responsibility versus liability. *Cultural Studies*. Science's impact on cultural belief.

Compare your descriptions with your classmates' in order to clarify the issues further for yourself and provide ideas for others. You will undoubtedly find some issues and perspectives more interesting and important than others, and that evaluation will help focus your research for the paper assignments below.

Critical Analysis Essay

Option a

See if you can find at least one academic article on your topic from each of the perspectives you have identified above. Compare their arguments with the potential contributions you have outlined and with each other, answering the following questions:

- In what ways does the article's perspective match the perspective you had predicted? How does the perspective differ?
- What new issues does the article raise?
- Does the article change or confirm your view of the potential contribution of that field to the resolution of the problem?
- How does the knowledge from different perspectives differ?
- Are all of the perspectives found equally important or necessary?

Write a critical analysis and evaluation of the academic work done so far (as evidenced in your articles) by the fields you have identified. You will need to discuss the way they identify the issues as well as the knowledge they contribute, and reach your own evaluation by comparing that knowledge to your own hypothesis about their contributions. If you were unable to find an article from a specific perspective, that too becomes a topic for discussion (for example, what might—or ought—the field contribute if it undertook to study it?).

Option b
Write an analysis of the rhetoric and arguments of two to three articles or media features produced for the general public. These may be from books, magazines, or newspaper feature sections, but should be long enough to contain substantial arguments—not simply news reports. The readings on global warming in the next chapter illustrate the kind of articles you need. Use the questions below to aid in your evaluation:

- What role does each of the disciplines you identified play in the argument?
- Judging from your own preliminary work, is the role each plays in the article adequate? Appropriate?
- Are perspectives you feel important omitted?
- Do the different articles define the problem in the same way?
- What perspective is implied by the way they define the problem and solution?
- Are the arguments logical and appropriate?
- Do they present sufficient evidence for their claims, and is the evidence appropriate to the discipline?

When you have finished the analysis above, you should be ready to draw some conclusions about both the importance of the problem and the work being done to resolve it. That conclusion will become your thesis. You may also want to include a judgment on the presentation of the problem to the public if you feel this is an issue—or a part of the problem.

Global Features

Purpose
To shed light on a current event in order to more clearly evaluate its importance and consequences to society, as well as the work being done to resolve it.

Audience
The general public. Essay to appear in *The Atlantic Monthly, Harper's, Scientific American* or some similar magazine that publishes lengthy analytical articles.

Form
- Introduction giving the issue and the articles under debate
- Thesis giving your evaluation of the importance of the problem and the work being done to resolve it
- Organization using your thesis as a road map to a logical ordering of your points

Local Features

Introduction
Should introduce the event to be studied, its significance for the world the readers live in, its complexity, and the importance of understanding it well.

Thesis
Option a. Your thesis should define the issue or event and evaluate the work of the various disciplines in its resolution.

> **Example:** Global warming, so far, has been treated largely as a scientific problem in the academy; its role in our political or ethical life has received far less attention.

Option b. Your thesis should evaluate the arguments of your articles on their effectiveness, and the soundness of their arguments from a multidisciplinary perspective.

> **Example:** Conflicting scientific evidence in public domain arguments about global warming reduces the credibility of such evidence, raising questions instead about the motives and interests of those employing it; Asimov's and Pohl's article alone seems to grasp both the science and human sides of the issue.

(Note: The assignments do not ask you to offer a resolution.)

Definition of Issue
Option a. The paper should define what sort of problem you think it is. You should describe the problem from multidisciplinary perspectives and make clear why you believe one or more to be the more important or significant than others.

> **Example topic sentence:** Science and politics certainly play critical roles in global warming, but the humanities hold the key to motivating human change.

Option b. You should outline the way the different articles define the issue and critique those definitions in light of your own assessment.

> **Example topic sentence:** Each author seems to define the problem from the point of view of his or her own interests in it.

Analysis of Arguments
Option a. For each article compare the focus, findings, and argument with your own expectations about the contribution of the field in question and its promise as a force for resolution. Critique the adequacy of the work in the different

fields (judging from your limited evidence, of course); discuss surprises, changes in your view, and omissions.

Option b: Analyze the logic and soundness of arguments presented in the articles from the appropriate disciplinary perspective (i.e., scientific claims should present scientific evidence, etc.). Critique the adequacy of the perspectives included, as well as the importance of those left out. Examine the adequacy, legitimacy, and appropriateness of the evidence presented.

Options a and b: As you write, review the principles of good writing below:

- Paragraph focus—take charge. Do not fall back into reporting the beliefs of others without making some statement of your own.
- Multiple voices—engage in dialogue with the authors and be sure they are identifiable.
- Utilize full paragraph development through evidence and/or quotations/paraphrases to support your claims.
- Logical flow is aided by transitions to establish and clarify the relationship between ideas.

Surface Features

Check your rough draft for all of the elements of "elegance" we have covered in this book:

- Word choice
- Clarity of sentence focus
- Efficiency—elimination of phrases and words that do no work
- Complexity—use of coordination, subordination, and modification to aid in focus, clarity, and precision
- Transitions that mark the logical flow
- Correct citation

MOVING ON

Throughout your work in this book, you may have noticed that the word "argument" has always been linked with inquiry. Often we think of argument only as convincing others, and we think of "rhetoric" as persuasion, often by any means necessary. Thus rhetoric has come to mean concealing facts and manipulating truth—to win debates rather than to resolve real issues. However, in this book, we have helped you develop *rhetorics of inquiry*, approaches to argument used by the disciplines in discovering and rediscovering "truths," or at least making credible claims. Such claims must be based upon openly shared and available evidence and be subject to critique and correction. They are not assertions of belief; they are problem-solving efforts and the products of ongoing curiosity. This is the kind of thinking we believe all citizens need to bring to their public and professional lives in the search for solutions to the complex situations we all face in the twenty-first century if we are to thrive. As you move on through and beyond your university education, we hope you will apply the rhetorical skills and attitudes of inquiry developed here to seek not just victories but resolutions.

eight

Readings for Critical Applications

INTRODUCTION

As indicated in the first chapter of this unit, the concepts and skills learned in this book can be applied in many ways: to papers written in other college courses, to current debates taking place in the public domain, to the world of media. The readings of this unit center on three possibilities only and relate to the three assignments given in Chapter 7. The student papers selected for revision workshop illustrate each of the three assignments: critical revision, Web site analysis, and disciplinary analysis of a public issue.

The Bell and Bartholomae articles are both drawn from books on what it means to be a college student and on what it takes to make that experience fruitful, advice we believe you can easily integrate with the discipline-specific skills and expectations addressed in this particular book. Sorapure et al. illustrate application of the skills and knowledge gained in university work to the Internet, and the three environmental articles are examples of public debate. We invite you to use those to practice your critical and analytical skills. We hope these will suffice to open the possibilities for other applications as you move on to other academic and professional tasks.

Everybody Hates to Write

Inge Bell

Biography: Inge Bell, a Professor of Sociology, draws on his years of experience in education at Pitzer College in the volume below. The book, which gives advice on the many pitfalls of college life and on how to use the experience productively, stems from Bell's academic concern with the larger issue of the different ways humans find to relate to society. His book Involvement in Society, *published in 1972, studies this issue.*

In this chapter, Bell reviews reasons people in general and students in particular hate to write and dash off only a single draft when forced to do so. He then argues for the importance of revision, beginning with instructor comments; he stresses revision for clarity (talking ideas out with someone), sound development of evidence, amplification of underdeveloped ideas. He ends with good advice for those confronted with oral reports and essay exams, as well. A very accessible essay that stresses students' own sense of satisfaction with their writing as the chief motivator for revision.

Nearly everybody I know, including professors, hates and fears the process of writing, and small wonder. Since we were in grammar school we have been forced to commit our precious thoughts onto paper where a red pencil might, at any moment, attack them. Where we were trying to develop intelligent ideas, we were regularly hassled about spelling and commas and semicolons;;; Our labors were usually returned to us crawling with corrections and a few well-chosen insulting remarks. When we did really well, however, we usually just got back a terse "good" and nothing more. When I first began teaching, I fell into the same thoughtless habit of giving more negative than positive feedback on papers. I had a feeling that if I gave a good grade, I didn't need to defend my position, whereas a low grade had to be accompanied by a lot of "explanation."

Then I had a very salutory experience. I taught a section of remedial writing. Here I discovered how utterly crushing and traumatizing our practices were, particularly for students who came to school speaking an ethnic or class-based dialect slightly different from the "King's English" (an interesting term, indicating the class snobbery involved in our notions of "proper" language). If you are Black, for instance, you probably grew up hearing a somewhat different language from academic English. Yours is a beautiful language full of imagery and rhyme and poetry. One has only to listen to the words of gospel music to see how vividly and with what wit Black poets illumined the King James version of the Bible. Yet more English teachers see it as their duty to expunge all traces of this native tongue in their Black students.

From *This Book Is Not Required.* Fort Bragg, CA: Small Press, 1985, 128–144.

What I discovered from my remedial writing students was that they so much hated writing that the old avoidance mechanism always set in. They resisted working on papers. When they did finally write them, they dashed them off quickly and never edited them. What did these students in was that they weren't properly enamored of their own creations—willing to read them to friends and relatives, to read them over and over, embellishing and correcting (and even looking up an occasional spelling) as they went. In our class we began to take one person's paper each week, editing it as a group. We made it a habit to give praise to every piece, as well as correction. We tried to show each person the strong points of her writing. From this experience I learned to give positive feedback. If I marked one paragraph "confusing," I would mark a better one "clearly written. Do you see the difference?" Gradually, the students warmed to the task until, by the end of the semester, I had at least induced most of them to exchange editing services with a friend. Somebody else can always see your errors more clearly than you can yourself. Reading your work out loud to yourself also helps you to catch clumsy phrasing.

In an interesting article on writing problems, Professor Howard Becker makes the essential point that time pressures in school force students to write only one draft. This runs counter to all good writing practices. Famous writers generally write many, many revisions of their original drafts. Not only do the drafts improve, but rewriting is perhaps the best way of increasing writing skills. Be advised, then, to knock out a first draft (it should not be perfect at this point) in time to revise, preferably with the help of a friend.

There are several common problems in student writing, and I want to say a word about a few of them. By remembering the kinds of comments you have received on your writing, you may be able to diagnose your own ills and take the advice that applies. Some students get lost in the earliest phase of the paper by beginning work before they thoroughly understand the professor's assignment. If the topic is unclear, you must talk to the professor. If you have a choice of topics, pick carefully to find a topic you like and which offers the chance to use material with which you are already familiar from personal experience or from other courses. If your subject matter is simply given as "Juvenile Delinquency in Urban Areas," try to develop a hypothesis or a theme. For example, your hypothesis might be that low income youngsters have higher rates of delinquency than higher income youths. Your title might then be "The Correlation Between Income and Juvenile Delinquency." Or, if you would rather use a theme, it might be "The Influence of Mass Media on Juvenile Violence." Developing a hypothesis or theme helps you to narrow down the topic and give direction to your research.

The most frequent and grade-losing problem with writing is lack of clarity. This is really not a writing problem, but results from a failure to think the issues you are writing about through to the point where they are clear to you.

Sometimes it may require you to ingest more information than you now have; sometimes you may need to discuss your confusion with a sympathetic friend. When I am in deep water, I may just drop the work for a few days, but if the going continues to be boggy when I return to it, I generally talk it out with someone. An outsider can frequently see the forest when you are lost in the trees.

Rewriting is also crucial here. First drafts generally contain some confusion, but the act of writing the confusion down is a major step in clarification. Often, you do not even know you are confused until you try to submit your thoughts to paper. What is most troubling to me is that many students don't seem to know when they are confused. I think this is because they have been confused so often at school that they have come to accept this mental state as natural. Because we teach people in batches of thirty to forty people with widely varying experience and ability, only the quickest and best prepared can insist on clarity, i.e., keep questioning the teacher until they really understand. Everybody else is going along pretending to understand until, finally, the line between understanding and confusion begins to blur and the student has lost the ability to practice self-correction. If this rings a bell with you, begin to make it a regular practice to insist on clarity in class. Keep asking questions until you understand. If you have to let something go, mark it clearly in the margin of your notes as "confusing." When you edit your writing, mark suspect sections in a similar way and then work them over with a friend or the professor, if you can corner her. In other words, either refuse to settle for confusion, or at least mark off your confusions where you can keep them from contaminating your whole thought process. Remember that something which is perfectly clear to you will come out clearly on paper. One of the reasons why writing is hard is that it is really thinking. Improving your writing is also a way of improving your thinking, which is why it is well worth laboring over.

A related, but slightly different, problem is the student who has fallen whole-hog for one of the many "secret languages" which are used in the academy. This is usually a student who doesn't think much of his own abilities and hopes to rescue himself by learning to write in the jargon of a discipline before the jargon is at all clear to him. These unfortunate folk are catching a disease which is so rampant in academia that many professors will even reward this type of behavior. I have discussed the function of the secret languages in an earlier section. Here I can only say, stay away from any jargon you don't feel completely at home with. Don't use long, complicated words and sentences where simpler ones will do. Good writing is simple writing. Academic writing is often lousy writing.

Another writing disease which is directly fostered in school is padding. Anyone who really knows literature will tell you that brevity is the very soul of poetry and prose. Yet we continue to demand certain quantities of writing ("Write a ten-page paper," etc.). Of course, this is an invitation to pad. I tell my students, "Write as if you were wording a telegram, as if each and every word, cost you money." When you edit your first draft, edit for brevity. If that results in too short a paper, according to your professor's lights, maybe you need to develop some additional ideas. If you just can't, take your chances with the shorter paper. Don't become a poor writer just to please your professors.

I want to tell you how not to write a lengthy term paper . . . from years of personal experience. I used to go at this type of assignment by proceeding to do all the research first. I would take voluminous notes just right: on an 8 by 5 card or half sheets of paper with the citation and subject at the top for easier sorting—one main item to a half sheet. This was fine, but I would invariably find myself nearing the end of the semester with a huge pile of unorganized notes, a loose collection of ideas, and a lot of anxiety about how the thing was ever going to come together. Before I could overcome my mounting fears and actually sit down to organize a paper, I would practice a ritual of self-torture. This took the form of a three- or four-day vigil in the college coffee shop where I would sit from morning till late afternoon consuming coffee and cigarettes while commiserating with my fellows in the same predicament until I was quite physically ill. Only then, when my discomfort became patent and physical, would I overcome my avoidance mechanism and sit down to the dreaded task. Such rituals of self-torture are, I discovered, quite common among students before they undertake a heavy assignment. You may have your own variation. Suddenly, we enlightened, twentieth-century folk find ourselves practicing a primitive rite to appease the angry academic gods. It is really hard for us to see that the ritual adds nothing whatsoever to our efforts. The only way I know to cure yourself of these rituals is just to dare it—just once—without the ritual. It's worth it, even if you chance a low grade. What will happen, of course, is that you will come out about as usual. It may take several such leaps of daring to overcome the ritual entirely. But it can be done. (It might be fun to do a study of such rituals, exploring the great variety of forms they take in different students.)

You can develop positive as well as negative rituals. In one of my writing courses, I had a student who told us that, before she sat down to write a paper, she always imagined herself to be a great expert on the subject under consideration. She imagined the many people who were waiting for enlightenment from her pen. In this way she jollied herself into a positive rather than a fearful frame of mind. She was, in fact, a very successful student, although she had to come from behind in terms of her earlier education. Perhaps you can develop your own variant of this fantasy. Imagining yourself to be a teacher may help. In fact, an interesting and subtle process sets in when one changes from the role of student to that of teacher. It is still the same process of mastering material, but now you are no longer the judged, but are among the judges. You feel very responsible to your class to give them a straight and clear rendition. But you are working from a position of power, and this adds wings to your typewriter.

Another type of positive ritual would be anything you can do to loosen up and relax your body and mind. Perhaps some exercise and meditation would work well for you. It may be easier to replace rituals of self-torture with positive rituals than just to give them up altogether. It is worth trying.

When doing library research for a paper, avoid the experience of going into the library cold. Most college and university libraries have huge collections in which you can easily lose your way. If at all possible, get some recommendations for sources from your professor. Sometimes you may have a topic on which your professor is not too knowledgeable. In that case, try to find another professor who knows the area. It is quite usual for students to ask for help from someone other than the professor teaching the course. Two sources of advice are always better than one. In some cases librarians will also be helpful.

If none of these methods has yielded a list of sources, you can sometimes use one or two current textbooks in the subject and begin by reading the relevant section and then following out the footnotes. With all these methods you are getting the benefit of advice from people who have already sifted through the mass of writing on the given subject, thus saving yourself hours of frustration.

I also learned some other ways of easing the burden of a research paper. One thing which I would strongly recommend to you is that you write little bits of your paper while you are in the research phase. Even if you don't yet know where or even whether the little section will eventually land, write it down as it occurs to you. By the time you finish your research and turn to your collection of little sections, you may find that you have your paper nearly half written. It is also the case that the process of writing forces you to clarify your ideas. You may discover, for example, that you are lacking a piece of information without which you cannot really make your point. Thus, your ongoing writing will add direction and precision to your research.

Finally, I would like to give you some advice about writing social science papers. (I cannot speak with authority in other areas.) Good social science writing has a lot in common with good fiction: It is the telling, concrete detail or example that makes a theory or generalization come to life. Never nurture, much less put down, a generalization which you don't understand well enough to translate into a specific case. Make it a mental practice to approach every theory with the question "How would this work in one individual's experience?" For example, voting studies show that husbands and wives who have opposite voting choices fail to vote more frequently than couples who agree. How would this actually look if you were peering into their living room? Perhaps you can imagine that, having just had some heated words with his spouse about the comparative venality of two candidates, Mr. A. decides, "This isn't worth quarreling about; the less said about it, the better." Henceforth, he avoids listening to the evening news and eventually conveniently forgets election day. Now you have the picture.

Or, let us say that you have just made the assertion that poor people have higher rates of mental illness than richer people. Here you want to throw in a few nice, startling statistics on rates of schizophrenia found in the latest study. There you have the illuminating fact. Now, can you see exactly why the poor might become ill more frequently and stay ill longer? You can see from your source material that the richer and better educated people are, the more likely they are to rush to a psychiatrist with the first symptoms, whereas poorer, less educated people might not know what was wrong or whom to go to until the symptoms became so severe that they come to the attention of some public agency like the schools or the police. Now, you can see the process in a little more detail.

Or, again, poor children who attend predominantly middle-class schools are likelier to go to college that similar poor children who go to schools where everybody is poor. Just what is the mechanism involved here? One is that the intellectually successful poor child may be excluded from his peer group which wishes to punish him for being more successful: "teacher's pet" might be the colloquial expression of this sentiment. Now, in a school where everybody is poor, the friendless child will usually respond to this exclusion by giving up the intellectual success in order to regain the acceptance of her peers. But in a more mixed school, she may begin to attach herself to a higher-class, higher-scoring peer group, take on their aspiration level, and make it to college. Once you can picture this youngster in the halls and at lunch time, you have understood the mechanism behind the generalization.

At times, a telling quotation or anecdote will illuminate the point. On this particular subject, I sometimes tell my students about a friend I had who had come from a very poor background to become a professor. When he was a young teenager and unusually studious for his group, his worried mother once placed a newspaper article on his bed which discussed the fact that homosexuals hang out in libraries. Wow! Now you really sense what it means to "break with the accepted working class role for males." If I were writing this up, I would make a direct quotation: Have my friend tell it in his own words. While you never want to let a paper become a collection of quotes, you do want to collect some nice, juicy ones as you research your subject, like ripe, plump raisins you can put in the final pudding. Don't hesitate to use examples from your own experience. Only a very pedantic professor will fail to appreciate this. Thus, your exposition in social science should always be brightened and sharpened with the concrete example (or even the hypothetical example), the nice, crisp fact and the telling quotation. If you have trouble doing this for a particular generalization, then you don't yet understand it.

If your college offers writing courses, it will be worth your time to see whether they have a good reputation and take one early in your college career. In most non-scientific fields writing is crucial to successful work. Writing courses are definitely not just for the weak student. If the course is at all well taught, even the A-student can learn a great deal from it.°

THE ORAL REPORT AS A CHINESE OPERA

Almost everybody hates to give an oral report. I believe this is because students fear each other's opinions even more than they fear the teacher's. You do not want to make an ass of yourself in front of your peers. In fact, many students never speak up in class for the same reason. It may help you a bit if you realize that everybody in the class probably shares your fears. Occasionally, I ask students to jot down on a piece of paper what people will think of them if they take part in the class discussion. Everybody fears disapproval from their fellows. Perhaps the most damning thing about education by coercion is the way it sets you against your peers. When we were younger and less socialized, we used to all gang up on the teacher—remember? But as some of us began to see that we could rise in the system by pleasing teachers, we also had to cut ourselves off from the body of our peers and begin competing with them instead. This is a fundamental betrayal which our fiercely competitive society exacts from each of us: We must break faith, must sell out our friends. From the day this process begins, fear of retribution grows in us. I used to try dealing with this by kidding around a little bit in class about oral reports and by letting everybody give immediate pro and con feedback on a report. This helped, but unfortunately most professors will not go this far. What they want from you is a coolly executed, highly "professional" performance.

It will help you to see the oral report for what it really is: as highly stylized a performance as a Chinese Opera. It doesn't follow the usual rules of daily communication, and your ability to execute it properly may have very little to do with your ability in ordinary conversation. A judgment on your report is in no way a judgment on your personality and mind.

A small positive ritual is recommended here. Before you start, you need to spend about ten minutes slowing down your physical and mental processes and lowering your tension level. This will help in every way but is particularly good for that most common of mistakes: overly fast presentation. If you are inclined to be very nervous, the best thing you can do is just to sit quietly with your eyes closed and get in complete touch with the physical sensations of nervousness. This is not at all a pleasant process, but you may be surprised at what can develop from it. If your anxieties are rather vague, you may wish to do some slow, deep breathing and some good physical stretching. Again, as you are about to begin your report in the classroom, allow yourself thirty seconds of quiet to col-

---

°For an unusual, creative way to enhance your writing skills, see Gabriele Lussor Rico, *Writing the Natural Way.*

lect your scattered self before you begin. Perhaps you can imagine yourself to be a famous professor, about to give the word to a collection of grateful, alert students. (Pure fantasy, under any circumstances.)

Never read an oral report verbatim. You will lose your audience instantly. Rather, prepare a fairly detailed outline. I find that, for a fifty-minute lecture, I need anywhere from four to ten pages of detailed outline. The outline has a "cue" phrase for each major idea; it is marked off so that I can see at a glance whether I am in Part I or Part III. If I plan to use quotes, I type them out verbatim. Nothing creates more anxiety than having to shuffle around in a huge sheaf of papers and books looking for a quotation or a statistic, while your listeners are waiting for you to continue.

A very effective way to break up the pace of your report and make a good impression all around is to have some material mimeographed to hand out. Sometimes an outline of your report may be in order; though more usually a set of statistics or some graphs or diagrams or maps may be better. Occasionally a dull subject may be made more lively by bringing in some illustrations. If you are working on some aspect of parent-child relations, for instance, it may be interesting to bring in some examples of the way these relationships are treated in advertising: "Have your mommy buy you a box of Super Sugar Chips." Rare is the professor who doesn't appreciate these signs of extra effort.

Always practice your report once or twice, timing yourself in the process. Students almost universally over-estimate what can be said in a given space of time. Nothing is so exasperating as having two students scheduled for a given date and having the first one take up three-quarters of the allotted time. This situation can be easily avoided, and you will have the added boon of discovering that you don't need as much material as you thought.

Now, let us assume that you have prepared your outline well, handed round your mimeoed material, and gone through your preparatory ritual. You have given yourself a few seconds to become centered and are about to begin. Here, precisely, is where most people blow half a grade. They begin with a little self-deprecating giggle, pull at their hair and say, "Well . . . I don't really know too much about this, but . . ."

That is not the way this particular Chinese Opera is played. You don't have to apologize or appease anybody. Instead, you look for a moment at your audience and then dive in crisply and clearly: "My topic today is the influence of foundations on the direction of medical research." Does it sound too daring? Do you fear that you can't deliver on the promise of such an opening? Be assured! The opening itself is worth half a grade. Your opener could be more original. I remember with particular pleasure the student who began his report on the Krupp family (the powerful owners of Germany's steel industry) with a picture of the Kaiser's whole family, which included a Krupp, placed strategically just at the Kaiser's right hand. It was a beautiful opener and the picture was worth a lot of words.

If your professor permits it, tell the class right at the beginning that you will welcome questions during your report. This helps vary the pace and keeps your audience involved and awake. Don't be terrified by the prospect of questions you can't answer. A simple "I'm sorry; I don't know that" is always permissible. Delivered in an unruffled, calm way, it can even raise your stock with the audience and the professor. The person who calmly admits she doesn't know seems, somehow, to be in special command of herself and her subject matter. (Look for professors who are not afraid to say "I don't know.") If you do wish to allow questions, allocate space for them when you time your presentation.

BLUEBOOKS AND OTHER SADISTIC MEASURES

Unfortunately, most of you will spend more time taking short-answer tests and writing three-hour bluebook exams than you will spend on writing term papers or giving oral reports. The latter at least have the virtue that they prepare you for much of the writing and speaking that you will probably have to do in the course of your professional work. Short answer tests and three-hour writing marathons, on the other hand, find no parallel in life outside the academy. In real situations you will always have more flexible time schedules, a typewriter, and access to books and notes.

It is difficult for me to write on these subjects because I discontinued these methods very early in my teaching career. I quit using short-answer tests after I allowed students to defend their answers in writing and discovered that half the right answers were for entirely wrong reasons. Three-hour bluebooks disappeared as soon as I found that most students' handwriting undergoes drastic collapse after two hours of writing. I could never dope out the last third of the effort. Since then, I have used only term papers and take-home exams.

Anyone who has suffered through a three-hour writing marathon must have suspected that there is a definite sadistic-harassment factor in most education. It really goes to extremes when you hit graduate school. In the sociology department at Berkeley where I did my graduate work, we had at one time an examination program which required five hours of writing per day for five consecutive days. It was truly dreadful to run into a friend in the middle of this exam week and see the stubble of beard, the red-rimmed eyes with their wild look and the general demeanor of exhaustion and suffering. Perhaps such measures are meant to ensure that only the physically toughest survive. More probably, our professors were merely repeating the treatment they themselves had received. Adults have an awful way of believing that, whatever their youthful sufferings, surely the next generation must benefit from their repetition.

If ever I write a final chapter to this book, entitled "Academic Chicken-shit," the three-hour bluebook exam must surely be granted center-stage. I cannot really offer you a way out. You can but know that, in this instance, you are victims of collective idiocy.

The only positive advice I can give you is slight. Some professors very much like bluebooks which have an outline at the beginning. If you go in for this idea, leave the first page of your bluebook blank and put the outline in at the end of writing—when you know what, in fact, you have said. It helps to write from an outline—but keep this one on the side to be thrown away.

When taking a bluebook exam, read the question very carefully and make sure your paper speaks directly to each part of the question. Take time to read through the entire exam and plan your answering schedule. Try to stick to your schedule. In general, the same advice applies as for term papers. Use as many facts and examples as you can. Don't "pad."

The other advice is tongue-in-cheek, though it may be suggestive. Very early in my undergraduate career I discovered "Weltanschauung." This is a German word—one of those "untranslatables"—which means "world view" or "ideology." I took to throwing one "Weltanschauung" (correctly spelled) into nearly every bluebook I ever wrote. I don't know for sure, but I always suspected that it raised me by half a grade. ⚬

Inventing the University

David Bartholomae

Biography: *David Bartholomae, Professor of English and former Director of Composition at the University of Pittsburgh, is a leading figure in the field of composition. He publishes widely in composition journals on the teaching of writing and is the author, along with colleague Anthony Petrosky, of several leading text books in the field. He is noted for the seriousness with which he takes students as learners and writers.*

Bartholomae discusses the hurdles students must overcome when learning to write in the university. Through interpretation of student examples, he illustrates the distance between writing about familiar personal experience and interpreting correctly the expectations of the many discourse communities of the university. He argues that many of the errors that students make are due to their lack of familiarity with these communities rather than incompetence with the language. Though he focuses on basic writers, the hurdles

From *When a Writer Can't Write: Studies in Writer's Block and Other Composing Process Problems.* New York: Guilford, 1985, 273–285.

remain valid for all novice academic writers. The essay also gives students a view of professionals in composition analyzing student work, which should reinforce the disciplinary expectations put forth in earlier chapters of this book.

> *Education may well be, as of right, the instrument whereby every individual, in a society like our own, can gain access to any kind of discourse. But we well know that in its distribution, in what it permits and in what it prevents, it follows the well-trodden battle-lines of social conflict. Every educational system is a political means of maintaining or of modifying the appropriation of discourse with the knowledge and the powers it carries with it.*
>
> —Foucault, "The Discourse on Language"

Every time a student sits down to write for us, he has to invent the university for the occasion—invent the university, that is, or a branch of it, like History or Anthropology or Economics or English. He has to learn to speak our language, to speak as we do, to try on the peculiar ways of knowing, selecting, evaluating, reporting, concluding, and arguing that define the discourse of our community. Or perhaps I should say the *various* discourses of our community, since it is in the nature of a liberal arts education that a student, after the first year or two, must learn to try on a variety of voices and interpretive schemes—to write, for example, as a literary critic one day and an experimental psychologist the next, to work within fields where the rules governing the presentation of examples or the development of an argument are both distinct and, even to a professional, mysterious.

The students have to appropriate (or be appropriated by) a specialized discourse, and they have to do this as though they were easily and comfortably one with their audience, as though they were members of the academy, or historians or anthropologists or economists; they have to invent the university by assembling and mimicking its language, finding some compromise between idiosyncrasy, a personal history, and the requirements of convention, the history of a discipline. They must learn to speak our language. Or they must dare to speak it, or to carry off the bluff, since speaking and writing will most certainly be required long before the skill is "learned." And this, understandably, causes problems.

Let me look quickly at an example. Here is an essay written by a college freshman, a basic writer:

> In the past time I thought that an incident was creative was when I had to make a clay model of the earth, but not of the classical or your everyday model of the earth which consists of the two cores, the mantle and the crust. I thought of these things in a dimension of which it would be unique, but easy to comprehend. Of course, your materials to work with were basic and limited at the same time, but thought help to put this limit into a right attitude or frame of mind to work with the clay.

In the beginning of the clay model, I had to research and learn the different dimensions of the earth (in magnitude, quantity, state of matter, etc.). After this, I learned how to put this into the clay and come up with something different than any other person in my class at the time. In my opinion color coordination and shape was the key to my creativity of the clay model of the earth.

Creativity is the venture of the mind at work with the mechanics relay to the limbs from the cranium, which stores and triggers this action. It can be a burst of energy released at a precise time a thought is being transmitted. This can cause a frenzy of the human body, but it depends on the characteristics of the individual and how they can relay the message clearly enough through mechanics of the body to us as an observer. Then we must determine if it is creative or a learned process varied by the individual's thought process. Creativity is indeed a tool which has to exist, or our world will not succeed into the future and progress like it should.

I am continually impressed by the patience and good will of our students. This student was writing a placement essay during freshman orientation. (The problem set to him was "Describe a time when you did something you felt to be creative. Then, on the basis of the incident you have described, go on to draw some general conclusions about 'creativity.'") He knew that university faculty would be reading and evaluating his essay, and so he wrote for them.

In some ways it is a remarkable performance. He is trying on the discourse even though he doesn't have the knowledge that makes the discourse more than a routine, a set of conventional rituals and gestures. And he does this, I think, even though he *knows* he doesn't have the knowledge that makes the discourse more than a routine. He defines himself as a researcher, working systematically, and not as a kid in a high school class: "I thought of these things in a dimension of . . ."; "had to research and learn the different dimensions of the earth (in magnitude, quantity, state of matter, etc.)." He moves quickly into a specialized language (his approximation of our jargon) and draws both a general, textbook-like conclusion ("Creativity is the venture of the mind at work . . .") and a resounding peroration ("Creativity is indeed a tool which has to exist, or our world will not succeed into the future and progress like it should"). The writer has even, with that "indeed" and with the qualifications and the parenthetical expressions of the opening paragraphs, picked up the rhythm of our prose. And through it all he speaks with an impressive air of authority.

There is an elaborate but, I will argue, a necessary and enabling fiction at work here as the student dramatizes his experience in a "setting"—the setting required by the discourse—where he can speak to us as a companion, a fellow researcher. As I read the essay, there is only one moment when the fiction is broken, when we are addressed differently. The student says, "Of course, your materials to work with were basic and limited at the same time, but thought help to put this limit into a right attitude or frame of mind to work with the clay." At this point, I think, we become students and he the teacher, giving us a lesson (as in, "You take your pencil in your right hand and put your paper in front of you"). This is, however, one of the most characteristic slips of basic writers. It is very hard for them to take on the role—the voice, the person—of an authority whose authority is rooted in scholarship, analysis, or research. They slip, then, into the more immediately available and realizable voice of authority, the voice of a teacher giving a lesson or the voice of a parent lecturing at the dinner table. They offer advice or homilies rather than "academic" conclusions. There is a similar break in the final paragraph, where the conclusion that pushes for a definition ("Creativity is the venture of the mind at work with the mechanics relay to the limbs from the cranium . . .") is replaced by a conclusion which speaks in the voice of an Elder ("Creativity is indeed a tool which has to exist, or our world will not succeed into the future and progress like it should").

It is not uncommon, then, to find such breaks in the concluding sections of essays written by basic writers. Here is the concluding section of an essay written by a student about his work as a mechanic. He had been asked to generalize about "work" after reviewing an on-the-job experience or incident that "stuck in his mind" as somehow significant: "How could two repairmen miss a leak? Lack of pride? No incentive? Lazy? I don't know." At this point the writer is in a perfect position to speculate, to move from the problem to an analysis of the problem. Here is how the paragraph continues, however (and notice the change in pronoun reference):

> From this point on, I take my time, do it right, and don't let customers get under your skin. If they have a complaint, tell them to call your boss and he'll be more than glad to handle it. Most important, worry about yourself, and keep a clear eye on everyone, for there's always someone trying to take advantage of you, anytime and anyplace.

We get neither a technical discussion nor an "academic" discussion but a Lesson on Life.[1] This is the language he uses to address the general question "How could two repairmen miss a leak?" The other brand of conclusion, the more academic one, would have required him to speak of his experience in our terms; it would, that is, have required a special vocabulary, a special system of presentation, and an interpretive scheme (or a set of commonplaces) he could use to identify and talk about the mystery of human error. The writer certainly had access to the range of acceptable commonplaces for such an explanation: "lack of pride," "no incentive," "lazy." Each would dictate its own set of phrases, examples, and conclusions, and we, his teachers, would know how to write out each argument, just as we would know how to write out more specialized arguments of our own. A "commonplace," then, is a culturally or institutionally authorized concept or statement that carries with it its own necessary elaboration. We all use commonplaces to orient ourselves in the world; they provide a point of reference and a set of "prearticulated" explanations that are readily available to organize and interpret experience. The phrase "lack of pride" carries with it its own account for the repairman's error just as, at another point in time, a reference to "original sin" would provide an explanation, or just as, in a certain university classroom, a reference to "alienation" would enable a writer to continue and complete the discussion. While there is a way in which these terms are interchangeable, they are not all permissible. A student in a composition class would most likely be turned away from a discussion of original sin. Commonplaces are the "controlling ideas" of our composition textbooks, textbooks that not only insist upon a set form for expository writing but a set view of public life.[2]

When the student above says, "I don't know," he is not saying, then, that he has nothing to say. He is saying that he is not in a position to carry on this discussion. And so we are addressed as apprentices rather than as teachers or scholars. To speak to us as a person of status or privilege, the writer can either speak to us in our terms—in the privileged language of university discourse—or, in default (or in defiance), he can speak to us as though we were children, offering us the wisdom of experience.

I think it is possible to say that the language of the "Clay Model" paper has come through the writer and not from the writer. The writer has located himself (he has located the self that is represented by the *I* on the page) in a context that is, finally, beyond him, not his own and not available to his immediate procedures for inventing and arranging text. I would not, that is, call this essay an example of "writer-based" prose. I would not say that it is egocentric or that it represents the "interior monologue of a writer thinking and talking to himself" (Flower 63). It is, rather, the record of a writer who has lost himself in the discourse of his readers. There is a context beyond the reader that is not the world but a way of talking about the world, a way of talking that determines the use of examples, the possible conclusions, the acceptable commonplaces, and the key words of an essay on the construction of a clay model of the earth. This writer has entered the discourse without successfully approximating it.

Linda Flower has argued that the difficulty inexperienced writers have with writing can be understood as a difficulty in negotiating the transition between writer-based and reader-based prose. Expert writers, in other words, can better imagine how a reader will respond to a text and can transform or restructure what they have to say around a goal shared with a reader. Teaching students to revise for readers, then, will better prepare them to write initially with a reader in mind. The success of this pedagogy depends upon the degree to which a writer can imagine and conform to a reader's goals. The difficulty of this act of imagination, and the burden of such conformity, are so much at the heart of the problem that a teacher must pause and take stock before offering revision as a solution. Students like the student who wrote the "Clay Model" paper are not so much trapped in a private language as they are shut out from one of the privileged languages of public life, a language they are aware of but cannot control.

Our students, I've said, have to appropriate (or be appropriated by) a specialized discourse, and they have to do this as though they were easily or comfortably one with their audience. If you look at the situation this way, suddenly the problem of audience awareness becomes enormously complicated. One of the common assumptions of both composition research and composition teaching is that at some "stage" in the process of composing an essay a writer's ideas or his motives must be tailored to the needs and expectations of his audience. A writer has to "build bridges" between his point of view and his readers'. He has to anticipate and acknowledge his readers' assumptions and biases. He must begin with "common points of departure" before introducing new or controversial arguments. There is a version of the pastoral at work here. It is assumed that a person of low status (like a shepherd) can speak to a person of power (like a courtier), but only (at least so far as the language is concerned) if he is not a shepherd at all, but actually a member of the court out in the field in disguise.

Writers who can successfully manipulate an audience (or, to use a less pointed language, writers who can accommodate their motives to their readers' expectations) are writers who can both imagine and write from a position of privilege. They must, that is, see themselves within a privileged discourse, one that already includes and excludes groups of readers. They must be either equal to or more powerful than those they would address. The writing, then, must somehow transform the political and social relationships between basic writing students and their teachers.

If my students are going to write for me by knowing who I am—and if this means more than knowing my prejudices, psyching me out—it means knowing what I know; it means having the knowledge of a professor of English. They have, then, to know what I know and how I know what I know (the interpretive schemes that define the way I would work out the problems I set for them); they have to learn to write what I would write, or to offer up some approximation of that discourse. The problem of audience awareness, then, is a problem of power and finesse. It cannot be addressed, as it is in most classroom exercises, by giving students privilege and denying the situation of the classroom, by having students write to an outsider, someone excluded from their privileged circle: "Write about 'To His Coy Mistress,' not for your teacher, but for the students in your class"; "Describe Pittsburgh to someone who has never been there"; "Explain to a high school senior how best to prepare for college"; "Describe baseball to a Martian."

Exercises such as these allow students to imagine the needs and goals of a reader, and they bring those needs and goals forward as a dominant constraint in the construction of an essay. And they argue, implicitly, what is generally true about writing—that it is an act of aggression disguised as an act of charity. What they fail to address is the central problem of academic writing, where students must assume the right of speaking to someone who knows Pittsburgh or "To His Coy Mistress" better than they do, a reader for whom the general common-places and the readily available utterances about a subject are inadequate. It should be clear that when I say that I know Pittsburgh better than my basic writing students, I am talking about a way of knowing that is also a way of writing. There may be much that they know that I don't know, but in the setting of the university classroom, I have a way of talking about the town that is "better" (and for arbitrary reasons) than theirs.

I think that all writers, in order to write, must imagine for themselves the privilege of being "insiders"—that is, of being both inside an established and powerful discourse, and of being granted a special right to speak. And I think that right to speak is seldom conferred upon us—upon any of us, teachers or students—by virtue of the fact that we have invented or discovered an original idea. Leading students to believe that they are responsible for something new or original, unless they understand what those words mean with regard to writing, is a dangerous and counterproductive practice. We do have the right to expect students to be active and engaged, but that is more a matter of being continually and stylistically working against the inevitable presence of conventional language; it is not a matter of inventing a language that is new.

When students are writing for a teacher, writing becomes more problematic than it is for the students who are describing baseball to a Martian. The students, in effect, have to assume privilege without having any. And since students assume privilege by locating themselves within the discourse of a particular community—within a set of specifically acceptable gestures and commonplaces—learning, at least as it is defined in the liberal arts curriculum, becomes more a matter of imitation or parody than a matter of invention and discovery.

What our beginning students need to learn is to extend themselves into the commonplaces, set phrases, rituals, gestures, habits of mind, tricks of persuasion, obligatory conclusions, and necessary connections that determine the "what might be said" and constitute knowledge within the various branches of our academic community. The course of instruction that would make this possible would be based on a sequence of illustrated assignments and would allow for successive approximations of academic or "disciplinary" discourse. Students will not take on our peculiar ways of reading, writing, speaking, and thinking all at once. Nor will the command of a subject like sociology, at least as that command is represented by the successful completion of a multiple choice exam, enable students to write sociology. Our colleges and universities, by and large, have failed to involve basic writing students in scholarly projects, projects that would allow them to act as though they were colleagues in an academic enterprise. Much of the written work students do is test-taking, report or summary, work that places them outside the working discourse of the academic community, where they are expected to admire and report on what we do, rather than inside that discourse, where they can do its work and participate in a common enterprise.[3] This is a failure of teachers and curriculum designers who, even if they speak of writing as a mode of learning, all too often represent writing as a "tool" to be used by [an] educated mind.

Pat Bizzell is one of the most important scholars writing now on basic writers and on the special requirements of academic discourse.[4] In a recent essay, "Cognition, Convention, and Certainty: What We Need to Know about Writing," she argues that the problems of basic writers might be

> better understood in terms of their unfamiliarity with the academic discourse community, combined, perhaps, with such limited experience outside their native discourse communities that they are unaware that there is such a thing as a discourse community with conventions to be mastered. What is underdeveloped is their knowledge both of the ways experience is constituted and interpreted in the academic discourse community and of the fact that all discourse communities constitute and interpret experience. (230)

One response to the problems of basic writers, then, would be to determine just what the community's conventions are, so that those conventions can be written out, "demystified," and taught in our classrooms. Teachers, as a result, could be more precise and helpful when they ask students to "think," "argue," "describe," or "define." Another response would be to examine the essays written by basic writers—their approximations of academic discourse—to determine more clearly where the problems lie. If we look at their writing, and if we look at it in the context of other student writing, we can better see the points of discord when students try to write their way into the university.

The purpose of the remainder of this paper will be to examine some of the most striking and characteristic problems as they are presented in the expository essays of basic writers. I will be concerned, then, with university discourse in its most generalized form—that is, as represented by introductory courses—and not with the special conventions required by advanced work in the various disciplines. And I will be concerned with the difficult, and often violent, accommodations that occur when students locate themselves in a discourse that is not "naturally" or immediately theirs.

I have reviewed five hundred essays written in response to the "creativity" question used during one of our placement exams. (The essay cited at the opening of this paper was one of that group.) Some of the essays were written by basic writers (or, more properly, those essays led readers to identify the writers as "basic writers"); some were written by students who "passed" (who were granted immediate access to the community of writers at the university). As I read these essays, I was looking to determine the stylistic resources that enabled writers to locate themselves within an "academic" discourse. My bias as a reader should be clear by now. I was not looking to see how the writer might represent the skills demanded by a neutral language (a language whose key features were paragraphs, topic sentences, transitions, and the like—features of a clear and orderly mind). I was looking to see what happened when a writer entered into a language to locate himself (a textual self) and his subject, and I was looking to see how once entered, that language made or unmade a writer.

Here is one essay. Its writer was classified as a basic writer. Since the essay is relatively free of sentence level errors, that decision must have been rooted in some perceived failure of the discourse itself.

> I am very interested in music, and I try to be creative in my interpretation of music. While in high school, I was a member of a jazz ensemble. The members of the ensemble were given chances to improvise and be creative in various songs. I feel that this was a great experience for me, as well as the other members. I was proud to know that I could use my imagination and feelings to create music other than what was written.
>
> Creativity to me, means being free to express yourself in a way that is unique to you, not having to conform to certain rules and guidelines. Music is only one of the many areas in which people are given opportunities to show their creativity. Sculpting, carving, building, art, and acting are just a few more areas where people can show their creativity.
>
> Through my music I conveyed feelings and thoughts which were important to me. Music was my means of showing creativity. In whatever form creativity takes, whether it be music, art, or science, it is an important aspect of our lives because it enables us to be individuals.

Notice, in this essay, the key gesture, one that appears in all but a few of the essays I read. The student defines as his own that which is a commonplace. "Creativity, to *me*, means being free to express yourself in a way that is unique to you, not having to conform to certain rules and guidelines." This act of appropriation constitutes his authority; it constitutes his authority as a writer and not just as a musician (that is, as someone with a story to tell). There were many essays in the set that told only a story, where the writer's established presence was as a musician or a skier or someone who painted designs on a van, but not as a person removed from that experience interpreting it, treating it as a metaphor for something else (creativity). Unless those stories were long, detailed, and very well told (unless the writer was doing more than saying, "I am a skier or a musician or a van-painter"), those writers were all given low ratings.

Notice also that the writer of the jazz paper locates himself and his experience in relation to the commonplace (creativity is unique expression; it is not having to conform to rules or guidelines) regardless of whether it is true or not. Anyone who improvises "knows" that improvisation follows rules and guidelines. It is the power of the commonplace (its truth as a recognizable, and, the writer believes, as a final statement) that justifies the example and completes the essay. The example, in other words, has value because it stands within the field of the commonplace. It is not the occasion for what one might call an "objective" analysis or a "close" reading. It could also be said that the essay stops with the articulation of the commonplace. The following sections speak only to the power of that statement. The reference to "sculpting, carving, building, art, and acting" attest to the universal of the commonplace (and it attests to the writer's nervousness with the status he has appropriated for himself—he is saying, "Now, I'm not the only one here who's done something unique"). The commonplace stands by itself. For this writer, it does not need to be elaborated. By virtue of having written it, he has completed the essay and established the contract by which we may be spoken to as equals: "In whatever form creativity takes, whether it be music, art, or science, it is an important aspect of *our lives* because it enables *us* to be individuals." (For me to break that contract, to argue that *my* life is not represented in that essay, is one way for me to begin as a teacher with that student in that essay.)

I said that the writer of the jazz paper offered up a commonplace regardless of whether it was "true" or not, and this, I said, was an example of the power of a commonplace to determine the meaning of an example. A commonplace determines a system of interpretation that can be used to "place" an example within a standard system of belief. You can see a similar process at work in this essay.

> During the football season, the team was supposed to wear the same type of cleats and the same type socks, I figured that I would change this a little by wearing my white shoes instead of black and to cover up the team socks with a pair of my own white ones. I thought that this looked better than what we were wearing, and I told a few of the other people on the team to change too. They agreed that it did look better and they changed their combination to go along with mine. After the game people came up to us and said that it looked very good the way we wore our socks, and they wanted to know why we changed from the rest of the team.
>
> I feel that creativity comes from when a person lets his imagination come up with ideas and he is not afraid to express them. Once you create something to do it will be original and unique because it came about from your own imagination and if any one else tries to copy it, it won't be the same because you thought of it first from your own ideas.

This is not an elegant paper, but it seems seamless, tidy. If the paper on the clay model of the earth showed an ill-fit between the writer and his project, here the discourse seems natural, smooth. You could reproduce this paper and hand it out to a class, and it would take a lot of prompting before the students sense something fishy and one of the more aggressive ones might say, "Sure he came up with the idea of wearing white shoes and white socks. Him and Bill White-shoes Johnson. Come on. He copied the very thing he said was his own idea, 'original and unique.'"

The "I" of this text, the "I" who "figured," "thought," and "felt" is located in a conventional rhetoric of the self that turns imagination into origination (I made it), that argues an ethic of production (I made it and it is mine), and that argues a tight scheme of intention (I made it because I decided to make it). The rhetoric seems invisible because it is so common. This "I" (the maker) is also located in a version of history that dominates classroom accounts of history. It is an example of the "Great Man" theory, where history is rolling along—the English novel is dominated by a central, intrusive narrative presence; America is in the throes of a great depression; during football season the team was supposed to wear the same kind of cleats and socks—until a figure appears, one who can shape history—Henry James, FDR, the writer of the football paper—and everything is changed. In the argument of the football paper, "I figured," "I thought," "I told," "they agreed," and, as a consequence, "I feel that creativity *comes from* when a person lets his imagination come up with ideas and he is not afraid to express them." The story of appropriation becomes a narrative of courage and conquest. The writer was able to write that story when he was able to imagine himself in that discourse. Getting him out of it will be a difficult matter indeed.

There are ways, I think, that a writer can shape history in the very act of writing it. Some students are able to enter into a discourse, but, by stylistic maneuvers, to take possession of it at the same time. They don't originate a discourse, but they locate themselves within it aggressively, self-consciously.

Here is one particularly successful essay. Notice the specialized vocabulary, but also the way in which the text continually refers to its own language and to the language of others.

> Throughout my life, I have been interested and intrigued by music. My mother has often told me of the times, before I went to school, when I would "conduct" the orchestra on her records. I continued to listen to music and eventually started to play the guitar and the clarinet. Finally, at about the age of twelve, I started to sit down and to try to write songs. Even though my instrumental skills were far from my own high standards, I would spend much of my spare time during the day with a guitar around my neck, trying to produce a piece of music.

Each of these sessions, as I remember them, had a rather set format. I would sit in my bedroom, strumming different combinations of the five or six chords I could play, until I heard a series which sounded particularly good to me. After this, I set the music to a suitable rhythm, (usually dependent on the mood at the time), and ran through the tune until I could play it fairly easily. Only after this section was complete did I go on to writing lyrics, which generally followed along the lines of the current popular songs on the radio.

At the time of the writing, I felt that my songs were, in themselves, an original creation of my own; that is, I, alone, made them. However, I now see that, in this sense of the word, I was not creative. The songs themselves seem to be an oversimplified form of the music I listened to at the time.

In a more fitting sense, however, I *was* being creative. Since I did not purposely copy my favorite songs, I was, effectively, originating my songs from my own "process of creativity." To achieve my goal, I needed what a composer would call "inspiration" for my piece. In this case the inspiration was the current hit on the radio. Perhaps with my present point of view, I feel that I used too much "inspiration" in my songs, but, at that time, I did not.

Creativity, therefore, is a process which, in my case, involved a certain series of "small creations" if you like. As well, it is something, the appreciation of which varies with one's point of view, that point of view being set by the person's experience, tastes, and his own personal view of creativity. The less experienced tend to allow for less originality, while the more experienced demand real originality to classify something a "creation." Either way, a term as abstract as this is perfectly correct, and open to interpretation.

This writer is consistent and dramatically conscious of herself forming something to say out of what has been said *and* out of what she has been saying in the act of writing this paper. "Creativity" begins, in this paper, as "original creation." What she thought was "creativity," however, she now calls "imitation," and, as she says, "in this sense of the word" she was not "creative." In another sense, however, she says that she *was* creative since she didn't purposefully copy the songs but used them as "inspiration."

The writing in this piece (that is, the work of the writer within the essay) goes on in spite of, or against, the language that keeps pressing to give another name to her experience as a song writer and to bring the discussion to closure. (Think of the quick closure of the football shoes paper in comparison.) Its style is difficult, highly qualified. It relies on quotation marks and parody to set off the language and attitudes that belong to the discourse (or the discourses) it would reject, that it would not take as its own proper location.[5]

In the papers I've examined in this essay, the writers have shown a varied awareness of the codes—or the competing codes—that operate within a discourse. To speak with authority student writers have not only to speak in another's voice but through another's "code"; and they not only have to do this, they have to speak in the voice and through the codes of those of us with power and wisdom; and they not only have to do this, they have to do it before they know what they are doing, before they have a project to participate in and before, at least in terms of our disciplines, they have anything to say. Our students may be able to enter into a conventional discourse and speak, not as themselves, but through the voice of the community. The university, however, is the place where "common" wisdom is only of negative value; it is something to work against. The movement toward a more specialized discourse begins (or perhaps, best begins) when a student can both define a position of privilege, a position that sets him against a "common" discourse, and when he can work self-consciously, critically, against not only the "common" code but his own.

The stages of development that I've suggested are not necessarily marked by corresponding levels in the type or frequency of error, at least not by the type or frequency of sentence level errors. I am arguing, then, that a basic writer is not necessarily a writer who makes a lot of mistakes. In fact, one of the problems with curricula designed to aid basic writers is that they too often begin with the assumption that the key distinguishing feature of a basic writer is the presence of sentence level error. Students are placed in courses because their placement essays show a high frequency of such errors and those courses are designed with the goal of making those errors go away. This approach to the problems of the basic writer ignores the degree to which error is not a constant feature but a marker in the development of a writer. Students who can write reasonably correct narratives may fall to pieces when faced with more unfamiliar assignments. More importantly, however, such courses fail to serve the rest of the curriculum. On every campus there is a significant number of college freshmen who require a course to introduce them to the kinds of writing that are required for a university education. Some of these students can write correct sentences and some cannot, but as a group they lack the facility other freshmen possess when they are faced with an academic writing task.

The "White Shoes" essay, for example, shows fewer sentence level errors than the "Clay Model" paper. This may well be due to the fact, however, that the writer of that paper stayed well within the safety of familiar territory. He kept himself out of trouble by doing what he could easily do. The tortuous syntax of the more advanced papers on my list is a syntax that represents a writer's struggle with a difficult and unfamiliar language, and it is a syntax that can quickly lead an inexperienced writer into trouble. The syntax and punctuation of the "Composing Songs" essay, for example, show the effort that is required when a writer works against the pressure of conventional discourse. If the prose is inelegant (although I'll confess I admire those dense sentences), it is still correct. This writer has a command of the linguistic and stylistic resources (the highly embedded sentences, the use of parentheses and quotation marks) required to complete the act of writing. It is easy to imagine the possible pitfalls for a writer working without this facility.

There was no camera trained on the "Clay Model" writer while he was writing, and I have no protocol of what was going through his mind, but it is possible to speculate that the syntactic difficulties of sentences like the following are the result of an attempt to use an unusual vocabulary and to extend his sentences beyond the boundaries that would be "normal" in his speech or writing:

> In the past time I thought that an incident was creative was when I had to make a clay model of the earth, but not of the classical or your everyday model of the earth which consists of the two cores, the mantle and the crust. I thought of these things in a dimension of which it would be unique, but easy to comprehend.

There is reason to believe, that is, that the problem is with this kind of sentence, in this context. If the problem of the last sentence is a problem of holding together these units—"I thought," "dimension," "unique," and "easy to comprehend"—then the linguistic problem is not a simple matter of sentence construction.

I am arguing, then, that such sentences fall apart not because the writer lacks the necessary syntax to glue the pieces together but because he lacks the full statement within which these key words are already operating. While writing, and in the thrust of his need to complete the sentence, he has the key words but not the utterance. (And to recover the utterance, I suspect, he will need to do more than revise the sentence.) The invisible conventions, the prepared phrases remain too distant for the statement to be completed. The writer must get inside of a discourse he can only partially imagine. The act of constructing a sentence, then, becomes something like an act of transcription, where the voice on the tape unexpectedly fades away and becomes inaudible.

Mina Shaughnessy speaks of the advanced writer as a writer with a more facile but still incomplete possession of this prior discourse. In the case of the advanced writer, the evidence of a problem is the presence of dissonant, redundant, or imprecise language, as in a sentence such as this: "No education can be *total,* it must be *continuous."* Such a student, Shaughnessy says, could be said to hear the "melody of formal English" while still unable to make precise or exact distinctions. And, she says, the prepackaging feature of language, the possibility of taking over phrases and whole sentences without much thought about them, threatens the writer now as before. The writer, as we have said, inherits the language out of which he must fabricate his own messages. He is therefore in a constant tangle with the language, obliged to recognize its public, communal nature and yet driven to invent out of this language his own statements (19).

For the unskilled writer, the problem is different in degree and not in kind. The inexperienced writer is left with a more fragmentary record of the comings and goings of academic discourse. Or, as I said above, he often has the key words without the complete statements within which they are already operating.

It may very well be that some students will need to learn to crudely mimic the "distinctive register" of academic discourse before they are prepared to actually and legitimately do the work of the discourse, and before they are sophisticated enough with the refinements of tone and texture to do it with grace or elegance. To say this, however, is to say that our students must be our students. Their initial progress will be marked by their abilities to take on the role of privilege, by their abilities to establish authority. From this point of view, the student who wrote about constructing the clay model of the earth is better prepared for his education than the student who wrote about playing football in white shoes, even though the "White Shoes" paper was relatively error-free and the "Clay Model" paper was not. It will be hard to pry the writer of the "White Shoes" paper loose from the tidy, pat discourse that allows him to dispose of the question of creativity in such a quick and efficient manner. He will have to be convinced that it is better to write sentences he might not so easily control, and he will have to be convinced that it is better to write muddier and more confusing prose (in order that it may sound like ours), and this will be harder than convincing the "Clay Model" writer to continue what he has begun.[6]

NOTES

1. David Olson has made a similar observation about school-related problems of language learning in younger children. Here is his conclusion: "Depending upon whether children assumed language was primarily suitable for making assertions and conjectures or primarily for making direct or indirect commands, they will either find school texts easy or difficult" (107).

2. For Aristotle there were both general and specific commonplaces. A speaker, says Aristotle, has a "stock of arguments to which he may turn for a particular need."

   If he knows the *topic* (regions, places, lines of argument)—and a skilled speaker will know them—he will know where to find what he wants for a special case. The general topics, or *common*places, are regions containing arguments that are common to all branches of knowledge. . . . But there are also special topics (regions, places, *loci*) in which one looks for arguments appertaining to particular branches of knowledge, special sciences, such as ethics or politics. (154–55)

   And, he says "The topics or places, then, may be indifferently thought of as in the science that is concerned, or in the mind of the speaker." But the question of location is "indifferent" *only* if the mind of the speaker is in line with set opinion, general assumption. For the speaker (or writer) who is not situated so comfortably in the privileged public realm, this is indeed not an indifferent matter at all. If he does not have the commonplace at hand, he will not, in Aristotle's terms, know where to go at all.

3. See especially Bartholomae and Rose for articles on curricula designed to move students into university discourse. The movement to extend writing "across the curriculum" is evidence of a general concern for locating students within the work of the university: see especially Bizzell or Maimon et al. For longer works directed specifically at basic writing, see

Ponsot and Deen, and Shaughnessy. For a book describing a course for more advanced students, see Coles.

4. See especially Bizzell, and Bizzell and Herzberg. My debt to Bizzell's work should be evident everywhere in this essay.

5. In support of my argument that this is the kind of writing that does the work of the academy, let me offer the following excerpt from a recent essay by Wayne Booth ("The Company We Keep: Self-Making in Imaginative Art, Old and New"):

> I can remember making up songs of my own, no doubt borrowed from favorites like "Hello, Central, Give Me Heaven," "You Can't Holler Down My Rain Barrel," and one about the ancient story of a sweet little "babe in the woods" who lay down and died, with her brother.
>
> I asked my mother, in a burst of creative egotism, why nobody ever learned to sing my songs, since after all I was more than willing to learn *theirs*. I can't remember her answer, and I can barely remember snatches of two of "my" songs. But I can remember dozens of theirs, and when I sing them, even now, I sometimes feel again the emotions, and see the images, that they aroused then. Thus who I am now—the very shape of my soul—was to a surprising degree molded by the works of "art" that came my way.
>
> I set "art" in quotation marks, because much that I experienced in those early books and songs would not be classed as art according to most definitions. But for the purposes of appraising the effects of "art" on "life" or "culture," and especially for the purposes of thinking about the effects of the "media," we surely must include every kind of artificial experience that we provide for one another. . . .
>
> In this sense of the word, all of us are from the earliest years fed a steady diet of art. . . . (58–59)

While there are similarities in the paraphrasable content of Booth's arguments and my student's, what I am interested in is each writer's method. Both appropriate terms from a common discourse (about *art* and *inspiration*) in order to push against an established way of talking (about tradition and the individual). This effort of opposition clears a space for each writer's argument and enables the writers to establish their own "sense" of the key words in the discourse.

6. Preparation of this manuscript was supported by the Learning Research and Development Center of the University of Pittsburgh, which is supported in part by the National Institute of Education. I am grateful also to Mike Rose, who pushed and pulled at this paper at a time when it needed it.

Works Cited

Aristotle. *The Rhetoric of Aristotle*. Trans. L. Cooper. Englewood Cliffs: Prentice, 1932.

Bartholomae, D. "Writing Assignments: Where Writing Begins." *Forum*. Ed. P. Stock. Montclair: Boynton/Cook, 1983, 300–12.

Bizzell, P. "The Ethos of Academic Discourse." *College Composition and Communication* 29 (1978): 351–55.

———. "Cognition, Convention, and Certainty: What We Need to Know about Writing." *Pre/text* 3 (1982): 213–44.

———. "College Composition: Initiation into the Academic Discourse Community." *Curriculum Inquiry* 12 (1982): 191–207.

Bizzell, P., and B. Herzberg. "'Inherent' Ideology, 'Universal' History, 'Empirical' Evidence, and 'Context-Free' Writing: Some Problems with E. D. Hirsch's *The Philosophy of Composition*." *Modern Language Notes* 95 (1980): 1181–1202.

Coles, W. E., Jr. *The Plural I*. New York: Holt, 1978.

Flower, Linda S. "Revising Writer-Based Prose." *Journal of Basic Writing* 3 (1981): 62–74.

Maimon, E. P., G. L. Belcher, G. W. Hearn, B. F. Nodine, and F. X. O'Connor. *Writing in the Arts and Sciences.* Cambridge: Winthrop, 1981.

Olson, D. R. "Writing: The Divorce of the Author from the Text." *Exploring Speaking-Writing Relationships: Connections and Contrasts.* Ed. B. M. Kroll and R. J. Vann. Urbana: National Council of Teachers of English, 1981.

Ponsot, M., and R. Deen. *Beat Not the Poor Desk.* Montclair: Boynton/Cook, 1982.

Rose, M. "Remedial Writing Courses: A Critique and a Proposal." *College English* 45 (1983): 109–28.

Shaughnessy, Mina. *Errors and Expectations.* New York: Oxford UP, 1977.

Web Literacy: Challenges and Opportunities for Research in a New Medium

Madeleine Sorapure, Pam Inglesby, and George Yatchisin

Biography: *Madeleine Sorapure and George Yatchisin are lecturers with the University of California, Santa Barbara Writing Program where they teach a wide range of academic, research, and technical writing courses. Pam Inglesby is a former colleague at the same institution. Madeleine Sorapure specializes in rhetorical analysis from the point of view of literature, Pam Inglesby is trained in communication and media, and George Yatchisin is a journalist and creative writer. Thus the three bring different disciplinary perspectives to their teaching of and writing on Web analysis.*

Sorapure et al. give a detailed and panoramic view of the opportunities and the hazards of the World Wide Web for the composition teacher and of the demands it puts upon composition professionals. They treat the Web as a new medium for rhetorical analysis, and demonstrate that many of the tools developed for library text evaluation can be transferred to this medium; this argues for both the intellectual and practical advantages (even necessity) of integrating Web analysis into the composition course. They argue that existing criteria for evaluating Web sites are rudimentary and chancy at best, and that professionals in composition are in the best position to tackle the challenge of Web literacy. The article gives teachers and students tools to open the Web to analysis.

Student researchers are turning in increasing numbers to the World Wide Web as a resource, though not necessarily with an understanding of how to assess the reliability or value of the information they find there. At all stages of the research process, but especially at the assessment stage, the Web poses challenges that writing teachers should address explicitly in guiding students to become skillful and discerning readers of Web sites. The Web literacy student need involves an

From *Computers and Composition* 15, 1998, 409–424.

ability to manage the diverse and largely unfiltered content of the Web and an attentiveness to the information conveyed in a site's nontextual features, most notably its images, links, and interactivity. Teaching students this literacy means
supplementing the evaluative criteria traditionally applied to print sources with
new strategies for making sense of diverse kinds of texts presented in hypertextual
and multimedia format. Assessing the value of information offered at Web sites
can enhance students' research and writing skills and is also an important step in
educating students to be critical users of the Web and the Internet.

INTRODUCTION

At this point in the age of the computer, it is nearly impossible to teach a writing class without having students ask, "Can we use the World Wide Web as a
source for our papers?" There is no easy answer to this question because Web
sites vary wildly in reliability and usefulness. To allow students to use the Web
as a resource without helping them judge the merits of the information they
find there is to invite trouble. But, a different trouble lurks if we prohibit students from drawing on Web sources. Indeed, they might be turning to the Web
for entirely valid and well-informed reasons, for instance to find up-to-date and
otherwise unpublished information from government agencies, corporations,
journalists, scholars, and others. Denying students access to such sources might
prevent them from doing the best research possible. Research, broadly conceived, involves not only finding relevant information but also assessing its quality and value for a specific project, and then determining how to integrate that
information, together with other sources, into one's own writing. At all stages of
the research process, but especially at the assessment stage, the Web poses
challenges that students may not recognize and that writing teachers should, we
argue, explicitly address. These challenges, in fact, are real opportunities for us
to enrich the curricula of writing courses, enhance the research and writing
skills of students, and expand our conception of literacy.

Two challenges in particular are posed by the Web as an information resource. The first arises from the fact that the Web offers many modes of writing, many rhetorical situations for students to assess. Web sites advocate causes,
sell products, entertain visitors, express opinions, present scholarly research; indeed, some sites try to do all of the above. The Web in itself provides little classification or categorization of these different modes, nor does it reject any
offerings; in this sense it is like a vast, open, and uncatalogued library, and one
in which reference librarians are nowhere to be found. Employing criteria developed for evaluating print sources (currency, bias, author's credentials, publisher, intended audience, and so on) is useful in sifting and assessing the
information one finds on the Web, but it is important that these criteria be ap-

plied flexibly to the Web's broad range of rhetorical situations. While library materials are organized and "filtered" (by publishing houses, peer reviewers, faculty, and librarians, for example), the Web presents mostly "unfiltered" material in an uncontextualized manner. Thus, it challenges students to do the kind of primary evaluative activity more often done by advanced researchers.

Web sites not only provide a range of rhetorical situations for students to assess but also do so in a multimedia, hypertextual, interactive format. The second challenge for student researchers, then, is to determine the effects of the medium on the message. For instance, what information do images and graphic design convey? How does the associative logic of a hypertextual Web site affect its content? How does interactivity affect the site's credibility and the audience's response? Answering these questions can help students determine the purpose of a Web site, its reliability, and its ultimate value for their projects; these features can be read as nontextual clues that facilitate evaluation of the text, just as the glossy pages, advertisements, and images in a popular magazine are one mark of its difference from an academic journal. But, what vocabulary do students have for discussing features such as images, links, and interactive technologies? As we suggest, these elements of Web sites have parallels in print documents—particularly, in aspects of print documents most often overlooked in their assessment—and so paying close attention to Web sites should return students to library sources with a keener eye and a wider range of questions. In addition, and no less importantly, reading, understanding, and evaluating the hypertextual and multimedia components of Web sites offer the opportunity to extend literacy skills—such as associative logic, visual rhetoric, and interactivity. This expanded conception of literacy is crucial in an increasingly technological and multimedia world, one in which the library is no longer the primary source of useful and reliable information for student researchers.

Web literacy, then, involves an ability to recognize and assess a wide range of rhetorical situations and an attentiveness to the information conveyed in a source's nontextual features. Teaching students this literacy means supplementing the evaluative criteria traditionally applied to print sources with new strategies necessary for making sense of diverse kinds of texts presented in hypertextual and multimedia formats.

WEB LITERACY AND COMPOSITION

Many scholars in our field believe that the viability of composition depends on such an expanded definition of literacy. Aside from benefiting students by expanding their repertoire of skills in evaluating different modes and media of communication, a broader conception of literacy invites us as scholars to make connections to other disciplines: film and art, graphic design, human-computer interface theories developed in computer science, and literary studies done in hypertext. Thus, it allows us to introduce rhetorical theory into an existing body of work focused on evaluating the content and form of Web sites.

Given these advantages to integrating the Web more fully into writing courses, and given the increasing importance of Web literacy for business, academic, and personal enterprises, there is surprisingly little research by composition specialists on the topic. Instead, the focus of research and of teaching practice has been on those computer and Internet uses that have more direct parallels than the Web to what instructors do in writing classrooms without computers: class discussions take place over local-area networks; drafts of papers are shared on electronic bulletin boards; grammar and revision exercises are done with Computer-Aided Instruction (CAI) programs; portfolios of student writing are compiled, stored, and evaluated electronically; and office hours are conducted via e-mail. In these instances, the computer facilitates new and (perhaps) improved ways of accomplishing familiar tasks. But, the Web is, in many respects, unfamiliar territory for us, bringing into the mix knowledge and experience we may or may not possess. Most writing teachers have notoriously little time and meager institutional support to become experts in this area, and the rewards of such expertise are as yet uncertain. Economic and logistical considerations come into play as well in causing skepticism about integrating the Web more fully into writing courses. Access to the Web is difficult at some institutions and for some students. Moreover, students enter our classes with different degrees of facility and experience with computers and with the Web, and we are rightly hesitant to penalize inadvertently those students already part of the "technological underclass."[1] We may also have ethical concerns about allowing into our classrooms the commercial and offensive material that seem an ineradicable part of the Web. Most broadly, writers such as Sven Birkerts (1994) and Neil Postman (1995) called our attention to the potentially detrimental effects of using the Internet and the Web, arguing that it promotes reduced attention span, poorer writing and communication skills, alienation from print documents, and isolation from human interaction.

These are valid concerns and are, with increasing regularity, topics of discussion at conferences and in journals both on the Web and in print. But, we need to recognize that the Web has already entered our classrooms even as we

---

[1] Cynthia Selfe and Richard Selfe (1994) pursued a related issue in their examination of computer technology's inscription in and complicity with dominant cultural and ideological constructions. They interpret computer interfaces in particular as promoting the grand cultural narratives that "foreground a value on middle-class, corporate culture; capitalism and the commodification of information; Standard English; and rationalistic ways of representing knowledge" (p. 494). Although Selfe and Selfe don't address the Web in their critique, a study of the cultural and ideological maps represented in the Web's interface(s) is clearly important. Moreover, we agree with their assertion that teachers and students should be encouraged to become "technology critics as well as technology users" (p. 484).

debate its value and its effects. Students access the Web not only to do research but also to be entertained, to shop, to be informed about current events, and in some cases to compose their own home pages. The activity of reading and creating Web sites will only increase as the software and hardware for it become more accessible. Therefore, it is important to defuse an uncritical acceptance of the Web and rather to guide students in becoming discerning, skillful readers of Web sites, particularly when they are drawing information from those sites for use in their own writing. The two major challenges posed by the Web as an information resource—its diverse and unfiltered content and its hypermedia format—are thus also opportunities for students to develop their critical thinking and research skills.

EXISTING CRITERIA FOR WEB EVALUATION

Resources currently exist on the Web itself and in print that can help students organize their search for information and evaluate both the content and the formal and nontextual elements of Web sites. On the Web, these guidelines fall into two broad categories: university library sites that focus on evaluating the content of Web sites, drawing on analogies to print documents and addressed to people using the Web as a research tool, and Web-authoring and human-computer interface guidelines that focus primarily on the design and technical elements of Web sites, drawing on analogies to graphic arts and broadcast media and addressed to people creating sites. We draw on both categories in the discussion that follows, suggesting that a rhetorical approach can bridge the content-form divide they represent. However, it is unlikely that students doing research on the Web would find either of these types of guidelines easily, or indeed, would even look for such guidance to help them assess Web sites. The evaluative guidelines students encounter most frequently on the Web are also, unfortunately, the least useful to them.

The least helpful but most pervasive evaluative term on the Web about the Web is *cool.* Web sites abound that index "cool sites of the day" or "Joe's top twenty cool sites," where *cool* is most often left undefined or only briefly explained.[2] Without clarification, the term "cool" is meaningless, and the complementary designation of *hot*—applied to frequently visited Web sites—tells us

---

[2]Alan Liu (1998), in his *Voice of the Shuttle* website (<http://humanitas.ucsb.edu>), remarked that cool is "one of the most single-minded and totalitarian aesthetics ever created. Why are there 'cool sites of the day' but no beautiful, sublime, or tragic sites?" In an attempt to clarify "cool," Liu's *Laws of Cool* page offers improvised categorizations such as "Ultra Graphical," "The Experience of the Arbitrary" (e.g., sites with random URL generators), "'Ordinary' Cool" (pages recording someone's grocery list or daily journal), "Corporate and Government Cool," "Technologically Advanced Pages," and "Cool Personal Home Pages." As these categories imply, "cool" allows for a wide range of interpretations dependent in large part on the purpose, audience, and content of the site.

nothing except that for some reason that site is popular. Knowing that a site is both cool and hot is not particularly helpful in assessing the quality of information it offers, merely making the Web seem like a weather map full of fronts about to clash. The other frequently encountered evaluation schema on the Web comes from search engines such as *Lycos, Infoseek,* and *Yahoo,* which provide ratings of certain sites, deeming some as excellent and others as unworthy of a visit. This evaluation process would seem quite helpful for student researchers because they could, in theory, confine their Web searches to only excellent sites, and thus gather only highly reliable information. In actuality, though, the criteria by which these sites are judged, as well as the qualifications of the reviewers making the judgments, are often left unspecified. When they are articulated, as in *Lycos'* Top 5% cite (see <http://www.lycos.com/help.top5-help2.html>), the evaluative categories are quite broad (content, design, and overall). Minimal information is given about the specific criteria in each category: for instance, what would it mean to deem the content of a site "interesting" or to say that its images are "well-chosen"? The categories are too vague and uncontextualized to be of much use to serious student researchers, and the reviews of individual sites are similarly superficial, intended primarily to be entertaining and catchy.

In short, the evaluation guidelines on the Web most accessible to and most frequently encountered by students are fundamentally flawed and only minimally helpful. In print, students might find that standard research writing textbooks give them good general advice for assessing sources, although these texts don't deal with the particular challenges posed by the Web; even the more recent composition textbooks that focus on electronic writing offer remarkably little guidance in this regard. For instance, Dawn Rodrigues' (1997) *The Research Paper and the World Wide Web* followed the lead of library Web sites in briefly covering the "internet applicability" of traditional print-oriented criteria for evaluation (pp. 13–15). Jeanette Woodward's (1997) *Writing Research Papers: Investigating Resources in Cyberspace* presented a similar list of print-oriented criteria but with no reference at all to the ways these criteria need to be adapted to address the different rhetorical situations of Web sites (pp. 130–133). In addition, neither of these textbooks, and neither of the Internet-oriented handbooks that have been published recently (Hairston, Ruszkiewicz, & Seward, 1997; Miller & Knowles, 1997), direct students' attention to the quite evident challenges that the Web's hypermedia format poses to an assessment of its offerings.[3]

---

[3]Mass-market paperbacks, such as *The Internet for Dummies* and *The World Wide Web Unleashed,* are available to guide students through the process of searching for information on the Web and on the Internet more broadly (FTP sites, Gophers, mailing lists, MUDs and MOOs, etc.). But, because they are not specifically addressed to academic researchers, these books generally don't concern themselves with how to evaluate the reliability of quality of information once it is found. A similar orientation guides Paul Gilster's (1997) *Digital Literacy.* Although Gilster stated that "critical thinking" is the most important "core compe-

The following sections propose a more thorough approach to evaluating Web sites and developing Web literacy, taking into account both the similarities of Web and print sources and their significant differences. Focusing first on the wide-ranging content of the Web, we suggest how two of its seemingly unreliable genres—the personal home page and the "infommercial" site—might be used productively by student researchers. In evaluating these sites and determining their value for a particular research project, students confront in an immediate way issues of authorial expertise, reliability, and bias, issues also crucial in assessing print sources. We turn next to several nontextual elements of Web sites—images, links, and interactivity—and suggest that assessing these features can also cultivate key critical thinking skills in students. Incorporating these new features into a rhetorically based analysis of a site's purpose and strategies can yield a more complete understanding of the site, as well as a broader and more sophisticated approach to assessing the value of information found within and beyond the confines of the library.

FROM THE LIBRARY TO THE WEB

The Web evaluation criteria most likely familiar to composition teachers have been developed by instructors and librarians engaged in helping students use the Internet as a research tool. These criteria tend to value Web sites similar in content and authorship to sources found in a typical academic library and treat the Web in general as an extension of the library, thus ignoring or denigrating new types of research sources the Web offers. The temptation to apply print-oriented evaluative criteria to Web sites is manifested by a site published by the library at Cornell University, a guide on "How to critically analyze information sources," which (the library suggests) can be applied to both print and Web texts (Ormondroyd, Engle, & Cosgrave, 1996). The guide posits two levels of evaluation: an "initial appraisal," which involves assessing the author's credentials and publisher's reputation, and a "content analysis," which involves assessing the text's intended audience, objectivity, coverage, writing style, and external evaluation. This approach draws directly from traditional print-oriented research writing textbooks such as Stephen Weidenborner's and Domenick Caruso (1996), which asked students to consider a source's depth of coverage, author's viewpoint, and currency of information, and Nancy Sommers' and Linda Simon's (1993), which focused on the status of the source's author and the strength of the evidence presented.

---

tency" demanded of Internet users, and although he advised checking an author's credentials and reading the address of a Web site for clues as to its reliability, Gilster mainly endorsed various Internet search tools and strategies as the primary solution to evaluating information. For instance, he advised that "you need to learn how to assemble this knowledge; that is, build a reliable information horde from diverse sources. You must choose an environment within which to work and customize it with Internet tools" (p. 3).

These traditional criteria are useful to some extent when evaluating Web sites for research purposes. For example, a student writing a paper on the critical reception of a movie for a popular culture class might turn to the Web rather than the library because of sites such as *The Internet Movie Database* (see <http://imdb.com>), which offers background information about thousands of movies and offers links to "commentary or reviews" for each one. The site fails to categorize or contextualize the reviews, however, which means students will need to draw on traditional print-oriented criteria to decide which ones represent serious critical commentary. For the movie *The Godfather*, for example, the Database offers a list of 18 reviews credited to sources as diverse as Roger Ebert, "Mr. Showbiz," *Box Office Magazine,* "Matt's Movie Reviews," and *The San Francisco Chronicle.* Using traditional evaluative criteria, the student would identify the author of each review, assess that author's credentials, and consider the nature of the publication and its target audience. Such an evaluation would likely lead the student to favor the kind of reviews typically found in a library (those written by professional critics and published in well-respected periodicals) and reject those with unclear authorship or sponsorship.

Although such an approach would not be problematic for that particular assignment, there are other situations in which dismissing Web sources just because of unclear or unusual authorship, sponsorship, currency, or other attributes might lead to an unwarranted rejection of useful information. In other words, there are potentially valuable Web sites available to student researchers that should not be dismissed just because they are dissimilar to sources found in the library. Because of this difference between the library and the Web, some research-oriented evaluative schemes have moved beyond positing the Web as equivalent to print, and instead, ask readers to become aware of special problems posed by the Web regarding content evaluation. A Web site composed by Jan Alexander and Marsha Tate (1996), reference librarians at Widener University, stated that although "traditional print techniques" are still appropriate for evaluating Web text, new techniques are also needed because of (among other things) the difficulty in identifying authors, the lack of gatekeeping or peer review, and the unclear use of dates. The librarians also call attention to the fact that the Web includes new genres of research sources not found in traditional print; two such genres, ubiquitous on the Web and worthy of particular attention, are personal home pages and infommercial Web sites.

The problem—and opportunity—posed by personal home pages is that almost anyone can create and maintain one on the Web. Indeed, many online services offer free space on the Web for members' home pages, and other Web-based organizations, such as Geocities, offer free Web space to anyone with access to a computer and a modem. This democratization of public communication poses a problem for a student who has been instructed to pay attention to an author's expertise and reputation because many people who create personal Web pages do so precisely because they do not have the cultural capital necessary to be published elsewhere. One way a student can solve this problem is by ignoring personal sites altogether or by extracting from them what seems the safest and most reliable information. For example, a student researching the current peacekeeping mission in Bosnia might encounter the *Bosnia Buddah Home Page* (see <http://members.aol.com/apstyle/bosnia.html>), created by Cesar Soriano, an America Online member who served for nine months in Bosnia-Herzegovina with the Maryland Army National Guard. Directing a student to see if there is "anything useful there," using traditional evaluative criteria, would lead the student to focus on the authoritative sources included or referenced in the site (a bibliography, wire service stories, and so on).

Such an approach, however, would neglect important resources that the Web—and in particular, personal home pages—have to offer, which in this case is the perspective and experiences of the individual constructing the site. At the *Bosnia Buddah Home Page,* the author provided a diary of his military experiences in Bosnia, a photograph album, and a Frequently Asked Questions (FAQ) section in which he gives his opinion on what the war is about, describes what it is like to live in Bosnia, explains the day-to-day dangers faced by peacekeeping troops there, and offers advice for partners of soldiers in Bosnia. This type of information could be used to enrich a research paper on Bosnia by providing an insider's perspective; the student could also use the site to contact other potential primary sources as it explains how to obtain a military pen-pal. Allowing students to use such Web sites as primary sources forces us to rethink what is meant by authorial expertise and reputation. Although we might legitimately demand certain educational or professional credentials of a secondary source, primary sources are often valued because of the author's unique experience and insight. The new availability of such sources on the Web can thus be regarded as an opportunity for student researchers, one which challenges them to distinguish between primary and secondary sources and to determine how they can be incorporated differently in a paper.

Although personal home pages may be difficult to assess in terms of authorial expertise, infommercial sites are problematic because their purpose is multiple—conflating educational and commercial goals—and therefore often unclear. An example of an unusual yet useful infommercial Web site is *Solar-Dome* (see <http://www.solardome.com>), "a solar theme park on the Web, designed for entertainment and education, along with complete solar components catalog and direct connection to hundreds of local renewable energy installation specialists around the globe." The site was found during a broad Web search using the search term *electric cars.* Librarians often caution students away from commercial sites because, it is argued, they are inherently persuasive and thus biased. We argue, however, that all texts are biased in one way or another; the wide range of texts available on the Web simply highlights this fact.

Therefore, sites should be evaluated on a case-by-case basis, by asking relevant questions about a particular site's purpose, authors, and target audience; by conducting follow-up research as necessary; and by balancing the information found in the site with information from other sites as well as from print sources with different rhetorical contexts.

The authors of the *SolarDome* site—Chris Jensen and Steve Lowe—are, respectively, an entrepreneur (an MBA-holding music store owner, who hopes to build a solar-vehicle theme park) and a "solar educator with twenty years of solar industrial experience." The site's sponsorship, purpose, and audience are unclear and difficult to categorize, as it is technically a commercial venture, offering products for sale, yet it appears predominantly educational and advocatory in tone. It would be a shame if a student researcher working on the topic of electric cars allowed this ambiguity to dissuade her from using the site, however, because it contains an informative article on electric and hybrid vehicles by Robert Q. Riley in which an argument advocating the use of electric cars is supported by a great deal of specific factual evidence. Unfortunately, the site contains no information about who Riley is, nor does Riley provide sources for most of his data; these are both common problems encountered on the Web. Students, however, need not decide at this point to accept or reject the source on its own ambiguous merits, because further research can answer some of the questions posed previously. For example, a new Web search on Riley himself reveals that he is a transportation design consultant located in Scottsdale, Arizona, with a great deal of experience in electric cars and provides his e-mail address and phone number if the student wanted to contact Riley. Additionally, students could conduct further Web or library research on electric cars, and compare the information found in other sources with different rhetorical missions to that of Riley's. The point here is that if Riley's article had been published in a reputable periodical such as *Technology Review* or *Automotive Engineering*, a student would not think twice about citing it in a paper. By encountering it on the Web, however, in an ambiguous context, a student is forced to evaluate the piece on its own merits, conduct further research into the credentials of the author, look to other elements on the Web site itself for clues as to its mode and value, seek sources that make an opposing argument to balance her information sources, and present an argument to the teacher as to that source's value. In other words, the challenging nature of Web sources creates new kinds of work for researchers but, as a result, highlights the fundamental critical and intellectual skills necessary for good research writing.

Invoking a set of Web evaluation criteria for students that is broader, more flexible, and more context-oriented than traditional print criteria can thus serve several functions in the research-oriented writing classroom. We can use it to call attention to the fact that there is no single set of criteria that can be used to evaluate all Web sites or indeed all print texts; instead, it is more useful to invoke a broad set of questions and ask questions as they become relevant. As Pixie Ferris (1997) pointed out, the only universal judgment that can be applied to any source of information is that, for a particular individual, it has value. Research exercises such as the one described previously have the immediate utility of helping students locate and evaluate Web information sources in a manner appropriate for the particular research they are conducting; in the long term, forcing students to decide on a case-by-case basis what contains value develops their ability to ask appropriate critical questions regarding the source, content, and presentation of information in any context, academic or not.

INTO THE WEB ... AND BEYOND

Analyzing and evaluating textual information from sources with diverse purposes and authors is not the only challenge faced by students using the Web. The medium through which this information is presented—specifically, the images, links, and interactivity on the Web—pose perhaps more obvious and more daunting challenges to student researchers and, correspondingly, opportunities for composition teachers. Images, links, and interactivity are not, strictly speaking, *new* elements in the reading and research experience; they have parallels in scholarly print texts and so compel us to revisit and give new emphasis to certain issues that have not previously played a large role in the evaluation of sources. Moreover, attention to the Web's hypermedia and interactive nature extends the horizon of rhetorical analysis in productive and intriguing ways.

Visual Literacy and the Web

Because of the ease with which high-quality images as well as text can be displayed, and because of its frequent use by entertainment and commercial organizations, the Web is a more visually-oriented place than the traditional library. Most Web sites incorporate images—photographs, charts, maps, original designs—as well as colors and other graphic elements (not to mention animation, video, and sound). The danger, of course, is that students get caught up in the coolness of a Web site's visual presentation; it is not too reductive to compare the Web to a con artist dangling shiny objects in front of a mark's eyes. But, although impressive, high-quality images may enhance the credibility of a Web site, conveying the impression that its author has the ability, interest, and resources to make a strong aesthetic appeal to readers, excellent images alone don't guarantee reliability or validity. Visual elements need to be read in two ways: as conveying information in themselves—information that may complement, complicate, or contradict the message conveyed by the text—and as providing clues to the overall rhetorical situation of the site. In both cases, visual elements are incorporated into a researcher's overall assessment of a site, yielding an analysis that acknowledges that the image as well as the text convey pertinent information.

A good starting point is to consider the relation between image and text. Although images themselves are rarely neutral, they become even less so when paired with words that can limit or alter their possible interpretations. A valuable example comes from John Berger's (1972) *Ways of Seeing*. Early in the book, Berger reprints a painting and asks readers to consider it. He then asks us to turn the page, and beneath the painting is written: "This is the last picture that Van Gogh painted before he killed himself" (pp. 27–28). Suddenly, the birds in the picture look more ominous, the wheat field more disturbed. Has the picture changed? Yes and no. What has become clear, though, is that seeing isn't just a physical process. In *The Language of Visual Art: Perception as a Basis for Design*, Jack Frederick Myers (1989) claimed that "perceptions are derived from: (1) biological structure; (2) experience; and (3) knowledge" (p. 9), and as teachers we must help students see how experience and knowledge shape the ways they read images. This experience and knowledge isn't limited to what we had before booting up our computers, either. Web sites teach us how they want to be read, in large part through visual, graphic, and layout elements, and we must be aware of that teaching process as we read.

Berger's (1972) example has particular relevance for the Web, where images are used in abundance and in widely varying ways. For example, students could easily find numerous Web versions of Edvard Munch's *The Scream*. Some are connected to personal home pages ("here are some paintings I like"), some are art reproduction companies selling posters or T-shirts, one is a site that matches Bob Dylan lyrics to famous paintings, one is the Ben and Jerry's site featuring the "Red Nose Day Museum" (touched-up famous images wearing red clown noses done in conjunction with *Comic Relief* (see <http://www.benjerry.com/rednose/6.html>), and one is a medical site that discusses Munch's clinical problems in light of his art. These sites present the painting cropped and full-sized, in both black-and-white and color, with and without title, artist, date, and museum information. If a student was working on an art history paper about Munch, she would have to be prepared to find the image in many different contexts and to consider what each of those contexts then does to the painting. A simple *Webcrawler* search and link to the Ben and Jerry's site could lead to disastrous conclusions ("Munch was a joyful painter who put clown noses on what might otherwise be startling images . . ."). The meaning of the image, in short, is dependent on the context in which it is presented.

Students must also be cognizant of the possible dissonance between image and text on a Web site. In an effort to discover a unified meaning of a site, students might miss the clues that make it easier to determine the site's validity. "The 'convention of unity' is a powerful ideological weapon," Mieke Bal (1990) theorized, "because of the pressure it exerts on the reader to choose one interpretation over another rather than to read through the conflict of interpretations" (p. 507). The conflict between seemingly dispassionate words and a quite emotionally charged visual, for instance, might be the key to determining the purposes of a Web site, and students must be encouraged to find and read such discontinuities.

Apart from their connection to the text, images themselves convey not only information but also possible bias. Michael Rock (1994) represented the concerns of graphic designers when he wrote that "images and charts seem to not imply an inherent point-of-view. They radiate a false objectivity because the concept of the image-as-opinion is difficult for most people to grasp" (p. 148). Students need, at the least, to be made aware of the possible ways visual information can be manipulated. Charts and graphs are not just neutral presentations of facts. Pictographs can "lie" if the base image doesn't equal a standard unit; bar graphs can "lie" if the y-axis has no zero point. Drawings and photographs can manipulate the eye through tricks of perspective and visual illusions. All these issues, obviously, also pertain to print documents. In an age when news magazines crop Saddam Hussein's mustache to make him look more like Hitler or darken O. J. Simpson's skin to heighten racial tensions, questioning where the truth meets the image is always worth doing, whether on the Web or off. Because the Web highlights these issues, it encourages us to reinvigorate our teaching about the graphic and visual components of print texts. Although the combination of graphics and text is far from new (illustrated manuscripts go back hundreds of years), the field of visual literacy is still relatively in its infancy, particularly in writing courses. The Web compels us to attend to it.

Links: Intertextuality and Structure on the Web

As with visual images, both Web sites and print documents incorporate intertextuality—implicit or explicit references to other sources—although a Web site's intertextuality, operating largely through its links, poses challenges for students in evaluating the source. In a print document, the references or bibliography section indicates the sources an author cited explicitly, and these resources can be tracked down and evaluated by student researchers to determine the credibility, comprehensiveness, and possible biases of the original source. Links in Web sites operate similarly to give readers clues about the value of the information the site presents. Although the mere existence of links in a Web site seems to imply that research has informed the site and that it is connected to a broader context of related and relevant information, links are only worth the information on the other side of the mouse click, just as an extensive bibliography doesn't necessarily indicate that the author has drawn on reliable, valid, or current information. In short, a necessary component of evaluation is assessing the sources to which an author refers.

Links pose certain challenges to students in making that assessment, some which stem from the Web's wide array of material; one is likely to find sites linked to other sites that have different purposes and different degrees of reliability. Although a status bar at the bottom of a Web browser generally will provide an URL (Universal Resource Locator) of a link when a Web-user puts the cursor over that link's name, URLs are rarely as descriptive and helpful as the publishing information of a reference page. Even the seemingly more trustworthy "edu" domain doesn't always mean that material has been sponsored by a university (let alone approved through some sort of peer review) because students and professors can display personal home pages through their university's server. In general, determining the value of a linked site is difficult without actually checking that site, and with the number of links on the Web, student researchers may find that their search for relevant information can become time-consuming and unfocused.

Students must also resist simplistically thinking that the number of links on a Web site correlates with the quality of the site. Obviously, a lack of links could signal that a source is not situated within its own particular research context; it could mean a source is lacking the equivalent of a literature review. However, students must also be aware that sites produced by academics frequently contain few links yet offer a reference page. Just because a source is not taking full advantage of being a Web document by using hypertextual links doesn't mean it presents unworthy information. Its value must be evaluated separately from its value as hypertext. On the other hand, a site could suffer from too many links. A technical writer and consultant, William Horton (1990) suggested that a writer link sparingly, citing Schneiderman's advice to link two to eight times per page (p. 310); an over-use of links can confuse researchers attempting to ascertain the priority and relevance of linked information. A Web site with too many links suggests an author's inability to discriminate: How can one trust an author who cannot seem to distinguish the valuable from the not valuable?

Links also present in a more forceful way a problem that exists in print material as well: Where does a source's borders exist? This question has troubled theorists writing on influence and intertextuality in print texts, but it is even more troubling in hypertext documents. Students can at least tell where articles begin and end in journals, but determining when a link merely goes to another page within a site as opposed to when it leaps to another Web document by different authors on a server far, far away is a trickier matter, and one at the heart of evaluating sources on the Web.

In the "Rhetoric of Hypermedia: Some Rules for Authors," George Landow (1991) provided nineteen rules for creating useful links, and one can read through his list to consider how sites should properly treat their readers. Landow prefaced his rules with three reader-centered reasons rules are necessary: 1) readers must be oriented as to their position in hyperspace, so they may "read efficiently and with pleasure;" 2) readers must be informed where links lead (a site must provide departure information); and, 3) readers must be made to feel at home in a document after using a link (a site must provide entrance information) (p. 82). Clearly, any site that cannot bother to do all three things is less trustworthy, given that consideration is one element of ethos.

Landow (1991) also stressed the active nature of hypertext, what most often gets called interactivity, particularly with rule four: "The author of hyper-media materials must provide devices that stimulate the reader to think and explore" (p. 86). He sees links as the way to encourage such thought and exploration, and so his rules offer ways to make links most helpful by creating context and relationships, by mapping links visually, and by leaning on existing metaphors of navigation (navigation itself is a metaphor he deconstructs in a footnote). Landow's work on hypertextual linking reveals that its significance extends beyond intertextuality into more broadly relevant rhetorical issues; links can become a means for stimulating and engaging readers, a Web-specific rhetorical strategy students should be encouraged to understand.

Links also compel students to attend to structure and organization. Through its capacity to link, a hypertext elicits associational, not linear thinking, a move that could seem a call for sloppiness of thought. However, linear thinking is just as much a construct as associational thinking can be; indeed, it has been suggested that the nonlinear, recursive way hypertext presents information is actually closer to the way certain non-Western cultures organize and process ideas. It has also been argued that hypertext is a more appropriate and effective way to structure certain kinds of information. Horton (1990) suggested the following as the best use for links: teaching concepts, writing highly annotated documents, creating problem-solving systems, providing loose collections of interrelated documents, and modeling and teaching organization itself (pp. 307–308). As they assess the way a site uses links, student researchers can consider the effectiveness of the structure of links within the context of the entire Web site as well as the effectiveness of individual links in providing related and reliable information. Hypertext links enable readers to create their own reading experience, and this in itself is a powerful tool for teachers. Discussing how and why links link can help us understand not only the value of a Web site, but also how ideas can connect, coordinate, and subordinate in any writing.

Interactivity on the Web

Although images and links on Web sites have some clear parallels to what we find in print texts, a feature such as interactivity, which is an essential element of the Web, would seem to manifest itself infrequently in print and so present a particular challenge to students as they evaluate Web sites during the research process. Some of the more popular, mass-market magazines and books occasionally include interactive elements such as quizzes, opinion polls, mail-in response forms, or membership applications. Scholarly writing, on the other hand, almost never requests such interaction from the reader, and indeed, is notable for the one-way direction of its communication. Of course, all critical readers do interact with scholarly writing in a variety of ways, ranging from intellectual engagement and response to material activities such as scribbling in the margins, writing letters to the author or editor, or publishing articles responding to other articles or calls for papers. The authors may not solicit this interaction, as they do on the Web, but it takes place nonetheless and is an important part of the process of understanding texts, an assumption that underlies the use of journal-writing exercises in conjunction with reading assignments. We might say, then, that the Web makes explicit and public the author-reader interaction that occurs with print sources and so draws students' attention to this component of evaluation, causing them to reflect on the kinds of interaction allowed or encouraged by a text. As students reflect on Web sources and determine how the interactive features of a site help indicate the quality, accuracy, bias, and overall value of the information it presents, they learn to give more consideration to the response of the reader in the overall rhetorical situation.

Simply browsing the Web makes one aware of the variety of interactive modes available there. As the discussion of links in the previous section made clear, the Web's hypertextual structure in and of itself enables a degree of interactivity. Readers can choose different paths through a Web site by making choices to follow certain links, thus personalizing their use of the site. An evaluation of a Web site's links necessarily includes an evaluation of the range and quality of choices the site offers for the reading experience. However, hypertextuality in itself is a relatively low order of interactivity, allowing the reader only to customize his or her own experience—an opportunity also offered in printed texts—and not to contribute to or affect the site in any way.[4] A higher order of interactivity is found in several other fairly common features of Web sites: It has become a rule of *netiquette,* for instance, to include an e-mail address or a "mail-to" at the bottom of a home page, allowing readers to contact authors with comments or questions. This possibility can lead students to do more primary research, and in so doing chip away at the notion of the unquestioned authority of the author. Advances in Web programming, driven largely by the development of commercial activities on the Web, also enable more complex types of interactivity: local search engines, questionnaires, application and pur-

---

[4]More interactive are those hypertexts that enable readers to make some contribution—for example, by adding plot elements or characters to a story. This is not yet a common feature of web sites, however, and is mostly found in CD-ROMs or special software programs.

chasing forms, guest books, bulletin boards, chat rooms, question-and-answer forums. In each case, a different kind of information is solicited from the reader, and for a different purpose. In assessing interactive features, then, student researchers need to consider why the site is soliciting interaction, from whom, and toward what end. In short, they need to read interactive elements as clues in determining a Web site's rhetorical mode and purpose.

For instance, membership applicants at nonprofit and advocacy organization sites, such as the NRA and Planned Parenthood, remind readers that the information offered there is, to some extent, intended as an advertisement for the organization, helping it to solicit members. Thus, the response sought from readers indicates that the information presented throughout the site should be regarded warily and should perhaps be double-checked for accuracy. The same is true for marketing and sales on the Web; interactive questionnaires and purchasing forms at these sites remind readers that the other information there is, at least in part, promotional. Chat rooms and discussion forums might also be used at a commercial site to generate increased customer contact and improve customer satisfaction; entertainment-oriented sites regularly provide this feature to increase the number of visitors and thus increase the Web sites' advertising revenue. The genre, purpose, audience, and persuasive strategies of the Web site, in other words, can be discerned through the interactive choices it offers.

However, not all interactivity on the Web has a promotional or commercial orientation, and indeed in some instances opportunities for reader input indicate that the site is produced and visited by exports in the field. In "Wired Science," Herb Brody (1996) noted that there are a number of Web sites where scientists, engineers, medical researchers, and technical professionals regularly post drafts of papers to solicit feedback from peers. Brody described the Internet as a virtual chalkboard for scientists, on which "theories, experimental results, shoot-from-the-hip notions are all shared, electronically, with the geographically dispersed community of people who find this information important" (p. 43). Similarly, the *Journal of Computer-Mediated Communication* (see <http://www.ascusc.org/jcmc>), an electronic publication affiliated with the Annenberg School of the University of Southern California and the Hebrew University of Jerusalem, includes in a recent issue several means to draw on the expertise of its readers: a readers' poll, a threaded message board to facilitate discussion of topics suggested by readers and editors of the journal, a list to which readers can submit addresses of important resources on the Web, and a newsletter that solicits submissions. In these examples of academically-oriented sites, the opportunities for reader interaction might be seen as enhancing the reliability, comprehensiveness, and authority of the information found therein. Through their interactive options we see that these sites are attempting to become loci for communities of experts and for the compilation and advancement of knowledge in certain fields, and therefore, they are dynamic and potentially rich sources of information for student researchers.

Authors of Web sites have a range of interactive possibilities from which to choose, and their choices both affect the experience of reading a Web site and afford insight into the site's overall purpose. Because interactive features directly address and solicit information from readers, assessing these features gives students quite direct experience in assessing audience. Indeed, the Web makes visible and legible the role of the reader in any rhetorical situation by making authors more accessible and readers' responses more public.

CONCLUSION

Clearly, the question "Can we use Web sources for this assignment?" opens up a series of teaching opportunities, particularly when our goal is to help students assess information and incorporate it into their own writing. Drawing the Web into the classroom enables us to teach more about rhetorical modes and strategies and to expand upon notions of literacy in general. We see it as a compelling and effective way to help students develop stronger research, reading, and writing skills, while enhancing their ability to perform useful primary and secondary research.

This is not to say, however, that we see the Web as some Panglossian answer to all of composition's ills. Indeed, any attempt to increase the presence of networked computing in writing classes brings to the fore certain very real material constraints affecting our field and academia generally; foremost among them is the unequal and inadequate distribution of resources, technological and otherwise. Within and across educational institutions, students do not have equal access to computers or to the internet, nor do most composition teachers have the equipment or the time for professional development in this area. Even if all departments and universities could rise above previously limitations of funding, providing computer and Internet access to every student and providing teachers the wherewithal to stay at least a step ahead of their students, it is still the case that the Web is not an ideologically neutral territory. It is inextricably bound to its time and place and to the ideologies of that time and place. The Web is unfortunately like the typical academic library, and like most of academia, in that it reflects and perpetuates inequalities of language, nationality, ethnicity, gender, and class. To these biases, the Web adds a heavy dose of capitalist values and consumerism.

However, it is unwise, we believe, to reject the Web for these reasons. We have outlined here how a close and careful reading of Web sites can enhance students' research and writing skills; it is also an important step in educating students to be critical users of the Web and the Internet. Assessing the value of information offered at individual Web sites leads naturally to a critical approach to the Web as a whole and invites students to enter important debates about the social, cultural, political, and economic implications of this new medium of communication. The Web has the potential to be shaped in some degree by its users; indeed, the Web users of this morning are the Web authors of this afternoon. Therefore, harnessing students' initial and perhaps uncritical enthusiasm for the Web, and cultivating in its place an attentive, thorough, and discerning approach, may ultimately lead to improvements in the Web itself.

REFERENCES

Alexander, Jan, & Tate, Marsha. (1996, October). The web as a research tool: Evaluation techniques. [Online]. Available: <http://www.science.widener.edu/~withers/evalout.htm> [1998, March 9].

Bal, Mieke. (1990). De-disciplining the eye. *Critical Inquiry, 16*, 506–531.

Berger, John. (1972). *Ways of seeing.* London: Penguin.

Birkerts, Sven. (1994). *The Gutenberg elegies.* Boston: Faber and Faber.

Brody, Herb. (1996). Wired science. *Technology Review, 99*, 42–52.

Ferris, Pixie. (1997). Writing in cyberspace. *CMC Magazine.* [Online]. Available: <http://www.december.com/cmc/mag/1997/jun/ferris.html> [1998, March 9].

Gilster, Paul. (1997). *Digital literacy.* New York: John Wiley & Sons.

Hairston, Maxine; Ruszkiewicz, John J.; & Seward, Daniel E. (1997). *CoreText: A handbook for writers.* New York: Longman.

Horton, William K. (1990). *Designing and writing online documentation.* New York: John Wiley & Sons.

Landow, George P. (1991). *Hypermedia and literary studies.* Cambridge, MA: MIT Press.

Liu, Alan. (1998, March). *The voice of the shuttle.* [Online]. Available: <http://humanitas.ucsb.edu> [1998, March 9].

Miller, Susan, & Knowles, Kyle. (1997). *New ways of writing: A handbook for writing with computers.* Upper Saddle River, NJ: Prentice Hall.

Myers, Jack Frederick. (1989). *The language of visual art: Perception as a basis for design.* Fort Worth, TX: Holt, Rinehart, and Winston.

Ormondroyd, Joan; Engle, Michael; & Cosgrave, Tony. (1996, October). *How to critically analyze information sources.* [Online]. Available: <http://www.library.cornell.edu/okuref/research/skill26.htm> [1998, March 9].

Postman, Neil. (1995, October 9). Virtual students, digital classroom. *The Nation, 261*, 377–382.

Rock, Michael. (1994). Since when did *USA Today* become the national design idea? In Michael Bierut, William Drenttel, Steven Heller & D. K. Holland (Eds.), *Looking closer: Critical writings on graphic design* (pp. 146–149). New York: Allworth Press.

Rodrigues, Dawn. (1997). *The research paper and the World Wide Web.* Upper Saddle River, NJ: Prentice Hall.

Selfe, Cynthia L., & Selfe, Richard, J., Jr. (1994). The politics of interface: Power and its exercise in electronic contact zones. *College Composition and Communication, 45*, 480–504.

Sommers, Nancy I., & Simon, Linda. (1993). *The HarperCollins guide to writing.* New York: HarperCollins College Publishers.

Weidenborner, Stephen, & Caruso, Domenick. (1996). Writing research papers: A guide to the process (4th ed.). New York: St. Martin's Press.

Woodward, Jeannette A. (1997). *Writing research papers: Investigating resources in cyberspace.* Lincolnwood, IL: NTC Publishing Group.

The Greenhouse Effect

Helen Caldicott

Biography: *Helen Caldicott is an Australian physician who cofounded Physicians for Social Responsibility and founded Women's Action for Nuclear Disarmament and International Physicians to Save the Environment. In the 1970s and 1980s, she taught at Harvard Medical School. She has written several books and won many international awards.*

Caldicott gives figures for the increasing carbon monoxide production and projects these figures fifty years into the future, predicting a range of possible consequences for the environment, including desiccation of wheat lands, rising sea levels, disruption of the food chain, and melting of the ice caps. She then outlines several possible steps to curtail the production of greenhouse gases. Caldicott bases her argument on science but uses a number of rhetorical and political appeals, making the article a good reading for rhetorical analysis.

The earth is heating up, and the chief culprit is a gas called carbon dioxide. Since the late nineteenth century, the content of carbon dioxide (CO_2) in the air has increased by 25 percent. Although this gas makes up less than 1 percent of the earth's atmosphere, it promises to have devastating effects on the global climate over the next twenty-five to fifty years.[1] Carbon dioxide is produced when fossil fuels—coal, oil, and natural gas—burn, when trees burn, and when organic matter decays. We also exhale carbon dioxide as a waste product from our lungs, as do all other animals. Plants, on the other hand, absorb carbon dioxide through their leaves and transpire oxygen into the air.

Carbon dioxide, along with other rare man-made gases, tends to hover in the lower atmosphere, or troposphere, covering the earth like a blanket. This layer of artificial gases behaves rather like glass in a glasshouse. It allows visible white light from the sun to enter and heat up the interior, but the resultant heat or infrared radiation cannot pass back through the glass or blanket of terrestrial gases. Thus the glasshouse and the earth heat up.

In one year, 1988, humankind added 5.66 billion tons of carbon to the atmosphere by the burning of fossil fuels, and another 1 to 2 billion tons by deforestation and the burning of trees. Each ton of carbon produces 3.7 tons of carbon dioxide.[2]

But carbon dioxide accounts for only half of the greenhouse effect. Other gases, the so-called trace gases, which are present in minute concentrations, are

From *If You Love This Planet: A Plan to Heal the Earth.* New York: W. W. Norton. 1992. [14pp]

[1] United Nations Environment Program (UNEP), *The Greenhouse Gases* (Nairobi, 1987).

[2] Lester R. Brown et al., *State of the World, 1990: A Worldwatch Institute Report on Progress toward a Sustainable Society* (New York: W. W. Norton, 1990), 18.

much more efficient heat trappers.[3] Chlorofluorocarbons (CFCs) are ten to twenty thousand times more efficient than carbon dioxide. Methane is also very efficient (twenty times more effective than carbon dioxide) and is released at the rate of 100 liters per day from the intestine of a single cow. For example, Australia's cows make an annual contribution to global heating equivalent to the burning of thirteen million tons of black coal (about half the coal used in Australia per year). The scientists Ralph Laby and Ruth Ellis, from the Australian Commonwealth Institute and Research Organization, have developed a slow-release capsule that diminishes by 20 percent the production of methane by bacteria in the rumen of cows. (Methane is also a wonderful gas for heating and lighting houses; for example, Laby and Ellis estimated that two cows produce enough methane to heat and light an average house!)[4] Further sources of methane are garbage dumps, rice paddies, and termites. Nitrous oxide is another greenhouse gas, a component of car and power plant exhausts, of chemical nitrogenous fertilizers, and of bacterial action in heated, denuded soil. Nitrous oxide has increased by 19 percent over preindustrial levels and methane by 100 percent.[5] A report from the World Wide Fund for Nature published in August 1991 stated that carbon dioxide emissions from aircraft flying at altitudes of ten to twelve kilometers account for 1.3 percent of the global warming. However, the nitrous oxide that aircraft also emit is an extremely efficient heat trapper at that height and may increase global warming by 5 to 40 percent.[6]

Within fifty years, the "effective carbon dioxide concentration" (CO_2 and trace gases) will probably be twice that of preindustrial levels, raising global temperatures 1.5° to 5.5°C (2.7° to 10°F).[7] Because many scientific variables—heat trapping by clouds, change in radiation over melting ice caps, and so on—are not well understood, this rise in temperature could be as high as 10°C (18°F). Other scientists say the earth could cool several degrees. But all agree that we are in trouble.[8]

Such a rapid change in climatic conditions has never occurred in human history. If global heating were at the lower predicted level, it would match the 5°C warming associated with the end of the last ice age, eighteen thousand years ago. But this change would take place ten to a hundred times faster.[9] And

[3] Stephen Schneider, "The Changing Climate," *Scientific American,* Sept. 1989, 70–79.

[4] Mike Seccombe, "An Ill Wind That Only Does Cows Good," *Sydney Morning Herald,* July 18, 1989.

[5] Brown et al., *State of the World, 1990,* 17.

[6] "Another Culprit of the Greenhouse Effect: Jet Aircraft," *Sydney Morning Herald,* Aug. 27, 1991.

[7] UNEP, *Greenhouse Gases;* Schneider, "Changing Climate"; Michael Lemonick, "Feeling the Heat," *Time,* Jan. 2, 1989.

[8] Phillip Shabecoff, "Cloudy Days in Study of Warming World Climate," *International Herald Tribune,* Jan. 19, 1989.

[9] Schneider, "Changing Climate."

at present temperatures, a 5°C increase would cause global temperatures to be higher than at any other time during the last two million years.[10]

What will happen to the earth? Let us look at a worst-case scenario. Changes of climate could have devastating consequences in the tropical forests and food-growing areas of the world, causing extinction of many plant and animal species over a few years, in evolutionary terms. Dust bowls could develop in the wheat belt of the United States, creating a situation like that described in *The Grapes of Wrath,* and the productive corn and wheat belt might migrate north into Canada and into the Soviet Union.[11]

Already the futures markets are speculating that productive banana and pineapple plantations will develop in the middle of arid Australia. Cyclones, tidal waves, and floods will almost certainly affect temperate areas of the world, which were previously immune to such catastrophes.[12]

Sea levels will probably rise as the warming oceans expand, and great areas of land will be flooded, particularly during storms. Rivers, lakes, and estuaries will have their courses and boundaries changed forever. This will disturb the hatching habitats of millions of fish.[13]

Because about one-third of the human population lives within sixty kilometers of the sea, millions, or even billions, of people will either be killed by floods or storms or be forced to migrate to higher levels, thereby severely dislocating other urban and rural populations. These refugees will create chaos as they move into established rural areas, towns, and cities. Food production will already have been disrupted by the change in climate, and a redistribution of the scarce remaining resources will probably not happen.[14]

As sea levels rise, beautiful cities, including Venice and Leningrad, will be submerged, and even Westminster Abbey and the houses of Parliament, in London, will be threatened. Many beautiful, exotic Pacific islands will be underwater. Sea levels could rise seven feet (2.2 meters) by the year 2010, according to the U.S. Environmental Protection Agency.[15]

It is possible that the polar ice caps will melt; alternatively, the Antarctic snow cover might increase in volume as warm air induces a buildup of snow-forming clouds over the South Pole.[16] (Warm air promotes the evaporation of water from the earth's surface, thereby thickening the cloud cover.)

---

[10]Walter H. Corson, ed., *The Global Ecology Handbook: What You Can Do about the Environmental Crisis.* (Boston: Beacon Press, 1990), 232.

[11]Lemonick, "Feeling the Heat."

[12]Ibid.

[13]Ibid.

[14]Corson, ed., *Global Ecology Handbook,* 233.

[15]Ibid., 232.

[16]UNEP, *Greenhouse Gases.*

The aquatic food chain will be threatened because the base of the pyramid of the ocean food chain—algae and plankton—will be seriously affected. These ubiquitous single-celled plants are food for primitive life forms and are themselves consumed by more evolved species of fish. Some forms of algae and plankton will be threatened by rising sea temperatures, and many are extremely sensitive to UV light. . . . Therefore, as the temperature rises and as the ozone diminishes,[17] this essential element of the food chain will be jeopardized.

Moreover, plankton and algae, together with trees and plants, are nature's biological traps for elemental carbon from atmospheric carbon dioxide, 41 percent being trapped in sea plants and 59 percent in land plants. Higher concentrations of atmospheric carbon dioxide will promote the growth of algae. But if algae are threatened by global warming and ozone depletion, this hypothetical fertilizer effect will become irrelevant. By increasing the atmospheric concentration of carbon dioxide from man-made sources, we are thus also threatening the survival of trees, plants, algae, and plankton.

Forests, too, are terribly vulnerable to climatic change and ozone destruction. Because temperature changes will be relatively sudden, specific tree species will not have thousands of years to migrate to latitudes better suited to their survival, as they did at the end of the last ice age. When the ice cap slowly retreated northward, the spruce and fir forests moved from the area of the United States into Canada at the rate of one kilometer per year. Although some plants that adapt rapidly will thrive under changed circumstances, most forests will die, and along with them many animal and bird species.[18]

Interestingly, although sudden global warming will kill large numbers of trees, increased carbon dioxide concentrations will actually stimulate the growth of those that remain, because the gas is a plant food during photosynthesis and thus acts as a fertilizer.[19] Therefore, as forests become extinct in the unusually hot climate, some food crops and surviving trees will grow bigger and taller. Unfortunately, many weeds are even more responsive to high carbon dioxide levels than crop plants are, and they will almost certainly create adverse competition.[20]

Another factor to consider in this rather dire biological scenario is that faster-growing crops utilize more soil nutrients. Hence more artificial fertilizer will be needed, and, since electricity is required for its production, more carbon dioxide will be added to the air. But nitrogen-containing fertilizers themselves

[17]**ozone:** A gas in the stratosphere that screens out most dangerous ultraviolet (UV) radiation. Many atmospheric scientists believe that the earth's protective ozone layer is being depleted primarily as a result of chlorofluorocarbon (CFC) emissions.—ED.

[18]Schneider, "Changing Climate."

[19]UNEP, *Greenhouse Gases.*

[20]Corson, ed., *Global Ecology Handbook,* 233.

release the greenhouse gas nitrous oxide into the air.[21] In addition, as soil heats, vegetable matter decays faster, releasing more carbon dioxide. These are just a few of the interdependent and variable effects of global warming that are so difficult to calculate.

When forests are destroyed by greenhouse and ozone deforestation, or by chainsaw and bulldozer deforestation, massive quantities of rich topsoil will be lost forever as floods and erosion wash it out to sea. Downstream waterways will overflow their banks as rain pours off the denuded high ground, and when the floods subside, the once deep rivers will be silted up from the eroded topsoil. Large dams designed for predictable rainfalls could collapse and drown downstream populations, and associated hydroelectric facilities would then be destroyed.

Decreased rainfall in other parts of the world will reduce stream runoff. For example, a rise of several degrees Celsius could deplete water levels in the Colorado River, causing severe distress for all communities that depend upon the river for irrigation, gardening, drinking water, and so forth. The water quality will also suffer, because decreased volumes will not adequately dilute toxic wastes, urban runoff, and sewage from towns and industry.[22] Until April 1991, when rain began to fall again in some quantity, California experienced a severe five-year drought, whose impact was rapidly becoming critical. After this April rainfall, the California drought continued unabated. That may be an omen of worse to come.

Cities will be like heat traps. For instance, Washington, D.C., at present suffers one day per year over 38°C and thirty-five days over 32°C (100°F and 90°F). By the year 2050, these days could number twelve and eighty-five, respectively.[23] In that case, many very young and many old and infirm persons would die from heat stress, and there would be a general temptation to turn on air conditioners, which . . . use CFCs and electricity, whose generation produces more carbon dioxide. People will thus be in a catch-22 situation— damned if they do and damned if they don't. . . .

How did the problem of atmospheric degradation become so alarming, and what are the solutions?

When CFC was first concocted, in 1928, nobody understood the complexities of atmospheric chemistry, and during subsequent decades scientists really believed that chlorofluorocarbons were ideal for refrigeration, air conditioners, plastic expanders, spray cans, and cleaners for silicon chips.[24] Industry became

[21]UNEP, *Greenhouse Gases;* Schneider, "Changing Climate."

[22]Schneider, "Changing Climate."

[23]UNEP, *Greenhouse Gases.*

[24]UNEP, *Action on Ozone.*

so heavily invested in its production that it now finds it very difficult to cut back, even though the environmental consequences of not doing so will be severe. . . .

In the early years of the Industrial Revolution, no person could have predicted the atmospheric havoc that the internal-combustion engine and coal-fired plants would wreak. Even during the 1930s and 1940s, when General Motors, Standard Oil, Phillips Petroleum, Firestone Tire and Rubber, and Mack Manufacturing (the big-truck maker) bought up and destroyed the excellent mass transit systems of Los Angeles, San Francisco, and most other large U.S. cities in order to induce total societal dependence on the automobile, global warming was a vague future threat.[25] These companies were subsequently indicted and convicted of violating the Sherman Antitrust Act.

But now that we understand the coming disaster, we are in a position to act. In order to act, we must be willing to face several unpleasant facts.

Fact Number One.   The United States, constituting only 5 percent of the earth's population, is responsible for 25 percent of the world's output of carbon dioxide.[26] It uses 35 percent of the world's transport energy, and an average-size tank of gasoline produces between 300 and 400 pounds of carbon dioxide when burned.[27] Together, the United States and the Soviet Union consume 44 percent of the world's commercial energy.[28]

In China, by contrast, there are 300 million bicycles, and only one person in 74,000 owns a car. Each year three times more bicycles than cars are produced. Domestic bicycle sales in 1987 came to 37 million—more than all the cars bought worldwide.[29] Motor vehicles globally produce one-quarter of the world's carbon dioxide, and in the United States transportation (cars, buses, trains, and trams [streetcars]) produces 30 percent of all the carbon dioxide. Transport consumes about one-third of all the energy consumed globally. The United States also produces 70 percent of the carbon monoxide gas (which leads to deoxygenation of the human blood), 45 percent of the nitrous oxides (which cause acid rain), and 34 percent of the hydrocarbon chemicals (many of which are carcinogenic).[30]

In 1985, there were 500 million motor vehicles in the world, 400 million of them cars. Europeans and North Americans owned one-third of these.[31]

[25]Jonathan Kwitny, "The Great Transportation Conspiracy," *Harper's,* Feb, 1981, 14–21.

[26]"What the U.S. Should Do," *Time,* Jan. 2, 1989, 65.

[27]Jeremy Leggett, ed., *Global Warming: The Greenpeace Report* (New York: Oxford University Press, 1990).

[28]Corson, ed., *Global Ecology Handbook,* 192.

[29]Brown et al., *State of the World, 1990,*120.

[30]Corson, ed., *Global Ecology Handbook,* 192; Leggett, ed., *Global Warming,* 261, 262.

[31]Leggett, ed., *Global Warming,* 269.

Fact Number Two.   In order to reduce carbon dioxide production, cars must be made extremely fuel efficient, and some computer models and proto-type automobiles can indeed achieve 60 to 120 miles per gallon (mpg) by means of lightweight materials and better design.[32] But these techniques are not being employed. In 1987, U.S. car manufacturers dropped most of their research on fuel-efficient cars, and in 1986 the fuel-efficient standard, or minimum mpg, in the States was only 26 mpg.[33] In 1991, it was still only 27.5 mpg, and the Bush administration has resisted any move to increase fuel efficiency in cars.[34] In fact, the president's new energy plan of 1991 barely deals with these issues, and does not deal at all with mass transportation. It is more efficient to transport hundreds of bodies in one train than hundreds of single bodies in hundreds of cars. Furthermore, the construction of sleek state-of-the-art trains would con-structively reemploy the one in eight people in California who currently are employed producing weapons of mass destruction.[35] Far more people will work in this wonderful new civilian industry than in the obsolete weapons industry, because the military sector is capital intensive, whereas the civilian sector is labor intensive. The corporation that first accepts this challenge could become the world's leading producer of global mass transit systems and could earn huge profits while saving the planet.

Cars can be fueled with solar energy. In 1990, an international solar car race across Australia was held. The cars achieved the acceptable speed of ap-proximately 60 mph. They were slow to accelerate, but who needs cars that go from 0 to 90 mph in a matter of seconds? Cars can also be fueled with natural gas, which generates less carbon dioxide than gasoline does, and with alcohol. By investing heavily in this form of energy, Brazil has been helped to become somewhat energy independent. In 1988, alcohol provided 62 percent of Brazil's automotive fuel. Although alcohol is relatively expensive, it gives off 63 percent less carbon emission than gasoline. This excellent form of energy production is renewable, and marginal land can be used to grow crops that can be converted into alcohol. The United States already produces twenty million barrels of alco-hol by the fermentation of corn. As oil prices climb, alcohol will obviously be-come a viable fuel alternative.[36]

Cars can also be fueled with hydrogen; the technology is available. One can drink the exhaust of a car powered by hydrogen, because when hydrogen burns it produces pure water. Unfortunately, major U.S. auto companies seem resistant to being inventive and creative. They stick to old, outdated designs and

[32]Ibid., 289.

[33]Corson, ed., *Global Ecology Handbook*, 205.

[34]Ibid.

[35]Helen Caldicott, *Missile Envy* (New York: Morrow, 1984), 208.

[36]Brown et al., *State of the World, 1990*, 26.

have even resorted to copying the latest Japanese designs—a rather sorry setback for an industry that once led the world in automobile technology. It could overtake the Japanese industry by manufacturing solar-, hydrogen-, and alcohol-powered cars, while helping to save the planet.

Fact Number Three. Bicycles use human energy and save global energy. They are clean, efficient, and healthful for human bodies. Roads must give way to bicycle tracks. In China, special bicycle avenues with five or six lanes are separated from motorized traffic and pedestrians.[37] This sort of planning is required by a large percentage of the population of the United States and of the Western world. The arrangement is simple, easy, cheap, and clean. Distant, large-scale supermarkets and shopping malls accessible only by car will become obsolete as people demand small, convenient shops within walking distance of their homes. We can reestablish small community shopping centers, where people meet each other and socialize and where the emphasis is on the community rather than on consumerism. What a healthy, exciting prospect!

Fact Number Four. Buildings can be made extremely energy efficient. Improved designs for stoves, refrigerators, and electric hot-water heaters can increase energy efficiency by between 5 and 87 percent. The sealing of air leaks in houses can cut annual fuel bills by 30 percent, and double-paned insulated windows greatly reduce energy loss. Superinsulated houses can be heated for one-tenth of the average cost of heating a conventional home. In the United States, 20 percent of the electricity generated is used for lighting, but new fluorescent globes are 75 percent more efficient than conventional globes. Theoretically, then, the country could reduce its electricity usage for lighting to 5 percent of the total.[38] This, together with other conservation measures, would cause the closing down and mothballing of all nuclear reactors in the States, because 20 percent of all the electricity used there is generated by nuclear power.[39]

I lived in the beautiful city of Boston for fourteen years and grew to love the old New England houses. But now that I am more aware of the fate of the earth, I realize that these are totally inappropriate dwellings. They are big, rambling, leaky, and inefficient. The vast quantities of oil required to heat these large volumes of enclosed air through a long Boston winter adds to carbon dioxide greenhouse warming. When these handsome houses were built, in the last century, no one imagined that the earth would someday be in jeopardy. Fuel supplies seemed endless, and the air was relatively clean.

[37]Ibid., 128.
[38]Corson, ed., *Global Ecology Handbook*, 203–4.
[39]Ibid.

Houses of that kind can be made somewhat fuel efficient by the insulation of walls, ceilings, and windows and by the sealing of all leaks. To encourage such reform, the federal government must legislate adequate tax incentives, for in the long run these will provide insurance for our children's future.

Actually, solar buildings are now in an advanced stage of design and development. The need is for legislation that requires all new buildings, residential and office, to be solar designed—with large heat-trapping windows oriented toward the south and with floors made of tiles and cement, which trap the sun's heat during the day, and appropriate window insulation, which retains the heat at night. Solar hot-water panels and solar electricity generation are relatively cheap and state-of-the-art. Firms that manufactured such equipment would make large profits. Householders would benefit because they would become independent of the utilities; they could even sell back electricity to the local utility at off-peak hours. Indeed, some Americans are already vendors of electricity.

Solar technology would then become highly efficient and cheap, and a huge market would open up in the Third World. The industrialized countries could assist billions of people to bypass the fossil-fuel era, so they could generate electricity from solar and wind power and use solar cookers and solar hot-water generators. This is a signal solution to the problem of ongoing global warming. The First World must help the Third World bypass the fossil-fuel era if the earth is to survive.

Attention should also be given to the strange high-rise buildings covered in tinted glass that seem to be in vogue in many U.S. cities. These are not solar buildings. The windows cannot be opened to allow ventilation during the summer, and they must be cooled with air conditioners, which use ozone-destroying CFCs and carbon dioxide-producing electricity. In the winter, heat leaks from the windows like water through a sieve. And these buildings are generally lit up like Christmas trees at night, for no apparent purpose, by energy-inefficient lighting. Dallas, Houston, and Los Angeles boast numerous of these monstrosities, many of which now sit empty and idle, built by speculators who cashed in on the savings and loan scandal. (I used to wonder as I traveled through the United States in the 1980s why the Sun Belt was thriving. Now we know! This prosperity was a by-product of the deregulation of the savings and loan industry by the Reagan administration.)

We all must become acutely conscious of the way we live. Every time we turn on a switch to light a room, power a hair dryer, or toast a piece of bread, we are adding to global warming. We should never have more than one light bulb burning at night in our house unless there are two people in the house in different rooms—then two bulbs. Lights must not be left on overnight in houses or gardens for show, and all lights must be extinguished in office buildings at night.

Clothes dryers are ubiquitous and unnecessary. In Australia, we dry our clothes outside in the sun, hung by pegs from a line. Americans can do the same in the summer, and in the colder climes, like Boston's, clothes can be hung on lines in the cellars in the winter. In some American cities there are laws prohibiting people from hanging clothes on lines outside, on grounds that it is not aesthetically pleasing. This method of drying offers, in fact, an easy and efficient step toward the reduction of atmospheric carbon dioxide and radioactive waste. Clothes dryers use over 10 percent of the electricity generated in the States,[40] a large fraction of that generated by nuclear power. And bear in mind that electrically operated doors, escalators, and elevators all contribute to global warming. . . .

Renewable energy sources (wind, solar, geothermal, and so on) could theoretically provide a total energy output equal to the current global energy consumption. Today these sources already provide approximately 21 percent of the energy consumed worldwide and are freely available to be developed further.[41]

Solar power will soon yield electricity as cheap as coal-fired electricity. In fact, scientists at the U.S. Solar Energy Research Institute estimate that photovoltaic solar systems could supply over half the U.S. electricity within forty to fifty years. This technology will decrease in price as it is mass produced, modified, refined, and made more efficient. Solar water and household heating is already widespread in Australia, Greece, and the Middle East.[42]

Wind power offers an obvious and benign technique that is being used to generate electricity in many countries, including Greece, China, Australia, Israel, Belgium, Italy, Germany, Britain, the United States, and Demark. Since 1974, fifty thousand wind machines have been built, mainly in California and Denmark. Wind "farms" cover areas of the desert between Los Angeles and Palm Springs, and by the year 2030 wind power could provide 10 percent of the world's energy.[43]

Geothermal power, which taps into the intrinsic heat and lava trapped below the earth's crust, is already being used to good advantage in New Zealand, Iceland, and Hawaii, and there is much potential for its use in the United States, Soviet Union, and Central America. Output is increasing by 15 percent per year.[44]

Tidal power utilizes the twice daily changes in sea level to generate electricity. It is suitable only for certain coastlines, but it certainly offers great

[40]Ibid.

[41]Leggett, ed., *Global Warming*, 231.

[42]Ibid., 25.

[43]Ibid., 24, 25.

[44]World Commission on Environment and Development (WCED), *Our Common Future* (New York: Oxford University Press, 1987), 193.

possibilities in places where the tides vary twenty to a hundred feet per day. Wave power is another dynamic area awaiting development.

Hydropower has been expanding by 4 percent annually worldwide, and the potential for further expansion is vast.[45] Hydroelectric and geothermal power provides over 21 percent of the world's electricity.[46] Electricity generated at dams and waterfalls crosses borders and can be used in other countries; for instance, New England uses Canadian hydroelectricity. Hydroelectric dams that flood large areas of natural forests are ecologically dangerous, and careful planning is essential before and during their construction.

Cogeneration is a wonderful method for harnessing heat usually wasted in factories. One technique, used extensively in the Soviet Union and in Scandinavia, is to heat water and pipe it to warm whole towns and cities. Another is to use waste steam to drive electricity-generating turbines, to run refrigerators, and to power industrial machinery. An ordinary power plant is 32 percent efficient, but a cogenerator consuming the same amount of fuel is 80 percent efficient.[47]

Conservation can save large quantities of energy. Society must invest in highly efficient light bulbs, refrigerators, stoves, cars, and street lighting. Energy-efficient equipment uses one-third to one-half less energy than does conventional technology. Much of it has already been invented, but monopolistic corporations tend to encourage distribution of inefficient equipment, thus leading to increased electricity consumption. For example, General Electric manufactures not only nuclear reactors but also hair dryers, toasters, stoves, and refrigerators. Is it not therefore in GE's best interests to encourage people to use more electricity with less efficient appliances and to use electric brooms, electric hedge clippers, and electric lawn mowers instead of ones operated by muscle power?

But energy-efficient investments are much cheaper financially and ecologically than the building and operating of coal or nuclear plants. Patents for wonderful energy-saving inventions abound, but most inventors lack the money to develop their product. And corporations seem uninterested in pursuing or financing such inventions.

Not least, utilities hide enormous government subsidies that they receive for fossil fuels and nuclear power. This deception makes renewable energy appear to be more expensive. Because utilities enjoy an almost total monopoly in energy advertising and technologies of energy production, it is very hard to understand and dissect their propaganda. Solar-heating systems and photovoltaic cells endow people with energy self-reliance, but clearly such self-sufficiency is not and will not be seen to be in the best interests of the utilities.

---

[45]Ibid., 192.

[46]Corson, ed., *Global Ecology Handbook,* 93.

[47]Ibid., 205; WCED, *Our Common Future,* 200.

Trees and other plants (biomass) are sources of energy mainly in the developing world. In India, people even burn pats of cow dung for cooking. But inhabitants of these countries often decimate their forests for short-term survival. I have seen Indian women spend a whole day walking to a patch of trees, gather the wood, and walk home for another day in order to cook food for their families. The burning of wood adds to atmospheric carbon dioxide.

Deforestation is leading to desertification in many countries—to creeping deserts and utter destruction of the land. Brazil is even using parts of the Amazon forest to fuel iron ore smelters.[48] So wood is not necessarily a good fuel and needs to be replaced by solar, wind, and other kinds of power. Still, garbage and agricultural wastes can be used to produce methane, an excellent gas for cooking and heating. Biomass supplies 12 percent of the energy worldwide and up to 50 percent in some poor countries.[49]

Industrial efficiency has been shown to have enormous potential. It must be developed on a massive scale, for industry uses 40 to 60 percent of the available energy in the developed countries and 10 to 40 percent in the developing countries.[50]

If all fossil fuels were taxed to avoid climate change, the ecosphere could be brought into a relatively stable equilibrium. In the United States, this tax would raise the price of electricity by 28 percent and that of a gallon of gasoline by seventeen cents, but it would produce $60 billion in revenue, and this money could then be earmarked for alternative-energy facilities and conservation. In India, the tax would raise $17.5 billion.[51] The international community within the United Nations must endorse this tax proposal. According to the Worldwatch Institute report of 1990, in order to stabilize atmospheric greenhouse gas concentrations by 2050, net carbon emissions will need to be reduced by two billion tons per year. So, given a probable global population of eight billion by then, all people will require levels of net carbon emissions similar to India's today, which is only one-eighth of the current levels in Western Europe. Furthermore, 20 percent of the global carbon tax could be diverted to Third World reforestation, benign energy production, and renewable energy sources.[52]

A 12 percent reduction in global greenhouse gas emissions by 2000 seems an appropriate interim goal if we are to achieve a stabilization of carbon dioxide concentrations by 2050. This means that the United States and the Soviet

---

[48]Sting and Jean-Pierre Dutilleux, *Jungle Stories: The Fight for the Amazon* (London: Barrie & Jenkins, 1989), 4.

[49]Brown et al., *State of the World, 1990,* 25.

[50]WCED, *Our Common Future,* 199.

[51]Lester R. Brown et al., *State of the World, 1990,* 36.

[52]Ibid., 37.

Union would have to reduce carbon dioxide production by 35 percent over the next ten years. To be fair, though, Kenya and India could actually increase carbon dioxide emissions, because they produce so little at present. If we fail to make these important decisions and if the industrial countries maintain present-day emission levels, the Third World, by emulating the First World, could increase the quantity of carbon dioxide by some 20 to 30 percent by the year 2000 and by 50 to 70 percent by 2010, as its fuel use and population base expand.[53]

I don't think we have any choice in these matters, and the sooner we knuckle down to the task, the sooner we can reassure our children that they will inherit a viable future. 🜂

[53]Ibid., 35, 36.

Greenhouse Earth

Dixie Lee Ray and Louis R. Guzzo

Biography: Dixie Lee Ray, a marine biologist and champion of nuclear energy, was governor of the State of Washington from 1977 to 1981. She chaired the Atomic Energy Commission under President Nixon and was assistant secretary of state for Oceans, the Environment and Scientific Affairs under President Ford. She died in 1994. Guzzo, a newspaper editor, reporter, TV commentator, and teacher, was a member of the AEC and public affairs director of Ray's bureau.

Ray and Guzzo argue that the "hysteria" over global warming is greatly overblown and that we do not understand enough of the science of warming to make sound predictions. They claim that scientists who have made dire predictions have ignored the effect of oceans in absorbing CO_2 and moderating temperature. They conclude that though steps should be taken to reduce emissions, there is no reason to believe draconian measures are needed or would be effective. They provide a scientific argument in opposition to Caldicott; the similarity and differences between the evidence and the interests of the authors make for good analysis and discussion.

T̲he year 1988 ended on a high note of environmental hysteria about global warming, fueled by an unusually hot, dry summer (in the United States). Testifying at a Senate hearing, NASA's James Hansen claimed that the high

From *Trashing The Planet: How Science Can Help Us Deal with Acid Rain, Depletion of the Ozone, and Nuclear Waste (Among Other Things)*. Washington, D.C.: Regnery Publishing. 1990 [12pp]

temperatures presaged the onset of the long debated "greenhouse effect" caused by increased carbon dioxide (CO_2) in the atmosphere.[1]

Forgotten was the harsh winter of 1982, or of 1978, when, for example, barges carrying coal and heating oil froze in river ice and more than two hundred people lost their lives in the cold weather.

Only days after *Time* magazine featured a doomed, overheated earth as its "man of the year" for 1988, Alaska experienced the worst cold in its history. The freezing weather set in on January 12, 1989. Twenty different locations in our most northerly state recorded their lowest-ever temperatures, mainly in the range of −50 to −65 degrees Fahrenheit. At Tanana, near Fairbanks, −75 degrees Fahrenheit was reached. (The all-time low recorded anywhere in Alaska was −80 degrees in January 1971 at a Prospect Creek pipeline station.) The cold persisted; it did not moderate and begin to move south until the first week of February. Old-timers agreed that no such cold had ever been experienced before, and they expressed amazement that the temperature remained a chilly −16 degrees Fahrenheit along the coast even with an 81-knot wind blowing. This was unheard of, since usually it is coldest when the wind is quiet. In early February, the cold seeped down from Alaska along both sides of the Rocky Mountains, bringing near-record lows both to the Pacific Northwest and throughout the Midwest south to Texas and eventually to the mid-Atlantic and New England states. Proponents of the "greenhouse-is-here-global-warming-has-begun" theory were very quiet during these weeks.

To be fair, even if the projected greenhouse warming should occur, no one would expect it to happen all at once or without intervening cold spells. So let's examine the situation more closely.

Of course, the earth, with its enveloping blanket of atmosphere, constitutes a "greenhouse." This fact has never been at issue. Indeed, were it not for the greenhouse function of air, the earth's surface might be like the moon, bitterly cold (−270 degrees Fahrenheit) at night and unbearably hot (+212 degrees Fahrenheit) during the day. Although the amount of solar energy reaching the moon is essentially the same as that reaching earth, the earth's atmosphere acts like a filter. Of the incoming solar radiation, about 20 percent is absorbed in the atmosphere, about 50 percent reaches and warms the earth's surface, and the rest is reflected back into space. As the earth's surface is warmed up, infrared radiation is emitted. It is the presence of CO_2 (and water vapor, methane, hydrocarbon, and a few other gases) in the atmosphere that absorbs the long wavelength infrared radiation, thereby producing the warming "greenhouse effect." This accounts for a net warming of the earth's atmosphere system of

---

[1]James E. Hansen, 1988, *The Greenhouse Effect: Impacts on Current Global Temperatures and Regional Heat Waves,* testimony given before the Senate Committee on Energy and Natural Resources, typewritten report.

about 55 degrees Fahrenheit. Without this natural greenhouse, it would be difficult to sustain life on this planet.

All the important "greenhouse gases" are produced in nature, as well as by humans. For example, CO_2 comes naturally from the respiration of all living organisms and from decaying vegetation. It is also injected into the atmosphere by volcanoes and forest and grass fires. Carbon dioxide from man-made sources comes primarily from burning fossil fuels for home and building heat, for transportation, and for industrial processes. The amount of CO_2 released into the atmosphere is huge and it is commonly believed that it is divided about evenly between natural and man-made sources.

Hydrocarbons come from growing plants, especially coniferous trees, such as fir and pine, and from various industries. In the transportation arena, hydrocarbons result from incomplete oxidation of gasoline. Both hydrocarbons and methane also enter the atmosphere through the metabolism of cows and other ruminants. It is estimated that American cows produce about 50 million tons of these gases per year—and there is no control technology for such emissions. Methane seeps into the air from swamps, coal mines, and rice paddies; it is often "flared" from oil wells. The largest source of greenhouse gas may well be termites, whose digestive activities are responsible for about 50 billion tons of CO_2 and methane annually. This is ten times more than the present world production of CO_2 from burning fossil fuel. Methane may be oxidized in the atmosphere, leading to an estimated one billion tons of carbon monoxide per year. All in all, the atmosphere is a grand mixture of gases, in a constant state of turbulence, and yet maintained in an overall state of dynamic balance.

But now this balance appears to be disturbed as CO_2 and the other major greenhouse gases are on the rise, increasing their concentration in the air at a rate of about 1 percent per year. CO_2 is responsible for about half of the increase. Analysis of air bubbles trapped in glacial ice and of carbon isotopes in tree rings and ocean sediment cores indicate that CO_2 levels hovered around 260 to 280 parts per million from the end of the last ice age ten thousand years ago) till the mid-nineteenth century, except for an anomalous rise 300 years ago. And these measurements also show that CO_2 concentrations have varied widely (by 20 percent) as the earth has passed through glacial and interglacial periods. While today's 25 percent increase in CO_2 can be accounted for by the burning of fossil fuels, what caused the much greater increases in the prehistoric past?

The present increase has brought the CO_2 level to 340 parts per million, up about 70 parts per million. If we add the greater amounts of methane, hydrocarbons, and so forth, there is now a total of about 407 parts per million of greenhouse gases. This is large enough so that from the greenhouse effect alone we should have experienced a global warming of about two to four degrees Fahrenheit. But this has not happened.

The observed and recorded temperature pattern since 1880 does not fit with the CO_2 greenhouse warming calculations. During the 1880s, there was a period of cooling, followed by a warming trend. The temperature rose by one degree Fahrenheit during 1900 to 1940, then fell from 1940 to 1965, and then began to rise again, increasing by about 0.3 degrees Fahrenheit since 1975. When all these fluctuations are analyzed, it appears unlikely that there has been any overall warming in the last fifty years. And if the temperature measurements taken in the northern hemisphere are corrected for the urban effect— the so-called "heat island" that exists over cities due mainly to the altered albedo[2] from removing vegetation—then it is probable that not only has there been no warming; there may have been a slight cooling. It all depends on whose computer model you choose to believe.

Clearly, there is still something that is not understood about global conditions and about the weather links between the oceans and the atmosphere. Have the experts fully taken into account the role of the sea as a sink or reservoir for CO_2, including the well-known fact that much more CO_2 dissolves in cold water than in warm? Interest in the greenhouse gases and projections of global warming has stimulated greater interest in the role that the oceans play in influencing moderately or even drastically changing global climate. The oceans hold more CO_2 than does the atmosphere, sixty times more. Complex circulation patterns that involve waters of different temperature, together with the activities of marine organisms that deposit carbonate in their skeletons, carry carbon dioxide to the depths of the ocean.

Recall that all the public furor about global warming was triggered in June 1988, when NASA scientist James Hansen testified in the U.S. Senate that the greenhouse effect is changing the climate now! He said he was 99 percent sure of it, and the "1988 would be the warmest year on record, unless there is some remarkable, improbable cooling in the remainder of the year."[3] Well, there was. Almost while Dr. Hansen was testifying, the eastern tropical Pacific Ocean underwent a remarkable, improbable cooling—a sudden drop in temperature of seven degrees. No one knows why. But the phenomenon is not unknown; it is called La Niña to distinguish it from the more commonly occurring El Niño, or warm current, and it has happened nineteen times in the last 102 years.

Dr. Hansen did not consider the possibility of La Niña, because his computer program does not take sea temperatures into account. Yet the oceans cover 73 percent of the earth's surface.

When people, including scientists, talk "global," it is hard to believe that they can ignore 73 percent of the globe, but obviously they sometimes do. It is all the more astonishing to ignore ocean-atmosphere interactions, especially in

---

[2]**albedo** The ratio of light reflected by a planet to that received by it.—ED.

[3]"Hansen vs. the World on the Greenhouse Effect," *Science,* Vol. 244, pp. 1041–43, 2 June 1989.

the Pacific, when it is well established that El Niño has profound and wide-spread effects on weather patterns and temperatures; does it not follow that La Niña may also? Indeed, some atmospheric scientists credit the severely cold winter of 1988-89 to the earlier temperature drop in the tropical Pacific.

Once again, since the greenhouse gases are increasing, what's keeping the earth from warming up? There are a number of possible explanations. Perhaps there is some countervailing phenomenon that hasn't been taken into account; perhaps the oceans exert greater lag than expected and the warming is just postponed; perhaps the sea and its carbonate-depositing inhabitants are a much greater sink than some scientists believe; perhaps the increase in CO_2 stimulates more plant growth and removal of more CO_2 than calculated; perhaps there is some other greenhouse gas, like water vapor, that is more important than CO_2; perhaps varying cloud cover provides a greater feedback and self-correcting mechanism than has been taken into account; perhaps. . . . The fact is, there is simply not enough good data on most of these processes to know for sure what is happening in these enormous, turbulent, interlinked, dynamic systems like atmosphere and oceanic circulation. The only thing that can be stated with certainty is that they do affect the weather. So also do forces outside the planet, and in a moment we'll look at the sun in this regard.

First, we must acknowledge that some zealots in the greenhouse issue make much of deforestation, especially in the tropical rainforests, but this topic is marked more by emotion bordering on hysteria than on solid scientific data. Good measurements on CO_2 uptake and oxygen production in tropical rain-forests are lacking. Such information could be critical, because we know that in temperate climates mature trees and climax forests add little in the way of photosynthetic activity and consequent CO_2 removal from the atmosphere. Mature trees, like all living things, metabolize more slowly as they grow old. A forest of young, vigorously growing trees will remove five to seven tons more CO_2 per acre per year than old growth.[4] There are plenty of good reasons to preserve old-growth forests, but redressing the CO_2 balance is not one of them. If we are really interested (as we should be) in reducing atmospheric CO_2, we should be vigorously pursuing reforestation and the planting of trees and shrubs, including in urban areas, where local impacts on the atmosphere are greatest.

Reforestation *has* been going on through enlightened forestry practices on private lands by timber companies and as a result of changes in agriculture and land use. In the United States, the average annual wood growth is now more than three times what it was in 1920, and the growing stock has increased 18

---

[4]John Rediske, 1970, "Young Forests and Global Oxygen Supply," *Weyerhauser World*, Vol. 2, No. 4, April 1970.

percent from 1952 to 1977. Forests in America continue to increase in size, even while supplying a substantial fraction of the world's timber needs.[5]

Finally, it should be kept in mind that when a tree is cut for timber, it will no longer remove CO_2 from the atmosphere, but it won't release its stored carbon either—until or unless it is burned or totally decayed. In the whole deforestation question, it would be interesting to try to determine what effect the deforestation of Europe had on temperature and climate in the nineteenth century, and, similarly, what the effect was of the earlier deforestation of the Mediterranean area and the Middle East.

If we study history, we find that there is no good or widely accepted explanation for why the earth's temperature and climate were as they were at any particular time in the past, including the recurring ice ages and the intervening warm periods. What caused the "little ice age" of the late seventeenth century and why was it preceded by 800 years of relative warmth? Is all this really due to human activity? What about natural phenomena? Recent studies of major deep-sea currents in the Atlantic Ocean suggest a causative relation to the onset of ice ages.[6] Occasional unusual actions by nature can release great quantities of CO_2 and other greenhouse gases [in]to the atmosphere.

I received my lesson in humility, my respect for the size and vast power of natural forces on May 18, 1980. For those who might not instantly recognize that date, it was a Sunday, a beautiful spring morning when at 8:31 Mount St. Helens erupted with the force of more than 500 atomic bombs. Gases and particulate matter were propelled 80,000 feet, approximately 15 miles, into the stratosphere and deposited above the ozone layer. The eruption continued for nearly twelve hours and more than four billion tons of earth were displaced.[7]

Because Mount St. Helens is relatively accessible, there were many studies conducted and good data are available on the emissions—at least those that occurred after May 18. For the remaining seven months of 1980, Mount St. Helens released 910,000 metric tons of CO_2, 220,000 metric tons of sulfur dioxide, and unknown amounts of aerosols into the atmosphere. Many other gases, including methane, water vapor, carbon monoxide, and a variety of sulfur compounds were also released, and emissions still continue to seep from the crater and from fumaroles and crevices.

Gigantic as it was, Mount St. Helens was not a large volcanic eruption. It was dwarfed by Mount St. Augustine and Mount Redoubt in Alaska in 1976 and

[5]Roger Sedjo and Marion Clausen (Resources for the Future), 1989, "Prices, Trade, and Forest Management," *Econ Update,* Reason Foundation, Vol. 3, No. 8, April 1989.

[6]Wallace S. Broecker and George H. Denton, 1990, "What Drives Glacial Cycles," *Scientific American,* Vol. 262, No. 1, p. 48ff.

[7]*The 1980 Eruptions of Mount St. Helens,* Washington Geological Survey Professional Paper 1250, Peter W. Lipman and Donald R. Mullineaux, editors, 1981.

1989 and El Chicon in Mexico in 1982. El Chicon was an exceptionally sulfurous eruption. The violence of its explosion sent more than 100 million tons of sulfur gases high into the stratosphere. Droplets of sulfuric acid formed; these continue to rain down onto the earth's surface. The earth, at present, appears to be in a period of active volcanism, with volcanic eruptions occurring at a rate of about one hundred per year. Most of these are in remote locations, where accurate measurements of the gaseous emissions is not possible, but they must be considerable. Some estimates from large volcanic eruptions in the past suggest that all of the air polluting materials produced by man since the beginning of the industrial revolution do not begin to equal the quantities of toxic materials, aerosols, and particulates spewed into the air from just three volcanoes: Krakatoa in Indonesia in 1883, Mount Katmai in Alaska in 1912, and Hekla in Iceland in 1947.[8] Despite these prodigious emissions, Krakatoa, for example, produced some chilly winters, spectacular sunsets, and a global temperature drop of 0.3 degrees Centigrade, but no climate change. From written records, we also know that the famous "year without a summer" that followed the eruption of Mount Tambora in 1816 meant that the summer temperature in Hartford, Connecticut, did not exceed 82 degrees Fahrenheit. No doom.

We can conclude from these volcanic events that the atmosphere is enormous and its capacity to absorb and dilute pollutants is also very great. This is no excuse, of course, to pollute the air deliberately, which would be an act of folly. But it does give us some perspective on events.

So far, we have considered only those phenomena that occur on earth that might influence global temperature, weather, and eventually the climate. "Weather" means the relatively short-term fluctuations in temperature, precipitation, winds, cloudiness, and so forth, that shift and change over periods of hours, days, or weeks. Weather patterns may be cyclic, more or less repeating themselves every few years. The "climate," on the other hand, is generally accepted to be the mean of weather changes over a period of about thirty years. Weather may change rapidly, but the climate may remain essentially the same over thousands of years, as it probably has for the last eight thousand years.

Now, what about the effects on weather of extraterrestrial phenomena? After all, it is the sun that determines the climate on earth—but the role of the sun, with its ever-shifting solar radiation, is generally ignored as being inconsequential in affecting shorter-term weather patterns. But is this really so?

Consider: the earth shifts in its position relative to the sun. Its orbit is eccentric, varying over a period of 97,000 years. The inclination of the earth's axis shifts with respect to the ecliptic over a cycle of 41,000 years, and the preces-

---

[8]Margaret Maxey, 1985, *Technology and a Better Environment*, National Council for Environmental Balance, Inc., P.O. Box 7732, Louisville, KY 40207.

sion of the equinox[es] varies over a period of 21,000 years.[9] How do these shifts affect the amount of solar radiation reaching the earth? Some astronomers believe that at least for the last 500,000 to one million years, these phenomena are related to the initiation and dissipation of glacial and interglacial intervals.

Although it may seem to us that the sun is stable and stationary, it is in fact whirling through the Milky Way galaxy, taking its family of planets with it. Activity on the sun itself goes through periods of relative quiet and then erupts into flares and protuberances, sunspots, and gigantic upheavals that "rain" solar material out into space.[10] One recent solar storm was measured at 43,000 miles across. This produced the largest solar flare ever recorded. Some of the increased solar radiation from such storms reaches the earth and disrupts radio communication and television transmission and increases the aurora borealis.[11] Solar activity in the form of storms seen as sunspots has a span of roughly eleven years. It seems that the sunspots whirl clockwise for about eleven years, then reverse and go counterclockwise for another eleven years. This interval is an average and may vary from seven to seventeen years. The controlling mechanism for this reversal is unknown.

Then there is another variable. The sun "flickers"; that is, it dims and brightens slightly over a period of about seventy years. When it dims, the sunspots attain lower maxima. When the sun brightens, the sunspots have higher maxima than "normal." Although this dimming and brightening has been suspected for some time, the first actual measurement of such a "flicker" was made on April 4, 1980, when a satellite measuring solar radiation outside the earth's atmosphere recorded a 0.2 percent drop in radiation. Changes in solar radiation are now routinely measured.

Coupled with the activity of the sun, there is the moon's gravitational force, to which the earth's waters respond daily and in twenty-eight-day cycles of tides. Also, there are twenty-year and sixty-year tidal cycles, as well as longer ones. Moreover, the solid land also responds to the moon's gravitational force, but because we move with the ground, we do not feel it. Recently, a 556-year variation in the moon's orbit around the earth was analyzed; some meteorologists believe that the occasional confluence of all these sun-and-moon cycles may trigger dramatic changes in ocean currents and temperatures. And it is now widely acknowledged that the oceans are a major influence on the climate.

[9]**ecliptic:** The sun's apparent annual path through the heavens. **precession of the equinoxes:** The change from year to year (precession) in the two dates when night and day are the same length (equinoxes).— ED.

[10]Doreen Fitzgerald, 1990, *Sun Meets Earth*, Vol. 8, Nos. 1 and 2.

[11]John Douglas et al., 1989, "A Storm from the Sun," *EPRI Journal*, July/August 1989.

There is also a 500-to-600-year cycle in volcanic activity, which appears to be near a peak at the present time.

Let's consider again. Does all this variability in solar activity really have anything to do with weather or climate? No one knows for certain. But studies are continuing, and Dr. John Eddy of the National Center for Atmospheric Research has found an interesting correlation between decades of low sunspot activity and cold periods, such as the "little ice age" of the seventeenth century, when there was a virtual absence of sunspot activity between 1645 and 1715, and decades of high sunspot activity with warm temperatures on earth.[12]

Since the sunspot cycle is not perfectly regular and varies considerably, how do scientists determine the extent of sunspot activity that occurred decades or centuries ago? This is a neat piece of scientific detective work that merits a brief explanation. It involves another extraterrestrial phenomenon—cosmic radiation.

Cosmic rays consist of high-energy particles that enter the earth's atmosphere from outer space. These energetic particles split the nuclei of atmospheric gases, giving rise to some of the background radiation to which all living organisms are exposed. Among the fission products are Potassium-40 and Carbon-14, which get into the food chain and are eaten (by animals) or absorbed (by plants), and that is one of the reasons that the bodies of all living organisms are radioactive. Of these two fission products, it is Carbon-14 that is the most interesting for tracing events in the past.

C-14, whose half-life is a relatively short 5,570 years, is being produced continuously in the atmosphere (through interaction with cosmic rays) and is continuously taken up by *living* organisms, but not by dead ones. Therefore, by measuring the amount of C-14 in dead or fossil material, one can infer the date of death. This is called carbon-dating. C-14 is a very good but not perfect clock of history, because the assumption is that the formation of C-14 is not only continuous but also that it occurs at a steady rate. But what Dr. Eddy has determined is that the rate of formation varies with the amount of cosmic radiation, which, in turn, varies with the amount of sunspot activity, because high solar activity also creates more solar wind that can compress the earth's magnetic field. This stronger field is more effective in shielding cosmic rays from the earth's atmosphere, which means that less C-14 is formed during periods of high sunspot activity. Less C-14 equates with warmer periods on earth.

Taking advantage of these phenomena, Dr. Eddy measured the C-14 radioactivity in tree rings in trees that are up to five thousand years old. Keep in mind that the years (rings) of low C-14 equate with years of high solar activity and warm temperatures. Dr. Eddy recorded twelve prolonged periods with ei-

[12]John Eddy, 1982, "C-14 Radioactivity in Tree Rings," *Access to Energy*, Vol. 9, No. 7, March 1982, Box 2298, Boulder, CO 80306.

ther unusually cold or unusually mild winters over the last five thousand years. These correlations between solar activity and weather on earth seem good; his measurements identified the terrible winter of 1683–84, also recorded in the novel *Lorna Doone,* when trees in Somerset, England, froze and many exploded from the buildup of internal ice.

If Dr. Eddy's work and theory hold up, the mid-twentieth century was an unusually warm period, and the earth may be set soon to enter a slow return to cooler temperatures. Besides, in geologically recent times, ice ages recur about every eleven thousand to twelve thousand years, and it is now eleven thousand years since the last one. How do all these complications interact with the greenhouse effect? Again, no one really knows. All we can say with confidence is that it is probably more complicated than many environmentalists seem to believe.[13]

When we consider all of the complex geophysical phenomena that might affect the weather and climate on earth, from changes in ocean temperatures and currents, volcanic eruptions, solar storms, and cyclic movements of heavenly bodies, it is clear that none of these is under human control or could be influenced by human activity. Is the "greenhouse effect" and its theoretical enhancement by increases in atmospheric CO_2 from human sources more powerful or capable of overshadowing all other planetary influences? Until the supporters of the man-produced-CO_2-caused-global-warming-theory can explain warm and cold episodes in the past, we should remain skeptical.[14] What caused the 80 parts per million increase in CO_2 during a hundred-year period three hundred years ago and the high peak—many times anything measured since—of 130,000 years ago?

The alteration of the chemical content of the air by *human* production of greenhouse gases, however, is something that man *can* control. And because no one knows what the ultimate consequences of heightened CO_2 might be, it is reasonable and responsible to reduce human contribution wherever possible.

Fortunately, there are ways to accomplish this. For starters, we can phase out the use of fossil fuel for making electricity and turn to the established and proven technology that has no adverse impact on the atmosphere—nuclear power. The energy of the atom now produces 20 percent of the electricity in the United States—more than the total of all electricity used in 1950. The number of nuclear power plants can be increased.[15]

[13]William Nierenberg, Robert Jastrow, and Frederick Seitz, 1989, *Scientific Perspectives on the Greenhouse Problems,* George C. Marshall Institute, 11 DuPont Circle, No. 506, Washington, D.C. 20036.

[14]Richard S. Lindzen, 1990, "Some Coolness Concerning Global Warming," *Journal of the American Meteorology Society,* Vol. 71, No. 3, March 1988.

[15]Support for nuclear power comes not only from the U.S. Council on Energy Awareness—1988 Midyear Report: *Taking Another Look at Nuclear,* 23 June 1988—but also from Robert M. White, president of the National Academy of Engineering, in testimony before the Senate Committee on Commerce, Science, and Transportation, 13 July 1988, and a news release from Senator Tim Wirth, 18 July 1988.

Second, we can shift to an essentially all-electric economy, utilizing electricity for direct heating of buildings and homes and extending the use of electric processes in industry. With enough electricity available, it can also be used to desalinate sea water and purify the fresh water sources that have become polluted. It can also be used to split water and obtain hydrogen, which has great potential as a clean fuel for transportation. Its "burning" produces only water vapor.

And we can turn, once again, to electric buses and trains, and eventually to electric automobiles.

None of these shifts away from fossil fuels will be easy or fast, but if we have an abundance of electricity from nuclear power plants, it can be done. That would leave fossil fuels for the important synthetics and plastics industries, and for the manufacture of medicinals, pesticides, and fertilizers.

There are also two important caveats; though steps to reduce CO_2 production may be possible for an advanced, highly technical, industrialized society with plenty of electricity, the infrastructure to make use of it, and money to spend, the story is different in the nonindustrialized world. In China, for example, 936 million metric tons of coal were burned in 1987. Who is going to tell China to stop or to change? What alternative do the Chinese have? No matter what we in the Western world do, the amount of CO_2 arising from human use of fossil fuel will not be significantly reduced.[16]

The second caveat is to remember that draconian measures intended to make rapid and large decreases in CO_2 formation won't do much good if they are so costly that they seriously impede the economy and degrade our standard of living without achieving the desired result. Certainly the level of atmospheric CO_2 is increasing, but nothing in all our knowledge of weather and climate guarantees that global warming will inevitably occur. It may, or it may not; the uncertainties are legion. The computer models are too simplistic and include too many estimates and guesses and too little about the role of the hydrosphere, both water vapor and the oceans.[17]

Notwithstanding all this, deliberate, reasoned steps can and should be taken to lower CO_2 emissions; responsible stewardship of the planet demands no less.

Finally, let's suppose that a worst case scenario does develop and that global warming does occur. If the warming caused polar ice to melt, only that on land, as in the Antarctic continent (or the glaciers of Greenland), would materially affect global sea level. When ice floats, as in the Arctic Ocean, it already displaces approximately the same amount of water that would result if it were

---

[16]Hugh W. Ellsaessar, 1989, "A Review of the Scientific American Article: Managing Planet Earth," *20th Century Energy and Environment*, November/December 1989.

[17]Warren T. Brookes, "The Global Warming Panic," *Forbes*, 25 December 1989.

to melt. (There would be some slight thermal expansion.) Whether Arctic ice stays solid or melts would no more cause the sea level to rise than ice cubes melting would cause a full glass of ice water to overflow.

Analysis of sea level data since 1900 indicates that the oceans may be rising at a rate of 10 to 25 centimeters per century (about 0.1 inch per year). The data are very sketchy and uncertain. The sea rise, if it is real, is not uniform and other phenomena, such as land subsidence or upthrust, the building and erosion of beaches by weather, and the variation of inshore currents, could all affect the few measurements that are available.

Some scientists postulate that the west Antarctic ice sheet, which is anchored on bedrock below sea level, could melt and add enough water to raise the world sea level by 6 or 7 meters. This would be disastrous for most coastlines, but if it should happen, it would probably take several hundred years, and there is currently neither observational evidence nor scientific measurements to indicate that it is under way. In fact, new measurements show that the glaciers in Antarctica are growing, not melting.[18]

Air temperatures in Antarctica average −40 degrees Centigrade. A five-degree rise in air temperature to −35 degrees Centigrade is certainly not enough to melt ice. But somewhat warmer sea water (above one degree Centigrade) might get under the ice sheet and start it slipping into the sea; then it would float and displace an enormous volume of water, causing the sea level to rise. But this is also a very unlikely "what if?" with no evidence to support it. . . .

The historian Hans Morgenthau wrote in 1946:

> Two moods determine the attitude of our civilization to the social world: confidence in the power of reason, as represented by modern science, to solve the social problems of the age, and despair at the ever renewed failure of scientific reason to solve them.
>
> The intellectual and moral history of mankind is the story of inner insecurity, of the anticipation of impending doom, of metaphysical anxieties.

John Maddox, editor of the prestigious British journal *Nature,* has said that "these days there also seems to be an underlying cataclysmic sense among people. Scientists don't seem to be immune to this."

Well, they ought to be. And we ought to remember that using our technology will go a long way toward averting those cataclysmic events and the "doom-is-almost-here" philosophy that seems to have so much appeal. Scientists owe it to society to show the way to a better life and an improved environment— through quality technology.

---

[18]Charles R. Bentley, 1990, "Recent Data from Measurements of Antarctic Glaciers," *Insight,* 15 January 1990.

Gaia and Global Warming

Isaac Azimov and Frederick Pohl

Biography: *Isaac Azimov and Frederick Pohl are both acclaimed science fiction writers with many novels to their credit. Azimov, who died in 1992, received his Ph.D. in Chemistry from Columbia University and was a professor of Biochemistry at Boston University School of Medicine. He wrote on subjects from biochemistry to the Bible to Shakespeare, to humor, to history.*

Azimov and Pohl first explore the science behind the Gaia hypothesis, which theorizes that the earth and its atmosphere form an interdependent organic whole, and like organic systems is, to a degree, self-regulating. They conclude the theory is credible, but caution against believing, therefore, that the system itself will take care of global warming. The theory predicts that the earth will take care of itself, they warn, not us, and the imbalance caused by CO_2 may be beyond the capacity of Gaia to counter in any case. Though stopping global warming, they argue, is beyond our capabilities, we can prevent the worst effects. This essay by two science fiction writers combines science with literature (mythology) in interesting ways and thus provides rich ground for disciplinary analysis.

We would all like to think that there was something—some benign and superior kind of *Something*—that would step in and save us from the things that are going wrong with our world.

Most people have always had a comforting belief of that sort. In most of human history their nominee for that "something" was usually their god—whatever god they chanced to worship in that time and place—which is why, in parched summers, farmers have long prayed for rain. They still do, but as scientific knowledge grew and began to explain more and more events as the working out of natural law, rather than divine caprice, many people began to wish for a less supernatural (and perhaps a more predictable) protector.

For that reason there was quite a stir in the scientific community when, about twenty years ago, an English scientist named James Lovelock came up with something that came close to filling that bill. Lovelock gave his hypothetical new concept a name. He called it "Gaia," after the ancient goddess of the earth.

When Lovelock published his "Gaia hypothesis" it shook up many scientists, especially the most rational-minded ones, who purely hated so mystical-sounding a concept. It was an embarrassment to them, and the most disturbing part of it was that Lovelock was one of their own number. He did have a reputation as a bit of a maverick, but his scientific credentials were solid. Among other accomplishments, Lovelock was known as the scientist who had designed

From *Our Angry Earth*, New York: Tom Doherty Assoc., 1991, [9pp]

the instruments for some of the life-seeking experiments that the American spacecraft *Viking* carried out on the surface of Mars.

Yet, in the eyes of his peers, the things that Lovelock was saying verged on the superstitious. Worse, he had the temerity to present his arguments in the form of the orthodox "scientific method." He had drawn the evidence for his proposal from observation and from the scientific literature, as a scientist is supposed to do. That evidence, he said, appeared to show the entire biosphere of the planet earth—which is to say, every last living thing that inhabits our planet, from the bacteria to the whales, the elephants, the redwood trees, and you and me—could usefully be described as one single, planet-wide organism, each part of it almost as related and interdependent as the cells of our body. Lovelock felt that this collective super-being deserved a name of its own. Lacking inspiration, he turned to his neighbor William Golding (author of *Lord of the Flies*) for help, and Golding came up with the perfect answer. So they called it "Gaia."

Lovelock came to his conclusions in the course of his scientific work while he was trying to figure out what signs of life the instruments he was designing should look for on the planet Mars. It occurred to him that if he had been a Martian instead of an Englishman, it would have been easy to solve that problem the other way around. All a Martian would need was a modest telescope, with a fairly good spectroscope attached, to get the answer. The very composition of earth's air proclaimed the undeniable existence of life. Earth's atmosphere contains a great deal of free oxygen, which is a very active chemical. The fact that it was free in such volume in the earth's atmosphere meant that something had to be constantly replenishing it. If that were not true, the atmospheric oxygen would long since have reacted with such other elements as the iron in the earth's surface and thus have disappeared—in just the same way that our own earthly spectroscopes have shown that whatever oxygen there ever was has long since been used up on all of our planetary neighbors, Mars included.

Therefore a Martian astronomer would have understood at once that that constantly oxygen-replenishing "something" could be only one thing. It had to be life.

It is life—living plants—which continually produces that oxygen in our air; it is that same oxygen which life—ourselves and almost every other living member of the animal kingdom—relies on to survive.

Lovelock's insight from that was that life—all terrestrial life combined—was interactive and had the capacity to maintain its environment in such a way that its own continued existence was possible. If some environmental change should threaten life, life would then act to counter the change, in much the same way that a thermostat acts to keep your home comfortable when the weather changes, by turning on the furnace or the air conditioner.

The technical term for this kind of behavior is "homeostatic." According to Lovelock, "Gaia"—the sum total of all life on earth—is a homeostatic system.

(To be more technically precise, the proper term is "homeorhetic" rather than "homeostatic" in this case, but the distinction would matter only to specialists.) This self-preserving system not only adapts itself to changes, it even makes changes of its own, altering the environment around it in whatever ways are necessary to its well-being.

With that speculation to spur him on, Lovelock began looking for other evidences of homeostatic behavior. He found them in surprising places.

Coral islands, for instance. Coral is made up of living animals. They can only grow in shallow water. Yet many coral islands are slowly sinking, and somehow the coral continues to grow upward just as much as it needs to remain at the proper depth for survival; that's a rudimentary kind of homeostasis.

Then there's the temperature of the earth. The global average temperature has stayed within fairly narrow limits for a billion years or more, although it is known that in that time the radiation from the sun (which is what basically determines that temperature) has been steadily increasing. Therefore the earth should have warmed appreciably. It didn't. How could that happen without some kind of homeostasis?

Even more interesting to Lovelock was the paradoxical question of how much salt there is in the sea. The present salt concentration in the world's oceans is just about right for marine plants and animals to live in. Any significant increase would be disastrous. Fish (and other sea life) have a tough job as it is in preventing that salt from accumulating in their tissues and poisoning them; if there were much more salt in the sea than there is, the job would be impossible and they would die.

Yet, by all normal scientific logic, the seas should be a lot saltier than they are. It is known that the rivers of the earth are continually dissolving salts out of the soil they run through and carrying more and more of those salts into the seas. The water itself which the rivers add each year doesn't stay in the ocean. That pure water is taken out by evaporation by the heat of the Sun to make clouds and ultimately to fall again as rain; while the salts those waters contained have nowhere to go and must stay behind.

We know from everyday experience what happens in that case. If we leave a bucket of salt water exposed in the summer, it will get more and more salty as the water evaporates. Astonishingly, that does not happen in the oceans. Their salt content is known to have remained at just about the same level for all of geological time.

So it is apparent that *something* is acting to remove excess salt from the ocean.

There is one known process that might account for it. Now and then, bays and shallow arms of the ocean are cut off. The Sun evaporates their water and they dry out to form salt beds—which ultimately are covered over by dust, clay, and finally impenetrable rock, so that when the sea ultimately returns to re-claim that area that layer of fossil salt is sealed in and is not redissolved. (When, later on, people dig them up for their own needs we call them salt mines.) In that way, millennium after millennium, the oceans get rid of the excess and keep their salt content level.

It could be simply a coincidence that that balance is maintained so exactly, no matter what else is going on . . . but it could also be another manifestation of Gaia.

But perhaps Gaia shows herself most clearly in the way she has kept earth's temperature constant. As we've mentioned, in the early days of earth the sun's radiation was about a fifth less than it is now. With so little warming sun-light the oceans should have frozen over, but that didn't happen.

Why not?

The reason is that then the earth's atmosphere contained more carbon dioxide than it does now. And there, Lovelock says, Gaia is at work. For plants came along to reduce the proportion of carbon dioxide in the air. As the sun warmed up, the carbon dioxide, with its heat-retaining qualities, diminished—in exact step, over the millennia. Gaia worked through the plants (Lovelock suggests) to keep the world at the optimum temperature for life. . . .

But we must not take too much personal reassurance from Lovelock's the-ory. The Gaia hypothesis does suggest that life is likely to continue, and even that many species will exist. However, there is nothing in the theory to say that the world will be safe for our grandchildren, because there is nothing in it which predicts that the assortment of species of living things which will survive the present assaults will necessarily include that particular species called *Homo sapiens sapiens*, which is ourselves.

James Lovelock said it himself one day, talking over a cup of coffee with the author of *The Hole in the Sky*, John Gribbin. As Lovelock put it, "People sometimes have the attitude that 'Gaia will look after us.' But that's wrong. If the concept means anything at all, Gaia will look after *herself*. And the best way for her to do that might well be to get rid of us."

Can natural checks and balances save us from the effects of the man-made greenhouse global warming?

No, they can't. They are certainly doing their best, in the face of greater challenges, due to our uncontrolled mining and burning of fossil fuels, than they ever had to face before, but their best is not good enough.

. . . There are many natural processes which operate to remove carbon dioxide from the air (they are technically called "sinks"), such as coal formation and the deep-freeze of dead plant material in the tundras. There are a great many of these natural sinks; but most of them are much too weak to resist the large-scale changes in the atmosphere.

Only two sinks, really, are big enough to make a dent in the problem. The first of them is the world aggregate of living plants, which suck carbon dioxide out of the air to turn it into vegetation. The other is the world's bodies of water, mostly the oceans, which dissolve large quantities of the carbon dioxide out of the atmosphere in much the same way that a cup of coffee dissolves a spoonful of sugar.

The world's living plants are our most valuable sink. When a plant takes in a molecule of carbon dioxide from the air, it uses sunlight to break the molecule down into its component elements, carbon and oxygen; the process is called photosynthesis. The plant uses the carbon that results to build into its own structure; that's how it grows. The plant has no use for oxygen, however, so it exhales the oxygen back to the air—that is how, billions of years ago when plants began to appear, the earth came to have an oxygen atmosphere for us to breathe in the first place.

Plant photosynthesis is a very satisfactory process for human needs—indeed, you could call it indispensable, not just for us but for almost all life on Earth. But we are killing the plants that do the job. We cut down our trees in vast numbers for such trivial reasons as to splinter them into disposable chopsticks for export to the Orient, as well as to use them for paper and lumber or simply to get them out of the way so we can build houses and plant farms.

The habit of destroying woodlands did not begin with our generation. Scientists tell us that the pristine world—the world that existed before the human race became numerous enough, and aggressive enough, to have much of an effect on it—contained almost twice as many forested acres as now remain; it was human beings who destroyed the missing half. But those ancient people who burned or cut down all those trees did not have our chain saws and bulldozers, so they were nowhere nearly as good at it as we are.

It isn't only trees that we are removing from the cycle. We take our toll of everything that is green. We destroy more of that indispensable plant life every time we drain a swamp, or bulkhead a shoreland, or construct a highway, or start a new suburban housing development, or lay a concrete parking lot for a shopping mall. And we do all this on so vast a scale that the vegetative sink is no longer large enough to handle the task of keeping the carbon-dioxide level in check.

As to the sink in the oceans: Water is very good at dissolving carbon dioxide—that's what makes our fizzy drinks like beer and ginger ale possible. Over the ages, the seas have dissolved enormous quantities of the gas, so that now there is far more carbon dioxide dissolved in the global ocean than is free in the atmosphere.

But there is a limit to how rapidly the oceans can take up excess carbon dioxide, and that limit depends on the temperature. If the seas should warm enough, more carbon dioxide will bubble out of solution than there is being dissolved—in just the same way that when you leave ginger ale out overnight it goes flat faster than the same beverage kept in the refrigerator.

In that case, the race that we call the carbon-dioxide exchange between the atmosphere and the oceans will go the wrong way. It will make the situation worse instead of better.

(Nor is the situation any better for the other greenhouse gases. The sinks for methane are similar to those for carbon dioxide, and equally threatened. For the synthetic gases like the chlorofluorocarbons [CFCs] there are no natural sinks at all. None ever arose, since those gases did not exist until we began to manufacture them.)

So Gaia alone can't do the job for us any more. It was primarily through these two carbon-dioxide sinks that she managed to keep the global climate so stable over so many millions of years, but now we've crippled her.

Which brings us to the second question: Is there anything we can do to restore Gaia to health—say, by inventing some technological fix?

That is the question with the "Yes, but" answer. There are a lot of things we might be able to *try* in the attempt to remove surplus greenhouse gases from the air, but no obvious good ones. Some would work too slowly to do us much good, some might not work at all, some might actually make the situation worse.

For instance, we can start planting new trees on the barren lands where the forests have been cut down.

That's the most obvious (and lowest-tech) of all the current proposals. It would probably help considerably, in the long run, but it is an enormous job. To replace the cut-over regions would mean planting the greatest forest in the world, covering an area about the size of Australia.

Reforestation on that scale may well be worth undertaking for many other reasons—for instance, in order to control soil erosion—but it can't solve our present problem. The atmospheric benefits of replanting logged-out areas come too slowly to help us now. It takes anywhere from forty years to several centuries for a newly planted sapling to grow big enough to match the carbon-holding capacity of a mature tree. We don't have that much time to spare.

There has been more technologically "sophisticated" proposals by the dozen. Some are grotesquely unrealistic, though they come from respected institutions: for instance, a Brookhaven National Laboratory project to catch all the carbon dioxide that comes from the world's smokestacks and pump it through vast pipes to the bottom of the sea, where it can dissolve and remain out of the air, at least for a while. (Think of the cost of such a program! Think of the extra carbon dioxide that would be produced by the power plants that ran the pumps that forced all that gas against the pressure of the deep sea.) Two Japanese scientists have a similar idea; they also want to catch all the stack emissions, but then their idea is to pump them through great tanks holding a soup of algae, letting the algae do what plants always do. (Expense again; plus the fact that suitable algae strains would have to be genetically engineered; plus the problem of how you then dispose of the slurry of dead algae that results.) Some are simply inadequate to the task, like the Environmental Protection Agency's March, 1989, suggestions of cutting down on cement production and finding alternative methods of producing rice, meat, and milk. (Again worth doing for other reasons, but not for dealing with the surplus carbon dioxide; the EPA plan would affect only the other greenhouse gas, methane, and only a small fraction of that.) Some might help to ameliorate the carbon-dioxide problem—like the EPA's other suggestion, of replacing fossil-fuel power plants with nuclear reactors—but create serious problems of another kind. (Such problems as the expense of constructing the nuclear plants; the long time delay involved in building such plants, which typically run to a decade or more; the dangers of nuclear plants—such as Chernobyl-style accidents[1]—and the equally worrisome but generally overlooked unsolved problems that afflict all such plants, such as the total lack of disposal facilities for their radioactive wastes.)

There are more speculative proposals, too. They represent wishes more than solid, realizable plans, but they are worth a look.

For instance: If natural trees grow too slowly, how about letting the molecular biologists build us some new kind of tree or shrub—one as good at surviving and growing as any weed—that will come to maturity very rapidly, and, what's more, will do it almost anywhere in the world without special care or irrigation, so that we could perhaps spray seeds out of airplanes over the bare Asian hills, or even over the empty Sahara? That's not quite impossible. Conceivably such new tree species could some day be bred. But we don't have them now, and no one presently knows how to start creating them; so that is a wish rather than a plan.

All right, then: How about dispensing with vegetation entirely and going right to inorganic chemistry?

We know that a lot of carbon dioxide does get taken out of the air by chemical means and turned into rocks like limestone. That doesn't happen fast enough naturally to be useful to our present needs, but perhaps science can find a way to speed it up. Can't we just spray some magic fairy dust into the air (let's not call it that; let's call the stuff by the more sober-sounding chemical name of "catalyst")—a high-tech catalyst, then, which would make the process happen quickly, creating great masses of carbon-containing rock which we could then bulldoze underground—or simply leave lying harmlessly around, or even use for building materials?

---

[1] **Chernobyl-style accidents:** On April 26, 1986, the worst commercial nuclear accident in history occurred at a nuclear power plant in Chernobyl. Chernobyl is located 80 miles north of Kiev, Ukraine, in the former Soviet Union.—Ed.

No. We can't. We don't know how; but even if we did we probably wouldn't dare. Like the sorcerer's apprentice, we would be tempting fate if we started things we might not be able to stop.

If we did have the capacity to speed up some such natural process we would risk it going beyond our control. Then it might keep on removing carbon dioxide past the point we intended it for—perhaps until it got down to that 200 parts per million level that means another Ice Age—or even beyond that, perhaps to the point where there is no atmospheric carbon dioxide at all. That would make our planet almost as cold as Mars. Then we would all die.

So we can't put back the lost trees in time, and we can't expect the inventors to give us a gadget that will make the process stop.

There's only one thing left. We're going to have to do it the hard way . . . if we are to have any hope of doing it at all. That is, we're going to have to cut down on the amount of fossil fuel we burn.

That doesn't mean we have to forswear the use of fossil fuel entirely. That wouldn't be sensible—there are applications to which fossil fuels are vastly better suited than any imaginable alternative—but fortunately it isn't necessary. What we have to do is *reduce* our burning of coal, oil, and natural gas to the point of our Steady-state Allowable Perturbation, or SAP.[2] So let's try to estimate just how much man-made interference we can inflict upon the environment in this area without making things worse.

That means we have to put numbers into the equation. Fortunately, in the race between our production of greenhouse gases and their removal from the atmosphere, we do know some of the necessary numbers. We know, for instance, that the human race now turns out some 50 billion tons of carbon dioxide a year from the burning of fossil fuels. And we know that that's too much.

It's doubtful that there is any way at all to stop the process of global warming entirely, whatever we do. The process has picked up too much momentum, and stopping or reversing it may be simply beyond our capacities. But perhaps we can do the next best thing by slowing it down. If we can do that adequately, then we can at least allow the world time to adjust to the coming climate changes.

We have a number for that. A pair of scientists, one from the Lawrence Berkeley Laboratories in California, the other a climatologist from West Germany, have prepared an estimate of what a tolerable rate of global warming should be. Their conclusion: no more than an increase of a twentieth of a degree every ten years. Any rate of global warming higher than that would result in unacceptable damage to forests and crops.

---

[2]**Steady-state Allowable Perturbation (SAP):** The level at which no further environmental damage occurs.—ED.

Even that is very rapid, as natural global change goes. (The warming after the last Ice Age took place at an average of about a *thirtieth* of a degree every ten years.) And it is certainly far less than our present practices would produce. According to a United Nations panel which studied the question in April, 1990, we're likely to experience an increase of about a whole degree every ten years between now and the year 2030. That's twenty times the proposed maximum level.

If we translate that one-twentieth of a degree level into what is produced by carbon dioxide production, holding our temperature rise to safe limits means that we have to make quite drastic cuts in our burning of fossil fuels. Our present discharge of 50 billion tons a year of carbon dioxide would have to come down to about 6 billion tons a year—about as much as we now produce every forty-four days.

So, as a first approximation, anyway, that can be our SAP for carbon-dioxide production. It's formidable. It means that for every gallon of oil we now burn, we have to restrict ourselves to a little less than a pint. (And that doesn't even take into account what has to be done about the other greenhouse gases—particularly methane and the CFCs.)

It isn't quite as bad as it sounds, though. We don't have to reduce our *energy* consumption to the same degree. . . . We can start taking advantage of nonpolluting energy sources to make up much of the slack; and we can save a good deal of the rest by using our energy more efficiently.

Still, reducing the rate of warming will certainly be a difficult task, and it is likely to be an expensive one as well.

Just how much this will cost us, in public and private funds, is almost as hard to predict as the fine-screen detail of what the climate changes will mean in your own neighborhood. Some studies are fairly scary. One such modeling of the probable cost of doing what is necessary to achieve this sort of steady state puts the price of change, for the United States alone, at anywhere from $800 billion to more than $3 trillion—and several times that when the changes for the rest of the world are taken into account.

But, in the event, it isn't going to be that bad. Those high cost-estimates show only the loss side of the ledger; there are gains as well.

The money we will save from, for example, more efficient use of energy will go a long way toward meeting those costs. Some estimates even suggest that a conversion to a steady-state energy economy will actually mean a *profit* for the world, in terms of cheaper bills forever after.

. . . It is possible to stave off at least the worst effects of the greenhouse disaster. The ways of doing it are known. It is only the dislocations and difficulties involved in making the transition to a steady-state world that are hard to face. ⚛

STUDENT PAPERS FOR REVISION WORKSHOP

This reflective commentary on the revision of a film studies paper reviews the original assignment, critically engages the instructor's comments, and describes a comprehensive reworking of the paper at global, local, and sentence levels. Where might the writer have used examples of his writing from various drafts to demonstrate the effects of his revision practice? Where might he have worked for greater sentence efficiency?

Critical Thinking and Revision for New Insight

Student E

In the process of rewriting and critical thinking, writers revisit their work and focus on the improvement of basic grammar, syntax, and the overall coherence in the asserted claims of the argument. Not only does rewriting require adjustments on the surface, local, and global levels, but it also incorporates a constructive rethinking and evaluation of the particular subject matter. Furthermore, revision requires a meticulous analysis of the paper to target areas in need of further clarification. By adding extensive explanations to support claims and incorporating new insight into one's paper, the writer can work to produce a stronger written assertion of the object of study and conclusions. Through revision of my general education film studies paper, I think I can gain a better understanding not only of the study of the particular film under analysis, but also I can get a feel for how to properly write in the humanities.

Building upon the particular criterion, I chose my first Film Studies 46 writing assignment for critical revision because it had much room for improvement. Initially, I did not completely follow the humanities writing guidelines when composing my paper. I failed to include a thesis statement in the introduction paragraph, which is where my problems began. My film paper had many constructive instructor criticisms that pertain to my now obvious mistakes and errors. I did not fully comprehend nor understand how to write a paper in the humanities at the time. My paper read very abruptly, and this is because there were no topic sentences that lead back to a sound thesis statement. This shakiness in my sentence structure caused confusion in the argument my paper set out to discuss.

Prior to taking on the task of revision, one must thoroughly reflect upon the original assignment criteria for the paper. My specific Film Studies paper assignment was to discuss and comment on the visual elements utilized in the film *Days of Heaven*. The paper called for a breakdown of the visual elements in the movie and a description of the significant aspects of *mise-en-scene* and cinematography. On the surface level, the requirements included correct spelling of key terms, coherent syntax of sentence structure, and accurate grammar throughout. Also stressed was the need for using proper citation to give credit to the original source of any incorporated reviews. The criteria for local level content included using examples of stylistic elements and pertinent evidence to support claims and incorporating correct technical terminology, key terms, and concepts.

The global level goals of my assignment were not explicitly defined by the instructor. In *The Harcourt Brace Guide to Writing in the Disciplines*, Bloom's Taxonomy is presented to further explore the different stages of thinking and to discuss the classification for purposes of understanding the relationships among the parts. Bloom's Taxonomy would define global level goals as the most complex and advanced of the cognitive areas of critical thinking, including, "synthesis: putting something together from disparate pieces . . . [and] Evaluation: judging, weighing, evaluating" (Bizzaro, Jones, & Selfe, 1997, p. 12). Since the assignment did not specify global level objectives, I was unclear at the time as to what was expected of me on a broader level. Was I to argue, in the spirit of evaluation, my critique of the movie against the review of a well-respected critic? Was I to make a claim about the cinematographer? I believe the instructor was more concerned with our acquisition of basic, fundamental knowledge of the process of film critiquing. Therefore, I believe she overlooked many global level goals to give us more time to focus in on demonstrating our ability to apply the knowledge of the cinematographer's techniques that we learned in our own personal evaluation of *Days of Heaven*.

Once I personally grasped the spirit of the assignment, I contrasted the paper objectives with the standard criteria for composing works in the discipline of Film Studies. I concluded that the assignment objectives outlined by the instructor failed to meet several of the applicable formal criteria for a paper written in Film Studies. The discipline of Film Studies surveys the fundamental aspects of cinema as an art form. The structure for analyzing a film entails an approach that leads to a complete understanding of the work. This approach begins with a detailed description of the individual scenes, an explanation of film production, a critical analysis of film theory, and drawing a relationship of the film art to its cinematographer (Bordwell & Thomson, 1997). The instructor did not ask for the global level goal of integrating film theory. I made it a goal to utilize a quotation concerning film theories in my paper from a well-known film critic to further my arguments about the cinematography in *Days of Heaven*.

Although the Film Studies paper has a loosely defined format for writing, the structure is similar to other papers written in the humanities disciplines. A productive method for discovering how to write in a particular subject is to gain an understanding of how to compose a paper in the particular discipline. As Bizzaro, Jones, and Selfe (1997) explain, "When you write in the humanities, you will not only be required to reflect personally on the people, institutions, occurrences, and ideas that in sum, constitute culture, but to interpret them as well" (142). In drafting a coherent humanities paper, it is essential that several key area are touched upon, including developing an interpretation, providing a rich detailed description, exploring technical and cultural values, and commenting on the stakes and critical implications of the interpretation.

Any form of peer editing or instructor comments should be assessed carefully to help in the revision process. The instructor for my General Education Film Studies 46 class made many constructive criticisms of my paper, which were helpful in rewriting. Through either underlines or short phrases, the instructor gave insightful feedback on how to bring my paper up to par and make it read more smoothly. The majority of the comments had to do with surface level adjustments such as spelling and misused key Film Studies words and phrases. The instructor also pointed out various problems with syntax and run-on sentences. Several unnecessary words and phrases were crossed out to indicate poor style. On the local level, the instructor suggested that I go into more detail when making claims about *mise-en-scene* and supporting them. This apparent lack of detail also attributed to the apparent incoherent structure of my entire argument. She also suggested that I elaborate on some of my examples and claims to make the argument more understandable and complete. The instructor did not make comments on the global level. All she asserted was a broad blanket statement of, "Poorly organized with inaccurate observations and little analysis." This comment goes to show that the instructor did not take the time to really specify more explicit areas that I could improve in. It would have been more productive if she had told me how to fix the problems, not just that they were wrong. I think she should have pointed out the exact areas where I made inaccurate observations and suggest a productive solution to revising those inconsistencies. In addition, she used several meaningless comments such as "What?" "Clarify," and "Awkward." Although I believe the instructor was trying to be helpful, I did not know how to use these comments to produce a different or better piece of writing. However, on the whole, her comments gave me another point of view, which in turn helped me to think further and edit or add to my paper.

When contrasting the abstract of my original paper to the abstract of my rewrite, I realized that my original paper was just a summary of the movie, preceded by several of my own opinions. The introduction paragraph lacked an assertion about the stylistic film techniques used in *Days of Heaven* and failed to mention how the cinematography played a role in the production of the film.

Based on the instructor's comments and the analysis of how to write in the discipline of Film Studies, I devised a plan for rewriting. I focused first on explicit grammar and syntax errors on the surface in order to interpret the movie accurately and distinctly. I then adjusted my paper to adhere to the Modern Language Association citation format, which is the style of documentation necessary for citing works in humanities classes. Focusing on the local level, I integrated quotations on film theory from professional film critics Charles Affron and Mirella Jona Affron to bring in a different viewpoint and perspective to the interpretation of *mise-en-scene* and its significance in the film *Days of Heaven*. Drawing from the quotation, I was able to assert that the film technique of *mise-en-scene* was intentionally utilized by cinematographer Nestro Almendros to bring out the innate qualities in ordinary scenes. The logical progression of my argument was further strengthened by adding such an assertion based on the foundation of the integrated quotation. Furthermore, on the global level, I reconstructed material and paragraph structure to strengthen the rational development of my thesis. Through the implementation of clear transitions between paragraphs, the reader can now follow the progress of my thesis. The rewrite achieved my goals and objectives of revising for a stronger thesis and logical progression of the argument.

In revising my paper I gained further insight into how film techniques were utilized to make the movie, and I learned how to write properly in Film Studies. I discovered how critical thinking about my paper can lead to a complete and coherent understanding of film analysis and the appropriate film stylistic techniques. In all honesty, for quite some time, I was very upset with the D grade my paper received. Although I did not like the grade, I now (after completing the critical thinking and revision) realize it is a fair grade in evaluating my lack of adherence to the objectives outlines by the instructor and the criteria for writing in the humanities. By reviewing the movie and incorporating more outside sources, I succeeded in attaining additional insight into my paper topic of cinematography in *Days of Heaven*. On a broader perspective, through this revision process I gained more movie critiquing skills that will enable me to appreciate the cinema more in my bimonthly movie outings with my friends. I also learned the critical revising skill of recognizing material and paragraphs to strengthen my thesis, which is an invaluable ability that will assist me further in my college academic writing.

References

Bizzaro, P., Jones, R. & Selfe, C. (1997). *The Harcourt Brace Guide to Writing in the Disciplines*. Fort Worth, TX: Harcourt Brace College Publishers.

Bordwell, D., & Thompson, Kristen. (1997). *Film Art: An Introduction*. New York: McGraw-Hill.

This critical comparison of two Web sites on global warming demonstrates skills introduced in the readings to apply academic evaluation to emerging information sources. It examines both technical and rhetorical features of the sites to assess their validity. Where might discussion of the sites' uses of scientific, social science, and humanities perspectives be relevant and deepen the analysis? How might the paper be strengthened by editing for repetition?

Evaluating the Reliability and Effectiveness of Web Sites

Student F

Over the past century, several drastic increases and decreases in the global climate temperature have occurred. In recent years, this global increase in temperature has reached new highs. According to Botkin and Keller, "the period from 1986 through 1998 have been the warmest in 138 years that global temperatures have been monitored" (446). Global warming has become the common term used to describe the natural or human-induced increase in global temperature. Is this global warming an effect of anthropogenic activities or just a natural change in climate? This question has become the cause of one of the most heated debates in the environmental field. Publications of all kinds have been created supporting and opposing the theory of global warming. Internet sources have become the most popular method used to address this issue. However, do these Internet sources provide objective and useful information? To discover the effectiveness and reliability of Internet resources, two Web sites with opposing viewpoints on the issue of global warming have been compared and evaluated.

In order to evaluate the validity of the information provided by the Internet, the United States Environmental Protection Agency's (EPA) Web site was compared with Rich Zipperer's "Global Warming Information Page." These two Web sites contained contradictory information on the global warming theory. The EPA believes that "the earth's climate is predicted to change because human activities are altering the chemical composition of the atmosphere." Through the emissions of greenhouse gasses into the atmosphere, humans are actively altering the composition of the atmosphere, and causing an increase in global temperature. The EPA also believes that such increases could have detrimental effects on ecosystems, wildlife, and even human health. Rich Zipperer disagrees with the EPA and argues that "climate models have consistently overestimated climatic warming, and new research has proved that mild warming will likely be beneficial to human beings and the planet." Since most of the warming is occurring in colder regions of the Earth during the winter season, a mildly warmer climate may have positive effects on ecosystems, wildlife, and human health, being that it is more suitable for life.

Not only did the two sites differ in opinion, but also in the overall setup. The EPA site contained a brief overview of global warming with concise text and informative graphics. The EPA site was also easy to navigate and understand. To make the information more accessible to the viewer, the EPA site was evenly divided into several sections such as climate, emissions, impacts, and actions. These sections were helpful in allowing the viewer to choose which information he or she wishes to view. The EPA site also contained a "Visitor's Center" which had subcategories directed toward a variety of interest groups. The "Visitor's Center" contained information on actions certain groups, such as concerned citizens, are taking. The "Visitor's Center" also provides information on what an individual can do to help. Each section of the "Visitor's Center" utilizes a different persona and language to appeal to each interest group. On the other hand, Rich Zipperer's "Global Warming Information Page" did not contain such a simple overview. Instead, Rich Zipperer's site had a link titled "Global Warming in Brief," but once the link was clicked on, no information appeared.

The "Global Warming Information Page" had a variety of links to other sources, with very little data provided by the author. This "intertextuality," defined by the authors of "Web Literacy" as the ability to go from text to text, made the Web site more difficult to navigate. According to "Web Literacy," this intertextuality can make the Web site difficult to evaluate (419). Through the use of intertextuality, the author's original work becomes mixed with works from other authors, creating difficulty in understanding the origin of the Web site. The authors of "Web Literacy" also believe that "a web site with too many links suggest an author's inability to discriminate ... between a valuable resource to one that is not valuable" (419). If an author cannot discriminate between a reliable resource and a resource that does not offer valid information, then how can the information presented by the Web site's author be trusted? Without further evaluation of the indirect resources, the information presented through the links cannot be considered reliable.

The links used by the EPA were not from other sources, but from sources either created by the EPA or affiliated with the EPA. The intertextuality utilized by the EPA was separated from the text itself so that it did not detract from the information being presented and increased the effectiveness of the page overall. Intertextuality should not substitute text itself and should instead use hypertext, more commonly known as links, to support an argument, or give extra insight into an issue. The arguments presented by Rich Zipperer against global warming lack supporting information, while the argument supporting global warming presented by the EPA includes much support. The use of hypertext without actual text creates a web of claims in an article without any support, which can easily confuse the viewer.

Another difference between the EPA Web site and Rich Zipperer's Web site is the source of information. In the EPA site, the information is gathered through governmental experiments and agencies. These agencies and programs are then cited in the section titled "About the Site." In this section, the EPA gives detailed explanations on how each program works and gives a detailed description of each agency. Rich Zipperer's site lacks this clear citation of information. The sources used in the site are not even listed. The only source that is cited is an interview with Dr. Patrick Michaels, but Rich Zipperer fails to mention what Dr. Michaels is a doctor of. Without the knowledge of where the information is coming from, the information cannot be taken as valid.

The analysis of the EPA Web site and Rich Zipperer's Web site has proved that certain Web sites can be considered reliable and effective, while other sites cannot. Since the EPA Web site has a clear path of logic, referenced resources, and is provided by the government, it can be considered to contain valid information. Furthermore, because this information is proved valid, the EPA Web page could be used as a reference in a research paper. Since Rich Zipperer's Web site lacks clarity, has a confusing path of logic, and does not contain support for the arguments presented, the "Global Warming Information Page" cannot be considered a valid resource for information on global warming, and should not be cited in research papers.

As the Internet continues to take the place of books and libraries, a careful evaluation of each Web site needs to take place before it can be cited in a reference paper. Students utilizing Internet resources need to become more critical of the source of their information, as anyone can publish an article on the Internet. University students need to become critical thinkers when researching for a paper. This critical thinking can begin with reviewing Internet resources and can then carry over into the world of published texts. If the student is critical of all the information going into his or her paper, then the information included within the paper will be more reliable and will increase the effectiveness of the final paper.

Works Cited

Botkin, Daniel and Keller, Ed. *Environmental Science.* New York, New York: John Wiley & Sons, Inc., 2000.

Environmental Protection Agency. *Global Warming.* 20, Jan. 2000. http://www.epa.gov/globalwarming/index.html.

Sorapure, Madeleine, Inglesby, Pamela, and Yatchisin, George. "Web Literacy: Challenges and Opportunities for Research in the New Medium." *Computers and Composition,* 15, 1998, 409-424.

Zipperer, Rich. *Global Warming Information Page.* 11 Nov. 1999. http://www.globalwarming.org/.

This interdisciplinary analysis evaluates the contribution of science and humanities to global-atmospheric theory in order to address a social science question. How do the writer's conclusions strengthen or weaken the preceding argument? Can you find places to strengthen the presentation through greater sentence efficiency?

The Realism of Gaia

Student G

Scientists and numerous individuals alike have tried for centuries to explain how this planet Earth works, how different organisms can coexist and survive together in such a relatively small space. People then try to understand and solve environmental problems based on these explanations. Theories presented have traditionally been completely scientific, explaining the way things work factually. However, James Lovelock presented a new sort of theory in 1992, naming it his "Gaia hypothesis." Lovelock explained Gaia as "the theory of an evolving system of two tightly coupled and indivisible parts: the living organisms of the earth and their material environment" (Azimov and Pohl, 207). He proceeded to defend this theory, explaining, "whether or not Gaia is an accurate description of the earth, it forces a different view from that of conventional wisdom, a view that could be crucial to understanding the consequences of pollution and other environmental disturbances." James Lovelock's "Gaia hypothesis" created friction in the scientific community as it intertwined social sciences and humanities, not only science, in its justification. Isaac Asimov and Frederik Pohl defend this theory in their article "Gaia and Global Warming," using techniques of attracting the audience to their opinion while expressing it in an effective manner. With its balance of science, social science, and humanities, the theory of Gaia and "Gaia and Global Warming" are both effective and well-rounded arguments.

Asimov and Pohl focus on the scientific aspects of Gaia, as it was a scientific theory and therefore needs much scientific evidence to justify it. Lovelock presented his theory following traditional "scientific method," drawing evidence from observation and other scientific literature, as a scientist is supposed to do (Asimov and Pohl, 208). His evidence was based on the entire biosphere of the planet earth. By using these scientific facts to back up his explanation, he could validate his arguments. Gaia is based on the scientific term "homeostatic behavior," defined as a self-preserving system, not only able to adapt to itself, but also even altering itself in whatever ways to preserve its own well-being. One specific example brought up by Lovelock, and then presented by Asimov and Pohl, is the paradoxical question of the salt content of the sea. The seas have the precise amount of salt in them to allow survival of its inhabitants. According to Lovelock, however, by all normal scientific logic, the seas should be a lot saltier than they are, from the evaporations of the rivers running into them. The scientific facts already known could not answer this phenomenon, but

Lovelock's theory could, saying the earth was acting through Gaia as a homeostatic system to maintain the correct balance.

Scientists, especially the most rational-minded ones, "purely hated so mystic-sounding a concept," claiming it was an embarrassment to science; most disturbingly, Lovelock was "one of them," with many strong scientific credentials behind him. The report was said to be on the verge of superstition, yet Lovelock still has the "temerity" to present his arguments in the form of the orthodox scientific method (Asimov and Pohl, 208). However, science is shown not to be able to explain everything, especially concerning naturally occurring phenomenon such as the lowered salt content of the sea. The mix of "mystical" insight as well as concrete scientific facts in Lovelock's theory can make sense of it all.

The "mystical" part of Lovelock's theory is where humanities ties in. Humanities is the expression of opinions, involving the ethical and creative side of arguments. Gaia is an expression of an individual's perspective of nature. As said before, scientists didn't like this mysterious creation, for it involved creativity and not only scientific facts in its formation. In this theory, humanities is first noticed in its title, which incorporated the use of Greek mythology. In naming it, Lovelock asked help from a friend, author William Golding, who proposed naming it after the Greek goddess of the earth, Gaia. Lovelock accepted this suggestion and proceeded to explain his opinion factually, but still using his imagination.

Just as Lovelock incorporated humanities in the development of his theory, Asimov and Pohl use this discipline in their explanation as well. Both authors are incredible thinkers and science fiction writers. They present their argument in the form of a story, making it fun and interesting to read, unlike the usual report of a theory. They use many comparisons to everyday life, relating to the audience's ethical and thinking side. By incorporating the audience into the theory, the ideas presented have a greater impact on each individual reader. This technique is used especially as they present proposed solutions to the global warming problem. One of these solutions suggested putting "magic fairy dust" into the air. This dust is scientifically known as a catalyst, an element that speeds up reactions. This catalyst would turn the element responsible for global warming, carbon dioxide, into limestone. This process is already naturally occurring, but it happens very slowly. However, in the effort to speed up the reaction, the risk is involved that it may get out of human control. Not being able to stop the catalysis would lead to complete decompression of carbon dioxide, killing off the human race and all other organisms on earth (Asimov and Pohl, 214). Asimov and Pohl explain: "Like the sorcerer's apprentice, we would be tempting fate if we started things we might not be able to stop." After hearing this comparison, one that brings a formidable and unethical image into the mind, no one would want to attempt using such a catalyst. Asimov and Pohl show there are no readily available solutions, and try to warn people about the harm of such ideas already proposed. Using the skills of humanities, which they both have mastered, they articulate their point well.

The entire article, "Gaia and Global Warming," is centered around social science, which is the attitudes and behaviors of society, and the attempt to change them. The opening states, "We would all like to think there was something—some benign and superior kind of *something*—that would step in and save us from the things that are going wrong in our world." Most of human history, people have believed in this something as their god (Asimov and Pohl, 207). Wanting a "superior being" to take care of them, and save them from problems that they have perhaps even created themselves, shows people's lack of responsibility in their behavior and attitudes, especially those towards nature. Although Gaia is the closest *something* that some people have ever reached, it does not solve these problems the way people want it to. Through this example, Asimov and Pohl show how Lovelock's theory attempts to change society's attitudes and behaviors by showing them that nothing will look after them but themselves.

Through their article, "Gaia and Global Warming," Asimov and Pohl make an attempt to change these same behaviors and attitudes. To do this, they involve Gaia's explanation of a specific environmental problem, global warming. This problem cannot be solved through scientific discovery. It is one that can only be solved through the change of society. This article is addressed to the public, offering solutions in an attempt to educate its readers, and lets them benefit from the information provided. It also invites people to form their own opinions; although the article tries to convince its audience to believe in its statements, the theory of Gaia allows room for other interpretations.

The presentations of Lovelock's theory Gaia and Asimov and Pohl's "Gaia and Global Warming" use science, social science, and the humanities to get across their perspectives. By using these three forms of discipline, they appeal to the reasoning of logos, ethos, and pathos. Logos is the logic behind and explanation of the crisp facts that science presents us with; ethos pertains to the ethical side of an argument, presented in the humanities; pathos is the emotional part, talking about human attitudes and behaviors, relating to the social sciences. To make an argument well rounded and clear, all three of these aspects must be incorporated into it. Because the arguments of Lovelock, and Asimov and Pohl contain strong ideas of all three, they are effective and persuasive. After reading these arguments, no questions remain in my head that would doubt the validity of their options; all sections are thorough and clear. Granted that I am not as educated as the three of them, I still cannot find any holes in their argument that anyone could refute with better knowledge than my own. By using all these techniques of persuasion, the reader is left affected by this article and definitely persuaded by it. There are no gaps left, no parts unturned. If there were any unclarified parts, the arguments would not be as convincing.

This article, and my newfound knowledge of Gaia, can and will be incorporated into my life, as I will now look for evidence of Gaia on a day-to-day basis. Questions and phenomena that may have been unexplained before, whether by science or myself, can now be explained by her. However, the power of this hypothesis is incredible to me. The part that scared me the most is when Lovelock says, "People sometimes have the attitude 'Gaia will look after us.' But that's wrong. If the concept means anything at all, Gaia will look after herself. And the best way for her to do that might well be to get rid of us" (Azimov and Pohl, 207). Many opinions orally presented in class deal with us trying to save the environment, attempting to fix the environmental problems that are the consequences of careless human behavior. I believe, however, that we are not trying to save the environment, but our environment, the one that humans can live and flourish in. In "The Case for Human Beings," Palmer declared that human life takes up only a hiccup of time compared to the entirety of the earth's existence (48). The Earth will continue after we are gone, just as it did the billion of years before we trampled on it. It scares me that society is so naïve in that they think that we are saving the environment, when in fact the only thing that we are saving is ourselves.

Works Cited

Asimov, Isaac and Pohl, Frederick. 1995 "Gaia and Global Warming." *The Environmental Predicament.* Boston: Bedford Books of St. Martin's Press. 1995.

Palmer, Thomas. 1995. "The Case for Human Beings." *The Environmental Predicament.* Carol Verburg, ed. Boston: Bedford Books of St. Martin's Press. 1995.

APPENDIX

Citation and Documentation Systems

PURPOSES OF CITATION AND DOCUMENTATION

Standards and features of citation and documentation systems for scholarly writing in various disciplines are established and revised by appropriate professional organizations such as the Modern Language Association (MLA), the American Psychological Association (APA), and the Council of Biology Editors (CBE) in order to facilitate the communication of knowledge in their fields. Though most citation and documentation systems share fundamental purposes and principles, they may handle certain details quite differently. Furthermore citation and documentation systems are regularly revised for increased efficiency and to address demands presented by emerging types and sources of information such as those made available by electronic media.

Though we have given some examples of the MLA and APA systems here, we recommend you consult current style guides (many are available on-line) for the particular citation and documentation systems required by your instructors. In this section we believe it is more important to focus on general purposes and principles of citation and documentation systems and compare some specific features of these two central systems. We hope our discussion of some of their distinguishing features will help you follow guidelines for these and other systems with a more comprehensive appreciation of their functions and a clearer understanding of the rationale for their specific requirements.

Most students assume that their purpose in using correct citation and documentation for their sources is to avoid plagiarism. In fact, most student handbooks on the topic emphasize ethical issues involved with inadequate acknowledgment of sources and quoted materials in student writing. Certainly appropriate acknowledgment of sources is a serious matter of academic integrity, and most educational institutions enforce strict policies and severe penalties to deter plagiarism among scholars. We strongly suggest you review your institution's policy and discuss any questions you may have about it with your instructor or with an academic advisor.

Knowing the actual policy bottom-line is crucial to avoiding unpleasant situations; however, we believe there are also more positive motivations for mastering scholarly practices for acknowledging one's sources. While academic integrity is certainly a matter of ethics, it is also a matter of etiquette, a matter of participating productively in a community of scholarship. We believe that understanding the purposes and principles of citation and documentation as a foundation for good scholarly manners will help you to join more fully and responsibly in the various academic conversations you may encounter across the disciplines.

The whole point of academic inquiry is to build upon what is known, to incorporate your discoveries with existing knowledge, to say something new in context of what has already been said. The production and communication of knowledge in any discipline is an ongoing conversation. As a new speaker in that conversation you must acknowledge and respond to previous speakers if you wish to be acknowledged and responded to yourself. You may remember how we previously applied the academic conversation analogy to our discussion of signal phrases in the section on supporting claims through well-integrated quotations in the humanities social science units. In those sections we discussed the use of signal phrases as a manner of writerly etiquette that helped to keep a conversation going and to identify the points of view of different participants. In this section we consider how signal phrases in your writing work more formally with parenthetical in-text references and bibliographic documentation systems to establish your scholarly credibility and to serve your readers.

Your readers will expect you to have done your homework on your topic. Your credibility with them on this count is another aspect of your academic integrity. Critical readers will want to know some things before they can decide how much to credit your contributions to a discussion or debate. Have you covered the ground before speaking on an issue? Have you studied the maps left by others? Have you identified the landmark positions? Have you surveyed the turf staked by critical opponents or longstanding antagonists in central arguments? In short do you know the territory? If not, why should a skeptical or already knowledgeable reader follow you into new terrain?

In addition to establishing credibility with already knowledgeable readers, citations lay out the area of your study. It helps them to orient quickly and accurately to your approach by providing a quick sketch of the topic which they can easily fill in from their prior familiarity with your sources. Furthermore your citation of important sources provides an even more essential service to readers less familiar with your subject who would like to pursue the topic even further.

These readers are able to grant you credibility—at least provisionally—because your use of citation will allow them to check your accuracy for themselves. Even more important, your citations provide them with a map of where they can go to learn more and to acquire greater background about the information and issues you address. Through your use of appropriate citations, you can become a guide for readers who might wish to explore the subject and to enter the conversation at hand themselves. In this way your inquiry incorporates your discoveries with existing knowledge *and* opens even broader frontiers for those who may follow.

For the reasons just explained—in addition to avoiding implications of even unintentional plagiarism—academic writers cite sources whether they quote them directly or paraphrase. Even when they translate an idea entirely into their own words, ethical and polite writers acknowledge and attribute ideas to their original sources. That is how a scholarly community continues to share and advance important conversations.

PRINCIPLES OF CITATION AND DOCUMENTATION SYSTEMS

Readers can track their way back to your sources through the bibliographic documentation of your *Works Cited* or *References* list through a combination of indicators embedded in your text itself and inserted into your text in parentheses. The most basic principle of citation to remember is that in-text parenthetical references supplement or complete information provided in signal phrases; together they provide only enough information necessary to locate corresponding entries in your bibliographic documentation. Your bibliographic documentation then provides the additional information necessary to locate the actual sources in a library or on-line.

The most important information your readers will need to locate your sources in your bibliographic documentation is the author's name. Frequently you will name the author whose work you draw from in the signal phrase introducing a quotation. This will likely be the case in instances when you rely strongly on the writer's statement in the development of your own inquiry or argument, or in instances when you will also draw subsequent citations from the same source. In such instances the author's name will not appear again in the parenthetical reference following the quotation. When you draw multiple quotations from a single source, you may perhaps choose not to repeat the author's name in all of the subsequent signal phrases. In other cases, such as in a literature review, you may cite sources without drawing quotations at all. In these cases, then, the sources' names will need to appear in the parenthetical references.

EXAMPLE 1A: IN-TEXT CITATION OF MULTIPLE AUTHORS WITHOUT QUOTATION IN MLA STYLE:

In Text

Contemporary ecofeminist scholarship has clearly mapped interdynamics of patriarchal power and environmental degradation (Griffin; Merchant; Shiva).

Works Cited

Griffin, Susan. *Woman and Nature: The Roaring inside Her.* San Francisco: Harper and Row, 1978.

Merchant, Carolyn. *The Death of Nature: Women, Ecology, and the Scientific Revolution.* San Francisco: Harper and Row, 1983.

Shiva, Vandana. "Development as a New Project of Western Patriarchy." *Reweaving the World: The Emergence of Ecofeminism.* Eds. Irene Diamond and Gloria Orenstein. San Francisco: Sierra Club Books, 1990. 189–200.

EXAMPLE 1B: IN-TEXT CITATION OF MULTIPLE AUTHORS WITHOUT QUOTATION IN APA STYLE:

In Text

Contemporary ecofeminist scholarship has clearly mapped interdynamics of patriarchal power and environmental degradation (Griffin, 1978; Merchant, 1983; Shiva, 1990).

References

Griffin, S. (1978).*Woman and nature: The roaring inside her.* San Francisco, CA: Harper and Row.

Merchant, C. (1983). *The death of nature: Women, ecology, and the scientific revolution.* San Francisco, CA: Harper and Row.

Shiva, V. (1990). Development as a new project of Western patriarchy. In I. Diamond and G. Orenstein (Eds.), *Reweaving the world: The emergence of ecofeminism.* (pp. 189–200). San Francisco: Sierra Club Books.

Often your signal phrases may include the titles of works from which quotations are drawn because they can help establish the relevance of sources to your inquiry. However, because readers can locate titles in your bibliographic documentation by authors' names, they are not generally required in in-text parenthetical references. Exceptions to this principle occur in the MLA system when you cite more than one work of the same authorship. In such cases, titles must appear either in a signal phrase or in an abbreviated form in the parenthetical reference. Because the APA system requires the year of publication for each citation, readers may distinguish multiple works of identical authorship by their dates and so this system never requires titles in signal phrases or in parenthetical references.

EXAMPLE 2A: CITATIONS OF MULTIPLE WORKS BY A SINGLE AUTHOR IN MLA STYLE:

In Text

In her earlier work, Susan Griffin argues that according to Western metaphysics, "Adam is soul and Eve is flesh" (*Woman* 17). In her more recent work, she explains that this metaphysical schism between the masculine and feminine reflects "a deeper schism in the shared vision of our civilization: the separation between the natural world and the spiritual world" (Griffin, "Curves" 87).

Works Cited

Griffin, Susan. "Curves Along the Road." *Reweaving the World: The Emergence of Ecofeminism.* Eds. Irene Diamond and Gloria Orenstein. San Francisco: Sierra Club Books, 1990. 87–99.

———. *Woman and Nature: The Roaring inside Her.* San Francisco: Harper and Row, 1978.

EXAMPLE 2B: CITATIONS OF MULTIPLE WORKS BY A SINGLE AUTHOR IN APA STYLE:

In Text

In her earlier work, Susan Griffin (1978) argues that, according to Western metaphysics, "Adam is soul and Eve is flesh" (p. 17). In her more recent work, she explains that this metaphysical schism between the masculine and feminine reflects "a deeper schism in the shared vision of our civilization: the separation between the natural world and the spiritual world" (Griffin, 1990, p. 87).

References

Griffin, S. (1978). *Woman and nature: The roaring inside her.* San Francisco, CA: Harper and Row.

Griffin, S. (1990). Curves along the road. In I. Diamond and G. Orenstein (Eds.), *Reweaving the world: The emergence of ecofeminism.* (pp. 87–99). San Francisco, CA: Sierra Club Books.

Precise page numbers for the sources of quotations, which almost never appear in signal phrases or in bibliographic documentation, are the most frequently included information found in parenthetical references. Because each citation system has particular requirements for their punctuation, you will want to consult appropriate style guides for specifications. And speaking of punctuation, one of the most common errors students make in citation is to put a period or other sentence end mark before—rather than after—a parenthetical reference. Parenthetical references always come after quotation marks, but they only follow the end mark of a sentence when you use a block format to incorporate a lengthy quotation.

EXAMPLE 3A: PUNCTUATING CITATIONS IN IN-TEXT AND IN BLOCK QUOTATION FORMATS IN MLA STYLE:

In Text

Griffin argues that our metaphysical separation of the natural and spiritual worlds contradicts reality as "all experience of material existence threatens the imaginary schism between nature and consciousness" (93).

Griffin uses language itself as an example of how our metaphysical separation of the natural spiritual worlds contradicts reality:

> All experience of material existence threatens the imaginary schism between nature and consciousness; even language, which is itself a material experience, reflects the acoustical shape of the mouth and tongue. The very world *culture* derives from the word for the cultivation of the soil. *Spirit* derives from the word for breath. (93)

Works Cited

Griffin, Susan. "Curves Along the Road." *Reweaving the World: The Emergence of Ecofeminism.* Eds. Irene Diamond and Gloria Orenstein. San Francisco: Sierra Club Books, 1990. 87–99.

EXAMPLE 3B: PUNCTUATING CITATIONS IN IN-TEXT AND IN BLOCK QUOTATION FORMATS IN APA STYLE:

In Text

Griffin (1990) argues that our metaphysical separation of the natural and spiritual worlds contradicts reality as "all experience of material existence threatens the imaginary schism between nature and consciousness" (p. 93).

Griffin (1990) uses language itself as an example of how our metaphysical separation of the natural spiritual worlds contradicts reality:

> All experience of material existence threatens the imaginary schism between nature and consciousness; even language, which is itself a material experience, reflects the acoustical shape of the mouth and tongue. The very word *culture* derives from the word for the cultivation of the soil. *Spirit* derives from the word for breath. (p. 93)

References

Griffin, S. (1990). Curves along the road. In I. Diamond and G. Orenstein (Eds.), *Reweaving the world: The emergence of ecofeminism.* (pp. 87–99). San Francisco, CA: Sierra Club Books.

As you can see, specifications for citations become fairly technical quite fast, and we have only touched a few basic principles here without even beginning to open up issues a number of special cases—such as sources with multiple authors, works in an anthology, Web sites, and personal interviews—can raise. We give examples of some of these variations at the end of this Appendix, but our purpose here, as we stated above, is to encourage you to use appropriate style guides to follow exact specifications and to help you understand the basic principles behind them. Remember, no matter how complex the details of different citation systems may seem, the goal is always the same and always simple: Provide your readers a track so they can find their own way back to your sources to check your accuracy or to study them further.

"Why, if the goals of citation are always the same," you might ask, "are there different systems with so many details to deal with?" "Why can't scholars just standardize their systems so students only have one to learn?" These are reasonable questions. Though our comparisons below of some particular features of the MLA and APA systems may not satisfy your desire for simple efficiency, we do hope they give you a working understanding of reasons behind their differences that allows you to appreciate the finer points of scholarly etiquette within particular disciplines.

FEATURES OF MLA AND APA CITATION AND DOCUMENTATION SYSTEMS

Differences in citation systems established by professional organizations in various disciplines result from differences in the ways that knowledge is produced, communicated, and valued among scholars in those fields. These differences can perhaps be seen most clearly in a comparison of the specifications for bibliographic documentation in two widely used systems. The MLA system, established by the Modern Language Association, is the accepted standard for literary scholarship and has also been adopted by scholars in many other disciplines of the humanities. The APA system, established by the American Psychological Association, is a common standard among scholars from the Social Sciences and also shares many features of the "name-year" system of the Council of Biology Editors used in the natural sciences.

As you consider the sample bibliographic entries below, think back to what you have learned from your work with earlier units of this book about similarities and differences in processes of inquiry in the sciences, social sciences, and humanities. What indicators can you identify of those differences in the specifications for bibliographic documentation? Which entry follows MLA specifications and which follows APA? How can you tell?

References

Sorapure, M., Inglesby, P., & Yatchisin, G. (1998). Web literacy: Challenges and opportunities for research in a new medium. *Computers and composition, 15,* 409–424.

Works Cited

Sorapure, Madeleine, *et al.* "Web Literacy: Challenges and Opportunities for Research in a New Medium." *Computers and Composition* 15 (1998): 409–424.

The first sample entry under the *References* heading follows APA specifications for an article with more than two authors in a journal paginated by volume, the second, under the *Works Cited* heading, follows MLA specifications. Aside from some differences in punctuation and capitalization—note the absence of quotation marks and capitalization for the article title in the APA version—what can a comparison of these entries tell you about the ways scholars produce, communicate, and value knowledge in different fields? What does the placement of the publication date near the beginning of the APA entry and near the end of the MLA entry suggest? What is suggested in the MLA entry by the substitution of *et al.* for the second and third authors' names? Why does one system use the heading *References* while the other uses *Works Cited?*

In the sciences and social sciences, new knowledge arises largely from empirical study, subsequent studies update, and may correct and even replace, knowledge gained from earlier observations. The relevance of information is closely related to its currency and scholars in these fields are keenly aware of the chronologies of research. This is why, as we explained above, publication dates are required by the APA system in either signal phrases or in-text parenthetical references for all citations. Though both APA and MLA systems organize authors alphabetically in their bibliographic documentation, multiple works with shared authorship are arranged chronologically in the APA References list while they continue to follow alphabetical order in the MLA Works Cited list.

Remember that knowledge produced in the humanities is the result of interpretations from various perspectives and no particular privilege is therefore given there to chronology. The relative merit of information in the humanities is more closely associated with an author's creditability, authority, and insights. This distinction is even reflected at the stylistic level of the text in the disciplinary preferences for verb tenses. In the sciences and social sciences, signal phrases introduce authors as speaking in the past tense: "Freud explained" or "Marx argued." In the humanities, however, these same authors, though long deceased, are treated as though they continue to contribute to the scholarly conversation along with present commentators: "Marx explains" or "Freud argues."

Scientific inquiry has always been a largely collaborative process and group authorship has traditionally been more common there than in the humanities. Also, in the case of many reported discoveries by research teams, "authorship" is often more a matter of membership than it is a matter of actual writing; lab technicians and computer programmers may be listed as authors of a report regardless of whether or not they helped to craft its prose. Scientists' advancement in their careers is in large part governed by their contributions to particular discoveries and the listing of every significant contributor's name in association with reported research is highly critical in this scholarly community.

Finally scientists and social scientists are expected to situate their new findings firmly within a comprehensive context of previous research on their topics. Their references list may provide bibliographic documentation of literature they have studied, though not necessarily cited, as a means of showing their broader familiarity with the existing body of relevant knowledge to which they are contributing. Humanities scholars, on the other hand, necessarily limit their bibliographies to sources actually cited since clear criteria of relevance such as those that govern selection of sources for the sciences do not necessarily exist. Though humanities scholars are also held accountable to situating their work in comprehensive contexts, philosophically speaking at any rate, almost any related perspective from any point in history could be considered somehow relevant to their topics. They must be able to draw a line of inclusion and exclusion somewhere and so they draw around the sources they have actually incorporated into their work.

As we have already stated, a complete coverage of even one of the principle citation and documentation systems used by scholars lies beyond the scope of this book. In fact professional organizations of scholars usually publish and regularly revise entire books on their systems. Fortunately many excellent handbooks and style guides for writers provide adequate explanations of the most frequently used systems and excellent on-line references are becoming more available.

We particularly recommend that you consult on-line references for suggestions on how to cite and document on-line sources incorporated into your research as these electronic information technologies and the systems for documenting their use are still evolving. You might study the citation of on-line sources in the article *Web Literacy* cited above for some basic examples of how to manage electronic source materials in your own scholarship.

Though we have not detailed here anything like a complete set of instructions for citing and documenting your sources, we provide below a list of citation styles for the most common types of sources. We hope the insight you have gained into the purposes and principles will be more useful in the long run than an endlessly complex list. We hope you will see both your incorporations of source materials and your citation and documentation of them as integral elements in your authentically motivated inquiries as you endeavor to produce new knowledge and to communicate your discoveries as a contributing member of a community of scholarship.

CITATION EXAMPLES

1. Book with one author

    MLA: Allport, Gordon. *The Nature of Prejudice.* Cambridge: Addison Wesley, 1954.

    APA: Allport, G. (1954). *The nature of prejudice.* Cambridge: Addison Wesley.

2. Book with two or three authors

    MLA: Ray, Dixie Lee and Louis R. Guzzo. *Trashing the Planet.* Washington D.C: Regnery Publ., 1990.

    APA: Ray, D. & Louis R. (1990). *Trashing the planet.* Washington, DC: Regnery Publ.

3. Book with four or more authors

    MLA: Bellah, Robert N., et al. *Habits of the Heart: Individualism and Commitment in American Life.* Berkeley CA: University of California Press, 1985.

    APA: Bellah, R., Madsen, R., Sullivan, W., Swidler, A., & Tipton, S. (1985). *Habits of the heart: Individualism and commitment in American life.* Berkeley, CA: University of California Press.

4. Author with an editor

    MLA: Bronowski, Jacob. *The Visionary Eye.* Ed. Piero E. Ariotti. Cambridge MA: MIT Press. 1978.

    APA: Bronowski, J. (1978). *The visionary eye.* P. E. Ariotti (Ed.). Cambridge, MA: MIT Press.

5. Edited book

    MLA: Stock, Patricia, ed. *Forum,* Upper Montclair, NJ: Boyton-Cook, 1983.

    APA: Stock, P. (Ed.). (1983). *Forum.* Upper Montclair, NJ: Boyton-Cook.

6. Translation

    MLA: Tocqueville, Alexis de. *Democracy in America.* Ed. J. P. Mayer; translated by George Lawrence. 1st Perennial Library edition. New York: Perennial Library, Harper & Row, 1988.

    APA: Tocqueville, A. (1988). *Democracy in America.* J. P. Mayer (Ed.). (George Lawrence, Trans.) (1988). 1st Perennial Library edition. New York: Perennial Library, Harper & Row. (Original work published 1830)

7. Corporate, institutional, or agency author

    MLA: Environmental Protection Agency. *Mitigating Global Climate Change Through the Adoption of Demand-side Technologies: Case Studies of the California South Coast and the State of Vermont.* Springfield, VA: The Associates, 1993.

    APA: Environmental Protection Agency. (1993). *Mitigating Global Climate Change Through the Adoption of Demand-side Technologies: Case*

Studies of the California South Coast and the State of Vermont. Spring-field, VA: The Associates.

8. Unknown author

MLA: Rand McNally. *Cosmopolitan World Atlas.* New York: Rand McNally & Co., 1981.

APA: Rand McNally. (1981). *Cosmopolitan World Atlas.* New York: Rand McNally & Co.

9. Two or more books by same author

MLA: Caldicott, Helen. *If You Love This Planet: A Plan to Heal the Earth.* New York: W.W. Norton, 1992.

——. *Nuclear Madness: What You Can Do.* Brookline, MA: Autumn Press, 1978.

APA: Caldicott, H. (1978). *Nuclear madness: What you can do.* Brookline, MA: Autumn Press.

Caldicott, H. (1992). *If you love this planet: A plan to heal the earth.* New York: W. W. Norton.

10. Edition other than first

MLA: Brown, M. Neil and Stuart M. Keeley. *Asking the Right Questions.* 3rd ed. Englewood Cliffs, NJ: Prentice Hall Publ. 1990.

APA: Brown, N. & Keeley, S. (1990). *Asking the right questions.* (3rd ed.). Englewood Cliffs, NJ: Prentice Hall Publ.

11. Multivolume work

MLA: University of Chicago College. *The People Shall Judge: Readings in the Formation of American Policy.* Ed. Staff of the University of Chicago College, Chicago, IL: University of Chicago Press, 1949, 2v.

APA: University of Chicago College. (1949). *The people shall judge: Readings in the formation of American policy.* Staff of the University of Chicago College (Ed.) (2 vols.) Chicago, IL: University of Chicago Press.

12. Encyclopedia or dictionary

MLA: "Toxicity." Encyclopedia of Environmental Biology. Ed. William A Nierenberg. San Diego, CA: Academic Press, 1995.

APA: "Toxicity." (1995). In *Encyclopedia of environmental biology.* W. Nierenberg (Ed.). San Diego, CA: Academic Press.

13. Work in an anthology

MLA: Solomon, Jack. "Masters of Desire: the Culture of American Advertising." *Signs of Life in the U.S.A.* Eds. Sonia Maasik and Jack Solomon. Boston: Bedford Books. 1997, 120-133.

APA: Solomon, J. (1997). "Masters of desire: The culture of American advertising." In S. Maasik & J. Solomon (Eds.), *Signs of life in the U.S.A.* (pp. 120–133). Boston: Bedford Books.

14. Magazine article

    MLA: Wallraff, Barbara. "What Global Language?" *The Atlantic Monthly*, November, 2000, 52–67.

    APA: Wallraff, B. (2000, November) What global language? *The Atlantic Monthly*, vol. 286, no. 5 pp. 52–67.

15. Journal article

    MLA: Martin, K.L.M.,Lawson, M.C., and Engebretson, H. "Adverse Effects of Hyposalinity from Stormwater Runoff on the Aggregating Anemone." *Bulletin of the Southern California Academy of Science*. 95(1), 1996, 46–51.

    APA: Martin, K. L. M., Lawson, M. C., & Engebretson, H. (1996). Adverse effects of hyposalinity from stormwater runoff on the aggregating anemone. *Bulletin of the Southern California Academy of Science*, 95(1), 46–51.

16. Newspaper article

    MLA: Gabler, Neal. "Celebrity Politics." *The Los Angeles Times*. 22 October, 2000, Sec. M:1+.

    APA: Gabler, N. (2000, October 22). Celebrity politics. *The Los Angeles Times*, pp. M:1+.

17. Electronic sources: Reference database

    MLA: Liu, Alan. *The Voice of the Shuttle*. [Online] Available: http://VoS.ucsb.edu March, 1998.

    APA: Liu, A. (1998). *The voice of the shuttle*. [Retrieved March 1, 1998 from On-line database] on the World Wide Web: http://vos.ucsb.edu.

18. Electronic sources: Web site

    MLA: Writing Program. University of California, Santa Barbara. http://www.writing.ucsb.edu, Nov. 2000.

    APA: Writing Program. University of California, Santa Barbara. (2000, November 15) Retrieved November 15, 2000 from the World Wide Web http://www.writing.ucsb.edu.

19. Electronic sources: On-line book or periodical

    MLA: Ferris, Pixie. "Writing in Cyberspace." *CMC Magazine*. [Online] Available: http://www.december.com/cmd/mag/1997/jun/ferris.html

    APA: Ferris, P. (1997). Writing in cyberspace. *CMC Magazine*. Retrieved April 2, 2000 from the World Wide Web: http://www.december.com/cmd/mag/1997/jun/ferris.html>

20. Work of Art

    MLA: Sargent, John Singer. *Fishing for Oysters at Cancale*. Museum of Fine Arts, Boston.

21. Musical composition

    MLA: Mahler, Gustav. *Symphony #4.*

22. Personal letter

    MLA: Kenyon, Megan. Letter to Judy Kirscht, 5 May, 2000.

23. Lecture

    MLA: Kabakov, Ilya. *Total Installation: How Art Shapes Our Experience of Space and Time.* University of California, Santa Barbara, Isla Vista Theater, 16 May, 2000.

    APA: Kabakov, I. (2000, May) *Total Installation: How Art Shapes Our Experience of Space and Time.* Lecture presented at the University of California, Santa Barbara.

24. Personal interview

    MLA: Tiffney, Bruce. Personal Interview, 5 May 1998.

25. Film or videotape

    MLA: *Pretty Woman.* Dir. Garry Marshall. With Richard Gere and Julia Roberts. Touchstone Home Video, 1990.

    APA: Goldstein, G. W. and L. Ziskin, Prod. (1990). *Pretty Woman.* Touchstone Home Video.

26. Live performance

    MLA: *The Rivals.* The Acting Company. Campbell Hall, University of California, Santa Barbara, 9 April, 2000.

27. Sound recording

    MLA: Mahler, Gustav. *Symphony #4.* Perf. Juliane Banse, Soprano, Cond. Pierre Boulez, Cleveland Orchestra. Deutsche Grammophon.

28. Map or Chart

    MLA: *Southern and Central California Campgrounds.* Automobile Club of Southern California, 1997.

STYLE GUIDES ON-LINE

Modern Language Association (MLA)
http://www.lib.ohio-state.edu/guides/mlagd.html

American Psychological Association
http://www.lib.ohio-state.edu/guides/apagd.html

Chicago Manual of Style
http://www.bedfordstmartins.com/online/cite7.html

References

Abrams, M. H. "Orientation of Critical Theories," *The Mirror and the Lamp: romantic theory and the critical tradition,* Ch. 1. New York: W. W. Norton Publ, 1958.

Allport, Gordon. "The Formation of In-Groups." *The Nature of Prejudice*, Ch. 3. Cambridge: Addison Wesley, 1954, 29–47.

Aristotle, *Ethics,* Book I, New York: Penguin Books.

Azimov, Isaac & Pohl, Frederick. "Gaia and Global Warming." *Our Angry Earth.* New York: Tom Doherty Assoc., 1991, [9pp].

Bacon, Francis. Idols of the Mind, *The Advancement of Learning, and Novum Organum.* New York: Wiley, 1944.

Bacon, Francis. "Tale of the Sphinx, Wisdom of the Ancients: a Series of Mythological Fables." *Bacon's Essays.* New York: A. L. Burt Co., 1883, 360–363.

Bartholomae, David. "Inventing the University." *When A Writer Can't Write: Studies in Writer's Block and Other Composing Process Problems.* New York: Guilford, 1985, 273–285.

Bell, Inge. "Everybody Hates to Write," *This Book is Not Required.* Fort Bragg, CA, Small Press, 1985, 128–144.

Bennett, Stephen Earl. Preface, Ch. 2, "Apathy in Political Theory and Political Behavior;" *Apathy in America, 1960–1984: Causes and Consequences of Citizen Political Indifference,* Dobbs Ferry, NY: Transnational Publishers, 1986.

Bronowski, Jacob. *The Visionary Eye.* Cambridge MA: MIT Press, 1978.

Caldicott, Helen. "The Greenhouse Effect." *If You Love This Planet: A Plan to Heal the Earth,* New York: W.W. Norton, 1992. [14pp]

Du Bois, W. E. B. "Introduction," Ch. 1 "Our Spiritual Strivings," *The Souls of Black Folk.* NY: A. C. McClurg, 86–103.

Ferrell, Jeff. Voodoo, "The Shadow," "Eye Six and Mac," "SPA (and Banshee)"; *Crimes of Style.* New York: Garland Publishing, 1993.

Fish, Stanley. "How to Recognize a Poem When you See One." *Is There a Text in This Class?* Cambridge, MA: Harvard University Press, 1980.

Gribbin, John. "Light," *In Search of Schrodinger's Cat: Quantum Physics and Reality.* New York: Bantam Books, 1984, 7–18.

Madison, James. *The Federalist #10. The Debate on the Constitution*, Part I, Library of America Series, NY: Library Classics of the United States, Inc., 1990, 404–411.

Mailloux, Stephen. "Interpretation." *Critical Terms for Literary Study.* Ed. Frank Lentricchia. Chicago: University of Chicago Press, 1990. 121–134.

Markstrom-Adams, Carol. "Attitudes on Dating, Courtship, and Marriage: Perspectives on In-Group Versus Out-Group Relationships by Religious Minority and Majority Adolescents." *Family Relations*, January 1991, Vol. 40, 91–96.

Martin, K. L. M., Lawson, M. C., and Engebretson, H. "Adverse Effects of Hyposalinity from Stormwater Runoff on the Aggregating Anemone." *Bulletin of the Southern California Academy of Science.* 95(1), 1996, 46–51.

Orr, David. Ch. V: "Ecological Literacy," *Ecological Literacy: Education and the Transition to a Postmodern World,* State University of New York Press, 1992.

Pagels, A. K. Wakefield and D. G. Fautin. "Symbiosis Between a Sea Anemone and a Scaphopod: Reducing the Difficulties of Deep Sea Life?" *American Zoologist,* v.34, n.5 (1994), 99A. Annual Meeting, American Society of Zoologists, 1994.

Quinn, Timothy. "Coyote (Canis Iatrans) Food Habits in Three Urban Habitat Types of Western Washington," *Northwest Science,* Vol. 71, No.1, 1997, 1–5

Ray, Dixie Lee & Guzzo, Louis R. "Greenhouse Earth," *Trashing The Planet: How Science Can Help Us Deal with Acid Rain, Depletion of Ozone, and Nuclear Waste (Among Other Things).* Washington D.C: Regnery Publ., 1990 [12pp].

Rimmerman, Craig A. Ch. 2, "Theoretical Perspectives on the New Citizenship." Ch. 3, "Civic Indifference in Contemporary American Politics." *The New Citizenship.* San Francisco, CA: Westview, 1997.

Shklar, Judith N. "Obligation, Loyalty, Exile." *Political Theory,* Vol. 21 #2: 181–197. 1993.

Solomon, Jack. "Masters of Desire: the Culture of American Advertising." *Signs of Life in the U.S.A.* Eds. Sonia Maasik and Jack Solomon. Boston: Bedford Books, 1997. 120–133.

Sontag, Susan. "Against Interpretation," *Against Interpretation and Other Essays.* New York: Farrar, Straus, & Giroux, 1966, 3–14.

Sorapure, Madeleine, Inglesby, Pam, & Yatchisin, George. "Web Literacy: Challenges and Opportunities for Research in a New Medium." *Computers and Composition,* 15, 1998, 409–424.

Steinbeck, John. *The Grapes of Wrath.* New York: Viking Press, 1939.

Toulmin, Stephen. *An Introduction to Reasoning.* New York: Macmillan. 1979

Wilson, Edward O. Storm over the Amazon, *The Diversity of Life.* New York: W.W. Norton, 1992, 3–15.

Credits

Index